European Welfare State Constitutions after the Financial Crisis

European Welfare State Constitutions after the Financial Crisis

Edited by

ULRICH BECKER

Director at the Max Planck Institute for Social Law and Social Policy

ANASTASIA POULOU

Senior Research Fellow at the Max Planck Institute for Social Law and Social Policy

OXFORD
UNIVERSITY PRESS

OXFORD
UNIVERSITY PRESS

Great Clarendon Street, Oxford, OX2 6DP,
United Kingdom

Oxford University Press is a department of the University of Oxford.
It furthers the University's objective of excellence in research, scholarship,
and education by publishing worldwide. Oxford is a registered trade mark of
Oxford University Press in the UK and in certain other countries

First Edition published in 2020

Impression: 1

Published in the United States of America by Oxford University Press
198 Madison Avenue, New York, NY 10016, United States of America

British Library Cataloguing in Publication Data

Data available

Library of Congress Control Number: 2020940065

ISBN 978–0–19–885177–6

DOI: 10.1093/oso/9780198851776.001.0001

Printed and bound by
CPI Group (UK) Ltd, Croydon, CR0 4YY

Preface

Hit by the European financial and economic crisis that erupted in 2008, several Member States of the European Union, namely Latvia, Rumania, and Hungary, and of the European Monetary Union, namely Greece, Ireland, Portugal, and Cyprus, were unable to refinance their gross government debt through the financial market. As a result, they asked for financial assistance not only from already established international institutions, such as the International Monetary Fund or the World Bank, but also from newly created European financial assistance mechanisms, such as the European Financial Stabilisation Mechanism (EFSM), the European Financial Stability Facility (EFSF), and the European Stability Mechanism (ESM). Other EU Member States, such as Italy and Spain, were not officially subjected to a financial assistance scheme, but received informal instructions for the reduction of social security benefits.

Despite their differences, strict conditionality represented a common ground for all types of financial assistance. The award of all loans was made dependent on the recipient state complying with economic policy conditions that were extremely broad in scope. Apart from budgetary discipline, the financial assistance conditions also related to what one would call the core of social policy, namely, cuts in pensions and social assistance, and reforms in public healthcare.

The far-reaching reforms in the field of social security and assistance were in many cases experienced as violations of human rights by the respective right-holders, who sought legal protection in national and international courts. As a result, many national constitutional courts, but also the Court of Justice of the EU and the European Court of Human Rights, issued a series of rulings on the conformity of the social protection reforms that were initiated during the eurozone crisis with constitutional law and human rights. This international and national jurisprudence and the mounting concern about the implications of the relevant reforms in social protection for the application of constitutional law motivated the launch of the proposed edited collection. Given that the majority of countries under examination have exited the crisis, the book seeks to unfold the legacy of the crisis, highlighting the lessons learned from it in the field of social protection and constitutional law.

This book aspires to offer a holistic approach that analyses both (1) the specific reforms in social protection introduced during the European financial crisis and (2) their implications for constitutional law. Against this background, its aim is twofold. First, it records and systematises the crisis-related reforms introduced in the field of social protection broadly understood, covering old-age benefits, social assistance allowances, unemployment benefits, and healthcare. This is done in a way that depicts the particular crisis experience of each country and links the crisis-related reforms with the overall national social policy developments. Second, the book aims to locate the social protection reforms within the constitutional framework of each country, by investigating the ways in which the application of constitutional law has changed during the crisis and the impact that this change has had on social democracy and the welfare state. More specifically, we were interested in investigating whether fundamental constitutional and democratic principles of the European welfare state, which traditionally recognises and protects social rights, were altered during the crisis.

At the same time, taking such an approach presents a certain challenge to legal scholarship. To gain a better understanding of the welfare state, it is necessary to dig deeply into the depths of—the often complex—social protection laws, but without losing sight of its constitutional foundations. Yet, social protection law on the one hand and constitutional or human rights law on the other are often dealt with as separate subjects, due to a high degree of specialisation in legal research. We are very grateful that the authors took up this challenge and brought both fields of law together in this project.

We would also like to thank Christina McAllister and Christian Günther for their valuable assistance in bringing this book into a readable and proper form. Finally, we have to thank Natalie Patey and Brianne Bellio from OUP for their kind support and help with the publication process.

Ulrich Becker
Anastasia Poulou
Munich, April 2020

Table of Contents

Table of Cases

CYPRUS: SUPREME COURT

CYPRUS: ADMINISTRATIVE COURT

CYPRUS: DISTRICT COURT

HUNGARY: CONSTITUTIONAL COURT

GERMANY: FEDERAL CONSTITUTIONAL COURT

GREECE: COUNCIL OF STATE

IRELAND: IRISH HIGH COURT

IRELAND: IRISH SUPREME COURT

ITALY: CONSTITUTIONAL COURT

LATVIA: CONSTITUTIONAL COURT

PORTUGAL: CONSTITUTIONAL COURT

ROMANIA: CONSTITUTIONAL COURT

ROMANIA: HIGH COURT

SPAIN: CONSTITUTIONAL COURT

UK: HIGH COURT OF JUSTICE

List of Contributors

Maria Bakavou, Dr, Judge at the Greek Council of State, Athens

Ulrich Becker, Prof Dr, Director at the Max Planck Institute for Social Law and Social Policy, Munich

Matteo De Nes, Dr, Post-Doctoral Researcher in Constitutional Law, University of Padova

Elaine Dewhurst, Dr, Senior Lecturer in Employment Law, University of Manchester

Elena-Luminiţa Dima, Dr, Professor at the Faculty of Law, University of Bucharest

Kristīne Dupate, Dr, Associate Professor at the Faculty of Law, University of Latvia

József Hajdú, Dr, Professor for Labour Law and Social Security Law at the Faculty of Law, University of Szeged

Athena Herodotou, Research Assistant at the Law Department, University of Cyprus

Constantinos Kombos, Dr, Associate Professor of Public Law at the Law Department, University of Cyprus

João Carlos Loureiro, Dr, Professor of Constitutional and Social Security Law, University of Coimbra

Juan Antonio Maldonado Molina, Dr, Professor of Labour and Social Security Law, University of Granada

Andrea Pin, Dr, Associate Professor of Comparative Public Law, University of Padova

Anastasia Poulou, Dr, Senior Research Fellow at the Max Planck Institute for Social Law and Social Policy, Munich

Juan Romero Coronado, Dr, Professor of Labour and Social Security Law, University of Granada

Suzana Tavares da Silva, Dr, Judge at the Portuguese Administrative Supreme Court and Professor of Constitutional, Administrative and Tax Law, University of Coimbra

José Carlos Vieira de Andrade, Dr, Full Professor of Constitutional and Administrative Law, University of Coimbra

1

Introduction

Ulrich Becker

I. Starting points

1. How did the European financial crisis change the constitution of welfare states?

The well-known background of this question can be summarised very briefly. The financial crisis, which reached Europe in 2008 in a time of economic recession, led to a debt crisis in 2009; a series of Member States of the European Union (EU) had to reduce their budgetary deficits. In this context, and more or less strongly influenced by European and international institutions, they undertook different measures to cut expenditure, and they reacted, in particular, with cutbacks in social rights.

These austerity measures continue to be highly disputed for good reasons. Their economic effectiveness and their political feasibility remain questionable. But this discussion will not be taken up here. We shall focus on the issue from a legal perspective. It is obvious that the financial crisis hit European states as an external shock, and the question we are interested in, and that the following chapters will deal with, is how the legal systems that can be understood as the backbones of welfare states have managed to cope with this shock. In this context, our understanding of the constitution of welfare states is twofold.

Ulrich Becker, *Introduction* In: *European Welfare State Constitutions after the Financial Crisis.* Edited by: Ulrich Becker and Anastasia Poulou, Oxford University Press (2020). © The Contributors. DOI: 10.1093/oso/9780198851776.003.0001

First, European states conceive of themselves as political communities that take care of the well-being of the people living in their territory.[1] There is a certain common understanding that they should do so, and the normative foundation for this can be found in the law of the European Union as well as in national constitutions. The so-called European social model[2] is based on a combination of guaranteeing individual freedoms and enabling their actual enjoyment, but it is a loose concept as far as the institutional settings and the level of social protection are concerned. States have to make political decisions in this respect,[3] and these decisions become tangible and receive a binding character once they have been transformed into legal documents. Social (protection) law is the instrument for putting social policy into practice. At the same time, it reflects fundamental ideas on the right and just construction of a political community, in particular on the legitimacy of public interventions, or how far governments should be entrusted with the task of influencing societal and individual behaviour. This is why modifications of social (protection) law are not a mere technicality but reveal, at least if they are of considerable importance and go beyond mere adjustments, changes in the very constitution of welfare states.

Second, it is constitutional law that forms and frames the welfare state. In the context of the financial crisis, the question arises as to whether and, if so, in what way it has been used in order to control and correct austerity measures and thus to stabilise the welfare state. And one might also expect with regard to its functioning that the financial crisis had some impact on its application.

2. It is this double-sided understanding of the constitution of welfare states that serves as a background to this book, which aims to provide a detailed analysis of crisis-driven changes in a comparative perspective. It concentrates on those nine EU Member States that were particularly affected by the financial crisis. We have subdivided them into three groups: the first consists of *Hungary*, *Latvia*, and *Romania*. All three are non-eurozone Member States that received financial assistance from the International Monetary Fund (IMF) and the World Bank, as well as from the EU in the form of a balance of payments according to article 143 of the Treaty on the Functioning of the EU (TFEU). These countries are of particular interest, since they were the first countries to receive financial assistance in the wake of the financial crisis and thus served as precedential cases for the bailout of eurozone Member

---

[1] It is noteworthy that this territorial responsibility is not restricted to their (own) citizens, although we do not elaborate on migration issues here; see for further explanations Ulrich Becker, 'The Challenge of Migration to the Welfare State' in Eyal Benvenisti and Georg Nolte (eds), *The Welfare State, Globalization, and International Law* (Springer 2003) 1.

[2] See Commission, 'European Social Policy, A Way Forward for the Union, A White Paper' COM (94) 333 final, 9, pointing at 'shared values' as a basis, 'held together by the conviction that economic and social progress must go hand in hand'.

[3] Which is the reason why different 'welfare state models' are under discussion, see Wil A Arts and John Gelissen, 'Models of the Welfare State' in Francis G Castles and others (eds), *The Oxford Handbook of the Welfare State* (OUP 2010)—even though most states do not follow one coherent social policy approach anyway.

States. The second group comprises *Greece, Ireland, Portugal,* and *Cyprus.* These are eurozone Member States that received financial assistance from the newly created European assistance mechanisms (EFSM, EFSF, ESM) and the IMF. The third group of country reports encompasses *Italy* and *Spain.* Both received instructions to reduce social protection benefits, even if in their case the crisis management measures were not formally prescribed by supranational organisations.

In its substance, the book combines two legal fields. On the one hand, the national reports document and systematise the crisis-related reforms introduced in the field of social protection as it is broadly understood, covering old-age benefits, social assistance allowances, unemployment benefits, family benefits, and healthcare. This part depicts the specific crisis experience of each country and links the crisis-related reforms to the overall national social policy developments. On the other hand, the national reports also investigate what role constitutional law played in controlling the social protection reforms and the ways in which the application of constitutional law has changed during the crisis. This allows an assessment of whether the fundamental constitutional principles of the European welfare state that traditionally protect social rights were altered during the crisis.

This study can build on previously collected information about recent changes of national social protection systems, such as reports from the World Health Organization (WHO) Regional Office for Europe,[4] the European Trade Union Institute,[5] or the European Social Observatory,[6] although they do not claim to offer a systematic and comprehensive legal analysis. Yet, they do highlight the practical outcome of the austerity measures, and the publications on the relationship between those measures and the now poor level of healthcare in various EU Member States hit by the financial crisis[7] are impressive. Recent research on concepts of the welfare state and their development throughout the years of the crisis concentrates on general theories of welfare state models rather than on a systematic assessment of reforms that were introduced as a reaction to the debt crisis.[8] It can serve as

---

[4] Anna Maresso and others, *Economic Crisis, Health Systems and Health in Europe* (Observatory Studies Series 41, WHO Regional Office for Europe 2014); Philipa Mladovsky and others, *Health Policy Responses to the Financial Crisis in Europe* (WHO Regional Office for Europe 2012).

[5] Furio Stamati and Rita Baeten, *Health Care Reforms and the Crisis* (European Trade Union Institute Report 134, 2014).

[6] Rita Baeten and others, 'Health Care Policies: European Debate and National Reforms' in David Natali and others (eds), *Social Developments in the European Union 2011* (European Social Observatory 2012).

[7] Gesellschaft für Versicherungswissenschaft und -gestaltung (GVG) (ed), *14. Euroforum: Auswirkungen der Euro-Krise auf die nationale Gesundheitspolitik: Dokumentation des GVG-Euroforums in Potsdam am 11. Oktober 2012* vol 72 (Schriftenreihe der GVG 2013); Marina Karanikolos and others, 'Financial Crisis, Austerity and Health in Europe' (2013) 381(9874) The Lancet 1323; Emmanuele Pavolini and others (eds), *Health Care Systems in Europe under Austerity* (Palgrave Macmillan 2013); David Stuckler and Sanjay Basu, *The Body Economic: Why Austerity Kills* (Gildan Media 2013).

[8] Jon Erik Dølvik and Andrew Martin (ed), *European Social Models from Crisis to Crisis: Employment and Inequality in the Era of Monetary Integration* (OUP 2014); Anton Hemerijck, *Changing Welfare States* (OUP 2012); Martin Rhodes (ed), *Southern European Welfare States: Between Crisis and Reform* (Routledge Chapman & Hall 2014); Maria Petmesidou and Ana Marta Guillén (eds), *Economic Crisis and Austerity in Southern Europe: Threat or Opportunity for a Sustainable Welfare State* (Routledge 2015).

background information as it hints at the already mentioned fundamentals of welfare states and their normative content. However, it documents rather generally the various welfare state transformations across European countries,[9] without taking legal instruments of implementation into account or showing a particular interest in the role of financial assistance.

While our study does not try to paint a general picture of recent social rights developments,[10] its focus and approach is, at the same time, different from the existing legal literature on these crisis-driven developments. We do not concentrate on an assessment at European level[11] or on the asymmetry between different political levels of regulation and the correspondent subject matters,[12] although the legal impact of this asymmetry has been discussed for a long time with regard to social protection.[13] Instead, we will provide, in Chapter 2, an analytical overview of the background of EU law. Actions at the international and European level served as a starting point for processes taking place at national level, namely, first and foremost, social protection law reforms and, second, their constitutional framing. The interplay between these processes shows the interaction of supranational and international measures in the framing of the national responses, as well as the interaction between crisis-induced reforms and previous processes of reforms.[14] It allows for insights into possible changes in the legal systems as such,[15] measured by the role of legal doctrine[16] and without a theoretical explanation of the role of

---

[9] Including Germany, Scandinavia, and the UK, see Peter Taylor-Gooby, Benjamin Leruth, and Heejung Chung (eds), *After Austerity: Welfare State Transformation in Europe after the Great Recession* (OUP 2017).

[10] Like Toomas Kotkas and Kenneth Veitch (eds), *Social Rights in the Welfare State, Origins and Transformations* (Routledge 2017), taking up a variety of different aspects.

[11] See for this approach Kaarlo Tuori and Klaus Tuori, *The Eurozone Crisis: A Constitutional Analysis* (CUP 2014); Andreas Fischer-Lescano, *Human Rights in Times of Austerity Policy: The EU Institutions and the Conclusion of Memoranda of Understanding* (Nomos 2014).

[12] See Juan Pablo Bohoslavsky and Letnar Cernic (eds), *Making Sovereign Financing and Human Rights Work* (Hart Publishing 2014).

[13] See for a—rather optimistic—summarisation Ulrich Becker, 'Sozialstaatlichkeit in der Europäischen Union' (2015) 19 Europarecht 25–26; for a different view Florian Rödl, 'Die dialektische Entwicklung des Sozialen im Prozess der europäischen Integration' in Ulrich Becker and others (eds), *Grundlagen und Herausforderungen des Sozialstaats* vol 1 (Erich Schmidt Verlag 2014).

[14] See for a more general approach Thomas Beukers, Bruno de Witte, and Claire Kilpatrick (eds), *Constitutional Change through Euro-Crisis Law* (CUP 2017).

[15] And not necessarily concentrated on social rights; see in this respect Aoife Nolan (ed), *Economic and Social Rights after the Global Financial Crisis* (CUP 2014), dealing with the global financial crisis in the post-2007 context and reflecting experiences from countries in a variety of global regions (Spain, USA, Colombia, Argentina, and South Africa) in different fields (including taxation or the labour market). See also Stefano Civitarese Matteucci and Simon Halliday (eds), *Social Rights in Europe in an Age of Austerity* (Routledge 2017) with a different selection of case studies (choosing the biggest European economies, namely UK, France, Germany, Italy, and Spain).

[16] And not so much the role of constitutional amendments; see for the incorporation of the 'golden rule' of the fiscal compact within national constitutions Maurice Adams, Federico Fabbrini, and Pierre Larouche (eds), *The Constitutionalisation of European Budgetary Constraints* (Hart Publishing 2014).

constitutions as such,[17] or an overall assessment of the role of a particular national constitution,[18] as we assume that this role not only depends on the given national institutions but also might change over time.

In particular, the actual effect of restrictions of social rights plays an important role in the application of the principle of proportionality. In most cases, this principle will serve as the doctrinal basis for court decisions on the constitutionality of restrictions,[19] and we may assume that the way it is applied can be influenced by the contextual background of these restrictions: courts might be more reluctant to correct measures if these measures react to situations of a severe and comprehensive financial crisis.[20] In order to test this hypothesis, one could try to collect all relevant case law and examine the various outcomes, although this method would not provide an explanation for any results. We would at least have to find out whether the application of the proportionality principle, especially of the necessity test, has changed over time, and whether the financial crisis could, at least with some degree of probability, be regarded as a relevant factor. To answer these questions, one would have to conduct qualitative empirical research and to compare cases before the times of crisis to those during the crisis, putting attention not so much on results as on the details of judicial control.[21] Such a historical-legal comparative method may also be used if we want to learn more about all other possible impacts of the financial crisis on welfare state constitutions. While it is a fastidious, even tedious, task, a detailed examination of the legal measures and of case law forms an unavoidable part of legal analysis in this context.

---

[17] See for that question Poul Kjaer, Gunther Teubner, and Alberto Febbrajo (eds), *The Financial Crisis in Constitutional Perspective: The Dark Side of Functional Differentiation* (Hart Publishing 2011).

[18] See Xenofon Contiades (ed), *Constitutions in the Global Financial Crisis: A Comparative Analysis* (Ashgate 2013) with globally collected examples and pointing at four different 'paths of constitutional reaction' (adjustment, submission, breakdown, stamina).

[19] If courts conduct a proportionality test at all, which very much depends on the institutional background and on the approach to every single social right at stake; see also Jeff King, 'Social Rights and Welfare Reform in Times of Economic Crisis' in Matteucci and Halliday (n 15) 214, 221–28.

[20] See eg ECJ of 13 June 2017, Case C-258/14 *Florescu* [2017] ECLI:EU:C:2017:448, paras 56 and 57: '... it should be noted that the purpose of [the restrictive law] is to rationalise public spending in an exceptional context of global financial and economic crisis ... As regards the suitability and necessity of the national legislation at issue in the main proceedings, it must be borne in mind that, given the particular economic context, Member States have broad discretion when adopting economic decisions ...'.

[21] In a certain way, this comes close to the comparison of 'prototypical cases', see Ran Hirschl, *Comparative Matters, The Renaissance of Comparative Constitutional Law* (OUP 2016) 258 with reference to Moshe Cohen-Eliya and Iddo Prodat, *Proportionality and Constitutional Culture* (CUP 2013). The difference here is that we do not aim at learning about different cultures but about the impact of external events on legal systems, and that we therefore do not suggest comparing jurisdictions but different periods of application within one jurisdiction.

II. The constitution of the welfare state under pressure

1. Social policy reforms and the financial crisis

It is not easy to know whether a specific social policy measure and the resulting legislative act is, or is not, to be considered as having been caused by the financial crisis. As a starting point, all social protection laws enacted within the period of analysis (see III.1) merit attention. Of course, the parallel in time between debt crisis and social law reforms is, generally speaking, not sufficient to ascertain causality between the two events. For methodologically sound empirical research, one would have to check the materials of every legal act and search for clear hints shedding light on the relevant motives. If draft bills or protocols of parliamentary debates contain a reference to the specific budgetary situation, it is safe to conclude that the resulting legislative act was a reaction to the debt crisis. In many cases, such causal relations may be established. In others, it will be difficult to find proper proof. But there is at least some plausibility that the economic situation played an important role for all reforms effected in times of the debt crisis, because this crisis has been perceived in most, if not all, Member States of the EU as a major challenge, with a strong impact on fiscal policies, in particular, and on all decisions of this time with relevance for public expenditure more generally.

Nevertheless, it is important to verify this general assumption that emphasises the role of the debt crisis as compared to the social policies that had been pursued before. To a certain degree, these policies had been in line with the general tendencies of developed countries to react to globalisation, changing labour markets, and demographic processes. One could argue that such tendencies must be regarded as an expression of neo-liberalism and that they were clearly meant to find a balance between social protection, individual freedoms, and markets. The Lisbon Strategy of the EU went in this direction, although the changes that were brought about were not as radical as they appeared to be.[22] In any case, one could observe common European trends in specific areas of social policy without being able to link these directly to one political actor on the European scene.[23]

---

[22] See for the so-called investive welfare state Nathalie Morel, Bruno Palier, and Joakim Palme, 'Social Investment: A Paradigm in Search of a New Economic Model and Political Mobilisation' in Nathalie Morel, Bruno Palier, and Joakim Palme (eds), *Towards a Social Investment Welfare State? Ideas, Policies and Challenges* (Policy Press 2012).

[23] See for pension policies Ulrich Becker, 'Alterssicherung im internationalen Vergleich' in Ulrich Becker and others (eds), *Alterssicherung in Deutschland, Festschrift für Franz Ruland* (Nomos 2007) 575 and for the difficulties in assessing the impact of the so-called Open Method of Coordination, Ulrich Becker, 'Die offene Methode der Koordinierung im Bereich Alterssicherung – eine Zwischenbilanz aus Sicht der Wissenschaft' (2011) 92 DRV Schriften 19.

It is true that austerity measures risked moving these tendencies into an ul-timately unbalanced situation.[24] Still, in several cases they were also the result of previous processes of reform, which at least produces mixed motives for cutbacks in social rights. In this respect, one can distinguish between different situations: (1) reforms had already been on their way but were extended, either concerning the material scope or the enhancement of the measures; (2) reforms had passed the process of decision-making but had not yet been implemented, and the debt crisis led to an accelerated implementation process;[25] (3) reforms had not been based on economic reasons but had been aimed at supporting political goals other than reducing budgetary deficits; they were just on the agenda in times of crisis, or the crisis might even have played a certain role in partly justifying reforms.[26] The last alternative reveals that often different policy motives collude. In these cases, it is hard to say which one had more weight than others, but we can still rely on the as-sumption mentioned above that consolidation measures during the time of crisis were, at least to a certain extent, also crisis-driven.

2. Constitutional protection of social rights

Reforming social protection law, and changing social rights based on this law, is foremost a task of the legislator and thus of parliaments. Their actions are, as is every legislative activity, framed by legal provisions. Those provisions form part of the constitution of a political community if we understand by this term, in a material sense, all legal norms aiming at establishing this community, enabling its functioning, and restricting public powers. In this context, it is advisable to briefly explain what is meant by social rights in terms of substance, dimensions, and nor-mative level (see II.2.a). Even if, in a formal sense, constitutional law may be re-garded as law following from a particular and fundamental sovereign decision and, in most cases, also following a specific procedure, there is an interplay between laws from different sources and different legal spheres that has the potential to re-strict legislative powers (see II.2.b). Human rights, also called fundamental or basic rights, are a powerful part of this as they limit the discretion of a legislator in order

---

[24] See Hemerijck (n 8) 373–98. Very sceptical with a view to increasing inequality Jon Erik Dølvik and Andrew Martin, 'From Crisis to Crisis' in Hemerijck (n 8) 325, 384 and with a view to the role of social rights also Colm O'Cinneide, 'Austerity and the Faded Dream of a "Social Europe"' in Nolan (n 15) 169, 184–201.

[25] An example being old-age pension reforms in Italy and Spain, see Ulrich Becker, 'Neuere Entwicklung der Alterssicherungssysteme in Europa – Reformen, Resilienz und rechtliche Aufarbeitung' (2014) 3 DRV 159, 169–70.

[26] An interesting case is the re-privatisation of old-age security schemes in some Central and Eastern European countries where ideological and economic motives concur; see for the reforms in Hungary András Simonovits, 'Pension Re-Reform in Hungary' (2012) 26 ZIAS 258; more generally Elaine Fultz and Kenichi Hirose, 'Second-Pillar Pensions in Central and Eastern Europe: Payment Constraints and Exit Options' (2019) 72(2) ISSR 3, 4–10.

to protect individual positions and to maintain individual freedoms. At every level of their formal construction, and notwithstanding the formal character of the respective legal basis (treaty of public international law, EU law, constitutional law in a formal sense), individual or human rights may protect social law positions via three different mechanisms (see II.2.c). Social rights as a subcategory of these human rights can serve as normative guidelines for legislators in various fields of social policy and impose certain obligations on legislative actions (see II.2.d). Yet, one should not concentrate on human rights only if the role of constitutional law is at stake. In times of crises, governments often feel the pressure to take immediate action. They may be tempted to react quickly to a given factual situation in order to avoid the risk of aggravation. This can, as a consequence, lead to the violation of constitutional provisions that aim to protect the principle of democracy and the rule of law by setting certain procedural requirements for governmental action (see II.2.e).

a) Starting points: different meanings of social rights

The term 'social rights' is, in different respects, open to interpretation, and a lack of clarity about what is understood by this term can easily lead to misunderstandings and sometimes misleading discussions. In order to avoid those, it is helpful to draw a distinction between dimensions and substance on the one hand, and between different levels of legislative actions on the other. And one should also, at least as a starting point, try to choose clear distinctive lines in order to emphasise the relevant categorial aspects.

As far as substance is concerned, social rights cover labour relations (or industrial relations, both individual and collective) and social protection, understood as a broad and recently widespread term embracing both social security and social assistance and thus a broad field of social benefits (see II.2.c) including different forms of governmental interventions (eg non-discrimination, regulation of private markets). As far as the dimension is concerned, social rights can be understood as placing an obligation on governments, and therefore as having a positive dimension.[27] How concrete this obligation actually is, and whether subjective, enforceable individual rights can be derived from the respective provisions, is a crucial question.[28]

This question also leads to the 'legal placement' of social rights, in terms of their rank in a hierarchy of legal sources. As part of constitutional law, EU law, and public international law, social rights aim at directing legislation (see II.2.d); as part of 'ordinary' national laws (acts of parliaments, statutory instruments), social rights

---

[27] 'Positive' in the sense of the necessity of action, and as opposed to a 'negative dimension'.
[28] See for a rough categorisation of the 'strengths' of economic and social rights Courtney Jung, Ran Hirschl, and Evan Rosevear, 'Economic and Social Rights in National Constitutions' (2014) 62 American Journal of Comparative Law 1043, 1049–53.

aim at implementing social policy (see II.1). It is not by chance that in practice the latter type of right is much more important when it comes to the actual granting of social benefits, and also that the character of social rights at the level of material constitutional law remains, generally speaking, doubtful. The reason for this is that any provision of social benefits not only requires state intervention but, in most cases, needs a certain public infrastructure. Regardless of the specific type of social benefits scheme,[29] it has to be based on up-to-date, specific legal relations between an administrative body—whether this be an undertaking or governmental body—and the individual beneficiary. In a nutshell, and despite a long-standing discussion on the nature and function of social human rights,[30] this is why many of those rights dealing with social security, social assistance, and other forms of social protection have a rather programmatic character[31] and can only be properly understood by taking their institutional and political context into account.[32]

b) Interplay between different legal levels
aa) It is the responsibility and within the competence of states to adopt and to implement social protection systems. Against this background, the most important source of law that may be applied in order to steer and control legal activities in this field is national constitutional law. How this works in practice depends very much on two circumstances. First, on a doctrinal approach, namely on the question of what legal effect follows from social rights according to national case law.[33] As already said, this might be a programmatic one, and in many cases courts do not derive rights to specific social benefits from constitutional social rights but they may be prepared to acknowledge some enforceable individual position and to protect such a position via the principle of proportionality or the assumption that a minimum core must always be left untouched. Second, and more importantly, there are very different legal cultures as far as the role of constitutional control is concerned. In Scandinavian countries, it does not play a role at all. When, for example, the Swedish old-age security system underwent a far-reaching structural reform,[34]

---

[29] See for typologies Neville Harris, 'The Shape and Characteristics of Social Security Today' in Neville Harris (ed), *Social Security Law in Context* (OUP 2000) 156 et seq; Ulrich Becker, 'Das Sozialrecht; Systematisierung, Verortung und Institutionalisierung' in Franz Ruland, Ulrich Becker, and Peter Axer (eds), *Sozialrechtshandbuch* (6th edn, Nomos 2018) 51, 57–60.

[30] See Christian Tomuschat, *Human Rights. Between Idealism and Realism* (3rd edn, OUP 2014) 136–48; in our context also Ignacio Saiz, 'Rights in Recession? Challenges for Economic and Social Rights Enforcement in Times of Crisis' (2209) Journal of Human Rights Practice 1, 277.

[31] And also why 'soft law' plays a considerable, or at least supplementary, role in implementation, see Alain Supiot, 'The Position of Social Security in the System of International Labor Standards' (2006) 2 Comp. Lab. L. & Pol'y. J. 27, 113, 116–18.

[32] See also Hirschl (n 21) 185. Of course, one may also argue that rights depend in a much more general way on a certain embeddedness in societal structures, see Christopher Thornhill, 'The Future of the State' in Kjaer, Teubner, and Febbrajo (n 17) 357, 381–84.

[33] See eg Portugal Quirin Vergho, *Soziale Sicherheit in Portugal und ihre verfassungsrechtlichen Grundlagen* (Nomos 2010) 251–300, 314–19.

[34] See Peter A Köhler, 'Die Reform der Alterssicherung in Schweden' in Becker and others (n 23) 691.

this had been prepared through the meticulous work of a standing commission of many years, but it had never been challenged before a court. To the contrary, nearly all welfare reforms taking place in Germany are subject to a constitutional law debate. One can assume that those different approaches on the relation between political decisions and constitutional law are strongly influenced by the national institutional background, even if the direction of this influence and all questions of causality remain to be investigated. Clearly, it makes a difference whether persons struck by a cutback in social rights have access to courts, how easily this can be realised, and whether courts are prepared to question the constitutionality of a reform and, if necessary, to correct the legislator.

bb) Because of its supremacy, EU law prevails over national law. Generally speaking, it is applied by national authorities and courts as forming part of one jurisdiction, and the reservations made by some national constitutional courts[35] do not play a role in the context of welfare reforms.

On the other hand, the EU has few powers to regulate social protection,[36] and there is no secondary legislation that would have a noticeable impact in this field. That does not mean that the European integration process did not have a so-called 'social dimension'. To the contrary, the EU has been establishing its own social policy since the 1970s.[37] Yet, while the relevant measures mostly come in the form of legally non-binding documents, we can observe a certain change in attitude towards substantial aspects of social protection. Whereas the most important EU social security legislation, the coordination regulations,[38] do not set up a common scheme of social security but allow different national social security schemes to exist,[39] there are two sources in particular that try to set up a normative framework for social protection. The first is the EU Charter of Fundamental Rights (EUCFR).[40] Within its chapter on 'Solidarity', it addresses social protection of families (Article 33), social security, and social assistance (Article 34) as well as healthcare (Article 35). It is clear that the respective provisions do not contain enforceable social rights for EU citizens, given the scope of application of the EUCFR[41] and the differentiation between 'rights' and

---

[35] See the case law of the Bundesverfassungsgericht (German Federal Constitutional Court), Decision of 30 June 2009 (*Lisbon*), 123 BVerfGE 267, paras 238; Decision of 6 July 2010 (*Honeywell*), 126 BVerfGE 268, paras 54; Decision of 14 January 2014 (*OMT*), 134 BVerfGE 366, paras 27.

[36] See art 153(2) TFEU.

[37] See Becker (n 13) 19, 21–31; for the development of social policy over the early decades of the Union and its open prospects Mark Kleinmann, *A European Welfare State?* (Palgrave 2002).

[38] Council Regulation (EC) No 3 on social security for migrant workers [1958] OJ 561/58; Council Regulation (EC) 1408/71 of 14 June 1971 on the application of social security schemes to employed persons, to self-employed persons and to members of their families moving within the Community [1971] OJ L149/2; Regulation (EC) 883/2004 of the European Parliament and of the Council of 29 April 2004 on the coordination of social security systems [2004] OJ L166/1.

[39] Standing case law, see eg ECJ of 7 December 2017, Case C-189/16 *Zaniewicz-Dybeck v Pensionsmyndigheten* [2017] ECLI:EU:C:2017:946, para 38.

[40] [2012] OJ C326/02.

[41] Art 51(1) sent 1 EUCFR; see ECJ of 6 March 2014, Case C-206/13 *Regione Siragusa v Regione Sicilia* [2014] ECLI:EU:C:2014:126, paras 24 and 25.

'principles'.[42] However, they may be used both in the context of interpreting EU law[43] and in order to put an emphasis on social rights as legitimate interests and grounds for justifying the restriction of economic rights.[44] In this sense, they are not so much part of a (new) European layer of law that—in a hierarchy of legal norms—lifts social rights up to a supranational level as they are helping to 'defend' national social rights against the integration dynamics of an internal (European) market that is driven primarily by economics. In practice, the EUCFR did not play a noteworthy role when it came to designing and negotiating financial assistance programmes for Member States (see, for these programmes, III.2)—although recent case law of the European Court of Justice (ECJ) makes it clear that the EUCFR is applicable when a Member State tries to comply with commitments made to the European Union set out in a Memorandum of Understanding.[45] That is one of the reasons why the EU organs solemnly proclaimed the so-called European Pillar of Social Rights at the Gothenburg Social Summit in November 2017.[46] According to the Commission, this document is 'about delivering new and more effective rights for citizens', although, at the same time, it describes its content as 'key principles'.[47] Indeed, the 'Pillar' is not as hard as stone but is a legally non-binding social policy programme.[48] Nevertheless, it formulates joint expectations for substantial social protection, and this comes as a comprehensive catalogue. The Pillar serves as a sort of concretisation of the EUCFR social rights, and as a basis for further action at EU level. Even in this respect, it will not lead to genuine EU social protection law as it does not shift the powers towards the EU.[49] But it may set future standards, and it may also develop a certain role in the context dealt with by this book, as the Pillar of Social Rights is also aimed at reacting to 'the social consequences of the crisis'.[50]

---

[42] Art 51(1) sent 2, art 52(2) and (5) EUCFR.

[43] And also contain subjective rights, see eg for art 31(2) EUCFR (annual period of paid leave) ECJ of 6 November 2018, Joined Cases C-569/16 and C-570/16 *Bauer and Willmeroth* ECLI:EU:C:2018:871.

[44] See for this construction Ulrich Becker, 'Schutz und Implementierung von EU-Sozialstandards' in Ulrich Becker, Bernd von Maydell, and Angelika Nußberger (eds), *Die Implementierung internationaler Sozialstandards* (Nomos 2006) 139, 178.

[45] ECJ of 13 June 2017, Case C-258/14 *Florescu* [2017] ECLI:EU:C:2017:448, paras 44–48.

[46] See for the booklet: https://ec.europa.eu/commission/sites/beta-political/files/social-summit-european-pillar-social-rights-booklet_en.pdf.

[47] Commission, 'The European Pillar of Social Rights in 20 Principles' <https://ec.europa.eu/commission/priorities/deeper-and-fairer-economic-and-monetary-union/european-pillar-social-rights/european-pillar-social-rights-20-principles_en> accessed 10 October 2019.

[48] See for a detailed analysis of its contents, character, and functions Ulrich Becker, 'Die Europäische Säule sozialer Rechte' (2018) 73 ZöR 525.

[49] The most prominent point on the present social protection agenda also comes as a non-binding instrument; see Council Recommendation of 8 November 2019 on 'access to social protection for workers and the self-employed' (2019/C 387/1).

[50] See recit 10 sent 2: 'However, the social consequences of the crisis have been far-reaching—from youth and long-term unemployment to the risk of poverty—and addressing those consequences remains an urgent priority.' And the implementation measures will play a role within the EMU; see for the plan to discuss progress in the implementation of access to social protection 'in line with the European Semester and the Open Method of Coordination for Social Inclusion and Social Protection' Council Recommendation (n 49), recit 21.

cc) Whereas EU law comes, as far as social protection is concerned, mainly in the form of soft law, international treaties contain some legally binding obligations in this field. To a small extent, this holds true for the European Convention on Human Rights (ECHR) (see II.2.c), which has a relatively strong impact on national policies as it can rely on its own institutions for implementation including the case law of the European Court of Human Rights (ECtHR).[51] Specific legal sources of social rights are the European Social Charter (ESC) of 1961 with its revision of 1996 (ESCRev)[52] and the International Covenant on Economic, Social, and Cultural Rights (ICESCR) of 1966. Although their binding character is undisputable, the role they actually play within domestic legal orders remains, to a large extent, in the hands of national institutions,[53] due to the weakness of international implementation and the openness of social rights. As a result, it is unsurprising that the ICESCR did not have any significant impact in the context of welfare reforms driven by the financial crisis, even though it should, as a matter of general principle, gain influence in exactly those times.[54]

c) Mechanisms: dimensions of human rights

Constitutional protection in a material sense through human rights is not, even in the field of social protection and social rights, restricted to the application of social human rights. Three different mechanisms of protection can be distinguished, and they each relate to a specific factual situation (in particular with regard to the implementation of social rights through legislation) and address a specific type of human rights, or at least a specific dimension of those rights.

First, human rights can oblige states to introduce (and to maintain) social protection systems. In every European constitution, specific constitutional provisions design, at least in general terms, the functions that are to be exercised by the welfare state in order to guarantee its citizens social protection. Some of them contain a respective general obligation in the form of a welfare or 'social state' clause. And most constitutions lay down social rights. As already mentioned, these may not provide for subjective rights (see II.2.a), but they will have a certain effect of 'fine-tuning' general welfare state obligations (see II.2.d). In addition, human rights aimed at protecting individual freedoms can also serve as a basis for a right to benefits.[55]

---

[51] See Christian Walter, 'Der Internationale Menschenrechtsschutz zwischen Konstitutionalisierung und Fragmentierung' (2015) 75 ZaöRV 753, 763–64.

[52] ETS No 35 and No 163. The ESCRev, and also the Additional Protocol to the ESC Providing for a System of Collective Complaints, ETS No 158, have not yet been ratified by all EU Member States (see: https://www.coe.int/en/web/european-social-charter).

[53] See Ulrich Becker, 'Der europäische soziale Rechtsstaat: Entstehung, Entwicklung und Perspektiven' in Julia Iliopoulos-Strangas (ed), *Die Zukunft des Sozialen Rechtsstaates in Europa* (Nomos 2015) 101, 114.

[54] See Mary Dowell-Jones 'The Sovereign Bond Markets and Socio-Economic Rights: Understanding the Challenge of Austerity' in Eibe Riedel, Gilles Giacca, and Christophe Golay (eds), *Economic, Social, and Cultural Rights in International Law* (OUP 2014) 51, 81–84.

[55] See for the right to human dignity (art 1(1) Basic Law) the famous decision of the Bundesverfassungsgericht (German Federal Constitutional Court), Decision of 9 February 2010

Second, constitutional provisions protect legal positions held by persons in specific situations of need, and thus the individual's claims under social security law. In this sense, the legislature does not remain entirely free to question a once gained position. Constitutional law may also protect the functioning of a social security system if this system is mandatory and affiliation to it can be regarded as a restriction of a legally protected individual freedom. In both cases, the so-called negative dimension of human rights is relevant, which refers to the function of those rights in protecting against any restrictions of rights to social benefits.[56] This is the reason why cases on cutbacks of social rights, and in particular of pension rights, play such an important role when it comes to controlling social policy retrenchments by way of constitutional law.[57] Of course, constitutional law does not restrain states from reforming their social security systems but, in the first place, calls for objective grounds and restrictions that pass a proportionality test. A provision which seems to be of specific importance in this context is the right to property. Its role is, especially in a European perspective, strengthened by the case law of the ECtHR. According to this, individual social security positions, understood as the promise of a state to grant a social benefit, can fall under the scope of article 1 of protocol no 1 to the ECHR.[58] The ECJ takes the same position on the interpretation of article 17 of the EUCFR.[59] The outcome of this assumption very much depends on the assessment of a given position and severance of the restrictions to these provisions. For example, the German Federal Constitutional Court had the opportunity to decide on more than 130 cases in which restrictions of pension rights had to be examined, but it has, over the last twenty years, not considered any of these restrictions unconstitutional. It is noteworthy, however, that the ECtHR has stressed the fact that cutbacks in pension rights must not go beyond a certain limit. In previous cases it stated: 'while a total deprivation of entitlements resulting in the loss of means of subsistence would in principle amount to a violation of the right to property, the imposition of a reasonable and commensurate reduction would

---

(*Arbeitslosengeld II*), 125 BVerfGE 175; also Decision of 23 July 2014 (social assistance for asylum seekers), 132 BVerfGE 134; reference made to this case law by the High Court of Justice (England and Wales) in *R (on the application of Refugee Action) v Secretary of State for the Home Department* [2014] EWHC 1033 (Admin).

[56] See in this context Ulrich Becker and others (eds), *Security: A General Principle of Social Security Law in Europe* (Europa Law Publishing 2010).

[57] And why it is not surprising that most cases within the context of the financial crisis and social rights dealt with the protection of acquired rights, but see also Claire Kilpatrick, 'Constitutions, Social Rights and Sovereign Debt States in Europe: A Challenging New Area of Constitutional Inquiry' in Beukers and others (n 14) 279, 289–90.

[58] *Gaygusuz v Austria* App no 17371/90 (ECtHR, 16 September 1996); *Azinas v Cyprus* App no 56679/00 (ECtHR, 28 April 2004); *STEC and Others v United Kingdom* App nos 65731/01 and 65900/01 (ECtHR, 12 April 2006); see also *Stefanetti and Others v Italy* App nos 21838/10, 21849/10, 21852/10, 21855/10, 21860/10, T-21863/10, 21869/10 and 21870/10 (ECtHR, 15 April 2014).

[59] With regard to art 52(3) EUCFR, see ECJ of 13 June 2017, Case C-258/14 *Florescu* [2017] ECLI:EU:C:2017:448, paras 49–51 (right to pensions).

not'.[60] In this sense, a minimum core of social rights may be protected, and we can assume that this result leads to a certain convergence with the protection of social human rights.

Third, equality or non-discrimination rules can have a certain protective effect for rights to social benefits. Even if we understand equality or non-discrimination rules as rather formal provisions, as far as they serve for comparisons between two different legal positions and for answering the question whether the relevant differentiation is justified (or the comparison between two different factual situations and one legal position, if an obligation to draw distinctions matters), those provisions can have a considerable impact on social rights.[61] In particular, they also ask for equal treatment with respect to cutbacks in such rights, and this is why the Portuguese Constitutional Court has, in a couple of decisions, held that some cutbacks of pension rights enacted in line with the annual budget law were unconstitutional.[62]

d) Substance: guidelines for social protection

Social rights in European constitutions and the EUCFR and ESC, as well as the ICESCR, indicate what kind of social protection shall be guaranteed by states, at least in general terms. A comparative overview of the respective rights shows that these essentially refer to five different fields or issues of social protection.[63] The first is work, in the sense of the possibility to earn a living.[64] Second, there is social security and social assistance or aid, understood as the organisation of transfer payments to cover social risks and to ensure the basic minimum living standard. These issues are handled separately in a significant number of countries.[65] In their

---

[60] *Da Conceição Mateus and Santos Januário v Portugal* App nos 62235/12 and 57725/12 [2013], para 24.

[61] See eg for Hungary Viktória Fichtner-Fülöp, *Einfluss des Verfassungsrechts und des internationalen Rechts auf die Ausgestaltung der sozialen Sicherheit in Ungarn* (Nomos 2012) 347–85, 400–402.

[62] Acórdão, Decisions of 5 April 2013, 187/2013, and of 19 December 2013, 862/2013.

[63] See for details and references Becker (n 53) 101, 107–10; for a different categorisation Jung, Hirschl, and Rosevear (n 28) 1043, 1053–55.

[64] On this, see for example art 1 n 2 of the European Social Charter (both in its revised and non-revised form), which connects the concept of worker with the possibility of earning one's own living. This idea can be found in a similar form in art 26(3) sent 1 of the Czech Charter of Fundamental Rights and Basic Freedoms; it is moreover comprised in the related concept of profession, inherent to which is the element of creating and preserving one's livelihood, cf Bundesverfassungsgericht (German Federal Constitutional Court), Decision of 11 November 1958 (*Apothekenurteil*), 7 BVerfGE 377, 397.

[65] cf Finland (§ 19(1): right to indispensable subsistence and care for a life of dignity; § 19(2): right to basic subsistence in the event of unemployment, illness, and disability and during old age); Bulgaria (art 51(1): social security and social assistance); Croatia (art 57(1): provision of social insurance; art 58(1): social assistance); Cyprus (art 9: right to a decent existence and to social security); Czech Republic (art 26(3) sent 2, 30(1), 31 sent 2: support for unemployment, old age, and inability to work; health insurance; art 30(2): support in the event of material need); Italy (art 38(1): entitlement to the necessary means of subsistence in the case of incapacity to work; art 38(2): entitlement in the case of accident, illness, disability, old age, and unemployment); Malta (art 17(1): social assistance; art 17(2): social insurance); Netherlands (art 20(2): anchoring of social security; art 20(3): right to social aid in the case of inability to provide for oneself); Slovakia (art 39(1): insurance against old age/inability to work; art 39(2): general assistance in case of material need).

context, the principle (sometimes expressly mentioned) of solidarity plays a role[66] as public social security systems are based on mandatory affiliation and financial redistribution. A subitem which is also relevant for the provision of social benefits is protection for families. The third issue, health, is enshrined separately, the protection of which, however, falls under social security in the wider sense or under social protection in the narrower understanding of the term. Issues four and five, namely education and housing, usually do not fall under the latter, although they concern central social functions.

e) Procedure: separation of powers and rule of law

Although most attention is, as a rule, paid to the protective (or non-protective) effect of human rights, one should not overlook that social protection reforms during times of crisis can also have an impact on welfare state constitutions in a different way.

Social protection and, in particular, the granting of social benefits is a complex task. It requires an elaborate institutional framework, and it is based on financial redistribution that relies not only on solidarity but also on a high degree of democratic legitimisation.[67] In this regard, external pressure on social policies stemming from financial assistance already poses severe problems. They may be solved, at least in a formal perspective, if national parliaments on their part assume responsibility by enacting welfare reforms.

Yet, by so doing in the course of consolidation programmes, more specific constitutional problems may arise.[68] One can assume that when reacting to strong economic pressure and to a situation of emergency, time pressures may occur. Governments often tend to take the necessary steps as quickly as possible. This can have a considerable impact on the legislative process,[69] and especially on the involvement of parliaments. Many national constitutions contain provisions for provisional governmental actions without parliamentary debates. If such provisional acts lead to cutbacks in social rights and therefore have a considerable impact on the living conditions of people, they can have a distorting effect on the separation of powers between executive powers or governments and parliaments,[70] and they

---

[66] See for the respective case law of the Greek Council of State Maria Bakavou, 'The Greek Social Security System: Legislation, Reforms and Jurisprudence' (2017) 31 ZIAS 148, 152–54.

[67] See Becker (n 1) 1, 5–13.

[68] And also constitutional reforms (in a formal or, rather often, material sense), see Xenophon Contiades and Alkmene Fotiadou, 'How Constitutions React to the Financial Crisis' in Contiades (n 18) 9, 22–30.

[69] And also on the role of administrative agencies and their relation to the legislative powers; see for the US case Steven M Davidoff and David Zaring, 'Regulation by Deal: The Government's Response to the Financial Crisis' (2009) 61(3) Administrative Law Review 463–541.

[70] See also for the general assumption that executive powers gain importance in times of crises but that these times actually lead to enforced cooperation between the powers Stefanie Egidy, *Finanzkrise und Verfassung* (Mohr Siebeck 2019) 155–401. For a comparative analysis on Ireland and Spain see Sonia Piedrafita, 'National Parliaments' Say on the New EU Budgetary Constraints: The Case of Spain and Ireland' in Adams and others (n 16) 319, 324–40.

can violate the principle of democracy[71] as well as the rule of law. Therefore, it is necessary to look not only at the outcomes of social protection reforms but also at the procedures used for their implementation.

III. Aim and outline of the Book

1. Aim

Overall, this book seeks to address the legacy of the financial crisis on social rights, on the application of constitutional law, and on the welfare state in general. What did the welfare state look like after the countries under examination came out of the crisis? Is the legacy of the crisis in the field of social protection of everlasting purport or were reverse measures adopted immediately after? In order to answer these questions, we were interested in collecting information on the following issues:

– the relationship between financial assistance and social protection reforms, based on the assumption that there was a conditionality in this regard but also that some of the reforms had already been planned for other reasons (demography, changes in societies and labour markets, general political goals); therefore, conditionality in the sense of financial assistance impact could also mean quicker, or more efficient, implementation;
– the impact of social protection reforms on the welfare state, and in particular whether they brought about changes in the concepts, structures, or principles of social protection;
– the impact of the financial crisis and the following restrictions of social rights on the constitution, in particular concerning the protection of human rights and the division of powers, taking into account the role of (constitutional or other) courts and thus the relationship between legislation and adjudication, looking for changes in the doctrinal background of the case law (in particular with respect to the principle of proportionality), but also for shifts in the division of powers between governments and parliaments;
– the legacy of the reforms, in particular whether these reforms have lasting effects or whether they have undergone re-reforms when economic pressure subsided or became less important for social policies.[72]

---

[71] See for the case of the German financial crisis management Egidy (n 70) 656–59.

[72] This understanding of impact is from a purely normative perspective and we do not try to base our assessment on a specific set of data. See for a recent stocktaking of crisis management in EU Member States, based on macroeconomic and financial variables plus some 'social variables such as social exclusion, happiness, health expenditures and wages', Joint Research Centre, *The Resilience of EU Member States to the Financial and Economic Crisis* (Science for Policy Report, Publications Office of the EU 2018)   <http://publications.jrc.ec.europa.eu/repository/bitstream/JRC111606/jrc111606_resilience_crisis_pilot_withidentifiers.pdf> accessed 10 October 2019.

If one wants to understand the legacy of the reforms, it is crucial to combine two perspectives and to analyse both (1) the specific reforms to social protection introduced during the European financial crisis, and (2) their implications for constitutional law. Accordingly, the aim of the book is twofold. First, it documents and systematises the crisis-related reforms introduced in the field of social protection as it is broadly understood, covering old-age benefits, social assistance allowances, unemployment benefits, family benefits, and healthcare. The country reports depict the particular crisis experience of each country under investigation and link the crisis-related reforms with the overall national social policy developments. Second, the book aims to embed the reforms in social protection in the constitutional framework of each country by analysing the ways in which the application of constitutional law has changed during the crisis, and the impact that this change has had on social democracy and the welfare state. By so doing, we expect to find answers to the question of whether fundamental constitutional and democratic principles of the European welfare state—which traditionally recognises and protects social rights—were altered during the crisis.

2. Time and area under analysis

In 2008, the financial crisis started—during a period of recession that began around one year earlier—with the breakdown of Lehman Brothers and the collapse of the housing bubble in the United States of America. In a certain way, and as far as the acquisition of real estate can be seen as an economic foundation for living, it reflected a welfare state model that builds on markets and the individual freedom to take up mortgages and loans, a model that had lost part of its public support.[73] Whereas the impact of social policy remained disputed, the main and directly relevant reasons for the critical reactions of financial markets were, as a matter of fact, the investment policy of many financial institutions, with high rates of uncovered credits, and the deregulation policies in many states that allowed for this investment policy. Due to the globally closed interrelationship between the institutions and the financial markets, it did not take long for the financial crisis to reach Europe where it turned, in late 2009, into a budgetary crisis and a debt crisis.

a) Countries
The Member States of the European Union were hit by the crisis in different ways and with very different outcomes. The following chapters give an account of the

---

[73] See for the context as to lacking state guarantees and contesting the argument that social politics promoting households' access to mortgage loans had led to the crisis Herman Schwartz, 'Housing, the Welfare State, and the Global Financial Crisis: What is the Connection?' (2012) 40 Politics & Society 35.

respective situation and the developments in those states that had to face particular crisis-related problems and took respective measures:

aa) The economic crisis, which started in *Hungary* in 2007, resulted in high public debt. This forced Hungary to apply for balance-of-payments assistance from the EU and the IMF in exchange for strict fiscal policies.[74] Between then and 2010, a series of austerity measures in social security benefits were adopted. The case law of the Hungarian Constitutional Court dealt with the legality of the age limit of retirement applicable to judges.

bb) *Latvia* received financial assistance from the EU and the IMF from 2008 until 2012,[75] and between 2012 and January 2015[76] it was subject to post-programme surveillance. As a result, Latvia reduced its social protection expenditure, especially in the fields of pensions and healthcare. In this context, the Latvian Constitutional Court issued a seminal ruling on the unconstitutionality of pension reductions due to violations of the right to social security.[77]

cc) *Romania* received three balance-of-payments assistance programmes from the EU, the IMF, and other international financial institutions (2009–2011 BoP;[78] 2011–2013 BoP;[79] 2013–2015

---

[74] Council Decision (EC) 2009/102 of 4 November 2008 providing Community medium-term financial assistance for Hungary [2009] OJ L37/5; 'Memorandum of Understanding between the European Community and the Republic of Hungary' (*europa.eu*, 19 November 2008) <https://ec.europa.eu/info/sites/info/files/economy-finance/publication13495_en.pdf> accessed 10 October 2019; 'Third addendum to the Memorandum of Understanding between the European Union and the Republic of Hungary' (*europa.eu*, January 2010) <https://ec.europa.eu/info/sites/info/files/economy-finance/mou_hu_20100121_en.pdf> accessed 10 October 2019.

[75] Council Decision (EC) 2009/289 of 20 January 2009 on granting mutual assistance for Latvia [2009] OJ L79/37; Council Decision (EC) 2009/592 of 13 July 2009 amending Decision 2009/290/EC providing Community medium-term financial assistance to Latvia [2009] OJ L202/52; 'Memorandum of Understanding between the European Community and the Republic of Latvia' (*europa.eu*, 28 January 2009) <https://ec.europa.eu/info/sites/info/files/ecfin_mou_bop_latvia_en.pdf> accessed 10 October 2019; 'Fifth supplemental Memorandum of Understanding between the European Community and the Republic of Latvia' (*europa.eu*, 21 December 2011) <https://ec.europa.eu/info/sites/info/files/ecfin_20111221_latvia_mou_en.pdf> accessed 10 October 2019.

[76] Commission, 'EU BOP assistance to Latvia – first review under post-programme surveillance' (*europa.eu*, 13 June 2012) <https://ec.europa.eu/info/sites/info/files/ecfin_lv_efc_note_pps_mission_en.pdf> accessed 10 October 2019; European Commission, 'EU BOP assistance to Latvia – sixth review under post-programme surveillance' (*europa.eu*, 25 November 2014) <https://ec.europa.eu/info/sites/info/files/ecfin_lv_efc_note_6th_pps_mission_en.pdf> accessed 10 October 2019.

[77] See on the decision in a comparative perspective Kilpatrick (n 57) 279, 299.

[78] Council Decision (EC) 2009/459 of 6 May 2009 providing Community medium-term financial assistance for Romania [2009] OJ L150/8; 'Memorandum of Understanding between the European Community and Romania' (*europa.eu*, 23 June 2009) <https://ec.europa.eu/info/sites/info/files/ecfin_publication15409_en.pdf> accessed 10 October 2019; European Commission, 'European Economy: Overall assessment of the two balance-of-payments assistance programmes for Romania, 2009–2013' (*europa.eu*, Occasional Papers 156, July 2013) <http://ec.europa.eu/economy_finance/publications/occasional_paper/2013/pdf/ocp156_en.pdf> accessed 10 October 2019.

[79] Council Decision (EU) 2011/288 of 12 May 2011 providing precautionary EU medium-term financial assistance for Romania [2011] OJ L132/15; 'Memorandum of Understanding between the European Union and Romania' (*europa.eu*, 29 June 2011) <https://ec.europa.eu/info/sites/info/files/ecfin_20110629-mou-romania_en.pdf> accessed 10 October 2019; Commission (n 76).

BoP[80]). Within the framework of this financial assistance, Romania reduced a number of social security benefits. Of particular interest in the Romanian case are the rulings of the Constitutional Court on the constitutionality of reductions in pension and unemployment benefits due to the threat of economic instability and the urgent need to reduce the budgetary deficit.

dd) In an attempt to contain the crisis, *Greece* signed three economic adjustment programmes with the European Commission, the European Central Bank (ECB), and the IMF in 2010,[81] 2012,[82] and 2015.[83] Within the framework of these agreements, Greece had to implement stringent social policies in return for financial support, such as pension reforms, reductions in existing old-age benefits, healthcare reforms, and reductions in salaries in the public sector.[84] The majority of these austerity measures were brought before the Greek Council of State and the European Committee of Social Rights as well as the European Court of Human Rights, the latter of which had to decide on the compatibility of the cuts with the fundamental principles of constitutional law.

ee) The banking and public financial crisis made its first appearance in *Ireland* in late 2008 and led to a crisis management policy. In the period of 2011–2013,[85] Ireland received financial assistance from the EU and the IMF with a strong emphasis on austerity with regard to public expenditures for social protection. And Ireland was the birthplace of the ECJ *Pringle* case , concerning the issue as to whether the bailout fund of the European

---

[80] Council Decision (EU) 2013/531 of 22 October 2013 providing precautionary Union medium-term financial assistance to Romania [2013] OJ L286/1; 'Memorandum of Understanding between the European Union and Romania' (*europa.eu*, 6 November 2013) <https://ec.europa.eu/info/sites/info/files/ecfin_20131106_mou_ecfin_en.pdf> accessed 10 October 2019; Commission, 'Balance of Payments Assistance Programme, Romania, 2013–2015, European Economy' (*europa.eu*, Institutional Paper 012, November 2015) <https://publications.europa.eu/en/publication-detail/-/publication/1daea1db-cbd3-11e5-a4b5-01aa75ed71a1/language-en> accessed 10 October 2019.

[81] Commission, 'European Economy, The Economic Adjustment Programme for Greece' (*europa.eu*, Occasional Papers 61, May 2010) <http://ec.europa.eu/economy_finance/publications/occasional_paper/2010/pdf/ocp61_en.pdf> accessed 10 October 2019.

[82] Commission, 'European Economy, The Second Economic Adjustment Programme for Greece' (*europa.eu*, Occasional Papers 94, March 2012) <http://ec.europa.eu/economy_finance/publications/occasional_paper/2012/pdf/ocp94_en.pdf> accessed 10 October 2019.

[83] 'Financial Assistance Facility Agreement between European Stability Mechanism and the Hellenic Republic and the Bank of Greece and Hellenic Financial Stability Fund' (*europa.eu*, 19 August 2015) <https://www.esm.europa.eu/sites/default/files/2015-08-19gr-esm-ffapublicationversion.pdf> accessed 10 October 2019; 'Memorandum of Understanding between the European Commission acting on behalf of the European Stability Mechanism and the Hellenic Republic and the Bank of Greece' (*europa.eu*, August 2015) <https://ec.europa.eu/info/sites/info/files/01_mou_20150811_en1.pdf> accessed 10 October 2019.

[84] Commission (n 80) 12 et seq; Commission (n 81) 31 et seq.

[85] Council Implementing Decision (NLE) 2010/0351 of 7 December 2010 on granting Union financial assistance to Ireland; Commission, 'European Economy, The Economic Adjustment Programme for Ireland' (*europa.eu*, Occasional Papers 76, February 2011) <https://publications.europa.eu/en/publication-detail/-/publication/49d48cfd-4680-4938-9780-65e9468f5a9e/language-en> accessed 10 October 2019.

Stability Mechanism ceded sovereignty, amounting to a breach of the Irish Constitution.[86] Although in December 2013 Ireland completed the programme by successfully achieving its fiscal targets, the majority of the social policy reforms seem to have had an ongoing impact.

ff) A restrictive framework for social protection benefits also resulted from the bailout agreement between *Portugal* and the EU and the IMF.[87] Some of the measures linked to the bailout were pension indexation, nominal cuts of pension benefits, taxation of all types of social transfers in cash, and increases of co-payments in the healthcare system. Against this background, the Portuguese Constitutional Court was very active and issued several rulings concerning the violation of the principles of equality and legitimate expectations in a series of reductions in pension benefits, and other courts also declared specific measures of social protection reforms as unconstitutional.

gg) In *Cyprus*, the social security reforms were strongly influenced by the financial crisis that hit the country in July 2011, when Cypriot banks experienced serious losses due to their exposure to Greek bonds. Against this background, an economic adjustment programme was signed between the European Commission, the ECB, the IMF, and the Cyprian State in 2013.[88] The financial assistance conditions included in this economic adjustment programme stipulated a pension reform designed to protect the sustainability of the system, the reduction of healthcare expenditures, and the introduction of a national healthcare system.[89]

hh) Although *Italy* did not formally receive financial assistance from the EU or the IMF, the financial crisis had a great impact on its already critical fiscal situation. In 2011, while in the midst of a severe recession, Italy received informal pressure from the ECB to reduce its public expenditure as a way

---

[86] ECJ of 27 November 2012, Case C-370/12 *Thomas Pringle v Government of Ireland and Others* [2012] ECLI:EU:C:2012:756.

[87] 'Portugal: Memorandum of Understanding of Specific Economic Policy Conditionality' (*europa. eu*, 17 May 2011) <http://ec.europa.eu/economy_finance/eu_borrower/mou/2011-05-18-mou-portugal_en.pdf> accessed 10 October 2019; Council of the European Union Press release of 17 May 2011 <https://www.consilium.europa.eu/uedocs/cms_data/docs/pressdata/en/ecofin/122047. pdf> accessed 10 October 2019; Commission, 'European Economy, The Economic Adjustment Programme for Portugal 2011–2014' (*europa.eu*, Occasional Papers 202, October 2014) <https:// ec.europa.eu/economy_finance/publications/occasional_paper/2014/pdf/ocp202_en.pdf> accessed 10 October 2019.

[88] 'Financial Assistance Facility Agreement between European Stability Mechanism and the Republic of Cyprus and Central Bank of Cyprus' (*europa.eu*, 8 May 2013) <https://www.esm.europa.eu/sites/ default/files/esm_ffa_cyprus_publication_version_final.pdf> accessed 10 October 2019; Commission, 'European Economy, The Economic Adjustment Programme for Cyprus' (*europa.eu*, Occasional Papers 149, May 2013) <https://www.esm.europa.eu/sites/default/files/theeconomicadjustmentprogrammefo rcyprus.pdf> accessed 10 October 2019.

[89] Commission (n 87) 39 et seq.

to combat the high Italian public debt and deficit. As a result, Italy adopted a number of legislative amendments aiming at the reduction of public expenditure on social protection.

ii) *Spain* received financial assistance from the ESM only for the recapitalisation of the country's banking sector.[90] However, due to high public debt and deficit, reductions in the amount of unemployment benefits and healthcare services were introduced and healthcare coverage shifted from universal to employment-dependent. Those measures have become a rather rich source of case law in Spanish courts on the constitutionality of cutbacks in social rights.

b) Time frame

The period of our investigations reaches into the present as it is an ongoing question whether, and to what extent, changes in social rights had an impact on the welfare state as such. This question asks for a comparison, and it starts, in a certain way, from an inherent assumption, namely that the recent era of crisis-driven reforms is already over. In reality, this is an open issue. In summer 2017, the European Commission announced that the EU was back on its road to recovery, ten years after the start of the crisis.[91] But the actual economic situation differs from one Member State to another. Therefore, it is helpful to use a further and more formal criterion in order to roughly mark the period of specific political pressure stemming from the financial crisis, and that is the time span between the first involvement of international institutions in crisis management and its formal coming to an end. The respective dates are quite different. Whereas, for example, Ireland completed the EU–IMF financial assistance programme in December 2013, it took more time for Greece to complete the ESM stability support programme, ie not until August 2018. And, in any case, this does not mean that the financial crisis and the hardships that came along with it are over.[92] Therefore, the country reports will also include observations on the aftermath of the crisis-related reforms.

---

[90] Commission, 'European Economy, The Financial Sector Adjustment Programme for Spain' (*europa.eu*, 118 Occasional Papers, October 2012) 25 et seq <http://ec.europa.eu/economy_finance/publications/occasional_paper/2012/pdf/ocp118_en.pdf> accessed 10 October 2019.

[91] European Commission Press release of 9 August 2017 <http://europa.eu/rapid/press-release_IP-17-2401_en.htm> accessed 10 October 2019.

[92] See for Greece the second enhanced surveillance report, Commission, 'Enhanced Surveillance – Greece, April 2019' COM (2019) 170 final, and with respect to social protection ('social welfare') the commitments of the Greek authorities set out in the annex to the Eurogroup statement of 22 June 2018, no 2 <https://www.consilium.europa.eu/media/35749/z-councils-council-configurations-ecofin-eurogroup-2018-180621-specific-commitments-to-ensure-the-continuity-and-completion-of-reforms-adopted-under-the-esm-programme_2.pdf> accessed 10 October 2019.

3. Structure of the country reports

The short overview on the country-specific background of crisis-driven reforms shows that each Member State necessarily had its own experience. Consequently, the following country reports are designed to 'tell their story', underlining the particularities of each national 'case', ie what is remarkable as regards the reactions of each country. In order for this to be achieved in a way that is not distortive for the coherence of the book, the chapters follow common general guidelines on the structure and the research themes to be developed, as far as this was relevant. Each report entails two big parts which connect the specific reforms of social protection laws with the broader constitutional framework of each country.

The first part of every country report presents the background of the reforms in social protection, and explains how the crisis-induced reforms came into existence and how they interacted with processes of reforms that had already existed before the crisis. In this respect, light is shed on the role of international and European actors especially as to their potential to influence the national responses to the financial crisis. After a very short introduction to the social security and healthcare system of the respective country (structure, financing), each report systematically unfolds the structural reforms and cuts introduced in the wake of the crisis. They cover different fields of social protection, ie old-age benefits, social assistance allowances, unemployment benefits, family benefits, and healthcare, as far as this is appropriate and relevant.

The second part of the country reports explores the impact of the crisis-related reforms in social protection on constitutional law and human rights. Particular attention is paid to the procedural particularities that might have occurred due to the adoption of the crisis reforms in each country. More precisely, it is investigated how contextual parameters, such as time pressure and budgetary constraints, have influenced the reaction of the national legal order (governments, parliaments, courts) and what instruments states used in order to respond to the time pressure (eg legislative decrees). Phenomena such as informality, lack of parliamentary control, and the rise of executive power to the detriment of the parliament are critically presented as indicators for the lack of democratic legitimacy in times of crisis.

Given that the majority of national courts issued a series of rulings on the conformity of the reforms with constitutional law, our project aims to first of all present the case law of each country in a way that explains the role of constitutional law during the crisis. At this point, it is worth noting that, while the case law of the Greek, Italian, Portuguese, and Spanish courts is, at least partially, quite well-known and discussed,[93] and also underwent some judicial control by the European

---

[93] See eg Cristina Fasone, 'Constitutional Courts Facing the Euro Crisis: Italy, Portugal and Spain in a Comparative Perspective' (EU Working Papers, MWP 2014/25) 17–50 <http://cadmus.eui.eu/handle/1814/33859> accessed 10 October 2019; Ulrich Becker, 'Security from a Legal Perspective' (2015) 3 Rivista del Diritto della Sicurezza Sociale 515, 519–21.

Court of Human Rights,[94] this does not hold true for all national courts that are included in the project. For example, the Latvian Constitutional Court has produced a vast collection of case law during the crisis that is not only little-known internationally but also rarely discussed domestically. The same holds true for case law produced in similarly small countries, such as Cyprus. When critically assessing the case law, we put emphasis on how institutional and procedural conditions and actual access to courts, or even the mere existence of a constitutional court, influenced the case law produced. We are also interested in finding out what the constitutional bases of the courts' decisions were and whether the absence of social rights in the constitution was an obstacle to the protection of social interests. A point of specific interest is to trace possible changes in the concrete application of constitutional law by courts, such as the use of the proportionality test. For example, the Greek and Portuguese courts often mentioned the temporal character of the measures as an element in favour of the proportionality of the interference caused, and they also made reference to the severity of the financial crisis.[95] Lastly, the country reports assess the actual implementation of the courts' decisions, as well as the reactions of other branches of power and of international lenders to the national case law.

---

[94] See eg concerning the deletion of a thirteenth and fourteenth rate of old-age pension benefits in Greece and Portugal *Koufaki and Adedy v Greece* App nos 57665/12 and 57657/12 (ECtHR, 7 May 2013); *Da Conceição Mateus and Santos Januário v Portugal* App nos 62235/12 and 57725/12 (ECtHR, 8 October 2013).

[95] See for an analysis of the early case law in Greece on cutbacks in old-age security Dafni Diliagka, *The Legality of Public Pension Reforms in Times of Financial Crisis* (Nomos 2018) 259–69.

2

Human Rights Obligations of European Financial Assistance Mechanisms

Anastasia Poulou

I. Introduction

Having been affected by the European financial crisis that erupted in 2008, several EU Member States required financial assistance beyond that available in the financial markets. In order to access financial assistance and to unlock successive tranches of bailout funds, EU Member States had to adopt structural adjustment programmes aiming, inter alia, at the reduction of public expenditure. As a consequence, a number of social security benefits were reduced and a great number of structural reforms were introduced, since expenditure on social security benefits and public healthcare was considered to have a strong impact on the public budget's macroeconomic balances. In this vein, the crisis management measures introduced in the wake of the European financial crisis constitute a new and highly significant source of social protection law for the countries involved.

The nine EU Member States most seriously affected by the demands for rapid fiscal consolidation and structural reforms can be classified into three groups. The first group comprises Hungary, Latvia, and Romania, which—as non-eurozone Member States—received financial assistance from the EU, the International Monetary Fund (IMF), and the World Bank in the form of a balance of payments

Anastasia Poulou, *Human Rights Obligations of European Financial Assistance Mechanisms* In: *European Welfare State Constitutions after the Financial Crisis.* Edited by: Ulrich Becker and Anastasia Poulou, Oxford University Press (2020).
© The Contributors. DOI: 10.1093/oso/9780198851776.003.0002

tied to conditionality of structural reforms.[1] The second group comprises the Member States of the Economic and Monetary Union (EMU) that entered into an economic adjustment programme, namely Greece, Ireland, Portugal, and Cyprus. The third group consists of Italy and Spain, which received instructions with regard to the reduction of social security benefits, even though the crisis management measures were not officially prescribed by supranational organisations. For example, the European Central Bank (ECB) informally put pressure on Italy to introduce reductions in their public expenditure, while Spain received financial assistance from the European Stability Mechanism (ESM) for the recapitalisation of its banking sector.

Despite their differences, these financial assistance schemes all combined supranational and international legal instruments and institutions. New financial assistance mechanisms, such as the European Financial Stability Facility (EFSF) and ESM, were created under international law and all financial assistance packages included the participation of the IMF. The hybrid nature of this European financial assistance raises the question of whether the actors involved in the award of the assistance are bound by EU and international human rights.

II. The EU financial assistance mechanisms

The decisions to grant financial support to Hungary (2008), Latvia (2008), and Romania (2009) were the first responses to the unfolding financial crisis in the EU. These countries are of particular interest since, to a great extent, they served as precedents for the bailout of eurozone Member States. According to article 143(1) and (3) of the Treaty on the Functioning of the EU (TFEU), Member States outside of the euro area might be granted financial assistance under certain conditions. Based on this article, the Medium-Term Financial Assistance (MTFA) Facility was established in 1988 by Council Regulation (EEC) 1969/88.[2] It was then modified in 2002 by Council Regulation (EC) 332/2002,[3] which sets out the details of the MTFA Facility. The Regulation requires the MTFA to be linked to the fulfilment of economic policy conditions, which are defined by the Council, acting by qualified majority on a proposal from the Commission.[4] On the basis of this decision, the Commission concludes with the Member State a Memorandum of Understanding (MoU), monitors compliance with the conditions, and decides the release of further instalments.[5]

---

[1] The World Bank did not participate in Romania's balance-of-payments programme.

[2] See Regulation (EEC) 1969/88 of the Council of 24 June 1988 establishing a single facility providing medium-term financial assistance for Member States' balances of payments [1988] OJ L178/1.

[3] See Regulation (EC) 332/2002 of the Council of 18 February 2002 establishing a facility providing medium-term financial assistance for Member States' balances of payments [2002] OJ L53/1.

[4] Art 3(2)(b) and art 8 Regulation (EC) 332/2002.

[5] Art 5 Regulation (EC) 332/2002. For more details on the role of the Commission in the MTFA facility see Michael Bauer and Stefan Becker, 'The Unexpected Winner of the Crisis: The European

In the midst of the financial crisis, the Council raised the loan ceiling of €12 billion anticipated in Regulation 332/2002 to €25 billion in December 2008[6] and then to €50 billion in May 2009.[7] The first country to receive financial assistance on the basis of Regulation 332/2002 was Hungary.[8] The balance-of-payments loan was up to €6.5 billion and was actually lowered to €5.5 billion. More importantly, Hungary was also the first country to receive financial assistance under the EU's MTFA Facility and the IMF.[9] The standby agreement with the IMF approved a loan of up to €12.5 billion, of which €8.7 billion was actually disbursed. The EU–IMF cooperation initiated new procedures to facilitate their joint missions negotiating financial assistance conditions and the monitoring of compliance. Latvia and Romania were the next non-eurozone states after Hungary to receive financial assistance from the MTFA Facility and the IMF. Latvia was offered a balance-of-payments loan of up to €3.1 billion, of which €2.9 billion was eventually disbursed.[10] The EU financial assistance package was complemented by a loan of around €1.7 billion from the IMF and €0.4 billion from the World Bank. In 2009 Romania received its first financial assistance programme of up to €5 billion under the MTFA Facility alongside €13 billion from the IMF and €1 billion from the World Bank.[11] In 2011 a follow-up joint EU/IMF precautionary financial assistance programme was requested to support the relaunch of economic growth, which consisted of up to €1.4 billion from the MTFA Facility and €3.5 billion from the IMF.[12] Finally, a third precautionary programme of €2 billion was agreed in 2013 and ran until 2015.[13]

When the financial crisis escalated in 2010, eurozone states started to become dependent on financial assistance beyond that available in the financial markets.

Commission's Strengthened Role in Economic Governance' [2014] Journal of European Integration 213, 217.

[6] See Council Regulation (EC) 1360/2008 of 2 October 2008 amending Regulation (EC) 332/2002 establishing a facility providing medium-term financial assistance for Member States' balances of payment [2008] OJ L352/11.

[7] See Council Regulation (EC) 431/2009 of 18 May 2009 amending Regulation (EC) 332/2002 establishing a facility providing medium-term financial assistance for Member States' balances of payments [2009] OJ L128/1.

[8] See Council Decision 2009/103/EC of 4 November 2008 providing Community medium-term financial assistance for Hungary [2009] OJ L37/5.

[9] Susanne Lütz and Matthias Kranke, 'The European Rescue of the Washington Consensus? EU and IMF Lending to Central and Eastern European Countries' [2014] Review of International Political Economy 310, 311.

[10] See Council Decision 2009/290/EC of 20 January 2009 providing Community medium-term financial assistance for Latvia [2009] OJ L79/39.

[11] See Council Decision 2009/459/EC of 6 May 2009 providing Community medium-term financial assistance for Romania [2009] OJ L150/8.

[12] See Council Decision 2011/288/EU of 12 May 2011 providing precautionary EU medium-term financial assistance for Romania [2011] OJ L132/15.

[13] See Council Decision 2013/531/EU of 22 October 2013 providing precautionary Union medium-term financial assistance to Romania [2013] OJ L286/1.

The quest for instruments to address the eurozone crisis brought a European constitutional crisis to the fore: the EU did not possess appropriate mechanisms to help the states in need and to guarantee financial stability within the EMU. As a reaction, the European Financial Stabilisation Mechanism (EFSM) was introduced, a new financial assistance mechanism modelled on the MTFA Facility.[14] Established on the basis of article 122(2) of the TFEU, the EFSM was an emergency funding mechanism reliant upon funds raised on the financial markets and guaranteed by the European Commission using the budget of the European Union as collateral. During its short-lived existence, the EFSM provided a loan of €22.5 billion to Ireland, €26 billion to Portugal, and a bridging loan of €7.16 billion to Greece.

The Member State seeking Union financial assistance had to discuss with the Commission, in liaison with the ECB, an assessment of its financial needs and submit a draft economic and financial adjustment programme to the Commission and the Economic and Financial Committee.[15] In practice, in all cases of financial assistance provided by the EFSM, the adjustment programme was drafted by the Member State in consultation with the so-called Troika, namely the Commission, the ECB, and the IMF. The decision to grant a loan under the EFSM was adopted by the Council, acting by a qualified majority on a proposal from the Commission.[16] Each Decision of the Council to grant a loan encompasses the general economic policy conditions that are attached to the Union's financial assistance, as defined by the Commission in consultation with the ECB, and an approval of the adjustment programme prepared by the beneficiary Member State to meet the economic conditions attached to the Union financial assistance.[17]

Moreover, the EFSM Regulation explicitly states that the Commission and the beneficiary Member State shall conclude an MoU detailing the general economic policy conditions laid down by the Council.[18] Although the EFSM Regulation mentions only the Commission as a negotiation partner, in practice the ECB and the IMF also participate in the preparation of the MoU. The loan is usually disbursed in instalments.[19] The release of further instalments is decided by the Commission on the basis of verifying whether the economic policy of the beneficiary Member State accords with its adjustment programme and with the conditions laid down by the Council.[20]

---

[14] See Council Regulation (EU) 407/2010 of 11 May 2010 establishing a European financial stabilisation mechanism [2010] OJ L118/1.
[15] Art 3(1) Regulation 407/2010.
[16] Art 3(2) Regulation 407/2010.
[17] Art 3(3)(b), (c) and (4)(b), (c) Regulation 407/2010.
[18] Art 3(5) Regulation 407/2010.
[19] Art 4(1) Regulation 407/2010.
[20] Art 4(2), (3) Regulation 407/2010.

III. The applicability of the Charter to EU institutions involved in the MTFA and EFSM

Both the MTFA Facility and the EFSM are clearly EU financial assistance mechanisms: they were established through EU Regulations on the basis of the EU Treaties and have an institutional underpinning, which entrusts major tasks to EU institutions. Financial assistance conditionality is laid down in two types of legal documents: on the one hand in an MoU, and on the other hand in Decisions of the Council of the EU. The MoU is signed by the recipient state and the European Commission. As EU institutions acting under EU law, the Commission, the ECB, and the Council of the EU are undisputedly bound by EU fundamental rights when negotiating, drafting, and monitoring financial assistance conditionality. The question of the application of EU fundamental rights is only partly complicated when it comes to MoUs containing financial assistance conditions. This is because the character of the MoUs as binding legal agreements is disputed. If the MoUs are not binding legal documents, how could they be measured against human rights standards?

The legal status and effects of MoUs in the context of the MTFA (article 143 TFEU) was addressed by the Court of Justice of the EU (CJEU) in *Florescu*,[21] a case that originated in the context of the first financial assistance programme to Romania, following Council Decision 2009/458/EC.[22] The core terms of the Romanian bailout were laid out in Council Decision 2009/459/EC[23] and subsequently elaborated in the MoU concluded between the European Union, represented by the Commission, and Romania.[24] The applicants in the main proceedings were judges who also held teaching positions at the university, as the law permitted at that time. The contested measure at issue in the main proceedings prohibited the combining of the net pension with income from activities carried out in public institutions if the amount of the pension exceeded a certain threshold, fixed at the amount of the national gross average salary. The persons affected sought to argue that article 17 of the Charter (right to property) should be interpreted as precluding national legislation, such as that at issue in the main proceedings, which prohibited the combining of a net public-sector retirement pension with income from activities carried out in public institutions if the amount of the pension exceeded a certain threshold.

---

[21] For a detailed analysis of the case, see Menelaos Markakis and Paul Dermine, 'Bailouts, the Legal Status of Memoranda of Understanding, and the Scope of Application of the EU Charter: *Florescu*' [2018] CMLR 643.

[22] Council Decision 2009/458/EC of 6 May 2009 granting mutual assistance to Romania [2009] OJ L150/6.

[23] Council Decision 2009/459/EC.

[24] Memorandum of Understanding between the European Community and Romania <https://ec.europa.eu/economy_finance/publications/pages/publication15409_en.pdf> accessed 31 July 2020.

In *Florescu* the Court ruled that the MoU 'gives concrete form to an agreement between the EU and a Member State on an economic programme, negotiated by those parties, whereby that Member State undertakes to comply with predefined economic objectives in order to be able, subject to fulfilling that agreement, to benefit from financial assistance from the EU'.[25] The Court held that the legal basis of the MoU lay in article 143 of the TFEU and Regulation 332/3002 and that it was concluded, in particular, by the European Union, represented by the Commission. Hence, the CJEU reached the conclusion that the MoU 'constitutes an act of an EU institution within the meaning of 267(b) TFEU' and may thus 'be subject to interpretation by the Court' through a preliminary ruling.[26] Furthermore, the Court added that the objectives set out in article 3(5) of Decision 2009/459, as well as those set out in the MoU, were sufficiently detailed and precise to permit the inference that the purpose of the prohibition on combining a public-sector retirement pension with income from activities carried out in public institutions, stemming from Law No 329/2009, was to implement both the MoU and that Decision and, thus, EU law, within the meaning of article 51(1) of the Charter; therefore the Charter was applicable to the dispute in the main proceedings.[27]

Building on the outcome of *Florescu*, one can reach the conclusion that the MoUs concluded within the EU legal order, meaning in the MTFA and EFSM framework, are to be qualified as Union acts within the meaning of article 267(1)(b) of the TFEU and, thus, are amenable to a request for interpretation under article 267.[28] Moreover, the EU institutions involved in the making and conclusion of those MoUs are unavoidably bound to respect human rights, since the Charter definitely applies to EU institutions undertaking Union acts. More difficult is the question of whether the Charter applies to MoUs concluded in the EFSF and ESM framework, as will be shown below.

IV. The hybrid European financial assistance mechanisms

The inadequacy of the EFSM budget to combat the long-lasting eurozone crisis necessitated the creation of additional funding mechanisms. The absence of suitable EU legal instruments and the confines of a limited EU budget led eurozone countries to fall back on the intergovernmental method in developing financial assistance mechanisms. The EFSF and ESM were created outside the institutional architecture of the EU. Moreover, the introduction of a third paragraph to article

---

[25] Case C-258/14 *Eugenia Florescu and Others v Casa Judeţeana de Pensii Sibiu and Others* [2017] EU:C:2017:448, para 34.

[26] ibid, para 35.

[27] ibid, para 48.

[28] For an updated analysis of art 267 TFEU, see Nils Wahl and Luca Prete 'The Gatekeepers of 267 TFEU: On Jurisdiction and Admissibility of References for Preliminary Rulings' [2018] CMLR 511.

136 of the TFEU established the use of intergovernmentalism as a permanent option, in the context of financial assistance, within EU primary law.[29] Nevertheless, in 2013 the framework of financial assistance had an EU component added to it, namely EU Regulation 472/2013,[30] which was brought into force as part of the so-called 'Two Pack' set of reforms and which aimed to ensure consistency between financial assistance conditionality and the economic and budgetary surveillance of eurozone states. Hence, the institutional framework of assistance to eurozone members is based on two parallel sets of rules. Firstly, it is based on the intergovernmental framework of the ESM and the EFSF Agreements. Secondly, it is based on the EU framework of Regulation 472/2013.

As a result, the two financially significant European financial assistance mechanisms, the EFSF and the ESM, combine such a variety of intergovernmental and supranational elements that they defy any easy categorisation as purely EU law mechanisms, such as the EFSM, or as international financial assistance mechanisms, such as the IMF. This hybrid nature of the European financial assistance mechanisms is illustrated by both institutional and substantive links between the international and the EU legal order.

With regard to the institutional underpinning of the EFSF and the ESM, EU institutions are officially involved in two ways. Firstly, the Commission and the ECB are entrusted by both frameworks with formulating and monitoring the conditions of loan arrangements as constituent parts of the Troika.[31] The Commission, in particular, has the additional role of signing the MoU (in which the conditions are set out) on behalf of the lenders.[32] Secondly, the adoption of a Council Decision containing the conditions for financial assistance was made obligatory by article 7(2) of EU Regulation 472/2013. Thus, the Council is obliged to approve the macroeconomic adjustment programme, prepared by the recipient state and the Troika, in the form of a Council Decision.

Moreover, given that financial assistance mechanisms aim at preserving the stability of the common currency, the Eurogroup experiences a *de facto* increase in its decision-making power in the context of financial assistance. As noted by the European Court of Justice (ECJ), the Eurogroup is a forum for discussion, at ministerial level, between representatives of the euro area Member States; it meets

---

[29] Art 136(3) TFEU reads: 'The Member States whose currency is the euro may establish a stability mechanism to be activated if indispensable to safeguard the stability of the euro area as a whole. The granting of any required financial assistance under the mechanism will be made subject to strict conditionality.'

[30] Regulation (EU) 472/2013 of the European Parliament and of the Council of 21 May 2013 on the strengthening of economic and budgetary surveillance of Member States in the euro area experiencing or threatened with serious difficulties with respect to their financial stability (Two Pack Regulation) [2013] OJ L140/1.

[31] Art 13(3)(7) ESM Treaty; art 7(1)(1) and 7(4)(1) Regulation 472/2013.

[32] Art 13(4) ESM Treaty; art 7(2)(2) Regulation 472/2013.

informally without having the power to take legally binding decisions.[33] This informality added to the benefits of the forum and made it the main body to decide on the adoption of the ESM Treaty, the modalities, and the volume of the financial assistance provided by the ESM.[34] Furthermore, although the ESM and the Eurogroup are separate institutions, the composition of the ESM's Board of Governance corresponds to that of the Eurogroup, and the Eurogroup President is elected to act as the President of the Board of Governance as well.[35] As a result, the Eurogroup enjoys an additional forum for its discussions within the ESM.

Numerous substantive links exist between the intergovernmentally established financial assistance mechanisms and EU law, evident in the dual legal nature of financial assistance conditionality. The EFSF and the ESM follow similar processes for awarding financial assistance. Domestic authorities negotiate, with the Troika, the macroeconomic adjustment programmes containing the conditions of financial support. Financial assistance conditionality is then laid down in two types of legal documents: an MoU and a Decision of the Council of the EU. The MoU is signed by the recipient state and the respective body entrusted with this task by the financial assistance mechanism. In both the EFSF and the ESM the body responsible is the Commission, which signs the MoU on behalf of the euro area Member States or on behalf of the ESM respectively.[36] The IMF receives the MoU only in the form of an annex to a Letter of Intent, which is signed by the country's finance minister and the president of the central bank and is addressed to the Managing Director of the IMF.[37] The IMF itself does not sign the MoU and does not consider it a legal agreement.[38]

At the same time, the Council of the EU adopts the main lending conditions in the form of Council Decisions directed at the respective recipient State. The legal basis for these Council Decisions has varied. In the case of the first countries receiving loans through the EFSF or the ESM, namely Greece (second assistance package) and Cyprus, Council Decisions were based on the excessive

---

[33] Joined Cases C-105–109/15 P *Mallis and Others v Commission and ECB* [2016] EU:C:2016:702, para 47. See generally René Repasi, 'Judicial Protection Against Austerity Measures in the Euro Area: Ledra and Mallis' [2017] CMLR 1123. In detail on the Eurogroup, see Uwe Puetter, 'Governing Informally: The Role of the Eurogroup in EMU and the Stability and Growth Pact' [2004] Journal of European Public Policy 854; Ulrich Häde, 'Art. 137 AEUV' in Christian Calliess and Matthias Ruffert (eds), *EUV, AEUV Kommentar* (5th edn, Beck 2016); Ulrich Palm, 'Art. 137 AEUV' in Eberhard Grabitz, Meinhard Hilf, and Martin Nettesheim (eds), *Das Recht der Europäischen Union* (67th edn, Beck 2019).

[34] Manuel Sarrazin and Sven-Christian Kindler, '"Brügge sehen und sterben" – Gemeinschaftsmethode versus Unionsmethode' [2012] Integration 215.

[35] Kaarlo Tuori and Klaus Tuori, *The Eurozone Crisis: A Constitutional Analysis* (CUP 2014) 95. See art 5 ESM Treaty.

[36] Art 2(1)(a) EFSF Framework Agreement; art 13(4) ESM Treaty.

[37] IMF, *Guidelines on Conditionality*, 25 September 2002, para 10 <http://www.imf.org/External/np/pdr/cond/2002/eng/guid/092302.pdf> accessed 31 July 2020.

[38] See Joseph Gold, *The Stand-By Arrangements of the International Monetary Fund* (IMF 1970) 44; Joseph Gold, 'The Legal Character of the Fund's Stand-By Arrangements and Why it Matters' (1980) 35 IMF Pamphlet Series 1. On the legal nature of the MoU see also Anthony Aust, *Modern Treaty Law and Practice* (3rd edn, CUP 2013) 46.

deficit provisions in articles 126(6) and (9) and 136 of the TFEU.[39] While done on an ad hoc basis to begin with, the adoption of a Council Decision containing the conditions for financial assistance was made obligatory on 21 May 2013 by the Two Pack Regulation,[40] so that, in cases of assistance given after this date, Regulation 472/2013 serves as the legal basis for Council Decisions approving financial assistance conditionality in the form of a macroeconomic adjustment programme (as for Cyprus, Portugal, Ireland, and the third assistance package to Greece).[41]

In terms of content, MoUs and Council Decisions do overlap, but are not identical. The MoUs are much longer and contain a more detailed description of the financial assistance conditions than the respective Decisions, which include only their most important elements. Temporally, MoUs and Council Decisions are adopted with a difference of a few days.[42] Thus, the temporal prioritisation of the one compared to the other seems to be of negligible importance. Instead, both manifestations of financial assistance conditionality are legally treated equivalently. The loan agreements concluded between the recipient states and the respective financial assistance mechanism include an explicit reference to both MoUs and Council Decisions, making the award of the loan conditional on compliance with both legal documents.[43] As a result, the obligations of the beneficiary countries in the context of European financial assistance to abide by financial assistance conditionality arise from both international and EU legal sources.

---

[39] See Council Decision 2010/320/EU of 10 May 2010 addressed to Greece with a view to reinforcing and deepening fiscal surveillance and giving notice to Greece to take measures for the deficit reduction judged necessary to remedy the situation of excessive deficit [2010] OJ L145/6; Council Decision 2013/236/EU of 25 April 2013 addressed to Cyprus on specific measures to restore financial stability and sustainable growth [2013] OJ L141/32. See also Ulrich Häde, 'Art. 136 AEUV – eine neue Generalklausel für die Wirtschafts- und Währungsunion?' [2011] JZ 337.

[40] Art 7(2)(1) Regulation (EU) 472/2013.

[41] See Council Implementing Decision 2013/463/EU of 13 September 2013 on approving the macroeconomic adjustment programme for Cyprus and repealing Decision 2013/236/EU [2013] OJ L250/40; Council Implementing Decision 2013/704/EU of 19 November 2013 approving the update of the macroeconomic adjustment programme of Portugal [2013] OJ L322/38; Council Implementing Decision 2013/373/EU of 9 July 2013 approving the update of the macroeconomic adjustment programme of Ireland [2013] OJ L191/10; Council Implementing Decision 2015/1411/EU of 19 August 2015 approving the macroeconomic adjustment programme of Greece [2015] OJ L219/12.

[42] See eg the cases of Greece, Portugal, and Cyprus. The first Greek MoU was signed on 3 May 2010 and Council Decision 2010/320/EU was issued on 10 May 2010. The Portuguese MoU was signed on 17 May 2011 and Council Implementing Decision 2011/344/EU was issued on 30 May 2011. The MoU of Cyprus was signed on 26 April 2013 and Council Decision 2013/236/EU was issued on 25 March 2013.

[43] See eg Master Financial Assistance Facility Agreement Between European Financial Stability Facility The Portuguese Republic as Beneficiary Member State and Banco de Portugal, recital 4 of the Preamble and arts 2(7) and 4(1) <http://www.efsf.europa.eu> accessed 31 July 2020; Financial Assistance Facility Agreement between European Stability Mechanism and the Republic of Cyprus and Central Bank of Cyprus, recital G of the Preamble and art 2(1) <http://www.esm.europa.eu> accessed 31 July 2020.

V. The applicability of the Charter to EU institutions involved in the EFSF and ESM

Given the important institutional and substantive links between the internationally embedded financial assistance mechanisms and the EU legal space, the initial question returns with even greater force. Is the Charter applicable in the context of European financial assistance or are the EU institutions involved freed from the obligation to respect the fundamental rights of the Union? In fact, as long as no limits are set in terms of the content of the conditions, the EU institutions retain a broad margin of appreciation with regard to the means and measures to be adopted.[44] At the same time, financial assistance conditionality intrudes on recipient countries' healthcare and pension systems, education, and labour sectors in such a detailed manner that violations of labour and trade unions rights and of the rights to property, social security and assistance, and healthcare are very likely to occur in practice.[45] Nevertheless, for reasons which relate either to the subject of action or to the act itself, not all bodies involved can be bound by the Charter. Hence, in the complicated framework of financial assistance, we have to assess separately which EU institutions and which of their acts are bound by the Charter.

1. The applicability of the Charter to the Eurogroup

In the context of European assistance, the Eurogroup is usually entrusted with general guidelines with regard to economic policy and not with the formulation of detailed financial assistance conditions. During the eurozone crisis, it determined the strategic choices of the economic adjustment programmes, such as the voluntary debt haircut in the case of Greece.[46] With regard to specific conditionalities though, it relied on the recommendations of the Troika. A notable exception to this rule was the case of Cyprus, in which the restructuring of the Cypriot banking sector was first decided by the Eurogroup before the Troika reached agreement with domestic authorities.[47] The Cypriot rescue package is of particular interest,

---

[44] See also Christoph Ohler, 'The European Stability Mechanism: The Long Road to Financial Stability in the Euro Area' [2011] German Yearbook of International Law 63; Friedrich Thießen, 'Stabilisierung oder Destabilisierung Europas: Was bringt der ESM?' [2012] Zeitschrift für das gesamte Kreditwesen 704; Angelos Dimopoulos, 'The Use of International Law as a Tool for Strengthening Economic Governance in the EU and its Implications on EU Institutional Integrity' in Maurice Adams, Federico Fabbrini, and Pierre Larouche (eds), *The Constitutionalization of EU Budgetary Constraints* (Hart Publishing 2014) 50.

[45] See Anastasia Poulou, 'Austerity and European Social Rights: How Can Courts Protect Europe's Lost Generation?' [2014] GLJ 1145.

[46] Eurogroup Statement on the European Stability Mechanism with respect to Greece, Doc No 128075, 21 February 2012 <http://www.consilium.europa.eu/uedocs/cms_Data/docs/pressdata/en/ecofin/128075.pdf> accessed 31 July 2020.

[47] See Eurogroup Statement on Cyprus, Doc No 136487, 25 March 2013 <http://www.consilium.europa.eu/uedocs/cms_Data/docs/pressdata/en/ecofin/136487.pdf> accessed 31 July 2020.

since it marks the first time that bank depositors were targeted as part of a European bailout deal. In exchange for the loans received by the ESM and the IMF, Cyprus had inter alia to wind up its second largest bank, the Cyprus Popular Bank (also known as Laiki Bank), and to recapitalise its biggest bank, the Bank of Cyprus, at the expense of shareholders, bondholders, and depositors. In the winding up of the Cyprus Popular Bank, uninsured deposits exceeding the amount of €100,000 were completely liquidated. In the recapitalisation of the Bank of Cyprus, the depositors lost 47.5 per cent of their uninsured deposits.[48]

Given their substantial financial losses—the result of the extensive write-off of their bank deposits—uninsured depositors sought judicial protection before the courts of the EU, challenging the validity of the Eurogroup statement outlining the conditions of the bailout. Nevertheless, all their actions for annulment have been unsuccessful.[49] In fact, in the ECJ case *Mallis and Others v Commission and ECB*, the Court confirmed the orders of the General Court holding that the Eurogroup, which is an informal forum for discussion between ministers of the Member States whose currency is the euro, cannot be classified as a body, office, or agency of the EU within the meaning of article 263 of the TFEU.[50] Thus, a statement by it cannot be regarded as a measure intended to produce legal effects with respect to third parties, [51] and can therefore not be annulled on the basis of article 263 of the TFEU. Moreover, in *Mallis* the ECJ rejected the argument that the Eurogroup is under the factual control of the Commission and the ECB, when it comes to meetings related to the ESM, and thus held that Eurogroup statements containing financial assistance conditions cannot be imputed to the EU institutions.[52]

In view of the serious interference with the fundamental rights of individuals, which might remain without legal remedy as is illustrated by the Cypriot case, the question arises whether the Eurogroup is bound by the Charter when formulating financial assistance conditionality. The scope of the Charter is determined by article 51(1) of the EUCFR, which reads: 'The provisions of this Charter are addressed

---

[48] Anastasia Poulou, 'The Liability of the EU in the ESM framework' Case note on Joined Cases C-8/15 P to C-10/15 P *Ledra Advertising and Others v Commission and ECB* [2017] Maastricht J. Eur. & Comp. L. 127, 129.

[49] See Case T-327/13 *Mallis and Malli v Commission and ECB* [2014] EU:T:2014:909; Case T-328/13 *Tameio Pronoias Prosopikou Trapezis Kyprou v Commission and ECB* [2014] EU:T:2014:906; Case T-329/13 *Chatzithoma v Commission and ECB* [2014] EU:T:2014:908; Case T-330/13 *Chatziioannou v Commission and ECB* [2014] EU:T:2014:904; Case T-331/13 *Nikolaou v Commission and ECB* [2014] EU:T:2014:905. For an analysis of these cases see Anastasia Karatzia, 'Cypriot Depositors Before the Court of Justice of the European Union: Knocking on the Wrong Door?' [2015] King's Law Journal 175 et seq.

[50] Joined Cases C-105–109/15 P *Mallis*, para 61. See also Opinion of AG Wathelet in Joined Cases C-105–109/15 P *Mallis* [2016] EU:C:2016:294, para 65.

[51] Joined Cases C-105–109/15 P *Mallis*, para 49.

[52] ibid, para 47. The question whether the Commission and the ECB are themselves bound by the Charter is addressed separately, see *infra* V.2.

to the institutions, bodies, offices and agencies of the Union with due regard for the principle of subsidiarity.' Not being one of the seven EU institutions listed in article 13(1) of the TEU, the Eurogroup may be bound by the Charter only if it could be regarded as a body, office, or agency of the Union or as a configuration of the Council of the EU. As pointed out in the explanation accompanying article 51 of the EUCFR, the expression 'bodies, offices and agencies' is commonly used in the Treaties to refer to all the authorities set up by the Treaties or by secondary legislation.[53] The Eurogroup is explicitly mentioned in article 137 of the TFEU, which, with respect to its composition and the arrangements for its meetings, refers to Protocol No 14 annexed to the TFEU. This Protocol provides that the Eurogroup consists of the finance ministers of the euro area Member States, who 'shall meet informally [...] to discuss questions related to the specific responsibilities they share with regard to the single currency'. As the Court has held, this provision presents the Eurogroup as 'a forum for discussion, at ministerial level, between representatives the Member States whose currency is the euro', and not as a 'decision-making body'.[54]

Furthermore, the Eurogroup is not among the different configurations of the Council of the EU provided by article 16(6) of the TEU and enumerated in Annex I to the Rules of Procedure of the Council.[55] Besides not being classified as such by the TFEU, the classification of the Eurogroup as a configuration of the Council would not be in line with the different functions that each of them performs. As Advocate General Wathelet observed in his Opinion on *Mallis*, while the Eurogroup is an informal forum for discussion between euro area Member States on questions specifically related to the single currency, the Council's functions pursuant to article 16(1) of the TEU are far broader and include the exercise, in conjunction with the Parliament, of legislative power within the EU and the other decision-making powers conferred on the Council alone by the TFEU.[56]

Since it can neither be equated with a configuration of the Council nor classified as a formal decision-making body, office, or agency of the EU,[57] the Eurogroup does not fall under the scope of the Charter as defined in article 51(1) of the EUCFR. In view of the fact that, despite its informal nature, the Eurogroup very often predetermines and shapes crucial decisions in the framework of financial assistance, the conclusion that its acts cannot be assessed against the Charter is very problematic from the perspective of human rights.

---

[53] Explanations relating to the Charter of Fundamental Rights [2007] OJ C303/17, 32.
[54] Joined Cases C-105–109/15 P *Mallis*, para 47.
[55] See Council Decision 2009/937/EU of 1 December 2009 adopting the Council's Rules of Procedure [2009] OJ L325/35.
[56] See Opinion of AG Wathelet in Joined Cases C-105–109/15 P, *Mallis*, para 61.
[57] Joined Cases C-105–109/15 P *Mallis*, para 61.

2. The applicability of the Charter to the Commission and the ECB

The Troika is a cooperation body and as such is not a subject that can be held accountable under international or EU law.[58] Its actions have to be regarded as joint measures of EU institutions and subjects of international law (Commission, ECB, and IMF), whose commitment to human rights must be investigated separately. As members of the Troika, the Commission and ECB always have an important say in formulating and monitoring financial assistance conditionality.[59] As a result, the question of whether they guarantee the compliance of the conditions with human rights has received increased attention both in the political and the legal discourse.[60] Indicative is the 2013 European Parliament (EP) investigation about the role of the Troika in euro area countries under financial assistance, in which both the ECB and the Commission were explicitly asked whether they assess the consistency of the measures negotiated with the Member States with EU fundamental rights obligations referred to in the Treaties.[61] Interestingly, their perceptions about the pertinence of fundamental rights commitments differ significantly.

The ECB held that 'it remains the responsibility of the Member State concerned to ensure the compliance of its national law and administrative practices with EU law. By the same token it is the responsibility of the Commission to initiate an infringement procedure against a Member State which it considers has failed to fulfil its obligations under EU law.'[62] As such, the ECB renounces for itself and the Commission any responsibility for ensuring the consistency of conditionality with EU law, and recognises solely the role of the Commission as guarantor of the Treaties against the Member State concerned. On the other hand, the Commission expressed a more positive approach, responding that '[w]hen negotiating the conditionality, the Commission [also] has a role in ensuring that the *acquis communautaire* is respected. It has also made sure that fundamental rights were complied with.'[63] On other occasions, the Commission has also explicitly claimed

---

[58] See also Andreas Fischer-Lescano, 'Troika in der Austerität: Rechtsbindungen der Unionsorgane beim Abschluss von Memoranda of Understanding' [2014] Kritische Justiz 7.

[59] Recital 3 of the Preamble and arts 2(1)(a) and 3(1) of the EFSF Framework Agreement; art 13(3) and (7) of the ESM Treaty; art 7(1)(1) and (4)(1) of Regulation 472/2013.

[60] See eg Daniel Sarmiento, 'Who's Afraid of the Charter? The Court of Justice, National Courts and the New Framework of Fundamental Rights Protection in Europe' [2013] CMLR 1273.

[61] European Parliament, Questionnaire supporting the own initiative report evaluating the structure, the role and operations of the 'troika' (Commission, ECB and the IMF) actions in euro area programme countries, Question No 18 <http://www.europarl.europa.eu/document/activities/cont/201401/20140114ATT77313/20140114ATT77313EN.pdf> accessed 31 July 2020.

[62] ECB's replies to the questionnaire of the European Parliament supporting the own initiative report evaluating the structure, the role and operations of the 'troika' (Commission, ECB and the IMF) actions in euro area programme countries, 7 <http://www.ecb.europa.eu/pub/pdf/other/140110_ecb_response_troika_questionnaireen.pdf> accessed 31 July 2020.

[63] Response of the European Commission to the questionnaire supporting the own initiative report evaluating the structure, the role and the operations of the 'troika' (Commission, ECB and the IMF) actions in euro area programme countries, Ref. Ares(2013)3736254, 16 December 2013, 12.

to be very attentive to ensuring the consistency of the MoU with EU law.[64] Thus, the EU institutions involved in the financial assistance scheme have remarkably different understandings of the relevance of human rights.

In the legal discourse, the applicability of the Charter to the Commission and ECB in the framework of financial assistance is often questioned for two reasons. First, on the ground that both in the EFSF and the ESM, the Commission and the ECB act under powers conferred on them by intergovernmental agreements and not under the mandate of the Treaties. Second, because of the fact that the character of the MoUs as binding legal agreements is disputed; if the MoUs are not binding legal documents, how could they be subsumed under the Charter? However, as will be shown, neither of these reasons suffices to rule out the applicability of the Charter in relation to the Commission and the ECB.

The first objection put forward, rejecting the applicability of the Charter to the Commission and the ECB (when they negotiate and conclude the MoU), failed dismally with the issuance of the *Ledra Advertising* judgment by the ECJ in September 2016.[65] On appeals against decisions of the General Court, which had dismissed as inadmissible actions for annulment and compensation raised after the restructuring of Cypriot banks, the ECJ clearly spelled out the obligation of EU institutions to respect human rights when formulating financial assistance conditionality. Filling the gap left on this issue in *Pringle*, the ECJ followed the Opinion of Advocate General Kokott,[66] explicitly stating that the Charter binds EU institutions in all circumstances, even when they act outside the EU legal framework.[67] In this vein, the Court clearly underlined that, in the context of the adoption of an MoU, the Commission is bound under both article 17(1) of the Treaty on European Union (TEU)—which confers upon it the general task of overseeing the application of EU law—and article 12(3) and (4) of the ESM Treaty—which requires it to ensure that the MoUs by the ESM are consistent with EU law—to ensure that such an MoU is consistent with the fundamental rights guaranteed by the Charter.[68]

Although article 51(1) of the EUCFR should have been mentioned in *Ledra Advertising*, together with article 17(1) of the TEU and article 13(3) of the ESM Treaty, among the provisions that oblige the EU institutions to ensure that the MoUs are consistent with EU fundamental rights, the clear reference to the pertinence of the Charter to actions of EU institutions in the making of financial

---

[64] See European Parliament, Joint answer given by Mr Moscovici on behalf of the Commission to written questions E-007535/14, E-007778/14, 1 December 2014 <http://www.europarl.europa.eu/sides/getAllAnswers.do?reference=E-2014-007535&language=EN> accessed 31 July 2020.

[65] For a detailed analysis of the judgement, see Paul Dermine, 'The End of Impunity? The Legal Duties of "Borrowed" EU Institutions under the European Stability Mechanism Framework: ECJ 20 September 2016, Case C-8/15 to C-10/15, Ledra Advertising et al v European Commission and European Central Bank' [2017] EuConst 369; Repasi (n 33); Poulou (n 48).

[66] See Opinion of AG Kokott in Case C-370/12 *Pringle* [2012] EU:C:2012:675, para 176.

[67] Joined Cases C-8-10/15 P *Ledra* [2016] EU:C:2016:701, para 67.

[68] ibid.

assistance conditionality constitutes a milestone for the protection of human rights in the context of post-crisis European financial assistance. *Ledra Advertising* leaves no doubt that—even if in the EFSF and ESM framework the Commission and the ECB act under powers conferred on them by intergovernmental agreements— their commitment to the Charter does not cease to exist. The fundamental rights commitment of the EU institutions irrespective of individual contexts is also re- peatedly stressed by the EP. In several of its Resolutions, the EP recalls that 'the EU institutions, even when they act as members of groups of international lenders ("troikas"), are bound by the Treaties and the Charter of Fundamental Rights of the European Union'.[69]

The second objection regarding the controversial nature of the MoUs signed in the context of European financial assistance goes back to the lending practices of the IMF. Receiving the MoU only as an annex to a Letter of Intent, the IMF perceives it as a unilateral declaration of the national policy programme of the re- spective government and this precludes the recognition of any legally binding ef- fects. Given its origin in IMF practice, heated discussions regarding the legal nature of the MoU were launched in eurozone countries receiving financial assistance. Besides minority opinions viewing the MoU as an international law agreement,[70] prevailing views in the legal discourse regarding its categorisation range from an instrument of soft law (in the form of a gentlemen's agreement)[71] to a policy statement[72] or a material act (*Realakt*).[73] Disagreement exists even within the ju- diciary of the states concerned. The Portuguese Constitutional Court (Tribunal Constitucional) affirmed the binding legal force of the Portuguese MoU,[74] whereas the Greek Council of State (Symboulio tis Epikrateias) described the Greek MoU as a mere national policy programme of the government.[75]

Nevertheless, any objection regarding the nature of the MoU has no effect on the applicability of the Charter to the Commission and the ECB. As pointed out in the explanation accompanying article 51 of the EUCFR, this provision 'seeks

---

[69] European Parliament Resolution of 10 September 2015 on the 30th and 31st annual reports on monitoring the application of EU Law (2012–2013), 2014/2253(INI), para 23. See also European Parliament Resolution of 13 March 2014 on the enquiry on the role and operations of the Troika (ECB, Commission and IMF) with regard to the euro area programme countries, 2013/2277(INI), para 81.

[70] Federico Fabbrini, 'The Euro-Crisis and the Courts: Judicial Review and the Political Process in Comparative Perspective' [2014] Berkeley Journal of International Law 111.

[71] Antonis Manitakis, 'Die Verfassungsfragen des Memorandums' [2011] Dikaiomata tou Anthrwpou 699 [in Greek].

[72] George Katrougalos, 'Memoranda sunt Servanda? Die Verfassungsmäßigkeit des Gesetzes 3845/ 2010 und des Memorandums für die Anwendung der Vereinbarungen mit dem IWF, EU und EZB' [2010] Efimerida Dioikitikou Dikaiou 151 [in Greek].

[73] Andreas Fischer-Lescano, *Human Rights in Times of Austerity Policy: The EU Institutions and the Conclusion of Memoranda of Understanding* (Nomos 2014) 60.

[74] See Tribunal Constitucional, Acórdão No 396/2011, judgment of 21 September 2011, para 5; Tribunal Constitucional, Acórdão No 353/2012, judgment of 5 July 2012, para 3; Tribunal Constitucional, Acórdão No 187/2013, judgment of 5 April 2013, para 29.

[75] Symboulio tis Epikrateias [StE], 668/2012, judgement of 20 February 2012, para 28; Symboulio tis Epikrateias [StE], judgement of 1283-6/2012, 2 April 2012, para 24.

to establish clearly that the Charter applies primarily to the institutions of the Union'.[76] These are defined under article 13(1) of the TEU and explicitly include the Commission and the ECB. Once it is established that an entity falls within the categories of legal subjects listed in article 51(1), any general or concrete individual act produced by it must comply with the Charter. This is because, unlike Member States (which are bound by the Charter only when implementing EU law), EU institutions must respect fundamental rights regardless of the specific framework or context in which they operate.[77]

Given that the commitment of EU institutions to fundamental rights is comprehensive and independent of the legal nature of the EU act,[78] all acts carried out by the Union in the exercise of public authority are covered. These of course include legislative, executive, and judicial acts.[79] Atypical and informal acts, such as resolutions, recommendations, or codes of conduct, are also encompassed as long as they are products of EU institutions and have legal effects.[80] Moreover, the comprehensive commitment of EU institutions signifies that they have to respect fundamental rights not only when they exercise public authority, but also when they act under private law.[81] In fact, it is only by including all types of acts that derive from EU institutions within the scope of article 51(1) that the Charter can effectively bind its primary addressees.[82] Against this background, regardless of its classification as an international agreement, gentlemen's agreement, or material act, the generation of the MoU by the EU institutions triggers the applicability of the Charter.[83]

Even more importantly, the MoUs adopted in the framework of European financial assistance possess distinct characteristics when compared to the MoUs of the IMF framework. Whereas the IMF does not sign the MoU and does not consider it a legal agreement, the MoU of the ESM framework is a separate document, which is signed by the Commission on behalf of the ESM. In fact, MoUs of this sort even have different names. The MoU of the ESM is the 'Memorandum on Specific Economic Policy Conditionality', while the MoUs of the IMF are

---

[76] Explanations relating to the Charter of Fundamental Rights, 32.

[77] See also Fischer-Lescano (n 74) 25.

[78] Walter Frenz, *Europäische Grundrechte* (Springer 2009), para 217; Armin Hatje, 'Artikel 51 EUCFR' in Ulrich Becker and others (ed), *Schwarze EU-Kommentar* (4th edn, Nomos 2019); Angela Schwerdtfeger, 'Artikel 51' in Martin Borowski and Sven Hölscheidt (eds), *Charta der Grundrechte der Europäischen Union* (5th edn, Nomos 2019).

[79] Hans-Werner Rengeling and Peter Szczekalla, *Grundrechte in der Europäischen Union: Charta der Grundrechte und allgemeine Rechtsgrundsätze* (Heymanns 2004), para 267; Michael Holoubek, Ulrike Lechner and Melina Oswald, 'Artikel 51' in Michael Holoubek and Georg Lienbacher (eds), *Charta der Grundrechte der Europäischen Union: GRC-Kommentar* (Manz 2019).

[80] See in detail Jan Klabbers, 'Informal Instruments Before the European Court of Justice' [1994] CMLR 997.

[81] Rengeling and Szczekalla (n 80) para 268; Hatje (n 79).

[82] See also Claire Kilpatrick, 'Are the Bailouts Immune to EU Social Challenge Because They Are Not EU Law?' [2014] EuConst 393, 405.

[83] Anastasia Poulou, 'Financial Assistance Conditionality and Human Rights Protection: What is the Role of the EU Charter of Fundamental Rights?' [2017] CMLR 991, 1011.

the 'Memorandum of Economic and Financial Policies' and the 'Technical Memorandum of Understanding'.[84] As a result, the fact that the MoU of the ESM is signed by the parties involved signifies the creation of something that is much closer to an agreement or a contract rather than a mere policy programme.

3. The applicability of the Charter to the Council of the EU

The Council of the EU approves financial assistance conditionality in the form of Council Decisions.[85] The applicability of the Charter with regard to financial assistance conditions included in the Decisions of the Council is less contested. The Council of the EU is undoubtedly included among the EU institutions which are bound by the Charter according to article 51(1) of the EUCFR read together with article 13 of the TEU. In addition, the Decisions of the Council fall under the types of secondary legislation listed in article 288(4) of the TFEU.[86] Thus, the Decisions of the Council adopted under the framework of European financial assistance are unilateral, legally binding acts of an EU institution and as such fall under the scope of the Charter.[87] The fact that their content arguably reflects a negotiated agreement between different actors does not impact on their legal nature as acts of secondary EU law within the meaning of article 288 of the TFEU.[88]

It is important to note that the applicability of the Charter with regard to the Decisions of the Council containing financial assistance conditionality should be distinguished from the ECJ case law arising from actions for annulment of those decisions, launched under article 263 of the TFEU. For example, the legality of Decision 2010/320/EU addressed to Greece was contested because of its provision stipulating a reduction of the Easter, summer, and Christmas bonuses and allowances paid to civil servants.[89] Similarly, Decision 2011/57/EU was challenged because of its provision on better management of public assets,[90] on means-testing of

---

[84] The three different MoUs are presented separately in the annex to the Economic Adjustment Programme for each country receiving financial assistance; see eg The Economic Adjustment Programme for Cyprus, Occasional Papers 149, May 2013, 66 et seq.

[85] Art 7(2) Regulation (EU) 472/2013.

[86] For a detailed analysis of the Decisions as forms of action in EU law, see Ulrich Stelkens, 'Die "Europäische Entscheidung" als Handlungsform des direkten Unionsrechtsvollzugs nach dem Vertrag über eine Verfassung für Europa' [2005] Zeitschrift für Europäische Studien 61; Matthias Vogt, Die Entscheidung als Handlungsform des Europäischen Gemeinschaftsrechts (Mohr Siebeck 2005) 335; Jürgen Bast, Grundbegriffe der Handlungsformen der EU (Springer 2006) 109.

[87] Poulou (n 84) 1012.

[88] This point can be compared with Council Decisions concluding external EU agreements. The fact that the Council Decisions do not add anything to the agreements is no obstacle against the legal challenge of these Decisions before the Court.

[89] Art 2(1)(f) Council Decision 2010/320/EU.

[90] Art 1(4)(k) Council Decision 2011/57/EU of 20 December 2010 amending Decision 2010/320/EU addressed to Greece with a view to reinforcing and deepening fiscal surveillance and giving notice to

family allowances,[91] and on the limitation of recruitment in the whole general government to a ratio of not more than one recruitment for five retirements or dismissals.[92] In order for the actions for annulment to be admissible, the applicants had to prove that the regulatory acts were of direct and individual concern to them pursuant to article 263(4) of the TFEU. The Court held that the challenged provisions were indeterminate and left a margin to the Greek State as to the way they were implemented, and thus could not directly affect the applicants.[93] As a result, both actions were rejected as inadmissible and no decision on their merits was taken.

Regardless of the quality of the reasoning of the ECJ in these cases with regard to the direct and individual concern,[94] it is not decisive for the application of the Charter to financial assistance conditions included in the Decisions of the Council. This is because the procedural question—whether the Decisions are of direct and individual concern to individuals, pursuant to article 263(4) of the TFEU—has to be held distinct from the substantive question of whether the Decisions fall within the scope of the Charter pursuant to article 51(1) of the EUCFR. The fact that the individuals concerned may experience procedural hurdles when launching an action for annulment against a decision entailing lending conditions does not change the fact that these decisions must be in conformity with the Charter.

VI. International human rights obligations of the ESM

There is a long and sordid history of the negative impacts on socio-economic rights, as well as political rights, arising from the interventions of international financial institutions in developing countries whereby human rights-holders have been left to direct claims to their enfeebled governments, as the traditional state duty-bearers under the relevant human rights treaties, while the international financial institutions, wearing their 'non-state' actor hats, have been able to claim that they possess no legal obligations in the area of human rights.[95] In this vein,

---

Greece to take measures for the deficit reduction judged necessary to remedy the situation of excessive deficit [2011] OJ L26/16.

[91] ibid, art 1(8)(s).
[92] ibid, art 1(8)(gg).
[93] Case T-541/10 *ADEDY and Others v Council* [2012] EU:T:2012:626, paras 70 and 72–73; Case T-215/11 *ADEDY and Others v Council* [2012] EU:T:2012:627, paras 81, 84, and 90. See also analysis of Kilpatrick (n 83) 416.
[94] This issue cannot be fully covered in this chapter. See further Anastasia Poulou, *Soziale Grundrechte und europäische Finanzhilfe* (Mohr Siebeck 2018) 153.
[95] See further Margot Salomon, 'International Economic Governance and Human Rights Accountability' in Margot Salomon, Arne Tostensen, and Wouter Vandenhole (eds), *Casting the Net Wider: Human Rights, Development and New Duty-Bearers* (Intersentia 2007) 153; François Gianviti, 'Economic, Social and Cultural Rights and the International Monetary Fund' in Philip Alston (ed), *Non-State Actors and Human Rights* (OUP 2005) 113.

the International Law Association took up the question of the accountability of international organisations in 1996, when it established a committee to consider what measures (legal, administrative, or otherwise) should be adopted to ensure the accountability of public international organisations to their members and third parties and of members and third parties to such organisations.[96] In its final report published in 2004, the conclusion of the Association was that international organisations should comply with basic human rights obligations.[97] Overall, there appears to be some consensus that international organisations have an obligation to respect those human rights that have attained the status of customary international law and/or general principles of law, and may be held responsible for respective breaches of those.[98] Nevertheless, uncertainty remains with regard to the sources and scope of their obligation to respect human rights standards.[99] Against this background, a lot has been written on the impact of the activities of the World Bank and the IMF on human rights.[100] Instead of focusing again on these actors, this chapter will address the problem of whether the ESM, which since June 2013 has assumed the tasks fulfilled by the EFSF and the EFSM in providing financial assistance to euro area Member States, could be bound by international human rights law.[101]

The ESM was announced by the European Council to be 'an intergovernmental organization under public international law'[102] located in Luxembourg. According to the ESM Treaty, the ESM is as an 'international financial institution' established by the ESM Members, ie the Member States of the euro area. The ESM is governed by the Board of Governors, which is formed by the Ministers of Finance of the

---

[96] International Law Association Report of the Seventy-First Conference (Berlin), 'Accountability of International Organisations: Final Report' (ILA 2004) 4.

[97] ibid 22.

[98] Matteo Tondini, 'The "Italian Job": How to Make International Organisations Compliant with Human Rights and Accountable for their Violation by Targeting Member States' in Jan Wouters and others (eds), *Accountability for Human Rights Violations by International Organisations* (Intersentia 2010) 177.

[99] Jan Wouters and others, 'Introductory Remarks' in Jan Wouters and others (eds), *Accountability for Human Rights Violations by International Organisations* (Intersentia 2010) 6.

[100] See for example Laurence Boisson de Chazournes, 'The Bretton Woods Institutions and Human Rights: Converging Tendencies' in Wolfgang Benedek, Koen de Feyter, and Fabrizio Marrella (eds), *Economic Globalization and Human Rights* (CUP 2007) 210; Daniel Bradlow, 'The World Bank, the IMF and Human Rights' [1996] Transnational Law and Contemporary Problems 63; Roberto Dañino, 'The Legal Aspects of the World Bank's Work on Human Rights' in Philip Alston and Mary Robinson (eds), *Human Rights and Development. Towards Mutual Reinforcement* (OUP 2005) 509; Mac Darrow, *Between Light and Shadow: The World Bank, the International Monetary Fund and International Human Rights Law* (Hart Publishing 2003); Sigrun Skogly, *The Human Rights Obligations of the World Bank and the International Monetary Fund* (Cavendish 2001). On the IMF in particular, see Daniel Bradlow, 'Operational Policies and Procedures and an Ombudsman' in Barry Carin and Angela Woods (eds), *Accountability of the International Monetary Fund* 89 (Ashgate and the International Development Research Centre 2005).

[101] See also Lisa Ginsborg, 'The Impact of the Economic Crisis on Human Rights in Europe and the Accountability of International Institutions' [2017] Global Campus Human Rights Journal 97, 111.

[102] See Conclusions of the European Council of 24/25 March 2011, Doc EUCO 10/1/11 REV 1, Annex II, 22.

euro area Member States.[103] The Board of Governors is responsible for fulfilling important tasks, such as providing stability support via the ESM, giving a mandate to the Commission to negotiate, in liaison with the ECB, the economic policy conditionality, or making adaptations to the ESM Treaty. Another important decision-making body of the ESM is the Board of Directors. Each Governor appoints one Director from among people of high competence in economic and financial matters to the Board of Directors, whose role is to ensure that the ESM is run in accordance with the ESM Treaty and the by-laws of the ESM adopted by the Board of Governors.[104] The voting rights of each ESM Member are equal to the number of shares allocated to it,[105] in practice giving two states (Germany and Italy) the right to veto.

The ESM is not a party to any international human rights law instrument, which means that, prima facie, it is not bound by any human rights treaty. Yet, becoming party to a treaty is not the only way to be bound by the rules stated therein, hence this section examines the means by which the ESM could be bound by international human rights law. One mechanism that would allow the ESM to be held accountable for any violations of human rights to which it contributes is self-regulation. In recent years, there has been a proliferation of initiatives through which international organisations voluntarily choose to develop procedures that aim to ensure that they will comply with human rights or, at least, with certain standards related to human rights, which are better adapted to their specific areas of activity. The World Bank and the IMF have developed a set of operational policies, comparable to internal codes of conduct regulating their activities, which integrate human rights considerations. For example, the IMF's own Guidelines on Conditionality promulgated in 1979 urge the Fund 'to pay due regard to domestic social and political objectives',[106] which has been interpreted as including the duty to consider the impact of IMF conditionality on basic human rights.[107] In addition, institutional mechanisms have been set up for monitoring compliance. Both the World Bank and the IMF have set up internal evaluation units to enhance accountability and improve the effectiveness of the strategies of these institutions, such as the Independent Evaluation Group for the World Bank and the Independent Evaluation Office for the IMF.[108] Nevertheless, with regard to the ESM there is no mention of international human rights, either in the ESM Treaty or in any of the ESM legal documents, hence one could not argue that the ESM is bound by human

---

[103] Art 5 ESM Treaty.
[104] Art 6 ESM Treaty.
[105] Art 4(7) ESM Treaty.
[106] IMF (n 37) para 10.
[107] Margaret Conklin and Daphne Davidson, 'The I.M.F. and Economic and Social Human Rights: A Case Study of Argentina, 1958-1985' [1986] Human Rights Quarterly 227, 247.
[108] Olivier de Schutter, 'Human Rights and the Rise of International Organisations: The Logic of Sliding Scales in the Law of International Responsibility' in Jan Wouters and others (eds), *Accountability for Human Rights Violations by International Organizations* (Intersentia, 2011) 95.

rights law by virtue of provisions included in its constituent instruments or further adopted documents.

Second, the ESM could be bound by those human rights standards that have become part of customary international law. In order to be established, custom in principle requires consistent identifiable state practice and evidence of a belief that this practice is rendered obligatory by the existence of a rule of law requiring it (opinion juris).[109] In particular in the field of human rights, evidence of custom could be based on the resolutions of the General Assembly of the United Nations and other international organisations, which demonstrate a clear commitment of the international community towards certain values,[110] while inconsistent state practice should not be an obstacle to the identification of such custom.[111] In fact, for the purposes of custom determination in the field of human rights 'state practice' is composed of official declarations,[112] participation in the negotiation of human rights instruments, and incorporation of human rights within national legal orders.[113] As a result, even if custom is traditionally associated with state practice, international organisations are generally considered to be bound by customary human rights law.[114]

The scope of customary human rights law is not clearly defined and, to a great extent, remains controversial. The majority of scholars agree that the rights included in the Universal Declaration of Human Rights (UDHR) can plausibly be regarded as part of customary international law.[115] On the twentieth anniversary

[109] See North Sea Continental Shelf, Judgement, ICJ Reports 1969, 3, para 77 'Not only must the acts concerned amount to a settled practice, but they must also be such or be carried out in such a way, as to be evidence of a belief that this practice is rendered obligatory by the existence of a rule of law requiring it. The need for such a belief, i.e., the existence of a subjective element, is implicit in the very notion of the *opinion juris sive necessitatis*. The States concerned must therefore feel that they are conforming to what amounts to a legal obligation. The frequency or even habitual character of the acts is not in itself enough.'

[110] See Military and Paramilitary Activities in and against Nicaragua, Merits, Judgement, ICJ Reports 1986, 14, para 188 'from, inter alia, the attitude of the Parties and the attitude of States towards certain General Assembly resolutions [...] The effect of consent to the text of such resolutions cannot be understood as merely that of a "reiteration or elucidation" of the treaty commitment undertaken in the Charter. On the contrary, it may be understood as an acceptance of the validity of the rule or set of rules declared by the resolution by themselves.'

[111] Theodor Meron, *Human Rights and Humanitarian Norms as Customary Law* (Clarendon Press 1989) 106.

[112] An important statement in this regard is the Proclamation of Teheran, Final Act of the International Conference on Human Rights, Teheran, 22 April to 13 May 1968, UN Doc A/CONF.32/41 (1968).

[113] Olivier de Schutter, 'The Status of Human Rights in International Law' in Catarina Krause and Martin Scheinin (eds), *International Protection of Human Rights* (2nd edn, Åbo Akademi University 2012) 42.

[114] Chittharanjan Felix Amerasinghe, *Principles of the Institutional Law of International Organizations* (2nd edn, CUP 2005) 21; B Ghazi, *The IMF, the World Bank Group and the Question of Human Rights* (Brill - Nijhoff 2005) 133; Cornelia Janik, *Die Bindung internationaler Organisationen an internationale Menschenrechtsstandards* (Mohr Siebeck 2012) 449.

[115] Hurst Hannum, 'The Status of the Universal Declaration of Human Rights in National and International Law' [1996] Georgia Journal of International and Comparative Law 322; Marc Cogen, 'Human Rights, Prohibition of Political Activities and the Lending Policies of the World Bank and the

of the adoption of the Declaration, a major international conference of nongovernmental organisations proclaimed unequivocally that the UDHR 'constitutes an authoritative interpretation of the Charter of the highest order, and has over the years become part of customary international law'.[116] More importantly, a governmental conference held in the same year at which eighty-four states were represented observed that the UDHR 'states a common understanding of the peoples of the world concerning the inalienable and inviolable rights of all members of the human family and constitutes an obligation for the members of the international community'.[117]

There is growing consensus that the recognition of the UDHR as an international customary human rights norm holds true for the civil and political rights entailed therein.[118] Prominent examples include the prohibitions against slavery, genocide, torture, mass murder, prolonged arbitrary imprisonment, and racial discrimination.[119] However, the question whether economic, social, and cultural rights are included in the scope of customary human rights norms still remains under discussion. Support for the view that at least the core of economic, social, and cultural rights forms part of customary law might be derived from a number of international soft law instruments. In its General Comment 8, the Committee on Economic, Social and Cultural Rights (CESCR) confirmed that a state and the international community itself must 'do everything possible to protect at least the core content of the economic, social and cultural rights of the affected peoples'.[120] Moreover, the Copenhagen Declaration on Social Development envisages social development and social justice as goals that cannot be attained 'in the absence of respect for all human rights and fundamental freedoms' .[121] In this vein, even if social rights do not universally enjoy the same level of legal protection, the core content of fundamental social rights, such as the right to work, the right to an adequate standard of living, and the right to education, should be regarded as part of customary human rights law and thus respected by international organisations. This is in line with the recent Guiding Principles on Foreign Debt and Human Rights of the Human Rights Council, which explicitly state that international financial organisations and private

International Monetary Fund' in Subrata Roy Chowdury and others (eds), *The Right to Development in International Law* (Nijhoff 1992) 387.

[116] Montreal Statement of the [Nongovernmental] Assembly for Human Rights (1968), reprinted in (1968) 9 Review of the International Commission of Jurists 94.
[117] Proclamation of Teheran, Final Act of the International Conference on Human Rights, Teheran, 22 April to 13 May 1968, UN Doc A/CONF.32/41 (1968) para 2.
[118] Meron (n 112) 93; Michael Lucas, 'The International Monetary Fund's Conditionality and the International Covenant on Economic, Social and Cultural Rights: An Attempt to Define the Relation' [1992] Revue Belge de droit international 104, 117; Economic, Social and Cultural Human Rights and the International Monetary Fund (prepared by F Gianviti), UN Doc E/C.12/2001/WP.5, 7 May 2001, paras 18–20.
[119] Lucas (n 119).
[120] CESCR General Comment 8 (1997), para 7.
[121] Copenhagen Declaration on Social Development, UN Doc A/CONF.166/9 (1995), para 5.

corporations have an obligation to respect international human rights based on the 'Ruggie principles'.[122] In particular, '[t]his implies a duty to refrain from formulating, adopting, funding and implementing policies and programmes which directly or indirectly contravene the enjoyment of human rights'.[123]

With regard to the content of the human rights obligations arising especially from economic and social rights, there is a need to distinguish between the negative obligations (to abstain from violations) and the positive obligations (to protect and fulfil human rights), which are traditionally imposed on the parties to international human rights treaties. Whereas, in order to be fulfilled, positive obligations require that the addressee possess the required competences to do so, negative obligations merely impose limits on how existing competences may be exercised. The implication is that, as eloquently put by De Schutter, when an international organisation is required to comply with human rights in the course of its activities, it is not asked to expand its powers beyond those which it has been attributed by its member states.[124] The international organisation is not even necessarily asked to exercise the powers it has been attributed with a view to ensuring the promotion of human rights, but rather to ensure that it will not negatively impact upon human rights when, and insofar as, it takes action.[125] In that sense, the danger of 'creeping competences' usually associated with the imposition of human rights responsibilities on international organisations should not be exaggerated: while such a danger cannot be ignored, it should not be considered an unavoidable consequence.

A third way to approach the obligation of international organisations towards human rights is through the lens of the human rights obligations of their member states. It has been argued that human rights obligations of international financial institutions derive from those of their member states.[126] However, international organisations do not become indirect parties to international human rights treaties—that are binding upon their member states—simply because they have been attributed certain powers that could be exercised in violation of the rights recognised under those treaties. International organisations are separate legal entities that do not themselves have to comply with the obligations of their member states. The member states, though, may not escape pre-existing human rights obligations through the establishment of an international organisation. A posterior treaty cannot be invoked against the parties to the earlier treaty, for whom it is a *res inter*

---

[122] The UN Guiding Principles on Business and Human Rights were proposed by the Special Representative of the Secretary-General on the issue of human rights and transnational corporations and other business enterprises, John Ruggie, and endorsed by the UN Human Rights Council in its Resolution 17/4 of 16 June 2011.

[123] Report of the Independent Expert on the effects of foreign debt and other related international financial obligations of states on the full enjoyment of all human rights, particularly economic, social, and cultural rights, Cephas Lumina, UN Doc A/HRC/20/23 (10 April 2011), para 9.

[124] De Schutter (n 109) 55, 128.

[125] ibid.

[126] Skogly (n 100) 106; Manisuli Ssenyonjo, *Economic, Social and Cultural Rights in International Law* (2nd edn, Hart Publishing 2016) 117.

alios acta.[127] As the articles on the Responsibility of International Organizations point out, '[a] State member of an international organization incurs international responsibility if, by taking advantage of the fact that the organization has competence in relation to the subject-matter of one of the State's international obligations, it circumvents that obligation by causing the organization to commit an act that, if committed by the State, would have constituted a breach of the obligation'.[128] In other words, states that share some human rights obligations (for example the European Court of Human Rights or the European Social Charter) must not violate them when participating in decision-making in international organisations.[129] This rule has an impact on international organisations, even if they are not bound themselves to comply with the human rights obligations of their member states: the international organisations should not create obstacles to compliance by its member states with pre-existing international human rights obligations.[130] Hence, a prohibition exists against an international organisations imposing obligations on its member states that would lead them to disregard prior human rights commitments. It is crucial to note that, since the obligation on the international organisation is simply defined as a prohibition on taking measures which, if they were adopted by its member states, would constitute a violation of the international obligations of the latter, there is no need for the organisation to have been delegated powers in the domain considered: rather, the prohibition applies to the exercise by the organisation of the powers it has been attributed.[131]

With respect to the ESM, this means that the representatives of the Member States sitting both on the Board of Governors and the Board of Directors should be bound by their state's human rights obligations in their approval vote, which constitutes a state act and, as such, is subject to human rights law.[132] Regardless of whether they are ministers of finance or experts in the field of finance, the members of the boards are representing their states in the context of the ESM. As such, the Member States of the ESM are bound to comply with their pre-existing human rights obligations in the formulation of their policies in recipient countries.[133] State decisions, with an extraterritorial effect taken under the auspices of the ESM, should not interfere with their core economic, social, and cultural rights obligations under international law.[134]

---

[127] De Schutter (n 109) 60.

[128] International Law Commission, Draft Articles on the Responsibility of International Organizations, 2011 (A/66/10) [hereinafter ARIO], art 61.

[129] Frédéric Mégret and Florian Hoffman 'The United Nations as a Human Rights Violator? Some Reflections on the United Nations Changing Human Rights Responsibilities' [2003] Human Rights Quarterly 318; Margot Salomon, 'Of Austerity, Human Rights and International Institutions' [2015] European Law Journal 521.

[130] De Schutter (n 109) 66.

[131] ibid 68.

[132] See art 61 ARIO.

[133] Salomon (n 130) 536.

[134] CESCR General Comment 19.

The international legal personality of the ESM does not imply that decisions adopted by the organs of the international organisation can only be attributed to the organisation and not to the states that participated in the organs: this argument fails to distinguish between the act of the state and the act of the international organisation. The question is not one of attributing the international organisation's act to the state, but rather of the responsibility of the state for its own act. Further, the argument that there can be no state responsibility where there is international personality creates a 'legal limbo', where states control the international organisation but are immune from legal responsibility for the consequences of such control. It appears that the better approach is to recognise the possibility of both the responsibility of the state for the acts of its organ, such as an executive director that votes to approve a project, as well as the responsibility of the organisation for the acts of its organs, for example, a board of directors that approves a specific measure.[135]

VII. Conclusion

The framework of European financial assistance opens new and incisive ways in which international actors can impose conditions that violate fundamental rights. So far, thorough research has been carried out on the evaluation of the measures implementing these conditions under aspects of national law and the fundamental rights of the states concerned. However, maintaining that absolute ownership and responsibility for implementing the proposed policies belongs to national authorities does not respond to the lending reality, and is thus democratically problematic. The conceptualisation of the dismantling of human rights guarantees as a problem with European origins aims to address this shortcoming, opening space for the application of supranational and international human rights.

The application of supranational and international human rights in this context is not only legally possible but also normatively desirable. Measuring financial assistance conditions against human rights standards would counterbalance the executive-expertise bias of the making of financial assistance conditionality and minimise the risk of a blind subordination of conditionality to purely market-driven choices, which already dominate the post-crisis European governance framework. Reliance on the supranational and international human rights would also induce actors preparing and enforcing lending conditions to more carefully assess the impact of their actions on human rights and to adopt more inclusive and responsive procedures, actively engaging civil society actors and social partners in the making of conditionality.

---

[135] International Financial Institutions and Human Rights Law, Legal Analysis by the Center for International Environmental Law, Public Hearing, Inter-American Commission on Human Rights (127th Regular Period of Sessions) (1 March 2007) 4; see also Salomon (n 96) 153.

3

The Transition from Welfare to Workfare in Times of Crisis

A Double-based Reform of the Hungarian Welfare State

József Hajdú

I. Introduction

As for the budgetary background, when the global financial crisis hit in 2008, Hungary was already in a difficult economic situation in spite of the previous Socialist government having introduced major austerity measures between 2006 and 2008. The restrictions and cuts, however, resulted in stagnating economic growth, which dropped further because of the spiralling global financial crisis.

The overheating of the Hungarian economy had been apparent since 2006. The main problem of the financial crisis was (1) large account deficits,[1] (2) large

---

[1] The financial crisis came as a shock to Hungary, long seen as a solid investor base in former communist Europe. Until 2008, the forint had enjoyed a strong standing because of the country's prospects of adopting the euro. As a result of a strong forint and high interest rates, many Hungarians took out mortgages in foreign currency loans. Hungary's heavy dependence on borrowing from abroad at a time

József Hajdú, *The Transition from Welfare to Workfare in Times of Crisis* In: *European Welfare State Constitutions after the Financial Crisis.* Edited by: Ulrich Becker and Anastasia Poulou, Oxford University Press (2020). © The Contributors.
DOI: 10.1093/oso/9780198851776.003.0003

foreign debt,[2] (3) currency mismatches, and (4) misaligned exchange rates.[3] On 15 September 2008, Lehman Brothers went bankrupt, and financial markets throughout the world froze up. Suddenly, Hungary found itself with little or no international finance. In early October 2008, Hungary applied for fresh financial support from the International Monetary Fund (IMF). In this situation the IMF agreed on new stand-by agreements for Hungary.[4]

As the crisis erupted, an ad hoc cooperation developed between the IMF and the European Commission (EC). The IMF had the staff, rules, and procedures for handling a financial crisis, while the EC had none, so it conceded and assisted instead. The EC has co-financed the IMF programmes for Hungary. The big question mark was how the EC and the European Central Bank (ECB) would adapt to the crisis. The EC increased its balance-of-payments fund for Member States from €12 billion to €50 billion in 2008, and it provided major loans to Hungary.[5] Immediate support from the IMF[6] and the ECB allowed Hungary to avert the worst economic scenarios.

Nevertheless, the crisis underscored several weak points in the Hungarian societal system which could no longer be ignored, which include: (1) an extremely high exposure to foreign currency debt (mainly in the private sector);[7] (2) high levels of external debt financing;[8] (3) low levels of employment combined with a high rate of long-term unemployment;[9] (4) low average monthly wages compared

of worldwide economic instability had caused investors to question whether the country's economy could continue to survive.

[2] For example, to reduce public debt and the budget deficit, the government grabbed about €13.5 billion worth of mandatory private pension fund assets. This step was highly questionable because it was a mandatory and fully funded system and every member had their own pension savings record. However, the Hungarian Constitutional Court and the European Court of Human Rights (ECtHR) did not find it illegal.

[3] The illusory safety of the pegged exchange rate attracted large inflows of short-term lending from European banks. The temptation for international banks was irresistible. But this was a dangerous speculative scheme. The foreign exchange inflows accelerated imports and boosted balance-of-payments deficits.

[4] The deal came with strings attached, with the IMF insisting on an introduction of austerity measures to curb high public spending. However, right-wing politicians said the agreement endangered Hungary's independence and was an attack on its sovereignty, while some experts warned budget cuts could lead to job losses, exacerbating the already bleak economic situation and increasing the chances of recession.

[5] <http://www.piie.com> accessed 21 April 2017.

[6] IMF, 'Dealing with Household Debt' in *World Economic Outlook* (April 2012) ch 3 <http://www.imf.org/external/pubs/ft/weo/2012/01/pdf/c3.pdf> accessed 24 April 2016.

[7] Hungarian households' indebtedness in foreign currency is among the highest in eastern Europe, although total household debt peaked at a relatively modest level, 40 per cent of GDP, and is concentrated in roughly 800,000 households (or 20 per cent of the total). (By the time the crisis arrived in 2008, 100 per cent of all new lending and 50 per cent of household loans outstanding were in Swiss francs and collateralised by housing.) With the sharp depreciation of the Hungarian forint after the start of the global financial crisis, concerns that the rising debt service was undermining private consumption compelled the authorities to help foreign-currency-indebted households.

[8] <http://www.socialwatch.org/node/15989 - _edn1> accessed 12 April 2017.

[9] Unemployment in Hungary rose very rapidly after the political change in 1989, but reduced to 7.8 per cent by 2008 (with a very low activity rate of 56.7 per cent). As a result of the last economic crisis, the unemployment rate rose again to 10 per cent by 2009, 11.2 per cent by 2010, 11.6 per cent by 2011, 11.7 per cent by 2012, 11.8 per cent by first quarter of 2013 and then continuously decreased from the second quarter of 2013 to reach 8.3 per cent by the first quarter of 2014. Source: <http://www.ksh.hu> accessed 12 April 2017.

to the productivity level; and (5) premature consumerism generated by the banks offering low interest rate credits denominated mainly in Swiss francs, which led to very high levels of household indebtedness.[10]

As for the labour market, more than 50,000 jobs were lost from 2008 to 2011, and an additional 90,000 jobs were converted from full-time into part-time. The crisis also affected those groups with fixed-term contracts. Most jobs were lost in the for-profit sector and most new jobs were created in the non-governmental organisation sector.[11]

As a precondition for a new IMF loan and to avoid the EU's excessive deficit procedure in October 2012, the government approved new austerity measures,[12] which hit the majority of enterprises (banks, public service providers, and telecom companies in particular). The Hungarian population was also directly affected by increased taxes on financial transfers and fringe benefits, since these measures are known to worsen the situation of the domestic economy, which was already in recession. The package was aimed at cutting the budget deficit, representing 1.2 per cent of the gross domestic product (GDP).[13]

The government presumed that welfare dependency was to be blamed for the crisis (at least partially). It hoped to achieve the work-based society by introducing a public work scheme for the poor (a necessary precondition to being entitled to a reduced[14] social assistance), cutting the duration of unemployment benefit (maximum of ninety days, which is the shortest period in Europe), tightening the eligibility criteria for disability benefits, repealing the disability pension, and criminalising homelessness by passing a bill that punished those living on the streets.

In sum, it is necessary to see that the democratic transition in 1990 and the accession to the EU all had the positive effects of establishing and reinforcing institutions that guaranteed the respect of social rights. The Hungarian post-communist

---

[10] *OECD Economic Surveys: Hungary* (March 2012) <https://read.oecd-ilibrary.org/economics/oecd-economic-surveys-hungary-2012_9789264127272-en#page4> accessed 24 April 2017.

[11] Luca Koltai, 'Work Instead of Social Benefit? Public Works in Hungary' (Peer Review on 'Activation Measures in Times of Crisis: The Role of Public Works', Riga, Latvia, 26–27 April 2012) Mutual Learning Programme: Peer Country Comments Paper—Hungary <http://ec.europa.eu/social/BlobServlet?docId=10515&langId=en> accessed 25 April 2017.

[12] The government's plans included a 200 billion forint (€735 million) (about 0.7 per cent of GDP) tax levy on the financial sector for both 2010 and 2011; a 15 per cent cut in public sector expenditure (saving €171 million); lower wage ceilings for public sector employees (and the elimination of the thirteenth-month payment); a 15 per cent cut in budget subsidies for political parties in 2010; and reductions of seats in parliament and local assemblies were possibilities. Additionally, measures implemented by the previous government in 2009 include a gradual three-year increase in the retirement age to sixty-five; a two-year freeze in public sector pensions; a temporary increase to 25 per cent in VAT rates; and cuts in the 'jubilee' bonuses for the prime minister, ministers, and state secretaries plus a 10 per cent cut in sick pay and suspension of a housing subsidy. <http://www.europeaninstitute.org/index.php/112-european-affairs/special-g-20-issue-on-financial-reform/1180-austerity-measures-in-the-eu> accessed 19 August 2019.

[13] The GDP share of social expenditure in Hungary was below the European average and it is more than it was in 2011 <https://2010-2014.kormany.hu/download/5/8f/a0000/edp%20progress%20report%20201210_hu.pdf> accessed 23 August 2019.

[14] Approximately €80 per month.

welfare state[15] in the 1990s and early 2000s was created under the neoliberal influence of international organisations (mainly the World Bank (WB) and IMF)
while retaining lots of elements of solidarity.[16] The growing social tensions in the
mid-2000s due to a second economic crisis in the new millennium led first the left-
then the right-wing governments to shift the post-communist welfare state into a
punitive type of workfare system. The post-communist Hungarian welfare state's
social policy had created welfare dependency that should be abolished and underscored the ideology of the workfare programme ('Pathway to Work Programme')
introduced by the Socialist government in 2009. A few years later (first in 2010
and in 2012) the Conservative government pursued this workfare programme[17]

---

[15] The post-communist state tried to compensate for the loss of jobs and the increasing rate of
poverty due to the economic transition; hundreds of thousands of people became entitled to various
social benefits, making them inactive on the labour market. The governments of the 1990s, besides
the relatively generous unemployment benefit system, provided early exits from the labour market
in the form of early retirement and disability pension, and introduced a system of assistance benefits, János Zolnay, *Long-term Exclusion from the Labour Market, Poverty, and Social Policy Response*
(Pro Cserehat Association 2012) <http://www.pillangokutatas.bffd.hu/kutatas_pdf/long-term-
exclusion-janos-zsolnay.pdf> accessed 24 August 2019, and Zoltán Fábián and others, 'Hungary.
A country caught in its own trap' in Brian Nolan and others (eds), *Changing Inequalities and Societal
Impacts in Rich Countries. Thirty Countries' Experiences* (OUP 2014) and Oxford Scholarship Online
<http://www.oxfordscholarship.com/view/10.1093/acprof:oso/9780199687428.001.0001/acprof-
9780199687428-chapter-14> accessed 24 August 2019. In brief, the high rate of inactivity is the
direct outcome of the social policy of the transition period, see Zsuzsanna Vidra, 'Hungary's Punitive
Turn: The Shift from Welfare to Workfare' (March 2018) 51(1) Communist and Post-Communist
Studies 73, 75.
[16] Besides these solidarity types of social policy instruments, the neoliberal influence on the
Hungarian post-transition welfare state can also be identified: a so-called bifurcated system of social
provisions was created, see Julia Szalai, *Hungary's Bifurcated Welfare State. Splitting Social Rights and
the Social Exclusion of Roma*, Conference Paper 2012 <https://cers.leeds.ac.uk/2013/05/11/global-
racisms-conference/> accessed 24 August 2019. Although a new Social (Assistance and Service) Act
was drafted in 1993 that contained reference to social rights—the concept introduced in the Hungarian
legislation for the first time—it also relied on the idea of 'social justice and efficiency' that paved the
way for a dual system of provisions. It was agreed by the political elite that public money should support only those who are in need, while the more fortunate ones had access to other provisions such as
contribution-based social insurance and/or voluntary private pension schemes. Thus, separating 'the
two sub-systems for providing efficient and just welfare exclusively for those in need was an inherent
part of liberal welfare reforms of the 1990s' (Szalai, 2013:9). The dual welfare system also reinterpreted
the concept of social citizenship in so much as it lost its universal, all-embracing meaning as the social rights of the employed and the inactive. The social policy instruments implemented by the post-
transition Hungary in the 1990s, such as the creation of various entitlements to social benefits aiming
to compensate for the loss of jobs, made a large proportion of the population dependent on state subsidies, especially the low-educated whose reintegration into the labour market, given the structural
specificities of the Hungarian economy, is a highly complex social policy challenge. These provisions
were, nonetheless, important to prevent a significant portion of the population from falling into extreme poverty (Vidra (n15) 75).
[17] The most serious of these measures was the radical reduction of the level of—already conditional—
social benefits for those who were not participating in public work. Similarly, the wage one could earn
in public work was also significantly lowered. Additionally, public workers do not enjoy any employee
rights and their behaviour, as assessed by local authorities, is a precondition to being engaged in
public employment, see Zsuzsanna Vidra, 'Önkormányzatok és segélyezettek a workfare szorításában.
A szociális segély csökkentésének hatásai a vidéki Magyarországon'(2012) Szociológiai tanulmány. Pro
Cserehát Egyesület <http://www.pillangokutatas.bffd.hu/kutatas_pdf/szociologiaLtanulmany-vidra-
zsuzsanna.pdf> accessed 24 August 2019; Dorottya Szikra, 'Democracy and Welfare in Hard Times: The
Social Policy of the Orban Government in Hungary between 2010 and 2014' (2014) 24 Journal of

while implementing stricter and more punitive rules.[18] It is questionable, though, whether Hungarian social citizenship in the post-1990 era had been fully guaranteed or not. Many would argue that the social rights of the most vulnerable have always suffered significantly[19] and that none of the successive governments have tried to face this challenge full-heartedly.[20]

II. The main reforms and developments of the social security systems in Hungary during the last financial crisis

1. Brief outlook of the Hungarian social security system

Hungary inherited a fairly comprehensive welfare model from the Socialist regime, which was further consolidated at the moment of entering the European Union (2004) and the adoption of the EU acquis. However, this system has been challenged by a number of reforms after the last crisis.[21]

As for the general framework, there are five main branches of the social security system.[22] Pensions and health services are still classified as social insurance, even though the term 'social insurance' was not mentioned in the new Fundamental Law.[23] The other three statutory branches are unemployment insurance, family support, and the social assistance system, which are outside of the scope of social insurance.

In Hungary, all persons who are gainfully employed and those of equivalent status are insured against all social insurance risks. This includes persons in

European Social Policy 486; Anikó Vida and Zsusza Vidra, "'Ez is segely, csak mashogy hfvjak" – helyi szegenypolitikak: segelyezesi gyakorlatok es a kozmunka' in: Tünde Virág (ed), *Toresvonalak: Szegenyseg Es Etnicitas Videki Terekben* (Argumentum 2015), 68.

[18] Vidra (n 15).
[19] The relative poverty rate (set at 60 per cent of the median equivalent income) rose steeply from the late 1980s and continued after the change of regime till 1996–97; it increased from 10 to 14 per cent. From then until the second half of the 2000s it remained more or less stable but since the mid-2000s it has been on the rise. Between 2009 and 2012 it grew from 13.6 to 17 per cent. Poverty also had an ethnic face: while about 5–10 per cent of the population belong to the Roma minority, 20 per cent of them were poor in 2007 while in 2012 one third of the poor were Roma, see Vidra (n15) 75–76.
[20] <http://www.citsee.eu/citsee-story/farewell-our-social-rights-hungarian-governments-and-their-most-vulnerable-groups> accessed 22 August 2019 and National Social Report Hungary 2014 <http://ec.europa.eu/social/BlobServlet?docId=11712&langId=e> accessed 22 August 2019.
[21] Ágota Scharle and Dorottya Szikra, 'Recent Changes Moving Hungary Away from the European Social Model' <http://real.mtak.hu/37009/1/hungarian_welfare_system_19902013.pdf> accessed 6 May 2018.
[22] The Hungarian social security system offers protection against sickness, maternity, old age, changed working capacity, survivorship, children's education, and unemployment.
[23] New name of the Hungarian Constitution.

paid employment (including those in public administration), the self-employed (including members of cooperative societies), numerous groups of persons of equivalent status, and persons receiving income subsidy, jobseeker's benefit, and jobseeker's aid.

Everyone is automatically affiliated to a social insurance scheme as soon as he/ she begins to work in Hungary and is not exempted from being compulsorily insured. Employers pay social tax (not contribution[24]) and employees pay health, pension, and unemployment contributions.[25] Economically inactive uninsured persons residing in Hungary may voluntarily pay a lump-sum amount in order to be covered against healthcare risks. Anyone who voluntarily subscribes to the health and/or pension system can sign an agreement with the competent social security institution.[26]

2. Pension system after the economic crises

Due to the financial crises there were several important changes in the pension system. For instance, the retirement age was raised from sixty-two to sixty-five years by parliament in 2009 and, in consequence, the pensionable age will increase by three years for both men and women—by half a year annually from the middle of the decade until 2022.

The package of reforms introduced in 2012 contained further significant measures for the restriction or termination of early retirement and concerned the entire range of early retirement schemes and the system of disability pension services.[27] Both measures promote a longer presence of older generations on the labour market, and thereby increase the average employment rate.[28] Extended presence on the labour market will also have a positive impact on the initial pension levels (resulting in 5 to 6 per cent higher initial pensions in real terms), which will equally improve the sustainability and adequacy of pensions.[29]

Furthermore, the thirteenth-month public pensions (bonus pensions) were eliminated, and the combined price–wage indexation of ongoing pensions was

---

[24] Since 1 January 2012. The social tax is the earmarking of a defined amount of revenues to finance social security. The shift from taxing labour to taxing consumption in order to finance social security is based on several premises: 1. reduce non-wage costs in order to improve competitiveness, 2. achieve sustainable revenues for the social security system, 3. share the tax burden of social security systems more equitably.

[25] The current (2018) individual contributions for the basic benefits package are set at 18.5 per cent (10 per cent for pension and 8.5 per cent for healthcare and unemployment) of gross earnings, and the employer's social tax is 19.527 per cent of the insured person's gross earnings.

[26] József Hajdú and Árpád Homicskó, *Bevezetés a társadalombiztosítási jogba* (Patrocinium Kiadó 2017) 60–61.

[27] National Social Report Hungary 2014 (n 20).

[28] In response to these measures, tens of thousands of people will delay their retirement by an annual average of three to four years over the next decade, improving the sustainability of pensions.

[29] National Social Report Hungary 2014 (n 20).

replaced by pure price indexation (ie, the rise in pensions is now to be linked purely to prices, which rise more slowly than wages in the long run).[30]

Two fundamental changes caused by austerity measures in the Hungarian pension system deserve particular attention, namely (a) the restructuring of the second pension pillar, and (b) the abolishing of early retirement pensions.

a) The transfer of the mandatory, private pension scheme (second pillar)

The Hungarian statutory pension insurance system was comprehensively reformed in 1997.[31] This reform[32] was deeply influenced by the WB and the IMF. The main aim was to introduce a mandatory second pillar, defined-contribution (DC) system with individual retirement accounts. After the reform the mandatory pension system consisted of two pillars. The reformed (old) first pillar remained as the mandatory state pension insurance scheme, which was publicly managed and financed on a pay-as-you-go basis. The newly introduced second pillar was a compulsory, privately managed and funded system.[33]

Until November 2010, the mandatory private pension scheme (second pillar) was regarded as an immanent part of the Hungarian old-age pension system.[34] The vast majority of the insured persons' 'contribution' was paid in the form of a membership fee into the private pension funds that agreed to award either one-off payments or monthly pension-type allowances under certain terms of the membership agreement.[35]

Due to the financial crises and a huge state deficit—in 2010—the Hungarian government returned to the original (pre-1997) pension scheme, based on the compulsory social insurance system, on the one hand, and voluntary savings, on the other hand.[36] The rest of the former—WB inspired—second pillar became a voluntary insurance from 1 November 2010, fully funded and run by authorised and independent private pension funds, which are supervised by the Hungarian Financial Supervisory Authority of the National Bank.[37] Currently, it has only

---

[30] ibid.

[31] The new act on the social insurance pension entered into force on 1 January 1998.

[32] The origin of this second pillar was based on the WB's so-called Chilean model.

[33] The membership in the second pillar was obligatory for those who commenced their career after 30 June 1998. Meanwhile, those who had paid contributions, ie who had already been insured during an earlier period of time, also had the opportunity to voluntarily join it. If they joined this mixed funded pension system, they automatically waived a quarter of their pension rights already acquired prior to the access.

[34] Before the reversal (end of 2010), approximately 3.1 million people (more than 70 per cent of the labour force) were members of the mixed system. After the reversal, only 102,000 scheme members decided to remain in the DC scheme. Since 31 December 2011, all of the social security contributions (employee's and employer's contributions) go to the Pension Insurance Fund.

[35] See <http://www.penzugyiszemle.hu/vitaforum/a-nyugdijreform-alapkerdesei-5-egy-uj-magyar-nyugdijrendszer-alapjai> accessed 9 September 2017.

[36] In practice, from 1 November 2010 to 31 December 2011 all payments to the mandatory funded, DC scheme were suspended, and almost all contributions were redirected to the public pension scheme.

[37] See <http://www.mnb.hu/letoltes/mnb-wp-2016-2-final.pdf> accessed 8 September 2017.

57,000 members[38] who are allocated in the former second pillar and pay the membership fee on a voluntary basis.[39]

Members of the DC scheme had to decide by 31 January 2011 whether to remain in the scheme or transfer back to the pay-as-you-go public pension system.[40]

The nationalisation of the mandatory second pillar, effected through a series of measures which started in October 2010, was the most spectacular feature of the centre-right pension strategy. By blackmailing 70 per cent of the workforce (telling them their future pension contributions to the public system would be fruitless if they kept sending part of their pension contributions to the private pillar), the government nationalised the bulk of the mandatory private pension system, constituting about 9 per cent of the country's GDP.[41] Not only can the legitimacy of this measure be questioned, one can doubt how economically sound it was.[42]

The official reasoning of the government was that the capitalised private pension scheme was regarded as part of the statutory pension scheme from 1998 to 2011, but that it did not meet the relevant requirements, deteriorated the budget balance on a long-term basis, and significantly exacerbated the increase in public debt.[43]

At the time of the 'nationalisation' of private pension accounts, the government promised to set up individual public pension accounts, copying the logic of the destroyed private pillar.[44] However, the abruptness and illegitimacy of the whole counter-reform process undermined the trust of the public in the public pension system.[45]

---

[38] <http://hvg.hu/gazdasag/20171116_Magannyugdijpenztari_tagok_dilemmaja_maradni_vagy_vissza_az_allami_rendszerbe> accessed 6 July 2018.

[39] See <http://www.onyf.hu/en/structure.html> accessed 12 April 2017.

[40] See <http://www.oecd.org/els/public-pensions/PAG2013-profile-Hungary.pdf> accessed 8 September 2017.

[41] The ECtHR found an application by an individual opting to stay in the private system, claiming a breach of her right to property under the ECHR, manifestly unfounded: *E.B. v Hungary* App no 34929/11 (ECtHR, 15 January 2013). It is worth noting that the Hungarian government had by then made modifications to the pension regime that applied to those retaining their private pension (only 2 per cent, 98 per cent having moved to the state regime) so that they could obtain entitlements based on both their private and state sector contributions.

[42] National Social Report Hungary 2014 (n 20).

[43] In addition, numerous elderly insured people joined the mixed system without thinking of the consequences; however, the investment performance of funds could not live up to expectations. These processes had dramatically deteriorated the benefit prospects for the majority of fund members. Meanwhile, the transitional costs of the reform and the reimbursement obligation concerning the shortfall of social security revenues burdened the state budget. As a result, the operation of the two-pillar system considerably contributed to the growth in state debt and the deficit in public finances.

[44] The individual public pension account is managed by the Hungarian Treasury <https://egyeniszamla.onyf.hu/> accessed 8 September 2017.

[45] József Hajdú, *Hungarian Pension System in Transition*, Studia Iuridica Caroliensia (Károli Gáspár Református Egyetem 2011) 34–52.

b) Fundamental changes in early retirement pension rights

Before 1 January 2012, several generous early retirement options were available within the public pension system. Due to the financial crisis the government has decided to curtail the early retirement benefits.[46] The theoretical starting point of the 2012 changes was that pensions prior to retirement age cannot be claimed from 2012 onwards. Early retirement pensions awarded *before 2012* for those under the retirement age on 1 January 2012 were transformed into social benefits—for a transitional period until reaching the retirement age. Their amounts were not altered and they remained subject to the annual pension increase.[47]

Prior to 2012, early retirement pensions had been awarded in the form of (a) advanced pensions, (b) early retirement pensions,[48] (c) early retirement pensions due to hazardous working conditions,[49] (d) miners' pensions,[50] (e) artists' pensions,[51] and (e) other special early retirement benefits.[52] It is worth mentioning the transition of service pensions for professionals of military organisations awarded under especially favourable conditions and—as a general rule—the significant decrease in their amounts until reaching the retirement age.[53]

The 2012 changes guarantee that the actual pension age (ie the age reached at retirement) of old-age retirement approaches or even meets the statutory retirement age. As a result, the measures facilitate the long-term sustainability of the pension system to a great extent and, at the same time, terminate the former diverse varieties of early retirement alternatives.[54]

---

[46] <http://www.oecd.org/els/public-pensions/PAG2013-profile-Hungary.pdf> accessed 21 April 2017.

[47] József Hajdú and others, 'Hungary' in Willy van Eeckhoutte (ed), *International Encyclopaedia of Laws: Social Security Law* (Kluwer Law International 2019) 189–90.

[48] This was a tripartite agreement among the Pension Fund, the employer, and the employee, who was within five years of his/her retirement age. The financial coverage of the early retirement pension was paid by the former employer until the statutory retirement age.

[49] Those entitled to an early retirement pension due to hazardous working conditions could claim a benefit prior to retirement age as many years before reaching the retirement age as the number of years of early retirement due to hazardous working conditions they acquired up to 31 December 2012 or, if the starting day of the benefit is in 2012, up to the day preceding the starting day of that benefit.

[50] The decision was not fully welcomed, hence the miners demanded to restore the previous disability pension for miners <http://www.boon.hu/s-hungary-miners-demand-restoring-disability-pensions/2003242> accessed 18 August 2019.

[51] Artists with 25 years of activity were also entitled to old-age pension irrespective of their age.

[52] For example, pension for war widows and retired members of former (Socialist type) cooperatives.

[53] See <https://ec.europa.eu/employment_social/empl_portal/SSRinEU/Your%20social%20security%20rights%20in%20Hungary_en.pdf> accessed 22 April 2017.

[54] Furthermore, a petition to the Hungarian Constitutional Court—referring to a violation of the right to property, the prohibition of discrimination, and the right to social security—objected that the law maker had terminated the pension entitlements that had already been obtained before reaching the retirement age. The new regulation disposed of benefits prior to retirement age. Former members of parliament and those who had had service pensions before considered it injurious that the sum of their benefits prior to retirement age and of their service allowance was less than the sum of their pension before. The Commissioner for Fundamental Rights also submitted a petition regarding the suspension of the service allowance.

The Constitutional Court has declared that—following the Closing and Miscellaneous Provisions of the Fundamental Law—s 3 of art 70/E of the former Constitution authorised the law maker to reduce the sum of the pension before reaching the general retirement age, to change it into a social allowance,

3. Challenges to the statutory healthcare system

Hungary's wobbly healthcare system exemplified the country's fiscal crisis. Healthcare has been one of the most conflicted policy fields in Hungary. The recent governing party (Fidesz) ascended to hitherto unknown levels of popularity in 2008 by attacking the Socialist-led government's efforts to raise the level of private-sector financing in the medical system. The party forced the Socialists to cancel their policy of requiring patients to pay a 300 forint (€1.06) co-payment for doctor's visits, then strong-armed the administration into revoking its plan to open the health insurance system to private investment.[55] Two years later, when they took power, the Orban government's organisational reforms were largely confined to the nationalisation of hospitals, which had previously been run by municipalities. This move has made it easier to reduce overcapacity and to reduce regional and local disparities, but has also raised the danger of over-centralisation and lowering the healthcare budget. Furthermore, due to the economic crises, the huge state debt of the country, and the high unemployment rate, the payroll contributions to the health insurance fund were nearly half in 2010 of what they were in 2007. The severe cuts in public spending on healthcare have further aggravated these problems.[56]

Basically, three outstanding problems of the Hungarian statutory healthcare system should be underlined during and after the financial crises: (1) financing (underfinancing), (2) lack of qualified medical staff (doctors, nurses, etc) in the public sector, (3) spread of private healthcare providers.

The share of healthcare expenditure in total government expenditure was one of the lowest in the EU: in 2014 it was 10.4 per cent, as compared to the EU average of 13.9 per cent. At the same time, the population's direct financing of nearly 30 per cent is high. Household expenditure includes particularly high medicine expenditure. In outpatient care, 43 per cent of the costs are financed directly by the population and about 53 per cent by the state. The role of the government subsidy is about 90 per cent in hospital care. However, most hospitals and clinics are struggling with huge debts, which cause daily shortages of materials and equipment.[57]

---

or to terminate the payment of the pension in case of ability to work. Due to the express constitutional authorisation, the violation of acquired rights, the right to property, and the right to social security had not been determined. However, the Constitutional Court has declared that the concerned regulation did not violate the prohibition of discrimination as the different legal regulations for the concerned groups of people had constitutional reason. Constitutional Court Order No. 23/2013 (IX. 25).

[55] Service fee (co-payment) introduced by Act LXXI of 2007 on amendment of some particular health related legislation (2007 évi LXXI törvény az egyes egészségügyi tárgyú törvények módosításáról).

[56] <http://hungarianspectrum.org/2015/08/01/the-failure-of-the-hungarian-healthcare-system-two-recent-stories/> accessed 25 November 2019.

[57] Péter Gyenes and others (eds), 'A magyar egészségügyi rendszer teljesítményértékelése 2013–15' (2016) Állami Egészségügyi Ellátó Központ 116–18.

According to polls,[58] Hungarians consider the state of public healthcare and social stability the most pressing issues facing the country.[59] This is not a new phenomenon, but the last economic crisis enhanced it.

In Hungary, the health system had already exhausted its (non-structural) efficiency reserves by the time the financial crisis began, meaning that health system goals were likely to be eroded much faster. Hungary cut the national health insurance budget in response to the financial crisis.[60] Cuts were partly caused by rising unemployment, which reduced revenue from social insurance contributions.[61] In parallel, Hungary lowered the contribution[62] rate[63] and the government increased its budget transfers[64] on behalf of non-contributing but eligible population groups to compensate the statutory health insurance fund for the loss of revenue.[65] To compensate for reduced revenues, the employee healthcare contribution rate was increased by one percentage point and the base for the proportional healthcare tax levied on non-wage-related income was broadened (2011).[66] Furthermore, Hungary reformed its fiscal policy to increase revenue for health system financing and introduced a public health tax. The new tax earmarked for health was levied on food products high in salt, sugar, or carbohydrates (2011).[67]

To protect the Hungarian health insurance fund the government introduced incentives for improved checks of eligibility for statutory coverage to identify and penalise those who avoid paying contributions. A system was established in 2008—and made obligatory in 2009—for the verification of eligibility. This is a 'variety of lights' system within the health service providers' IT network. The 'green light' means that the patient's TAJ (social insurance) number is valid and the legal

---

[58] Standard Eurobarometer 81, Spring 2014, *Public Opinion in The European Union Report 2014* <http://ec.europa.eu/commfrontoffice/publicopinion/archives/eb/eb81/eb81_publ_en.pdf> accessed 22 August 2019.

[59] This is in contrast to European trends, where the citizens of most EU Member States consider unemployment the most important issue.

[60] In contrast, the new government announced it would increase public spending on health (2010) but the centrally set statutory health insurance budget did not change much nominally between 2008 and 2012, resulting in a decline in real terms.

[61] Philipa Mladovsky and others, 'Health Policy Responses to the Financial Crisis in Europe' in World Health Organization and European Observatory on Health Systems and Policies (eds), *Policy Summary 5* <https://apps.who.int/iris/handle/10665/108608> accessed 22 August 2019.

[62] The employer social insurance contribution (which includes the health insurance contribution) was renamed 'social contribution tax' (2012). This change seems to be playing with words, but in reality there is a significant difference: 'contribution' is earmarked state revenue that must be used to cover social insurance benefits and services, while 'social contribution tax' ends up in the central budget and it can be used for financing any expenditure of the state.

[63] Health insurance contributions paid by employers was reduced from 5 per cent to 2 per cent between 2008 and 2011.

[64] Tax transfers as a share of the statutory health insurance budget rose in 2009 and exceeded 50 per cent for the first time in 2010, before reaching an estimated 60 per cent in 2011 and remaining above an estimated 50 per cent in 2012.

[65] Mladovsky and others (n 61).

[66] <https://mafiadoc.com/economic-crisis-health-systems-and-health-in-europe-_5a0f31f41723dd55a2cdd891.html> accessed 22 August 2019.

[67] <https://ado.hu/ado/a-nepegeszsegugyi-termekado-chipsado/> accessed 22 August 2019.

status is in good order. A 'red light' means that the TAJ number is valid, but the legal status is 'unsettled'; in that case, the practitioner cannot refuse to provide care, but the patient must contact the local office of the health insurance administration to settle the 'legal status'. A 'blue light' signifies that the patient is insured abroad and that the TAJ card is temporarily invalid. A 'brown light' signifies that the TAJ card is 'invalid for other reasons', and in this case, the patient must pay a fee in order to receive healthcare services. A 'yellow light' indicates that the TAJ card is valid, but that the patient is eligible only for limited medical services; in that case, the patient is entitled to medical care through an agreement with the health insurer and the patient is not entitled to dental care unless it is deemed urgent, nor can they be placed on a waiting list for a transplant.[68]

The nationalisation of all hospitals, hoping to decrease costs after the crisis, turned to the opposite direction, hence year after year practically all Hungarian hospitals accumulated huge debts that had to be paid, at least in part, from the central budget. But, the quality of care has decreased and the number of doctors and nurses seeking employment abroad has been growing.

The fact that high numbers of medical professionals left the statutory healthcare institutions jeopardised the basic right to health in Hungary. There are three main reasons behind the external and internal migration of medical staff: (1) wages (underpayment of medical staff), (2) overwork, and (3) working conditions (underfinanced healthcare system). Furthermore, due to the economic crisis, it is commonly believed that many physicians went abroad to work for better remuneration and working conditions, but in reality, rather than leaving the country, considerably more physicians left public healthcare for the sake of private healthcare.[69] The internal migration of healthcare workers from the public healthcare system into the private sector is ever intensifying. Meanwhile, neither general practitioners nor public healthcare dentists can maintain their practices from the little income they have. Technical and economic staff in hospitals are also migrating into the private sector.[70]

4. Transformation of 'disability pension' to 'rehabilitation benefits'

The issue of disability was dealt with through a two-sided approach with a very similar target:[71] (1) the UN Convention's *integration approach* and (2) the *budget*

---

[68] <http://www.neak.gov.hu/felso_menu/lakossagnak/ellatas_magyarorszagon/jogosultsag_az_ellatasra/ellatasra_jogosultsag_igazolasa> accessed 22 August 2019.

[69] The current trend is that capital flows into private healthcare. While outpatient care and private practices were previously developed, today inpatient capacities are invested in.

[70] See <http://www.azenpenzem.hu/cikkek/kulfold-szivja-el-az-orvosok-tobbseget-egy-fenet/4399/?=hirkereso> accessed 3 October 2017.

[71] Most of the formerly disabled persons should be active and return to the labour market.

savings approach. The aim was multifaceted, aiming on the one hand to reintegrate those into the job market whose conditions allow them to work (the government estimated that out of the 900,000 disabled[72] about 220,000 could be reintegrated) and, on the other hand, to save some €300 million annually.

As for the former, originally the disability pension could be found in the Social Insurance Pension Act.[73] The first reform of the disability pension system was introduced in 2008. In a second phase, the disability benefits' system was reformed with Act CXCI of 2011 on the 'benefits for persons with changed working capacity and amendments of certain acts', which entered into force on 1 January 2012. From this date on, the social insurance-based invalidity pension scheme was completely closed,[74] and was replaced by disability and rehabilitation allowances.

The new benefits substituting the invalidity pensions aim at the reintegration of persons with changed working capacity into the labour market and focus on rehabilitation.[75] The new system of invalidity insurance offers two types of benefits by virtue of the health status and the remaining working capacity of the person claiming the benefit.[76] The aim of the complex rehabilitation procedure is to revise those entitlements that are based on the working capacity of persons who were in receipt of any benefit on the basis of damaged health until 31 December 2011.[77]

As part of the implementation of the reform, all disabled persons are obliged to go for a medical check-up to have their level of disability re-examined and revised. Due to the fact that the disability pension has been replaced by a disability and rehabilitation allowance, entitled persons have been deprived of their earlier protected status as pensioners[78] (eg the amount of pension cannot be changed whereas

---

[72] Even though this figure is not proved, one of the reasons for producing such a high figure was an unfortunate legacy (or we can call it abuse) of the past: after the Socialist regime changed in 1989, it became a widespread practice to get entitlement to disability pension that basically substituted unemployment insurance. A disability pension was an escape route to avoid unemployment.

[73] In fact, previously too many older workers chose this escape route (qualifying as a disabled person) rather than being unemployed or non-employed.

[74] Consequently, from this date new invalidity pensions and accident-related invalidity pensions (pensions for accidents at work or occupational diseases), rehabilitation annuities, regular social annuities for persons with ill health, temporary invalidity annuities, and health damage annuities for miners could not be awarded.

[75] The basic aim of the new disability benefits is, from one part, to guarantee incomes for those persons who are not able to work because of their state of health. From the other part, the aim of the rehabilitation is to reintegrate persons with changed working capacity into the labour market, to prepare them for employment in a suitable workplace, and to ensure such employments concerning their working capacity.

[76] 1. The person is entitled to rehabilitation benefit if he/she can be rehabilitated. Rehabilitation benefit may be provided for the period required for rehabilitation, within the limit of three years from the start of the benefit. 2. A person with changed working capacity is entitled to disability benefit if rehabilitation is not recommended, or he/she cannot be rehabilitated, or the person reaches the retirement age within five years.

[77] See <http://www.onyf.hu/hu/> accessed 12 April 2016.

[78] This practice was questioned by the Hungarian Constitutional Court in its Decision No 21/2018 (XI. 14). Acting ex officio, the Constitutional Court states that the Parliament failed to fulfil its legislative duty resulting from an international treaty by ordering the application of Section 12 (1) a) of the Act CXCI of 2011 on Benefits for Persons with Altered Working Ability and Amendments of Certain Acts in the cases under Section 33/A (1) a), without adopting, at the same time, rules allowing to take

the amount of allowance can easily be modified) and, with the new law, they are no longer entitled to free public transport and other reduced fees from which pensioners were benefiting. Furthermore, it should be underlined that depriving pensioners of their earlier legal status is contradictory to the principles of the constitutional state[79] in Hungary.[80]

The government policies trying to reintegrate disabled people into the labour market had a well-intended and legitimate aim. However, figures show that 90 per cent of those who are now entitled to rehabilitation allowance—their health condition having been assessed as improvable—were not able to find a job. The Secretary General of the Confederation of Hungarian Employers and Industrialists said this about the job market reintegration of disabled persons: 'in the middle of the crisis only very few employers can take disabled employees even if they get tax reduction. Just because it is the government's will to reintegrate the disabled into the job market, there will be no more new jobs.'[81]

5. Challenges to family policy

The financial crisis hit the cornerstone of Hungarian society: the financial and emotional stability of family. Hence, the Hungarian population is steadily decreasing. Highlighting the issue's importance, the Fundamental Law promulgated in 2011 affirms state support for 'the family as the basis of the survival of the nation' (article L(1)),[82] while on the economic side, the government spends almost 3.1 per cent of the GDP on financial support for families, compared to an average of 2.2 per cent among the twenty-eight Member States of the European Union.[83]

---

into account, during the determination of the benefit amount, the extent of the improvement of the actual physical condition substantially determining the conditions of the beneficiary's life, as well as the amount of the benefit determined before 1 January 2012.

[79] See for more detail Hungarian Constitutional Court's Decision No 1228/B/2010, AB of June 2011, and *Béláné Nagy v Hungary* App no 53080/13 (EctHR, 13 December 2016). (The applicant alleged that she had lost her means of support, guaranteed only by a disability allowance, as a result of legislative changes applied by the authorities without equity, in spite of the fact that there had been no improvement in her health.)

[80] See for more detail Hungarian Constitutional Court's Decision No 21/2018, AB of 14 October 2018, on how the lack of a regulation allowing for the appraisal of the actual condition of a person with a reduced ability to work violates Hungary's international obligations. In its decision the Hungarian Constitutional Court invalidated the regime of disability assistance as a violation of international human rights obligations, echoing earlier judgments of the European Court of Human Rights.

[81] See   <http://www.vg.hu/vallalatok/egeszsegugy/rokkantkartya-a-kiadas-sem-csokkent-tobb-munkahely-sem-lett-390714> accessed 19 August 2019.

[82] József Hajdú, 'The Right to Social Security in the Hungarian Fundamental Law (Constitution)' in *The Right to Social Security in the Constitutions of the World: Broadening the Moral and Legal Space for Social Justice* (ILO Global Study, Volume 1: Europe, International Labour Organization 2010) 89–106.

[83] ibid.

In spite of the economic crisis, the Hungarian family policy is fundamentally based on the assumption that most children under age three will be cared for at home; ie, that the vast majority of mothers will suspend their participation in the labour market for several years after giving birth. During this period, families were supported by four main types of allowances, which until 2014 were mainly granted to parents who were not in paid employment.[84] From 1 January 2014 on-wards, the system has been more flexible to allow for a combination of work and child-raising.[85]

Between 2010 and 2013, the government's family policy also provided debt re-lief and stimulated job growth. In line with this target, the government launched the Job Protection Action Plan in 2013,[86] offering tax incentives to employers for hiring mothers with small children.[87] The results were clearly evidenced by the statistical data: the employment rate of women was the highest in more than 20 years.[88] Simultaneously, the Labour Code is also supporting the development of a more flexible and family-friendly labour market.

6. Employment and unemployment policies

The economic crisis hit the labour market participants as well. The official rhetoric of the government was to create a strong national middle class based on the prin-ciple of a firm work ethic. The government suggested that increasing unemploy-ment and welfare dependency was to be blamed for the crisis (at least partially).[89] In fact, the basic financial aim was to save on the social security and assistance budget and the disciplinary aim was to activate welfare dependents to return to the labour market.

In Hungary, which has historically had a strong welfare state, only 54.6 per cent of the working age population was employed in 2011, the lowest number in Europe for that year. In 2010, the unemployment rate reached 11.8 per cent, one of the highest in the country's history. By 2014, it had shrunk to 7.3 per cent and then

---

[84] See József Hajdú, 'The Hungarian Maternity/Paternity and Family Cash Benefits System' in Görög Márta and Hegedűs Andrea (eds), *Lege duce, comite familia: Ünnepi tanulmányok Tóthné Fábián Eszter tiszteletére, jogászi pályafutásának* (Iurisperitus Bt. 2017) 60, 159–61.

[85] Nóra Jakab, Gábor Mélypataki, and Bernadett Szekeres, *A szociálpolitika jogi alapjai a XXI. század társadalmi kihívásainak tükrében* (Bíbor Kiadó 2017) 113–19.

[86] <http://rsm.hu/en/rsm-intelligence/job-protection-action-plan> accessed 21 March 2017.

[87] In 2014, allowances of a total amount of 9.3 billion forint were granted for a total number of 37,000 parents with young children. In March 2015, within the framework of the Job Protection Action Plan, contribution allowance was granted for employers of 39,803 parents returning from their child home care allowance/fee period.

[88] In 2014, the employment rate of women of 15–64 years of age was 55.9 per cent. At the time of the change of government in 2010, it was around 50 per cent.

[89] <http://www.citsee.eu/citsee-story/farewell-our-social-rights-hungarian-governments-and-their-most-vulnerable-groups#_ftn1> accessed 24 August 2019.

went to 4.5 per cent in January 2017. The government decided to change this trend and to transform the welfare-based society into a work-based society by creating opportunities and incentives to return to work and boost productivity, supporting disadvantaged groups[90] (from welfare to workfare).[91] However, the above-mentioned 'employment miracle' reflects some discrepancies.

First, employment data also include most Hungarian citizens who *work abroad*.[92] However, the dramatic turn-around occurred after 2014–2015. As a consequence of a massive labour migration, during and after the crisis, Hungary experienced a lack of skilled workers in many sectors. This has become one of the major obstacles to attracting foreign and domestic capital, upgrading economic activities, and sustaining international competitiveness (beyond the well-known anti-capital government policies).

Second, employment figures also cover people employed in *public work*. Even during the crisis, the previous Socialist government introduced the 'Road to Work' programme in 2009. It put emphasis on job creation instead of social assistance. While the idea was to help the unemployed reintegrate into the labour market, many experts warned that this scheme was very expensive for the state and that it was a completely useless instrument to enable the unemployed to find work on the primary labour market (mainly because the majority are low-skilled, long-term unemployed and live in poor, remote geographical areas with no job opportunities). At the same time, this labour policy measure resonated well with those who believed that there should be no social assistance without work.

The first public work programme of the Fidesz government (2010–2014) was introduced in 2010 and reformed by the Széll Kálmán Plan 1.0[93] in 2011.[94] From 2012, a new type of public employment system was introduced by which the state organises temporary employment schemes for people who cannot profit from their physical and mental skills but are eager and able to work. Therefore—instead of social assistance—via the public employment system they can receive higher wages. However, unskilled full-time public workers had to work for approximately 60 per cent of the minimum wage per month,[95] which is actually more than many people

---

[90] For those hardest hit by the economic downturn, where the unemployment for some has lasted decades and spanned generations, the government created a public work programme. Instead of a welfare cheque, the programme has brought those who are able to work back into the real labour market, giving them experience and self-respect.

[91] <http://abouthungary.hu/issues/stability-growth-jobs-the-hungarian-model-of-economic-recovery/> accessed 24 August 2019.

[92] Their number has increased in the last decade and reached about 400,000–600,000 persons (about 4–5 per cent of the population and 7–9 per cent of the active population).

[93] The Széll Kálmán Plan 1.0 was introduced in March 2011. As a structural reform plan, its main objectives were to reduce the public debt and foster the economy's growth through twenty-six objectives.

[94] Éva Nagy, 'On Poverty in Hungary and the Formation of a Penalistic State' (27 March 2014) <http://budapestbeacon.com/public-policy/on-poverty-in-hungary-and-the-formation-of-a-penalistic-state/> accessed 24 August 2019.

[95] This is 59.1 per cent of the minimum wage.

receive, as most are not employed on an eight-hour work contract or are only employed on a temporary basis. While they are out of the public work scheme, they receive social assistance that is around €86 per month.

However, the public work programme has its critics.[96] It has been maligned as some kind of forced labour or 'harsh' workfare, the provided jobs do not pay high wages, and the work is often menial labour. But the main point of the programme is to break the cycle of long-term welfare dependency and restore some sense of self-esteem. The basic question is: 'which is better: collecting a welfare cheque or getting paid for doing work?'[97] In fact, it cannot be used to bring unemployed people back into the labour market (almost totally financed by EU sources). However, these mainly unskilled people cannot be integrated into a competitive labour market without active labour market policies, which are mainly lacking from the current public work scheme.[98]

Third, a technical change in the legislation *cut the duration of unemployment benefits* to ninety days (down from nine months). The Hungarian jobseeker's benefit became the shortest among the Member States of the EU.

In sum, Hungary's level of employment statistically rose back to pre-crisis levels[99] but this state was achieved via public work programmes and an ever-higher number of Hungarians working abroad. Employment remains below pre-crisis levels in the private sector,[100] although corporates have not just cut their head-count, but also reduced working hours in order to avoid layoffs.[101]

[96] According to some experts, this model is expensive and ineffective and it criminalises the unemployed, but it looks good in the statistics: two-thirds of the new jobs in the country come from the public work figures that reduced the unemployment rate significantly.

[97] On poverty in Hungary and the formation of a penalistic state, see Nagy (n 94).
Regular participants in public work, who are usually registered jobseekers between the closure of a programme and the start of a new programme, do not necessarily accurately remember their status during a specific week, and it is also possible that they also consider themselves public work participants in between programmes. Uncertainty is further increased if, instead of the person concerned, another adult member of the household provides information.

[98] András Inotai, 'Looking Behind the Curtain: What About the Hungarian "Economic Miracle"?' (2015) 20 CIFE note de recherché 4–5.

[99] There were 4.053 million people employed in Hungary in the December 2013 to February 2014 period, the Central Statistical Office (KSH) has reported. The employment rate in the fifteen–seventy-four age group rose to a new ten-year high (53.2 per cent), whereas the unemployment rate dropped further to 8.6 per cent. The favourable set of figures is no surprise in light of the fact that, as a result of the winter public work scheme, there were 165,000 more fostered workers in January than in the same month of 2013.

[100] The National Bank of Hungary sees the rate of unemployment at around 10 per cent both in 2013 and 2014, because the rising labour supply cannot be taken up by the market.

[101] Gergő Rácz, 'Public Work Programs, Jobs Abroad Drive Down Unemployment' (2013) Budapest Business Journal <http://www.bbj.hu/economy/public-work-programs-jobs-abroad-drive-down-unemployment_69816> accessed 22 August 2019.

III. The impact of constitutional law on the content of social security rights

1. Transition from Constitution to Fundamental Law

One of the constitutional reactions to the economic crisis was that the Hungarian parliament passed Hungary's Fundamental Law[102] on 18 April 2011.[103] The Fundamental Law, which entered into force on 1 January 2012, supersedes the previous constitution (hereinafter the '1989 Constitution'), which, in keeping with the requirements of democratic constitutionalism during the 1989–1990 regime change, comprehensively amended the first written Constitution of Hungary (Act XX of 1949).[104]

The Fundamental Law—according to the declaration set forth in article B—seeks to maintain that Hungary is an independent, democratic state governed by the rule of law, and furthermore—according to article E—that Hungary contributes to the creation of European unity. However, in some respects it does not comply with the standards of democratic constitutionalism and the basic principles set forth in article 2 of the Treaty on the European Union.[105]

The new Fundamental Law provides for some issues to be decided by the governing majority, while it requires a two-thirds majority for others. This made it possible for the government (2010–2014 and 2014–2018), enjoying a two-thirds majority support, to write in stone its views on economic and social policy. A subsequent government possessing only a simple majority will not be able to alter these even if it receives a clear mandate from the electorate to do so. In addition, the prescriptions of the Fundamental Law render fiscal policy especially rigid since significant shares of state revenue and expenditure will be impossible to modify without obtaining a two-thirds majority. This hinders good governance since it will make it more difficult for subsequent governments to respond to changes in the economy and in society. The very possibility created by the Fundamental Law of regulating such issues of economic and social policy by means of two-thirds statutes is incompatible with parliamentarism and the principle of the temporal division of powers.[106]

---

[102] The drafting of the Fundamental Law took place without following any of the elementary political, professional, scientific, and social debates. The Council of Europe's Venice Commission also expressed its concerns related to the document.

[103] For the 'official' English translation of the Fundamental Law, see <http://www.kormany.hu/> accessed 10 March 2017.

[104] For the official English translation of the Opinion, see <http://tasz.hu/files/tasz/imce/2011/opinion_on_hungarian_constitutional_questions_enhu.pdf> accessed 24 August 2019.

[105] Balogh Zsolt and Hajas Barnabás, 'Rights and Freedoms' in Schanda Balázs, Varga Zs András, and Csink Lóránt (eds), *The Basic Law of Hungary: A First Commentary* (Clarus Press 2012).

[106] For example, pensions: the Fundamental Law itself excludes the possibility that a subsequent governing majority create a compulsory funded pension scheme based on capital investment. It is not compatible with the functions of the constitution that the governing majority excludes the application of

2. Right to social security: state goals instead of social rights

The 1989 Constitution set forth that citizens have the right to social security[107] and that they are entitled to the support required to live.[108] Even though it is outside of the examined period, there was a milestone decision[109] of the Hungarian Constitutional Court concerning social security, where the Court established as a general constitutional requirement that the right to social security obliges the State to secure a minimum livelihood, through all of the welfare benefits, necessary for the realisation of the right to human dignity.

Here the institutional guarantees of social security must be mentioned. The 1989 Constitution mentioned the social insurance system and the system of social institutions in relation to implementing social security, while the new Fundamental Law talks about a general state pension system and a system of social institutions. Besides the state pension system, the Fundamental Law allows for the 'operation of voluntarily established social institutions'[110]—which also promotes the livelihood of the elderly. Thus the two-pillar pension system (first pillar: statutory state pension and second pillar: voluntary pension funds) was stabilised by the Fundamental Law.[111] However, the text of the Fundamental Law rules out the reinstatement of

one of the available public policy solutions in the Fundamental Law without having been empowered by the electorate to do so. In addition, art 40 of the Fundamental Law assigns the basic rules of the pension system to a cardinal act, which, as mentioned above, requires a two-thirds majority. In any case, the Fundamental Law makes it possible that the retirement age and other conditions of eligibility as well as the basis for calculating pensions will be modifiable only by a two-thirds majority. In addition, art L of the Fundamental Law specifies that the regulation of family welfare support is also to be subject to two-thirds statutory regulation. It is clear, however, that the pertaining prescriptions of the Fundamental Law create the possibility that every detailed issue of the family welfare support will only be modifiable subsequently by a two-thirds majority.

[107] Trócsányi László (ed), *A mi alkotmányunk* (Complex Kiadó 2006) 483–84.

[108] However, for the sake of accuracy it must be mentioned that the provisions of the 1989 Constitution relating to social rights were the subject of debate in the practice of the Constitutional Court too (see Constitutional Court Order No. 24/1991 (V. 18.)). The issue under debate was whether these (social rights) were rights or were formulated only as a state objective. Finally, the practice of the Constitutional Court reinforced the latter position, ie that the Constitution's rules on social rights served only as guidance for the state and no right can be derived from the Constitution (in spite of being worded as a right), and at best they can be secondary, subjective rights created by legislation. The consideration underlying this opinion was that they shall not be fundamental rights because they depend on the economic performance of the state. If the economic performance declines, there are two options: either the state does not observe the provisions of the Constitution and thus the Constitution will be devalued, or it observes them and impending state bankruptcy will follow.

[109] Decision No 32/1998 (VI. 25), AB decision. The Hungarian Constitutional Court establishes that the right to social security contained in art 70/E of the Constitution entails the obligation of the state to secure a minimum livelihood through all of the welfare benefits necessary for the realisation of the right to human dignity.

[110] These are the voluntary and supplementary pension funds.

[111] However, the two-pillar pension system implied by the Fundamental Law is not the same as the two-pillar (statutory social insurance pension and compulsory private pension) model proposed earlier by the WB.

the previously eliminated compulsory private pension fund (which was originally the second pillar under the WB concept) and there is absolutely no mention of social insurance.[112]

As for the content and legal enforcement of social security rights, the new Hungarian Fundamental Law, in keeping with the spirit of the old Constitutional Court decisions, treats social security not as a right, but as a state goal. The second sentence of paragraph (1) of article XIX is virtually a word-by-word repetition of the second phrase of article 70/E of the 1989 Constitution, but while this clearly only lists examples of those entitled to receive assistance, the new text can be interpreted as an exhaustive list of the entitled persons, from which it can be concluded, for example, that the state only needs to concern itself with creating social security protection for the persons included in the list[113] (and not persons unemployed through their own fault, for example). Another change is reflected in the fact that the assistance to be provided is no longer of the extent 'necessary for subsistence' but just the extent 'determined by law'.

Furthermore, 'social insurance' has been completely removed as a means of social security and only the system of social institutions and measures remains in the text. The Fundamental Law contains regulations which aim to restore balance by reducing social security, public welfare, and public services. These provisions aim to ensure that there are no constitutional barriers to introducing measures to make benefits dependent on the performance of work or other activity regarded as socially beneficial, in keeping with the new social policy approach. At the same time, in connection with the new Fundamental Law, it must be noted that it adds to the state goals within the scope of social rights. The state aims to provide every person with decent housing[114] and access to

---

[112] Juhász Gábor, 'A gazdasági és szociális jogok védelme az Alkotmányban és az Alaptörvényben' (2012) évi 1 szám Fundamentum 35 <http://www.fundamentum.hu/sites/default/files/12-1-02.pdf> accessed 14 March 2017.

[113] 'Every Hungarian citizen shall be entitled to assistance in the case of maternity, illness, disability, handicap, widowhood, orphanage and unemployment for reasons outside of his or her control, as provided for by an Act.'

[114] The Constitutional Court examined the issue within the framework of constitutional interpretation whether the right to housing can be deduced from the Constitution. The parliamentary commissioner for civil rights and the ombudsman for national and ethnic minority rights submitted a petition to the Constitutional Court asking the Court to interpret art 70/E of the Constitution on the right to social security and to decide whether the right to housing forms a part of the right to social security. According to art 70/E.1 of the Constitution, citizens of the Republic of Hungary have the right to social security. In the case of old age, sickness, disability, being widowed or orphaned, or unemployment through no fault of their own, they are entitled to assistance necessary for their subsistence. Art 70/E.2 of the Constitution requires the Republic to implement the right to assistance through the social security system and the system of social institutions.

The Constitutional Court's jurisprudence has made it clear that the legislature has a relatively wide discretion in determining the methods and degrees by which it enforces constitutionally mandated state goals and social rights. A violation of the Constitution may arise only in borderline cases when the enforcement of a state goal or a protected institution or right are clearly rendered impossible by either interference by the State or, more frequently, by its omission. Above that minimal requirement, however, there are no constitutional criteria—except for the violation of another fundamental right—to

public services, which were not included in the 1989 Constitution (article XXII).[115]

Under the provisions of the Fundamental Law on social rights it is clearly possible to interfere with existing rights,[116] to rearrange them, and ultimately to transform the social security system. According to the Fundamental Law, the state enjoys a great degree of freedom in the field of social rights, and this may result in social and economic policies which are more flexible and better suited to the relevant circumstances. A recent affirmation of this freedom can be seen in the Constitutional Court's decision on the preferential treatment of women in relation to early retirement, allowing only them to receive an old-age pension after forty years of service.[117] The Constitutional Court held that Hungary's Supreme Court (the Curia) had been wrong to overrule the refusal of the National Election Committee to authenticate the question 'whether men and women should be entitled to the same rights to early retirement' for a referendum. Given that lowering the age of early retirement for men would increase the demands on the state budget, the Court argued (rather permissively) that the question falls within a category on which no referendums are allowed under the Fundamental Law.[118] Accordingly,

determine whether legislation providing for a state goal or a social right is constitutional or not. In its Decision No 43/1995 (Bulletin 1995/2 [HUN-1995-2-004]) the Constitutional Court pointed out that the state meets its obligation specified in art 70/E of the Constitution if it organises and operates a system of social insurance and welfare benefits. Within this, the legislature can itself determine the means whereby it wishes to achieve the objectives of social policy. It is important, however, that social assistance as a whole may not be reduced to below a minimum level which may be required according to art 70/E of the Constitution.

The Hungarian Constitutional Court held that the constitutional right to social security includes the duty of the state to guarantee minimum conditions of subsistence, therefore the state is obliged to provide accommodation for the homeless if human life is in imminent danger. The obligation to provide shelter, however, is not identical with ensuring the right to housing in a broader sense, because the state is only required to provide a roof if human life is directly threatened by lack of accommodation.

To realise the citizen's right to minimum subsistence, the state is obliged to operate and maintain a social security system. The protection of human life and dignity (art 54 of the Constitution) is a fundamental principle to be upheld when creating this system of social provisions. The Constitutional Court reached a negative answer, at the same time maintaining that in the case of imminent danger to life the state shall provide a dwelling (Constitutional Court Decision No 42/2000 (XI. 8).

[115] Gábor (n 112).
[116] One might venture to say that the prohibition set up by Constitutional Court Decision No 43/1995 (VI. 30), according to which the abrupt change of a social insurance service or its downgrading from insurance to assistance qualifies as interference into a fundamental right, no longer exists in this form. The Constitutional Court declared that the partial shifting of burdens to insured persons and to employers on the grounds of difficulties encountered in the operation of the social security system, provided that it is proportionate and that the reasons behind it are constitutional, is not necessarily unconstitutional. In such matters, however, it is a constitutional requirement that those concerned learn of the risk of such a shift in burdens early enough to be able to calculate further risks and to make arrangements for insurance cover.
[117] Constitutional Court Decision No 28/2015 (IX. 24).
[118] According to art 8.3.b of the Fundamental Law, no referenda may be held on the central budget, the implementation of the central budget, central taxes, duties, contributions, customs duties, or the content of Acts determining the central conditions for local taxes. The preferential treatment of women also did not violate the principle of equality under art XV.2 of the Fundamental Law, which stipulates that 'Hungary shall guarantee the fundamental rights to everyone without any discrimination,

the provisions of the Fundamental Law do not impede the efforts of the state in a poorer economic situation, and the rules on social security alone will not bankrupt the state merely because they shall be observed under all circumstances. However, the ultimate limit lies not in the regulations on social rights but in the realisation of human dignity.[119]

As for the institutional protection of fundamental rights the government elected in 2010 quickly restricted the competence of the Constitutional Court. There were two limitations introduced to the access to the Constitutional Court: (1) constitutional complaint system[120] and (2) budgetary constraint.[121] However, the limitations of the Court's powers on central budgetary issues has been a subject of strong criticism: 'Although it is undoubtedly the constitution-making power's competence to amend the competences of the Constitutional Court, their curtailing is hardly in line with the rule of law. It is definitely not acceptable if an entire sector (finances and taxation) is exempted from the requirement of compliance with the constitution.'[122]

in particular on grounds of sex'. Rather, it followed from the special protection to which women are entitled under arts XV.5 and XIX.4 of the Fundamental Law. Under provision art XV.5 of the Fundamental Law, Hungary shall take special measures to protect, among others, women and art XIX.4 of the Fundamental Law reads that 'Hungary shall contribute to ensuring a livelihood for the elderly by maintaining a unified state pension system based on social solidarity and by allowing for the operation of voluntarily established social institutions. The conditions of entitlement to state pension may be specified by an Act also in view of the requirement for increased protection for women'. A successful referendum would violate this constitutional right.

[119] See <http://projektjeink.birosag.hu/sites/default/files/allomanyok/e-learning/alaptorveny_birok/at_szabadsag/> accessed 20 February 2020.

[120] From 1 January 2012 abstract posterior constitutional review can be initiated by (1) the government, (2) one-quarter of the members of parliament, (3) the Commissioner for Fundamental Rights (upon the recommendation of the Venice Commission, which urged to keep an indirect access mechanism through which an individual could reach the Constitutional Court), (4) the head of the highest judicial authority (Kúria), and (5) the Prosecutor General. However, before that date the Hungarian Constitutional Court was accessible to literally everybody ('actio popularis'), without the requirement to show any legal interest in challenging any legal regulation in the Hungarian legal system.

[121] Art 37(4) of the Fundamental Law:

As long as the state debt exceeds half of the Gross Domestic Product, the Constitutional Court may, within its powers set out in Art 24(2)b) to e), review the Acts on the central budget, the implementation of the central budget, central taxes, duties and contributions, customs duties and the central conditions for local taxes for conformity with the Fundamental Law exclusively in connection with the rights to life and human dignity, to the protection of personal data, to freedom of thought, conscience and religion, or the rights related to Hungarian citizenship, and it may annul these Acts only for the violation of these rights.

Accordingly, there is a conditional limitation—as long as the state debt exceeds half of gross domestic product (GDP)—for reviewing Acts on the central budget, the implementation of the central budget, central taxes, duties and contributions, customs duties, and the central conditions for local taxes for conformity with the Fundamental Law <http://www.venice.coe.int/WCCJ/Seoul/docs/Hungary_CC_reply_questionnaire_3WCCJ-E.pdf> accessed 24 August 2019.

[122] Opinion of the President of the Constitutional Court, see Péter Paczolay, 'Limits and Possibilities of Expansion' (26 September 2013) International Conference on Jurisdiction of the Constitutional Court in Riga.

IV. Conclusion

The last financial crisis urged Hungary to enact several laws, including the new Constitution (Fundamental Law), which is the fundamental basis and framework of legislation relating to basic human (social) rights during the last decade. However, some pieces of this bulk legislation (eg transforming the second pension pillar, changing the immanent principle of disability, banning early retirement, and introducing a controversial public work programme) revealed a two-sided nature. On the one hand, the traditionally developed social insurance system, including the work-based proportional benefit system, is gradually disappearing from the Hungarian social security scheme. On the other hand, the Fundamental Law contains regulations which aim to restore balance by reducing social security, public welfare, and public services. These provisions aim to ensure that there are no constitutional barriers to introducing measures to make benefits dependent on the performance of work or other activities regarded as socially beneficial, in keeping with the new social policy approach. This is the Hungarian workfare model.[123]

Pursuant to the provisions of the Fundamental Law, the state has a greater and more flexible freedom in providing social rights. Therefore it treats social security not as a right, but as a state goal. Furthermore, it inherits the constitutional basis for introducing austerity measures during the crisis period, which might assist in the marginalisation of the traditional solidarity- and income-based social insurance system. Due to the fundamental changes in the unemployment and social assistance system[124] and the fact that the amount of the social assistance did not change for many years, an increasing number of marginalised populations is living in poverty.[125]

---

[123] As a 'preventive' action to save pension budget the early retirement system was abolished (2012) and the ancient disability pension was transferred to an (activation-based) invalidity benefit system (1998 and 2011), which left many disabled persons abandoned and the registered jobseekers were not entitled to jobseeker's benefit after ninety days. The public work programme—offering salary below the minimum wage—tried to absorb the redundant former and recent long-term unemployed social assistance receivers.

[124] Due to the fact that jobseeker's benefit is payable up to a maximum of ninety days, the number of registered jobseekers without jobseeker's benefit has increased (in 2010 it was 38 per cent and in 2017 it was 48 per cent). Besides the exclusion from the benefit, the additional problem was that the monthly amount of the basic social assistance had not changed since 2008, and it was and still is only 28,500 forint (€90). It is only 18 per cent of the monthly minimum wage in 2020.

[125] Due to the low activation rate (among disabled, unemployed, and social assistance receivers) and gloomy demographic trends and economic situation, the austerity measures were undoubtedly the correct actions in Hungary. The main problem in the last ten years' social policy was that it supported mainly the middle class families with two or more children. However, the vulnerable population who had not received an increase in real income was persistently marginalised and the public workers of the workfare model were indirectly stigmatised <https://g7.hu/kozelet/20171017/csak-a-legszegenyebbekrol-feledkezett-meg-a-kormany-mikozben-nekiesett-a-szocialis-halonak/> accessed 10 February 2020.

It is difficult to decide the roots of these changes and whether the financial crisis[126] or the changing economic[127] and political reality determined them. Sometimes one could have the impression that these changes are Janus-faced norms, which seemingly provide social rights but substantially do not provide progressive social security.

---

[126] <http://www.attac.hu/2017/11/austerity-measures-in-central-and-eastern-europe-especially-in-hungary/> accessed 18 August 2019.

[127] As for economic policy, the so-called 'unorthodox economic policy' was launched in 2010 by breaking off cooperation with the IMF, whose aid of €20 billion the government intended to replace with investment from eastern countries such as Azerbaijan, China, and Russia, which seemingly would not demand strict terms for money. However, the decision turned out to be a somewhat poor one, since the 'eastern opening' never brought the economic fruit expected. In fact, it also included a mixture of steps that the IMF highly recommended and some that the IMF clearly opposed. The former included a reduction of many social benefits, such as unemployment benefits and pension pillars, and aimed to bring the budget under control.

4

The Latvian Response to Its First Economic Crisis under a Free Market Economy

Kristīne Dupate

I. Introduction

At the end of 2008 Latvia had hardly been hit by the global economic crisis and yet, by the second quarter of 2009, the decrease in its gross domestic product (GDP)—a change of a staggering 18.7 per cent between the first halves of 2008 and 2009—was the fourth highest among European Union (EU) Member States. More specifically, while the state budget's expenditure rose by 7.2 per cent in the first half of 2009, its revenue dropped by 15 per cent. To overcome this crisis Latvia had to fall back on the help being offered by foreign donors and, as a result, its external debt increased by 33.2 per cent in the second half of 2009.

Internally, this situation led the government to make sharp cuts in public expenditure in general and in the social security system in particular. It is a

Kristīne Dupate, *The Latvian Response to Its First Economic Crisis under a Free Market Economy* In: *European Welfare State Constitutions after the Financial Crisis*. Edited by: Ulrich Becker and Anastasia Poulou, Oxford University Press (2020).
© The Contributors. DOI: 10.1093/oso/9780198851776.003.0004

contentious matter among economists whether this 'belt-tightening' policy was a failure, since Latvia experienced a huge wave of emigration, losing around 15 per cent of its working-age population, or it was real success story,[1] since the Latvian economy began to recover in 2010 and was demonstrating the fastest growth of any EU Member State by the first three quarters of 2012.

Although there was a rise in unemployment and a dramatic decrease in income, which led to the bankruptcy of numerous households after credits 'skyrocketed' in 2007–2008, there was no major public response to the relevant measures in the form of demonstrations or protests. This phenomenon may be explained by Latvia's history. First, the population had experienced far more severe economic difficulties after the collapse of the Soviet Union, which had necessitated at least a decade-long period of rebuilding the economy; replacing the absolutely state controlled model with a free market capitalist one. Second, due to the Soviet regime there was no developed tradition of protesting against political decisions.

From a legal perspective the crisis did not have a structural influence on Latvia's social security system because the measures adopted constituted only temporary expenditure cuts. At the same time some cuts, in particular those relating to pensions and allowances, were contested before the Constitutional Court. These decisions represent valuable developments in Latvian constitutional law doctrine, especially serving to clarify the legislator's procedural obligations when it wishes to restrict already acquired rights.

In order to evaluate these matters in the requisite depth, this chapter will introduce the Latvian social security system, assess the austerity measures taken in this field, and highlight the impact of international loan agreements. It will also analyse the manner in which such measures were contested before the Constitutional Court, focusing particularly on the impact of different human rights and international law and on identifying developments in national constitutional law doctrine. Lastly, the chapter also describes the response of parliament to the decisions of the Constitutional Court where it found the relevant restrictions to have been unconstitutional.

---

[1]   See, for example, Anders Åslund and Valdis Dombrovskis, *How Latvia Came Through the Financial Crisis* (Peterson Institute for International Economics 2011); Olivier J Blanchard and Mark Griffiths, 'Gruss International Monetary Fund, Boom, Bust, Recovery: Forensics of the Latvia Crisis' (fall 2013) *Brookings Papers on Economic Activity* <https://www.brookings.edu/wp-content/uploads/2016/07/2013b_blanchard_latvia_crisis.pdf> accessed 5 April 2020.

II. Reforms in national social security systems

1. Overview on the social security and healthcare system

The Latvian social security system in principle includes the right to education, healthcare, social insurance, social flat-rate allowances, and social assistance.[2] Statutory social insurance schemes cover the following risks: old age, unemployment, accidents at work and occupational diseases, disability, maternity, paternity, and parenthood.[3] All employees must make mandatory social insurance contributions with respect to all of these risks.[4] Self-employed persons are only required to make such mandatory social insurance contributions if they earn above a certain minimum annual income[5] and their insurance only covers the risks of old age, disability, sickness, maternity, paternity, and parenthood.

Statutory social insurance schemes are financed by the contributions made by economically active persons. There is a specific statutory social insurance budget for each type of social risk.[6] There is only one exception—old-age pensions, which are also financed by the state budget.[7] The old-age pension scheme is based on a two-tier model, whereby a certain part of the contributions paid by economically active persons does not go to the special social insurance budget but gets invested in financial markets. A person may choose an investment scheme that is provided by private organisations.[8] Apart from the general old-age pensions there are statutory occupational pensions or long-term service pensions for persons who were public service employees. In particular, it applies to officials who served in the ministry of the interior,[9] the military,[10] or as judges,[11] prosecutors,[12] diplomats,[13]

---

[2] Law on Social Security (*likums 'Par sociālo drošību'*), OG (Official Gazette) No 144, 21 September 1995.

[3] Art 4 of the Law on Statutory Social Insurance (*likums 'Par valsts sociālo apdrošināšanu'*), OG No 274/276, 21 October 1997.

[4] Art 5 of the Law on Statutory Social Insurance (n 3).

[5] The Cabinet of Ministers Regulation No 1478 'Regulations on minimum and maximum amount of mandatory statutory social insurance contribution object' (*Noteikumi par valsts sociālās apdrošināšanas obligāto un brīvprātīgo iemaksu objekta minimālo un maksimālo apmēru*), OG No 250, 20 December 2013.

[6] Arts 7–11 of the Law on Statutory Social Insurance (n 3).

[7] See also the Law on State Pensions (*likums 'Par valsts pensijām'*), OG No 182, 23 November 1995.

[8] State Funded Pension Law (*Valsts fondēto pensiju likums*), OG No 78/87, 8 March 2000.

[9] Law on Pensions for Employees of the System of the Ministry of Interior Affairs with Special Ranks (*Par izdienas pensijām Iekšlietu ministrijas sistēmas darbiniekiem ar speciālajām dienesta pakāpēm*), OG No 100/101, 16 April 1998.

[10] Law on Pensions for the Military (*Militārpersonu izdienas pensiju likums*) OG No 86, 1 April 1998.

[11] Law on Long-Term Service Pensions for Judges (*Tiesnešu izdienas pensiju likums*) OG No 107, 7 July 2006.

[12] Law on Pensions for Prosecutors (*Prokuroru izdienas pensiju likums*) OG No 181, 3 June 1999.

[13] Law on Long-Term Service Pensions for Diplomats (*Diplomātu izdienas pensiju likums*), OG No 183, 15 November 2006.

officials of the anti-corruption bureau,[14] officials of the constitution bureau,[15] and artists employed by the state or municipalities.[16] The aim of the long-term service pensions is to provide a fair pension and, where necessary because of the specific nature of the service, before the general statutory pensionable age. The long-term pensions are funded by the state budget.

The Latvian social security system, aside from statutory social insurance allowances, provides universal (ie non-income dependent), flat-rate, and non-contributory statutory allowances fully financed by the state budget. Such allowances predominantly aim to support families with minor children. For example, parental allowance, family allowance, and fostering allowance. Allowances that do not have this aim are universal and flat-rate allowances, and take the form of either an allowance for the care of a severely disabled person or a funeral allowance.[17]

The social assistance system in general envisages two types of assistance: an income-test-based allowance and the provision of social services.[18] If a person is legally recognised as poor, he or she is entitled to a minimum subsistence and housing allowance. Such allowances are provided by the municipalities, although ultimately the state budget provides the requisite funds.[19] Social services for specific groups with specific purposes are provided and financed by the state. For example, those for the rehabilitation of disabled persons or for victims of violence or trafficking. Other social services are provided by the municipalities within the limits of the available municipal budget.

All Latvian citizens (and a specific category of non-Latvian citizens: migrants from the former Soviet Union that were not automatically entitled to Latvian citizenship) are subject to statutory health insurance, universally without any conditions. However, for certain types of statutory medical treatment, the payment of a reasonable amount (calculated on the basis of the average income in the country) may be required.[20]

---

[14] Law on the Long-Term Service Pensions for the Officials of the State Anti-Corruption Bureau (*Korupcijas novēršanas un apkarošanas biroja amatpersonu izdienas pensiju likums*), OG No 164, 22 October 2008.

[15] Law on the Long-Term Service Pensions for the Officials of Constitution Protection Bureau (*Satversmes aizsardzības biroja amatpersonu izdienas pensiju likums*), OG No 2, 7 January 2004, repealed on 17 June 2015, replaced by Law on Long-Term Pensions of the Officials of the State Security Institutions (*Valsts drošības iestāžu amatpersonu izdienas pensiju likums*), OG No 107, 3 June 2015.

[16] Law on Pensions for Artists of State and Municipal Orchestras, Choirs, Concert Organisations, Theatres, and Circuses (*Valsts un pašvaldību profesionālo orķestru, koru, koncetrorganizāciju, teātru un cirka mākslinieku izdienas pensiju likums*), OG No 106, 7 July 2004.

[17] State Social Allowances Law (*Valsts sociālo pabalstu likums*), OG No 168, 19 November 2002.

[18] Social Services and Social Assistance Law (*Sociālo pakalpojumu un sociālās palīdzības likums*), OG No 168, 19 November 2002.

[19] The Cabinet of Ministers Regulation No 1251 'Regulation on allocation of the state budget resources for the municipalities to provide minimum subsistance allowance and housing allowance' (*Noteikumi par valsts budžeta līdzekļu piešķiršanu pašvaldībām garantētā minimālā ienākumu līmeņa pabalsta un dzīvokļa pabalsta izmaksām*), OG No 181, 13 November 2009.

[20] Art 17 of Medical Treatment Law (*Ārstniecības likums*), OG No 167/168, 1 July 1997. The right to state paid health case does not apply with regard to third country nationals possessing temporary

2. Structural reforms and the cuts introduced
after the crisis

Following the economic crisis the social security system was mainly subjected to cuts, rather than sweeping structural reforms.

On 16 June 2009 the parliament adopted the Law on the Payout of State Pensions and State Allowances for the Period 2009–2012.[21] This law, along with amendments to specific laws on long-term service pensions in particular public sectors, purportedly imposed many restrictions on social security rights.[22] The most considerable and contested ones were temporary 10 per cent cuts of old-age and long-term service pensions, a temporary 70 per cent cut of the old-age pension for pensioners in active employment, and cutting parental allowance by 50 per cent for persons in active employment. The law entered into force two weeks after its adoption on 1 July 2009.

Further, on 1 December 2009 the Parliament adopted amendments to this law that restricted the amount of unemployment, sickness, maternity, paternity, and parental allowance.[23] In particular, the respective persons would be entitled to a daily social insurance allowance that did not exceed LVL 11.51 (€16.37) in total. Those receiving a higher allowance were granted 50 per cent for the sum exceeding LVL 11.51 (€16.37).[24]

residence permits, except third country nationals who are family members of EU citizens residing in Latvia. The universal health care system is, however, under revision currently. It is planned to introduce a statutory health-insurance scheme, namely, additional risk under statutory social insurance system, leading to the situation where persons who are not economically active without due reason will be entitled to the minimum state paid healthcare services.

[21] *Par valsts pensiju un valsts pabalstu izmaksu laika periodā no 2009.gada līdz 2012.gadam*, OG No 100, 30 June 2009.

[22] Amendments to the Law on Long Service Pensions of Military Persons (*Grozījumi Militārpersonu izdienas pensiju likumā*), OG No 100, 30 June 2009; amendments to the Law on Long-Term Pensions for Diplomats (*Grozījumi Diplomātu izdienas pensiju likumā*), OG No 100, 30 June 2009; amendments to the Law on Long-Service Pensions for Ministry of the Interior System Employees with Special Service Ranks (*Grozījumi likumā 'Par izdienas pensijām Iekšlietu ministrijas sistēmas darbiniekiem ar speciālajām dienesta pakāpēm'*), OG No 100, 30 June 2009; amendments to the Law on Long Service Pensions for Public Prosecutors (*Grozījumi Prokuroru izdienas pensiju likumā*), OG No 100, 30 June 2009; amendments to the Law on Long-Term Service Pensions for Judges (*Grozījumi Tiesnešu izdienas pensiju likumā*), OG No 100, 30 June 2009; amendments to the Law on Long-Term Service Pensions for the Officials of Corruption Prevention and Combating Bureau (*Grozījumi Korupcijas novēršanas un apkarošanas biroja amatpersonu izdienas pensiju likumā*), OG No 100, 30 June 2009; amendments to the Law on Long-Term Service Pensions for the Officials of the Constitutional Protection Bureau (*Grozījumi Satversmes aizsardzības biroja amatpersonu izdienas pensiju likumā*), OG No 100, 30 June 2009; amendments to the Law on Long-Term Service Pensions for Artists of the State and Municipal Orchestras, Choirs, Concert Organisations, Theatres, and Circuses (*Grozījumi Valsts un pašvaldību profesionālo orķestru, koru, koncertorganizāciju, teātru un cirka mākslinieku izdienas pensiju likumā*), OG No 100, 30 June 2009.

[23] The amendments to the Law on the Payout of State Pensions and State Allowances for the Period from 2009 till 2012 (*Grozījumi likumā 'Par valsts pensiju un valsts pabalstu izmaksu laika periodā no 2009.gada līdz 2012.gadam'*), OG No 200, 21 December 2009.

[24] By amendments to the Law on the Payout of State Pensions and State Allowances for the Period from 2009 till 2014 (*Grozījumi likumā 'Par valsts pensiju un valsts pabalstu izmaksu laika periodā no*

The basic social assistance, providing guaranteed minimum income, was not affected. On 1 October 2009 the Cabinet of Ministers raised the amount of guaranteed minimum income from LVL 37 (€52.65)[25] to LVL 40 (€56.91) for an adult and
LVL 45 (€64.03) for a child.[26] The rest was the competence of the municipalities
who provided social assistance and services according to the available municipal
budget.

The parliament also adopted amendments to the State Funded Pension Law.[27]
These cut the share that had to be transferred from the statutory social insurance
old-age budget to the second tier of the statutory old-age pension. Before the cuts,
the share that had to be transferred to the second tier of the old-age pension (also
called 'state funded pension') was 8 per cent of the contributions made to the statutory old-age insurance. That share was decreased to 2 per cent of contributions
made to the statutory old-age insurance.[28]

Due to the financial crisis, municipalities also suffered from limited financial
means to provide minimum social assistance, in particular minimum subsistence
allowance and housing allowance, as required under the Social Services and Social
Assistance Law.[29] Thus on 3 November 2009 the Cabinet of Ministers adopted a
regulation[30] that clearly stipulated the share to be provided to the municipalities
from the state budget to comply with these obligations. Hereby municipalities were
entitled to be compensated for 50 per cent of the minimum subsistence allowances
and for 20 per cent of the housing allowances they provided.

Statutory healthcare expenditure was also cut. In 2008 the healthcare budget
was LVL 516 million (€734 million), in 2009 it was LVL 471 million (€670 million), and in 2010 LVL 423 million (€601 million).[31] These numbers attest to the

---

2009.gada līdz 2014.gadam'), OG No 192, 6 December 2012, the daily maximum amount of the allowance was increased respectively from €16.37 to €32.75.

[25] The Cabinet of Ministers Regulation No 693 'Regulation on the level of guaranteed minimum
income and amount of the allowance for the provision of the level of guaranteed minimum income' (*Noteikumi par garantēto ienākuma līmeni un pabalsta apmēru garantētā ienākuma līmeņa
nodrošināšanai*), OG No 176, 12 December 2003, entered into force on 1 January 2004, in force till 1
October 2009.
[26] The Cabinet of Ministers Regulation No 1070 'Regulation on amount of guaranteed minimum income' (*Noteikumi par garantēto minimālo ienākumu līmeni*), OG No 154, 29 September 2009, entered
into force on 1 October 2009, in force till 1 December 2009; also Regulation No 1489, OG No 201, 22
December 2009, entered into force on 23 December 2009, in force till 1 January 2013.
[27] (n 8).
[28] Amendments to the State Funded Pensions Law (*Grozījumi Valsts fondēto pensiju likumā*), OG No
66, 29 April 2009.
[29] Social Services and Social Assistance Law (n 18).
[30] The Cabinet of Ministers Regulation No 1251 'Regulation on allocation of the state budget resources for the municipalities to provide minimum subsistance allowance and housing allowance'
(*Noteikumi par valsts budžeta līdzekļu piešķiršanu pašvaldībām garantētā minimālā ienākumu līmeņa
pabalsta un dzīvokļa pabalsta izmaksām*), OG No 181, 13 November 2009.
[31] The data on healthcare expenditure years 2005–2010 and comparative analysis of healthcare budget for years 2005–2010 are available from the website of the Ministry of Health in Latvian
<http://www.vm.gov.lv/lv/ministrija/budzets/veselibas_aprupes_budzets_20062011gads/> accessed 5
April 2020.

considerable cut in funds that were allocated to the statutory healthcare system. In addition, starting from 1 March 2009 the patients' co-payments were raised,[32] for example, co-payment for visiting family doctors was raised from LVL 0.5 (€0.71) to LVL 1 (€1.42), for a day spent in hospital from LVL 5 (€7.11) to LVL 12 (€17.7).[33]

3. Elements in the making and implementation of the reforms

a) Overview

The cuts in social security expenditure were directly influenced by the international donors that Latvia had turned to in order to tackle the economic crisis and to cover the state budget deficit. The biggest lender was the EU. On 20 January 2009 the Council of the EU adopted a Decision (2009/290) to make medium-term financial assistance of up to €3.1 billion available to Latvia. It was to be provided for a period of three years starting from the first day after the Council Decision entered into force. The EU assistance was provided in conjunction with a loan from the International Monetary Fund (IMF) of SDR 1.5 billion (1,200 per cent of Latvia's IMF quota, around €1.7 billion) under an IMF standby arrangement approved on 23 December 2008. The Nordic countries (Sweden, Denmark, Finland, Norway, and Estonia) contributed €1.9 billion together, the World Bank €0.4 billion, and the European Bank of Reconstruction and Development, the Czech Republic, and Poland a total of €0.4 billion, bringing the total to €7.5 billion over the period to the last quarter of 2011.[34]

The reforms and cuts in the field of social security were initiated, supervised, and controlled by international lenders. This is well recorded in six memorandums of understanding between the European Community and the Republic of Latvia.[35] The Initial Memorandum of Understanding was concluded on 28 January 2009 and does not envisage any particular obligations of a fiscal nature with regard to the social security system. It provides only general obligations for cuts in public expenditure.[36] The Supplemental Memorandum of Understanding concluded

---

[32] The Cabinet of Ministers Regulation No 91 'Amendments to the 19 December 2006 Regulation No 1046 "The organisation and funding of the health care"' (*Grozījumi Ministru kabineta 2006.gada 19.decembra noteikumos Nr.1046 'Veselības aprūpes organizēšanas un finansēšanas kārtība'*), OG No 25, 13 February 2009.

[33] Informative report of the Ministry of Health Care on the effect of the budget cuts to the accessibility of the healthcare for poor persons and further measures, 15 February 2010.

[34] See para 1 of Initial Memorandum of Understanding between European Community and Republic of Latvia concluded on 28 January 2009, available in English at the webpage of the Ministry of Finance <http://www.fm.gov.lv/files/files/MoU_ENG_versija.pdf> accessed 5 April 2020.

[35] Available in English at the webpage of the Ministry of Finance <http://www.fm.gov.lv/lv/sadalas/ starptautiska_finansu_sadarbiba/starptautiska_aizdevuma_programma/saprasanas_memorands_ar_ eiropas_savienibu/> accessed 5 April 2020.

[36] (n 34).

on 13 July 2009[37] stipulates the commitment to make further reductions of LVL 500 million to the budget deficit in 2010 and that additional structural measures are required in the areas of pension, remuneration, and local government systems.

The Second Addendum to the Memorandum of Understanding concluded on 22 February 2010[38] approved of the measures that had been taken to balance the state budget. In particular, it mentioned how the 2010 budget contributed LVL 500 million (over 4.2 per cent of GDP) to this end. This approval was conveyed despite the fiscal costs that arose from the Constitutional Court ruling of the 21 December 2009, which had held that the pension cuts introduced in the June 2009 supplementary budget were not in accordance with certain procedural principles deriving from the Constitution. As to future tasks, the Second Addendum to the Memorandum of Understanding listed the following measures to be taken. First, there was a commitment to allocating appropriate financing, or to increasing state co-financing of local governments to meet increased social needs. Further, all significant Cabinet of Ministers decisions and other decisions with a fiscal impact, including on social security or any guarantee scheme, were to be announced and undertaken after discussions with the EC and the IMF, and in consultation with the National Tripartite Cooperation Council. Second, fiscal consolidation was to be achieved through a review of social insurance benefits and pension systems and consequent proposals for medium-term reform of these systems. In particular, by the end of June 2010, with technical assistance from international organisations and in cooperation with social partners, Latvia had to propose changes to the pension system to be implemented by 2011 in order to preserve the future sustainability and adequacy of the three pillars of the pension system. In this context, all special pension regimes and retirement ages were to be reviewed. By the end of June 2010 Latvia also had to review the social insurance benefits system, considering economic and demographic forecasts, so that appropriate changes could be implemented after 2012.

The Fourth Addendum to the Memorandum of Understanding was concluded on 8 June 2011.[39] It established that the budget adopted by the parliament on 21 December 2010 was to include reforms regarding revenue and expenditure. The list of measures to cut expenditure included cuts to healthcare expenditure. Reference was also made to the concept paper on social security prepared by the authorities, which was to be the basis for a comprehensive pension reform to be introduced in the 2012 budget. It also provided that the authorities were committed to preserving the sustainability of the three pillars of the pension system

[37] Available in English at the webpage of the Ministry of Finance <http://www.fm.gov.lv/files/files/Supplementary_MoU_13%2007%202009_ENG.pdf> accessed 5 April 2020.
[38] Available in English at webpage of the Ministry of Finance <http://www.fm.gov.lv/files/files/201002_LV-ES_memoranda_2papildinajums_eng.pdf> accessed 5 April 2020.
[39] Available in English at the webpage of the Ministry of Finance <http://www.fm.gov.lv/files/files/SMOU_4_08_06_2011_eng.pdf> accessed 5 April 2020.

and to restoring contributions to the second pillar to 6 per cent of gross salaries by 2013, provided that the budgetary situation improved in line with the (then) current forecast.

The Fifth Addendum to the Memorandum of Understanding was concluded on 21 December 2011[40] and stipulated that the key measures to be taken under the 2012 budget must include a reduction in expenditure by the Ministry of Health (LVL 2.7 million), as well as the Ministry of Welfare. The latter was to be achieved by (i) implementing controls to limit the duration of sick leave (LVL 3 million) and (ii) submitting a proposal to the parliament to reduce replacement rates for long-term sickness benefits. As regards already existing measures the authorities had to: (i) continue to limit the maximum amount of maternity, paternity, parental, unemployment, and sickness benefits until the end of 2014; (ii) submit to parliament—together with the 2012 budget—a proposal to continue to cap the replacement rate of maternity and paternity benefits at 80 per cent starting from 2013 (LVL 5.3 million in 2013); (iii) keep in place the ceilings on social contributions for high income earners beyond 2014, to limit the maximum amount of social insurance that high income earners could receive. The Fifth Addendum also stipulated that further audits would be performed to rationalise and increase the efficiency of social benefits. Moreover, Latvia was required to increase the statutory retirement age and the qualification period for retirement and to consider measures to extend the period during which pension indexation was suspended and ways of linking statutory retirement age to life expectancy.

With regard to social assistance provision, the Fifth Addendum required Latvia to assess the feasibility of its social assistance scheme, considering particularly whether it served to activate those receiving benefits, and to allow local governments access to relevant administrative databases (recording income and assets of 'social assistance clients') to prevent a misuse of the system.

b) Reasons for reforms

It follows that all cuts and reforms in the field of social security were elaborated and implemented under the supervision of international donors, primarily the IMF and the EU.

The explanatory note[41] of the Law on the Payout of State Pensions and State Allowances for the Period 2009–2012[42] provides that the aim of the law is not only to serve the interests of the state budget in the context of the economic recession, but also to balance the expenditure of the special social insurance budgets in order

---

[40] Available in English at the webpage of the Ministry of Finance <http://www.fm.gov.lv/files/files/FBB68C37295900132929968467 1343.pdf> accessed 5 April 2020.

[41] Explanatory note to the draft legislative, available in Latvian at <http://titania.saeima.lv/LIVS/SaeimaLIVS.nsf/0/0BEB9E49A7761574C22575D6003F8248?OpenDocument> accessed 5 April 2020.

[42] (n 21).

to provide social rights in accordance with article 116 of the Constitution.[43] It was submitted that, if no measures were taken, all funds of the special social insurance budgets would be exhausted within the following couple of years.

Before the Constitutional Court the government and parliament claimed that this law was based on the need to prevent a budget deficit from arising with respect to the social insurance special budget. Such a deficit, it was argued, would result from the drop in the revenue of the social insurance special budget that was precipitated by a decrease in wages and increase in unemployment, and a concomitant increase (of approximately LVL 86 million) in social insurance special budget expenditures.[44]

It follows that all possible grounds were put forward for the justification of the cuts regarding social insurance benefits. Namely, economic emergency, financial stability, and the protection of society's interests in general.

c) Procedural particularities in the making of the reforms

The central legal document providing for cuts in the field of social security—the Law on the Payout of State Pensions and State Allowances for the Period 2009–2012[45]—was adopted in an extremely short period of time. According to the explanatory note, the draft law was adopted in the meeting of the State Secretaries on 12 June 2006, in the extraordinary meeting of the Cabinet of Ministers on 14 June 2009, and submitted to the parliament on 15 June 2009. It was adopted by the parliament on the next day, ie on 16 June 2009, published in the Official Gazette 'Latvijas Vēstnesis' on 30 June 2009, and entered into effect on 1 July 2009. Within this timeframe there was no room for debates on whether to withdraw or amend any particular provision.

It is noteworthy that none of the international loan agreements was ratified by the parliament as required by the Latvian Constitution. They were concluded directly between the Latvian government and its international donors in the form of private law agreements. Some scholars argue that, taking into account especially the extent to which these agreements affected the lives and rights of Latvia's inhabitants, the international loan agreements should have been classified as public international agreements. As such, ratification by parliament in accordance with the procedure set out by the Constitution would have been necessary. However, it must also be pointed out that factually the state was on the verge of bankruptcy and in such a situation almost any measure seems justifiable. In particular, the

---

[43] Respective art stipulates: 'The rights of persons set out in Articles ninety-six, ninety-seven, ninety-eight, one hundred, one hundred and two, one hundred and three, one hundred and six, and one hundred and eight of the Constitution may be subject to restrictions in circumstances provided for by law in order to protect the rights of other people, the democratic structure of the State, and public safety, welfare and morals. On the basis of the conditions set forth in this Article, restrictions may also be imposed on the expression of religious beliefs.'

[44] Decision in case no 2009-43-01, 21 December 2009, para 27.1.

[45] (n 21).

procedure of ratification may require some time, while international aid was necessary in a very short period of time.[46] In any case, this fact indicates the questionable legitimacy of the measures undertaken later on (even by parliament) to comply with the conditions that were set by international donors.

III. Human rights affected by social security reforms

1. National case law referring to the social security reforms

a) Overview

The social security reforms were challenged before the Constitutional Court. All together there were six decisions (these will respectively be referred to as the: Pension Indexation Case,[47] Old-Age Pension Case,[48] Parental Allowance Case,[49] Ministry of the Interior Long-Service Pension Case,[50] Military Long-Service Pension Case,[51] Prosecutors' Long-Term Service Pension Case[52]). Five of

---

[46] Mārlis Lejnieks, 'Latvijas Republikas starptautisko aizņēmumu tiesiskie aspekti' (The legal aspects of the international loans of the Republic of Latvia) (2 February 2010) No 5 Jurista Vārds.

[47] Decision in case no 2009-08-01 'On Compliance of the Words "State Pensions Shall Not Be Revised in 2009" of Section 2 of Law "On Amendments to Law On State Pensions" of 12 March 2009 with Article 1 and Article 109 of the Satversme (Constitution) of the Republic of Latvia', 27 November 2009 <http://www.satv.tiesa.gov.lv/web/viewer.html?file=/wp-content/uploads/2009/04/2009-08-01_Spriedums_ENG.pdf#search=> accessed 5 April 2020.

[48] Decision in case no 2009-43-01 'On Compliance of the First Part of Article 3 of the Law "On State Pension and Allowance Disbursement from 2009 to 2012" insofar as it Applies to State Old-Age Pension with Article 1, Article 91, Article 105 and Article 109 of the Satversme (Constitution) of the Republic of Latvia', 21 December 2009 <http://www.satv.tiesa.gov.lv/web/viewer.html?file=http://www.satv.tiesa.gov.lv/wp-content/uploads/2009/07/2009-43-01_Spriedums_ENG.pdf#search=> accessed 5 April 2020.

[49] Decision in case no 2009-44-01 'On Compliance of Section 5 (1) of Law On Payment of State Allowances during the Time Period from 2009 to 2012 with Article 1, Article 91 and Article 109 of the Satversme (Constitution) of the Republic of Latvia', 15 March 2010 <http://www.satv.tiesa.gov.lv/web/viewer.html?file=http://www.satv.tiesa.gov.lv/wp-content/uploads/2009/07/2009-44-01_Spriedums_ENG.pdf#search=> accessed 5 April 2020.

[50] Decision in case no 2009-76-01 'On Compliance of Point 20 of the Transitional Provisions of the Law "On Long-Service Pensions for Ministry of the Interior System Employees with Special Service Ranks" with Article 1 and 109 of the Satversme (Constitution) of the Republic of Latvia', 31 March 2010 <http://www.satv.tiesa.gov.lv/web/viewer.html?file=http://www.satv.tiesa.gov.lv/wp-content/uploads/2009/08/2009-76-01_Spriedums_ENG.pdf#search=> accessed 5 April 2020.

[51] Decision in case no 2009-88-01 'On Compliance of Points 14, 16 and 17 of the Transitional Provisions of the Law "On Long Service Pensions of Military Persons" with Article 1, Article 91 and Article 109 of the Satversme (Constitution) of the Republic of Latvia', 15 April 2010 <http://www.satv.tiesa.gov.lv/web/viewer.html?file=http://www.satv.tiesa.gov.lv/wp-content/uploads/2009/09/2009-88-01_Spriedums_ENG.pdf#search=> accessed 5 April 2020.

[52] Decision in case no 2009-86-01 'On Compliance of Point 8 of the Transitional Provisions of the Law on Long Service Pensions for Public Prosecutors with Article 1, Article 91 and Article 109 of the Satversme (Constitution) of the Republic of Latvia', 21 April 2010 <http://www.satv.tiesa.gov.lv/en/cases/?case-filter-years=[2009]&case-filter-status=&case-filter-types=&case-filter-result=&searchtext=&page=2> accessed 5 April 2020.

them—Old-age Pension Case, Ministry of the Interior Long-Service Case, Military Long-Service Pension Case, Prosecutors' Long-Term Service Pension Case, and Parental Allowance case—related to the cuts of pensions and social security benefits following the adoption of the Disbursement Law[53] and special laws regulating long-term service pensions in certain sectors of service. Amongst them, four decisions dealt with cuts of pensions and one with the cut of parental allowance for parents remaining in active employment during parental leave. The first decision was in the Pensions Indexation Case and related to the 'freezing' of the annual indexation of pensions. The decision was negative for the claimants. The second and most important one was a decision on general old-age pension cuts, followed by three decisions on long-term pension cuts for officials in certain fields of public service (officials of the interior ministry, prosecutors, and military). In all cases the Constitutional Court found the restrictions incompatible with the Constitution. The sixth decision, in the parental allowance case, was a negative decision for applicants. The first decision on the 'freezing' of pension indexation is not discussed in detail in this chapter because the restricted rights did not lead to any major decrease of the rights to social security. As the Constitutional Court stressed in that decision—the issue of pension indexation, unlike in pension and allowance cases, did not concern already acquired rights.

The respective constitutional complaints were submitted by individuals or members of parliament, since Latvian constitutional law[54] grants legal standing not only to constitutional and state/municipal institutions and certain officials, but also to private persons (natural and legal) if they consider their fundamental rights, as provided by the Constitution, have been violated.[55]

b) Outcome

In all cases, the claimants argued that the restrictions on their social rights were incompatible with general principles of law and with the substantial social rights provided by the Constitution.

In the Old-Age Pension Case, the applicants claimed incompatibility of the cuts, as provided by Disbursement Law, with the principles of legitimate expectations, proportionality, the rule of law as deriving from article 1 of the Constitution, and

---

[53] Law on the Payout of State Pensions and State Allowances for the Period 2009–2012 (n 21).

[54] Satversmes tiesas likums (The Law on the Constitutional Court), OG No 103, 14 June 1996, art 19².

[55] ibid. Art 17(1) provides that the following institutions, officials, and personas have the right to submit the claims before the Constitutional Court: the President of the State; the parliament (*Saeima*); not less than twenty deputies of the parliament (*Saeima*); the Cabinet of Ministers; the Prosecutor General; the Council of the State Audit Office; a local government council; the Ombudsman, if the authority or official who has issued the disputed act has not rectified the established deficiencies within the time period specified by the Ombudsman; a court, on adjudicating a civil matter, criminal matter, or administrative matter; the Land Registry Office judge in performing an entry of immovable property or associated corroboration of rights thereof in the Land Register; a person in the case of the fundamental rights being infringed upon as defined in the Constitution; and the Board of Justice within the scope of the competence stipulated in the law.

equal treatment as provided by article 91, as well as the principles of the socially responsible state, good governance, and social solidarity. They also claimed that substantive social rights under the Constitution—the right to social security in case of old age (article 109) and the right to property (article 105)—had been breached.

In the long-term pension cases, the applicants' claims proceeded on a similar legal basis, although the relevant rights were combined in differing ways. In the claim regarding the long-term pensions of officials of the interior ministry, it was argued that there had been a disproportionate restriction of the right to social support in the case of old age and inability to work as provided by article 109 of the Constitution (Ministry of the Interior Long-Term Service Case), while in the application regarding prosecutors' long-term service pensions the claim was that general principles of law—principle of legal certainty and proportionality and equality—had been breached (Prosecutors' Long-Term Service Pension Case). In the case concerning long-term service for members of the military (Military Long-Service Pension Case) the applicants claimed that principles of legal certainty, proportionality, and equality, as well as the substantive rights under article 109 of the Constitution, had been breached.

The Constitutional Court decided to assess these applications only with respect to the principles of legal certainty and proportionality, taken in conjunction with article 109.

In the Parental Allowance Case, the applicants contested the compatibility of the Disbursement Law with article 110 (the state's obligation to protect and support families, parents, and children) and the principles of legal certainty and proportionality as derived from article 1 and equality as provided by article 91. The Court in substance evaluated the compatibility of the contested norms of the Disbursement Law with the principle of equality and with the principle of legitimate expectations in conjunction with article 110 of the Constitution.

In the Old-Age Pension Case, the Constitutional Court found that the restrictions as provided by the Disbursement Law were incompatible with article 109 of the Constitution on the grounds that the legislator failed to find the least restrictive means for the attainment of a legitimate aim. Moreover, the restrictions were also incompatible with the principle of legal certainty, stemming from article 1 of the Constitution, because the legislator did not envisage different treatment of persons in different situations, nor compensation or a transition period. In this case the compatibility with article 109 and the principle of legal certainty were assessed separately.

In the Ministry of the Interior Long-Service Case, the Constitutional Court found an incompatibility with articles 1 and 109 of the Constitution. However, it did not provide extensive and structured argumentation as to which argument proved decisive in this regard.

In the Military Long-Service Pension Case, the Court applied a different approach. It decided to review the case under article 109 in conjunction with the

principle of proportionality and legal certainty. The Constitutional Court established that the contested norm had a legitimate aim and that the measures chosen
were a suitable means of attaining it. Then it went on to analyse the compatibility
with the principle of legal certainty, albeit that its argumentation was structured in
a way that mirrored an analysis of necessity under the principle of proportionality.

In the Prosecutors' Long-Term Service Case, the structure was again different.
The Constitutional Court decided to review the case under article 109 in conjunction with the principle of proportionality and legal certainty. However, unlike in
the Military Long-Service Pension Case, the Court evaluated the compatibility of
the contested norm with article 109 by going through all the steps of the proportionality analysis and found that the legislator did not choose the least restrictive
means of achieving its legitimate aim. The analysis of the principle of legal certainty
was provided separately.

In all pension cases, the contested restrictions were declared void from the moment that they had purportedly entered into force.

In the Parental Allowance Case, the Court assessed the compatibility of the
relevant restriction with article 110, article 91, and the principle of legitimate expectations in conjunction with article 110 separately. The Court found that the
contested norm was compatible with article 110 of the Constitution, since the state
still provided the parents with parental allowance, although on changed conditions. Then it went on to assess its compatibility with the principle of equal treatment, as provided by article 91 of the Constitution, and found that parents on
parental leave are not in a comparable situation with parents who remain in active
employment. Thus article 91 is not breached by treating these groups differently.
Consequently, the restriction on the amount of parental allowance for parents who
remain in active employment was found compatible with both articles 110 and 91
of the Constitution.

2. Analysis of the case law

a) Role of constitutional rights

aa) Right to property

The Old-Age pension case was the only one where it was claimed that there had
been a breach of the right to property.[56] The Constitutional Court heard the case
on this ground, but did not address it in substance. First, the Constitutional Court
held that article 109 of the Constitution provided for a more specific right—the
right to social security, which is a kind of *lex specialis* in relation to the right to
property, provided by article 105 of the Constitution. It held that article 109

---

[56] Old-Age Pension Case (n 48), point 2.3.

afforded the right to a pension a higher level of protection than article 105. The only argumentation provided by the Constitutional Court for this finding was the fact that article 9 of the International Covenant of Economic, Social and Cultural Rights (ICESCR) provided a specific right to social security, while the European Convention on Human Rights (ECHR) did not contain similar rights. Thus social security issues were addressed under the right to property as provided by article 1 of Protocol 1 of the ECHR. Although the Constitutional Court decided to hear the case on the basis of the right to social security, not the right to property under the Latvian Constitution, it nevertheless stated that the compatibility with article 1 of Protocol 1 of the ECHR would also be analysed.[57]

Finally, in the Old-Age Pension Case, after finding that the contested norm was not compatible with the right to social security provided under article 109, the Court stated that there was no need to review the compatibility under other provisions of the Constitution, including the right to property as provided by article 105.[58]

The legal doctrine underpinning the relationship between article 109 and article 105, as they relate to social security rights, is not clear and was not further clarified by the Constitutional Court. In the Old-Age Pension Case the Constitutional Court stated that article 109 provided greater protections to the right to a pension than article 105. At the same time, in the case concerning the constitutionality of the deduction of income tax from pensions, the Constitutional Court stated that pensions fell within the concept of 'property' under article 105 irrespective of the date of award and the source of financing. However, the caveat was added that, in this respect, social security rights did not enjoy the same level of protection as property in its 'classical sense'.[59] It follows that the relationship between the right to social security and the right to property is not clearly established in Latvian constitutional legal doctrine. On the other hand, when looking at this relationship from the perspective of the case law of the European Court of Human Rights (ECtHR) on article 1 of Protocol 1 it becomes clearer—formally, according to the ECtHR, the right to property does not entail that an individual must receive social security benefits or a pension, unless it is provided for in national law. Thus the ECHR does not guarantee any pension or social security benefit.[60] Consequently, article 105 of the Constitution also does not oblige the state to provide social security rights.

---

[57] ibid, point 20.

[58] ibid, point 33.

[59] Decision in case no 2007-01-01 'On Compliance of words "until 1 January 1996" Article 13(1)(2) and Article 13(1)(3) "On Residents' Income Tax" with Article 91 of the Satversme of the Republic of Latvia', 31 March 2010, point 21, available in Latvian at <http://www.satv.tiesa.gov.lv/wp-content/uploads/2016/02/2007-01-01_Spriedums.pdf> accessed 5 April 2020. See also Ringolds Balodis (ed), *Latvijas Republikas Satversmes Komentāri. VIII nodaļa. Cilvēka pamattiesības (Commentaries to the Constitution of the Republic of Latvia Section VII The Basic Human Rights)* (Latvijas Vēstnesis 2011) 554.

[60] Pieter Van Dijk and others (eds), *Theory and Practice of the European Convention on Human Rights* (5th edn, Intersentia 2018) 858; *Carson and Others v the United Kingdom* App no 42184/05 (Grand Chamber, 16 March 2010), paras 64 and 65.

At the same time article 109 of the Latvian Constitution imposes a constitutional obligation to provide social security benefits and, as stated by the Constitutional Court, since such rights are included in the basic law the state cannot refuse to provide them.[61] The fact that, if a state creates a social security system, the rights and interests of an individual fall within the ambit of article 1 of Protocol 1 of the ECHR and so the proportionality of any restriction must be ensured, as well as the compatibility with general principles of law,[62] has secondary importance in this context.

bb) Right to social security

Regarding the obligations of the state with respect to fundamental rights in general, the Constitutional Court has stated following: 'The State has a threefold duty in the area of each fundamental right: to respect, to protect and to guarantee the rights of persons. Acting in conformity with human rights, the State should enact a range of measures—both passive, for example, non-interference with the rights of persons, and active, for example, satisfaction of persons' individual needs'.[63]

As regards the content of the right to social security under article 109, the Constitutional Court by recalling its own established case law has stated following. In the field of social rights the state must take positive measures by creating an effective, fair, and sustainable social security system[64] in order to guarantee the social rights of a person taking into account his/her individual need, but the state does not have an obligation to grant social rights that are equivalent to a specific amount,[65] and the state must refrain from interfering excessively with the financial relations of its citizens.[66]

In particular, it is the state itself that is responsible for the system of social and economic protection, namely the types and amounts of allowances, the persons or groups to whom such allowances must be provided, and the maintenance of such rights. The state has a wide margin of appreciation regarding this matter. The decisions of the legislator in the field of social rights have significant political dimensions. In particular, the decisions are taken primarily on the basis of political, rather than legal, considerations, which are dependent on the principles specified by the legislator for the provision of social services and regarding society's, or a particular group's, need for state aid and support.[67] Provision of such rights depends on the resources at the disposal of the state. However, if any rights are declared

---

[61] Ministry of the Interior Long-Service Pension Case (n 50) point 5.5, by referring to the decision in case no 2000-08-0109, 13 March 2001.

[62] Van Dijk and others (n 60) 859.

[63] Old-Age Pension Case (n 48), point 24, by referring to the decision in case no 2007-23-01, 3 April 2008, point 7; also Balodis (n 59) 562.

[64] Prosecutors' Long-Term Service Pension Case (n 52), point 8.

[65] Old-Age Pension Case (n 48), point 20.

[66] ibid, point 24.

[67] ibid.

fundamental then the state may not waive their enactment because they have constitutional value. According to article 109, if the state has provided particular social rights through the law then a person obtains subjective rights to them.[68]

The state's margin of appreciation in providing or restricting social rights under article 109 is not unlimited, it has to comply with other norms and general principles of law,[69] including principles of legitimate expectations and proportionality.[70] In addition, the state has an obligation to provide core social rights. Under article 109 this core consists of the minimum financial support necessary to secure a decent living.[71]

As stressed by the Constitutional Court, the specific character of the social rights determines the limits of judicial control. In implementing social rights the legislator enjoys a wide margin of discretion, ie as far as it is reasonably connected with the economic situation of the state.[72] The judicial power has an obligation to assess if the legislator has observed its margin of discretion.[73]

In order to establish if the state has complied with its positive obligations under the Constitution in the field of social rights, the following aspects must be assessed: (1) if the legislator has taken measures that provide persons with the opportunity to implement their social rights; (2) such measures are appropriate, ie, such measures allow implementation of social rights at least to a minimum level; (3) general principles of law have been observed,[74] or, in the words of the court, 'the rights granted by Article 109 of the Constitution may be restricted if such a restriction is established by the law, justified by a legitimate end and conforms to the principle of proportionality'.[75] According to the Constitutional Court 'if, while assessing a legal provision, it can be established that it does not comply with at least one of these criteria, it follows that the legal provision in question does not comply with the principle of proportionality and therefore is unlawful'.[76]

With regard to the obligations of the state during the economic crisis, the Constitutional Court stressed that in the situation of economic crisis the state is compelled to cut budget expenses. Consequently the amount of pensions could be decreased and the state has a margin of appreciation to change the conditions regarding the pension, but only in the course of ensuring a socially just social security system.[77] This means that during the economic crisis each citizen has to

[68] Prosecutors' Long-Term Service Pension Case (n 52), point 10, reference to 2001-12-01, point 2; 2009-08-01, point 15.

[69] Ministry of the Interior Long-Service Pension Case (n 50), point 8.

[70] Prosecutors' Long-Term Service Pension Case (n 52), point 10.

[71] Old-Age Pension Case (n 48), point 31.2.

[72] ibid, point 24.

[73] Prosecutors' Long-Term Service Pension Case (n 52), point 9, reference to case Nos 2006-07-01, points 13, 14, and 2007-13-03, point 8.4.

[74] ibid by reference to the decision in case no 2006-10-03, point 16.1.

[75] Old-Age Pension Case (n 48), point 26; Prosecutors' Long-Term Service Pension Case (n 52), point 9, reference to case Nos 2004-21-01, point 10, and 2009-43-01, point 26.

[76] Old-Age Pension Case (n 48), point 28.

[77] Military Long-Service Pension Case (n 51), point 9; Old-Age Pension Case (n 48), points 24, 29.2.

carry a proportionate responsibility and obligation to prevent the consequences of the crisis.[78] However, all measures taken on account of the economic crisis—and the related restrictions on the rights of persons—must comply with the principles of a state governed by the rule of law.[79] The legislator's chosen solution must also be socially responsible, which means that 'legal interests of certain person must be balanced with those of the society'.[80] In other words, the state can restrict benefits if it is necessary in order to balance the interests of society with the rights of other persons receiving financial support from the state.[81] Such balancing also entails ensuring the sustainability of the social security system.[82] The Constitutional Court repeated its statement from previous judgements that article 109 obliges the state to provide at least a minimum or 'core' of social rights, ie an amount ensuring a decent living.[83]

The Court also repeated its statements regarding the concept of the socially responsible state. In particular, 'measures chosen by the legislator may be regarded as proportionate for reaching the legitimate aim only if they are in compliance with the principle of the socially responsible state'.[84] And continued that 'the State has the duty to coordinate not only the rights of persons in the social field but also the necessity to ensure welfare of the entire society with its economical possibilities, as well as it must elaborate such legal regulatory framework that would be aimed at sustainable development of the State'.[85]

In the Old-Age Pension Case, the Constitutional Court elaborated on the concept of the 'core' or minimum level of social rights. It stated that there were several international methods for assessing the minimal level of social security. These were based on the needs of households (depending on their size and composition) and they determined the level of income required to meet the basic needs of each person. It emphasised a range of factors that influenced the choice of a particular yardstick (economies of scale in consumption, the priority to be assigned to certain groups such as the elderly, the effect on inequality, etc) and concluded: 'Since the results may differ depending on the method chosen, a substantiated choice of the method which is most suitable to the situation in Latvia is a matter of political choice of the legislator.'[86]

At the same time the Constitutional Court did not elaborate on the actual amount of old-age pensions. It only noted that the poverty risk of lonely pensioners

---

[78]   Military Long-Service Pension Case (n 51), point 9, reference to 2009-11-01, point 10.3.
[79]   ibid, point 9, reference to 2009-08-01, points 17.2, 23, 25; 2009-11-01, point 10.3; Ministry of the Interior Long-Service Pension Case (n 50), point 6.2.
[80]   Parental Allowance Case (n 49), point 22.
[81]   Prosecutors' Long-Term Service Pension Case (n 52), point 12.
[82]   Parental Allowance Case (n 49), point 16.
[83]   Old-Age Pension Case (n 48), point 31.2.
[84]   Parental Allowance Case (n 49), point 22.
[85]   ibid.
[86]   Old-Age Pension Case (n 48), point 31.2.

had also increased during a period of economic growth. It also did not refer to the method used under article 12(1) of the European Social Charter to establish the 'core' or minimum amount of old-age pension, namely that the income should not fall below the poverty threshold, defined as 50 per cent of median equalised income.[87]

In the Ministry of the Interior Long-Service Case, the Constitutional Court had to deal for the first time with the question of whether such a specific type of pension fell within the scope of article 109 of the Constitution. The Court found that long-service and old-age pensions 'are not absolutely similar'. They differed in the following respects. First, they had different aims—old-age pension was granted because of the loss of employability, while long-service pension may have several aims—compensation for the partial loss of employability, including employability in specific conditions, and it may also be granted as a compensation for employment in specific conditions, like additional restrictions and workload, and also promote the quality of work of respective state services.[88] It was also taken into account that this service pension was not basic but an additional social guarantee.[89] Therefore, rights to an old-age pension were 'core' basic rights while rights to a long-service pension did not concern minimum social rights.[90] Second, the service pensions were partially paid from the state budget and from the statutory insurance budget and they were calculated differently. However, this fact did not exempt service pensions from the scope of article 109.[91] The Court did not provide further clarification on why long-service pensions fell within the scope of article 109. For example, the Constitutional Court did not explain the significance of the fact that long-service pensions were partially financed from different sources than old-age pensions and were also calculated differently. It just pointed out that neither the applicants nor Parliament contested the fact that long-service pensions fell within the scope of this provision. Further the Court simply went on to hold that if the legislator had decided to establish such a specific type of pensions, then they had become a part of the statutory social security system. Thus article 109 was also applicable to long-service pensions. However, on the basis of the aforementioned difference, that the cases at hand did not affect 'core' or minimum rights,[92] the entitlement to a long-service pension enjoyed a lesser level of protection and the legislator had a wider margin of appreciation when restricting long-service

---

[87] *Digest of the Case Law of the European Committee of Social Rights* (2018) 138; also Balodis (n 59) 565.

[88] Ministry of the Interior Long-Service Pension Case (n 50), point.5.1; Prosecutors' Service Pension Case (n 52), point 8, reference to 2006-13-103, point 7.2; Military Service Pension Case (n 51), point 8, reference to 2003-14-01, point 7.

[89] ibid, point 5.2, reference to 2003-14-01, point 7.

[90] ibid, point 6.1.

[91] ibid, points 5.1, 5.2; Prosecutors' Long-Term Service Pension Case (n 52), point 8, reference to 2009-76-01, points 5.1, 5.2; Military Long-Service Pension Case (n 51), point 8, reference to 2009-76-01, points 5.1, 5.2.

[92] Ministry of the Interior Service Pension Case (n 50), point 6.1.

pension rights.[93] None of the three decisions provide more extensive argumentation for this finding. The present author finds no basis for reaching such a conclusion with regard to all recipients of long-service pensions, since the following is
listed among the aims of long-service pensions: loss of employability, either due to
specific service conditions experienced or because ageing may affect one's ability to
be employed in specific conditions. It follows that long-service pensions may also
be granted in cases where a person has lost employability and then such a specific
pension is the only source of income. In such a situation there is no factual difference between an old-age and a long-service pension.

According to the well-established case law of the Constitutional Court, the social rights envisaged for families with children are provided by article 110 of the
Constitution. Thus the restrictions on the amount of parental allowance for parents
in active employment was assessed under this provision. With regard to article 110
the Court repeated that it implied the positive duty of the state to establish and
maintain a social and economic protection and support system for families.[94] The
state must undertake a broad range of measures for the support of families and
children. It specifically applied to the first years of a child's life, because during that
period a child needs specific care and thus parents are not able to earn a living at
the same level as before childbirth. The state was, however, not under an obligation to grant the family all financial means necessary for the child, because such
a system would be contrary to the traditional structure of relationships within a
family, according to which it is parents who have the primary obligation to take
care of a child's economic and emotional welfare. The state's obligation was to provide reasonable support to the family, especially in situations where they were not
able to ensure all necessary means for a child.[95]

At the same time the ability of the state to form and provide an effective and
functioning social system for the families depends on the available resources, ie
the economic situation of the state,[96] and under article 110 the legislator has a wide
margin of appreciation in deciding which groups of persons are entitled to support
and regarding the amount of such support.[97]

In the Parental Allowance Case, the Constitutional Court found that, with this
background in mind, the provision of parental allowance in different amounts to
some groups of parents did not, by itself, lead to a breach of article 110. The state's
support of families with young children was ensured even under the contested
norm. However, the wide competence of the legislator regarding this issue was not
unlimited. The legislator must comply with the general principles of law, including
that of universal equality.[98]

---

[93] Military Service Pension Case (n 51), point 14.
[94] Parental Allowance Case (n 49), point 8.
[95] ibid, point 11.
[96] ibid.
[97] ibid.
[98] ibid.

cc) Equality

The breach of the principle of equality was raised by the applicants explicitly or implicitly in all constitutional complaints. However, the Court only heard cases on this ground in four out of five cases. In the Ministry of the Interior Long-Service Case the Court did not even mentioned article 91. In the Old-Age Pension Case and two other long-service pension cases the Court did not formally address the issue under the principle of equality or article 91, because it had already established the incompatibility of the contested norms with article 109 and the general principles of law. Thus, as stressed by the Court, there was no need to address the compatibility with additional norms or principles. At the same time, in all cases one of the central issues discussed was unequal treatment. In old-age and long-service pension cases the restriction of the rights under article 109 were found disproportionate exactly because there was no differentiation in cuts of the pensions, taking into account different amounts of pension and different amounts of income from employment. This was the central argument for the court's finding that the least restrictive means had not been chosen for attaining a legitimate aim.

Only in the Parental Allowance Case did the Constitutional Court review the compatibility of the contested norm with the principle of equality as provided by article 91 of the Constitution. As already mentioned, article 110 of the Constitution provides the legislator with a wide margin of appreciation in deciding which groups of persons are entitled to support and the amount of such support. However, such competence is not unlimited. The legislator must comply with the general principles of law, including that of universal equality.[99]

The principle of equality under the Latvian Constitution is a 'classic' example of such a right. Article 91 of the Constitution requires equal treatment of the persons who are in equal and comparable circumstances and different treatment of the persons who are in different situations. Only if there are reasonable and objective grounds may persons in similar situations be treated differently and persons in different situations similarly.[100] This means that the Court must establish if the persons are in a comparable (or different) situation, if there is a legitimate aim, and whether the principle of proportionality has been observed.

The argumentation on the compatibility of the contested norm with the principle of equality is unclear if not mistaken. First, it is not clear on what theoretical basis the Constitutional Court arrived at the conclusion that parents in active employment and parents on leave are in different situations. According to Latvian legal doctrine the comparability of the situation must be analysed on the basis of primary common characteristics and circumstances[101] and not secondary ones. In the Parental Allowance Case, the Court first found that all parents of children

---

[99] ibid.
[100] ibid, points 13, 14.
[101] Balodis (n 59) 95.

under the age of one were in comparable situations, but then went on to say that parents in active employment and parents on parental leave were not in comparable situations, because the income of working parents remains the same, unlike that of parents on parental leave. This conclusion is mistaken. If both parents remain in active employment, then the financial situation of the family deteriorates in comparison with parents where one remains in full-time work and another takes full-time parental leave. In the case where both parents remain in active employment they either both have to work part-time, thus decreasing their income from work, or they have to hire a childminder. At the same time the 'traditional' family does not suffer a loss of income—one parent continues working full-time and the other is entitled to the full amount of parental allowance, which in practice almost corresponds to the previous salary. Therefore, even if the characteristics and circumstances chosen by the Constitutional Court for comparison of the situation of parents in active employment and parents on parental leave might be considered as theoretically correct, the reasoning on why those two groups of persons are in different situations is factually mistaken. On this mistaken basis, the Court reached the conclusion that, since the contested norm envisaged differential treatment of persons who were not in similar and comparable situations, it was not contrary to article 91. This formulation of the conclusion also deserves criticism because differential treatment of persons who are not in similar and comparable situation in fact falls outside the scope of the principle of equality. In light of this, the present author considers that the correct theoretical approach would be to establish that parents in active employment and parents on parental leave are in comparable situations and then establish if unequal treatment could be justified.

It follows that, first, in the only case where the principle of equality was applied it was done in an incomplete if not an incorrect manner and, second, that, while it was not addressed formally in all pension cases, the principle of equality played a significant 'role' in finding the restrictions incompatible with article 109.

b) Role of general principles
aa) Relation to rights
The general principles of law—such as the rule of law, proportionality, legitimate expectations, and others—are not provided by the Constitution explicitly but, according to the case law of the Constitutional Court, derive from article 1, providing that Latvia is a democratic republic. The only principle explicitly stated in the Constitution is the principle of equality and non-discrimination provided by article 91. The compatibility of national legal norms of a lower rank with the general principles may be invoked in isolation or in the context of the rights provided by the Constitution. The legal doctrine applicable in the latter cases is not yet well established. In some cases the Constitutional Court analyses the compatibility of the contested norm with the general principles of law within the material constitutional rights, as in the Ministry of the Interior Long-Service Pension Case, Military

Long-Service Pension Case, and Prosecutors' Long-Term Service Pension Case. In other cases the Constitutional Court addresses the constitutionality of the restriction of material rights and the compliance of the contested norm with general principles of law separately, like it did in the Old-Age Pension Case. In the Parental Allowance Case the Court analysed separately the rights to parental allowance under article 110, the compatibility with the principle of equality under article 91, and the compatibility of the restriction with the principle of legal certainty in conjunction with article 110. Irrespective of the review technique that is applied, the substance and addressed issues under each of the general principles of law are the same. This is well reflected in the five decisions analysed in this chapter.

As regards the content and effect of the general principles of law the Constitutional Court has stressed that 'manifestation of these principles in different fields of law might differ. The character of the Contested Norm, relation with other norms of the Satversme, and its place in the legal system impacts the control provided by the Constitutional Court. Namely, freedom of action of legislator, when regulating a particular question, can be either broader or narrower, and the Constitutional court has the duty to assess whether the extent of freedom of action realized by the Saeima complies with the established limits.'[102]

From this it follows that the manifestation of the general principles of law may differ depending on how broad the margin of appreciation of the legislator is regarding the particular question. In this respect the Constitutional Court has stated that in the field of civil and political rights the legislator has a narrow margin of appreciation and in the field of economic, social, and cultural rights it is broad, because in the former field it concerns a negative obligation—non-interference—while in the latter field it concerns a positive obligation.[103] In addition, the fact that the provision of social rights depends on the available financial resources of the state, the needs of society, or the needs of the specific groups of society entails that decisions taken in this field have a greater political than legal dimension. Consequently, the legislator cannot be subject to the same requirements when implementing economic, social, and cultural rights as when complying with the obligation of non-interference in civil and political rights.[104]

As regards the status of proportionality, the decisions of the Constitutional Court have always referred to it as a general principle of law that derives from article 1 of the Constitution, which states that Latvia is a democratic republic.[105] The academic literature also holds that the proportionality test is a general principle

---

[102] Parental Allowance Case (n 49), point 15, by referring to the earlier decision of the Constitutional Court in case no 2006-04-01, points 15.2, 15.3.

[103] ibid, point 16, by referring to the earlier decision of the Constitutional Court in case no 2006-10-03, point 14.1.

[104] ibid, point 16, by referring to the earlier decision of the Constitutional Court in case no 2006-04-01, point 16.

[105] For example, see the decisions in case nos 04-03(98); 04-07(99), also Military Long-Service Pension Case (n 51), point 7, Prosecutors' Long-Term Service Pension case (n 52), point 7.

of law.[106] The principle of proportionality has in practice been used as the test for checking if the restriction of the relevant basic right could be justified. It has the same 'classic' content as under international agreements like the ECHR.[107] At the same time, checking the compatibility of a restriction theoretically has more elements than just the principle of proportionality. Article 116 of the Constitution lists the rights provided which may be restricted as well as the legitimate aims which may be used for the restriction. Under this provision it has to be established that the restriction is provided for by law and that it is necessary in democratic society.[108]

bb) Legitimate expectation

Concerning the principle of legitimate expectations the Constitution Court held that 'government institutions are obliged to act consistently with respect to the normative acts issued and to respect the legitimate expectations that persons could have developed under a specific legal provision', and that this principle 'requires the State, when it changes an existing legal order, to observe a reasonable balance between persons' confidence in the currently effective legal order and those interests for the sake of which this legal order is being changed ...'.[109]

Consequently, in order to establish if the principle of legitimate expectations has been complied with, it has to be established whether legitimate expectations arise with regard to any particular rights of a person and whether a reasonable balance has been struck between the protection of that person's legitimate expectation and the interests of society. In the course of this assessment it should be taken into account whether a lenient or reasonable transition to new legal regulations or compensation has been provided.[110] Moreover, for a successful claim, the relevant right must 'have been determined to the person' (ie their legal status must have been or may be worsened), the person's trust in the relevant legal norms must be 'legitimate, well-grounded and reasonable' and the legal regulation must be reasonably definite and constant.[111]

Where a person has already been awarded an individual social security benefit they have clearly acquired the right to rely on the legal regulation in force.[112] However, as stressed in the Pension Indexation Case, a person may obtain the right to legal security not only from an individual administrative act, sufficiently constant actions of the executive institutions, or a legal norm, but also from a legal norm not yet applied, if it provides for planned rights.[113] However, 'the extent of

---

[106] Daiga Rezevska, *Vispārējo tiesību principu nozīme un piemērošana (The meaning and application of the general principles of law)* (Riga 2015); Balodis (n 59) 780–81.
[107] For example, see Old-Age Pension Case (n 48), point 28.
[108] Balodis (n 59) 738–82.
[109] Old-Age Pension Case (n 48), point 32.
[110] Prosecutors' Long-Term Service Pension Case (n 52), points 14, 14.2.
[111] Parental Allowance Case (n 49), point 17, referring to the decision in case no 2006-04-01, 8 November 2006, point 21.
[112] ibid, point 17.1.
[113] Pension Indexation Case (n 47), point 24.

safeguarding of legal security differs depending on the fact whether a person has trusted into already conferred rights or those to be conferred'.[114] It follows that in cases restricting rights that are yet to be conferred, the balance test between the legal security of a person and the interests of the society is less strict.

c) Changes of constitutional doctrine

The doctrine on the principle of legal certainty, with regard to the right to change existing legal regulations, was extended in response to the economic crisis, although the Constitutional Court had already recognised the right to change existing legal regulation before the economic crisis, stating that acquired rights may not last forever and that the principle of legal certainty does not provide a basis for believing that the legal situation will never change.[115] In the cases regarding restrictions of social rights due to the economic crisis, the Court extended this doctrine by stating that the principle of legal certainty required a fair balance to be struck between the protection of the legal security of a person and the interests of society, adding that in the situation of exceptional circumstances the importance of the interests of the society increase. The Constitutional Court rejected the argument put forward by Parliament that during the economic crisis, or other exceptional circumstance, the substance of the principle of legal certainty is different.[116] In the Pension Indexation Case the Constitutional Court recognised that the principle of legal certainty does not always require a transitional period or the provision of compensation for the lenient transition to new regulations. Such a transition may also be provided for by other means. Such a finding was supported by previous decisions of the Court itself, as well as by decisions of the Federal Constitutional Court of Germany.[117]

In the long-service pension cases the Constitutional Court for the first time established that such pensions fall within the scope of article 109. Although there had been several decisions on long-service pensions before, none of them had addressed this issue. Since the Court decided that long-term service pensions fall within the scope of not only article 105 (right to property), but also article 109, such pensions are afforded a higher level of protection. In addition, the Constitutional Court has stated that if the social rights are provided by the basic law—the Constitution—then the state cannot refuse to implement them. This statement may cause problems in future, especially when one considers emerging discussions on the future ability of the state and the state social security budget to

---

[114] ibide, point 25.

[115] Decision in case no 2004-03-01, 25 October 2004, point 9.3; Ringolds Balodis, *Vispārējie tiesību principi: Tiesiskās drošība un tiesiskā paļāvība (General Principles of Law: Principle of Legal Certainty and Principle of Protection of Legitimate Expectations)* (Tiesu Nama Aģentūra 2017) 60.

[116] Balodis (n 115) 59.

[117] In particular, Judgment of 8 February 1977 by the Federal Constitutional Court of Germany in the case no 1BvR 79, 278, 282/70, published in BVerfGE 43, 242, pp 286–89 and Judgment of 19 November 1980 in the case no 1BvR 228, 311/73, published in BVerfGE 55, 185, pp 203–04.

provide long-service pensions and the need to ensure sustainability of the entire social security system.

In the Old-Age Pension Case the Court clarified the previously used term 'minimum level rights' or 'core rights' with regard to level of social security benefits. It referred to different methods for assessing the household income level, as applied by international institutions. Other aspects of these cases had already been developed in previous decisions taken before the economic crisis.

3. Critical assessment of the decisions

The fact is that the Constitutional Court found the legislator's fault to lie more in the procedural aspects of adoption of the contested norms than in the substantive sources of unconstitutionality.[118]

Although the Constitutional Court formally explored all relevant rights and principles in each of the cases, the decision in the Parental Allowance Case deserves criticism when compared to the Pension cases.

The first critique concerns the reasoning around the compliance with the principle of legitimate expectations. This criticism is evident in the partially dissenting opinion by judge Gunārs Kūtris.[119] He agrees with the finding of the Constitutional Court with regard to the compliance of the contested norm with articles 91 (principle of equality) and 110 (the state's obligation to protect family and children). However, he finds the reasoning and finding on the compliance with the principle of legitimate expectations to be mistaken. In particular, the principle of legitimate expectations requires the assessment of two aspects: (1) if a person has been conferred a legitimate expectation with regard to any particular rights and (2) whether reasonable balance has been insured between the protection of the legitimate expectation of a person and interests of the society. The Constitutional Court itself established that parents had legitimate expectations with regard to the right to parental allowance for a particular amount, because such a right was provided not only by the law but also by individual administrative acts.[120] At the same time the Constitutional Court failed to apply its own interpretation regarding the level of protection under the principle of legitimate expectations. Namely, persons who have already acquired rights enjoy a higher level of protection to legitimate expectations than those who only expect to enjoy respective rights in the future.[121] Taking

[118] See to this regard R Razumovskis, 'Atšķirīgais 1999. un 2009.gada lēmumos "Pensiju lietās"' ('The Differences in the Decisions of 1999 and 2009 in the "Pension Cases"'), available in Latvian at <http://www.tvnet.lv/4753115/atskirigais-1999-un-2009-gada-lemumos-pensiju-lietas> accessed 5 April 2020. See also Second Addendum to the Memorandum of Understanding concluded on 22 February 2010 (n 38).

[119] 26 March 2010, available in Latvian at <http://www.satv.tiesa.gov.lv/web/viewer.html?file=/wp-content/uploads/2016/02/2009-44-01_Atseviskas_domas.pdf#search=> accessed 5 April 2020.

[120] Parental Allowance Case (n 49), point 17.

[121] By referring to interpretation given in Pension Indexation Case (n 47), points 24, 25.

into account this and also the fact that the principle of legitimate expectations secures a person the chance of planning his/her future, the enforcement of a norm cutting parental allowance by 50 per cent within two weeks after adoption cannot be considered as complying with the principle of legitimate expectations. In the pension cases, one of the arguments put forward for finding non-compliance with the principle of legitimate expectations was the fact that labour law does not allow the employment relationship to be terminated within two weeks. In the Parental allowance case such an argument is 'skipped'. In particular, the Constitutional Court 'forgot' to mention that labour law requires a parent wishing to go on parental leave (in order to remain entitled to 100 per cent of parental allowance under to the new legal regulation) to inform an employer a month in advance. The Constitutional Court, unlike in Pension cases, also 'forgot' to mention one more argument. Namely, that there was a public announcement of the prime minister a month before the adoption of the contested norm that the 'cut of parental allowances is acceptable, neither from legal, nor emotional point of view'.[122]

The second point of criticism arises because the situations of recipients of pensions and of the parental allowance were not compared. The decisions in the pension cases are primarily based on the assumption that, for the majority of pension recipients, their pension amount is so low that in reality their decrease would run contrary to the obligation to provide sufficient means for decent living. As the Constitutional Court pointed out, according to Eurostat in 2007, 33 per cent of persons below the age of sixty-five were at risk of poverty and according to Latvian research the percentage of lonely pensioners grew from 45 per cent in 2005 to 69 per cent in 2006 and to 75 per cent in 2007.[123]

In the Parental Allowance Case no similar assessments were made to determine if a parent (family) after the birth of a child has sufficient income. The Constitutional Court simply concluded that if a working parent is entitled to parental allowance in the full amount of his/her salary, it provides extra income for the family in addition to their pay from active employment. Consequently, even after the cut of parental allowance by 50 per cent, the remaining 50 per cent forms extra income to their normal income and the family would be entitled to the income which is higher than their normal working income.[124] Such reasoning is only partially true and cannot be applied to the majority of families as in the absolute majority of families one parent is on childcare leave while the other remains in full-time employment. Under the legal regulation in force until 1 July 2009 parental allowance was

---

[122] Partially dissenting opinion in Parental Allowance Case (n 49), point 6.

[123] Old-Age Pension Case (n 48), point 31.2. The official statistics on the average old-age pension provides the following data: €114.58 in 2005; €136.52 in 2006; €157.64 in 2007; €200.33 in 2008; €232.50 in 2009, Central Statistic Bureau of Latvia, database on average amount of different types of state pensions <http://data1.csb.gov.lv/pxweb/lv/sociala/sociala__socdr__pensijas__ikgad/SDG030.px/> accessed 5 April 2020.

[124] Parental Allowance Case (n 49), point 23.

received in full by parents who remained in full-time employment. The situation was that one parent took child-care leave and did not work while another parent (usually the one with the higher salary) applied for parental allowance. In such a situation the total income of a family was higher than normally. In the situation where parental allowance is cut by 50 per cent, the income of the family remains at the same or higher level as before (before child-care leave when both parents were working) only if the salary of the parent on child-care leave is 50 per cent or lower of that of the other parent—the recipient of parental allowance. Consequently, it is only partially true that the entitlement to the full amount of parental allowance to any parent—even those remaining in full-time employment—always constituted a higher or extra income to the family. A further aspect of this point relates to the factual amount of parental allowance and the decent living standard. According to statistical data provided by the Ministry of Welfare the average amount of parental allowance in 2008 was €483. In the factual situation described above this would mean that one parent is on childcare leave without income from working while another is working and receiving a salary of €483 and parental allowance in amount of €483. In total €966. If this sum is divided to all family members—in most cases four persons (mother, father, new-born, and older child) the income per person would be €241.50. In the case of a family with three or more children the income per person would fall below the average amount of the old-age pension, which in 2008 was €200.33. This aspect was not discussed by the Constitutional Court. In contrast, the Constitutional Court specifically mentioned the amount of parental allowance received by the applicants before the cut—€1,168, €1,367, €2,430, €599, and €2,455. This gives the impression that due to the fact that most applicants were high earners, the Constitutional Court got 'lost' with regard to the majority of other parents who were not high earners at all. Also the fact that many families have more than one child that has to be maintained has been constantly 'forgotten' by the Constitutional Court in numerous decisions on issues concerning allowances during the childcare period.[125] The fact that families with three or more children were subject to the risk of poverty just as much as lonely pensioners was not mentioned.[126] This leads to the conclusion that the Constitutional Court did not approach the Parental Allowance and Pension cases in a similar way. In particular, unlike in the pension cases, in the Parental Allowance Case it failed to establish the legislator's failure to find different and alternative solutions for different level income groups.

---

[125] Kristīne Dupate, 'Reform of the Labour and Social Security Law in Latvia with Regard to the Rights of Employees in Connection with Parental Leave' in Thomas Davulis (ed), *Labour Law Reforms in Eastern and Western Europe* (Peter Lang 2017) 453–69.

[126] Ministry of Welfare, *National Report on Social Protection and Social Inclusion Strategy for 2006–2008* (2006), available in Latvian at <https://view.officeapps.live.com/op/view.aspx?src=http%3A%2F%2Fwww.lm.gov.lv%2Fupload%2Fsociala_aizsardziba%2Fsociala_ieklausana%2Flmzino_150906.doc> accessed 5 April 2020.

The third criticism regarding the decision in the Parental Allowance Case is that, in the end, parents were the only group that suffered from the relevant cuts, although the crisis in the social security budget occurred not so much on account of the economic crisis as on account of populistic decisions. The Constitutional Court in the Old-Age Pension Case stressed that the deficit in the statutory social insurance budget was the consequence of irresponsible decisions taken by the legislator during times of economic growth. In particular, new social risk 'parenting' was included among social insurance risks, granting the right to parental allowance, while no balancing measures were taken in relation to the revenue and expenditure of the statutory social insurance budget. Namely, there were no increases in contributions. This resulted in a situation where the statutory social insurance budget had to bear €94 million extra expenses in 2008 and, in 2009, such expenses were planned in the amount of €118 million.

The fourth aspect for criticism arises from the fiscal impact of the cuts of parental allowance by 50 per cent and the unconstitutionality of the cuts of pensions. In the decision in the Parental Allowance Case it is indicated that during the six months after the entry into force of the contested norm (cut of parental allowance by 50 per cent for parents in active employment)—the second half of 2009—the savings were €14 million.[127] By contrast, in the Old-Age Pension Case, the projected savings from the cut in pensions were in the amount of €125 million. Consequently, the fiscal impact of the cuts of parental allowances was ten times less than the cuts of pensions.

4. Role of international law

Article 89 of the Latvian Constitution explicitly requires the application of human rights provisions contained in binding international treaties and this was reflected in the 'economic crisis decisions', where the Constitutional Court made direct references to different international legal sources. Yet it is doubtful whether such obligations actually played a significant role in the positive outcome of those cases.

In the Old-Age Pension Case the Constitutional Court stated that, under article 89, it must seek to interpret constitutional rights in line with international human rights norms, but only if such an interpretation did not lead to a restriction of the rights provided by the Constitution.[128] In this respect, reference was made to relevant international legal sources and policy documents.

---

[127] Parental Allowance Case (n 49), point 22.
[128] Old-Age Pension Case (n 48), point 20.

a) ECHR

First, the Constitutional Court addressed the restriction of social rights under the ECHR. In particular it noted that the ECtHR addresses such cases under article 1 of Protocol 1 (the right to property); for instance referring to *Stec and Others v the UK*.[129] Although the Latvian Constitution also contains a right to property in article 105, the pursuant analysis was complicated by the fact that the proper national norm under which to consider the case is article 109, since it provides a more specific right to social security. Nevertheless, it was stressed that this—and by extension the contested norm—still had to be evaluated under the ECHR's right to property.[130] A more in-depth analysis of the contested norm's consistency with this obligation was not provided, but substantively the Constitutional Court appears to have followed the ECtHR's jurisprudence on the state's obligations and margin of appreciation in the field of social rights. This represented a continuation of the approach adopted by the court in previous decisions, where ECHR obligations had already been utilised in the examination of relevant social rights.[131] However, some novel insights still emerged from the consideration of the ECtHR's case law in these cases.

The Constitutional Court addressed the issue of 'untouchable core social rights' for the first time by referencing the ECHR and other international sources. It held that, while pensions may be reduced to an extent during an economic crisis, the state had an obligation to provide a certain minimum amount. This was supported by the ECtHR's finding that the essence of a recipient's pension rights must not be infringed.[132]

Further the Constitutional Court referred to the ECtHR decision in *Moskal v Poland* in its assessment of whether alternative solutions were properly considered in the adoption of the contested norms. It was emphasised that, while the legislator enjoyed a wide margin of appreciation in reducing pensions (or similar payments) and in defining the relevant 'public interest', the respective action must not obviously lack any reasonable basis.[133]

With regard to the principle of proportionality, the Constitutional Court referred both to the concurring opinion of judge Thomassen in *Asmundsson v Iceland*, to support the state's right to change the entitlement conditions for pensions to ensure a just social insurance system in times of economic hardship,[134] and to the decision.[135] It held that delay, unpredictability, and a lack of implementation

---

[129] App nos 65731/01 and 65900/01 (ECtHR, 12 April 2006), para 51.
[130] Old-Age Pension Case (n 48), point 20.
[131] Van Dijk and others (n 60) 858–59; Old-Age Pension Case (n 48), point 24, by referring to the decision in case No 2007-23-01, 3 April 2008, point 7; Prosecutors' Long-Term Service Pension Case (n 52), point 8, by referring to the decision in case No 200-08-0109, 3 March 2001.
[132] Judgement in *Kjartan Asmundsson v Iceland* App no 60669/00 (ECtHR, 30 March 2005), para 39.
[133] Decision in *Moskal v Poland* App no 10373/05 (ECtHR, 15 September 2009), para 61.
[134] (n 132).
[135] See para 40 of the decision.

of the contested norms were indicative of a breach.[136] This was supported by the statement of the ECtHR in *Broniowski v Poland* that, in assessing the compliance with the right to property, the public authorities must act in good time and in an appropriate and consistent manner.[137] This jurisprudence reinforced the argument that the contested norms were adopted in haste, without proper consultations, and without an assessment of alternative solutions.

When analysing the principle of legitimate expectations, the Constitutional Court also referred to ECtHR case law. It found that, when amending existing legal regulations, the state had to observe a reasonable balance between the individual's reliance on the permanence of the norm and those interests underlying its change.[138]

Numerous decisions of the ECtHR were also relied on to establish that, where the state had withheld financial resources from an individual, they must be reimbursed in reasonable time, taking into account the particular situation and involved interests.[139] However, since it is not apparent that the ECtHR in fact made such pronouncements with regard to withheld social security payments, this use of international law by the Constitutional Court is questionable.

It follows that the Constitutional Court introduced certain aspects of ECtHR jurisprudence to national law for the first time, such as the notion of core social rights and the specific protection afforded to legitimate expectations.

b) ICESCR

In the Old-Age Pension Case the Constitutional Court also referred to article 9 of the ICESCR. It served to outline the principles that states are obliged to observe in their social security systems. More specifically, General Comment No 19 of the UN Committee on Economic, Social and Cultural Rights (CESCR) was drawn up to establish that it was a legitimate aim to seek to ensure that the pension system was sustainable, so as to preserve the right to an old-age pension for the present and for future generations.[140]

---

[136] Referring to David Harris and others, *Law of the European Convention on Human Rights* (2nd edn, Oxford University Press 2009) 676.

[137] Decision of the ECtHR in *Broniowski v Poland* App no 31443/96 (22 June 2004), para 151: 'indecisiveness—no matter whether it has come about as a result of legislation or administrative or institutional practice—is a factor to be considered in adjudicating an action of the state. Indeed, in the case of dealing with a matter of common interest, the public authorities have a duty to consider this matter in due and coordinated manner for a reasonably long period of time.'

[138] Referring to Harris and others (n 136) 675.

[139] The Constitutional Court referred to ECtHR decisions in *Lithgow v UK* App no 9006/80 (8 July 1986), paras 120–22; *Guillemin v France* (art 50) App no 105/1995/611/699 (2 September 1998), para 24; *Jucys v Lithuania* App no 5457/03 (8 January 2008), paras 37, 39; *Broniowski v Poland* App no 31443/96 (22 June 2004), para 151.

[140] Adopted on 23 November 2007, point 11 <https://tbinternet.ohchr.org/_layouts/15/treatybodyexternal/Download.aspx?symbolno=E%2fC.12%2fGC%2f19&Lang=en> accessed 5 April 2020.

The Constitutional Court also relied on the Limburg Principles on the Implementation of the ICESCR in its proportionality analysis, recalling that according to them a state must provide a minimum level of social rights irrespective of its financial capacities and that laws restricting social rights may not be unjust or discriminatory. The CESCR General Comment further supported this position and the Constitutional Court stated that even if a state was suffering from a considerable lack of resources it had a duty to protect the most vulnerable members of society, emphasising that the CESCR General Comment specifically referred to elderly people as such a vulnerable ground. However, this is subject to criticism because it ignored other statements of the CESCR. Namely, that the elderly may also be in good health and in an acceptable financial situation and that, as such, they do not automatically belong to the most vulnerable.

General Comment No 19 was also referred to by the court to establish the state's obligation to define groups that deserve specific protection in cases where a scarcity of resources does not allow it to offer minimum protection to all risk groups. This reference was made in the context of considering Eurostat data from 2007, which held that in Latvia 33 per cent of persons above the age sixty-five were at risk of poverty.[141]

c) Other sources and conclusions

While the ECHR and the ICESCR were considered, what is conspicuously absent from the Constitutional Court's crisis jurisprudence is the European Charter of Social Rights.

The Constitutional Court utilised various international policy documents to outline the basic principles of social security systems, even though their status as sources for constitutional doctrine remains unclear. Specifically, reference was made to the three principles for securing the long-term sustainability of pension systems that had been endorsed by the European Council: safeguarding the capacity of systems to meet their social objectives, maintaining their financial sustainability, and meeting changing societal needs.[142] Basic elements of pension systems were also cited from the EU Social Protection Committee's 2000 report on adequate and sustainable pensions, which included adequacy, justice, and solidarity as well as the opportunity to react to the changing needs of individuals and society.[143] Further, the European Commission's Communication on national strategies for safe and sustainable pensions was drawn on, as it required

---

[141] Old-Age Pension Case (n 48), point 31.2.

[142] Council of the European Union, 'Joint report of the Social Protection Committee and the Economic Policy Committee on objectives and working methods in the area of pensions: applying the open method of coordination' 14098/01, 10672/01 ECOFIN 198 SOC 272 (23 November 2001) <https://ec.europa.eu/economy_finance/publications/pages/publication_summary6584_en.htm> accessed 5 April 2020.

[143] Social Protection Committee, *Adequate and Sustainable Pensions* (2000).

the state to provide all elderly persons with a standard of living that ensured their human dignity and the opportunity to participate actively in the state's public, social, and cultural life.[144] Taken together, these references demonstrate that soft law did influence the court's understanding of what constitutes an appropriately functioning social security system, albeit ultimately this does not appear to have resulted in specific legal consequences.

Overall, international law was used to reinforce general principles that related to the state's obligations in the field of social security rights. However, such principles were already prevalent in the pre-crisis case law of the Constitutional Court. The novelty of the crisis decisions' analysis of international law was their in-depth consideration of the sustainability of the social security systems, as well as the obligations to protect the most vulnerable groups.

IV.   Conclusion

It is clear that the measures that were taken in response to the economic crisis did not lead to any structural changes in the social security system. Rather, they constituted temporary cuts of various social insurance benefits, which ultimately did not include any kind of pension. The right to parental allowance was the only one which was restricted permanently. However, it would be misleading to see even this as a structural change in response to the crisis because the relevant entitlement criteria had already been subjected to numerous changes since the 1990s and they were altered again in 2014.

Meanwhile, the Constitutional Court in its 'crisis' decisions appears to reaffirm the view that old-age pensions are a kind of 'untouchable' benefit, since all relevant cuts were deemed unconstitutional. This may be explained by the fact that the average old-age pensions are low. By contrast, in the only 'crisis' case dealing with another type of benefit, the Parental Allowance Case, the relevant changes were upheld. Nevertheless, it was outlined above why this divergent case was problematic. Namely, because both the legislator and the Constitutional Court adopted the relevant measures on the assumption that all parents live in couples and that they have no more than one child. Based on such an assumption, the income for one person in a family is indeed higher than the average old-age pension per retired person. However, the reality is often different—there are many one-parent families and families with more than one child. As a result the latter group have even less income per person than the recipients of an average level old-age pension.

---

[144] European Commission, 'Communication on supporting national strategies for safe and sustainable pensions through an integrated approach' COM (2001) 362 final.

From a legal perspective the Constitutional Court decisions also represented new developments in constitutional law doctrine. First, the Constitutional Court clarified the scope of the legislator's competence in the field of social rights, specifically also in a situation of crisis. The Court drew the conclusion that it is for the legislator to decide how to allocate the state's budget, but that the Constitutional Court retains a role in evaluating if the norms are reasonable and coherent, if the state has the necessary resources to implement them, if they are balanced, flexible, and ensure short-term and long-term needs, and if they are transparent and known to society.[145] Further, a reasonable balance must be maintained between the relevant legitimate aim and the measures used to attain it, and the latter must be proportionate to the financial crisis and the interests affected by them.

Second, with respect to the development of substantive rights, the Court established the concept of a 'core' or minimum pension amount. This was crucial because the state could not depart from its obligation to meet this minimum level of rights. Furthermore, the Constitutional Court established for the first time that long-term service pensions are protected under the constitutional right to social security, adding, however, that only rights to an old-age pension—and not rights to a long-service pension—are 'core' basic rights.[146]

Third, the Constitutional Court developed the substance of the principle of legal certainty. The Court held that the principle of legal certainty requires a fair balance to be struck between the protection of the legal security of a person and the interests of society, adding that in exceptional circumstances the importance of society's interests increases. In the Pension Indexation Case, the Constitutional Court further recognised that the principle of legal certainty does not always require a transitional period or alternative compensation for a lenient transition to new regulations. Such a transition may also be provided for by other means.

As for the impact of international law, the Constitutional Court introduced certain aspects of ECtHR jurisprudence to national law for the first time, such as the notion of core social rights and the specific protection afforded to legitimate expectations. Apart from this, the Court also referred to the ICESCR and related sources, as well as to some international policy documents and academic literature.

The response of parliament and the government was immediate—the withheld pensions were paid out before the date indicated by the Constitutional

---

[145] Old-Age Pension Case (n 48), point 29.2 referring to Pius Langa, 'Taking Dignity Seriously. Judicial Reflections on the Optional Protocol to the ICESCR' (2009) 27(1) Nording Journal of Human Rights 33.

[146] Ministry of the Interior Long-Service Pension Case (n 50), point 6.1.

Court and there were no further attempts to restrict the rights to social insurance benefits.

The present situation demonstrates that the Latvian politicians have learned some of the lessons of 2008 regarding the social security system. So far, no patently populistic decisions have been made to increase—or make additional awards of—social security benefits. When proposed, or even adopted, such decisions have since been discussed beforehand with the sustainability of the social security system in mind and with an awareness of the need to make further savings in case another crisis should materialise.

5

Upholding the Welfare State During the Financial Crisis

The Pivotal Role of the Constitutional Court of Romania

Elena-Luminiţa Dima

I. Introduction

In Romania, both components of the social protection system (social insurance and social assistance) were influenced by the global economic crisis that occurred in 2008, mainly due to the increasing deficit of the social insurance funds and of

Elena-Luminiţa Dima, *Upholding the Welfare State During the Financial Crisis* In: *European Welfare State Constitutions after the Financial Crisis*. Edited by: Ulrich Becker and Anastasia Poulou, Oxford University Press (2020). © The Contributors.
DOI: 10.1093/oso/9780198851776.003.0005

the general public budget, the increase in the number of unemployed persons, and the increase in the number of persons in need of social assistance. Changes were adopted and implemented in respect of both fields.

On the one side, the crisis itself required the implementation of some fiscal, financial, and economic measures to prevent and/or diminish its effects towards the Romanian economy and society. On the other, the global measures taken at the European and international level have also included Romania who benefited from financial assistance from the European Union (EU), International Monetary Fund (IMF), and World Bank (WB) through the International Bank for Reconstruction and Development (IBRD).

Thus, Romania signed a Memorandum of Understanding (MoU) with the European Community for medium-term financial assistance of up to €5 billion[1] and Stand-by Arrangement (SBA) documents with the IMF for about €12.95 billion,[2] as well as financial borrowing documents with the WB for €1 billion and the European Investment Bank and European Bank for Reconstruction and Development for another €1 billion. Such financial assistance was conditional upon the implementation of a comprehensive economic policy programme, encompassing fiscal, financial sector, and structural reform measures in order to enable the economy to withstand short-term liquidity pressures while improving competitiveness and supporting an orderly correction of imbalances in the medium term, hence bringing the economy back on a sound and sustainable footing.

Romania undertook to decrease the public expenditure and decrease the public deficit through various fiscal, economic, financial, and structural measures expressly included in general terms in the above-mentioned documents signed with the European and international institutions, some of them affecting the social protection system. For example, one such measure initially undertaken was to reform key parameters of the pension system to help improve the long-term sustainability of public finance.[3]

---

[1] Memorandum of Understanding between the European Community and Romania of 23 June 2009 <https://ec.europa.eu/info/sites/info/files/ecfin_publication15409_en.pdf>, Council Decision 2009/459 of 6 May 2009 <https://eur-lex.europa.eu/LexUriServ/LexUriServ.do?uri=OJ:L:2009:150:00 08:0010:EN:PDF> accessed 1 December 2019.

[2] The SBA framework allows the IMF to respond quickly to countries' external financing needs and to support policies designed to help them emerge from crisis and restore sustainable growth. When a country borrows from the IMF, it agrees to adjust its economic policies to overcome the problems that led it to seek funding in the first place. These commitments, including specific conditionality, are described in the member country's letter of intent <http://www.imf.org/en/About/Factsheets/Sheets/2016/08/01/20/33/Stand-By-Arrangement> accessed 1 December 2019. IMF approved SBA for Romania on 4 May 2009.

[3] For example, the MoU signed with the European Community mentioned that 'changes will include moving toward indexing public pensions to consumer prices, limiting the scope for discretionary pension increases and gradually increasing the retirement age beyond the currently agreed plans (particularly for women), taking into account the evolution of life expectancies. In addition, groups of public employees currently excluded from pension contributions will have such contributions phased-in. The programme foresees the continuation of the implementation of the second pension pillar with regularly scheduled increases in contributions as originally planned'.

However, the approval of a new law on the public pension system was not the only measure envisaged and taken. The elaboration and approval of this law took a rather long time and could not have immediate effects. There were also a large number of immediately effective measures that decreased the expenses within the social protection system. Such measures were not initially envisaged, but they were discussed, adopted, and implemented later on when it was considered that such additional measures were necessary, such as: decreasing the amount of the pensions, decreasing the value of the pension point on the basis of which the pension is calculated, removing special pensions and recalculating them according to the rules applicable to the general ordinary public insurance pension system, and decreasing other social insurance and social assistance benefits.

All such measures were adopted and implemented over a period of time when measures taken by Romania were monitored by the European and international institutions granting the above-mentioned financial assistance. The documents subsequently issued reveal that this control of the observance of the obligations undertaken by Romania was continuous, occurring alongside adjustments and amendments to the documents relating to the granting and payment of the financial assistance amounts involved.

For example, the medium-term financial assistance granted by the European Community was intended to be paid in a maximum of five instalments, payment requirements being laid down within the MoU. However, the economic crisis context and its related effects were changing and therefore the MoU was subsequently complemented by four Supplemental MoUs,[4] according to the further economic developments in the fields encompassed. When a significant worsening of the economic outlook for 2009 and 2010 was acknowledged, the specific criteria for the payment of further instalments were supplemented, including measures such as: 'a nominal freeze in the level of pensions compared to the level reached by end-2009, except for the minimum pensions which can be indexed according to inflation', 'in case envisaged measures are not on track to deliver the expected consolidation, contingency measures will be implemented to close any anticipated gap',[5] and '15% reduction in all social benefits with the exception of pensions and allowances for those accompanying handicapped people with a first degree handicap'.[6]

The other financial assistance-related documents were also amended to adjust the implementation requirements to the evolution of the economic context. For example, the SBA documents, relating to the amounts borrowed from the IMF,

---

[4] <https://ec.europa.eu/info/business-economy-euro/economic-and-fiscal-policy-coordination/ eu-financial-assistance/which-eu-countries-have-received-assistance/financial-assistance-romania_ en> accessed 1 December 2019.

[5] The first supplemental MoU signed on 18 February 2010 <https://ec.europa.eu/info/sites/info/ files/ecfin_2010-02-25-smou_romania_en.pdf> accessed 1 December 2019.

[6] The second supplemental MoU signed on 2 August 2010 <https://ec.europa.eu/info/sites/info/ files/ecfin_2010-07-20-mou-romania_en.pdf> accessed 1 December 2019.

were subsequently revised through an average of four reviews per year,[7] detailing additional similar measures to be implemented to obtain the payment of the borrowed amounts: 'streamline the social benefit system by consolidating some of the more than 200 benefits currently existing and by improving targeting of the remaining programs', 'keep the minimum wages and pensions unchanged to protect the more vulnerable members of society and no wage or pension will be cut below that level', 'reform of the social support programs with a view toward improving their effectiveness and targeting them better on the poor and needy', etc.

Under close monitoring from the EC, IMF, and WB, the measures affecting the public social insurance and social assistance system—included in the official documents as requirements for payment of financial assistance instalments—were adopted. Sometimes adoption of such measures was affected by delays and, therefore, consecutive adjustments were agreed. Most of the measures were subject to constitutionality control and some were removed from the list of official requirements due to being invalidated as contrary to provisions of the Romanian Constitution (eg decrease the amount of pensions by 15 per cent), influencing the general adjustment thereof for payment of further instalments.[8]

Within the above-described context, the first part of the present analysis will focus on the reforms implemented in the Romanian social protection system, starting from the economic background and its evolution and describing the areas of the social protection system and the specific measures taken in respect of each area over the past decade. The second part of the study is dedicated to analysing to what extent the reforms affected human rights, with particular reference to some of the procedural issues that arose and were overcome, the arguments invoked for the legal amendments, and their conformity with the constitutional norm, as they were assessed by the Constitutional Court, High Court of Justice, and regular courts, and the effects of such assessments and court decisions towards the respective measures. Finally, the study presents some conclusions specific to the context and measures adopted and implemented in Romania.

II. Reforms in Romania's social protection systems

1. Background and stages of reform

The public social insurance systems cover old-age benefits, healthcare benefits, maternity allowances, and unemployment benefits. The access to such benefits is

---

[7] <http://www.imf.org/en/Countries/ROU> accessed 1 December 2019.

[8] See Letter of Intent and Technical Memorandum of Understanding of 16 June 2010 (item 8) in relation with Supplementary Letter of Intent and Technical Memorandum of Understanding of 29 June 2010 (item 29).

granted mainly on the basis of the principle of contribution to the respective insurance systems, and the respective benefits represent allowances meant to replace professional incomes.

On the other side, the social assistance benefits are not based on the contribution of the respective persons to an insurance system, but on the constitutional right of the citizens to be granted a minimum income for living by the state. Benefits granted to persons with disabilities, family allowances, and other social assistance benefits are included in this category.

Both categories of benefits were affected by the profound global financial and economic crisis and the measures implemented to prevent and/or diminish its effects.

a) First stage

In the first stage, in 2008, the legislative measures adopted for the next year were elaborated taking into consideration the following context:

- The pressure and risks determined by the internal and external economic changes.[9]
- The need to sustain economic growth and reduce inflation.[10] In order to maintain budgetary balances, some measures were needed to keep the volume of budget expenditures at a level that allowed for the internal and international commitments made by the Romanian Government, including the level of the budget deficit.[11]
- Ensuring co-financing of the projects with European funding sources and Romania's contribution to the EU budget.[12]
- Taking into consideration the opinions and recommendations of the European Commission, as well as those of the rating agencies delivered on

---

[9] The negative effects of the international economic crisis were already manifested in Romania and, in particular, regarding the revenues of the consolidated state budget, by diminishing these revenues, even in the context of an economic growth of over 8 per cent in 2008. The general consolidated budget deficit was estimated in 2008–2009 at 3.5 per cent of gross domestic product (GDP), beyond the limits set by the Maastricht Treaty.

[10] Supporting economic growth and reducing inflation were the objectives for the main features of fiscal-budgetary policy, with the purpose of reaching a budget deficit at a level correlated with macroeconomic objectives, as well as supporting the process of convergence of the Romanian economy with the European economies.

[11] The gradual reduction of the personnel expenditures in the central and local public administration by up to 20 per cent compared to the 2008 level was a priority listed in the Government Programme and the measures included in this project adhere to the objectives set for the achievement of savings to the state budget.

[12] Since 2007, Romania has benefited from financial transfers within the framework of EU cohesion policy, which requires priority to be given to the funds needed to co-finance these transfers, thus ensuring the commitments of the Romanian government undertaken during the accession negotiations, as well as ensuring a high degree of absorption of the funds allocated to Romania and the achievement of a high absorption rate of the cohesion and structural funds.

the occasion of periodic evaluations, showing that in order to avoid the high-lighted risks it is necessary to adopt policies that aim to reduce the public budget expenditures. In this context, it was intended to allocate the budgetary resources for priority areas such as: infrastructure projects, education, health, social protection/safety, agriculture, and co-financing related to the funds received from the European Union and Romania's contribution to the EU budget.

b) Second stage

In the second stage, starting 2010, in spite of slight improvements to the economic status, the financial conditions proved to be more difficult than initially antici-pated, the economic activity in Romania being continuously marked by recession because of the reduced internal demand and a slow return of commercial partners of Romania.[13]

The extensive anti-crisis plan supported by the IMF, the EU, and the WB Group was considered to serve as the mechanism leading to the standardisation/normal-isation of the Romanian financial conditions, which are meant to reverse the effect of the economic imbalances, as well as to prepare the economic recovery.

The financial data, as well as the prognosis carried out by the specialised au-thorities, outlined the image of a severe economic crisis, which could have jeop-ardised Romania's economic stability and, through this, it could also have had consequences as regards public policy and national security. Also, as a result of the assessment mission completed by the European Commission departments, along with the IMF experts and the WB Group between 26 April and 10 May 2010, ana-lysing the progress made regarding the specific conditions attached to the third share, amounting to €1.15 billion within the financial assistance programme, and taking into account the current policies, it was envisaged that the fiscal deficit target (6.4 per cent from GDP) could not be met.

The Romanian government reached the conclusion that this situation had been caused by the deterioration of the economic conditions, some difficulties with the col-lection of revenue, as well as slippage regarding the expenses sector. The government

---

[13] According to the latest evaluation conducted by the European Commission, economic activity in Romania was still at a low level and, contrary to initial expectations, most likely, economic growth continued to be negative during the first trimester of 2010. This displayed mainly the weak domestic demand from the beginning of 2010.

An improvement of the economic growth was expected in the second half of 2010, although the un-certainties regarding the external markets were still significant. However, all year round, in 2010, eco-nomic growth was expected to be close to zero or slightly negative, considering that the inflation rate decreased from 4.7 per cent, by the end of 2009, to 4.2 per cent by the end of March 2010, these values remaining within the domestic range of the inflation rate, as established with the IMF.

By the end of 2010, it was estimated that the inflation rate would continue to decrease to approxi-mately 3.75 per cent, as a result of the low domestic demand and of the application of a cautious mon-etary policy. The weak recovery of the domestic demand reduced the level of import and, therefore, the prognosis illustrated a current account deficit of approximately 5 per cent from the GDP of 2010, as compared to the initial 5.5 per cent.

was committed to taking additional countervailing measures, which had to be adopted and implemented before the European Commission's issuance of the third share from the EU loan. These additional measures referred to:

- a 25 per cent reduction of salaries, salary increments, and other amounts of this nature, for all public sector employees, starting from the date when the law became enforceable;
- a 15 per cent reduction of the indemnities granted as support to families for raising a child, as well as to the pensions and unemployment allowances. The social programmes that are not designated for the disadvantaged groups of society will contribute more to this reduction;
- the freezing of early retirement pensions, starting from June 2010, until a reform law regarding the pension system enters into force.

Also, it was discussed that in case such measures were not implemented until June 2010 or did not lead to the expected consolidation, additional measures to increase the budgetary revenue would be implemented, including measures regarding an increase in taxation rates, in order to eliminate any anticipated budgetary difference. These measures were also undertaken in accordance with financial assistance documents and adopted by a specific law regarding some necessary measures for the restoration of the budgetary balance.

c) Third stage

In a third stage, by the end of 2010, attention was focused on the unemployment situation and unemployment insurance budget since the local labour market continued to be influenced by the effects of the economic and financial crisis, such effects leading to the rapid increase in the number of unemployed persons and the rate of unemployment registered in December 2008—March 2010.

The situation on the labour market reflected correspondingly on the budgetary level by having a significant financial impact on the unemployment insurance budget and generating difficulties in ensuring necessary financial resources for the payment of unemployment indemnity, as well as for financing active measures to stimulate the employment of the workforce, given that the number of unemployed persons and of persons searching for a place of work was increasing.[14]

Practically, in 2010 the effects of the crisis were already transpiring and the pressure on the unemployment insurance budget was very high due to a large number

---

[14] Statistics of the National Agency of Workforce Deployment show that the number of unemployed beneficiaries exceeded the number of unemployed persons that did not benefit from the unemployment allowance (the statistics indicated on 31 October 2010 the fact that 329,182 persons had been unemployed beneficiaries, whereas 316,271 unemployed persons did not benefit from this indemnity).

of dismissals, especially collective dismissals, which affected a very large number of employees.

Such effects of the economic-financial crisis upon the labour market in Romania caused a perpetuation of low-level revenues for the unemployment insurance budget, with immediate difficulties in ensuring sufficient resources for financed programmes from this budget. It was estimated that such difficulties would be amplified if the minimum base salary level in 2011 was set higher than in 2010.

Considering the necessity of protecting the rights of unemployed persons, to ensure effective observance of the rights granted by the legislation in force, it was necessary to avoid a situation where raising the limit of the minimum base salary for 2011 could lead to the impossibility of granting such rights. On the other side, multiple recommendations of international financial organisations regarding the maintenance of actions for reducing unemployment were analysed, in order to strive for the employment of the beneficiaries of unemployment indemnity and to stimulate them to take up work. In this context the conclusion was reached that it was necessary to change the modality in which the unemployment allowance is established, by eliminating the reference to the minimum gross base salary when calculating the unemployment indemnity. The 'social index of reference' established the new reference, a fixed amount, not related to the minimum gross base salary.

2. Specific reform measures

a) Old-age benefits
The old-age insurance system of Romania is based on three pillars.

aa) Pensions pillar I
Since 2001 the public pension system has been an autonomous state-owned public system of insurance for pensions and other benefits, based on the principles of equal treatment and social solidarity, the granting of benefits being conditional on the payment of contributions and the mandatory character of the contribution payments.[15] The public pension system budget is administrated by the National House of Public Pensions and receives its income from: social insurance contributions, interest, increases, and other incomes, as well as other amounts allocated from the state budget.

The categories of beneficiaries mainly include persons who are insured by operation of law and for whom the payment of the contribution is mandatory (eg employees, civil servants, freelancers, shareholders of companies)—from 2001

---

[15] Law 19/2000 on the public system of pensions and other social insurance rights [2000] Official Gazette (OG) 140, entered into force on 01 April 2001.

the contribution quota was split between the employer and employee[16] and it was calculated based on the employee's gross monthly income. As regards the persons who benefit from unemployment payments from the unemployment budget, the contribution quota was the one applicable for normal work conditions, paid from the unemployment budget. The persons insured in the public pension system enjoy the benefit of retirement pensions, anticipated retirement pensions, invalidity pension, inheritor pension, and death allowances. The amount of the pension is calculated by multiplying the value of a pension point (provided by the law[17]) on the date of retirement, using the annual average score (number of points) accumulated by the respective individual.[18]

The amounts of the contribution quotas were changed (diminished) starting 2009.[19] For that year the initial value of a pension point was 763 lei (approximately €211) but the piece of legislation that provided for this amount was immediately repealed and the new value adopted for a pension point was 697 lei (approximately €193). Starting 2010, the contribution quotas increased again.[20] The income that serves as the basis for the calculation of these quotas was capped at five times the average gross monthly income at the national level. Another change was adopted in 2014, when the contribution quotas were decreased again[21] and remained in force until the end of 2017.[22]

---

[16] In 2008 the split was as follows: 29 per cent for normal work conditions—19.5 per cent owed by the employer and 9.5 per cent by the employee; 34 per cent for harmful work conditions—24.5 per cent owed by the employer and 9.5 per cent by the employee; 39 per cent for hazardous work conditions—29.5 per cent owed by the employer and 9.5 per cent by the employee.

[17] The value of a pension point in 2008 was approx. €160.

[18] By monthly payment of the contribution, the individual person accumulates in a month a number of points equal with the insured income divided by the gross average monthly income at the national level corresponding to the respective month. For a complete year the average score is represented by the total number of points cumulated by the respective person each month, divided by twelve (months) while for the entire contribution period the annual average score is calculated by dividing the total amount of the annual scores by the complete period of contribution provided by the law (thirty-five years).

[19] In 2009 the split was as follows: 28 per cent for normal work conditions—18.5 per cent owed by the employer and 9.5 per cent by the employee; 33 per cent for harmful work conditions—23.5 per cent owed by the employer and 9.5 per cent by the employee; 38 per cent for hazardous work conditions—28.5 per cent owed by the employer and 9.5 per cent by the employee (Governmental Emergency Ordinance 226/2008 on some financial budgetary measures [2008] OG 899).

[20] In 2010 the split was as follows: 31.3 per cent for normal work conditions—15.8 per cent owed by the employer and 10.5 per cent by the employee; 36.6 per cent for harmful work conditions—20.8 per cent owed by the employer and 10.5 per cent by the employee; 41.3 per cent for hazardous work conditions—25.8 per cent owed by the employer and 10.5 per cent by the employee (Law 12/2010 on the public insurance budget for 2010 [2010] OG 61).

[21] In 2014 the split was as follows: 26.3 per cent for normal work conditions—20.8 per cent owed by the employer and 10.5 per cent by the employee; 31.3 per cent for harmful work conditions—25.8 per cent owed by the employer and 10.5 per cent by the employee; 36.3 per cent for hazardous work conditions—30.8 per cent owed by the employer and 10.5 per cent by the employee (Law 123/2014 amending the Fiscal Code [2014] OG 687).

[22] From 2018 the social insurance system was fundamentally changed as regards owing and payment of the contributions.

Another measure affecting the public pension system was a prohibition on re-ceiving the public pension cumulatively with the income from an employment relationship with a public institution, public administration authority, or state-owned company. Such a measure had initially been adopted through Government Emergency Ordinance no 230/2008,[23] as it was considered necessary to adopt spe-cific provisions pursuant to which retired persons would not be allowed to cumu-late the pension with incomes obtained from positions paid from the state budget. This necessity arose as a result of taking into account the financial situation which determined budgetary constraints, the need to reduce personnel-related public expenditures, and the notion that the failure to adopt such measures may lead to difficulties in the implementation of other measures to alleviate the economic and financial crisis assumed by the government. In the event of being hired within such a legal entity, the pension income of the respective person was suspended by effect of the law. A couple of days after this piece of legislation entered into force it was declared to have breached the constitutional norms by the Constitutional Court, following advice received from the Romanian Ombudsman, and it ceased to pro-duce its effects.

Furthermore, in the same year, parliament adopted Law no 329/2009,[24] which included some provisions limiting the possibility to cumulate the public pension with the income from an employment relationship with a public institution, public administration authority, or state-owned company. According to this law, the beneficiaries of a right to a pension who also have salary incomes, or incomes as-similated to the salaries from employment relationships with legal entities within the public sector or private sector of the state, may cumulate the net amount of the pension with such incomes only if such an amount does not exceed the amount of the average gross salary income used for the elaboration of the public social in-surance budget. In cases where this requirement is not met, the individual has the right to choose between the suspension of the payment of his pension or termin-ation of the employment relationship. Failure to exert this option right terminated the employment relationship of the respective individual by effect of law. The com-pliance of these provisions with the constitutional norms was also challenged, both before and after its entry into force, but the Constitutional Court found them to be compliant with the Romanian Constitution. The respective provisions were re-pealed later on by Law no 134/2014.[25]

The restrictions on cumulating a public pension with the income from an em-ployment relationship paid from state funds was not enough and, therefore, other

[23] Government Emergency Ordinance 230/2008 amending certain normative acts in the area of pen-sions granted within the public insurance system, state pensions and special pensions [2008] OG 4.
[24] Law 329/2009 on the reorganisation of some public authorities and institutions, rationalizing the public expenses, sustaining the business environment and observance of the framework agreements with European Commission and International Monetary Fund [2009] OG 761.
[25] Law 134/2014 on repealing certain provisions of Law 329/2009 [2014] OG 753.

measures were adopted. The parliament issued Law no 118/2010 on certain measures necessary to restore budgetary balance.[26] Among other measures, regarding mainly wages, benefits granted to public sector employees, and social protection benefits, the law affected the area of pensions by reducing the amount of pensions by 15 per cent, as well as reducing the allowance for the person accompanying the beneficiary of a severe invalidity pension and decreasing the value of the pension point. Before this law entered into force the compliance of these provisions with the constitutional norms was challenged and the Constitutional Court found them in breach of constitutional norms (see details in section III below). Consequently, these provisions did not enter into force. Further, as such measures were taken into consideration and included in the documents signed as requirements for the payment of various instalments of the financial assistance agreed with the European and international institutions, following the decisions of the Constitutional Court such requirements had to be amended by taking into consideration other measures (eg in the area of VAT).

Another specific piece of legislation was adopted to remove the special pensions. The special pensions were calculated as a percentage of the individual person's last month gross salary incomes, and the difference between the amount the respective person would have benefited from under the public system of social insurance for pensions, based on their contribution, and the amount of the pension they were in fact entitled to was covered from the state budget. Such special pensions were granted to some particular categories of retired persons such as persons employed in the army, police, judges, public prosecutors, persons employed as auxiliary personnel within the courts and prosecutors' offices, diplomatic personnel, members of the parliament and public officers within the parliament structures, civil aviation aircrew, and personnel of the Court of Accounts.

Parliament adopted Law no 119/2010[27] to establish some measures in the area of pensions. The effect of this law was to recalculate the pensions granted to those particular categories of retired persons who benefited from special pensions by taking into consideration, for them as well, the general rules applicable to all those pensions granted on the basis of contributions to the public system of social insurance for pensions and, practically, remove from such pensions that amount which was covered from the state budget. The provisions of this law were also challenged in front of the Constitutional Court, both before and after its entry into force. Most of its provisions were found to be compliant, the exception being those referring to the special pensions of the magistrates and the personnel having similar legal status (based on similar restrictions, interdictions, and incompatibilities recognised at the constitutional level). After this, there were changes in the provisions of

---

[26] Law 118/2010 on certain measures necessary to restore budgetary balance [2010] OG 441.
[27] Law 119/2010 on certain measures in the area of pensions [2010] OG 441.

this law, for example as regards the state pensions granted to persons retired from the army.[28]

In addition to all the above-mentioned measures, the adoption of a new law on public pensions was agreed with the borrower institutions as a general measure to be implemented. In 2010, parliament adopted a new law on the public pension system, Law no 263/2010.[29] This law did not fundamentally change the vision of the previous law. The contribution quotas and rules for their calculation were moved to the Fiscal Code. The income basis used for the calculation of the contribution quota was capped to five times the gross average monthly income at the national level. This law was adopted with some delay and, by reference to the above-mentioned obligations undertaken by Romania to obtain financial assistance, increased in a gradual manner the retirement age of women (from sixty-two years, ie the retirement age for women under the previous law, to sixty-three years) and included in the system (with the obligation to make contribution payments) groups of public employees who were previously excluded from pension contributions (for example, persons employed in the army and police).[30] Additional measures were also included in the reform such as: a freeze on pension amounts, suspension of early retirements until the entry into force of the new law, elimination of disability pensions obtained through fraudulent claims, and greater control on disability pension claims, keeping the minimum pensions unchanged to protect the more vulnerable members of society.

bb) Pensions pillar II

As regards the compulsory insurance for pensions within a private administrated system,[31] the contribution quota paid within such a system is deducted from the individual contribution to the public system of pensions and redistributed to the private insurance pension fund chosen by the insured person. In 2008 and 2009, this quota was 2 per cent, but it was increased from 2010 by 0.5 per cent per year, as undertaken by the government in the financial assistance-related documents, up to 5 per cent in 2015. For 2016 and 2017 it was further increased, but only slightly to 5.1 per cent, while for 2018 it was 3.75 per cent.

cc) Pensions pillar III

The third system of insurance for pensions, characterised by optional insurance to a private pension fund, was not affected by any change. The only relevant

---

[28] Law 223/2015 on state military pensions [2015] OG 556.

[29] Law 263/2010 on the public pension system [2010] OG 852.

[30] Such provisions were amended and the respective categories were excluded from insurance within this general ordinary public pension system and excluded from the payment of related contributions by the Governmental Emergency Ordinance 103/2017 [2017] OG 1010. Previously, specific legislation was adopted providing for the granting of special pensions for certain categories (eg Law 223/2015 on state military pensions (n 28)).

[31] Law 411/2004 regarding the pension funds under private administration [2007] OG 482.

provision in this respect is that a maximum amount of €400 paid to such pension insurance funds is deducted from the income subject to taxation.[32] No changes were implemented in respect of the legislation regulating this pillar of insurance for pensions.

b) Unemployment benefits

Unemployment benefits are granted within another autonomous public insurance system regulated by Law no 76/2002.[33] The unemployment insurance budget is administrated by the National Agency of Workforce Deployment. The income of this budget comes from: social insurance contributions, interest, increases, and other income, such as income from the training performed by the territorial agencies of workforce deployment, as well as other amounts allocated from the state budget.

The categories of beneficiaries mainly include persons who are insured by effect of the law and for whom the payment of the contribution is mandatory (eg employees, civil servants)—the contribution quota is split between the employer and employee[34] and it is calculated based on the employee's gross monthly income. Persons who are insured within this system benefit from unemployment allowance for:

- six months in the case of at least one year of contributions,
- nine months in the case of at least five years of contributions,
- twelve months in the case of more than ten years of contributions.

The amount of the unemployment allowance is calculated as follows: 75 per cent of the gross monthly salary at the national level in force on the date the allowance is calculated for the beneficiaries having at least one year of contributions, to which there is added a percentage (applied to the average of the monthly gross base salary over the last twelve months of contribution payment), set at (i) 3 per cent in case of at least three years of contributions, (ii) 5 per cent in case of at least five years of contributions, (iii) 7 per cent in case of at least ten years of contributions and (iv) 10 per cent in case of at least twenty years of contributions.

The law also provides for measures to prevent unemployment and measures to stimulate employment.[35] A new measure that was intended to stimulate

---

[32] Law 204/2006 on the voluntary insurance for pension [2006] OG 470.

[33] Law 76/2002 on the unemployment insurance system and stimulation of employment [2002] OG 103.

[34] In 2008 the split was as follows: 1 per cent owed by the employer and 0.5 per cent by the employee (Law 387/2007 on the public insurance budget for 2008 [2007] OG 901).

[35] As regards the measures to prevent unemployment, for example, Law 76/2002 (n 33) states that employers who organise professional training for their own employees may benefit from the unemployment insurance budget by only having to bear 50 per cent of the costs of the professional training if at least 20 per cent of the employees participate in the respective professional training programme.

employment, introduced at the beginning of December 2008,[36] provided for a subvention for employers who hired persons unemployed for at least three months, benefiting them by around €1,000 for each such person hired, but it was immediately repealed in the same month of December 2008. The same piece of legislation that repealed this measure changed the contribution quotas starting 2009, decreasing the contribution of the employer.[37]

Starting July 2010, all unemployment allowances as well as any other rights granted from the unemployment insurance budget were reduced by 15 per cent through Law no 118/2010. The same diminution was also applied to the subventions and other payments granted to employers to stimulate employment after the entry into force of the new law. The provisions regarding the subventions granted for the development of local communities were repealed and the subvention agreements already signed remained in force until their expiry. All such provisions were applicable until 31 December 2010. Claims of non-constitutionality in respect of such provisions were all rejected by the Constitutional Court.

Starting January 2011, the unemployment benefits started to be calculated by reference to a 'social index of reference' (500 lei—approximately €120) instead of the minimum gross average salary at the national level (670 lei—approximately €160).[38] The value of this social index of reference has not increased since that time up to the present. On the other side, the subventions granted were capped to the total amount approved as having such destination within the unemployment insurance budget.

c) Family allowances
Family allowances are granted either as social assistance benefits or as social insurance allowances.

aa) Social assistance benefits
In the area of social assistance benefits the Romanian law provides for: children state monthly allowances (a fixed amount granted to each child until they reach the age of eighteen years—amounting to 42 lei—approximately €12 in 2008, and 200 lei for children up to two years of age—approximately €55); allowance for families with children (a fixed amount granted to families with net incomes below a specific level per each family member, which is provided by the law—approximately €45 in 2008—its amount depending on the number of children—amounting to 36–52

---

[36] Government Emergency Ordinance 192/2008 on certain measures for relating the tax regime in view of economic growth and increase of job number [2008] OG 103.

[37] In 2009 the split was: 0.5 per cent owed by the employer (diminished), 0.5 per cent by the employee, and 1 per cent owed by persons who were not obliged to pay the contribution but who were insured based on an insurance agreement (Governmental Emergency Ordinance 226/2008 on some financial budgetary measures [2008] OG 899).

[38] Governmental Emergency Ordinance 108/2010 amending Law 76/2002 on the unemployment insurance system and stimulation of employment [2010] OG 830.

lei—approximately €10–€15 in 2008); and allowance to stimulate the family in raising a child of up to two years of age (granted without it being conditional on the payment of contributions and, therefore, covered by the state budget).

The children state monthly allowance was maintained at a uniform amount until January 2012. From then on, the children state allowance was fixed by reference to the social index of reference (SIR): a higher amount for children of up to two years of age (0.4 SIR—200 lei) and lower amounts for older children (0.084 SIR—approximately 42 lei—and 0.168 SIR). In these two latter cases there were no increases until 2015. The allowance for families with children was also fixed by reference to the SIR. During the crisis such amounts were not to be increased by the relevant measures.

As regards the allowance to stimulate the family in raising a child of up to two years of age, any individuals who received income subject to taxation for a period of twelve months in the year before the date of the child's birth were entitled to leave to raise the child up to two years of age, as well as leave for raising a child with disabilities up to three years of age, as well as a fixed monthly allowance since the respective parent was thus deprived of his/her salary income. In addition, in cases where the beneficiary received income subject to taxation until the child turned two or three years of age, the allowance for the leave to raise the child was suspended and the individual was paid a fixed amount called 'insertion incentive'. The benefit of such rights was granted to one of the child's parents, meaning that they had the possibility of choosing which one of them would benefit from the respective leave and allowance. Also included in the category of beneficiaries were individuals who adopted the child, who were legally entrusted with the respective child, or who were appointed as the child's guardian.

In 2008, this allowance for raising a child was initially fixed (600 lei—approximately €160) and was subsequently, during the same year, regulated in an alternative manner: either in terms of a fixed amount (600 lei) or 85 per cent of the average of the incomes received during the past twelve months. The latter amount was not capped and the beneficiary was allowed to choose. The 'insertion incentive' was fixed at 300 lei—approximately €85).

Starting 1 January 2009, the allowance for the leave to raise a child of up to two years of age—85 per cent of the average of the incomes received during the past twelve months—was capped to 4,000 lei (around €1,000). The 'insertion incentive' was maintained at the same value of 300 lei. In July 2010, the allowances and insertion incentive benefit were decreased by 15 per cent until end of 2010. If the final amount was less than 600 lei, the beneficiary was granted 600 lei. On 1 January 2011, the regulation was again changed to provide for three categories of leave and related allowances, but for all of them the maximum limit was lower than the previous one. The quota of 75 per cent was subsequently changed again in October 2012 to 85 per cent. The insertion incentive was fixed at 500 lei, corresponding to 1 SIR. In 2016, before an electoral period, there were some substantial changes to encourage the middle class to give birth to children and to increase the birth rate.[39] The allowance was 85 per cent of the average of the income subject to taxation received during the past twelve months and it was not capped. Only a minimum limit was provided—at least 85 per cent of the minimum wage at the national level. In 2017, the legislation was changed again[40] and the allowance became 85 per cent of the average of the net income received during the past twelve months before giving birth, but it was again capped to 8,500 lei (approximately €1,800).

In 2008, the social assistance legislation also granted a birth allowance to any mother for each of her first four children (213 lei—approximately €60), if requested within twelve months from the date of birth, and an allowance for the wives of persons who are on military compulsory service in cases of: pregnancy of more than 4 months, taking care of children under seven years of age who they financially support or who fall under grade I or II of disability (195 lei—approximately €55).

With respect to the other two benefits granted within the social assistance system, the birth allowance was insignificantly increased in 2009 and repealed in 2010. The allowance for the wives of persons who are on military compulsory service was repealed starting January 2011.

bb) Social insurance allowances
Two further allowances are granted within the public system for health insurance leave: maternity leave allowance and leave allowance for taking care of a sick child. The budget is distinct from the health insurance budget but also administrated by the National Health Insurance House.

Until the end of 2017, the compulsory contribution quota within this insurance system was owed and paid by the employers, amounting to 0.85 per cent of the salary income subject to taxation received by the insured persons. The length of contribution payments in order for the insured persons to benefit from said allowances was one month during the twelve-month period preceding the first day of leave. The duration of maternity leave is 126 days, while the duration of the leave for taking care of a sick child is forty-five calendar days per year for each child.

The amount of both allowances has been established at 85 per cent of the average gross monthly salary income according to which the contribution to the social insurance system was calculated over the past six months before the first day of leave. The monthly calculation basis is capped to the total amount of twelve gross minimum wages at the national level multiplied by the total number of employees of a specific employer. Consequently, the amount of maternity allowance was capped to 85 per cent of twelve gross minimum wages at the national level.

---

[39] Law 66/2016 amending Government Emergency Ordinance 111/2010 on the leave for raising a child and related monthly allowance [2016] OG 304.
[40] Government Emergency Ordinance 55/2017 amending and supplementing Government Emergency Ordinance 111/2010 on the monthly allowance and leave for raising children [2017] OG 644, entered into force on 07 August 2017.

As regards maternity leave allowance and leave allowance for taking care of a sick child, there were no changes in the wake of the economic and financial crisis.

d) Healthcare benefits

Healthcare benefits are granted within two public insurance systems: (1) public health insurance and (2) the public system for health insurance leave. These systems have two distinct budgets which are administrated by the National Health Insurance House. In 2008, the contribution quota to the public health insurance system was split between employers and employees.[41] The persons insured in this system benefited from the medical services designated by law as services financed through the public health insurance budget.

Within the second insurance system, in addition to maternity leave, allowance and leave for taking care of a sick child, and related allowance, the beneficiaries of this system may also access leave and allowances for: temporary work incapacity (sick leave) due to usual diseases and accidents unrelated to work, prevention of sickness, and recovery of the capacity to work, as well as risks related to maternity at the workplace. The main rules applicable to insurance and payment of the contribution quota have been presented above, as well as those regarding access to such benefits.

With respect to the public health insurance system, starting January 2009 the contribution quota decreased.[42] There were no relevant changes concerning the benefits granted within this system. As well, no changes were noted regarding the benefits granted within the public system for health insurance leave.

e) Social assistance benefits

Under the Romanian legislation a large number of social assistance benefits are granted.

The main benefit is the social assistance allowance. Based on the principle that families and individuals who are Romanian citizens are entitled to a social solidarity benefit of social assistance, those families and individuals with a net income below the monthly level of the minimum guaranteed income are entitled to a social assistance allowance calculated as the difference between the monthly level of the minimum guaranteed income and the net income of that family or individual. The monthly level of the minimum guaranteed income is fixed depending on the

---

[41] Persons insured owed 6.5 per cent of their incomes, employers owed 5.5 per cent of the total salary fund, and persons insured based on signing an insurance agreement owed 13.5 per cent of the value of two times the gross monthly basic salary at the national level; the quotas decreased during the year (Law 95/2006 on the reform of the health system, as subsequently amended and supplemented).

[42] Persons insured owed 5.5 per cent of their incomes, employers owed 5.2 per cent of the total salary fund, and persons insured based on signing an insurance agreement owed 10.7 per cent of the value of two times the gross monthly basic salary at the national level; the quotas decreased during the year (Law 95/2006 on the reform of the health system, as subsequently amended and supplemented).

number of family members. In 2008, this was 100 and 372 lei (for one- to five-member families)—approximately between €30 and €100.

Other social assistance benefits are granted to persons with disabilities, including: access to medical devices, access to accommodation in medical facilities, balneary treatment free of charge, and free access to transportation, parking, museums, shows, etc. Such persons also benefit from some allowances for themselves and for their accompanying persons (in case of persons with serious disabilities).

The monthly level of the minimum guaranteed income, represented by a fixed amount, depending on the number of family members, was slightly increased in 2009. In 2008, this was 100 and 372 lei (for one- to five-member families)—approximately between €30 and €100. Starting January 2012, the minimum guaranteed income was fixed by reference to the SIR, but still depending on the number of family members.

As regards the benefits granted to persons with disabilities, no relevant changes occurred as a result of the economic and financial crisis.

Some social assistance benefits, such as allowances granted to persons participating in the 1989 Revolution and anti-communist actions and to their heirs, were suspended successively until 2016.

III. Human rights affected by social protection reforms

To a certain extent, the measures taken during and following the economic crisis came in conflict with constitutional law. From a procedural perspective, they have raised specific issues given the emergency character of their elaboration and adoption. As regards conformity with the constitutional norms, since the elaboration and adoption of the relevant legislative measures, the elaboration commission has anticipated such issues and presented arguments sustaining their conformity with constitutional rights.

Most of the measures adopted by parliament in the context of the economic crisis underwent the constitutionality control of the Constitutional Court. In some cases it was a control performed by the Constitutional Court before the promulgation of the relevant laws, a priori, while in other cases the Constitutional Court was asked to assess the compliance of some provisions after their entry into force through an a posteriori control.

For the most part, the legal provisions were considered to be in compliance with the Romanian Constitution, but some were found in breach of it. Those provisions found to be contrary to the constitutional norms in the case of a priori controls were removed from the laws and did not enter into force. In those cases where legal provisions were considered contrary to the Constitution on the occasion of an a posteriori control, such legal provisions ceased to be applicable going forward (*ex tunc*).

It is to be noted that the legal literature is rather scarce. The main debates were included in the jurisprudence of the Constitutional Court, High Court of Justice, and ordinary courts. Therefore, the relevant legal literature mainly reflects the opinions of the judges involved in the relevant case law of either the Constitutional Court or the regular courts, as they are, for the most part, the authors of the respective published papers. The most relevant arguments invoked before the above-mentioned courts of law in the examination of compliance with the Romanian Constitution are further analysed.[43]

1. Procedural issues

Some of the measures were adopted via an emergency procedure (specific to GEOs), through specific individual pieces of legislation, generally under time pressure, with late parliamentary control, since such pieces of legislation were only subject to the approval of parliament after their adoption and entry into force.

However, in one of these cases, Government Emergency Ordinance no 230/2008, on the basis of which retired persons were not allowed to cumulate their pension with income obtained from a position paid from the state budget, was assessed as unconstitutional for breaching the constitutional rules on the adoption of such measures within a couple of days of entering into force. After a couple of days of this piece of legislation having entered into force, the Constitutional Court declared that it breached constitutional norms, having received advice from the Romanian Ombudsman, and it stopped producing its effects.

The Court stated that this piece of legislation imposed on persons who were in the relevant situation the obligation to make a choice between the pension and the income resulting from professional activity. More exactly, an obligation to either waive the right to pension in order to continue the professional activity or to put an end to the professional activity, which results in lack of income. Thus, it placed a limitation on both the right to a pension and the right to work, as provided by article 47(2) and article 41 of the Romanian Constitution. By taking into consideration the provisions of article 115(6) of the Romanian Constitution,[44] according to

---

[43] Puskas Valentin Zoltan, *Main Aspects Retained Within the Case Law of the Constitutional Court with Respect to the Non-Constitutionality Objections Raised in the Area of Wages and Social Insurance Benefits* (2012) <http://www.ccr.ro/uploads/RelatiiExterne/2012/Puskas.pdf> accessed 1 August 2018; see also <https://www.yumpu.com/ro/document/view/48554138/lucrarea-prezentata-de-domnul-judecator-puskas-valentin-zoltan> accessed 1 August 2020;; Dana Apostol Tofan, 'Commented Case Law—Constitutional Court: Decisions 871/2010, 872/2010, 873/2010, 874/2010' (2010) 7 Curierul Judiciar 391.

[44] Romanian Constitution art 115(6): 'Emergency ordinances cannot be adopted in the field of constitutional laws, or affect the status of fundamental institutions of the State, the rights, freedoms and

which the emergency ordinances cannot affect the rights and freedoms provided by the Romanian Constitution, the Constitutional Court reached the conclusion that the provisions of Government Emergency Ordinance no 230/2008 were unconstitutional because they affected the above-mentioned fundamental rights.[45]

Nevertheless, the Constitutional Court framed its analysis of the constitutional norms as a procedural one and stated that the government was not prevented from further promoting the necessary measures regarding the manner in which pensions may be cumulated with work-related income, as long as it complied with the constitutional provisions, the principle of non-retroactivity of the law, the principle of non-discrimination, the principle of equality of rights, and all the other provisions and principles regulated by the Constitution.

From this point onwards, most measures were adopted as laws, as normative acts adopted by parliament. Also in such cases, the respective laws were subject to objections of unconstitutionality before the law was promulgated and also after the law entered into force. Most provisions of such laws were found to be in compliance with constitutional norms, while some others were considered as breaching the constitutional provisions, with most of the latter being removed from the law before their entry into force.

However, in case of other government emergency ordinances (extending the duration of the suspension of some rights initially operated by means of Law no 118/2010), which pertained to the possibility of the government using a government emergency ordinance to suspend, or deprive of effect, provisions of law, the Court has stated that the relevant piece of legislation allows the government, under the control of parliament, to cope with an extraordinary situation and is justified by the necessity and emergency of regulating such a situation in adopting immediate solutions in order to avoid severe damage to the public interest. On the other side, regarding the constitutional prohibition on the government adopting emergency ordinances to hinder a law adopted by parliament from producing its effects, the Court reached the conclusion that such prohibition does not refer to the government's power to adopt regulations regarding the rights that are not provided by the Constitution.[46] Therefore, the principle of the state's separation of powers is not breached.

Regarding the claim that the constitutional prerequisites for issuing the emergency ordinances were not met by the government when it adopted the criticised emergency ordinances, the Court concluded that the arguments invoked by the

---

duties stipulated in the Constitution, the electoral rights, and cannot establish steps for transferring assets to public property forcibly'.

[45] Decision 82/2009 OG 33/16.1.2009.

[46] Decision 1221/2008 OG 804/2.12.2008, Decision 842/2009 OG 464/6.7.2009, Decision 984/ 2009 OG 542/4.8.2009, Decision 989/2009 OG 531/31.7.2009, Decision 278/2015 OG 447/23.6.2015, Decision 443/2016 OG 580/29.7.2016, Decision 681/2017 OG 148/16.2.2018.

government within the background note did meet the requirements of there existing an extraordinary and urgent situation that objectively justified the issuance of an emergency ordinance (ie the need to establish in due time clear directions with regard to extremely important areas such as wages in the public sector and areas having major financial implications, within the context of setting up the newly elected parliament and investment of the new government, do represent reasons justifying the legislative intervention of the Government to avoid severe damage to the public interest).[47]

Another procedural aspect that was raised on the occasion of such unconstitutionality claims referred to the fact that by identifying the economic crisis as a problem of national security it would have been mandatory that the procedure for declaring the occurrence and termination of the state of emergency, as provided in Government Emergency Ordinance no 1/2009,[48] be complied with.[49] The Constitutional Court has rejected such claims, stating that for the correct application of article 53 of the Romanian Constitution the situation at hand is sufficient to justify the measures taken, as it affects the national security, and that not only a situation involving the armed forces engages the application of article 53, as there are other aspects involving the state that can be regarded as situations of national security, such as economic, financial, or social ones, which could even affect the existence of the state itself, through their dimension and severity.[50]

2. Pensions

a) Restrictions in cumulating the pension with salary income paid from state budget

According to Law no 329/2009,[51] the beneficiaries of the right to a pension who also had salary incomes or incomes assimilated to the salaries from employment relationships with legal entities within the public sector or private sector of the

---

[47] Decision 42/2014 OG 210/25.3.2014, Decision 443/2016 OG 580/29.7.2016, Decision 681/2017 OG 148/16.2.2018.

[48] Emergency Government Ordinance 1/1999 on the regime of the siege state and the regime of the emergency state [1999] OG 22.

[49] The authors argue that by being the expression of the national security defence, art 53 of the Constitution must be read in connection with the Emergency Government Ordinance no 1/1999 on the regime of the siege state and the regime of the emergency state. According to art 3(a) of this piece of legislation, national security is regarded as a situation which imposes declaring the occurrence of the emergency state and the government must not appropriate the role of the president and that of the parliament to take measures involving the national security while breaching arts 53 and 93 of the Romanian Constitution. Therefore, the austerity measures taken by the government in this situation were claimed to be unconstitutional.

[50] Decisions 872/2010 and 874/2010 OG 433/28.6.2010.

[51] Law 329/2009 on the reorganisation of some public authorities and institutions, rationalising the public expenses, sustaining the business environment and observance of the framework agreements with European Commission and International Monetary Fund [2009] OG 761.

state could cumulate the net amount of the pension with said incomes if such an amount did not exceed the amount of the average gross salary income used for the elaboration of the public social insurance budget. In the case where this require-ment is not met, the individual has the right to choose between the suspension of the payment of his pension or termination of the employment relationship. Failure to exert this option right terminated the employment relationship of the respective individual by effect of law.

Initially, an objection of unconstitutionality was raised by members of parlia-ment before promulgation of this law, based on article 41(1) on the right to work, article 16(1) on equality of rights, and article 44 on the right of private property of the Romanian Constitution.

The Court has rejected the objection of unconstitutionality,[52] determining that the law's provisions are constitutional to the extent that they do not refer to the persons for whom the Constitution provides the duration of their terms of office, because in cases involving a failure to exert the right of option the ter-mination of the mandate of such persons is incompatible with the constitutional provisions.[53]

According to previous decisions of the Constitutional Court, no constitutional provision prohibits the legislator from removing the right to cumulate pension with salary, provided that such a measure applies equally to all citizens, and eventual dif-ferences of treatment are based on lawful reasoning.[54] The provision on the basis of which the pension cannot be cumulated with the salary complies with the require-ments imposed by the non-discrimination principle: objectiveness (expressly pro-vided by the law, predictable, and determinable) and reasonableness (the national average gross salary income represents a fair and balanced option). As regards the proportionality between the intended purpose and measures used, the purpose de-clared is combating the effects of the profound economic crisis that endangers the economic stability and, therefore, public order and national security. The restric-tion of the right to cumulate pension with salary is one of the measures taken to relieve the state budget and public social insurance budget in such a manner as not to affect the incomes of the respective person so that they would fall below the level of the national average gross salary income. Therefore, the measure is proportional with the situation that caused it and it is applied in a non-discriminatory manner to all persons found in the situation referred to by the legal norm. Neither the authors

---

[52] Decision 1414/2009 OG 796/23.11.2009. Such arguments and conclusions were also maintained on the occasion of analysing exceptions of non-constitutionality raised after the law came into force (Decision 297/2011 OG 513/2.7.2011).

[53] See comments on the arguments of the Constitutional Court in Dragoş Călin, 'Legal Regime of Cumulating the Pension with Salary Income Aimed at Reducing the Public Expenses, According to Law 329/2009 Does Not Breach Art 14 of ECHR and Article 1 of Protocol 1—Decision Ionel Panfile v Romania' (2012) 4 Social Law Review 47.

[54] Decision 375/2005 OG 591/8.7.2005.

nor the Court presented arguments regarding the claimed breach of the constitutional provisions on the right to private property.[55]

b) Decrease in the amount of pensions

Law no 118/2010 concerns some measures necessary to restore the budgetary balance and provides for a series of reductions of budgetary expenses such as: decreasing salary incomes for individuals employed in the public sector by 25 per cent and reducing by 15 per cent pensions, unemployment benefits, and other social insurance or social assistance benefits. Objections of unconstitutionality were raised by the High Court of Justice and, respectively, members of the parliament.

Most of these objections were rejected, the Court ascertaining that the respective provisions of the new law were in compliance with the provisions of the Romanian Constitution given the challenges already addressed, with the exception of some of the law's provisions (regarding pensions) in respect of which an unconstitutionality objection was upheld and the respective provision was rejected from the law before its promulgation and entry into force.[56]

aa) Right to property (article 44 of the Constitution and article 1 of Protocol 1 to the ECHR)

The High Court of Justice underlined that the provisions of the criticised law fell under article 1 of Protocol 1 to the European Convention on Human Rights (ECHR), as the rights resulting from the contributions made for social protection (such as the right to pension) represent rights of property, which are protected. Within their objections, the members of parliament added to such arguments the fact that under European Court of Human Rights (ECtHR) case law the concept of 'goods' encompasses any interest of economic value belonging to a person subject to private law, so that the rights to social insurance and social assistance allowances can be assimilated to rights of property (*Büchen v Czech Republic*) and, consequently, the restrictions imposed on these rights affect the very substance of the right of property (*Gaygusuz v Austria*; *Stubbings et al v The United Kingdom*; *Akdeejeva v Latvia*; *Müller v Austria*).

The authors reminded the Court that the ECtHR emphasised that the authorities must maintain a fair balance between the general interest and the prerequisites of protection owed to the individual fundamental human rights. The reduction in the rights to pensions (assimilated to a right to property) was excessive and disproportionate and did not follow the aforementioned balance. Therefore, the

---

[55] However, with respect to the claimed breach by Law 329/2009 of art 14 of ECHR and art 1 of protocol 1 through measures adopted in the area of cumulating the pension with salary income, by Decision of 20 March 2012 (*Ionel Pamfile v Romania*) the ECtHR has ascertained that there is no such breach, see Călin (n 53).

[56] Decisions 872/2010 and 874/2010 OG 433/28.6.2010.

breach of article 1 of the Protocol resulted from the measure failing to have the proportional[57] and reasonable nature that any such restriction must have (*Kjartan Asmundssonv Iceland*; *Moskal v Poland*; *Sporrong and Lonnroth v Sweden*; *Mellacher et al v Austria*; *James et al v The United Kingdom*).

It was also maintained that the criticised law constituted an expropriation, according to article 44(3) of the Romanian Constitution, but without providing fair and preliminary compensation. Moreover, the legislator had not even justified these measures by invoking a situation of public utility.

In relation to all these arguments, the Constitutional Court recalled that in *Stec et al v The United Kingdom*, the ECtHR established that article 1 of the Protocol does not apply to rights of property concerning systems of social protection. Any state may freely assess and decide on an applicable social protection policy and on the type and amount of allowances or benefits granted as part of the chosen policy. The only condition imposed on the state is to comply with the provisions of article 14 of the ECHR, regarding non-discrimination. However, if the state enforces a set of laws which regulate the rights resulting from the social insurance system, irrespective of the contributory or non-contributory nature of these rights, this set of laws must be regarded as generating an interest of economic value, as provided by article 1 of the Protocol.

bb) Right to a decent living standard and right to benefits

The claims of the Members of Parliament emphasised that the criticised law failed to consider the living standards of those social categories of persons affected by austerity measures. The subjects of this law are therefore forced to live with barely sufficient means to stay alive. Neither the living conditions nor the purchasing power of these individuals have been improved by the enactment of this law and the restrictions it imposes. These measures might violate the right to a decent living standard and therefore drastically influence the constitutional rights of people with low income.

However, the Constitutional Court allowed the unconstitutionality objection regarding the decrease in the amount of pensions, grounding its arguments mainly on the provisions of article 47 of the Constitution. The Constitutional Court notes that the right to a pension is based on contribution, meaning that the persons who contributed to the system of social insurance for pensions throughout parts of their active lives are entitled to contributory pensions. Article 47(2) of the Romanian Constitution classified the right to a pension as a fundamental right that leads to

[57] Laura Maria Crăciunean, 'Protection of the Wages and Social Benefits Within the Economic Crisis Context: The Answer of ECHR' (2016) Universul Juridic <http://www.universuljuridic.ro/protectia-salariului-prestatiilor-si-alocatiilor-sociale-contextul-crizei-economice-raspunsul-curtii-europene-drepturilor-omului/> accessed 1 December 2019.

additional constitutional duties of the state, such as a duty on the state to ensure a high level of protection of this right.

The right to a pension is a previously acquired right, based on the contributory period of a person's life. Therefore, during retirement the person is entitled to a pension calculated on the basis of contributions paid to the state social insurance budget. Even if these sums do not represent a deposit and do not create a debt of the state, the pension must reflect the level of income received during the active period of life. The reduction of pensions cannot be accepted or deemed constitutional, not even if it is of a temporary nature, as it would affect an already-acquired right. The Court held that the objection raised was therefore justifiable.

This does not indicate that the state is prevented from rearranging the contribution-based pension system in the future. Otherwise, the evolution of legislation in this field would be prevented. Accordingly, if further modifications resulted in a reduction of pensions, then the previously calculated amount would have to be maintained for payment.

Given the high protection granted by the Constitution to the pension right and the above-mentioned reasons, neither the decrease of pensions that are calculated on the basis of contributions, nor the decrease of the pension point, on the basis of which the pension to be paid is calculated, may be accepted, regardless of the percentage or duration of such a decrease. Therefore, article 53 of the Constitution could not represent grounds for such a decrease.

The Constitutional Court also remarked that the reduction by 15 per cent of the allowances for the attendants of persons retired on grounds of invalidity (first grade) violated the provisions of article 47(1). The state failed to comply with its duty to take appropriate social protection measures.

c) Removal of the non-contributive part of the special pensions

The effect of Law no 119/2010 was to recalculate the pensions granted to some particular categories of retired persons who benefited from special pensions by taking into consideration, also for them, the general rules applicable to all retired persons within the public system of social insurance for pensions based on the contribution principle.

The law was challenged by members of parliament before its promulgation. However, regarding this challenge, the Constitutional Court ascertained that the new law complied with the relevant provisions of the Romanian Constitution. The High Court of Justice submitted another objection of unconstitutionality of this law to the Constitutional Court and this claim was upheld and the provision under review was rejected from the law before its promulgation and entry into force.[58]

---

[58] Decisions 871/2010 and 873/2010.

aa) Retroactive effect (article 15(2) of the Constitution)
One argument supporting the objection was that the obligation to recalculate all special pensions, which the provision under review imposed, violated the principle of non-retroactivity of civil law. It was pointed out that the special pensions already being paid represented rights that preceded the law on the establishment of measures in the field of pensions, that they therefore represented previously acquired rights, and that their modification constituted a flagrant violation of the aforementioned constitutional principle. Moreover, the authors of the first objection submitted that the Constitutional Court had already ruled that a new law could not affect the already-established amount of pensions, which represented a previously acquired right, and could only have effects for the future, starting from the date when the law becomes enforceable (Decision 375/2005; Decision 57/2006; Decision 120/2007).

By assessing the arguments raised, the Constitutional Court noted that special pensions constituted a different legal regime to pensions granted in the public pension scheme. Thus, unlike the latter, the special pensions were composed of two elements, regardless of the specific method of calculation established by the provisions of the special laws, namely: the pension based on contributions and a supplement from the state which, by being added to the pension based on contributions, reflected the amount of the special pension stipulated by the special law. The contributory part of the special pension was covered from the state social insurance budget, while the part exceeding this amount was covered from the state budget.

The Constitutional Court stated that the special pension constituted 'partial compensation for the inconveniences resulting from the rigor of the special statuses'.[59] This compensation, not being dependant on the contribution to the social insurance system, was related to the state's policy in the field of social insurance and it was not covered by the constitutional right to a pension.

The Romanian Constitution refers separately to the right to a pension, as opposed to the right to other forms of public or private social insurance, under article 47(2) of the Constitution. The legislator has the exclusive right to decide, depending on the social policy and the available funds, whether to grant these other forms of public or private social insurance, as well as on the amount and conditions thereof. Moreover, considering that these benefits, which are granted by the state, are not influenced by the contribution of the insured person to the fund from which they are granted, it is evident that obtaining the right to a pension does not create an everlasting obligation on the state to grant this right. The only acquired right is the right to the benefits that were received before the new legislation entered into force.

Therefore, the legal texts that were objected to did comply with the provisions of article 15(2) of the Romanian Constitution, as they would only prospectively

---

[59] Decision 20/2000 OG 72/18.2.2000.

influence the special pensions and only with respect to their amount. All the other conditions relating to their grant were not affected. Particularly, the newly adopted law did not affect the benefits already obtained prior to its entry into force. The Constitutional Court considered that such a right could only be eliminated, ultimately diminishing the pension, on the basis of a sufficiently strong motivation. Regarding the law at hand, the necessity of reforming the pension system to rebalance it, the elimination of injustices of the system, and, last but not least, the economic and financial crisis that the state faced (affecting both the state budget and the state social insurance budget) represented a sufficiently strong motivation. In addition, this measure did not impose an excessive burden on the beneficiaries, as it would be applicable to all special pensions, without any distinction.[60]

bb) Right to property

The main argument was that, according to the ECtHR (as ruled in *Büchen v Czech Republic*), in relation to article 44 of the Constitution and article 1 of Protocol 1 of the ECHR, the notion of property, as related to goods, also covers any interest of economic value belonging to a person, subject to private law. Therefore the right to a pension can be assimilated to the right to property and the pension itself to a good which represents private property. The recalculation and reduction of special pensions could thus be equated to an expropriation, for which the legislator did not provide grounds of public utility.[61] The High Court of Justice added that the criticised law led to an 'irreversible loss' regarding the special pension and that the reduction in the patrimonial rights was excessive and disproportionate, thus breaching article 1 of Protocol 1 of the ECHR (with reference to ECtHR cases *Kjartan Asmundsson v Iceland, Moskal v Poland*).

Responding to these objections the Constitutional Court restated the already analysed distinction between the two constituent elements of the special pension, namely the contributory and the non-contributory elements, as well as the fact that the latter was subject to the requisite financial resources being available to the

---

[60] The arguments were also maintained on the occasion of analysing an exception of non-constitutionality of Law 119/2010 after its entry into force (a posteriori constitutionality control), regarding in particular one category of the special pensions the amount of which is reduced through this law. The Court also added that the criticised law affects neither the status as pensioners of the retired persons nor the amount of the pensions already granted and received (cashed) and that it does not affect the amounts legally calculated and already paid. The new law may produce effects for the future, namely on the amount of the future successive payments (Decision 1380/2011 OG 847/29.11.2011).

[61] As support to these arguments, the author of the objection also relies on ECtHR cases such as *Gaygusuz v Austria; Stubbings et al v Great Britain; Andrejeva v Latvia;* and *Müller v Austria.* In such cases, the ECtHR ruled that the right to a pension is a right to property and the recalculation of pensions, with the effect of decreasing the pension, represents a violation of an already-acquired right. Also according to these ECtHR cases, 'a substantial decrease in the amount of pension could be considered a serious breach in the mere substance of the right to property and even in the right to remain a beneficiary of the old age social insurance system' (Decision 871/2010 of the Constitutional Court, section I.2. of the preamble).

state to grant social insurance benefits other than those expressly provided by the Romanian Constitution.

Given all this, despite the fact that the non-contributory part of the special pension could be identified as a 'good', subject to the right to property, it nevertheless represented, from this perspective, an acquired right only with regard to the social insurance benefits obtained up to the date that the new law entered into force. The fact that these benefits would no longer be granted in the future did not represent an act of expropriation.

When rejecting the second objection the Court also invoked the ECtHR decision issued in *Müller v Austria* in 1972 stating that, even if article 1 of the Protocol granted rights to a person who contributed to the social protection system, this legal provision could not be interpreted as granting a certain pension amount.[62]

cc) Decent living standard and securing conditions to increase the quality of life
The author of the objection remarked that the state's obligation to ensure a decent living standard for its citizens (article 47(1) of the Constitution) and to increase the quality of life (article 135(2)(f)) were objectives reached through the measures taken in the field of social protection and also by guaranteeing the right to a pension. Nevertheless, given the economic and social context at the time, the recalculation of special pensions placed pensioners in a detrimental position because the insufficient funds allocated for special pensions and a failure to correlate the pensions with inflation did not safeguard the income of those retirees whose only income was their pension. To the contrary, it put them rather in danger of social exclusion. Moreover, it was submitted that the decrease of special pensions engaged the principle that establishes protection for the legitimate expectations of the citizens towards a certain level of social security and social protection.

The Constitutional Court noted that this purported principle did not enjoy constitutional recognition. Moreover, the rights that result from retirement were predictable, representing the entitlement to the amount of the general ordinary public pension system, while the supplementary amount was subject to the variable elements mentioned above, namely the state's policy and financial resources that could be allocated to this objective.[63]

---

[62] In order to sustain this argument, on the occasion of a subsequent control of constitutionality after the law entered into force, the Court also invoked other ECHR cases (such as *Munoz Diaz v Spain, Maggio v Italy, Kopecky v Slovakia*) and reached the conclusion that the partial decrease of the amount of the special pensions did not represent an excessive individual burden, especially given that its purpose was to equalise a factual situation and calculate the amount of the pension based on the contributions and not on the amount of the wages (Decision 1380/2011).

[63] Later on, when analysing an exception of non-constitutionality of Law 119/2010 after its entry into force, regarding in particular one category of the special pensions the amount of which had been reduced through this law although it did not invoke non-compliance with the constitutional provision guaranteeing the right to pension, the Court stated that the Constitution does not provide the right to a special pension but the right to a pension based on the contributions paid according to the law. Also, the retirement act does not determine the right to a specific amount of the pension *ad aeternum*.

dd) Necessity of acts of parliament

It was argued that the failure to provide a ground that would justify the restrictions imposed on the right to a pension, as well as to the right to a decent living standard, meant that these measures were not covered by the exceptions under article 53—which states that the exercise of certain rights or freedoms may only be restricted by law under the conditions provided therein (in a number of exceptional cases expressly mentioned in the body of article 53, if necessary in a democratic society, and if the measure shall be proportional to the situation having caused it and it is applied without discrimination and without infringing on the existence of such right or freedom)— since it did not follow that those restrictions were necessary and proportional to the situation that necessitated them. As mentioned in the explanatory statement of the law in question, it was adopted in the context of the protraction of the economic crisis throughout 2010, in order to maintain the budget deficit within sustainable limits and to ensure the continuity of the agreements with international financial institutions. However, these mere facts did not objectively justify the impact on the fundamental rights to social protection and to a decent living standard.

Moreover, the measures instituted were not temporary, which is a constitutional prerequisite for restrictions that could be imposed on certain rights or fundamental freedoms. Finally, the restrictions laid down by the law at hand did not comply with the requirements of proportionality of the measure to the situation that necessitated it, as the effect on the right to pensions considerably exceeded the benefit to society that could result from the imposed measures.

Within its claim, the High Court of Justice invoked previous statements of the Constitutional Court (Decision 1414/2009) to sustain the argument that the criticised law imposed a permanent restriction on the right to a pension, as the recalculation of special pensions did not correspond with a time limitation. Moreover, the restrictions provided by the criticised law were not of an exceptional nature, as they represented a second measure of this kind, adopted within a period of about six months. In addition, the substantial decrease of pensions imposed by the new law did not comply with the constitutional requirements of proportionality and reasonability, as these related to the exercise of rights under other forms of public or private social insurance provided by article 47(2) of the Romanian Constitution.

Taking into consideration the above-mentioned arguments, the Constitutional Court stated that the reference to article 53 of the Romanian Constitution was of no relevance, as the right to pension concerned the pension obtained through the general ordinary public pension system and there was no constitutionally acknowledged right to special pensions or, more exactly, to the financial supplement granted by the state.

ee) Breach of other constitutional provisions

The criticised law was claimed to represent a regulation of the special pensions that was parallel to the one embedded in the already existing special laws. This was claimed to conflict with the principles of unique enactment and the prevention of legislative parallelism.

The Constitutional Court rejected these arguments and explained that the legislator intended to maintain the provision of the previous laws, but established, through article 12 of the criticised law, a mere interpretation. More precisely, the persons whose pension rights would be established under the new law would automatically become subject to the recalculation process as regulated by this law, following the date of its entry into force. The other aspects of retirement, apart from the amount of the pension, remained subject to the previous laws and therefore did not lead to a violation of constitutional provisions.

With regard to the principle of equality (article 16 of the Romanian Constitution), the criticised law did not include the pensions of the members of the Romanian Court of Accounts in the category of special pensions subject to recalculation. This created a different and preferential treatment for this group. The Constitutional Court noted that, considering an interpretation of all applicable legal provisions in conjunction, the provisions of the new law were also applicable to the members of the Court of Accounts and, thus, article 16 of the Constitution was not breached.

According to article 20 of the Romanian Constitution, the constitutional provisions concerning the citizens' rights and liberties shall be interpreted and enforced in conformity with the Universal Declaration of Human Rights and with the conventions and other treaties that Romania is a party to. Where any inconsistencies exist between the conventions and treaties on fundamental human rights that Romania is a party to and national law, the international regulations shall take precedence, unless the provisions of the Constitution or national laws are more favourable. The authors of the claim also maintained that article 20 of the Constitution was breached by the new law, as it violated the above-mentioned articles of the Universal Declaration of Human Rights and the Charter of Fundamental Rights of the European Union. Considering all the arguments presented by the Constitutional Court in response (described above), the Court noted that there was no violation of the international treaties. However, although the legal provisions regarding the recalculation of certain special pensions as contributory pensions (and removal of their non-contributory part) was declared not to breach the constitutional provisions, in practice, in most of the litigation concerning the cancellation of decisions to recalculate such pensions, the regular courts have cancelled the relevant decisions. This is because they maintain that the Constitutional Court cannot assess the conformity of the law with the ECHR and that the regular courts, where they consider such instruments to have been breached in a specific case, are empowered[64] to directly apply European legislation, to interpret decisions of the Constitutional Court, and to ignore domestic legislation and the interpretation given to it by the Constitutional Court if this contravenes the international instruments and the competent international courts' decisions.[65]

ff) Independence of the judiciary

The financial independence of judges is an essential component of the independence of the judiciary. The criticised law contradicted this fundamental principle by eliminating the special pensions of judges. Such a measure ignores the fact that the special pension is part of the professional career of the judge, along with his/her appointment, continuous vocational training, evaluation, and promotion. Retirement is the final step of the judge's career and the pension has the legal nature of an acquired right that shall generate legal effects, regardless of the circumstances.

The High Court of Justice argued that the special pensions granted to magistrates compensated for the absence of some fundamental rights, such as those of a political nature (the right to be elected into the Senate or into the Chamber of Deputies, as Romania's president, into the local administration bodies, or as member of the European Parliament) and socio-economic rights (the right to collective bargaining in terms of work, the right to strike, economic freedom), as well as the constitutionally acknowledged incompatibilities for the magistrates. The strict absence of these rights and the existence of incompatibilities and interdictions provided by the Constitution or by special laws, as well as the responsibilities and risks involved, dictated the granting of the right to special pensions.[66] After an

---

[64] Elena Mădălina Nica, 'Constitutionality Control. Conventionality Control. Article 1 of the First Additional Protocol to the Convention for the Protection of Human Rights and Fundamental Freedoms. Interference. Proportionality of the Interference with the Aimed Legitimate Purpose. Precise Analysis of the Proportionality. Right to Pension. Free Access to Court' (2012) 4 Pandectele Române Review 133.

[65] Ciprian Diaconaru, 'Brief Observations on the Conflict Between Law 119/2010 and International Instruments' (2011) 1 Social Law Review 5; Tiberiu Medeanu, 'Vulnerability of the Last Regulations Regarding Certain Special Pensions' (2011) 9 Curierul Judiciar 446.

[66] The European legislation, more exactly Directive 86/378/EEC of 24 July 1986, as amended by Directive 96/97/EC of 20 December 1996, is an example of a legal basis for the right to special pensions granted to a number of professions, including judges. This directive creates the EU legal framework so that the Member States may establish for a specific professional sector, considering its place and role, a specific professional regime of social security, with the observance of the principle of equality of treatment between men and women. Thus, the special pension for judges takes into consideration the place and role of the judiciary in a state governed by the rule of law, as well as the European legislation on professional regimes of social protection.

Other such examples invoked by the High Court of Justice are the European Charter on the Statute of Judges (art 6.4) and Notice no 1/2001 of the Consultative Council of European Judges. According to these provisions, the state grants judges who reach the legal age of retirement in their position the right to a pension, the amount of which shall be as close as possible to the amount of the last salary received during the judicial activity.

Also, it is argued that the elimination of the special pensions for magistrates violates the internationally established requirements regarding the rights of the magistrates, considering the importance of the role they play in the protection of the rule of law (The UN Basic Principles on the Independence of the Judiciary, Milan 26 August-6 September 1985; Recommendation no R (94) 12 regarding the independence, efficiency, and role of judges).

analysis of the special status of the magistrates, the Court noted that article 124(3) of the Romanian Constitution did not expressly require the special pension for magistrates. It is beyond doubt that the principle of judicial independence cannot be reduced to the amount of their salary and pension. This principle includes a series of guarantees such as the statute[67] (conditions of access, procedures of appointment, promotion, transfer, suspension, and termination of office), the stability and the irrevocability of the magistrates, financial guarantees, administrative independence of the magistrates, and the independence of the judiciary in relation to the legislative and executive powers. On the other side, the independence of the judiciary includes their financial security, which also requires that social guarantees, such as their special pension, be guaranteed.

In conclusion, the Court determined that the principle of the independence of the judiciary protected the special pension of the magistrates, as a component of their financial stability, to the same extent that it protected any other guarantees of this principle.

Moreover, the Court also stated that the special pension granted to the magistrates did not represent a privilege and was objectively justifiable, as it partially compensated for the inconveniences that result from the strict aspects of the special status of the magistrates. This special status has a highly restrictive nature and imposes duties and restrictions that are not imposed on other groups subject to social insurance. The magistrates are prohibited from activities that could result in additional income and which could guarantee a standard of living during retirement similar to that enjoyed during the active part of their life.

In addition, the Court referred to examples of decisions issued by other Constitutional Courts on the unconstitutionality of similar legal provisions that had been adopted in their countries, demonstrating that financial security was a guarantee of the independence of judges (Decision of 18 January 2010 of the Constitutional Court of Latvia, Decision of 12 July 2001 of the Constitutional Court of Lithuania, Decision of 14 July 2005 of the Constitutional Court of the Czech Republic) and ECtHR case law (*Cooper v The United Kingdom*).

Finally, the Constitutional Court held that the constitutional status of magistrates necessarily entailed their right to special pensions, as an element of independence of the judiciary, a guarantee of the rule of law stated by article 1(3) of the Romanian Constitution.

Based on the above arguments, all the objections of unconstitutionality against the law establishing relevant measures in the area of pensions were rejected, except for those providing for the recalculation of the special pensions of judges,

---

[67] Marin Voicu, '20 Years of Constitutional, Legal and Legitimate Regime of Pension of the Judges' (2017) Universul Juridic <http://www.universuljuridic.ro/20-de-ani-de-regim-constitutional-legal-si-legitim-al-pensiilor-de-serviciu-ale-judecatorilor-1997-2017/> accessed 1 December 2019; <http://www.juridice.ro/essentials/1423/20-de-ani-de-regim-constitutional-legal-si-legitim-al-pensiilor-de-serviciu-ale-judecatorilor-1997-2017/> accessed 1 December 2019.

prosecutors, and the assistant-magistrates of the Constitutional Court according to the rules applicable to the calculation of pensions within the general ordinary public pension system. The latter was considered to breach the constitutional principle of the independence of the judiciary.[68]

After the entry into force of Law no 119/2010, several objections of unconstitutionality were raised as regards the removal of the special pensions (recalculation of the amount of such pensions under the general ordinary rules applicable to the public pension insurance system) for some categories of personnel of the Court of Accounts (public external auditors[69] and counsellors of accounts[70]). The authors of the claims argued that the legal status of the specific personnel of the Court of Accounts was similar to the status of the magistrates, due to the existence of some incompatibilities and obligations provided both through legal and constitutional norms, the said individuals having benefited from a special pension calculated as per the legal provisions applicable to the magistrates.[71]

The Constitutional Court followed these arguments, stating that, to the extent that their legal status requires it, the personnel of the Court of Accounts must benefit from the same legal treatment regarding the special pension as magistrates.

While this is not the position for public external auditors with regard to the counsellors of accounts, the Court has stated in previous decisions that the latter benefit from a distinct constitutional and legal framework and a distinct legal status from other categories of personnel of the Court of Accounts.[72] They are independent in exercising their mandate, irremovable during this exercise, and they are subject to the same incompatibilities provided for by the law for the judges and,

---

[68] A contrary opinion was also registered by one of the nine judges of the Constitutional Court, stating that not only the above-mentioned provisions but the entire law was non-constitutional, as it violated the provisions and principles provided by the Romanian Constitution (separate opinion to the Decision 871/2010 OG 443/28.6.2010).

It is argued that the provisions of the law under analysis violate the provisions of art 15(2) of the Constitution, which enshrines the principle of non-retroactivity of the law. The special pensions are acquired rights that cannot be recalculated on the basis of a new law and cannot be changed, as the law would apply retroactively.

It is stated that the Court previously held that 'the recalculation operation inevitably concerns the past because the contribution period was made in the past, but has effects only for the future. In the cases when the recalculation results in a higher amount of the pension, it will be paid, and if the new amount is lower, the previously determined pension will continue to be granted, without any prejudice to the legal rights previously acquired' (Decision 120/2007 OG no. 204 of 26.03.2007).

[69] Decision 1283/2011 OG 826/22.11.2011.

[70] Decision 297/2012 OG 309/9.5.2012.

[71] When Law 119/2010 entered into force such rights were eliminated for the said personnel of the Court of Accounts while they were maintained for the magistrates, thus breaching (i) art 15 on the universality of the Constitution and the applicability of the civil law only for the future, (ii) art 16(1) on the constitutional principle of equality of rights, (iii) art 140(4) stating that the members of the Court of Accounts shall be independent in exercising their term of office and irremovable throughout its duration and subject to the incompatibilities the law stipulates for judges, and (iv) art 14 of the ECHR and art 1 of the First Additional Protocol.

[72] Decision 1283/2011 OG 826/22.11.2011.

therefore, they have a legal status similar to that of the judges,[73] the counsellors of accounts being assimilated with the magistrates through a constitutional norm.

Based on the same analysis, the unconstitutionality objections submitted in respect of those provisions of Law no 119/2010 removing the special pensions for other categories of personnel (such as speciality auxiliary personnel within the courts and prosecutor's offices, members of the parliament)[74] were rejected by the Court, stating that the differences regarding their constitutional legal status justified a different legal treatment of the magistrates and the respective categories of personnel.

3. Unemployment benefits

The amount of unemployment allowance was decreased by 15 per cent through Law no 118/2010, effective until the end of 2010. The High Court of Justice argued that by submitting this draft law, the Romanian Government resorted to the provisions contained in article 53 of the Romanian Constitution and diminished for a second time in six months the exercise of some rights laid down in the Romanian Constitution, such as the right to a pension, the right to unemployment allowance, and the right to other social assistance measures. However, the motivation behind these measures, namely to cushion the effects of the economic crisis, did exceed the legal frame of article 53—the economic crisis and the high amount of budgetary expenses did not represent arguments to apply article 53 of the Constitution as the economic crisis did not represent a threat to the national security.

The provisions of the criticised law do not require these restrictions to be of a temporary nature. Despite the fact that these restrictions are announced to be effective only until 31 December 2010, another paragraph of the same article allows the institutions of the state to put social and personnel policies into applications starting from 1 January 2011, so that the budgetary expenditures resulting from the previous restrictions are not exceeded. In other words, this last provision granted permission to the state to further restrict the exercise of the above-mentioned rights. Consequently, this restriction acquired a permanent nature, opposed to the temporary character required by the Romanian Constitution in article 53.

The criticised provisions also violate essential legal and constitutional requirements, such as the accessibility and predictability of the law. Further, the restrictions imposed and the manner in which they are enacted do not allow the recipients of this law to estimate the extent of their rights to pensions, to unemployment

---

[73] Decision 1094/2008 OG 721/23.10.2008.
[74] Decision 1284/2011 OG 838/25.11.2011, Decision 1285/2011 OG 828/23.11.2011, Decision 1286/ 2011 OG 845/29.11.2011.

allowances, and to social protection measures, thus breaching the principle of legitimate expectations.

The members of parliament added that the right to a pension and the rights that are due from social protection represent already-acquired rights, which excludes the possibility of restrictions or reductions.

On the other side, article 53 of the Romanian Constitution corresponds to the provisions of article 15 of the ECHR, which was previously applied only in the case of war, siege, or the fight against terrorism, which was not the case at the time. The author of the objection noted that the Government wrongfully invoked the case *Lawless v Ireland* in order to justify the measures taken. Even if the present justification based on national security was accepted, the law would still be unconstitutional because it should have imposed only temporary restrictions.

Finally, the authors of the objection noted that there were other solutions that could have led to a decrease in budgetary expenditures and that could have ensured the sustainability of the state budget, such as the reduction of sums designated for public acquisitions.

In response, the Constitutional Court remarked that not only a situation involving the armed forces engaged article 53. There were other aspects involving the state that could be regarded as situations endangering national security, such as economic, financial, or social problems, which could even be of such severity as to affect the existence of the state itself. As previously stated (Decision 1414/2009), the global financial crisis may affect, in the absence of suitable measures, the economic stability of the country and, therefore, also national security.

The Constitutional Court referred to the explanatory statement corresponding to this law or, more exactly, to the evaluation of the European Commission on which it was based. Based on this evaluation, the Constitutional Court noted that if this threat to economic stability persisted, then the Government was entitled to take the appropriate measures to lower its impact. Under article 53 of the Romanian Constitution the situation at hand was sufficient to justify the measures taken because it affected national security. Moreover, the restrictions imposed were necessary in a democratic society in order to guard the existence of the state and to protect democracy. As for the proportionality requirement, the Constitutional Court acknowledged that an appropriate balance had been struck between the means utilised by the state and the anticipated results and that this was also reflected in the balance between the general interests and the protection owed to the individual fundamental human rights.

The Constitutional Court further explained that the restrictions imposed by the criticised law were indeed of a temporary nature, so they complied with this constitutional requirement, and the substance of the rights referred to by the authors of the objection was not affected. The measures were meant for a limited period of time, namely until 31 December 2010. From 1 January 2011, if the level of budgetary expenditures remained within the estimated limits, the level of pensions and unemployment allowances would return to that before the restrictions of the criticised law.

However, it is contentious that the Court found such provisions, providing for the decrease of unemployment allowance, to be constitutional while those decreasing the amount of pensions were considered unconstitutional, since both categories of allowances are granted and calculated on the basis of beneficiary contributions to a specific insurance fund (respectively the unemployment and public pension funds, which are based on similar rules and principles and determine the acquisition of specific insurance rights based on contribution).

4. Other social protection benefits

As regards other social protection benefits, the Constitutional Court did not find the provisions of Law no 118/2010 to breach constitutional norms.

The Constitutional Court stated that the legislator could decide in respect of any social protection allowances that were not provided by the Constitution whether to grant them or not, depending on the available budgetary funds. The removal or the reduction of such allowances did not breach the provisions of the Constitution.[75]

The objection of unconstitutionality was raised for normative acts that were adopted to extend the period when some social protection allowances were not granted, or were granted but based on different calculation rules than other social protection benefits that recovered to a greater extent from their decrease. This was based on the lack of predictability of such legal provisions, their unreasonable character given the very long-term suspension of their grant, and the disproportionate protection between state and beneficiary interests, given that such allowances enjoyed the protection granted to property rights, although not expressly provided for by the Constitution.[76]

It was argued that such laws breached Constitutional provisions—such as those on the rule of law, the observance of the supremacy of the Constitution and the laws

---

[75] On the occasion of a subsequent control of constitutionality determined by the submission of an exception of non-constitutionality after the entry into force of Law 118/2010 (n 26), the authors invoked the breach of the constitutional norms by the provisions decreasing by 15 per cent the amount of the allowance granted from the state budget during parental leave for raising a child up to the age of two years. However, through the exception of non-constitutionality, which was in fact referring to several legal provisions, the authors did not indicate the specific constitutional norms that were breached by such a specific decrease and, consequently, the Constitutional Court did not make a particular analysis of the constitutionality of such specific legal provisions. Nevertheless, the exception of non-constitutionality was rejected by the Court (Decision 346/2014 OG 591/7.8.2014) based on general arguments regarding observance of equality of rights and prohibition of forced labour (practically not related to this particular social security benefit issue) stated within its previous decisions (Decision 447/2012, Decision 379/2011).

[76] It was also argued that the ECtHR jurisprudence calling for the clarity, accuracy, and predictability of legal norms was also breached (cases *Păduraru v Romania*, *Beian v Romania*, *Rotaru v Romania*, *Petra v Romania*).

of Romania, equality of rights, the right to live and to physical and mental integrity, the right to social protection, the right to a fair trial, the right of defence, the role and structure of parliament and government, and article 53 (regarding the constitutional requirements for restrictions on the exercise of certain fundamental rights or freedoms)—as well as article 1 of the First Additional Protocol to the ECHR and article 17 of the Universal Declaration of Human Rights.

The Constitutional Court has stated[77] that such benefits do not have a constitutional basis, that there is no constitutional obligation on the legislator to regulate the grant of such benefits, and that the legislator is free to decide on the content, limits, and conditions of their grant, including the decrease or cessation of their grant without being obliged to follow some constitutional requirements. In addition, the Court recalled the findings of the High Court of Justice in a decision issued on the interpretation of legal provisions, according to which the provisions analysed did not refer to the existence of the right itself, but to the suspension of its exercise over a specific period of time.[78]

The Constitutional Court has also stated[79] that the principle of equality of rights was not breached because the beneficiaries were not in similar legal situations. The legislator was free to decide the measures through which it would ensure a decent living standard for the citizens, the conditions and requirements for granting such rights depending on the state's policy, financial resources, intended purposes, and observance of other constitutional obligations. The particular rights referred to were also not provided for by the constitution and, therefore, the requirements for restrictions on the exercise of certain fundamental rights and freedoms were not applicable. The constitutional provisions on the right to live and to physical and mental integrity were not considered to be connected to the criticised legal provisions.

IV. Conclusion

Romania was affected by the global economic crisis and was compelled to adopt and implement measures to decrease public expenditures and the public budget deficit.

Such measures were taken within a context of accessing mid-term financial support from the European Community, IMF, and WB, under some specific requirements provided within the documents signed in view of accessing the respective

---

[77] Decision 541/2015 OG 622/17.8.2015, Decision 170/2015 OG 354/22.5.2015, Decision 443/2016 OG 580/29.7.2016, Decision 681/2017 OG 148/16.2.2018.

[78] Decision of the High Court of Justice 16/2015 OG 525/15.7.2015.

[79] Decision 193/2013 OG 416/10.7.2013, Decision 482/2014 OG 848/20.11.2014, Decision 441/2015 OG 571/30.7.2015, Decision 508/2015 OG 618/14.8.2015, Decision 660/2015 OG 891/27.11.2015, Decision 644/2015 OG 899/3.12.2015.

funds, documents ratified by Romania's parliament. All the measures were constantly monitored and analysed by the European and international institutions and adjusted, amended, and supplemented by additional documents signed as necessary in connection with the evolution of the crisis, the results of the implementation of previous measures, procedural delays and delays due to the political context, and other objective economic reasons.

On the other side, the measures were adopted under the close control of parliament and the Constitutional Court. Therefore, some measures were found to be in breach of the Romanian Constitution before being promulgated and entering into force. The draft laws were easily accessible and various stakeholders (members of parliament, the High Court of Justice, and Romania's Ombudsman) were monitoring them and were active in claiming their non-compliance with the Constitution. Also, a large number of individuals were raising objections of unconstitutionality on the occasion of their claims submitted to the regular courts. Most of these individual (or collective) claims were submitted in respect of measures decreasing salary incomes, but were also challenging the decrease of the pension amounts and removal of special pensions. A small number of claims referred to the unemployment allowance, allowance for raising a child up to the age of two years (decreased only for several months in 2010), or other social protection benefits (suspended by successive normative acts for several years).

The non-constitutionality claims took into consideration all relevant constitutional provisions (right to a pension, right to unemployment benefits and to other forms of social assistance, right to a decent living, protection of the right to property, restriction of the exercise of certain rights or freedoms only by law under the imperative conditions provided therein, compliance with the international instruments regulating fundamental rights, equality of rights, etc).

Some provisions were found to be contrary to the constitutional norms, most of them before the law was promulgated (ie decreasing the amount under the right to a pension and of the pension point used for the calculation thereof was found contrary to the constitutional provisions guaranteeing the right to a pension; removal of the special pension for the magistrates was found to breach the constitutional norm guaranteeing the independence of the judiciary), and some others after the law entered into force (removal of the special pension for persons whose legal regime was similar to that of the magistrates was found to breach the constitutional norm of equality of rights).

Both the unconstitutionality claims submitted and the decisions of the Court make express reference to ECtHR and European Court of Justice case law, as well as to the jurisprudence of constitutional courts of other states that had analysed similar claims.

The decisions of the Constitutional Court were observed by all the stakeholders. Moreover, due to some findings of non-unconstitutionality, the requirements within the financial assistance documents relating to the payment of further instalments were amended accordingly with the agreement of the respective international and European institutions.

However, although the recalculation of certain special pensions as contributory pensions (and removal of their non-contributory part) was declared to not breach the constitutional provisions, the regular courts have cancelled the respective decisions in most of the particular litigation on the cancellation of the decisions to recalculate such pensions. The regular courts argued that the Constitutional Court could not assess the conformity of the law with the ECHR and that the regular courts, where they considered such instruments to have been breached, were empowered to directly apply European legislation and to ignore domestic legislation and the interpretation given to it by the Constitutional Court if this contravened the international instruments and the competent international courts' decisions, so long as this approach of the court did not breach the constitutional principle of the division of powers.[80] This was the interpretation of the regular courts, although in some particular cases that reached the ECtHR, the Court has stated that the new legislation transforming the special pensions into public pensions is compatible with article 1 of Protocol 1 of ECHR (eg decision *Frimu et al v Romania*).[81]

On the other side, it is to be mentioned that the Constitutional Court was not itself consistent in assessing the compliance of various social protection rights with the Constitution, since decreasing the amount of contributory pensions was considered unconstitutional (because the right to a pension benefits from constitutional protection and represents an acquired right) while decreasing the unemployment allowance was found by the Court to be in compliance with the Constitution, even though both categories of allowance are based on contributions and benefit from the same constitutional protection. Regarding the assessment of the legal norms reducing the unemployment benefit, along with the other tests required by the Constitution, the Court has applied the proportionality test but has generally adopted a more generous interpretation than in other previous cases.

All the other benefits, which do not benefit from express constitutional protection, were considered not to breach constitutional norms. Their absence from the constitutional provisions was practically an obstacle to their protection.

The welfare state was not seriously affected after the crisis. Most of the measures that were assessed as not breaching the Constitution were temporary and the respective benefits returned to their previous amounts. The special pensions recovered their place as the categories benefiting from such pensions applied the

---

[80] Cecilia Jabrea 'Court Decision Regarding Claims Submitted for Cancellation of the Decisions Issued for the Recalculation of the Pensions of Persons Retired from the Army' (2012) 3 Social Law Review 39; Medeanu (n 65).

[81] Dragoş Călin, 'Reform of the Pension System by Transforming the Special Pensions into Public Pensions, According Law 119/2010 is Compatible with Article 1 of Protocol 1—Decision Frimu et al v Romania' (2012) 3 Social Law Review 30; Tiberiu Medeanu and Adrian Crăciunescu, 'Breach of Certain Fundamental Rights Through the Normative Acts Regarding the Recalculation and Revision of the Professional Pensions' (2013) 4 (supplement) Romanian European Law Review 129.

necessary pressure to regain their legal establishment. The amount of pensions has even increased for some individuals due to certain fiscal measures so that, in these cases, the net amount of the special pension is higher than the net amount of the last working month's salary of the respective person.

On the other side it must also be mentioned within this context that the amounts of all the other social protection benefits, including the contributory pensions, are rather low, but they were also low before the crisis.

Unfortunately, Romania did not give up the old habit of adopting and implementing extreme measures, including in the area of social protection, and it continues to search for the right balance between the interests of the individuals in general, the interests of some categories of individuals, and, finally, the public interest.

6

Salus Rei Publicae Suprema Lex Esto? Welfare State Reforms Before the Greek Courts

Maria Bakavou

I. Introduction

The global financial crisis of 2007 had a negative effect on the public finances of all state members of Organisation for Economic Cooperation and Development (OECD). Greece was the first member state of both OECD and the eurozone to face a rapid maximisation of its sovereign debt.[1] Being unable to access financing from the markets, Greece had to seek financial aid from other European Union (EU) Member States,[2] dependent on bilateral state agreements, which came to be

---

[1] Kevin Featherstone, 'The Greek Sovereign Debt Crisis and EMU: A Failing State in a Skewed Regime' (2010) Journal of Common Market Studies 193–217.
[2] Georgia Kaplanoglou and Vassilis T Rapanos, 'The Greek Fiscal Crisis and the Role of Fiscal Governance' (June 2011) Hellenic Observatory European Institute, Greece Paper no 48 - Hellenic Observatory Papers on Greece and Southeast Europe; Shinji Takagi and others, 'The IMF and the Crisis in Greece, Ireland and Portugal: An Evaluation by the Independent Evaluation Office of the International Monetary Fund' (retrieved 28 July 2016); Richard Baldwin and Francesco Giavazzi (eds),

Maria Bakavou, *Salus Rei Publicae Suprema Lex Esto? Welfare State Reforms Before the Greek Courts* In: *European Welfare State Constitutions after the Financial Crisis.* Edited by: Ulrich Becker and Anastasia Poulou, Oxford University Press (2020). © The Contributors. DOI: 10.1093/oso/9780198851776.003.0006

known, especially in Greek public discourse, as 'Memoranda Agreements'. These agreements linked the financial aid provided to Greece with a package of measures that aimed to remedy some of the country's deep systemic problems.

One must note, however, that fiscal adjustment means different things for each state and depends on several factors, such as the composition of the public deficit, the potential growth of the economy, the (in)capability to access the markets, and the political and legislative decisions to enforce tax policies and combat tax evasion[3] or assume whatever structural reforms are deemed necessary. In the case of Greece, the need for fiscal adjustment was often underestimated in relation to the social unrest it caused,[4] since the implemented measures resulted in a major shrinking of the welfare state. Greek public opinion has often maintained that the Memoranda measures were ultimately enforced, despite the deep recession and the violent downsizing of the welfare state, to secure the country's ability to pay its creditors back.

In April 2010, Greece requested financial assistance from its European and international partners. In May 2010, the Greek authorities signed a financial assistance programme with the European partners,[5] as well as a standby arrangement from the International Monetary Fund (IMF). This came to be known as the First Memorandum Agreement. Financing from European partners was provided through the Greek Loan Facility. The financing of the welfare state, especially the funding of pensions, the healthcare system, and pharmaceutical expenditure, was considered to contribute significantly to the Greek public deficit, so large-scale cuts were considered indispensable to achieving the required adjustment.[6]

Several factors derailed the implementation of the measures of the First Memorandum: political instability,[7] social unrest, issues of administrative capacity, and a very deep recession that had been grossly underestimated. Important fiscal targets were missed, which led to the adoption of additional consolidation measures throughout 2010 and 2011. Even so, Greece achieved a substantial reduction in the general government deficit from 15.75 per cent of gross domestic

---

The Eurozone Crisis: A Consensus View of the Causes and a Few Possible Solutions (CEPR Press 2014) accessed 26 September 2016.

[3] Katerina Savvaidou, 'The Combination of Fiscal Adjustment Measures is a Major Factor of Prolonged Financial Viability' (2017) 129 (3-4) Journal of Theory and Practice of Administrative Law 229 (in Greek); Featherstone (n 1).

[4] Maria Markantonatou, 'The Social Consequences of the Financial Crisis in Greece: Recession, Insecurity and Welfare Deregulation' (2012) 27(3) International Journal of Anthropology.

[5] Memorandum of Economic and Financial Policies, 3 May 2010 <https://ec.europa.eu/economy_finance/publications/occasional_paper/2010/pdf/ocp61_en.pdf> accessed 29 January 2020; International Monetary Fund, 'Letter of Intent, Memorandum of Economic and Financial Policies, Technical Memorandum of Understanding and Memorandum of Understanding on Specific Economic Policy Conditionality (European Commission and European Central Bank)' (August 2010) <http://www.imf.org/external/np/loi/2010/grc/080610.pdf> accessed 29 January 2020.

[6] European Commission Directorate-General for Economic and Financial Affairs, 'The Economic Adjustment Programme for Greece' (2010) Occasional Papers No 61, 15.

[7] IMF, *Country Report 13/20 Greece: First and Second Reviews Under the Extended Arrangement Under the Extended Fund Facility* (January 2013) <http://www.imf.org/external/pubs/ft/scr/2013/cr1320.pdf> accessed 29 January 2020 .

product (GDP) in 2009 to 9.25 per cent in 2011, an adjustment much larger than most other fiscal consolidation programmes in EU countries observed in the past. In spite of that, Greece signed a second financial assistance programme in March 2012 (Memorandum II[8]). This financial assistance was also accompanied by measures to restructure private sector debt, including the bonds held by public social security institutions (PSI Agreement), leading to a reduction in Greece's debt stock. In a letter of intent addressed to the IMF, the Greek government vowed to uphold the path of reforming the welfare state and cutting health spending. Given the high share of pensions and pharmaceutical expenses in Greek government spending, the large remaining fiscal adjustment involved further pension adjustments, as well as bringing the pharmaceutical spending closer to levels in other European countries, and the continued reform of health system governance.[9] Considerable progress in correcting imbalances and implementing reforms was made up to the closure of the fourth review of the European Financial Stability Facility (EFSF) programme in mid-2014. The EFSF programme expired without being completed in June 2015[10] and that led, amongst other things, to the imposition of capital controls in Greece, which were lifted only on 1 September 2019. After that, Greece signed a third agreement, known as Memorandum III, for stability support in the form of a loan from the European Stability Mechanism (ESM) in August 2015, which ended on 20 August 2018.[11]

Being the first EU member to succumb to the financial crisis, Greece suffered the longest, for it was not only the fiscal policies that needed adjusting, but also the social and administrative ones. Greece may have come with a unique package of challenges, but the endemic deficiencies were not the sole reason for the long duration of the crisis. The EU reaction was hardly swift and comprehensive.[12] The

---

[8] European Commission Directorate-General for Economic and Financial Affairs, 'The Second Economic Adjustment Programme for Greece - March 2012' (2012) Occasional Papers No 94 <https://ec.europa.eu/economy_finance/publications/occasional_paper/2012/pdf/ocp94_en.pdf>   accessed 29 January 2020. Unlike the first programme, which was based on bilateral loans, the financing of the second programme came through the EFSF, fully operational since August 2012.

[9] Letter of Intent of the Greek Government of 9 March 2012 <http://www.imf.org/external/np/loi/2012/grc/030912.pdf> accessed 29 January 2020.

[10] On 17 July 2015, the Council adopted a decision granting up to €7.16 billion in short-term financial assistance to Greece under the European Financial Stabilisation Mechanism (EFSM) <http://www.consilium.europa.eu/en/press/press-releases/2015/07/17/efsm-bridge-loan-greece/> accessed 29 January 2020.

[11] Greece signed a Memorandum of Understanding with the European Commission, acting on behalf of the ESM, on 19 August 2015. On this basis, the Greek authorities signed a financial assistance facility agreement with the ESM to specify the financial terms of the loan. At the same time, the Council of the European Union adopted decisions approving the stability support programme and the updated fiscal path for Greece. This paved the way for mobilising up to €86 billion in financial assistance over three years (2015–18), see <https://ec.europa.eu/info/business-economy-euro/economic-and-fiscal-policy-coordination/eu-financial-assistance/which-eu-countries-have-received-assistance/financial-assistance-greece_en> accessed 29 January 2020.

[12] Kyriakos Mikelis and Dimitrios Stroikos, 'Hierarchies, Civilization, and the Eurozone Crisis: The Greek Financial Crisis' in John Marangos (ed), *The Internal Impact and External Influence of the Greek Financial Crisis* (Palgrave Macmillan 2017) 126: 'the response to the GRFC [Greek Financial Crisis]

consequent recession was deep and long term, in part because there had been no other precedents of EU institutions handling a crisis of this magnitude. Indeed, the EU learned some profound lessons during the Greek crisis about how to safeguard and guarantee the fiscal solidarity of the Union. Still, this initial inexperience did cost Greece dearly, the only country that eventually signed three Memoranda Agreements. This fact alone is a testament to the necessity of permanent EU mechanisms.

Every Memorandum Agreement contained an extensive list of measures that had to be implemented in order to secure financial aid from the creditors. The Greek government bore the obligation to introduce these measures to the Greek parliament, which in turn would specify their content, by passing the respective law. It has been a point of ongoing dispute in Greece as to who is accountable for selecting the measures that were implemented in exchange for the financial aid the country received through the loans from other European countries and the ESM. The Troika and the Court of Justice of the EU (CJEU) have long maintained that 'the Greek authorities have a wide discretion, provided that the final objective of reducing the excessive deficit is pursued.'[13] On the other hand, in the face of the great social unrest that followed the majority of the enforced measures, the various Greek governments often argued that even though the Memoranda measures were harsh and even inflexible, enacting them into law was the only way to avoid a default. Consequently, it was widely debated before courts whether the contested legislative acts were dictated by the Troika or whether it was the Greek government who ultimately chose which measures to implement, given that the forefront argument for their legality was the economic and temporal emergency and the undisputed public interest to avoid a state bankruptcy.

II. Overview of the Greek social security protection systems and their reforms

Even before the effects of the crisis surfaced, there had been many fruitless efforts to reform the public social security system, whose costs consumed a significant portion of the state budget, in the form of pensions, medical costs, and pharmaceutical expenditure. The systemic deficiencies of the Greek public social security

marks a significant departure from previous EU policies. This is because a member country is presented as a negative signifier. This has important implications not only for the future of Greece and its people, but also for the prospects of the EU project in general'.

[13] For other EU Member States see the analysis of Tito Boeri, Axel Börsch-Supan and Guido Tabellini, 'Pensions Reforms and the Opinions of European Citizens' 92(2) The American Economic Review; Papers and Proceedings of the 114th Annual Meeting of the American Economic Association (May 2002) 396, 396: '[...] citizens are aware of unsustainability but lack information about the cost of the PAYG system ...'.

system were not singular:[14] uninsured employment, unemployment or part-time employment, public budget deficit,[15] and unpaid contributions affected most countries; most importantly, inaccurate predictions were made about the future of the system, ignoring the future needs in favour of satisfying current demands[16] or succumbing to the complaints of the public,[17] following the path of least resistance.[18] The peak of the financial crisis has given grounds to many aggressive articles on the generous Greek pensions or the insufficient number of hard-working employees, choosing to focus on the high returns of selected groups, and thus ignoring the vast majority. Not to mention that, as most Europeans would attest, a pension or a salary of €384[19] or €586[20] respectively may be above the threshold of poverty, but it does not allow for much.

1. Overview of the Greek social security system

The Greek social security system has strong Bismarckian origins[21] and is organised in compliance with the three-pillar system. The first pillar consists of the public, constitutionally protected, pension system. The contributory, earnings-related,

---

[14]   Bernhard Ebbinghaus and Mareike Gronwald, 'The Changing Public-Private Pension Mix in Europe: From Path Dependence to Path Departure' in Ebbinghaus (ed), *The Varieties of Pension Governance: Pension Privatization in Europe* (OUP 2011) 23–56.

[15]   For a detailed analysis see Tassos Giannitsis and Stavros Zografakis, 'Crisis Management in Greece—The Shaping of New Economic and Social Balances' (January 2018) Study no 58 IMK Studies (IMK at Hans Boeckler Stiftung (Foundation), Macroeconomic Policy Institute) 50: 'A more detailed breakdown of government expenditure (excluding interest payments and spending under the Public Investment Programme) into salaries and pensions shows that expenditure related to social security (pensions to public sector employees plus transfers to cover the deficits of social security funds) was a significant factor in the emergence of the crisis. ... social security expenditure (public sector pensions and deficits of the pension funds) ... had an upward effect ... on deficits, thus more than offsetting the positive effect of all other categories on fiscal consolidation'.

[16]   That meant, inter alia, the provision of very generous benefits compared to the contributions paid, or a low standard retirement age.

[17]   According to an explanatory note of 18 March 2010 addressed to the Committee of Social Cases of the Parliament and accompanying the draft legislation of Law 3863/2010, the ratio of insured persons had reached 1.7:1, rendering the system unviable, see <https://www.hellenicparliament.gr/UserFiles/7f4d3181-8c97-4d49-8212-57bdfe7ff860/7070676_Ασφαλιστικο.pdf> accessed 29 January 2020.

[18]   R Kent Weaver, 'The Politics of Blame Avoidance' (1986) Journal of Public Policy 371–98, Giuliano Bonoli, 'Pension Politics in France: Patterns of Co-Operation and Conflict in Two Recent Reforms' (1997) West European Politics 111–24.

[19]   Data derived from the site of EFKA (Unified Social Security Fund) <http://www.efka.gov.gr/el/syntaxe-logo-geratos-poso> accessed 27 August 2019.

[20]   From 1 February 2019, the minimum gross wage of €586 increased to €650, see Ministerial Decision 4241/127/2019 Hellenic Government Gazette 173 B 30 January 2019 (<http://www.et.gr> National Printing House accessed 29 January 2020).

[21]   According to Gosta Esping Andersen's *Distinction in Three Worlds of Welfare Capitalism* (Polity Press and Princeton University Press 1990), Greece belongs to a 'subtype' of the Bismarckian system, namely the Southern European or Mediterranean systems where the gaps in social protection are covered by the family. See also Maurizio Ferrera, 'The European Welfare State—Golden Achievements, Silver Prospects' (January 2008) West European Politics; Arjan Soede and Cok Vrooman, 'A Comparative Typology of Pension Regimes' (April 2008) ENERPI Research Report no 54.

statutory pension scheme is a mandatory pay-as-you-go (PAYG) system, where the current contributions finance the current pensions. The system is benefits-defined, and the principle of foreseeability is respected, so the insured have an educated guess of the pension they will receive and may plan their lives accordingly. Even though proportionality must be preserved, contributions are not accumulated in a personal account, so there is no full equivalence between contributions and benefits. In recent years, there has been a shifting towards a system of defined contributions, particularly concerning the supplementary pensions.

The first pillar complies with the principle of solidarity, which entails that sources are redistributed amongst the members of the insurance community from the financially powerful to the weaker ones.[22] The participation of employers and employees to the system is obligatory and the costs are distributed between them and the state.[23] According to the jurisprudence of Greek courts, the principle of solidarity is transgenerational, which allows the reduction of current pensions to ensure the future viability of the pension system, provided that the reduction is due to objective and foreseeable reasons.[24] Notably, after the crisis, the Council of State ruled that the reduction of certain pension benefits is required to ensure the transgenerational solidarity,[25] as the main pension system remains PAYG. The first pillar is characterised by a unique feature, as compared to all the other public social security systems of the EU. It provides not one but two kinds of pension benefits: the main pension, covering around 80 per cent of the total pension amount, and the supplementary pension, which is a top-up and only received by the recipients of a main pension. Second-pillar occupational pensions have been introduced primarily after incorporating the Institutions for Occupational Retirement Provision (IORP) Directive, but the state is in any case obligated to provide a public, supplementary pension.[26] The public funds of supplementary pensions are equally mandatory, non-profit, respect the principle of solidarity, and they too fall under the scope of article 22 paragraph 5 of the Constitution. The only notable difference between the public main pension and supplementary pension is that the state is constitutionally obliged to finance only the main pension, whereas the supplementary pension is financed by the contributions of employers and employees.

The first pension scheme in Greece was established in 1836 and started its operation in 1861. In 1934, the most inclusive social security institution in Greece, IKA (Social Security Institution for private sector workers)[27] was established. There

---

[22] Council of State Judgment 1010/2019.

[23] Council of State Judgments 241/1989, 1689/2009, 2024/2009, 1891/2019 (plenary session).

[24] Council of State Judgments 3410, 3663/2014 (7-member chamber), 2288–2290/2015, 1891/2019 (plenary session).

[25] Council of State Judgments 1374, 2126/2019.

[26] Council of State Judgment 5024/1987 (plenary session).

[27] For the full history of main pension funds see Patrina Paparrigopoulou-Pechlivanidi, *Social Security Law* (Nomiki Vivliothiki Publications 2013) (in Greek); Maria Bakavou, 'The Greek Social Security System: Legislation, Reforms and Jurisprudence' (2017) Zeitschrift fuer auslaendisches und internationales Arbeits- und Sozialrecht 148, 151.

were also funds for craftsmen and small trades, farmers, etc. Meanwhile, social security institutions for supplementary pensions have also been established.[28] Since this is a singularity of the Greek system, it must be underlined that in Greece the supplementary pension is not viewed simply as a top-up for the pension offered by the first-pillar schemes.[29] In contrast, it is an integral part of the pension benefits of a pensioner, because the main pension alone could not achieve the income replacement purpose of the PAYG system.

Worldwide, a mandatory 'second pillar' is typically described as an individual savings account with a wide set of design options. Defined contribution plans establish a clear linkage between contributions, investment performance, and benefits; they support enforceable property rights and may be supportive of financial market developments. When compared to defined benefit plans, they can subject participants to financial and agency risks as a result of private asset management, the risk of high transaction and administrative costs, and longevity risks unless they require mandatory annuitisation. In Greece, the second pillar falls under the scope of article 12 of the Constitution and consists of mutual aid unions and occupational pension funds established by Law 3029/2002, which incorporated the IORP Directive. These private-law legal persons provide additional pension benefits and are financed by the contributions of employers and employees. The primary goal is to preserve the different financial statuses of various professions even after retirement and respect the equivalence principle[30] (linking contributions to benefits). The third pillar of the Greek social security system refers to private insurance and can cover individuals or specific groups, ie the employees of a certain company. The main difference between a scheme of the second pillar and a scheme of the third pillar is that the second-pillar schemes are strictly non-profit.

Overall, the Greek Constitution includes three articles relevant to the organisation of the social security system. Article 22 paragraph 5 embodies both the principle of the welfare state[31] and the principle of solidarity. It imposes on the legislation the commitment to create, maintain, finance, and define a public system of social security, but does not give rise to specific entitlements.[32] The regulatory nature of

---

[28] The first one was founded under Law 281/1914 but the concept of the supplementary systems as part of the social security system was not introduced until art 13 Law 6298/1934. Finally, the various supplementary funds were merged into one by Law 4052/2012.

[29] Bank of Greece, 'Greece's Economic Performance and Prospects' (2001) 363; Helene Petridou, 'Supplementary Pensions in Greece' in Emmanuel Reynaud and others (eds), *International Perspectives on Supplementary Pensions, Actors and Issues* (Quorum Books 1996) 24.

[30] Greek Courts unwaveringly hold that the principle of direct equivalence is not supported by art 22 para 5 of the Constitution, where the social security system is grounded. That entails that the pension is not directly linked, but analogous to the contributions paid, see Council of State Judgments 3487/2008, 2188/2015, 1891/2019 (plenary session). On the other hand, the second pillar applies the principle of equivalence directly, meaning that the benefits correspond directly to the contributions.

[31] Wolfgang Abendroth, *Zum Begriff des demokratischen und sozialen Rechtsstaates im Grundgesetz der Bundesrepublik Deutschland, in Rechtsstaatlichkeit und Sozialstaatlichkeit* (Fortschoff 1968) 115–16.

[32] Frans Pennings and Gijsbert Vonk (eds), *Research Handbook on European Social Security Law* (Edward Elgar Publishing 2015) 7.

social rights compels the state to provide decent social services to the citizens, comparable to those of the private market, especially given the people's growing inability to afford them. The quality of the services rendered should be the main criterion and not the reduction of the costs.[33] The social welfare state at its core requires the transfer of resources, therefore participation is mandatory. The principle of solidarity, under article 22 paragraph 5 aims to establish a social balance and fulfil the transgenerational contract: contributions are proportional to financial ability, benefits are analogous to financial needs.[34] The Constitution outlines the limits of the legislator's discretion, so that the rights of the insured and the pensioners are not impaired. The right to social security binds both the state and the legislator, to ensure the continuation of the public social security system, along with a modicum of welfare for the citizens. Even though the jurisprudence of the Greek courts has yet to openly use this heavily implied term, in recent cases it was emphasised that article 2 of the Constitution preserves a subsistence minimum for all.

2. Suggested and implemented reform measures

In terms of how social security financing mechanisms proved able to weather the economic crisis, European social models fared quite differently.[35] While corporatist/continental-model countries that managed to maintain steady employment were quite successful at stabilising public revenues, Sweden—an example of the universal model—experienced a steep drop in revenue. Even more severe were the consequences in the UK with its Beveridge system. The Bismarckian-type systems introduced cost-cutting by decreasing the benefits. To counteract that, most countries encouraged the introduction of second-pillar pension funds.

Greece was bound by the First Memorandum to reform, inter alia, its public social security system. A severe budget cut was implemented, which, in turn, led to a significant reduction of the pensioners' income. It was suggested that the participation in the second- or third-pillar pension schemes would balance out this loss,[36] even though it is questionable if, in a time of recession and rising unemployment, people would truly be able to afford it.

The First Greek Memorandum took into consideration the deterioration of the finances of the public pension institutions and the consequent burden on the country's GDP.[37] A series of fiscal and social reforms were agreed on, particularly

[33] Council of State Judgment 1749/2016 (plenary session).

[34] Council of State Judgments 4387/1997, 241/1989.

[35] Norman Wagner, 'Financing Social Security—Business as Usual?' (2011) 9 ETUI WP 19.

[36] David Natali, 'Pensions After the Financial and Economic Crisis: A Comparative Analysis of Recent Reforms in Europe' (2011) 7 ETUI WP 9.

[37] According to data derived from the Commission in 2009, by 2040 Greece would need to spend 21.4 per cent of its GDP to cover pension benefits.

with regard to the reformation of the public pension system.[38] Aggravating factors such as the continued ageing of the population, the evasion of tax and contributions, and the already high costs of contributions were taken into account. It was determined that the main pension schemes would merge into three, since the extreme fragmentation of the system exacerbated its finances,[39] and a new way to calculate pension benefits should be introduced (automatic indexation, greater equivalence between contributions and benefits, curbing of costs, and raising the standard retirement age at sixty-five in line with life expectancy). It was also suggested that the public pension system should provide the pensioners with a basic pension to cover the risk of poverty, and with a pension based on one's contributions. Discussed cuts in pensions consisted of the abolition of the Easter, summer, and Christmas bonuses and their replacement by a flat bonus for certain monthly pensions. The pension award formula would be amended in the contributory-based scheme to strengthen the link between contributions paid and benefits received, and penalties would be imposed for early retirees. Before the presentation of the draft bill in parliament, the National Actuarial Authority produced pension spending projections for the period 2010–2060.

Many guidelines were issued in the field of public social security policy. It was determined that the main pension schemes would merge into three, and that the calculation of pension benefits had to be changed (automatic indexation, more equivalence between contributions and benefits, curbing of costs, and raising the standard retirement age to sixty-five).[40] In lieu of two distinct pensions,[41] a total pension was introduced, consisting of the 'basic' sum (€360 for all insured persons) and a part related to earnings, hence proportionate to the whole working life's contributions. The system remained PAYG, but significantly lower pensions were afforded.

The standard retirement age was set to sixty-five (or sixty with a lower pension benefit) and later elevated to sixty-seven.[42] Costs were reduced by lowering pensions, discontinuing the family allowance, and eliminating Christmas and Easter allowances for pensioners younger than sixty years old. The benefit became means-tested for older pensioners. Furthermore, only the basic public pension (€384) remained state-guaranteed, while a distinction between social security and social assistance benefits was introduced and is believed to have ultimately allowed the abolition of certain means-related subsidiary benefits. A 'solidarity levy' on all pensions was imposed to help finance the public pension system, as well as a 'solidarity

[38] Tassos Giannitsis, *The Social Security System and the Financial Crisis* (Polis Publications 2016) 112 (in Greek).

[39] George Symeonidis, 'The Case of Greece: Through the Wormhole' in József Mészáros (ed), *Pension Systems in Crisis: Response and Resistance National Pension Insurance* (Budapest, 2013).

[40] See Laws 3845/2010, 3863/2010 (private sector workers), 3865/2010 (public servants).

[41] Aaron G Grech, 'The Financial Crisis and Differences in State Pension Generosity Across EU Countries' (2015) 2 CESifo DICE Report 37.

[42] Laws 4337 and 4342/2015.

levy for the unemployment', reducing the income of pensioners further. The contributions further increased at 6 per cent, 7 per cent, 9 per cent, 10 per cent, 12 per cent, 13 per cent, and 14 per cent of the wage and the aforementioned solidarity levy.[43]

The struggle between the principle of solidarity and the principle of equivalence was also manifested in the legislation for the supplementary public pension schemes.[44] The Greek public supplementary pension schemes are mainly financed by employers and employees. Nonetheless, the state is constitutionally obliged to guarantee their continued existence. Actuarial reports in 2011 showed that only nine out of thirty-eight public schemes could be considered financially viable. Viability of the system being the ultimate goal, Law 4052/2012 merged all remaining supplementary pension funds into one, called ETEA, and mingled their distinctive resources. ETEA is a public supplementary pension fund, with managerial and financial autonomy. It is a notional defined contribution system,[45] a hybrid between a PAYG and a funded system:[46] There is a notional account for every insured person, but the contributions are used to pay the current pensions (PAYG system) and not invested (fully funded system). Benefits are calculated using several criteria outlined in the law, such as biometric data, the years of contributions paid, and retirement age.[47]

Public pension funds resisting the integration into ETEA, which entailed the loss of their financial autonomy, were converted into mandatory occupational pension schemes to preserve their viability.[48] They were transferred from the first to the second pillar, but participation remained mandatory, as with first-pillar schemes.[49]

---

[43] Law 3896/2011.

[44] For a comprehensive juxtaposition of the two principles see Maria Bakavou, *Supplementary Pension Schemes for Workers* (Nomiki Vivliothiki Publications 2015) 281; Maria Bakavou, 'Changes in the Public Supplementary Pension Schemes According to Law 4052/2012—Creation of Notional Pension Schemes' (2015) 12 Journal of Theory and Practice of Administrative Law; Franco Modigliani, Marialuisa Ceprini, and Arun Muralidhar, 'A Solution to the Social Security Crisis' (August 2000) Sloan WP 4051, 10. Later, the Council of State would recognise in Judgment 1891/2019 (plenary session) that, even though no constitutional protection is afforded to the principle of equivalence, it is a derivative of the principle of proportionality, which is constitutionally protected. Therefore, a certain correlation between contributions and benefits must be observed.

[45] Milton Nektarios, 'Greece: The NDC Paradigm as a Framework for a Sustainable Pension System' in Edward Palmer, Robert Holzmann, and David Robalino (eds), *Non-Financial Defined Contribution Systems: Progress and New Frontiers in a Changing Pension World* (World Bank 2010) 259.

[46] Axel Börsch-Supan, 'What Are NDC Systems? What Do They Bring to Reform Strategies?' in Robert Holzmann and Edward Palmer (eds), *Pension Reform* (The World Bank 2006) 38.

[47] Robert Holzmann, *Toward a Reformed and Coordinated Pension System in Europe: Rationale and Potential Structure* (Social Protection Discussion Paper Series 18, The World Bank 2004).

[48] Platon Tinios, *Social Security System, A Method of Reading* (Kritiki Publications 2010) 448 (in Greek).

[49] A case of annulment was rejected by the Council of State Judgment 960/2017. The Court ruled that art 22 para 5 C allows the legislator a broad range of discretion to create, organise, and abolish public pension schemes, in the general policy framework, in order to ensure the ongoing adaptability to the circumstances at hand. Reforms are deemed constitutional if they are proportionate, fair, reasonable, and predictable and respect the public character of pension schemes. Provided that the mandatory occupational pension schemes fulfil the requirements set by art 22 para 5 C., the application was unanimously rejected.

Other measures were more cost-oriented. Pursuant to the Second Memorandum, the PSI Agreement was enacted,[50] which drastically reduced the reserved assets of the public pension funds, which were obligated by law to hold Greek bonds. This amplified the strain on their staggering budget balance. The total amount of the main and supplementary pensions was further reduced (5 per cent for those above €1,000, up to 20 per cent for pensions above €3,000). Additionally, aiming to 'rationalize the policy of family allowance provisions', a standard family allowance for all recipients was introduced and, thus, pre-existing ones were abolished.[51]

The Third Greek Memorandum noted that the pension system was still fragmented, costly, and required significant annual transfers from the state budget.[52] To address these challenges, a fully committed implementation of the existing reforms and an introduction of further reforms was required in order to reinforce long-term sustainability, targeting savings by creating, inter alia, strong disincentives for early retirement through increasing early retirement penalties and eliminating the grandfathering of rights to retire before the statutory retirement age. It was noted that the authorities had already increased health contributions of pensioners to 6 per cent on their main pensions and applied health contributions of 6 per cent also to supplementary pensions from 1 July 2015. Furthermore, it was mandated that all remaining supplementary funds would integrate into ETEA by 1 September 2015 and would only be financed by their own means from 1 September 2015. Monthly guaranteed contributory pension limits in nominal terms would freeze until 2021. Most importantly, people retiring after 30 June 2015 would receive the basic, guaranteed, contributory and means-tested pension 'only at the attainment of the statutory normal retirement age of currently 67 years'. It was also stipulated that authorities must modernise the contribution and pension base for all self-employed, including by switching from notional to actual income subject to minimum required contribution rules, and must revise and rationalise all different systems of basic, guaranteed contributory and means-tested pension components, taking into account the incentives to work and contribute. The phasing out of Epidoma Koinonikis Allileggyis Syntaxiouxwn (EKAS)[53] until December 2019 was also dictated. More tellingly, it was also stated that 'the Greek government will identify and legislate by October 2015 equivalent measures to fully compensate the impact of the implementation of the Court ruling on the pension measures of 2012; and repeal the amendments to the pension system introduced in Laws 4325/2015 and 4331/2015 in agreement with the institutions'.

Consequently, the income replacement rate was decreased to 50–55 per cent for every retiree after 2011 and the penalties for early retirees were increased.

---

[50] Law 4046/2012.
[51] Law 4093/2012.
[52] <https://ec.europa.eu/info/sites/info/files/01_mou_20150811_en1.pdf> accessed 29 January 2020.
[53] Stands for Social Solidarity Allowance for Pensioners.

Pursuant to the Third Memorandum, a new public pension system leaning towards Beveridgian principles was introduced.[54] The reform's ratio was the introduction of a single social security organisation for the coverage of all employees irrespective of their professional activity/identity. EFKA 'Unified Social Security Institution' incorporates all existing main social security institutions, as of 1 January 2017. Common rules applied for the calculation of contributions and benefits. The accompanying report declares the departure from the common Bismarckian conception of the pension as income replacement, since 'it allows the continuation of inequalities of working life to the pensioners' life'. In truth, since the contributions are earnings-related but the benefits are not, the pensions were decreased. The stipulation of the Third Memorandum to fully compensate for the impact of the recent judgments of the Greek Council of State,[55] which ruled that further reductions on the pensions were unconstitutional, was thusly achieved. The rulings were sidestepped by revamping the organisation of public pension schemes and the method of calculating pensions.

The pension consisted of two parts: (a) National Pension, paid to those for whom has been established a direct or disability pension entitlement or transfer pension entitlement in accordance with the relevant provisions. The beneficiaries must have permanently and lawfully resided in Greece for at least fifteen years, between the age of the fifteenth year and the year of lawful retirement age. National Pension amounts to €384 and is paid in full if the beneficiary was insured for at least twenty insurance years; (b) Contributory Pension, namely the contributory, earnings-related part of the main pension. The monthly contribution of entrepreneurs/self-employed persons is calculated based on their gross income. It has been argued that, combined with taxation, they were charged 60–70 per cent of their earnings. The law was controversial enough that every trade union/professional association filed an application of annulment. The Council of State rendered eighteen judgments where many aspects of Law 4387/2016 were overturned. EFKA sought to clarify the effect of these judgments, initiating a 'pilot trial', which was heard on 10 January 2020. Judgments 1439–43/2020 were delivered on 14 July 2020 and generally maintained the precedents set by Judgments 2287–90/2015 and 1891/2019.[56]

After signing the Third Memorandum, in cooperation with Troika, certain legislative measures to alleviate the minimisation of the welfare state were enacted. Their underlying common feature is that they addressed social groups at the threshold of poverty and are financed by the various solidarity levies imposed on

---

[54] Law 4387/2016, which introduced a single social security institution, called 'EFKA'.
[55] Judgments 2287–90/2015 in plenary session, under part C.
[56] Pensioners were awarded additional benefits for the period from June 2015 until May 2016, when EFKA, the new public pension system, was introduced.

slightly better-faring citizens.[57] In an effort to battle rising unemployment, access to employment was facilitated by introducing flexible working conditions, company-level collective bargaining, and a reduction of labour costs by introducing the minimum wage and reducing the severance payment.[58]

3. The Greek healthcare system

The Greek Constitution contains two provisions relevant to healthcare. Article 21 paragraph 3 provides that 'The State shall care for the health of citizens and shall adopt special measures for the protection of youth, old age, disability and for the relief of the needy', whereas article 5 paragraph 5 states that 'All persons have the right to the protection of their health and of their genetic identity. Matters relating to the protection of every person against biomedical interventions shall be specified by law'. Every reform concerning the public healthcare system must conform to article 21.

The healthcare system in Greece was primarily influenced by Beveridgian principles. The system was characterised by a lack of infrastructure or adequate funding, with great inequalities in access to healthcare and it being one of the least developed amongst OECD countries until the 1980s. The Ethniko Systima Ygeias (ESY),[59] a universal healthcare system, was considered one of the most influential reforms of the 1980s,[60] since the state bore the obligation of providing all citizens with a healthcare system, irrespective of their social, financial, or professional status. Admittedly, immediate access to healthcare was drastically improved. Article 1 specifically stated that. The capital, human, and technological infrastructure of the public healthcare sector was improved.[61] The ESY was, and is still, financed by general taxation[62] and social security contributions.

---

[57] For instance, Law 4320/2015, amended by Law 4472/2017, introduced humanitarian aid allowances (rent allowance up to €220/month, food and electricity bill vouchers), while Law 4389/2016 (art 235) introduced the Social Solidarity Supplement (KEA), in part to counterbalance the abolition of the aforementioned EKAS. It is a solidarity allowance for poorer households and homeless people, is tax-free, and is not offset against unemployment levies.

[58] Laws 4024/2011 and 4046/2012.

[59] Stands for National Health System.

[60] Law 1397/1983. See Charalampos Ekonomou, 'The Performance of the Greek Healthcare System and the Economic Adjustment Programme: "Economic Crisis" versus "System-Specific Deficits" Driven Reform' (2012) 2 Koinoniki Theoria (Social Theory) 38; World Health Organisation, 'Healthcare Systems in Transition' (1996) 4 <http://www.euro.who.int/__data/assets/pdf_file/0020/120278/E72454.pdf> accessed 29 January 2020. For an extensive presentation of the Greek Healthcare System see Konstantinos Kremalis, *Health Law, vol 1: General Principles of the Social Healthcare Services; vol 2: Legislature and Case Law* (Nomiki Vivliothiki Publications 2011) (in Greek); Maria Mitrosyli, *Health Law* (Papazisis Publications 2009) (in Greek); Patrina Paparrigopoulou-Pechlivanidi, *Public Law of Health* (Nomiki Vivliothiki Publications 2017) (in Greek).

[61] In 2000, the ESY ranked fourteenth worldwide in the overall assessment conducted by the World Health Organisation <http://www.who.int/whr/2000/en/whr00_en.pdf> accessed 29 January 2020.

[62] Nikos Tatsos, 'The Funding of Social Policy in Welfare State and Social Policy in Greece' in Panagiotis Getimis and Dionysis Gravaris (eds), *Social State and Social Policy—Current Issues* (Themelio Publications 1993) (in Greek).

The ESY consists of general and specialised hospitals, providing emergency, outpatient, and inpatient care. There are also military and university hospitals, managed and funded by the Ministries of Defence and Education respectively. The public healthcare system also comprises primary care health centres and rural medical surgeries for primary care services in rural areas, also funded by the state budget.

Apart from the state budget, some expenses are supposed to be covered by service charges to the insurance funds and patients, calculated on the basis of a complicated reimbursement system, which accounts in some cases only for the duration of hospitalisation and in others for the consumables and medications dispensed; cover for other expenses is based on a pre-fixed fee for the intervention undertaken, depending on the social security system of the patient.

The ESY, characterised by an outdated organisational structure dominated by clinical medicine and hospital services, produced deficits annually. Governance was characterised by a high degree of centralisation in decision-making and administrative processes, ie suboptimal managerial structures lacking adequate information management systems. Health service planning was not based on needs assessment, priority-setting mechanisms, or health technology assessment. Funding was regressive, with high out-of-pocket payments. The retrospective reimbursement system and problematic pricing created incentives for supplier-induced demand and prevented cost containment.[63] The financial crisis threw a sharp focus on all those deficiencies.

The legal frame primarily addressed the delivery side of the healthcare system. It did that by expanding the public hospital sector and improving primary healthcare by establishing the aforementioned rural and semi-urban primary care centres. More importantly, the state covered the greater portion of the pharmaceutical costs. Despite that, the ESY failed ultimately to unify the social insurance funds into a single one. As was the case with the pressure groups concerning the proposed social security reforms, the trade unions of the privileged social groups who enjoyed better coverage strongly rejected the idea.[64]

There had already been a need for structural, long overdue changes in the healthcare sector,[65] especially given the failure to control health spending.[66] At the onset

---

[63] World Health Organisation, *Regional Office for Europe Assessment Report Monitoring and Documenting Systemic and Health Effects of Health Reforms in Greece* (2019) <http://www.euro.who.int/__data/assets/pdf_file/0011/394526/Monitoring-Documenting_Greece_eng.pdf?ua=1> accessed 29 January 2020.

[64] Elias Mossialos, Sara Allin, and Konstantina Davaki, 'Analysing the Greek Health System: A Tale of Fragmentation and Inertia' (2005) Health Economics, published online at Wiley InterScience, DOI: 10.1002/hec.1033 <http://www.interscience.wiley.com> accessed 29 January 2020.

[65] European Parliament Directorate-General for Internal Policies, Policy Department C—Citizen's Rights and Constitutional Affairs, 'The Impact of the Crisis on Fundamental Rights Across Member States of the EU, a Comparative Analysis' (2015) 38.

[66] Charalampos Economou and others, *The Impact of the Financial Crisis on the Health System and Health in Greece* (WHO and European Observatory on Health Systems and Policies 2014) 7

of the crisis, the health sector was cited as 'a major factor' in the country's economic derailment and as such came under intense scrutiny from the Troika.[67] The health policy responses to the crisis were, as was the case with the social security system, twofold: on the one hand, much-needed operational and structural reforms, designed to address the weaknesses in the healthcare system, were implemented. On the other hand, complying with the overlying cutting-of-costs philosophy of the Memoranda, the measures stipulated were, by and large, fiscal consolidation measures.[68] Some aimed to achieve both goals of structural reform and fiscal consolidation. Major cuts to hospital and pharmaceutical expenditure were ensured by imposing clawbacks and rebates to rebalance the budget.

Law 3918/2011 introduced a major restructuring of the health system. The Greek social health insurance system provided universal coverage for almost 100 per cent of the population through a network of several funds. The system was, and remains, linked to employment status and type of employment. In 2011, as it was stipulated, almost all social health insurance funds were merged into one unified fund, the National Health Services Organisation (EOPYY). The explanatory notes accompanying the draft legislation state that EOPYY aims to ensure equal access to a universal healthcare system, providing certified medical services, exams, and pharmaceuticals and to create a common network of health services for all insured persons. EOPYY was designed to act henceforth as a unique buyer of medicines and healthcare services for all those insured, thus acquiring higher bargaining power against suppliers.

EOPYY covers the vast majority of the population (workforce, dependants, and pensioners), assuming the presence of only short-term unemployment. The basis for entitlement is the respective insurance status. Persons unemployed for less than twelve months continue to have access to sickness benefits for a year after the commencement of unemployment with the prerequisite proof of at least fifty working days in the previous year.[69] Unemployment rose rapidly, though, to reach 27.5 per

---

<https://www.euro.who.int/__data/assets/pdf_file/0007/266380/The-impact-of-the-financial-crisis-on-the-health-system-and-health-in-Greece.pdf?ua=1> accessed 17 June 2020; Lycourgos Liaropoulos, 'Greek Economic Crisis: Not a Tragedy for Health' (2012) BMJ 345.

[67] Furio Stamati and Rita Baeten, 'Health Care Reforms and the Crisis' (2014) ETUI 31.

[68] After the introduction of extensive austerity measures, Greece had one of the lowest ratios in the EU in public health expenditure by 2012, not exceeding 11.5 per cent compared with the EU average of 15 per cent, (see Health Expenditure Series; OECD 2013; WHO Regional Office for Europe 2014).

[69] Given the universal nature of the Greek healthcare system, uninsured persons have never been left without access to healthcare. After the expiry of the one-year continuation for the unemployed, health coverage is provided for (a) the long-term unemployed over fifty-five years old, according to art 10, Law 2434/1996; (b) long-term unemployed aged twenty-nine to fifty-five years old are covered for a period of up to two years according to art 5 para 4, Law 2768/1999; (c) young unemployed persons (up to twenty-nine years old) are covered for six months according to art 18, Law 2639/1998. For a more detailed presentation see Charalampos Ekonomou and others, 'Impacts of the Economic Crisis on Access to Healthcare Services in Greece with a Focus on the Vulnerable Groups of the Population' (2014) 9(2) Social Cohesion and Development 99–115.

cent in 2013 and 26.8 per cent in 2014,[70] so a great part of the population was left uninsured. In June 2014, new amendments were introduced, so that uninsured persons and their families were entitled to primary and in-hospital health services as well as pharmaceutical care.

Reduction of costs was proposed by other means such as: (a) procurement of health supplies, achieved through the Regional Programmes for Goods and Services that was introduced by the National Central Authority for the Procurement of Health Services;[71] (b) rationalisation of licensing, pricing, and reimbursement systems for medicines, by relaxing population-based restrictions, increasing opening hours, allowing new pharmacists to form partnerships with incumbents; (c) reduction of the profit margin for pharmacies and pharmaceutical companies through a system of rebates and clawback measures; and (d) the Ministry of Health becoming the sole author of pharmaceutical policies.[72] Additional measures adopted concern the governance, monitoring, and financing of the health system, as well as of hospitals and pharmaceuticals.[73] Furthermore, reductions in pharmaceutical expenditure are being pursued mainly by price reductions, increased rebates (clawbacks imposed on private pharmacies and pharmaceutical companies for both inpatient and outpatient drugs), and the promotion of generic medicines and prescription control mechanisms.

Current reforms tend to focus on operational, financial, and managerial dimensions. Reductions in public spending by sector were conserved throughout the crisis, indicating that cuts were made across the board in order to achieve the targets set under the Memoranda, without an effort to support services that may prove more efficient in the long term (eg primary care services).[74] Additionally, more than 2.5 million people lost their social health insurance rights and thus faced insurmountable barriers to accessing healthcare. Even worse, the financial crisis negatively affected the health status of the population,[75] with beneficiaries complaining about a steep deterioration of the level of health services. Nevertheless, important positive steps include the standardisation of the health benefits package for all citizens, new monitoring tools for hospital management, a prospective

---

[70] Hellenic Statistical Authority (ELSTAT) <http://www.statistics.gr/en/statistics/-/publication/SJO02/2013-M12> accessed 30 August 2019.

[71] Art 21, Law 4472/2017.

[72] Until the introduction of Law 398/2011, the National Organisation for Drugs (EOF—Ethnikos Organismos Farmakon) was responsible for licensing and pricing new drugs.

[73] Arts 1, 11, Law 4052/2012. See also amendments by Law 4472/2017.

[74] Charalambos Ekonomou, 'The Impact of the Crisis on the Health System and Health in Greece' in World Health Organisation Observatory Studies Series 41, *Economic Crisis, Health Systems and Health in Europe, Country Experiences* (2015).

[75] Notably, the numbers of infant and maternal deaths have increased, as have suicides and homicides (for males only). World Health Organisation, Regional Office for Europe, *Greece, Profile for Health and Well-Being 2016* <http://www.euro.who.int/__data/assets/pdf_file/0010/308836/Profile-Health-Well-being-Greece.pdf> accessed 29 January 2020.

payment system for hospital care, and the implementation of the System of Health Accounts of the OECD.[76]

In conclusion, one observes that the unwavering commitment to cost-containment measures has by necessity been applied in the form of horizontal cuts rather than a more targeted resource allocation. In addition, reforms have often been implemented rapidly, without sufficiently considering potential side effects, including people's inability to afford healthcare.

III. Constitutional and human rights affected by social security reforms

1. Procedural particularities in the adoption of the reform measures

Each of the three Memoranda contained detailed terms and conditions for cutting costs, such as the abolition of family and holiday allowances, the increase of the pension eligibility age, e-prescription of pharmaceuticals, and so forth. This was also the case with taxation. In this sense, the discretion the Greek government enjoyed when introducing those measures to the parliament was not particularly large, given that the Memoranda included not only the desired goals (reduction of costs) but also specific suggestions on how to achieve them.

Still, unless national legislation was enacted, the measures suggested by the Memoranda could not be incorporated in the national legal order. In most cases, these suggestions were introduced to the parliament via the ultra-fast-track procedure, normally reserved for emergencies, which did not permit an extensive discussion on the matters at hand. That, naturally, led to many complaints on the part of the MPs who felt pressured to vote for the legislation, under the threat of the looming default, but who did not have adequate time to study the suggested measures in depth or contemplate alternatives. During all voting procedures, each government invariably invoked the public interest, which consisted of avoiding a public default at all costs, to secure parliamentary majority, even though (especially up to 2015) at times there was no unanimity.

In other cases, hoping to avoid an inflammatory parliamentary conflict, the government invoked article 44 of the Constitution, which stipulates that under extraordinary circumstances of an urgent and unforeseeable need, the President of the Republic may, upon proposal of the Cabinet, issue acts of legislative content. Such acts shall then be submitted to parliament for ratification, as specified in the provisions of article 72 paragraph 1, within forty days of their issuance or within forty

---

[76] Ekonomou (n 74).

days from the convocation of a parliamentary session. That was the case with legislative act 6/2012, which regulated collective bargaining.

Consistently, the state argued against every application of annulment before the courts that the Memoranda law is 'législation d'exception' or 'emergency law', established to preserve the public interest, more specifically the state financial interest to avoid default and ensure the refinancing of the public deficit. The courts consistently refused to hear the cases on the basis of emergency law, contrary to the consideration given to the 'extraordinary financial straits'.

2. Constitutional protection of the welfare state

The welfare state is a type of governance where the state actively provides for the social and financial growth and protection of its citizens. Social rights create a bond between the individuals living in a given society and the state. Enacting measures to protect individuals[77] from the negative effects of the financial crisis falls within this scope. Within the EU, the welfare state principle is integrated in the European Social Model ideal, which aims to guarantee social protection and employment through financial growth, good working conditions, and an emphasis on high standards of living, as compared to the USA, for instance.[78] The outbreak of the crisis threatened the fundamental clauses of the social contract between European citizens and their governments.[79] In that sense, the courts were often regarded as the last champions for the welfare state and social rights.

The Greek Constitution may protect the right to social security and healthcare but it does not provide specific entitlements. It serves as a guideline[80] for the legislator to create, develop, and sustain a social security and healthcare system, while simultaneously awarding the freedom to choose and implement provisions correlating to the current needs and the political, social, and financial framework. With this in mind, one will have a clearer perception of the 'financial crisis case law'.

Since 2012, many applications have been brought before Greek and European courts, on the grounds that the Memoranda and the implemented measures violated the social rights guaranteed by the Constitution, the European Convention of Human Rights (ECHR), and the Charter of Fundamental Rights of the European Union.

---

[77] Torben Andersen, 'The Welfare State and the Great Recession' in Centre for European Policy Studies, *The Welfare State After the Great Recession* (6 December 2012); Georges Menahem, 'The Decommodified Security Ratio: A Tool for Assessing European Social Protection Systems' (October– December 2007) 60 International Social Security Review 69–103.

[78] Tony Judt, *Postwar: A History of Europe Since 1945* (Penguin Press 2005).

[79] Tassos Giannitsis and Stavros Zografakis, *Poverty, Inequality and Economic Disruption in Times of Financial Crisis* (Polis Publications 2016) (in Greek).

[80] Ulrich Scheuner, 'Die Funktion der Grundrechte im Sozialstaat. Die Grundrechte als Richtlinie der Staatstaetigkeit' (1971) DOV 513.

It is widely known that the EU courts ruled the relevant cases inadmissible,[81] since the applicants were not deprived of the right to effective judicial protection, nor did they meet the conditions for admissibility[82] requiring direct concern. So did the European Court of Human Rights (ECtHR),[83] reasoning that the imposed reduction did not expose the applicant to subsistence difficulties incompatible with article 1 of Protocol 1, noting also 'the particular climate of economic hardship in which it occurred'.[84] This throws into sharp relief the difficulties[85] the Greek Council of State faced when the first application of annulment was heard.[86] There was no judicial precedent to fall back on. It was the first Supreme Administrative Court with constitutional review to hear a case where the social rights of people, the rule of law, the country's eminent default, and its subsequent relationship with other EU Member States were at stake.[87]

Interestingly, as time passed, fewer cases were brought before the courts, due to the high cost of litigation and the 'financial crisis case law' of the Greek courts, which more often than not upheld the legality of the contested act on grounds of the public interest to avoid default, given the 'dire financial straits' and 'extraordinary emergency' that befell the Hellenic Republic.[88] Consequently, it was felt that the courts were powerless to prevent the erosion of the welfare state.[89]

---

[81] For Greece, see General Court Orders in Case T-541/10 *Anotati Dioikisi Enoseon Dimosion Ypallilon (ADEDY) v Council of the European Union* [2012] EU:T:2012:626 and Case T-215/11 *Anotati Dioikisi Enoseon Dimosion Ypallilon (ADEDY) and Others v Council of the European Union* [2012] EU:T:2012:627.

[82] Art 263(4) TFEU.

[83] *Koufaki* and *ADEDY v Greece* App no 57665/12 and 57657/12 (ECtHR, 7 May 2013).

[84] Thomas Beukers, Bruno de Witte, and Claire Kilpatrick (eds), *Constitutional Change Through Euro-Crisis Law* (CUP 2017) 297; George Gerapetritis, *New Economic Constitutionalism in Europe* (Hart Publications 2019) 135.

[85] Edoardo Chiti and Pedro Gustavo Teixeira, 'The Constitutional Implications of the European Responses to the Financial and Public Debt Crisis' (2013) 50(3) Common Market Law Review 683–708; Deirdre Curtin, 'Challenging Executive Dominance in European Democracy' (2014) 77(1) Modern Law Review 1–32; and Kilpatrick, 'On the Rule of Law and Economic Emergency: The Degradation of Basic Legal Values in Europe's Bailouts' (2015) Oxford Journal of Legal Studies.

[86] Constantin Yannakopoulos, *La Déréglementation constitutionelle en Europe* (Sakkoulas Publications 2019) preface.

[87] Xenophon Contiades (ed), *Constitutions in the Global Financial Crisis: A Comparative Analysis* (Ashgate 2013) and Claire Kilpatrick and Bruno de Witte (eds), 'Social Rights in Times of Crisis in the Eurozone: The Role of Fundamental Rights' Challenges' Working Paper, EUI Law 2014/05.

[88] Backlash consciousness is an important feature of the judicial attitude towards the financial crisis dilemma, as was obvious in the Greek and Portuguese case law (for a comprehensive analysis see Alexia Herwig and Marta Simoncini (eds), *Law and the Management of Disasters: The Challenge of Resilience* (Routledge 2016)).

[89] George Karavokyris, 'The Role of Judges and Legislators in the Greek Financial Crisis: A Matter of Competition' in Lina Papadopoulou, Ingolf Pernice, and Joseph HH Weiler (eds), *Legitimacy Issues of the European Union in the Face of Crisis* (European Constitutional Law Network Series, vol 9, Nomos 2017) 117 ff.

3. Overview of the Greek system of judicial review

Greece has adopted the system of diffused (exercised by all courts) and concrete (exercised within the frame of a specific case) constitutional review. Every person with a legitimate interest may be heard. In such a judicial system, it is even more difficult for the strategic framework that was adopted, based on the relevant legislative decisions of the Parliament, to be taken into account by the judge in a comprehensive manner and to be—ultimately—challenged.[90] The court that was primarily called to deal with the onslaught of cases, especially those concerning the reforms of the public social security system, was, per the systemic structure of the Greek judicial system, the Council of State, namely the Supreme Administrative Court of Greece (in Greek, Symvoulion tis Epikratias).[91] The judgments of the Council of State provide the highest authority on legal precedent for the lower administrative courts and set the standards for the interpretation of the Constitution and the laws and for the advancement of legal theory and practice. Still, the Council of State is not a constitutional court. Its judicial authority has certain boundaries: it is vested with the power to declare the contested act unconstitutional[92] but not the authority to suggest alternatives to the state, or effectively legislate,[93] pursuant to article 26 of the Constitution (Distinction of Powers).[94] It is not a matter of deference to the parliament[95] or judicial restraint but of lack of authority. 'Concrete judicial review' means that the judge evaluates strictly the legality of the measures pertaining to the

[90] Evangelos Venizelos, 'State Transformation and the European Integration Project—Lessons from the Financial Crisis and the Greek Paradigm' (February 2016) CEPS Special Report, available for free downloading from the CEPS website <http://www.ceps.eu> accessed 29 January 2020.

[91] The Greek Constitution establishes two jurisdictions, the administrative and the civil/criminal, which are organised in three instances: the courts of first instance (lower courts), the courts of appeals (higher, appellate courts), and the Supreme Courts. The Council of State is at the top of the hierarchy of ordinary administrative courts. The Council of State and the ordinary administrative courts decide on all matters of administrative law disputes: money claims, the function of the civil service, social security claims, public works and supplies competitions, compensation claims against the state, challenges to the legality of administrative acts in general. Law 3900/2010 also established a system of 'pilot trials' and preliminary reference concerning constitutionality from lower courts when it is deemed that the matter at hand affects a great number of persons.

[92] The Greek legal system prohibits an application of annulment directly against a law, and only permits applications against administrative acts (presidential decrees, ministerial decisions etc).

[93] This is the position generally held by Constitutional Courts, see Bundesverfassungsgericht of 7 September 2011, 2 RvR 987/10 and others: 'Die Entscheidung über Einnahmen und Ausgaben der öffentlichen Hand ist grundlegender Teil der demokratischen Selbstgestaltungsfähigkeit im Verfassungsstaat (vgl. BVerfGE 123, 267, 359)'.

[94] Art 26, 1. The legislative powers shall be exercised by the Parliament and the President of the Republic. 2. The executive powers shall be exercised by the President of the Republic and the Government. 3. The judicial powers shall be exercised by courts of law, the decisions of which shall be executed in the name of the Greek People.

[95] Cristina Fasone, 'Constitutional Courts Facing the Euro Crisis: Italy, Portugal and Spain in a Comparative perspective' EUI MWP 2014/25.

case at hand, which effectively hinders a complete evaluation of the whole package of the measures implemented to tackle the crisis. For the erosion of the welfare state this proved critical: the accumulated burden of decreased income, increased taxation and contributions, and the imposition of new solidarity levies imposed a burden that was known to the courts but could not be taken into consideration, as not all of them together could pertain to the same case[96]—even more so as the Greek Constitution does not provide for the fate of constitutional rights in times of public deficit, as does the German or Swiss Constitution. Moreover, there is no provision for permanent advisers/technical consultants in the Greek courts, so there is no external input on the effectiveness of the contested acts or the possibility of the implementation of equivalent measures other than whatever data the parties can provide. And yet, the Greek courts heard cases of extreme financial complexity, such as the PSI Agreement case, deriving knowledge from the relevant legal documents.

Despite these parameters, the violent conflict of rights revived the always relevant discussion on the limitations of judicial review. Contrary to the pre-crisis case law, where the state's fiscal interest did not suffice to uphold the legality of the measures, it has been argued that the Greek courts have invoked the public interest (of avoiding default) to avoid exercising constitutional review.[97]

Still, the courts in Greece do not create law. The judge is constitutionally bound to search for and apply the law, even if it is ineffective, or bad, as long as it adheres to the Constitution, the EU, and ECHR law. In Greece, all constitutional clauses are held equal to each other. When two rights clash, the court strives to balance them out,[98] when upholding both proves impossible. An analytical approach to the relative case law shows that the deliberation of the Court sought to find the balance between fiscal consolidation and the limitation of social rights. The dilemma between the public interest and the welfare state reflects the agony of the Court to safeguard the welfare state, all the while being mindful that a state bankruptcy serves no legal interests.

---

[96] There has been a notable exception in Judgments 2287–90/2015 (plenary session) of the Council of State. The Court cited all the reductions that had been imposed on citizens under the aegis of participation in public burdens so far, in order to sustain the argument that the legislator ought to seek other alternatives than perpetually reducing people's incomes and, as a result, to keep minimising their living standards.

[97] George Gerapetritis, 'Judicial Review on Financial Choices—Projections of New Deals' (2011) Gazette of Administrative Law 464 (in Greek).

[98] Blanca R Ruiz, 'Discourse Theory and the Addressees of Basic Rights' (2001) 32 Rechtstheorie 87, 115.

4. Social protection reforms before the Greek courts

a) The initial phase of judicial self-restraint

The first major case brought before the Council of State contested the first reform of the public social security system,[99] regarding reductions imposed on pensions.[100] The applicants were trade unions and other socio-economic structures, bar associations, and natural persons, arguing that the pension reductions and the holiday-allowance discontinuation were in violation of article 1 of the First Additional Protocol to the ECHR.

The Council of State[101] examined the nature of the contested legislative acts. If they were considered as the product of an international treaty, per article 28 paragraph 2[102] of the Constitution, they should be ratified by three-fifths of the parliament. The Court determined that the First Memorandum and its annexes may have been 'a product of cooperation of the Greek authorities, the European Commission, the European Central Bank and the International Monetary Fund and irrespective of the obligations assumed by the Greek State toward the other members of the Eurozone' but, in essence, it was the Greek government's general policy framework, defining the objectives of its fiscal policy.[103] The Council of State therefore ruled that the Greek legislator took ownership of the policies introduced to handle the financial crisis effects[104] as the state was obliged to honour the bilateral state agreements. This position has been tacitly maintained ever since.

The Court then addressed the claims for the violation of article 1 of the First Additional Protocol to the ECHR. Invoking the well-known ECtHR's case law, the Council of State acknowledged that the state's wide margin of appreciation of the

---

[99] It was agreed, expressis verbis, that the reduction of public spending would be primarily achieved through the reduction of the financing of the welfare state, see Sotirios Rizos, 'The Council of State Between the Principle of the Welfare State and the Political Commandment of "You Shall Not Receive by the One Who Has Nothing"' (2015) Theory and Practice Administrative Law Review 289 ff (in Greek). Giannitsis (n 38) (in Greek) remarks that in extreme circumstances, as such, the problems should be immediately solved, while restricting the unfavourable effects of the chosen solutions.

[100] Art 3(10)–(15), Law 3845/2010.

[101] Judgment 668/2012 in plenary session.

[102] 'Authorities provided by the Constitution may by treaty or agreement be vested in agencies of international organizations, when this serves an important national interest and promotes cooperation with other States. A majority of three-fifths of the total number of Members of Parliament shall be necessary to vote the law ratifying the treaty or agreement'.

[103] Dimitrios V Skiadas, 'Greek Fiscal Governance: The EU's Impact on Fiscal Sovereignty in Spyridon Litsas' in Aristotle Tziampiris (ed), *Foreign Policy under Austerity—Greece's Return to Normality* (Palgrave McMillan 2017) 189.

[104] Judgment 668/2012 has often been criticised as having adopted the 'emergency rhetoric' used by the government and translating it in legal terms. See for example Afroditi Marketou, 'Greece: Constitutional Deconstruction and the Loss of National Sovereignty' in Beukers, de Witte, and Kilpatrick (n 84) 188, Konstantinos Giannakopoulos, 'The Public Interest in the Light of the Economic Crisis' (2011) JAdmL 100 ff. (in Greek).

public interest on social or economic grounds allowed only for a borderline judicial review.[105] It was subsequently held that the imposed measures sought to manage the reduction of the GDP deficit by 2.5 per cent, as part of the government's broader programme of fiscal adjustment. In this context, the financial public interest had become a 'compelling national interest'.[106] Therefore, the adoption of measures which ensured the viability of the country's economic system was compatible with the general objectives of the ECHR. The public social security institutions are a part of the general government, so a reasonable relation of proportionality[107] between the legitimate aim of reducing public deficit and the adopted measures is established. The Court also rejected the argument that the state had the obligation to contemplate milder measures, by counterclaiming that the aforementioned measures were only a part of the general framework adopted by the government to contain the public deficit. Lastly, the Court held that the reduction of the pension benefits adhered to the principle of proportionality, since the Christmas and Easter allowances were still maintained for pensioners aged older than sixty years and for pension benefits above €2,500 (gross). The alleged violation of article 2 of the Constitution (right to personal dignity) was also summarily rejected, because the Court held that a right to a pre-fixed amount of pension was not guaranteed, except if the subsistence minimum was violated, which was not the case.

Two more cases, filed by the Public Power Corporation's unions and natural persons against new pension reductions, were brought before the Council of State.[108] The Court maintained that, even though legal expectations against social security institutions are protected according to ECHR law,[109] pension cuts were equally distributed to all the pensioners, pursuant to the constitutional obligation to contribute without distinction to public charges in proportion to one's means. The increase of the statutory retirement age was also deemed legitimate, justified, and objective, because it respected the transgenerational contract: the burden to

---

[105] *National and Provincial Building Society and Others v UK* ECHR 1997-VII, para 80 and *Stec and Others v UK* ECHR 2006-VI, para 52.

[106] This distinction has been made because the case law of the Court before the crisis did not view the fiscal interest of the state as a legitimate reason to allow the restriction of fundamental rights (see, for example, Judgment 1663/2009 in plenary session).

[107] Xenophon Contiades and Alkmene Fotiadou, 'Social Rights, Proportionality and Fiscal Crisis' < www.constitutionalism.gr/2377-koinwnika-dikaiwmata-analogikotita-kai-dimosionomi/> accessed 29 January 2020 (in Greek); Costas Chrysogonos and Akritas Kaidatzis, 'The Reformation of the Pension System and the Constitution' <http://www.constitutionalism.gr/ast/cov/su/suntaxiodotikimetarruthmisi.pdf> accessed 29 January 2020 (in Greek); Athina Petroglou, 'The Significance of the Judgment of the Conseil d'Etat 668/2012 for the Protection of Social Rights in Circumstances of Crisis' (2012) 1(636) Social Security Law Review 580 ff (in Greek).

[108] Pension reductions introduced by Law 3863/2010. Judgments 1285–6/2012 in plenary session.

[109] However, ECtHR's case law uses the criterion of foreseeability of a judicial success in a slightly different manner. In the case of *Ichtiaroglou v Greece* (Decision of 19 June 2008) the Court held that in social insurance law, the protection of the legitimate expectations of the pensioners, when a welfare law clause changes, is linked not only to a foreseeable prospect of success according to the national courts' case law, but also to the person's inability to predict this amendment through art 1 of the First Additional Protocol.

current pensioners is a reduced income. The burden to future pensioners is a rise in contributions and decreased benefits.[110]

The Greek courts unilaterally deny a direct correlation between a person's contributions and the pension received, due to the PAYG nature of the social security system. The principle of direct equivalence is not constitutionally imposed,[111] so pension reductions are considered, prima facie, legitimate. In the face of looming default, the Court remained loyal to the previous case law, ruling that the preservation of the social security institutions' capital was more protection-worthy than the pensioners' income, in the balance of clashing rights. This stance is in conformity with social security law, which views social security as a community against common dangers. In this sense, the viability of pension funds comes first. In light of that, no violation of the right to property either under article 1 of the First Additional Protocol or article 17 of the Constitution was found.[112]

A claim based on the violation of article 34 of the Charter of Fundamental Rights of the EU was also rejected given the measures' 'national character'. The contested acts were, ultimately, legislative acts voted on by the Greek parliament and implemented by the Greek government, so they fell outside the scope of the Charter. The Court also held that article 51 paragraph 2 must not be interpreted as allowing the scope of the Charter to be implemented outside the scope of EU law, thus article 6 of the ECHR cannot be invoked through the Charter. In this, the Council of State echoed the jurisprudence of the CJEU.[113]

b) The milestone decisions on cuts in pensions

A notable exception from the previous case law was made with Judgments 2287–90/2015[114] in plenary session. For the first time, the Court held that the responsibility to contain the public deficit rested primarily with the legislation and enactment of appropriate measures and not with the citizens' participation in contributing to public charges. Judicial review in Greece is concrete; this means that the courts have no authority to suggest alternative measures. Still, the Council of State held that the reduction of pensions was an initial, swift, and direct response to the 'unpredictability and ferocity of the crisis', but it could not be accepted as a permanent

---

[110] Dafni Diliagka, 'The Legality of Pension Reforms in Times of Financial Crisis, The Case of Greece' in *Studien aus dem Max-Planck-Institut für Sozialrecht und Sozialpolitik* (Nomos 2018) 118.

[111] Olga Angelopoulou, 'Country Report: Greece' in Ulrich Becker and others (eds), *Security: A General Principle of Social Security Law in Europe* (Europa Law Publishing 2010) 175.

[112] It is noteworthy that the minority opinions in these judgments were in favour of the violation of art 1 of the First Additional Protocol, as the imposed reductions exceeded the legitimate foreseeability demanded by this provision and arts 2, 4(1) and(5) (equality and equal participation in public charges) and 22(5) (social security rights) of the Greek Constitution. They argued that the principle of equivalence and proportionality were not respected: reductions were determined by criteria unrelated to social security law (link between contributions and benefits) and solely referred to life expectancy/age.

[113] Case C-249/96 *Grant v South-West Trains Ltd* [1998] ECR 1998 I-00621, para 45.

[114] The applications of annulment were brought against measures implemented by Law 3896/2011.

solution.[115] The right to a pension entails the state's obligation to provide social insurance for the working population and to safeguard the social capital, with two additional caveats: to ensure the viability of pension funds and a living standard for the pensioners, not limited to the subsistence minimum but equivalent to the one before retirement. The second caveat had not been respected.

These judgments signify a shift from the previously established case law of the Court, where the dire fiscal need of the state superimposed the protection of certain social rights.[116] By that time, Greece was five years down the road of continuous fiscal adjustment. The cumulative effect of income reductions and rising taxation had exhausted people's resources. The judgment, in an unusual move, breaks away from the traditional approach that the Court examines the facts of only the case it hears: it enumerates all the reductions that were imposed on pensioners,[117] to make the case that the legality of the initial measures was tied to the public interest of avoiding a sudden and messy default, responding to matters of utmost energy. But in the face of ongoing financial austerity, the legislator must examine and adopt other solutions than continuing to impose reductions (decrease of wages, pensions, elevated taxation, etc) on the citizens' income in perpetuum, thus eventually violating the subsistence minimum. The Court, citing the Judgment of the German Federal Constitutional Court (Bundesverfassungsgericht) of 9 February 2010,[118] stressed that the state was allowed to introduce unfavourable reforms to the public social security system, in order to ensure its viability, but it must act in accordance with other constitutional provisions, such as article 4 paragraph 1 (equality) and article 2 paragraph 1 (respect and protection of the value of the human being). The freedom to choose methods of financing the system is constrained by the obligation to ensure the pensioners' decent income replacement, which should allow

---

[115] See Athina Petroglou, 'The Judicial Protection of Social Rights during a Prolonged Financial Crisis and Ongoing Reductions of Social and Pension Benefits' (2014) 2(644) Social Security Law Review 268 (in Greek), where the reasoning of Judgment 2192/2014 in plenary session of the Council of State is mentioned: the legislator must respect the obligations arising from the Constitution when implementing measures of fiscal policy.

[116] Anastasia Poulou, *Soziale Grundrechte und europäische Finanzhilfe* (Mohr Siebeck 2017) 289.

[117] See European Parliament Directorate-General for Internal Policies, 'The Impact of the Crisis on Fundamental Rights across Member States of the EU' (2015) 87. 'In Greece, the contribution was imposed on both private and public sector pensions, and was determined on a sliding scale between 3% and 10%, which later increased to between 6% and 10%. This contribution was initially imposed on principal pensions but was later extended to supplementary pensions. ... Additional cuts were imposed in Greece on pension lump-sums paid from specific pension funds. Furthermore, additional reductions between 20% and 40% (depending on the amount of pension and the age of the pensioner) for principal pensions that exceed a certain amount were introduced on the amount exceeding a certain threshold amount of pension. Supplementary pensions were also subject to a reduction on a sliding scale between 10% and 20%—depending on the total amount of the supplementary pension.' See also United Nations, 'Independent Expert on the Effects of Foreign Debt and Other Related International Financial Obligations of States on the Full Enjoyment of All Human Rights, Particularly Economic, Social and Cultural Rights', Mr. Cephas Lumina: Mission to Greece 22–26 April 2013 (26 April 2013).

[118] Bvl 1/09, 1 Bvl 3/09, 1 Bvl 4/09.

them to fully participate in social life.[119] Article 2 of the Constitution was interpreted in conjunction with article 22 paragraph 5, to highlight the correlation between the living standards before and after exiting the workforce. The Court did not specify this correlation, as it falls in the legislative sphere, but observed that the principle of proportionality must be respected.[120] Finally, the Court stressed that the imposed reductions were not corroborated with actuarial reports that reflected the financial status quo of the pension funds, thus violating the Constitution.

c) Current developments

It could be argued that the context of these judgments was overturned by Judgment 734/2016, which handled reductions imposed on the lump-sum payments pensioners receive when they exit the workforce. The case was brought before the Council of State in the context of a pilot trial.[121] The applicant was a pensioner of the public sector, 204 other pensioners lodged statements as interveners. The Court reiterated its case law that the lump sum, called 'ef apax',[122] was considered a pension benefit and that the insured capital was entirely contributory.[123] However, the reduction was deemed legitimate and proportionate in order to secure the viability of the public social security institutions in extremely adverse economic circumstances. This reduction may also be retroactive, regarding the applications that were pending at the time of the legislative reform, since the Constitution prohibits the retroactive effect of laws only in certain circumstances, as long as the principle of proportionality is respected.[124] This seemingly different treatment originates from the different perception of the pension benefits, with the latter being considered as ensuring the pensioners' living standard, while the lump sum is received by the pensioner only once.

The consequences of the accumulative measures were also not addressed in Judgments 1880–1897, 1900–1904/2019 in plenary session of the Council of State, which were delivered in cases against the introduction of EFKA. The judgments rule on five important aspects of the law: (a) the unification of the social security

---

[119] It is no coincidence that a discussion of establishing a framework for a guaranteed European minimum income has begun after the outbreak of the crisis. See Ramón Peña-Casas and Denis Bouget, 'Towards a European Minimum Income? Discussions, Issues and Prospects' in David Natali, *Social Developments in the European Union* (ETUI 2013) 156.

[120] Olga Angelopoulou, 'The Core of the Social Security Rights as a Limit to the Reduction of Pension Benefit—A Comment on Judgments 2287–8/2015 of the Council of State' (2015) Social Security Law Review 459 (in Greek).

[121] Art 1 para 1 Law 3900/2010 introduced the notion of the 'pilot trial': if a case falls within the jurisdiction of a court of first instance but the legal issue at hand is expected to affect a lot of people—and thus generate a lot of trials—the case can be directly referred to the Council of State.

[122] It literally means 'once and for all' and is the terminology used for the lump sum the pensioners receive when exiting the workforce. If they die immediately after the working relationship is terminated and before they claim it, their relatives have a right to it.

[123] Judgment 2679/2011 in plenary session.

[124] For reference, see the previous case law of the Council of State Judgments 3478/2008 in plenary session, 2999/2009, 3613/2013.

institutions into a single legal entity; (b) the integration of public servants into EFKA; (c) the calculations of the contributions of the entrepreneurs; (d) the calculation (reduction) of the main pension; and (e) the calculation (reduction) of supplementary pensions and the funding of the supplementary pension schemes.

The landmark judgments circumscribe the social security institution in Greece, in line with the constitutional principles of the welfare state, solidarity, and the rule of law, and outline the legal borders for the legality of the legislator's choices. In general, the judgments treated the contested reforms as the introduction of a new pension system: the old system relied on creating a different pension fund for different categories of workers, thus resulting in different rules for contributions, retirement age, and benefits for insured persons. The unification of all social security institutions into one was not simply a logistical matter, as it led to the application of universal rules for all. According to the judgments, article 22 paragraph 5 of the Constitution endows the legislator with a vast margin of appreciation for the organisation, funding, and function of the social security system, which can be only be marginally reviewed by the courts, as long as it is provided by the state or public legal persons. Therefore, the unification of all social security institutions into one was deemed constitutional, both for the main and the supplementary pension funds. The Court reiterated that social security in Greece was based on the principle of solidarity. Insured persons are obliged to contribute to the system, whereas beneficiaries receive a benefit which must ensure the enjoyment of a living standard as close as possible to pre-retirement time. Beyond that, social solidarity is achieved by the redistribution of capital, in order to defuse social inequalities. On the other hand, the Court noted that the principle of equivalence may not be constitutionally protected but that it derived from the principle of proportionality. Therefore, a certain correlation between contributions and benefits must be observed. In this vein, the Court stressed that the social security system must be organised in such a way that the obligation for contributions does not drastically reduce the insured persons' income and the awarded benefits allow for participating in social life, thus preserving the subsistence minimum, whereas the principle of equality prohibits similar treatment of different cases. On these grounds, the Court ruled that the law's provisions that specific categories of workers (entrepreneurs, farmers, self-employed persons) enjoy the same benefits as public servants, even though they are burdened with higher contributions, defies the principle of equality and these provisions are, therefore, annulled. Furthermore, the provisions that held that workers with shorter insured periods enjoy greater replacement rates than those who worked longer were also deemed unconstitutional. It was also examined if the reductions in pensions, established as a result of the new calculation method of the pensions, were sustained by actuarial reports. This was not the case for supplementary pensions, so they were deemed unconstitutional. The Court reiterated Judgments 2287–88/2015 to overturn the reductions on grounds of not being supported by actuarial reports, but refrained from making an accumulative assessment, as did the previous judgments. Lastly, the Court addressed the matter of funding social security institutions from the public budget. It was held that the state was obliged to guarantee the viability of the main and supplementary pension funds, and this obligation entailed the coverage of their deficits if other measures (restructuring, cutting down of benefits) failed to accomplish that. As mentioned above (see II.2), EFKA sought to clarify the effect of these judgments. As a result, the Council of State delivered judgments 1439–43/2020 on 14 July 2020, awarding additional pension benefits for the period June 2015 to May 2016.

d) The decision on the Greek PSI LM Facility Agreement

Judgments 3016 and 3724/2014[125] in plenary session are not directly linked to social security rights but are crucial in the general context, as they upheld the Private Sector Involvement Liability Management (PSI LM) Facility Agreement. The agreement included a haircut to the value of the Greek bonds and therefore entailed significant losses for all bond holders, including public social institutions/ pension schemes in Greece, which are obliged under law to maintain their capital and assets in the Bank of Greece. The assets are mingled in the 'Common Fund' and the assets are invested as the bank sees fit, including the purchase of state bonds. The Court held that although the choice to participate in the PSI Agreement rested solely with the Bank of Greece, the pension schemes, as owners, bore the financial risk and the subsequent loss. Given the extremely adverse financial circumstances, the state may invoke the clause of 'rebus sic standibus', strongly linked to the principle of 'pacta sunt servanda'. To adopt the opposite interpretation, the Court held, was to expect that a state's solvency was absolute and perennial, 'a fact disproved by reality and the aforementioned 17 February 2012 opinion of the European Central Bank'. And while many will argue that the PSI Agreement was unavoidable, it put an even greater strain on the pension schemes' budgets, which, in turn, meant a greater strain on the working population's contributions.

5. Assessment of the courts' approach to social protection reforms

The landscape of the protection of the social security rights was shaped by the aforementioned judgments of the Council of State.[126] The cases brought before the Court by private natural and legal persons (current workers, pensioners, and their

---

[125] The Court rendered many judgments concerning the PSI agreement, but those two affected public social security organisations as bond holders.

[126] Athina Petroglou, 'Providing Social Security Rights under the Constitution, according to the recent case law of the Council of State' (2016) 1(651) Social Security Law Review 82 (in Greek); Konstantinos Kremalis, 'Possible Influence of the International and Comparative Law in the Reform of the Social Security System' (2016) Social Security Law Review 37.

unions) affect the entirety of the working population in the country. Since trade unions and other forms of association have the right to file applications on behalf of their members, it can be supported that in the Greek financial crisis there has been no social group whose rights have not been litigated. These judgments portray the 'violent' wakeup call of those tasked with the managing of public finances and, legally speaking, present many similarities. The contested measures were not only fiscal (reduction of costs) but also promoted structural changes (increase of standard retirement age, unification of pension funds). The Council of State sought to establish their legality on the public interest, which 'in times of extreme financial need' aligns with the fiscal interest of the state, a fact proved by the current inadequacy of the public budget, the inability to achieve the same result with other, milder legislative acts, and the deficiency of the insured capital of the pension schemes. In every single case, the Court underlined the fact that, in these cases, the judicial review can be only borderline, due to the Constitution's separation of powers. Nevertheless, the Court set procedural and substantial boundaries for the reformative legislation of the public social security state,[127] by reinforcing the need for recent actuarial reports and studies of the possible outcomes and insisting on respecting the core of the social security rights adhering not just to the subsistence minimum but preserving, as much as possible, the pre-retirement living standard, along with the principles of proportionality and equality. More importantly, the Court upheld the public nature of the social security system, which, in turn, entails the obligation of its funding by the public budget. The wide discretionary margin of the legislator was recognised, as far as the shaping and the organisation of the system is concerned, provided that the core values of the welfare state, human dignity, solidarity, equality, and proportionality are respected. It was further ruled that the transgenerational contract is still embedded at the heart of the social security system, so the legislative choices may not sacrifice the needs of future generations to preserve the benefits of current pensioners. In this vein, the importance of the—not yet constitutionally protected—principle of equivalence was heavily emphasised by annulling provisions which burdened certain categories of workers with elevated contributions for the same benefits others enjoyed. In general, it can be argued that the Council of State abided with its core case law both in procedural and substantial matters: bound by the rules of concrete review, every case was examined within its specific frame (with the aforementioned exception of Judgments 2287–90/2015). The wide margin of legislative appreciation was respected, provided that the core rights were respected. And it was underlined that for all the reforms, the nature of the social security system must remain public.

---

[127] Antonis Manitakis, 'The Impressive Resilience of the Greek Constitution in the Current Financial Crisis in Europe' in Lina Papadopoulou, Ingolf Pernice, and Joseph Weiler (eds), *Legitimacy Issues of the European Union in the Face of Crisis* (European Constitutional Law Network Series, vol 9, Nomos 2017) 217 ff.

6. The healthcare reform before the Greek courts

As was the case with the public welfare state, the reforms of the healthcare system aimed more at the cutting of costs than at a truly structural change.[128] Certain healthcare services were provided only by doctors with a contract with the EOPYY,[129] so patients wishing to receive certain healthcare services were asked to only address doctors contracted by the EOPYY, otherwise they were expected to finance healthcare services all by themselves. The Panhellenic Medical Association argued that this imposed an illegitimate burden on the patient's freedom to choose their doctor.

The Council of State[130] stressed that the state and the public healthcare services bear the obligation to provide patients with high quality health services and fully cover their needs (including diagnosis, medication, surgery etc). Still, the legislator may impose limitations on the enjoyment of these rights, provided that they do not undermine the right to health, echoing previous case law.[131] Furthermore, it ruled that those limitations fall under the scope of article 22 paragraph 5 of the Constitution, which safeguards, inter alia, the viability of the public social security institutions by controlling the general expenditure on the healthcare services they provide. The judgment also stated that since the contested legislative act allowed the doctors the freedom to choose whether to enter into a contract with the EOPYY in order to be eligible to provide specific healthcare services, it respected their financial freedom and was thus in line with article 5 paragraph 1 of the Constitution.

In line with the shift in the social security reforms jurisprudence, jurisprudence for the healthcare reforms gradually evolved. Of course, the impact of the contested measures was more detrimental to the patients' interests in the second case; a ceiling on the monthly pharmaceutical expenditure of the healthcare divisions of the public social security institutions was imposed along with a clawback clause for pharmaceutical companies in accordance with the Second Memorandum

---

[128] Council Decision 2011/257/EU of 7 March 2011 amending Decision 2010/320/EU addressed to Greece with a view to reinforcing and deepening the fiscal surveillance and giving notice to Greece to take measures for the deficit reduction judged necessary to remedy the situation of excessive deficit [2011] OJ L110/26: 'implementation of the comprehensive reform of the healthcare system started in 2010 with the objective to keep public health expenditure at or below 6 % of GDP; measures yielding savings on pharmaceuticals of at least EUR 2 billion relative to the 2010 level, of which at least EUR 1 billion in 2011; improvement in the accounting and billing systems of hospitals, through: finalising the introduction of double-entry accrual accounting systems in all hospitals; the use of the uniform coding system and a common registry for medical supplies; [...] and ensure that at least 50 % of the volume of medicines used by public hospitals by the end of 2011 is composed of generics and off-patent medicines by making it compulsory for all public hospitals to procure pharmaceutical products by active substance'.

[129] Laws 3896/2011 and 4046/2012. This further entailed a serious cut to the doctors' fees. According to the EOPYY, the doctor is reimbursed with €5–€10 per visit.

[130] Judgment 3962/2014 (plenary session).

[131] Judgment 1187–8/2009 in plenary session, 1812/2013.

Agreement.[132] The state provided patients with the most inexpensive medicine, since doctors were forced to prescribe only the international non-proprietary name ones. Otherwise, the patients bore the additional costs all by themselves. The Panhellenic Medical Association filed an application of annulment against these legislative acts, due to concerns for not addressing the needs of patients, especially severely or chronically ill ones.

The Council of State took the opportunity to highlight the respect for human dignity and the protective scope of articles 22 paragraph 5 (principle of the welfare state, principle of solidarity) and 21 paragraph 3 of the Constitution (social right to healthcare).[133] The regulatory nature of social rights compels the state to provide at least decent—if not high quality—social services to its citizens, even if the market offers the same. Additionally, the social right to health tasks the legislator with the obligation to take all necessary precautions and measures to safeguard this right.[134] In the context of the case, this was interpreted as an obligation to provide public social services comparable to at least the standard services provided by the market, given the people's growing inability to afford them.[135] Moreover, it is noted that the state's main criterion should be the quality of the services rendered and not the reduction of the costs. The Court stressed that the state and the public pension schemes were obliged to provide the citizens with high quality health services, so that their needs for the best medical care and treatment could be fully met.

Another case concerned the distribution of certain medicines for severe illnesses exclusively through pharmacies operating within hospitals or belonging to EOPYY. The pharmacists' union contested the measure, claiming that it violated article 5 paragraph 1 of the Constitution (financial freedom), by restricting the pharmacists' financial freedom to distribute the whole range of medicines for severe illnesses. According to Judgment 2677/2016 of the Court, the balance between the financial interest of pharmacists and the public interest of reducing the medical cost was not violated. It was held that the effects of this measure, which did not impose a universal ban on private pharmacists to distribute the aforementioned medicines, were not disproportionate.

---

[132] Anastasis Poulou, 'Financial Assistance Conditionality and Human Rights Protection: What is the Role of the EU Charter of Human Rights?' (2017) 54 Common Market Law Review 993; Poulou, 'Austerity and European Social Rights: How Can Courts Protect Europe's Lost Generation?' (2014) 15 GLJ 1145, 1199.

[133] Judgment 1749/2016 in plenary session.

[134] Konstantinos Chrysogonos and Spyridon Vlachopoulos, *Individual and Social Rights* (Nomiki Vivliothiki Publications 2017) 268 (in Greek).

[135] See Hans Dubois and Robert Anderson, 'Impacts of the Crisis to Healthcare Services in the EU' <http://digitalcommons.ilr.cornell.edu/int/324> accessed 29 January 2020; Maria Zafiropoulou, 'Exclusion from Healthcare Services and the Emergence of New Stakeholders and Vulnerable Groups in Times of Economic Crisis: A Civil Society's Perspective in Greece' (2014) 12 Social Change Review 35.

In the matter of containing the pharmaceutical expenditure laid down in Memoranda I and II,[136] the Court stressed, time and again, that the legislator bears the obligation to achieve a viable balance between the financial and the social aspect of the right to healthcare; the restriction of pharmaceutical costs is monitored by strictly financial factors, but the social aspect of (public) healthcare should not be minimised. Thus far, the relevant applications of annulment have been rejected,[137] barring the case for orphanmedicinal products.[138]

IV. Conclusion

Undoubtedly, the financial crisis put great pressure on countries with high social expenditures.[139] Greece was a prime example of that, but one should keep in mind that the baby boomer generation is expected to claim their pensions between 2020 and 2030 throughout Europe. Understandably, this cannot be brushed aside as a national problem,[140] but is one that will affect all EU countries.

The social impact of the financial crisis is deeply worrying. In Greece, unemployment is currently averaging at 20.8 per cent, and at 45 per cent for young people according to Eurostat.[141] These trends should worry policymakers: doing nothing or enacting only incremental changes should not be an option. Yet despite the worrying statistics, EU political institutions have not effectively addressed these problems,[142] instead transferring the responsibility to the judiciary. Moreover, they have not assumed responsibility for not providing a swift and united response at the outbreak of the crisis, when it would have mattered the most.

In Greece, the financial crisis highlighted that the state was ill-equipped to absorb the effects of the financial crisis and thus unable to safeguard the welfare state.[143] It is an undesirable fate, both for the legislative and the judicial power, to be tasked with the equal distribution of poverty. The stipulation of the Memoranda that the state must enact alternative measures when a court rules in favour of social

---

[136] See also Xenofon Contiades and Kyriakos Souliotis, *The Policy of Medicines in Greece in the Financial Crisis* (Papazisis Publications 2017) (in Greek).

[137] Judgments 1580–1/2017, 3047–8/2017, 1784/2019.

[138] Judgment 1785/2019 in line with Regulation 141/2000 of the European Parliament and of the Council of 16 December 1999 on orphan medicinal products [2000] OJ L18/1.

[139] Ulrich Becker, 'Security from a Legal Perspective' (2015) 3 Rivista del Diritto della Sicurezza Sociale 515.

[140] Maria Petmetsidou and Ana Guillén, 'Economic Crisis and Austerity in Southern Europe: Threat or Opportunity for a Sustainable Welfare State?' (2014) 19(3) South European Society and Politics.

[141] <http://ec.europa.eu/eurostat/statistics-explained/index.php/Unemployment_statistics> accessed 29 January 2020.

[142] David Natali, Bart Vanhercke and Riley Johnson, 'The EU and the Social Legacy of the Crisis: Piecemeal Adjustment or Room for a Paradigm Shift?' in David Natali and Bart Vanhercke (eds), *Social Policy in the European Union: State of Play* (ETUI 2015) 13–14.

[143] Manos Matsaganis, 'The Welfare State and the Crisis: The Case of Greece' (December 2011) 21(5) Journal of European Social Policy 501–12.

rights is indicative. Moreover, the Memoranda stipulation that the recipient state must enact alternative measures in the case of unfavourable judicial review signals that judicial review is secondary to fiscal adjustment.

In the face of this struggle, the Council of State reiterated that under the welfare state principle social rights are preserved. All citizens must be allowed to participate in social life.[144] The shift between the first and the second wave of Memoranda-related case law aligns with the declining imminence of a state default. When the danger receded, the social rights protection came front and centre, in tandem with the obligation to serve the public interest.

Indeed, it is not the judicial power's task to finance or budget the welfare state. That falls to the legislative and executive authorities. But it is a judge's sworn duty to ensure that the constitutional rights are protected and fulfilled. The need for fiscal adjustment, without adhering to the Constitution's principles, strongly opposes European social law. The conflict between the public interest, which for a long time was identified as the state's fiscal interest, and social rights is a brutal one when there is not enough capital for funding. It is a balancing act, often on a knife-edge: no matter how considerate the balancing of opposing interests, or how adherent to social and human rights law the ruling is, the sense of justice can never be fully satisfied.

The financial crisis seems to be receding after ten years. The restoration of the welfare state and the correction of social imbalances, while respecting the doctrines of financial stability, is finally possible. Given the course of human history, another financial crisis may come to pass in future. Hopefully, the EU, founded on the ideal of peaceful coexistence and prosperity for all Europeans, will exercise its authority to guarantee the citizens' social rights and, along with them, the European Social Model.

---

[144] Bakavou (n 27) 148, 164.

7

The Financial Crisis as a Turning Point for Constitutional Rights Jurisprudence

An Assessment of the Absence of Social Rights Protection in the Irish Constitution

Elaine Dewhurst

I. Introduction

After years of unprecedented economic growth, the Celtic Tiger finally met its demise. In 2008, Ireland faced an 'economic crisis without parallel in its recent history'.[1] To address this crisis, a large programme of financial assistance was obtained from the European Union (EU) and the International Monetary Fund (IMF), and the Irish government set about the process of reforming the structure and financing of social security benefits and the healthcare system to ameliorate the effects of the crisis. The first part of this chapter analyses these crisis-related reforms and their rationales (section II), while the second part addresses the legacy of the crisis on the Irish constitutional system (section III). There is a dearth of case law in Ireland challenging the social protection and healthcare reforms imposed as a

---

[1] Letter of Intent, Ireland to the International Monetary Fund, 3 December 2010 <http://www.imf.org/external/np/loi/2010/irl/120310.pdf> accessed 1 September 2019.

Elaine Dewhurst, *The Financial Crisis as a Turning Point for Constitutional Rights Jurisprudence* In: *European Welfare State Constitutions after the Financial Crisis.* Edited by: Ulrich Becker and Anastasia Poulou, Oxford University Press (2020).
© The Contributors. DOI: 10.1093/oso/9780198851776.003.0007

response to the crisis. To assess the impact of the crisis on the Irish Constitution, analogous case law (case law which involved challenges to other crisis-related reforms unconnected to social protection or healthcare) has been utilised.[2]

Following an analysis of this case law it is contended that the economic crisis had a fourfold impact on Irish constitutional and human rights law. First, it highlighted practical obstacles in pursuing constitutional and human rights challenges to social protection reforms, such as the necessity of bringing such claims before the High Court with the associated costs and legal complexities attached to such actions. Second, the most commonly invoked rights were the right to property and the right to equality. In the case of property rights, the proportionality test stood as the greatest hurdle to applicants. The courts in these cases appeared to grant a wide margin of deference to the legislature given the unprecedented economic constraints. More particularly, the courts identified the existence of safeguards within the impugned legislation, however theoretical or impractical these safeguards may be, as being of importance in determining proportionality. The equality guarantee was also invoked, although not as frequently, but the presumption of constitutionality attaching to legislation presented an almost insurmountable burden for applicants in these cases. What was remarkable in these cases was the consistent judicial deference to the legislature and the reluctance of the courts to second-guess the rationales and the operation of such reforms given the very extraordinary nature of the economic crisis. Third, while administrative doctrines, such as legitimate expectations, were invoked, the courts were keen to point out once again that protecting the public interest, given the perilous state of the public finances, would qualify any administrative protections held. Finally, the Irish Constitution does not expressly or impliedly protect a right to social security or a right to healthcare, and it is considered here whether this lack of protection was detrimental to affected individuals during the financial crisis. Comparisons are drawn with the right to dignity which has implicit protection in the Irish Constitution as well as the rights to property and equality. It is concluded that during this particular economic crisis, public interest arguments would almost always have superseded any potential protections available to affected individuals. However, in spite of this, it is undeniable that express protection of social rights may have had other more tangible benefits outside of judicial action. Given that future economic threats, such as Brexit or the global pandemic arising from Covid 19, may involve similar impacts on social rights, it is concluded that the economic crisis should be recognised, from a constitutional perspective, as a low point for Irish constitutional rights jurisprudence. Judicial deference to the legislature has weakened the content of the rights and left affected individuals unarmed in the absence of express social rights protection against legislative incursions on their social rights. Constitutional reform and

---

[2] The case law chosen focuses on constitutional rights challenges to crisis-related reforms.

more robust judicial protection of rights in times of crisis would provide welcome relief to affected individuals.

II. The economic crisis and crisis-related reforms

1. Economic crisis in Ireland

After many years of economic prosperity, the Irish economy, in response to the global economic downturn, suffered severe dips in economic growth, the banking system was in crisis (which led to a controversial bank bailout), the international markets lacked confidence in the economy, and the government had real concerns about its fiscal sustainability.[3] On 1 December 2010, the then Minister for Finance, Mr Brian Lenihan, and the Governor of the Central Bank, Mr Patrick Honohan, applied to the EU and the IMF for an €85 billion bailout. The eurozone area contributed €40.2 billion, the UK and Sweden contributed €4.3 billion, the IMF contributed €22.8 billion, and the rest was made up of released funds mostly from the National Pensions Reserve Fund (€17.5 billion). This much-needed financial injection of funds into the struggling economy was to be granted over a three-year period (2010–2013), which would be released incrementally on the basis of Ireland meeting certain economic commitments quarterly. Set out in the Memorandum of Economic and Financial Policies and the Technical Memorandum of Understanding, there were three essential elements upon which the Irish government had to focus their concern: financial sector reforms and fiscal and structural reforms. The latter reforms were the most pertinent with respect to the impact on social rights in Ireland.

2. Structure, administration, and funding of social protection and healthcare

Distinct from other systems in Europe, both the Irish social security and healthcare systems are hybrid models involving a mix of insurance-based, means-tested, and universal arrangements[4] provided for by a variety of actors from the public, private, and voluntary sectors.[5] This has the effect of creating a rather diffuse model of social security and healthcare protection, which is administratively complex and expensive, albeit practically effective.

---

[3] For more detailed examination see Donal Donovan and Antoin Murphy, *The Fall of the Celtic Tiger: Ireland and the Euro Debt Crisis* (Oxford University Press 2013).

[4] National Economic and Social Council, *The Developmental Welfare State* (Report No 113, 2005) 35.

[5] National Economic and Social Council (n 4) 35.

a) Structure

Structurally, the social security system is centrally administered by the Department of Employment Affairs and Social Protection,[6] which provides for three types of income support: social insurance payments (contributory), social assistance payments (non-contributory), and universal payments.[7] Contributory payments are available to those individuals who have contributed a sufficient number of social insurance contributions (pay-related social insurance contributions), based on the number of weeks they have worked, earning more than a minimum amount per week. These payments require the establishment of a link between the raising of revenue through work by employees, employers,[8] and the self-employed[9] and the expenditure on social protection.[10] Voluntary contributions can also be made to increase the number of contributions under certain conditions.[11] The system allows for the making of credited contributions in the event of a contingency occurring such as the individual becoming sick or unemployed. Payments will accrue where the individual can demonstrate that they have made a sufficient number of contributions and also that they satisfy other conditions which vary depending on the payment being claimed (eg being unemployed for the purposes of Jobseeker's Benefit). Payments tend to be flat-rate payments, with additions allowed for adult or child dependants. Contributory payments in Ireland are generally referred to as 'benefits' and include a wide variety of payments including: Illness Benefit, Partial Capacity Benefit, Maternity Benefit, Health and Safety Benefit, Adoptive Benefit, Paternity Benefit, Jobseeker's Benefit, Occupational Injuries Benefit (including Injury Benefit, Disablement Benefit, and Death Benefit), Carer's Benefit, State Pension (contributory), State Pension (transition), Invalidity Benefit, Widow/ Widower and Surviving Civil Partner Pension (contributory), Guardian's Payment (contributory), Bereavement Grant, Widowed or Surviving Civil Partner Grant, and Treatment Benefit.[12]

Non-contributory payments are paid out on the occurrence of a certain contingency and where a means test is satisfied.[13] Payments tend to be flat rate, with additions allowed for adult or child dependants. Non-contributory payments in Ireland are referred to as 'allowances' and include: Jobseeker's Allowance,

---

[6] For further information see the website of the Department of Employment Affairs and Social Protection: <http://www.welfare.ie/en/Pages/Overview%20of%20the%20Department.aspx> accessed 1 September 2019.

[7] National Economic and Social Council, (n 4) 142.

[8] Social Welfare Consolidation Act 2005, s 13.

[9] ibid, s 20.

[10] See the discussion of this topic in more detail in Mary P Murphy and Fiona Dukelow (eds), *The Irish Welfare State in the Twenty-First Century: Challenges and Change* (Palgrave MacMillan 2012).

[11] Social Welfare Consolidation Act 2005, s 24 which provides that where a person ceases to be an employed contributor or a self-employed contributor, otherwise than by reason of attaining pensionable age, and the person has qualifying contributions in respect of not less than 260 contribution weeks, he or she shall be entitled to become an insured person paying contributions voluntarily.

[12] Social Welfare Consolidation Act 2005, s 39 (1) as amended.

[13] ibid, s 139 as amended.

Pre-Retirement Allowance, State Pension (non-contributory), Blind Pension, Blind Welfare Allowance, Widow/Widower and Surviving Civil Partner Pension (non-contributory), Guardian Payment (non-contributory), Widow/Widower and Surviving Civil Partner Grant, One-Parent Family Allowance, Carer's Allowance, Domiciliary Care Allowance, Supplementary Welfare Allowance, Family Income Supplement, Disability Allowance, and Farm Assist.

The contributory and non-contributory social security system is supported by a number of universal benefits which are paid out to all qualifying individuals regardless of their contribution history and regardless of their means. Once again these payments are made on a flat-rate basis and are generally referred to as 'benefits'. These payments include Child Benefit,[14] Free Travel Scheme,[15] Fuel Allowance Scheme,[16] Early Childhood Care and Education Scheme,[17] Back to School Clothing and Footwear Allowance,[18] Respite Care Grant,[19] Carer's Support Grant,[20] and Household Benefits Package.[21]

Another hybrid[22] model, the Irish healthcare system comprises a centralised, heavily regulated national health service with private health insurance operating in parallel with the system. It has been described as 'Beveridgian' in nature, involving a 'single-payer system' where 'financing and provision are handled within one organisational system, i.e. financing bodies and providers are wholly or partially within one organisation'[23] as compared to the 'Bismarckian' nature of the continental social health insurance systems.[24] Healthcare is essentially provided to all individuals on a two-tiered basis: category 1 and category 2. Persons who are in category 1 have full eligibility to free healthcare.[25] They are issued with a medical card, have free-at-point-of-use access for primary and hospital care, and have limited prescription charges. Category 1 persons include anyone over the age of seventy years with earnings less than €500 a week and anyone under the age of seventy years who is

[14] ibid, pt 4 and continued payment for a qualified child in pt 7.
[15] See Scheme details <http://www.welfare.ie/en/Pages/204_Free-Travel.aspx> accessed 1 September 2019.
[16] See Scheme details <http://www.welfare.ie/en/Pages/Fuel-Allowance.aspx> accessed 1 September 2019.
[17] See Scheme details <http://www.welfare.ie/en/Pages/Early-Childcare-and-Education-Scheme. aspx> accessed 1 September 2019.
[18] See Scheme details <http://www.welfare.ie/en/Pages/Back-to-School-Clothing-and-Footwear-Allowance.aspx> accessed 1 September 2019.
[19] Social Welfare Consolidation Act 2005, pt 5.
[20] ibid, s 225 as amended by the Social Welfare and Pensions Act 2015, s 5 and sch 2.
[21] See Scheme details <http://www.welfare.ie/en/Pages/Household-Benefits.aspx> accessed 1 September 2019.
[22] Sarah Thomson, Matthew Jowett, and Philippa Mladowsky (eds), 'Health System Responses to Financial Pressures in Ireland' (2014) 33 Observatory Studies Series (WHO and European Observatory on Health Systems and Policies) 38.
[23] Arne Bjornberg, Euro Health Consumer Index 2012 Report (Health Consumer Powerhouse May 2012) 11.
[24] Elliot Bidgood, Healthcare Systems: Ireland and Universal Health Insurance—An Emerging Model for the UK? (CIVITAS 2013) 1.
[25] Health Act 1970, s 45.

on a low income which is means-tested.[26] All other persons have limited eligibility and are entitled to category 2 healthcare.[27] This essentially provides 'limited free maternity and infant services' but individuals are 'required to pay in full for GP and other primary care services and to pay user charges for treatment in public hospitals'.[28] They must pay for primary care (unless they have a General Practitioner (GP) visit card which provides free funded GP services for anyone over the age of seventy years,[29] under the age of seventy years who meets a means test, and anyone under the age of six years[30]). They must also pay for all prescriptions (although there is a Drugs Payment Scheme which provides for ceiling charges under certain conditions). As a result, many Irish people pay for private health insurance, which gives them faster access to services and refunds on charges incurred. As of March 2020, 46.2 per cent of the Irish population have private health insurance.[31]

b) Administration

Administration of both the social security system and the health system lies with the relevant government departments (with some overlap), namely: the Department of Employment Affairs and Social Protection and the Department of Health, reflecting the centrally administered nature of these systems. With respect to the decision to grant social security payments, this decision is made by a Deciding Officer within the Department of Employment Affairs and Social Protection.[32] Appeals can be made to an Appeals Officer.[33] A slightly different scheme is run with respect to decisions regarding Supplementary Welfare Allowance. Decisions are made by Community Welfare Officers on behalf of the Health Service Executive (under the remit of the Department of Health).[34] An appeal of a decision of a Community Welfare Officer lies with the Health Service Executive Appeals Officer. Further appeal to the Social Welfare Appeals Officer is also available.[35] A statutory body called the Health Service Executive was established in 2004 to effectively run the Irish health service,[36] providing all the public health services in hospitals and communities across Ireland. The Health Service Executive is supported in its work by four Regional Health Forums made up of representatives of local government from each area. It is managed by a directorate encompassing a director general and directors of various services such as primary care or hospital care. Nine Community

[26] ibid.
[27] ibid.
[28] Thomson, Jowett, and Mladowsky (n 22) 38.
[29] Health Act 1970, s 58A as inserted by Health (Alteration of Criteria for Eligibility) Act 2013, s 7.
[30] Health Act 1970, s 58 as amended by Health (General Practitioner Service) Act 2014, s 4, 5.
[31] Health Insurance Authority, Market Figures March 2020, <https://www.hia.ie/sites/default/files/Market%20Figures%20Mar%202020.pdf> accessed 3 August 2020.
[32] Social Welfare Consolidation Act 2005, s 300.
[33] ibid, s 311(1) and s 326.
[34] ibid, s 322.
[35] ibid, s 323.
[36] Health Act 2004.

Healthcare Organisations across Ireland deliver community and primary care services on behalf of the Health Service Executive and seven Hospital Groups deliver hospital care.

c) Funding

Funding is also centralised for both the social security and health systems in Ireland. There is a centrally administered Social Insurance Fund for all contributory payments, which was set up in 1952 and is made up of employment contributions (employer and employee contributions), self-employed contributions, optional contributions, and voluntary contributions.[37] Most other social welfare payments are financed by general taxation measures.[38] The Irish healthcare system is also funded from general taxation and, more specifically, from the income-related Universal Social Charge, which is essentially a healthcare-related tax introduced in 2011 and applied on gross incomes over a certain defined amount, which varies annually.[39] Hospital services are provided by three different hospital types: (a) public hospitals provide publicly funded care (they can also provide private care but they must distinguish between public and private beds); (b) voluntary hospitals are funded partly by general taxation and partly by private bodies (eg religious institutions) and can provide both public and private care; and (c) private hospitals are exclusively privately funded and are dependent on income from private health insurance. The National Treatment Purchase Fund is a corporate body[40] which purchases beds or treatment in private hospitals for public patients who have been waiting more than a legally defined period for certain procedures.[41] This funding can also be used to purchase treatment in other EU jurisdictions. Primary care is provided for by GPs, who are reimbursed for treating public patients and may charge on a fee-per-service basis for all other patients.

3. Justifying crisis-related reforms

In the years following the crisis, significant structural and fiscal alterations were made to the social security and healthcare systems in Ireland. These modifications took four main forms: alterations to the eligibility/qualification criteria required

---

[37] Social Welfare Consolidation Act 2005, s 6(1)(a)–(d).
[38] ibid, s 139.
[39] Finance Act 2011, s 3(1)(a) which inserts Taxes Consolidation Act 1997, pt 18D.
[40] National Treatment Purchase Fund (Establishment) Order 2004, SI 179/2004.
[41] All public hospitals have the responsibility to ensure they meet the maximum waiting time guarantees for their patients. For patients requiring admission to hospital these are: maintaining an eight month maximum wait time target for adults; maintaining a twenty week maximum wait time target for paediatrics; maintaining a thirteen week maximum wait time target for GI endoscopy. The maximum waiting time target for a first out-patient appointment is twelve months.

to access protections; alterations to the model of calculation of protections; abolition of protections; and cuts to the financial rate of protection available. There were a number of justificatory rationales proffered with respect to these changes including adherence to the bailout agreements, the importance of restoring confidence in the Irish economy, the necessity to bring about economic stability for the common good, the need to ensure stability for older people, the requirement to reduce unemployment, and the need to reduce public sector spending more generally. These justifications were referred to in Budget speeches annually during the crisis, in the Dáil and Seanad debates leading up to the passage of relevant emergency legislation, and in the preambles to the legislation introduced to make the necessary alterations.[42]

Certainly, many of the structural changes to social security payments can be directly attributed to the conditions of the financial assistance agreements. The EU/IMF Memorandum of Understanding set out a number of specific quarterly targets which required structural and rate changes to many social security protections as outlined in the table below.

Quarter	Target	Response
1	*A reduction of existing Public Service Pensions on a progressive basis averaging over 4% will be introduced.*	A reduction of existing Public Service Pensions on a progressive basis averaging over 4% was introduced.
1	*The government will reform the unemployment benefit system in such a way as to provide incentives for an early exit from unemployment.*	The government reduced the amount and length of payment of both Job Seeker's Benefit and Allowance to meet this target (as well as other measures).
2	*The authorities undertake to introduce legislation to increase the State Pension age.*	The pension age was increased to 66 years in 2014, 67 in 2021, and 68 in 2028. However, the most recent Government are currently placing these changes on hold pending a pensions review.

[42] For a more political examination of the reforms see Rod Hick, 'Enter the Troika: The Politics of Social Security during Ireland's Bailout' (2018) 47 (1) Journal of Social Policy 1.

Quarter	Target	Response
3	*Pension entitlements for new entrants to the public service will be reformed with effect from 2011. This will include a review of accelerated retirement for certain categories of public servants and an indexation of pensions to consumer prices. Pensions will be based on career average earnings.*	A career average earnings model was introduced and severe reductions in Public Service Pensions were introduced.
12	*The nominal value of the State Pension should not rise over the period of the programme*	There was no rise in State Pension over this period.

Other structural changes and rate cuts, while not expressly mentioned in the conditions of the bailout agreement, can also be attributed by implication to the financial assistance programme which required current expenditure reductions to be implemented. The size of the budget deficit was a clear rationale for social security spending reductions. In 2011, the Minister for Finance in his budget speech indicated that 'further reductions in social welfare spending are unavoidable if we are to reduce the budget deficit'.[43] Tied to this need for economic stability was the admission that reductions would depend entirely upon the 'rate of decline in unemployment; the effectiveness of anti-fraud and control measures; and the reform of the benefits system',[44] all of which were linked to the conditions set by the bailout agreements. It is worth noting that the preambles to both the 2010 and the 2013 Financial Emergency Measures in the Public Interest Acts expressly stated that the measures introduced in the legislation were 'necessary ... as part of a range of measures provided for in those [financial assistance] programmes to address the economic crisis in the State and to restore domestic and international confidence and to prevent a sovereign debt crisis affecting the State'.[45]

Maintaining confidence in the Irish economy appeared to be equally decisive in introducing various measures. In 2010 (prior to the application for financial assistance), the Budget Speech indicated the importance attached to international confidence. It was announced with a sense of relief that the 'measures we

---

[43] Minister for Finance, 'Budget Speech 2011' (Dublin, December 2010) <http://www.budget.gov.ie/Budgets/2011/2011.aspx> accessed 1 September 2019.

[44] ibid.

[45] Financial Emergency Measures in the Public Interest Act 2010, Preamble. See also the Financial Emergency Measures in the Public Interest Act 2013, Preamble.

have taken have been commended by international bodies such as the European Central Bank, the European Commission, the IMF and the OECD. They have also won the approval of the international markets'. Indeed the measures imposed in the Financial Emergency Measures in the Public Interest Acts 2009, 2010, and 2015 were all explicitly stated to be connected to a need 'to demonstrate to the international financial markets that public expenditure is being significantly controlled'[46] and to ensure 'ongoing access to international funding and improve competitiveness'.[47] Clearly, securing the economic stability and the economic future of the state was central to the reform agenda.[48] Even prior to the application for financial assistance, the Minister for Finance indicated that the 2010 Budget was not captured by any sectional interest. The focus of the reforms was essentially 'the common good'.[49] Admitting that the reforms introduced (particularly to public sector workers) were drastic, the Minister for Finance indicated that the Irish government was 'determined to meet the immediate fiscal problems Ireland faces and, at the same time, to make far-reaching reforms for the future'.[50] Indeed the 2009 and 2010 Financial Emergency Measures in the Public Interest Acts also identified the 'serious disturbance in the economy' as a threat to the 'well-being of the community'.[51] This need for financial stability to protect the well-being of Irish residents during this economic emergency appeared to remain a key, and possibly an even greater, concern even after the financial assistance programme had been agreed. During this time, the Minister for Finance acknowledged that Ireland was in a 'traumatic and worrying time', and that there were legitimate concerns with seeking 'external support to help us with our economic and financial difficulties' and the 'impact of this momentous and difficult decision'. Indeed in 2011, the Minister for Finance indicated that the 'number one priority for 2011 and onwards must be economic growth and maximising employment creation'[52] with a view to returning Ireland to economic stability and ensuring the well-being of the state.

An analysis of old-age, social assistance, family, unemployment, and healthcare protections identifies the structural and fiscal reforms introduced in pursuance of these aims, and identifies additional subsidiary aims where they exist.

---

[46] Financial Emergency Measures in the Public Interest Act 2009, Preamble.

[47] Financial Emergency Measures in the Public Interest Act 2010, Preamble. See also the Financial Emergency Measures in the Public Interest Act 2015, Preamble.

[48] Minister for Finance, 'Budget Speech 2010' <http://www.budget.gov.ie/Budgets/2010/FinancialStatement.aspx> accessed 1 September 2019.

[49] ibid.

[50] ibid.

[51] Financial Emergency Measures in the Public Interest Act 2009, Preamble. See also the Financial Emergency Measures in the Public Interest Act 2010, Preamble.

[52] Minister for Finance, 'Budget Speech 2011' (n 43).

a) Old-age benefits

Structural changes to social security protections for older persons were extensive throughout the economic crisis. Such changes were preferred to more obvious rate cuts which would have been politically unpalatable. The changes were introduced incrementally, on a transitional basis and in a manner which meant that the impact of the changes was, to a limited extent, hidden. A number of strategies were employed to structurally reduce the social security spend.

Alterations to eligibility/qualification criteria to access protections were introduced to many old-age benefits. Perhaps the most significant qualification amendment, in terms of the widespread impact of the measure, introduced during this period was the alteration of the definition of 'pensionable age' with the effect of increasing the pension age to sixty-six years in 2014, to sixty-seven years from 1 January 2021, and to sixty-eight years from 1 January 2028.[53] The increase in the pension age can be attributed directly to the reforms proposed in the government's National Pension Framework 2011[54] as set out in the EU/IMF Programme of Financial Support for Ireland. It was expressly stated that the reforms were necessary as a result of demographic changes in Ireland, most specifically that people were living longer and healthier lives.[55] Interestingly, the most recently elected government have decided to put the impending pension age increases on hold pending a pensions review. In addition to the alteration of the state pension age there were changes to the contribution conditions for access to a State Pension (contributory) or a State Pension (transition) that meant that many individuals previously entitled to a certain rate of pension either became ineligible to claim a State Pension (contributory) or a State Pension (transition) or remained eligible but at a much reduced rate. Originally, any person who had a yearly average of at least forty-eight contributions over his or her working life qualified for a State Pension (contributory) at the maximum rate. If a person had less than forty-eight contributions on average a year, the State Pension (contributory) was paid at a reduced rate. Prior to 2012, there were four reduced rates of State Pension (contributory) related to the person's yearly average contributions (contribution bands): five to nine contributions, ten to fourteen contributions, fifteen to nineteen contributions, and twenty to forty-seven contributions. In the case of State Pension (transition) there was one reduced rate of pension that applied where a claimant had a yearly average of between twenty-four and forty-seven contributions. In 2012, alternations to these contribution bands effectively meant that anyone who had less than ten contributions a year on average was no longer eligible to a State Pension (contributory). The remaining contribution bands were altered to include five bands (ten–fourteen,

---

[53] Social Welfare Consolidation Act 2005, s 2 as amended by Social Welfare and Pensions Act 2011, s 7.

[54] Irish Government, *National Pension Framework*, (Government Publications 2011), 23.

[55] Ibid.

fifteen–nineteen, twenty–twenty-nine, thirty–thirty-nine, and forty–forty-seven). These subtle movements in the bands meant that a person who had been achieving a higher-rate pension now received a reduced-rate pension. The State Pension (transition) (abolished in 2014) was also affected in the same way, introducing more bands in the reduced-rate categories (twenty-four–twenty-nine, thirty–thirty-nine, and forty–forty-seven).[56] Similar alterations to qualifying criteria were employed with respect to Widow/Widower and Surviving Civil Partner (contributory) Pensions, where the number of qualifying contributions required for receipt of the pension was almost doubled from 156 contribution weeks[57] to 260 contribution weeks,[58] with significant impacts on entitled individuals.

Complete structural overhaul as to method of calculation of an old-age payment only occurred in the case of Public Sector Pensions. The Public Service Pensions (Single Scheme and Other Provisions) Act 2012 introduced a career average earnings model of pension calculation, which provides that the value of pensions attributable to new entrants to the civil/public service will be calculated in accordance with their average career earnings and not their salary at the date of retirement (which was originally the case). This was a very significant change in the calculation of pension entitlements and had a potential freezing effect on public sector recruitment. In addition, public sector workers had to pay a 'pension levy', which was essentially an increased tax on their salary to pay for Public Sector Pensions (although this money was not ring-fenced for that purpose).

Abolition of old-age benefits was for the most part avoided except with respect to the State Pension (transition) in 2014[59] and the Bereavement Grant. In terms of actual rate cuts to the old-age benefits, these were limited mainly to non-contributory and universal payments. For example, the State Pension (contributory and transition) remained stable between 2008 and 2015 and since 2016 has seen yearly increases. The Widow/Widower and Surviving Civil Partner Pension (contributory) and Invalidity Pension did see a drop in 2010 and in 2011 but this has been steadily rising again since 2016, although it is not yet at the same level as it was before the crisis. The one exception to this relative rate stability with respect to contributory payments was Public Sector Pensions which were perhaps the most drastically affected. Beginning in 2010, the Financial Emergency Measures in the Public Interest Act 2009 reduced the annualised amount of a Public Sector Pension, in some cases by up to 12 per cent.[60] In 2013, further cuts were introduced[61] by section 5 of the Financial Emergency Measures in the Public Interest Act 2013, in some cases up

---

[56] Social Welfare (Consolidated Claims, Payments and Control) (Amendment) (No 8) (Reduced Rates) Regulations 2012, SI 321/2012.
[57] Social Welfare Consolidation Act 2005, s 125(1)(a).
[58] ibid, s 125(1) as amended by Social Welfare Act 2011, s 6.
[59] ibid, s 114(9) as inserted by Social Welfare and Pensions Act 2011, s 6.
[60] Financial Emergency Measures in the Public Interest Act 2009, s 2. Up to €12,000, exempt; €12,000–€24,000, a 6 per cent cut; €24,000–€60,000, a 9 per cent cut; over €60,000, a 12 per cent cut.
[61] Financial Emergency Measures in the Public Interest Act 2013, s 5.

to 28 per cent.[62] For those becoming pensioners after 29 February 2012, reductions up to 8 per cent were introduced.[63] As of 1 January 2018, the reduction in the annualised amount of Public Service Pension could be up to 28 per cent in certain cases.[64] Non-contributory and universal payments also saw drastic rate cuts. There were cuts made to the Widow/Widower and Surviving Civil Partner (non-contributory) Pension during the height of the crisis (2010–2011). The household benefits package (which is available to all persons over the age of seventy years regardless of their means and to all persons below the age of seventy years if they satisfy a means test) was severely affected: certain aspects of the package were abolished (eg the Telephone Allowance was discontinued in 2014) and cuts were made to the level of the allowances given (eg Fuel Allowance). The Free Television Allowance, the Living Alone Allowance, the Free Travel Scheme, and the Over-80 Increase for all social welfare payments remained unaffected.

Stability for older persons 'in recognition of the contribution they have made to the State'[65] was a central tenet of the reform agenda with respect to old-age benefits. Even at the height of the crisis, it was confirmed that the State Pension would remain unchanged given the 'security this has brought to older people'.[66] However, such altruism was not extended to Public Service pensioners who experienced drastic cuts and structural changes in the way the pension was paid. The Minister for Finance in 2011 admitted that '[r]educing the income of pensioners is an exceptional measure. But these are exceptional times. The Government has to make savings and pensions costs are a very significant part of public expenditure. Failure to reduce the cost of pension provision could undermine the longer-term viability of the public service pension system.'[67] The Financial Emergency Measures in the Public Interest Act 2009 referred explicitly to the equity in ensuring that the public sector shared the burden of the financial constraints the state found itself in. With respect to Public Sector Pensions, the 2009 Act expressly stated that the value of 'the public service pensions is significantly and markedly more favourable than those generally available in other employment' making amendments not only necessary but ostensibly 'fair'.[68] Similar sentiments were expressed in the Financial Emergency Measures in the Public Interest Act 2010.

b) Social assistance

Social assistance payments in Ireland include Supplementary Welfare Allowance, Disability Allowance, Invalidity and Blind Pensions, and Farm Assist. These are all

---

[62] Rates of 8 per cent, 12 per cent, 17 per cent, and 28 per cent cuts.
[63] Rates of 2 per cent, 3 per cent, 5 per cent, and 8 per cent cuts.
[64] Financial Emergency Measures in the Public Interest Act 2015, s 2.
[65] Minister for Finance, 'Budget Speech 2010' (n 48).
[66] Minister for Finance, 'Budget Speech 2011' (n 43).
[67] ibid.
[68] Financial Emergency Measures in the Public Interest Act 2009, Preamble.

non-contributory flat-rate payments that are means-tested. There were no major structural reforms of these payments during the crisis but there were significant rate cuts which impacted on the levels of payments individuals received. In terms of Supplementary Welfare Allowance, drastic reductions were seen in 2009 and 2010 and the rates have not yet recovered to pre-2009 levels. Similar patterns have been repeated with respect to Farm Assist payments. Younger adults were particularly affected as reductions were made to Supplementary Welfare Allowance in 2009 with respect to reducing the level of payment to new claimants under twenty years of age.

c) Family allowances

There are a number of contributory, non-contributory, and universal family allowances in Ireland. As regards structural changes, the modification of eligibility criteria was the most commonly chosen method of reform in pursuance of reducing public expenditure. Three examples are illustrative. First, in an effort to restrict access to the contributory Health and Safety Benefit, earnings limits were increased (excluding certain people from the benefit in 2009) and minimum contribution records were introduced (ie an individual had to demonstrate that they had paid a minimum of thirteen social insurance contributions in the relevant tax year). Second, there was also a twofold increase in the total number of contributions needed to be eligible for the Health and Safety Benefit payment (52 to 104 contributions). Third, non-contributory allowances also fell victim to eligibility alterations. While originally the One-Parent Family Allowance was payable to an individual who had a child under the age of fourteen years, this was amended to restrict the payment to those individuals who had a child under twelve years in 2012 (excluding previously entitled new claimants from the payment). It has been further reduced to seven years on a phased basis.[69] In addition, in 2009 the age at which a child qualified for the universal Child Benefit was reduced to under the age of eighteen years.[70] Higher rates for a third and subsequent child were phased out from 2012. A compensatory measure was put in place to assist certain low-income families affected by this change but this ended on 31 December 2010.

Abolition or phased abolition of certain payments was also introduced. Early Childcare Supplement was introduced in 2006 to assist families with the cost of childcare.[71] The Early Childcare Supplement was originally halved in May 2009, and its application restricted to those under five and a half years (as opposed to six

---

[69] Social Welfare Consolidation Act 2005, s 172(1) as amended by Social Welfare and Pensions Act 2011, s 9(2) as amended by Social Welfare and Pensions Act 2012, s 4(1)(A) which reduces entitlement to those with children under twelve years from 2012, ten years from 2013, and seven years from 2014.

[70] Social Welfare (Miscellaneous Provisions) Act 2008, s 20.

[71] Social Welfare Consolidation Act 2005, pt 4A as inserted by Social Welfare Law Reform and Pensions Act 2006, s 28.

years). This was followed by complete abolition in 2010.[72] It has been very recently replaced to a limited extent by a free pre-school year of Early Childhood Care and Education Scheme for all children between the ages of three years and five years.

Rate cuts were also introduced alongside these structural reforms. Reductions were seen in 2010 and 2011. In 2014, these benefits took a further, rather drastic cut, reducing them to pre-2008 levels. While the benefits have been increasing since 2017, they are still below or only marginally exceeding pre-2008 levels.

While many of the measures introduced were clearly linked to the financial assistance agreements, other alternations to social security and medical benefits were more tenuously linked. It would be more correct to assume that these alterations arose from a political desire to reduce public expenditure which had existed prior to the agreements. For example, alterations to Child Benefit payments were justified not by reference to economic stability or public interest but on the grounds that the current regime was unfair. Due to the fact that Child Benefit was a flat-rate payment, it had long been argued that it should be means-tested or taxable so that those who needed more received more. However, it appears that this would have been politically, potentially legally, and certainly logistically difficult. For this reason, the payment at the lower and higher rates was reduced but welfare-dependent families and low-income families were compensated by an increase elsewhere.[73] The economic crisis provided further encouragement and necessity to speed through these types of changes. As Burke noted, the economic crisis was 'used as a lever to introduce change that ha[d] been long planned but very slow to take effect'.[74]

d) Unemployment benefits

Once again, both structural changes and rate cuts were commonplace throughout the crisis in all forms of unemployment payments, including Jobseeker's Benefit and Jobseeker's Allowance. There was a perceived need to encourage those who were unemployed (and particularly those who were young and unemployed) to 'stay close to the labour market' ie discourage reliance on welfare and encourage people back into the labour market.[75] Drawing on the 'bitter experience' of the recession in Ireland during the 1980s, the Minister for Finance indicated in 2010 that reductions in Jobseeker's Allowance and Supplementary Welfare Allowance for young people was targeted at ensuring that the welfare system would not be 'out of step with labour costs in the rest of the economy' and 'trap people in protracted joblessness'.[76] A cohesive part of this policy was also removing disincentives by

---

[72] Social Welfare (Miscellaneous Provisions) Act 2010, s 24.

[73] Increases in qualified Child Allowance and Family Income Supplement.

[74] Sara Burke, 'Boom to Bust: Its Impact on Irish Health Policy and Health Services' (2010) 2 (1) Irish Journal of Public Policy.

[75] Minister for Finance, 'Budget Speech 2010' (n 48).

[76] ibid.

removing poverty traps and ensuring that those who were unemployed would not be discouraged from returning to work.

The most common model of structural rearrangement in contributory unemployment payments was the alteration of eligibility so as to restrict access to the payment. This can be identified with respect to Jobseeker's Benefit. In 2009, new requirements were introduced which provided that if a new claimant (or a person who had been in receipt of the payment for less than six months) had more than 260 contributions, they would have access to the payment but only for a period of twelve months, as opposed to fifteen months previously. Those with less than 260 contributions were only entitled to the benefit for a period of nine months. These time periods were further reduced in 2013 and now a new claimant can only receive the benefit for a period of nine months and six months respectively depending on their contribution record. In order to qualify for Jobseeker's Benefit in the first instance, the number of social insurance contributions was also increased from 52 to 104 contributions. In order to claim the benefit, a claimant now has to have a minimum of thirteen paid social insurance contributions in the relevant tax year.

Non-contributory payments (Jobseeker's Allowance) were not structurally altered during this period, although they were subject to significant rate cuts. Beginning in 2010, both the contributory Jobseeker's Benefit and the non-contributory Jobseeker's Allowance were severely cut. They faced further cuts in 2011 but remained stable until 2017. While some increases have been introduced in 2017, this has not restored the payments to pre-crisis levels. Younger individuals were more acutely affected as further rate cuts were introduced in 2014 for those claiming Jobseeker's Allowance who were under the age of twenty-five years.

e) Healthcare
Naturally, like other forms of social security, healthcare also faced structural and rate changes during the recession.

One of the most important aspects of the healthcare system in Ireland is access to a medical card. Since the 1970s anyone over the age of seventy years, and anyone who met a certain means-tested income level, was entitled to a free medical card. In the early stages of the crisis, these medical cards and the eligibility requirements generally remained untouched. However, in late 2009, income limits were introduced for those aged over seventy years, which essentially meant that if a person had an income of over a certain limit they were no longer entitled to a medical card.[77] This was a drastic change to medical provision which had been a staple old-age benefit since the 1970s and, to ameliorate any hardship, a discretionary scheme was introduced that allowed those who were over the income limit to apply for a medical card on a discretionary basis. These weekly income limits were again

---

[77] Health Act 1970, s 45 as amended by Health Act 2008, s 3 and s 4.

reduced further in 2013[78] and 2014. Where an individual would have been entitled to a medical card under the old limits, a GP visit card (a limited form of medical card) was made available, once again to reduce the hardship caused by the reduction in income limits. This coincided with the introduction of free GP care to children under the age of six years and those over the age of seventy years, which was finally initiated in 2016. Medical cards are provided free to all children (regardless of age) who are in receipt of a Domiciliary Care Allowance in 2017.[79]

Prescription charges also underwent significant alterations during the crisis. The Drugs Payment Scheme (which limits the amount a family or an individual have to pay monthly on prescription drugs) saw year-on-year increases in the limit payable by individuals and families. In addition, in 2010 a charge (€0.50 per prescription) was introduced for individuals on medical cards and those on long-term illness cards subject to a monthly limit per family (€10). Over the course of the crisis, this charge increased incrementally from the original €0.50 to €2 in 2018 with a ceiling limit of €25 (€20 if over seventy years).

f) Overall assessment

At the outset of the financial crisis in Ireland, there was a distinct decision made by the Irish government that a reduction of public expenditure (in addition to revenue raising initiatives) was to be first line of action in ameliorating the effect of the financial crisis. The finance raised through such reductions was earmarked to recoup the budget deficits and to meet the terms of the financial assistance programme.[80] These public expenditure reductions were brought about in four main ways: alterations to the eligibility/qualification criteria required to access protections; alterations to the model of calculation of protections; abolition of protections; and cuts to the financial rate of protection available. The cumulative effect of the public expenditure reforms, whether these involved tightening conditions with respect to eligibility[81] or structurally altering pension provisions,[82] was to directly impact on the everyday lives of Irish residents.

Due to the worsening financial situation in Ireland (heightened by increased unemployment) there was an increased demand for social protection but there were also reduced resources available. Reductions in public services had a significant and direct impact on individuals. The Irish report to the European Anti-Poverty Network in 2009 indicated that 'there ha[d] been a reduction in the level of services

[78] ibid, s 45A as amended by Health (Alteration of Criteria for Eligibility) Act 2013, s 1(3) and s 3(a).
[79] ibid, s 45 as amended by Health (Amendment) Act 2017, s 2.
[80] Council of the European Union, *Second Joint Assessment by the Social Protection Committee and the European Commission of the social impact of the economic crisis and of policy responses – Full Report* (2009) Brussels (16169/09 ADD 1 SOC 715 ECOFIN 808) 69.
[81] Council of the European Union, *Update of the Joint Assessment by the Social Protection Committee and the European Commission of the social impact of the economic crisis and of policy responses – Full Report* (2010) Brussels (16905/10 SOC 793 ECOFIN 786) 10.
[82] ibid 14.

to all groups' including 'care supports for older people and people with disabilities'. In addition, 'Rural Transport Programmes' and general health services, particularly those with an outreach function, were being curtailed 'with proposals to stop them completely'.[83] Such cuts to public services, compounded by the other effects of the crisis, such as unemployment, over-indebtedness, and homelessness, were to have serious consequences. For example, provisional data with respect to Ireland in 2009 indicated a 'sharp and clear increase in suicides between 2008 and 2009 (24%). The level of suicide is the highest level ever recorded in the country'.[84] The effect of public expenditure reduction fell hardest on certain groups of individuals particularly those who were either unemployed or on low incomes, such as lone parents. Young people were also disproportionately affected. There was a focus on 'activation policies', which were designed to tighten the group of individuals entitled to certain benefits in an effort to force them back into the labour market, even though the labour market was severely constrained at the time.[85] Overall, the assessment of the European Anti-Poverty Network with respect to the social protection reforms introduced in 2008–2009 cannot be disputed: 'social protection schemes ensuring minimum income and specific support for the most vulnerable' were 'insufficient to cushion the impact of the crisis'.[86]

As to the longer-term effects, the report of the National Economic and Social Council[87] in 2013 is instructive. Alongside issues such as unemployment and income reduction, they highlight the social protection impacts of the crisis. They indicate that pensioners have been less affected than other groups as a result of the strategic decision to maintain the State Pension. However, they recognise some stark patterns of economic vulnerability arising from the crisis: '7 per cent of the population can be classified as "poor and vulnerable" (people who are long-term unemployed, people who are ill and disabled, and lone parents); 7 per cent as "poor but not vulnerable" (many older people and some of the self-employed); and 11 per cent as "non-poor but vulnerable" (people with debts whose outgoings exceed their current income). The "non-poor but vulnerable" is a new "at risk" group that has emerged with the economic crisis.'[88] In addition, the numbers of those in poverty has increased since the onset of the economic crisis. While the National Economic and Social Council describe the annual budgets as 'broadly progressive' they did note that 'reductions in social welfare payments and increases in indirect taxes, such as VAT, impact those on low incomes most'.[89]

---

[83] European Anti-Poverty Network, *Social Cohesion at Stake: The Social Impact of the Crisis and of the Recovery Package* (Brussels 2009) 14.
[84] Council of the European Union, *Update of the Joint Assessment* (n 81) 15.
[85] European Anti-Poverty Network (n 83) 17.
[86] ibid.
[87] National Economic and Social Council, *The Social Dimensions of the Crisis: The Evidence and its Implications Executive Summary* (Dublin, 2013).
[88] ibid, vi.
[89] ibid, vi.

III. Crisis and the Constitution

The crisis-related reforms raised some interesting issues in constitutional law in Ireland. Firstly, it uncovered some institutional and procedural barriers within the constitutional structure to accessing justice in Ireland. It would be pertinent to clarify at this juncture that the crisis had no impact on the constitutionally pre-scribed legislative process. While emergency legislation was passed, the normal procedures were firmly adhered to and therefore the crisis did not interfere with the democratic legislative process. However, the fact that there were no reported cases directly challenging any of the social protection or healthcare reforms is evi-dence of both the incremental encroachment of social protection reductions and the practical obstacles to pursuing constitutional challenges in Ireland. Secondly, when analogous cases are examined (those which challenged other types of crisis-related reforms), other constitutional impacts come to light. Many of these cases challenge reforms by invoking civil and political rights such as property rights and the right to equality. These cases were unsuccessful as a result of the application of the proportionality test where the state was given a wide margin of deference with respect to the implementation of measures in the public interest at a time of crisis. More particularly, it reveals that as long as theoretical safeguards are in place to protect individuals from state action, the state has a wide discretion as to the types of measures it may impose in pursuance of its aims. In addition, the case law re-flects long-established difficulties with respect to shifting the burden of proof in equality law cases. Thirdly, and in addition, the case law reflects that administrative protections are also weak in the face of economic crisis. Finally, the dearth of cases challenging the crisis-related social protection reforms does raise the question as to whether the lack of social rights protection in the Irish Constitution effectively leaves applicants unprotected or whether existing protections could fill this gap. The chapter concludes that even if such rights had a justiciable basis in the Irish Constitution, the deference which the courts gave to the state in a time of crisis may render these rights merely illusory. However, that does not mean that their inclusion in the Constitution would not be welcome. On the contrary, their ex-press inclusion would have, at the very least, a constraining effect on parliament in enacting legislation that potentially infringes constitutional rights, and would provide individuals with a platform upon which to consider challenging reforms of this nature in the future.

1. Institutional and procedural conditions

The crisis highlighted rather starkly certain institutional and procedural obstacles to pursuing constitutional and human rights claims in Ireland. The impact of these obstacles is evidenced by the fact that there were no cases directly challenging any of the many social protection and healthcare reforms introduced during the crisis. Analogous case law, which pursued actions against other crisis-related reforms, such as the pension levy or student grant eligibility, indicate that that these cases present huge obstacles to applicants with respect to legal standing, legal representation, and cost. The first major hurdle is presented by the Constitution itself which provides that any judicial review of legislation requires that the claim must be made before the High Court in Ireland.[90] While applicants may represent themselves, such a challenge would be legally complex and would generally require legal representation. This would have serious cost implications for most applicants. The Constitution does provide legal standing to 'some other person for whom he is deemed by the court to be entitled to speak',[91] such as a representative organisation. This has been the conduit through which some of the cases challenging the imposition of the pension levy in Ireland have been conducted with representative organisations or trade unions stepping in to represent individuals affected by the reforms. Considering that litigants who are reliant on social security or healthcare benefits tend to have lower socio-economic means, it is no surprise that the number of cases challenging the crisis-related social protection reforms have been limited.

2. Constitutional rights impact

The legal basis of most challenges taken to reforms introduced during the crisis tended to centre on more traditional civil and political rights such as the right to equality, property rights, or certain personal rights.[92]

What is striking is that in all the analogous cases studied, where the right to property was invoked, the determination of the proportionality test inevitably leads to negative outcomes for applicants. The state was almost always granted a wide margin of deference with respect to measures taken in the interests of the common good. This is not unusual if one examines previous case law on the right to property but the financial crisis gave the courts the opportunity to solidify the principle. The right to property is protected by article 40.3.2 of the Irish Constitution which states that the 'State shall, in particular, by its laws protect as best it may from unjust attack, and in the case of injustice done, vindicate the ... property rights of every citizen'. This is supplemented by article 43 which ensures the protection of private property. The case law rarely focused on whether property rights were affected or whether there had been infringements, but rather whether the interferences

---

[90] Arts 15 and 34.3.1 Irish Constitution.

[91] *Cahill v Sutton* [1980] IR 269.

[92] For further assessment of this question see Aoife Nolan, 'Welfare Rights in Crisis in the Eurozone: Ireland' (2014) 1 European Journal of Social Law 37.

identified could be justified and were proportionate in the circumstances. Prior to the crisis the courts had dealt with many cases involving challenges to taxation measures.[93] In these cases the courts were generally slow to intervene and would only find disproportionate action where the measures in question were 'capricious in operation.'[94] It was therefore not unexpected that during the economic crisis the courts would take an equally deferential approach.

The courts have found that the imposition of many crisis-related reforms (eg the pension levy,[95] the acquisition of loans by the National Asset Management Agency (NAMA),[96] the reduction of rates payable under pharmacy contracts[97]) were legitimate and proportionate mainly because of the existence of inbuilt safeguards to protect against unwarranted interference. With respect to the acquisition of loans by the NAMA,[98] the court identified certain safeguards in the legislation, including the need for the relevant bank to opt into the scheme and the fact that the NAMA had to determine not only the eligibility of the loan for inclusion but also the necessity of including it. Similar sentiments were raised with respect to the potential attack on property rights arising in the case of *Haire*.[99] A company who had contracted with the state to provide pharmacy services at certain rates saw those rates significantly reduced by legislation. The court showed some sympathy for the applicants but once again indicated that the state was acting in 'the light of the unusual economic crisis' 'whereby the State is forced to introduce drastic economies and cuts across the board. These economic realities must inform the interpretation of the constitutional phrases in assessing what the State can do and what distributive measures it must take to ensure not only the stability of the economy, but the stability of the State itself. It is also relevant to mention in this context that whatever the State's duty is in relation to property rights under the Constitution, these have always to be balanced against "other constitutional duties" that the State may have to uphold.' With this in mind, it was accepted by the court that the legislative provisions challenged were exceptional but were 'measured, proportionate and carefully drawn ... with a number of significant safeguards inbuilt'. Once again the court appeared to firmly reiterate the importance of safeguards, including, in this case, the inclusion of provisions in the legislation with respect to consultation processes, the provision of a list of matters to be considered in implementing rate reductions, the fact that any regulations introduced under the legislation have to be laid before

---

[93] *Brennan v Attorney General* [1985] ILRM 355; *Madigan v Attorney General* [1986] ILRM 136.

[94] Elaine Dewhurst, Noelle Higgins, and Los Watkins, *Principles of Irish Human Rights Law* (Clarus Press 2013) 244.

[95] *Garda Representative Association (GRA) v Minister for Finance* [2010] IEHC 78; *Unite the Union and Paul Gallagher v Minister for Finance* [2010] IEHC 354.

[96] *Dellway Investments Limited and Others v National Asset Management Agency* [2011] 4 JIC 1202.

[97] *J & J Haire & Company Ltd and Others v Minister for Health and Children and Others* [2009] IEHC 562.

[98] *Dellway* (n 96).

[99] (n 97).

both Houses of the Oireachtas and are subject to annulment by resolution by either House, and the fact that the Minister for Health and Children must annually review the operation, effectiveness, and impact of the amounts and rates fixed by the regulations and is obliged to consider the appropriateness of the amounts and rates having regard to any change of circumstances and, in particular, any alteration of relevant matters. In addition, the Minister for Finance has an obligation to annually review the regulations and a health professional is also entitled to terminate his/her contractual obligations by giving thirty days' notice. While in this case it was argued that these safeguards were merely 'theoretical' with little or no practical value, the court held that there was no real evidence to support this contention and reiterated the fact that without such safeguards the legislation would be open to strong criticism from an objective standpoint. This statement indicates two very distinct points: (a) that inbuilt safeguards within legislation provide some immunity from challenge in such cases and (b) that whether these safeguards are practically effective is not especially important to a finding of proportionality unless there is some strong evidence to indicate the impracticality of the safeguards.

Another striking impact of the case law arising during the crisis has been the fact that it has highlighted the almost insurmountable hurdle presented by the burden of proof in cases where the right to equality has been invoked. Article 40.1 of the Irish Constitution provides that '[a]ll citizens shall, as human persons, be held equal before the law. This shall not mean that the State shall not in its enactments have due regard to differences of capacity, physical and moral, and of social function.' However, due to the fact that all legislation enjoys the presumption of constitutionality, the applicant has the burden of proving that the particular measure falls foul of the equality guarantee. There may be cases where the burden may shift but in constitutional jurisprudence this has been reserved for cases involving discrimination on the basis of some essential attribute of the human personality, such as race or sex. The majority of cases challenging crisis-related reforms do not fall within this category and have left applicants with extraordinarily high burdens to overcome. In the case of *Haire*,[100] which challenged reductions in rates payable under pharmacy contracts, the applicants argued that the cuts introduced affected their income by at least 24 per cent (as opposed to the 8 per cent cut on other health professionals) and that this evidence of disparate treatment was sufficient to discharge the burden of proof in the case. However, the court was not convinced and stated that in order to form a conclusion as to whether the applicants had been subject to arbitrary or unequal treatment, more information on the nature of these other health professional contracts and the state objectives with respect to these contracts would be required. A mere contrasting of figures would not be sufficient to discharge the burden of proof. The court will require 'comparative evidence' that will allow them to fully assess whether unequal treatment has occurred. Similarly

---

[100] ibid.

in the case of *Unite*,[101] the court held that the burden was on the applicant to establish that the members of its union were victims of unequal treatment in having to pay the pension levy when compared with other public servants who are exempt from that requirement for various reasons. The court indicated that discharging this burden of proof would require 'expert evidence on the manner in which pensions are paid across the public service and evidence of how pension schemes operate in the commercial semi-state sector in comparison'. As no such evidence was advanced, the applicant failed to establish unequal treatment.

The impact of these decisions effectively means that utilising the equality guarantee will be ineffectual unless clear and unequivocal comparative evidence of unequal treatment can be proffered. Discharging the presumption of constitutionality will only occur where such evidence can be clearly provided. This is a substantial hurdle for applicants and weakens significantly the usefulness of the protection.

3. Administrative protections

While administrative arguments, such as legitimate expectation or unreasonableness of decision-making, were raised in some cases, these were almost universally overridden by the public interest in protecting the state from economic disaster, which was particular to the financial crisis.

In the case of *GRA*,[102] the Garda Representative Association argued that the failure of the Minister for Finance to exercise his discretion and exempt certain groups of public sector workers (namely Gardaí in the *GRA* case) from the pension levy was unreasonable. The court held that the discretion granted to the Minister by the relevant legislation was considered to be both 'policy-based and fiscal' and 'places policy and financial responsibility on the respondent in the exercise of this discretion'. It was felt by the court that it was difficult to argue that the Minister had acted improperly in failing to exempt the applicants under the discretionary procedure and the Minister had to be just and equitable in the exercise of that discretion. The Minster essentially had an unfettered discretion in this respect and it was not unreasonable for the Minister to decide that the Gardaí should not be excluded. The judge noted that ultimately the challenge in 'alleviating the nation's problems lies with those who are elected to Dáil and Seanad Éireann and who, in turn, have chosen the Government'. He specifically noted that the court 'cannot, and does not, have any view in the executive or political sphere'. However, he did caution this deference to the state was not absolute and stated that if the 'imposition of any austerity measure' involved a 'legal error' then this clearly 'may be subject to the possibility of judicial review'.

---

[101] (n 95).
[102] (n 95).

The doctrine of legitimate expectations has also been raised by applicants with respect to challenging certain crisis-related reforms but it has in equal measure been tempered with respect to the public interest in ensuring the fiscal sustainability of the state. In the case of *McCarthy v Minister for Education and Skills*,[103] the applicants were students who ordinarily qualified for student support grants. These grants are payable to students in full-time third-level education and the rate paid varies depending on a number of factors, including the distance between the student's ordinary residence and the third-level institution. The Minister altered the distance criteria and also removed a provision that automatically entitled mature students to a higher rate of grant. The applicants submitted that they had a legitimate expectation that the higher rate would continue throughout their studies (having embarked on their studies before the alterations were made) and that they relied on this expectation to their detriment. The court held that the applicants must establish three criteria: (a) the public authority must have made a representation; (b) the representation must be addressed or conveyed either directly or indirectly to an identifiable person or group of persons; and (c) it must be such as to create an expectation reasonably entertained and it would be unjust to permit the public authority to resile from it.[104] The court held that no representation could be said to have been made to the applicants by their own admissions. While the court accepted that the students were an identifiable group, whether the applicants could have expected the regular practice to continue, the court was less convinced. In particular, the court indicated that the applicants 'must have been aware of the worsening economic situation' and that student grants had been subject to reductions in previous years. These changes had been signalled in the 2010 Budget and therefore the court held it was not reasonable for the applicants to expect this practice to continue. However, even if the applicants had a legitimate expectation, the court held that an 'expectation legitimately held may be qualified by considerations of the public interest'. This had previously been the heart of the decision in *Curran*[105] where a decision to withdraw an early retirement scheme was challenged on the grounds of legitimate expectations. The court in that case referred to the bleak state of the public finances and the worsening economic circumstances as factors that could qualify a claim for legitimate expectations. In the *McCarthy* case, there was clear evidence of the 'perilous state of the public finances at the time this decision was taken'. The court referred to the fact that the state was in an 'unprecedented economic emergency' with national debt standing at €119 billion, an 'unsustainable gap' between the 'State's income and its expenditure', and a 'challenging economic background'. With this in mind, the court held that the 'obvious requirement for reduction in public expenditure' illustrated a 'clear public policy basis' for the actions of the Minister.

---

[103] [2012] IEHC 200.
[104] *Glencar Exploration plc v Mayo County Council (No. 2)* [2002] 1 IR 84.
[105] *Curran v Minister for Education* [2009] 4 IR 300.

4. Social protection and healthcare rights

It is well established that while certain economic and social rights are protected by the Irish Constitution (eg right to earn a livelihood and right to education), the right to social protection and healthcare are not expressly or impliedly protected.[106] Article 45 of the Irish Constitution provides for certain 'Directive Principles of Social Policy' which provide general guidance for the legislature but are not justiciable. These guidelines include safeguarding the economic interests of the weaker sections of the community and contributing where necessary to the support of the 'infirm, the widow, the orphan and the aged'.[107] At the Ninth Plenary Meeting of the Constitutional Convention,[108] the strengthening of the economic, social, and cultural rights provisions of the Constitution was discussed. In principle, a sizeable majority of the Convention (85 per cent) were in favour of strengthening the protection of economic, social, and cultural rights in the Constitution. Further, the Convention recommended that a provision should be inserted into the Constitution to the effect that the state shall progressively realise economic, social, and cultural rights, subject to maximum available resources and that this duty is cognisable by the courts. In addition, a large majority also voted to enumerate the right to social security (78 per cent) and essential healthcare (87 per cent) in the Constitution, indicating a preference for express protection of these rights. Four separate attempts have been made to amend the Constitution to include an express reference to economic, social, and cultural rights but these have been defeated on three occasions.[109] There has not been until recently the political appetite to engage with this topic. The most recent attemptproposed amending article 45 of the Constitution by inserting a provision that would commit the state to progressive realisation, subject to its maximum available resources and without discrimination, of the rights contained in the International Covenant on Economic, Social, and Cultural Rights.[110] This duty would be cognisable by the courts. The Bill has now lapsed with the recent dissolution of Parliament and it is unclear whether another Bill of a similar nature will be brought again. .

The real question, perhaps, is whether the inclusion of such protections would have had any impact during the crisis in terms of altering the trajectory of the

[106] For more information on this point see Nolan, 'Ireland: The Separation of Powers Doctrine vs Human Rights' in Malcolm Langford (ed), *Social Rights Jurisprudence: Emerging Trends in Comparative and International Law* (CUP 2008) 295.

[107] Art 45.4.1 Irish Constitution.

[108] The Convention on the Constitution, *Eighth Report of the Convention on the Constitution: Economic, Social and Cultural Rights* (2014) <http://escr-irl.org/wp-content/uploads/2016/01/CC_ESC_Report. pdf> accessed 1 September 2019.

[109] Thirty-First Amendment of the Constitution (Economic, Social and Cultural Rights) Bill 2012; Thirty-Fourth Amendment of the Constitution (Economic, Social and Cultural Rights) Bill 2014; Thirty-Fifth Amendment of the Constitution (Economic, Social and Cultural Rights) Bill 2016; Thirty-Seventh Amendment of the Constitution (Economic, Social and Cultural Rights) Bill 2018.

[110] Thirty-Seventh Amendment of the Constitution (Economic, Social and Cultural Rights) Bill 2018.

reforms, or whether it would have led to more applicants directly challenging the crisis-related reforms. More importantly, would the inclusion of such provisions in the Constitution have changed the outcome of decisions in the courts? It is this author's opinion that, given the current framing of the potential constitutional amendment which would provide for progressive realisation and the judicial reluctance to intervene in legislative action during the crisis, it is likely that the express protection of social protection and healthcare rights would not have led to different outcomes during the crisis. An analogy can be drawn with the right to dignity. The Constitution protects a justiciable right to dignity[111] in article 40.3, with actions of both a positive and negative nature capable of constituting an interference that must be justified and proportionate. However, even this very important right can be restricted in the interests of the common good and the rights and freedoms of others, and it is entirely possible that this reference to the common good could be justified by reference to the economic crisis.

However, this is not to say that the protection of a right to social security or healthcare would not be useful. On the contrary, the protection of such rights has the effect of increasing cognisance and understanding of the importance of such rights both within the legislature and in the general public. Indeed, Nolan has commented that the crisis has 'raised the profile' of social rights language and concepts in Ireland.[112] It assures accountability of government action and would highlight shortcomings in government policy. It would provide a more direct avenue of redress for individuals affected by legislative action or inaction. The value of public awareness and understanding should also not be underestimated. While the presence of express protection of rights to social security and healthcare may be trumped by the common good, not having protection of these rights at all has led to a situation whereby legislative reform in these areas is practically unchallengeable.

IV.   Conclusion

The financial crisis was a huge shock to the Irish state and the centralised and flat-rate nature of the social security and healthcare systems were exposed as being particularly vulnerable to the severity of the austerity measures. The crisis-related reforms introduced both rate cuts and structural changes to social security and healthcare systems. These structural changes included changing eligibility conditions, models of calculation of payments, and in some cases required abolition of certain payments. While certain reforms can be expressly linked to the financial assistance programme conditions, others were more implicitly linked

---

[111] , 'The Right to Human Dignity in the Irish Constitution' in Paolo Becci and Klaus Mathis (eds) *Handbook of Human Dignity in Europe* (Springer 2018) 431.
[112] Nolan, 'Welfare Rights in Crisis' (n 92) 48.

through their contribution to reducing the budget deficit. Other reforms had been considered for many years prior to the financial crisis but the crisis gave the legislature the impetus to proceed with the reform. The legislature rarely referred explicitly to the conditions of bailout in justifying the introduction of reforms but rather preferred to defend the measures by reference to the need to restore confidence in the economy, to secure economic stability for the common good, to ensure stability for older persons, to reduce unemployment, and to reduce public sector spending.

There were no cases taken which challenged any of the social security or healthcare reforms in Ireland. There were some cases which challenged the imposition of other crisis-related reforms so it is possible to draw some conclusions by analogy as to how these cases may have proceeded and been resolved. The case law points to four conclusions as to the impact of the crisis on the Irish Constitution. First, there are significant practical obstacles to taking constitutional and human rights challenges in Ireland, which are even more profound in social protection and healthcare cases. Second, there was a clear judicial reluctance to interfere with the legislative intentions in most cases. The courts referred to the clear public interest in easing the state's finances and this legitimised the actions of the legislature. Provided that there were theoretical safeguards in place, the courts appeared to accept that the actions of the legislature were proportionate in the circumstances. Third, administrative protections were also trumped by public interest in times of crisis and therefore their effectiveness in such situations is limited. Finally, the lack of express enumeration of a right to social protection and essential healthcare would most likely not have altered the mind-set of the courts during this crisis and there would have been an equal judicial reluctance to intervene given the severity of the crisis.

However, express social rights protection, as envisaged by the Constitutional Convention, may have had other, more tangible benefits such as acting as a tool to hold the government to account, ensuring greater transparency of decision-making, increasing the public knowledge around the content of their rights, and providing more obvious grounds for challenge under the Constitution. Given future potential threats to social protection and healthcare rights, for example from Brexit or the global pandemic caused by Covid 19, it is concluded that we are now at a turning point in Irish constitutional jurisprudence whereby existing constitutional protections have proved ineffective and where express rights to social protection and healthcare ought to be included in the Constitution to ensure that individuals are not unarmed against legislative incursions on their social rights, particularly during times of crisis.

8

Legal Changes and Constitutional Adjudication in Portuguese Social Law in Consequence of the European Financial Crisis

José Carlos Vieira de Andrade, João Carlos Loureiro, and Suzana Tavares da Silva

I. Introduction

Crisis law in Portugal, which sought to respond to the European financial crisis that erupted in 2008, focused mostly on the legal scheme of social security, including the regime of various non-contributory benefits.

José Carlos Vieira de Andrade, João Carlos Loureiro, and Suzana Tavares da Silva, *Legal Changes and Constitutional Adjudication in Portuguese Social Law in Consequence of the European Financial Crisis* In: *European Welfare State Constitutions after the Financial Crisis*. Edited by: Ulrich Becker and Anastasia Poulou, Oxford University Press (2020).
© The Contributors. DOI: 10.1093/oso/9780198851776.003.0008

Portugal was simultaneously affected by an economic, financial, and budgetary crisis, and this fact should be taken into account when interpreting and critically analysing the measures adopted. The fiscal crisis was particularly severe, which explains why counter-cyclical and social support measures could not be taken to mitigate the effects of the economic crisis. So, as has been expressly established in the agreement on the programme formally adopted,[1] measures to curb budget expenditures were to be implemented and these measures had to include cuts on social expenses in wages, pensions, and other benefits of an 'assistentialist' nature.

Legislative amendments carried out on social security schemes mostly sought to respond to the following issues: (1) guarantee the sustainability of the system in the framework of the social security reform; (2) ensure equality in the implementation of fiscal tightening measures, particularly with regard to civil service pensions as historically they involved more benefits and were higher; (3) promote distributive justice.

At the end of 2015, an age of reversion began, with the rise to power of the Socialist Party (*Partido Socialista*), supported by the Communist Party (*Partido Comunista*) and Left Bloc (*Bloco de Esquerda*). One of the main points of the political platform was to repeal some of the social protection-related changes[2] in fields such as social aid (eg, Social Insertion Income—*Rendimento Social de Inserção*; Solidarity Supplement for the Elderly—*Complemento Solidário para Idosos*) implemented during the Troika (European Commission, European Central Bank, International Monetary Fund) intervention.

In this chapter, we will first describe the Portuguese national social security system and the reforms implemented on it during the crisis; then we will focus on the human rights affected by these reforms and analyse the Portuguese Constitutional Court (CC) case law. In our critical assessment of the constitutional jurisprudence we shall follow a time criterion instead of a material or substantive

---

[1] The programme embraced two instruments: the International Monetary Fund (IMF) Memorandum and the European Institution Memorandum of Understanding (MoU). On the different approaches of the two documents, see José M Magone, 'Portugal as the "Good Pupil of the European Union". Living under the Regime of the Troika' in José M Magone (ed), *Core-Periphery Relations in the European Union: Power and Conflict in a Dualist Political Economy* (Routledge 2016) 182. For the text of documents, see *Portugal: Memorandum of Understanding on Specific Economic Policy Conditionality*, 3 May 2011 <http://www.jn.pt/infos/pdf/Memorando_troika.pdf> accessed 31 July 2019 and, for IMF, *Portugal: Letter of Intent, Memorandum of Economic and Financial Policies, and Technical Memorandum of Understanding*, 17 May 2011 <http://www.imf.org/external/np/loi/2011/prt/051711.pdf> accessed 31 July 2019. On their juridical nature, see Eduardo Correia Baptista, 'A natureza jurídica dos Memorandos com o FMI e com a União Europeia' (2011) 71 Revista da Ordem dos Advogados 477; Francisco Pereira Coutinho, 'A natureza jurídica dos memorandos da *Troika*', *Themis. Revista da Faculdade de Direito da UNL*, 13 (2013/24–25) 147; see also Francisco Pereira Coutinho, 'Austerity on the Loose in Portugal: European Judicial Restraint in Times of Crisis' (2016) 8(3) Perspectives on Federalism 105, 116–17 <https://ssrn.com/abstract=2933261> accessed 15 August 2019; Giovanni Vagli, 'Portogallo – Profili costituzionalistici dell'accordo tra Portogallo e FMI/EU' (2017/4) 8 Diritto Pubblico Comparato ed Europeo <http://www.dpceonline.it/index.php/dpceonline/article/view/312> accessed 15 August 2019.

[2] For an overview, see Law No 113/2017 of 29 December 2017 (Grandes Opções do Plano) para 2018.

one—on the one hand, because there were few issues for discussion (social security benefits, pensions, and labour conditions) and, on the other hand, because the Court used its own decisions as some 'functional precedents'. We will finish our assessment by pointing out the main theoretical achievements from this period, mainly for the Portuguese constitutional doctrine on the judicial protection of social rights and legitimate expectations principle.

II. Reforms in national social security systems

1. Overview of the social security and healthcare system in Portugal

The Portuguese constitutional framework for social security and healthcare systems gives us a first idea of its main features. The Carnation Revolution, on 25 April 1974, ended a dictatorship and started what Samuel Huntington called the 'third wave of democratization'.[3] Until then, social security and healthcare mostly followed a Bismarckian model.[4] Especially in its last years, the corporative regime presented itself as a social state (*Estado Social*), extending coverage to the rural population, ending a pensions cap, and reducing the insurance period required for entitlement to an old-age pension. Access to healthcare was obtained either through affiliation with an institution (*Caixas de Previdência*), or social assistance (coverage for the poor).

After the Revolution, the approval of a new Constitution (CRP—*Constituição da República Portuguesa*) in 1976 changed the system. First, following the British model, article 64 laid down a National Health Service (*Serviço Nacional de Saúde*) as the principal mode of implementing the right to health protection. Universality and gratuity were some of the constitutional features of this public service.[5] This separation between social security and healthcare protection is a paradigmatic revolution in Portuguese history. The fundamental law has other norms expressly relevant to social security: beyond the human dignity principle,[6] a right to social security must be mentioned,[7] as well as other norms concerning the protection

---

[3] Samuel Huntington, *The Third Wave: Democratization in the Late Twentieth Century* (University of Oklahoma Press 1991).

[4] For an overview, see Ilídio das Neves, *Direito da Segurança Social* (Coimbra Editora 1996) 188–204.

[5] Art 64(2) CRP [now Art 64(2)(a) CRP].

[6] Art 1 CRP.

[7] Art 63 CRP:
1. Everyone has the right to social security.
2. The state is charged with organising, coordinating and subsidising a unified and decentralised social security system, with the participation of the trade unions, other organisations that represent workers and associations that represent the other beneficiaries.
3. The social security system shall protect citizens in illness and old age and when they are disabled, widowed or orphaned, as well as when they are unemployed or in any other situation that entails a lack of or reduction in means of subsistence or the ability to work.

of particular groups (such as children and young people, and disabled or elderly persons[8]) or budgetary requirements (the obligation of a social security budget[9]).

Different from other countries (eg, France or Germany), where there has been a general codification of social security law, Portugal is still waiting for a similar process (there is only partial codification regarding contributions).[10] However, there is a Framework Law on Social Security (*Lei de Bases da Segurança Social*) that maps the field.[11] Following its systematisation, there are three major fields of social security: (1) Social Insurance System (*Previdência*); (2) Citizenship Social Protection System (*Sistema de Proteção Social da Cidadania*); (3) Complementary or Supplementary System (*Sistema Complementar*). The first and the third are contribution-based;[12] the Citizenship Social Protection System is tax-funded.

Besides, a public service civil servant's social protection system (CGA—*Caixa Geral de Aposentações*)[13] and a few special schemes[14] exist, such as the System for Lawyers and Solicitors (CPAS—*Caixa de Previdência dos Advogados e Solicitadores*).[15]

a) Social security

Previdência is the part of the system based on social insurance, being a pay-as-you-go system.[16] Despite the existence of voluntary social insurance (*seguro social voluntário*),[17] the Social Insurance System is mainly mandatory for both employed and self-employed persons. In the case of dependent workers, employers pay the most significant amount of the contribution.[18] It is a cash-based response to losses

---

4. All periods of work shall, as laid down by law, contribute to the calculation of old age and disability pensions, regardless of the sector of activity in which they were performed.
5. With a view to the pursuit of the social solidarity objectives that are particularly enshrined in this Article and in Articles 67(2)(b), 69, 70(1)(e), 71 and 72, the state shall, as laid down by law, support and inspect the activities and modus operandi of private charitable institutions and other not-for-profit institutions that are recognised to be in the public interest

English version available at <https://dre.pt/part-i> accessed 14 October 2019.

[8] Arts 69 (Childhood), 70 (Youth), 71 (Disabled Persons), and 72 (Elderly) CRP.

[9] Art 105(1)(b) CRP.

[10] Law No 110/2009 of 16 September 2009 (*Código dos Regimes Contributivos do Sistema Previdencial da Segurança Social*, hereafter CRCSPSS), as amended, most recently by Law No 71/2018 of 31 December 2018.

[11] Now Law No 4/2007 of 16 January 2007, as amended by Law No 83-A/2013 of 30 December 2013.

[12] Although the Social Insurance System (*Previdência*) mainly relies on contributions, there is the possibility of state budget transfers, 'when the financial situation of the social security system justifies it': see Decree-Law No 367/2007 of 2 November 2007 (last amendment: Law No 55-A/2010 of 31 December 2010), art 14(3).

[13] For more information, including the relevant norms, see <https://www.cga.pt> accessed 14 October 2019.

[14] Law No 4/2007 (n 11), art 103.

[15] Decree-Law No 119/2015 of 29 June 2015, last amendement:Decree-Law No 116/2018 of 21 December 2018. For more information, see <http://www.cpas.org.pt> accessed 14 October 2019.

[16] On the financing of Social Security, see Law No 4/2007 (n 11), arts 85–93; Decree-Law No 367/2007 (n 12).

[17] Law No 4/2007 (n 11), arts 51(2) and 53; CRCSPSS (n 10), arts 169–84.

[18] Usually, 23.75 per cent (employers) and 11 per cent (employees): see art 53 CRCSPSS (n 10).

of revenues and/or an increase in costs, playing a replacement function. The system is mostly comprehensive, providing against the usual contingencies (sickness, invalidity, old age, parenthood, death, occupational diseases, and unemployment).[19] Private mandatory insurance still covers work accidents (*Acidentes de trabalho*).[20]

In contrast with other countries, the Complementary System is not mandatory.[21] There is a publicly funded scheme,[22] with little impact, as well as collective (mainly professional) schemes and individual complementary mechanisms of protection (eg, pension saving plans, life insurance, mutualistic solutions).

The Citizenship Social Protection System is an essential part of the Portuguese Social Security System. Its primary purposes are, according to article 26 (1) of the Framework Law on Social Security, 'to guarantee the basic rights of citizens and the equality of opportunities, as well as to promote social welfare and social cohesion'. As laid out, it embraces three subsystems: the Social Action Subsystem;[23] the Solidarity Subsystem;[24] the Family Protection Subsystem.[25]

The Solidarity Subsystem has a vital role in the sphere of social aid or assistance, also integrating several schemes based on low or residual contributions (eg, old systems of protection related to agricultural activities).[26] One central benefit is the Social Insertion Income,[27] which replaced the seminal Guaranteed Minimal Income (*Rendimento Mínimo Garantido*). In a framework of activation, as a rule, it requires (with some exceptions[28]) the subscription of a social insertion contract (*contrato social de inserção*).[29]

---

[19] For an overview, see, in English, Portuguese Public Finance Council, *Social Protection Systems: Notebook No 2/2014* (Lisbon, October 2014) <http://www.cfp.pt> accessed 31 July 2019; explaining the main features of benefits, see European Commission, *Your Social Security Rights in Portugal* (European Commission 2018).

[20] Labour Code (*Código do Trabalho*), art 284; Law No 98/2009 of 4 September 2009, art 79.

[21] Law No 4/2007 (n 11), arts 81–86.

[22] See Decree-Law No 26/2008 of 22 February 2008 (as amended by Law No 82/2018 of 16 October 2018).

[23] Law No 4/2007 (n 11), arts 29–35

[24] ibid, arts 36–43.

[25] ibid, arts 44–49.

[26] ibid, art 39.

[27] Law No 13/2003 of 21 May 2003, as amended by Law No 45/2005 of 29 August 2005, Decree-Law No 70/2010 of 16 June 2010, Decree-Law No 133/2012 of 27 June 2012, Decree-Law No 1/2016 of 1 January 2016, Decree-Law No 90/2017 of 28 July 2017, and Decree-Law No 126-A/2017 of 6 October 2017. See, on the benefit, Departamento de Prestações e Contribuições, *Guia Prático Rendimento Social de Inserção* (Instituto de Segurança Social 2019). On the impact of the constitutional jurisprudence, see José Carlos Vieira de Andrade, 'O "Direito ao Mínimo de Existência Condigna" como Direito Fundamental a Prestações Estaduais Positivas—Uma Decisão Singular do Tribunal Constitucional: Anotação ao Acórdão do Tribunal Constitucional n.º 509/02' (2004) 1 Jurisprudência Constitucional 21; Pedro Fernández Sánchez, 'Breve Nota sobre uma Inovação na Jurisprudência Constitucional Portuguesa: entre o Fortalecimento da Tutela dos Direitos, Liberdades e Garantias com Recurso ao Princípio da Igualdade e o Reconhecimento da Garantia de um Mínimo Existencial' (2015) 56 Lisbon Law Review/Revista da Faculdade de Direito da Universidade de Lisboa 93.

[28] Law No 13/2003 (n 27), art 6-A (exemption of the entitlement conditions): for instance, in cases of persons temporarily unable to work or the support carers (those 'providing an indispensable support to members of their family household').

[29] ibid, arts 3, 6(1)(f), 6-A(7), 17/13, 18, 18-A, 21-A, 21-C(1)(b), 22-A, 25(1), 29, 30, and 31.

The Social Action Subsystem, in addition to complementary mechanisms relevant in the social aid domain (covering risks not protected by the Solidarity Subsystem), plays a vital role in the field of care, ensuring personalised social benefits. In the Portuguese case, some of the relevant players here are non-profit entities that are part of the civil society (mainly *Instituições Particulares de Solidariedade Social*[30]), providing services primarily for the most vulnerable persons (eg, children, young people, older people, disabled persons). Their core task is to provide access to social facilities (eg, home or residential care).

Finally, in contrast with the latter (Social Action Subsystem), the Family Protection Subsystem centres on cash benefits related to family burdens or expenses (*encargos familiares*), disability expenses (*encargos no domínio da deficiência*), and dependency expenses (*encargos no domínio da dependência*).[31]

b) Civil servant's social protection system: convergent social protection scheme

The civil servant's social protection system has organisational autonomy and includes specific schemes. First, one should point out that there has been a significant revolution: since 1 January 2006,[32] newly hired civil servants have been covered by the general system (Social Security). That is to say, the civil servants' scheme and its specific institution (CGA) are transitory, even if 'transitory' may mean a duration of some decades if no additional reform is undertaken, and the idea is to promote convergence between the Social Security and CGA schemes.[33]

Established in 1929,[34] the system mainly covers old-age pensions, survivor's pensions, and invalidity pensions. Usually, benefits such as old-age pensions were better than the general coverage of Social Security. In 1993, there was a fundamental reform: for public servants hired since 1 September, the applicable material scheme (not the institution, which remains CGA) would be the regime of Social Security.[35]

c) Healthcare system

An overview of the Portuguese healthcare system shows the centrality of the National Health Service (*Serviço Nacional de Saúde*). The Portuguese Constitution underlines this relevance, confirmed by the Framework Health Act (*Lei de Bases*

---

[30] Decree-Law No 119/83 of 25 February 1983, substantially amended by Decree-Law No 172-A/2014 of 14 November 2014 (last amendment: Law No 76/2015 of 28 July 2015). On this point, see Licínio Lopes Martins, *As Instituições Particulares de Solidariedade Social* (Almedina 2009); Licínio Lopes Martins, 'Breves Nótulas sobre o "Novo Estatuto" das Instituições Particulares de Solidariedade Social no Direito Nacional e no Direito da União Europeia' (2014–2015) 37 Cooperativismo e Economia Social 139.

[31] Law No 4/2007 (n 11), art 46.

[32] Law No 60/2005 of 29 December 2005, art 2.

[33] Law No 4/2007 (n 11), art 104; Law No 4/2009 of 29 January 2009.

[34] Decree No 16:667 of 27 March 1929.

[35] Decree-Law No 286/93 of 20 August 1993.

da Saúde),[36] stressing that a National Health Service based on universality shall enforce the right to health protection and, 'with particular regard to the economic and social conditions of the citizens who use it, shall tend to be free of charge'.[37] Taxes finance the National Health Service almost in its entirety. There are also user charges (*taxas moderadoras*), but they have a very secondary role in funding the system.[38]

Furthermore, ADSE (*Assistência na Doença dos Servidores do Estado*),[39] a health subsystem for the public service founded in 1963,[40] permits, among other things, access for its beneficiaries to medical assistance outside the National Health Service.

2. Structural reforms and cuts introduced after the crisis

a) Old-age benefits
aa) Old-age benefits: a brief introduction
Old-age benefits embrace a set of social benefits, in particular old-age pensions. To start with, for old-age coverage, one must distinguish between social insurance and social assistance benefits. The former is usually dependent on a minimum contribution period of fifteen years[41] (shortened in the case of voluntary social insurance[42]), which is a clear break with the minimalist framework that dominated the system some decades ago.[43]

The Solidarity Subsystem is still essential for old-age social protection. Those who have not fulfilled the legal prerequisites of Social Insurance Pension (*Previdência*) can apply for Social Old-Age Pensions (*Pensões Sociais de Velhice*),[44] a non-contributory benefit based on need and dependent on a means test (*condição de recursos*). Besides, for those who contributed under the *Previdência* schemes, minimum amounts of pensions are guaranteed based on the length of

---

[36] Law No 95/2019 of 4 September 2019.

[37] Art 64(2)(a) CRP.

[38] See II.2.e.bb.1.

[39] See, for more information, <https://www2.adse.pt> accessed 14 October 2019. There are other public health subsystems for the police (SAD—*Serviços de assistência na doença da GNR e da PSP*) and the Army (ADM—*Assistência na doença aos militares das Forças Armadas*).

[40] Decree-Law No 45002 of 27 April 1963 (now see Decree-Law No 7/2017 of 9 January 2017).

[41] Decree-Law No 187/2007 of 10 May 2007 (last amended: Decree-Law No 79/2019 of 14 June 2019), art 19.

[42] To 144 months (Decree-Law No 40/1989 of 1 February 1989, art 47(1)(b)).

[43] In some periods sixty months (Regulation/Decreto-Regulamentar No 25/77 of 4 May 1977) or even three years (Decree-Law No 486/73 of 27 September) were enough for persons to be entitled to an old-age pension.

[44] See Centro Nacional de Pensões, *Guia prático Pensão social de velhice* (Instituto de Segurança Social, IP 2019).

contributions paid.[45] Taxes finance the difference between the amount collected under the rules of social insurance and the guaranteed minimums. This benefit, called Social Complement (*Complemento Social*),[46] is not dependent on a means test,[47] which is under criticism.[48] The retirement age (pensionable age) is sixty-six years and five months (2019),[49] following automatic mechanisms of adjustment.

Another significant old-age benefit is the Solidarity Supplement for the Elderly,[50] aiming to ensure a minimum level of revenues to aged persons. It is a means-tested benefit, based on a subsidiary intervention of the state: only if it is impossible to ensure the component of family solidarity is there room for this benefit. Beneficiaries of Solidarity Supplement for the Elderly also have access to other advantages, such as social benefits related to health and energy.[51]

A Long-Term Care Supplement (*Complemento por Dependência*)[52] exists, with two different degrees of dependence, but it is part of the Family Protection Subsystem.[53]

---

[45] In 2019 the picture is as follows: contribution period of under fifteen years, €273.39; of fifteen to twenty years, €286.78; of twenty-one to thirty years, €316.45; of thirty-one years or more, €395.57: see Regulation (*Portaria*) No 25/2019 of 17 January 2019, art 4.

[46] Decree-Law No 187/2007 (n 41), art 46.

[47] ibid, art 47.

[48] Ilídio das Neves, *Lei de Bases da Segurança Social Comentada e Anotada* (Coimbra Editora 2004) 126; Ulrich Becker, 'Leistungen für langjährig Rentenversicherte in Südeuropa—eine rechtsvergleichende Analyse' (2012) 1 Zeitschrift für ausländisches und internationales Arbeits- und Sozialrecht 1, 14; Fernando Ribeiro Mendes, 'Prefácio' in Miguel Coelho, *Segurança Social: Situação Actual e Perspectivas de Reforma* (Diário de Bordo 2013) 15, 21–22.

[49] Regulation (*Portaria*) No 23/2018 of 18 January 2018 (for 2020, there will be no changes: Regulation No 50/2019 of 8 February 2019). There are some exceptions for some professions, such as miners or embroiderers from Madeira. For a European insight, with comparative references, see *Retirement Regimes for Workers in Arduous or Hazardous Jobs in Europe: A Study of National Policies* (European Commission 2016).

[50] Decree-Law No 232/2005 of 29 December 2005 (as amended by Decree-Law No 236/2006 of 11 December 2006, Decree-Law No 151/2009 of 30 June 2009, Decree-Law No 167-E/2013 of 31 December 2013, Law No 7-A/2016 of 30 March 2016, Decree-Law No 126-A/2017 of 6 October 2017, Law No 71/ 2018 of 31 December 2018); Regulation (Decreto Regulamentar) No 3/2006 of 6 February 2006 (as amended by Regulation (Decreto Regulamentar) No 14/2007 of 20 March 2007, Regulation (Decreto Regulamentar) No 17/2008 of 26 August 2008, Decree-Law No 151/2009 of 30 June 2009, and Decree-Law No 126-A/2017 of 6 October 2017). See Centro Nacional de Pensões (n 44); Paula Távora Vítor, 'Solidariedade Social e Solidariedade Familiar: Considerações sobre o Novo "Complemento Solidário para Idosos"' in José Manuel Moreira, Carlos Jalali, and André Azevedo Alves (eds), *Estado, Sociedade Civil e Administração Pública: para um Novo Paradigma do Serviço Público* (Almedina 2008); João Paulo Remédio Marques, 'Em Torno do Estatuto da Pessoa Idosa no Direito Português: Obrigação de Alimentos e Segurança Social' (2007) 83 Boletim da Faculdade de Direito 183–217, esp 204–06, 210–11, 213–16; João Paulo Remédio Marques, *Algumas Notas sobre Alimentos (Devidos a Menores) "Versus" o Dever de Assistência dos Pais para com os Filhos (em Especial Filhos Menores)* (2nd edn, Coimbra 2007), 254–58.

[51] See II.2.b.

[52] Decree-Law No 265/99 of 14 July 1999, as amended by Decree-Law No 309-A/2000 of 30 November 2000, Decree-Law No 13/2013 of 25 January 2013, Law No 6/2016 of 17 March 2016, and Decree-Law No 126-A/2017 of 6 October 2017.

[53] Although for the amount of the benefits it is relevant whether one is, or is not, a recipient of the general scheme of social insurance. Therefore, those receive less who are covered by the special scheme for agriculture activities, a non-contributive scheme, or equivalent.

Social protection for old persons also includes access to facilities as part of the benefit in kind, including home care (*apoio domiciliário*), daycare centres (*centros de dia*), and different types of residential care.[54]

bb) Reform and cuts during the intervention

Taking into account the growing burden of pension expenditures, the attempt to limit the costs in this crucial field of social security does not come as a surprise. Government and parliament approved two groups of measures: one affecting future pensions and another aiming at pensions already in payment.

(1) Changing the legal framework for future pensioners A sensitive question concerning old-age pensions is the age of access to a pension that changed on the basis of an automatic system. Actually, the normal pension age was raised in connection with longer life expectancy at 65.[55] This rule concerning the age applies to both contributory and non-contributory pensions.[56] Furthermore, the reference year for the factor of sustainability has changed:[57] it was fixed to be 2000 instead of 2006, and this had a substantial impact on the pension amount.

Furthermore, in 2012, the anticipation of old-age pensions (early retirement based on the flexibilisation of the age to access the benefit) was suspended for the majority of workers[58] (those from Social Security, with the exception of the long-term unemployed[59]), and it was only public servants under the special scheme (CGA) for whom early retirement was still a possibility. This difference of treatment was justified based on the purpose of reducing the number of persons working for the state. For 2015, a transitional regime was put into force,[60] offering the option of early retirement for recipients of sixty years of age and older with a contribution history of at least forty years (with reductions laid down for anticipation of retirement[61]).

(2) Pensions in payment Pensions in payment were a hot topic of the reforms during the Troika intervention. The legislator suspended the mechanisms for

---

[54] For further information, see João Carlos Loureiro, 'Cidadania, Proteção Social e Pobreza Humana' (2014/I) 90 Boletim da Faculdade de Direito 71, 122–23.

[55] Decree-Law No 167-E/2013.

[56] ibid, art 2.

[57] ibid.

[58] Decree-Law No 85-A/2012 of 5 April 2012.

[59] ibid, art 1(3).

[60] Decree-Law No 8/2015 of 14 January 2015, art 4. After the elections the new government transitorily adopted the restrictive regime in force in 2015, by stressing the need to reform the old-age pension legal framework and avoid a negative impact on recipients (Decree-Law No 10/2016 of 8 March 2016).

[61] There is now a more favourable system (non-enforcement of the factor of sustainability in these cases) for sixty-year-old recipients with a contribution history of at least forty years: see Decree-Law No 119/2018 of 27 December 2018; for public servants covered by CGA, see Decree-Law No 108/2019 of 13 August 2019.

updating the pension amount as well as the thirteenth and fourteenth months of pensions in 2012.[62] However, the war scenario in public discussion came from the attempt to reduce the amount of pensions in payment, affecting the so-called acquired or vested rights. The creation of an Extraordinary Solidarity Contribution (ESC—*Contribuição Extraordinária de Solidariedade*), affecting not only pensions above €1,500 but also other revenues, was strongly contested.[63] Afterwards, two reforms were also approved: one applicable only to the recipients of CGA;[64] another—Contribution of Sustainability (*Contribuição de Sustentabilidade*)—for the beneficiaries both of Social Security and CGA.[65]

b) Social assistance

During the crisis period, some measures affecting family allowances and unemployment benefits were also approved. There is a social unemployment benefit (*subsídio social de desemprego*), initial or subsequent, subject to a means test that integrates the social solidarity subsystem.[66]

The relevant measures in the field of social assistance were either to improve the quality of life of those primarily affected by crisis, or to reduce social assistance benefits to spare money. The former is represented by some measures of the Programme of Social Emergency (*Programa de Emergência Social*), including, for instance, social canteens as part of the fight against poverty. Other social benefits entitled the beneficiaries to social support in fields such as energy[67] (Extraordinary Social Support to the Energy Consumer, a Social Tariff for Gas, and a Social Tariff for Electricity), health,[68] and transportation.[69]

The latter is well illustrated by the Social Insertion Income,[70] a central social assistance benefit. Decree-Law No 133/2012 modified the Social Insertion Income regulation and worked as a kind of global reform. The Preamble sums up the significant issues, namely emphasis on duties regarding the active search for employment, occupational training, and socially useful work,[71] and changing of access conditions to this social benefit regarding the means test.

---

[62] Law No 64-B/2011 of 30 December 2011.
[63] See below (III.1.b) Decision No 187/2013.
[64] See below (III.1.b) Decision No 862/2013.
[65] See below (III.1.c) Decision No 572/2014.
[66] Art 41(1)(c) Law No 4/2007 (n 11); Decree-Law No 220/2006 of 3 November 2006 (as last amended by Decree-Law No 53/2018 of July 2018), art 3(b), art 24, and art 30 (amount); art 31 (changing of the amount); art 38 (duration of the social unemployment benefit subsequent to the unemployment benefit).
[67] Concerning energy social tariffs, see Centro Nacional de Pensões (n 44) 8–10.
[68] See Centro Nacional de Pensões, *Guia Prático Benefícios Adicionais de Saúde* (Instituto de Segurança Social, IP 2017).
[69] Social Pass (*Passe Social*).
[70] Law No 13/2003 (n 27) (as last amended by Decree-Law No 126-A/2017 of October 6).
[71] See also Decree-Law No 221/2012 of 12 October.

c) Family allowances

Decree-Law No 133/2012 of 27 June provides for the possibility of a re-evaluation of the family revenues to determine the level of Child Allowance (*Abono de Família*) at any time (contrasting with the rule of annual evaluation).[72] Given the increase of unemployment during that period, this was a measure designed to help the most affected families.

A cap was also introduced to the Death Grant (*Subsídio por Morte*),[73] reducing the maximum amount to six times the indexing reference for social support (IAS—*Indexante dos Apoios Sociais*) in 2012, [74] and to three times in 2013.[75] In the field of dependency and disability, according to its revised regime, if the global amount of pensions (with a few exceptions, such as those generated by work accidents) exceeds €600, the Long-Term Care Supplement is excluded.[76]

For the contingencies of maternity, paternity, and adoption, Decree-Law No 133/2012[77] declared that Christmas and holiday allowances should no longer be taken into account for the determination of the reference income, thus reducing the level of benefits. New rules introduced a reduction in the amount of the Survivor's Pension too (*Pensão de Sobrevivência*).[78]

d) Unemployment benefits

In terms of unemployment benefits, some measures are worth mentioning.[79] Favouring unemployed persons, a temporary 10 per cent increase in the unemployment benefit was established in case of unemployment of both parents or single-parent families.[80] The guarantee period (insurance period) was reduced from 450 to 360 days.[81]

As foreseen in the agreement with Troika, the personal scope of unemployment benefit was increased to cover independent workers who worked mainly for just

---

[72] Decree-Law No 176/2003 of 2 August 2003 (as amended by Decree-Law No 133/2012), art 14/7.

[73] Concerning the reimbursement of funeral expenses (*reembolso das despesas de funeral*), a similar solution was adopted: Decree-Law No 322/90 of 18 October 1990 (as amended by Decree-Law No 13/2013 of 25 January 2013), art 54(2) (Decree-Law No 133/2012 has already limited the amount paid to four times the indexing reference of social support).

[74] Decree-Law No 322/90 (n 73) (as amended by Decree-Law No 133/2012), art 32.

[75] ibid (as amended by Decree-Law No 13/2013 of 25 January 2013), art 32.

[76] Decree-Law No 265/99 (n 52) (as amended by Decree-Law No 13/2013 of 14 July 2013), art 6(2).

[77] Decree-Law No 89/2009 (as amended by Decree-Law No 133/2012), art 22(5); Decree-Law No 91/2009 (as amended by Decree-Law No 133/2012), art 28(3).

[78] See below (III.1.c) Decision No 413/2014.

[79] See the Preamble of Decree-Law No 64/2012 of 15 March 2012; a synthesis of the measures is also available in OECD, *Labour Market Reforms in Portugal 2011–2015: A Preliminary Assessment* (OECD Publishing 2017), 37–38.

[80] ibid, art 2.

[81] Decree-Law No 220/2006 (n 66) (as amended by Decree-Law No 64/2012), Art 22(1).

one entity.[82] Independent workers with entrepreneurial activity and members of the governing bodies of legal persons were also covered.[83] To stimulate the return to work, accepting a full-time low-paid job is an admission criterion for the possibility of receiving an amount equivalent to part of the unemployment benefit for some time.[84]

However, the legislator likewise adopted measures to reduce expenditure regarding the unemployment benefit, such as a 10 per cent decrease in the amount of unemployment allowance after the first six months;[85] the reduction of the maximum sum of the benefit;[86] shortening of the duration of unemployment benefit receipt;[87] and reinforcement of activation policies, stimulating the return to the labour market.[88]

A recent report assessing the reforms from a comparative perspective concludes that they 'brought the generosity of Portuguese unemployment benefits closer to the OECD average, although maximum duration remains high'.[89]

e) Healthcare
In healthcare, some of the impacts of the crisis result from the diminution of economic resources affecting a part of the population.[90]

aa) Sickness benefits
Decree-Law No 133/2012 of 27 June provides for a reduction in the replacement rate of lost revenues, affecting a period of sick leave (*período de baixa*) of up to thirty days. To protect socially vulnerable persons, the measures adopted include an increase of 5 per cent for beneficiaries whose reference remuneration is €500 or less, with three or more descendants under sixteen (age twenty-four, if they receive Child Allowance) who are part of the household, where the household includes persons receiving the Disability Allowance.[91] Another measure provided for the

[82] Decree-Law No 65/2012 of 15 March 2012 (last amendment: Decree-Law No 53/2018 of 2 July 2018); see also CRCSPSS (n 10), art 141(2).

[83] Law No 12/2013 of 25 January 2013 (amended by Decree-Law No 53/2018 of 2 July 2018); see also CRCSPSS (n 10), arts 65(2) and 141(3).

[84] On the previous legal framework, see OECD (n 83), 38, fn 21. See Portaria (Regulation) No 207/2012 of 6 July 2012, art 4.

[85] Decree-Law No 220/2006 (n 66) (as amended by Decree-Law No 64/2012), art 28. Decree-Law No 53-A/2017 of 31 May 2017 established limits to this reduction of the amount.

[86] ibid, art 29(1) changed the replacement rate from three times the IAS to two-and-a-half times the IAS.

[87] ibid, art 37.

[88] On activation policies and, more broadly, reforms to improve employability, OECD (n 83).

[89] ibid 38.

[90] See Carlos Farinha Rodrigues, Rita Figueiras, and Vítor Junqueiras (eds), *Desigualdade do Rendimento e Pobreza em Portugal* (Fundação Francisco Manuel dos Santos 2016).

[91] Decree-Law No 28/2004 (as amended by Decree-Law No 133/2012), art 17.

possibility of taking into account, for the determination of reference remunerations, the working days until the date prior to the day of incapacitation, supposing
the standard rules are unenforceable.[92]

A contribution on sickness benefits was approved,[93] but it did not survive constitutional review.[94]

bb) Healthcare: National Health Service and ADSE

(1) **National Health Service** The legal framework of the user charges changed,
raising the amounts that users must pay in order to access to healthcare services.
Decree-Law No 113/2011 of 29 November establishes the increase in fees and enshrines an automatic indexation clause based on the inflation rate. The exemptions
were also reviewed, reflecting the positive discrimination of socially vulnerable
persons. Rules also reformulated the procedure for ensuring the charging of fees to
guarantee sufficient payment, thus reducing major debts. Strategically, immediate
payments replaced deferred ones.

(2) **ADSE (public servants' system)** Auto-sustainability became the structural
principle of ADSE, and this was one of the major reforms undertaken. Although
contribution-based, the system was significantly dependent on budgetary
state transfers. The *Memorandum of Understanding on Specific Economic Policy
Conditionality*[95] pointed towards the end of this subsidisation process. Therefore,
there were significant rises in the contribution rates of the recipients and a reduction of the employers' charges (state and other public entities).[96] Since 2015, ADSE
has been relying only on the contributions of the recipients.[97]

3. Relationship between the reforms and financial assistance commitments

Considering the crisis and the impact on social benefits, we can identify different
key moments. Even before the intervention of the so-called Troika, after the 2008
crisis, some measures were adopted to diminish the harmful effects of the recession.[98] The other side of the coin was the cut in social expenditures to reduce public

---

[92] ibid, art 18.
[93] Law No 66-B/2012 of 31 December 2012.
[94] (n 78).
[95] (n 1).
[96] Decree-Law No 105/2013 of 30 July 2013; Law No 30/2014 of 19 May 2014.
[97] Art 260(e) of the State Budget Law (Lei do Orçamento do Estado) for 2015: see Law No 82-B/2014
of 31 December 2014.
[98] Even before the MoU, the Government adopted some measures on social security to fight the
crisis. First, the temporary exemption from the payment of contributions in cases such as 'ajudas de
custo TIR' (subsistence allowance—International Road Transport) (see Regulation/Portaria No 932/

debt. Different paths are possible: reducing the personal scope (eg, from univer-sality to selectivity; or changing the criteria of the means test, making access to social benefits harder); eliminating some social benefits; or, at least, reducing the amount.

Decree-Law No 133/2012 of 27 June begins as follows: 'The economic and finan-cial situation of the country requires a reassessment of the legal schemes (*regimes jurídicos*) for benefits of the social security system ... to ensure that social protection is effectively provided to the neediest (*mais carenciados*) citizens without undermining the sustainability of the social security system.' The economic and financial situation was therefore presented as a critical element of the social security cut rhetoric, also illustrated by other statutes. Sustainability (usually more associated with the environ-ment) got a second breath at both political and juridical levels. Public interest, as will be shown below, was the central argument to be considered in balancing processes in the judicial control of constitutionality. The idea of emergency also played a role in legal argumentation (with a discussion on the application of the constitutional norms of state of exception[99]). Rereading the statutes of this period,[100] these kinds of argu-ments are recurrent.

Time pressure determined all these 'reforms'. The tightly scheduled visits of the so-called Troika functioned as a kind of sword of Damocles, impairing the possibility of deep and extended political modifications. Besides, the climate of confrontation made it almost impossible to find a broad consensus on structural reforms in fields such as old-age pensions.

One of the reforms proposed as to social insurance was defeated in the streets (on 15 September 2012) by a movement called *Que se lixe a Troika* (Screw the Troika).[101] The Government had tried to change the percentage of social security contributions to be paid by employees, transferring onto them some costs from the employers. In

---

2009, 19 August). Second, the suspension of the automatic indexation clause of some benefits, to avoid their decrease, since the inflation rate was negative (see Regulation/Portaria No 1458/2009, 31 December). Third, in light of the negative variation of the nominal gross domestic product per capita in 2009, the non-use of it to update Complemento Social para Idosos (see Regulation/Portaria No 1457/ 2009, 31 December). Fourth, cuts concerning child allowance (abono de família) (see Decree-Law No 116/2010, 22 October) and unemployment benefit (subsídio de desemprego) (see Decree-Law No 15/ 2010, 9 March). Fifth, reinforcing the social protection of the recipients (ie, ensuring an increase of six months in the period of award of the allowance to the beneficiaries of the social unemployment benefit whose benefit would cease in 2010). Finally, presenting a new framework on access to non-contributory social benefits: see Decree-Law No 70/2010, 16 June. These are just some examples of the measures adopted before the MoU.

[99] eg, Suzana Tavares da Silva, 'Sustentabilidade e solidariedade em tempos de crise' in José Casalta Nabais and Suzana Tavares da Silva (eds), *Sustentabilidade fiscal em tempos de crise* (Almedina 2011) 61.

[100] eg, Decree-Law No 64/2012 (n 79).

[101] Tiago Fernandes, 'Late Neoliberalism and Its Discontents: The Case of Portugal' in *Late Neoliberalism and its Discontents in the Economic Crisis: Comparing Social Movements in the European Periphery* (Palgrave Macmillan 2017).

Portugal, in contrast with other countries (eg, Germany), employees pay only about one-third of the social security contributions.

In short, the Portuguese government obliged itself to reduce public expenditures in some areas,[102] with quantified aims (eg, health sector, €375 million; health systems for civil servants—*trabalhadores em funções públicas*), but the measures were to be chosen by national authorities following the constitutional framework. In some cases, however, the MoU went a step further: besides the quantification of the expenditures to be reduced, there were specific impositions (no indexation of pensions, except for the reduced ones[103]). To spare costs and increase efficiency, particular measures were also set for the reorganisation of social security.[104] There was also an imposition of 'taxation of all types of cash social transfers and convergence of personal income tax deductions for pensions and labour income.'[105]

---

[102] See *Letter of Intent* (Portugal/IMF) (n 1): 'Better means-testing procedures will protect lower in-come families while making savings in social security non-contributory benefits'; 'the domestic tax ad-ministration, customs administration, and the information technology service will be unified. We will complete a study by the end of September 2011 to assess the feasibility of the new structure taking over the collection function of the social security administration'; 'We will reduce the maximum dur-ation of unemployment insurance benefits to no more than 18 months, and cap unemployment bene-fits at 2.5 times the social support index and introduce a declining profile of benefits after six months of unemployment (a reduction of at least 10 percent in benefits), without reducing accrued-to-date entitlements. To extend social safety nets, we will reduce the necessary contributory period to access unemployment insurance from 15 to 12 months, and present a proposal to extend eligibility for clearly defined categories of self-employed. Training opportunities will be strengthened, especially for the low-skilled'; 'A critical goal of our program is to boost competitiveness. This will involve a major reduction in employer's social security contributions. This measure will be fully calibrated by the time of the first review (end of July 2011, structural benchmark)'; 'ensure that changes to social security contributions are compensated by allocating equivalent revenues in order to not jeopardize the sustainability of the pension system'.

[103] See *Memorandum of Understanding on Specific Economic Policy Conditionality* (n 1) 1.29. ix: 'maintain the suspension of pension indexation rules except for the lowest pensions in 2013'. See also 1.30: 'the government will extend the use of means testing and better target social support achieving a reduction in social benefits expenditure of at least EUR 350 million'.

[104] See ibid 2.19: 'The authorities will also take the necessary actions to authorise the tax and so-cial security administrations to use a wider range of restructuring tools based on clearly defined cri-teria in cases where other creditors also agree to restructure their claims, and review the tax law with a view to removing impediments to voluntary debt restructuring'. See also 3.3 on reporting on budgetary execution.

[105] See ibid 1.31.iii.

III. Human rights affected by social security reforms and constitutional theoretical achievements from this period

1. National case law

The measures adopted during the crisis affected foremost, in 2011,[106] public employees,[107] and in 2012 they were extended to many pensioners. As we have said previously, we will analyse the case law based on a timeline because it is essential to understand the development of the reasoning of the Portuguese CC. The Court considered that its own decisions could be a reasonable base for legitimate expectations.[108]

---

[106] In 2010, the State Budget Law for 2011 (Law No 55-A/2010 of 31 December 2010) created measures that provided for 'reduction of remuneration for persons who receive salaries from public entities above €1,500, including judges and public prosecutors' (arts 19, 20, and 21). Under the rules governing abstract *ex post facto* reviews, a group of Members of the Assembly of the Republic asked the Constitutional Court for a declaration with generally binding force of the unconstitutionality of arts 19, 20, and 21. The Constitutional Court considered the differential treatment between public and private employees resulting from these norms not in breach of the Constitution. According to the Court (Decision No 396/11): (i) this difference of treatment (between public and private employees) was a transitional measure founded on the conditions of financial assistance (suitable for reducing the budget deficit to a level, respecting the limit established by the European Union, within the framework of the rules of economic and monetary union); (ii) the rules were not labour measures, so the constitutional norms respecting the guarantee of participations from representatives of workers' organisations and trade unions did not apply; (iii) the Portuguese Constitution did not expressly grant a fundamental right of the non-reduction of salary, and the constitutional right to a salary (which has long been ruled by the constitutional jurisprudence as an individual fundamental right, *see* Decision No 620/2007) could not be interpreted as a right to a certain amount of salary independent from economic and financial conditions; and although the measures frustrate legitimate expectations, there was an overriding public interest (the financial crises) that neutralises infringement of the principle of the protection of legitimate expectations.

[107] All changes of labour law approved during this period as a direct consequence of the MoU are beyond the scope of this chapter. However, it is worth highlighting some of the most controversial ones. The most contentious measure was the extension of the public employees' working week to forty hours, approved by Law No 68/2013 of 29 August 2013, and revoked by Law No 18/2016 of 20 June 2016, which restored the thirty-five-hour working week. The thirty-five-hour working week for public employees was also restored after the recognition, by the Constitutional Court (see Decision No 494/2015), that the local entities were not obliged by Law No 68/2013, which represented a break (and a breach) on the homogeneity of their legal statutes and an inadmissible different treatment among public employees.

[108] On the jurisprudence of crisis, see, inter alia, Gonçalo de Almeida Ribeiro and Luís Pereira Coutinho (eds), *O Tribunal Constitucional e a Crise* (Almedina 2014); Carlos Blanco de Morais, *Curso de Direito Constitucional: Teoria da Constituição em Tempo de Crise do Estado Social*, t. II, vol. 2 (Coimbra Editora 2014) VII, ch II; Jorge Reis Novais, *Em Defesa do Tribunal Constitucional: Resposta aos Críticos* (Almedina 2014); José Melo Alexandrino, 'O Impacto Jurídico da Jurisprudência da Crise' (2014) 11 Revista da Faculdade de Direito da Universidade do Porto 159; Jorge Miranda, 'Estado Social, Crise Económica e Jurisdição Constitucional' (2014) 55 Revista da Faculdade de Direito da Universidade de Lisboa 375; Gonçalo de Almeida Ribeiro, 'Judicial Activism Against Austerity in Portugal' *Iconnectblog.com* (2014) <http://www.iconnectblog.com/2013/12/judicial-activism-against-austerity-in-portugal> accessed 15 August 2019; Romano Orrù, 'Crisi economica e responsabilità dei giuridici costituzionali: riflessioni sul caso portoghese' (2014) 20 Diritto Pubblico Comparato ed Europeo 1015; Ana Guerra Martins, 'Constitutional Judge, Social Rights and Public Debt Crisis: The Portuguese Constitutional Case Law' (2015/5) 22 Maastricht Journal of European and Comparative Law 678; Mariana Canotilho, Teresa Violante, and Rui Lanceiro, 'Austerity Measures Under Judicial Scrutiny: The

a) State Budget Law 2012

One of the first measures was the suspension of the Christmas-month (thirteenth-month) and holiday-month (fourteenth-month) payments from annual salaries for persons who received retirement pensions from the public social security system. But, under the rules governing abstract *ex post facto* reviews, a group of Members of the Assembly of the Republic asked the CC for a declaration with generally binding force of the unconstitutionality of article 25 contained in the State Budget Law (Lei do Orçamento do Estado) for 2012, Law No 64-B/2011 of 30 December.[109] According to article 25, the suspension of the so-called thirteenth and fourteenth months of pay applied to persons who received a pension above €1,100 per month. Pensioners who received pensions above €600 and below €1,100 were also affected, but only by a cut in the quantum of these thirteenth and fourteenth months of pay. Non-payment of the whole of this quantum represented, in some cases, a 14.3 per cent reduction in the annual value of retirement pensions. In its assessment, the CC did not consider this measure solely; instead it ruled on its cumulated effect with the ESC adopted in 2011 (article 162, Law No 55-A/2010 of 31 December, amended by article 20(1), Law No 64-B/2011 of 30 December). The ESC appeared in the State Budget Law for 2011 as a new type of tax ('special contribution') applicable only to pension incomes over a certain amount and based on the following rates: (i) 25 per cent on pension incomes above €5,030 and below €7,545; (ii) 50 per cent on pension incomes above €7,545.[110]

Applicants claimed that this measure was unconstitutional because it violated the principle of equality between citizens (article 13 of the Portuguese Constitution), and both the principle of equality concerning public costs and the

---

Portuguese Constitutional Case-Law' (2015) 11 European Constitutional Law Review 155; Jorge Silva Sampaio, Filipe Brito Bastos, and Afonso Chuva Brás, 'New Challenges to Democracy: The Portuguese Case' (2015/1) 27 Revue européenne de droit public = European Review of Public Law = Eur. Zeitschrift des öffentlichen Rechts = Rivista europea di diritto pubblico 387; Ana Raquel Gonçalves Moniz, 'Socialidade, Solidariedade e Sustentabilidade: Esboços de um Retrato Jurisprudencial' in João Carlos Loureiro and Suzana Tavares da Silva (eds), *A Economia Social e Civil: Estudos* (Instituto Jurídico 2015); Mariana Canotilho, 'Austeridad y Derechos Fundamentales en Portugal: Episódios de una Crisis Interminable' in Francisco Balaguer Callejón (ed), The Impact of the Economic Crisis on the EU Institutions and Member States = El Impacto de la Crisis Económica en las Instituciones de la UE y los Estados Membros (Aranzadi 2015); Mario Iannella, 'Condizionalita e diritti sociali: spunti dal caso portoghese' (2016) 1 Diritto e società 107; Caterina Drigo, 'La Grammatica Giurisprudenziale dei Diritti ai Tempi della Crisi: le Corti Costituzionali nel Gorgo della Politica: Legittima Ingerenza o Influenza Eccessiva sulla Forma di Governo? Alcune Riflessioni sui Casi Portoghese e Italiano' in Germán Manuel Teruel Lozano, Antonio Pérez Miras, and Eduardo C. Raffiota (eds), *Constitución e Integración Europea: Derechos Fundamentales y sus Garantías Jurisdiccionales* (Dykinson 2017); Teresa Violante, 'The Eurozone Crisis and the Rise of the Portuguese Constitutional Court' (2019) 39 Quaderni costituzionali: Rivista italiana di diritto costituzionale 208.

[109] They also asked the Constitutional Court for a declaration with generally binding force of the unconstitutionality of art 21 contained in the same Law, which established the suspension of the same payments for persons who receive salaries from public entities. The request was based on the violation of the principles of equality, proportionality, and the protection of legitimate expectations.

[110] The Court applied the same criteria to art 21, considering also in its assessment of this measure the effects of the 'reduction of remuneration for persons who receive salaries from public entities above €1,500, including judges and public prosecutors'.

principle of 'fiscal justice' (article 103(1) of the Portuguese Constitution). However, the Court did not base its decision on a violation of any of these articles. Instead, it considered the accumulation of this measure with the measures adopted in previous years, such as ESC and pension freezing (pension amounts had been the same since 2010), as well as the fact that these conditions should remain the same for three budget years. All this together inflicted a particular injury to pensioners' financial situations and had no connection with financial contributions required from other categories of citizens, such as workers in private economic sectors or those who lived on financial incomes.

Thus, the Portuguese CC, in its Decision No 353/12,[111] considered that 'the difference between the degree of sacrifice undergone by those affected by this measure and those who are not must be subject to limits, and in this case the sacrifices were not equally distributed among citizens. In its assessment, the state could achieve the same results (reducing public deficit) by spreading the sacrifices more comprehensively and concentrating measures within some categories of people (pensioners and persons who receive salaries from public entities). The measure was adopted for efficacy-related reasons, because measures based on the expense (instead of the revenue side) could quickly reduce the public deficit.

So, in this case, the Court founded the unconstitutionality of the measure on a doctrinal grounding: the violation of the principle of proportional equality. Although, bearing in mind that the execution of the 2012 Budget was already well underway, the CC considered that the consequences of an unqualified declaration of unconstitutionality could endanger the maintenance of the agreed financing and thus the state's solvency. It therefore restricted the effects of the declaration of unconstitutionality as permitted by article 282(4) of the Constitution and did not apply them to the suspension of payment of the Christmas and holiday bonuses or any equivalent payments in 2012.[112] Three dissenting opinions opposed the restriction of the decision effect.[113]

---

[111] Miguel Nogueira de Brito, 'Comentário ao Acórdão nº 353/2012 do Tribunal Constitucional' (2012) 1 Direito & política/Law & Politics 108; Ricardo Branco, '"Ou Sofrem Todos, ou Há Moralidade": Breves Notas sobre a Fundamentação do Acórdão do Tribunal Constitucional n.º 353/2012, de 5 de Julho' in *Estudos em Homenagem a Miguel Galvão Teles*, vol. I (Almedina 2012).

[112] Some pensioners challenged this measure—the restriction of the effects of the declaration of unconstitutionality—in the European Court of Human Rights (App nos 62235/12 and 57725/12), claiming violation of art 1 of Protocol No 1. In its ruling, the Court referred to Council Opinion on the updated stability programme of Portugal, 2011–2014, issued in June 2011 [SEC (2011) 730 final] and the overall economic situation in Portugal to conclude that the applicants did not bear a disproportionate and excessive burden. See Hans-Joachim Reinhard, 'Portugal in der Sozial- und Finanzkrise: Rentenkürzungen verfassungswidrig aber kein Verstoß gegen die EMRK' (2014) 28 Zeitschrift für ausländisches und internationales Arbeits- und Sozialrecht 92.

Other pensioners had also challenged this measure in labour courts, claiming that the administrative pension entity (CGA) should not suspend the payment of the thirteenth and twenty-fourth month because the measure was unconstitutional, but as in the meantime the Constitutional Court published its decision, the labour courts merely referred to that decision—see Case 715/12.0TTCBR.C1; 3530/12.8TTLSB.L1-4; 822/12.0TTPRT.P1.

[113] The decision on the unconstitutionality of art 21 (the suspension of the same payments for persons who receive salaries from public entities) was based on the same grounds and the restricted effects also applied in this case.

b) State Budget Law 2013 and definitive cut in amount of the pensions
of CGA beneficiaries

In 2013, the President of the Portuguese Republic, two groups of Members of the Assembly of the Republic,[114] and the Ombudsman asked the CC for a declaration with generally binding force of the unconstitutionality of different norms of the State Budget Law for 2013 (Law No 66-B/2012 of 31 December).

These norms aimed at overcoming the financial crisis, and ruled for the partial suspension of the holiday month for pensioners (article 77), the contribution payable on unemployment and sickness benefits (article 117(1)), the extension of the scope of application of the ESC (article 78), and changes in the personal income tax code.[115] Although not all applicants challenged the same norms and based them on the same grounds, the Court merged them into a single action with a view to Decision No 187/2013.[116]

Despite some (not remarkable) differences in their grounds, all applicants challenged the partial suspension of the holiday month for pensioners,[117] mainly based on the violation of the equality principle and the previous decision of the CC on Decision No 353/2012. Once again, the CC ruled the unconstitutionality of the measure founded on the violation of the equality principle. In this case, although the pensioners were deprived of a lower amount of money and on a transitory basis, the accumulation of these effects with the extension of the scope of application of the ESC aggravated an already unequal situation, not only in relation to other pensioners whose fourteenth-month payment was not suspended, but also compared with other forms of income.

Applicants also challenged the extension of the ESC.[118] They essentially argued the violation of the unified taxation of personal income, mandatory under article

---

[114] A group of deputies of the Socialist Party and a group of deputies of the left parties.

[115] Mainly limitations on tax-deductible items (art 186 amending art 78 of the personal income tax code).

[116] Suzana Tavares da Silva, 'O Problema da Justiça Intergeracional em Jeito de Comentário ao Acórdão do Tribunal Constitucional n.º 187/2013' (2013) Cadernos de Justiça Tributária 3; Luís Manuel Teles de Menezes Leitão, 'Acórdão do Tribunal Constitucional n.º 187/2013: Lei do Orçamento do Estado para 2013' (2012/4) 72 Revista da Ordem dos Advogados 1483; Miguel Nogueira de Brito and Luís Pereira Coutinho, 'A Igualdade Proporcional, Novo Modelo no Controlo do Princípio da Igualdade?' (2013/4) Direito & política/Law & Politics 182; Tania Abbiate, 'Il Tribunale costituzionale portoghese al tempo della crisi: una nuova pronuncia in materia di bilancio' (2013/2) 33 Quaderni costituzionali: Rivista italiana di diritto costituzionale 438.

[117] The measure consisted of the suspension of 90 per cent of the holiday-month (fourteenth-month) or any equivalent payment for pensions above €1,100 and a suspension of a lower amount for pensions between €600 and €1,100. The same measure was established for public administration staff (art 29) and for the same types of amount payable under teaching and research contracts (art 31), and the Court also considered this measure unconstitutional as violating the principle of equality.

[118] According to art 78 of the Law No 66-B/2012 (n 93), the ESC was applicable to monthly pension incomes above €1350 based on the following rates: (i) 3.5 per cent on pension incomes above €1350 and below €1800; (ii) 3.5 per cent on €1800 and 16 per cent on a remaining pension income value between €1800.01 and €3750, which amounts to an overall rate of between 3.5 per cent and 10 per cent; (iii) 10 per cent on pension incomes above €3750. In the last case, an extra rate is also applicable: 15 per cent on the amount above €5,030.64 and below €7,545.96; and 40 per cent on amounts above €7,545.96.

104 of the Portuguese Constitution, the violation of the ability-to-pay principle and the principle of equality and its sub-principle of equality with regard to public costs, the violation of the principle of the protection of legitimate expectations, and, lastly, the violation of property (fundamental) rights. Although the measure has been primarily challenged[119] and socially contested, the CC did not rule its unconstitutionality.

In its decision, the Court recognised that this parafiscal contribution frustrated pensioners' legitimate expectations on the continuity of the legislative framework and their incomes. However, it could be considered a proportionate measure because it was appropriate to the goals pursued by the legislator, fulfilled the principle of necessity (there were no alternative measures), and, simultaneously, caused less damage to the holders of the legal positions at stake (they were exceptional and transitory) and served the public interest to the same extent.

Only the group of deputies of the left parties challenged the contribution payable on unemployment and sickness benefits (article 117(1)). This contribution was also extraordinary and transitory, and applicable to unemployment and sickness benefits to the rate of (i) 5 per cent on sickness benefits and (ii) 6 per cent on unemployment benefits. Claimants argued the violation of the principle of proportionality. Although the Constitution does not guarantee a certain amount of social benefits and the legislator can fix its quantum, they claimed that this kind of benefit protected people in vulnerable conditions, and that they were usually in line with the minimum material assistance, and thus a cut in these benefits might put the beneficiaries in a more vulnerable position. In this Decision, the Court went a step further in recognising the existence of a guarantee of a right to a minimum level of subsistence (a combination of the principle of the dignity of the human person and the right to social security in situations of need).

Finally, the same parliamentary group from the left parties also challenged some changes in the personal income tax code, especially limitations on tax-deductible items (article 186 amending article 78 of the personal income tax code). The constraints on tax-deductible items prevented taxpayers from deducting social expenses on health, education, and housing, which represented an increase in taxes.

---

[119] Art 78 of Law No 66-B/2012 (n 93) has also been challenged by individual claims in administrative courts, but the Supreme Administrative Court of Portugal affirmed in all cases that this was a constitutional issue, so it was not competent to rule on the question—see process No 0729/14 (22/09/2016); 0922/15 (20/10/2016); 01518/13 (31/10/2013); 0998/14 (30/10/2014); 0729/14 (22/04/2015); 0577/15 (24/09/2015); 0317/15 (1/10/2015).

Some pensioners also challenged the extension of the scope of application of the ESC in the European Court of Human Rights (App no 13341/14), claiming violation of art 1 of Protocol No 1. Once again, in its ruling, the Court referred to the Portuguese economic situation and the reasoning of the Constitutional Court in its decisions of 2013 and 2014, in which it considered that the ESC, in general, was not unconstitutional and thus fulfilled the requirement of lawfulness. Thus, it decided that, observing the overall public interests at stake in the respondent state at the material time and given the limited extent and the temporary effect of the ESC applied to the applicant's pension, the impugned measure was proportional.

On this issue, the CC, based on the exceptional and transitory nature of the measures, considered that there was no violation of the alleged principles of the ability to pay taxes and the constitutional rule that taxes on personal income must be unitary (article 104(1) of the Portuguese Constitution).

It is important to note that Decision No 187/2013 was a hard decision for the Court. Ten of its thirteen justices presented dissenting opinions or statements of the vote, pointing out not only different interpretations or decisions but also different reasoning for the decisions.

Also in 2013, and somewhat as a requirement for finding alternatives for the measures considered unconstitutional in Decision No 187/2013, the parliament approved a decree to amend the statute governing the retirement of public sector staff. That decree revoked norms that added extra time to the periods service people have worked in specific, exceptionally demanding situations, to calculate their retirement entitlements in pensions paid by CGA. Some of these norms were subjected, by the President of the Republic, to prior (*ex ante*) review to determine whether they were in breach of the Constitution.

According to those measures, pensioners who received a pension income of above €600 (gross value) would have a cut of 10 per cent in their pensions, which would apply to all pensions, not only to retirement pensions but also to disability and survivors' pensions, and other persons would have their pensions recalculated downward.

In Decision No 862/2013[120] the Court had considered, unanimously, that these measures were in breach of the constitutional principle of the protection of trust.[121] Unlike with Decision No 187/2013, in this case justices have tried to find some common grounds for their decision, but probably because of that, the reasoning for the decision is not so clear. On the one hand, the Court considered that this was not a tax (as the President of the Republic had argued) and the measure was not retroactive, but just retrospective, as it would apply to future payments, even though affecting pensions for which the quantum had been previously determined and was also in payment. Thus, there was no violation of article 103(3) of the Portuguese

---

[120] In this decision the Constitutional Court analysed a measure of the definitive cut in the amount of the pensions of CGA beneficiaries. See Nazaré da Costa Cabral, 'Convergência do Regime e Proteção Social da Função Pública com o Regime Geral da Segurança Social: Comentário ao Acórdão do Tribunal Constitucional n.º 862/2013, de 7 de Janeiro' (2013) 4(6) Revista de Finanças Públicas e Direito Fiscal 255; Nazaré da Costa Cabral, 'Redução de Pensões em Curso de Atribuição e o Princípio da Protecção da Confiança: algumas Reflexões sobre o Modo de Superação do Acórdão do Tribunal Constitucional n.º 862/2013' (2014) 7 Direito & política/Law & Politics 90; João Carlos Loureiro, 'Sobre a (In)Constitucionalidade do Regime Proposto para a Redução dos Montantes de Pensões da Caixa Geral de Aposentações' (2013) 89 Boletim da Faculdade de Direito 159; João Carlos Loureiro, 'Sobre a chamada Convergência das Pensões: o Caso das Pensões de Sobrevivência' (2013) 89 Boletim da Faculdade de Direito 603.

[121] The constitutional principle of the protection of trust is a broad fundamental principle and it can be used to express both a general trust in the durability of the legal order (legal certainty) and the individual trust in a subjective protection against abrupt changes in legal regimes (legitimate expectations).

Constitution. On the other hand, the Court recognised that it had already stated that it was not unconstitutional to decrease the amount of the pensions of CGA beneficiaries, but added that the reasons underlying its earlier findings could not apply in this case. Moreover, the decision included some political grounds when it considered that it was necessary to evaluate whether the public interest in reducing the transfers from the State Budget used to finance the CGA's structural deficit justified cutting the pensions of the CGA's beneficiaries, and ruled negatively. To briefly summarise, as two of the justices pointed out in their statements, the Court based its decision on the violation of the protection of the trust but did not provide any proportionality test to sustain that violation and entered into political considerations on the reform of the statute governing the retirement of public sector staff.

c) Decisions of 2014 and 2015

In 2014, the CC was asked by a group of deputies of the left parties for a declaration with generally binding force of the unconstitutionality of norms contained in the State Budget Law for 2014, Law No 83-C/2013 of 31 December, as amended by Law No 13/2014 of 14 March. Once again, the main focus was on the extension of the scope of application of the ESC and the increase in its rates (article 76).[122]

The Court decided, in Decision No 572/2014, that this new regime of the ESC was not unconstitutional. As it had ruled earlier, this contribution, implemented in 2011, was not per se unconstitutional, and the fact that its norms were constantly changing could not be considered a violation of the principle of the protection of the trust (legal certainty) because people expected those permanent changes. The Court also invoked the economically exceptional context and the international financial obligations (mainly, the financial assistance program) to base its ruling. Finally, we notice that in this case the Court demonstrated self-restraint in its analysis, considering that the measure remained within limits outlined by the proportionality principle. Furthermore, there was nothing that would allow the Court to conclude that expanding the ESC base was not indispensable to the ability to safeguard the budgetary balance in the 2014 budget year. However, this measure represented an interim response to solve the social security financial problem, and was directly motivated by the Court's Decision No 862/2013.

Finally, and still in 2014, under the rules governing the abstract *ex ante* review, the President of the Republic asked the CC to pronounce the norms which defined the scope of application of a new contribution—the Sustainability

---

[122] In this new revision of the ESC its scope of application was extended to pension incomes of above €600/month and rates were also increased. Thus, in 2014 the ESC was calculated as follows: (i) 3.5 per cent on the total pension incomes between €1,000 and €1800; (ii) those with pensions above €1800 would pay 3.5 per cent on €1800 and 16 per cent on the remaining amount between €1800 and €3750 (which corresponds to a global rate of between 3.5 per cent and 10 per cent); (iii) those with pensions above €3750 would pay 10 per cent on the total amount, plus an extra tax of 15 per cent on amounts between €4611 and €7126 and 40 per cent on amounts above €7126.

Contribution—approved by a parliamentary decree, to be in breach of the Constitution.

Parliament based this new contribution, on the one hand, on the need to accomplish international financial obligations under the Stability and Growth Pact and the Treaty on Stability, Coordination and Governance in the Economic and Monetary Union and, on the other hand, on the financial deficit of the social security system. The Sustainability Contribution (unlike the ESC) was a permanent contribution on pension incomes already in payment calculated according to the following rules: (i) 2 per cent on the total amount of pensions up to €2000/month; (ii) those receiving pensions above €2000/month and up to €3,500 would pay 2 per cent on €2000 and 5.5 per cent on the excess; (iii) those receiving pensions above €3500/month would pay 3.5 per cent on the total amount. In this legal precept, there was also a safety guarantee clause to ensure that no pensioner would receive less than €1000/month (gross value).

In Decision No 575/2014,[123] the CC pronounced these norms unconstitutional, reasoning that the Sustainability Contribution consisted of a pension-cutting measure in the strict sense, which affected legal positions that deserved full constitutional protection within the overall framework of the control of the protection of the trust (legal certainty). As it was a permanent measure and not a transitory one, the Court considered that pensioners' economic rights, in this case, deserved stronger protection under certainty parameters of the protection of the trust. The Court also considered that the measure raised difficulties in terms of equality, and the public interest provided by the legislator was not strong enough to prevail over the intensity imposed on private subjects, which means that it was not strong enough under the proportionality test.

In 2014, a group of deputies of the Socialist Party asked the CC for a declaration with generally binding force of the unconstitutionality of norms contained in the State Budget Law for 2014. First, this referred to the suspension of the payment of pension supplements in state-owned business sector enterprises that had returned net losses in the last three financial years, and, second, to the new ways of calculating and reducing survivors' pensions when accumulated with income from other pensions.[124] In Decision No 413/2014, the Court, once again in a decision with many dissenting opinions, considered the first measure not in breach of the principles of protection of the trust, equality, and proportionality, as was alleged by the applicants, but declared unconstitutional the second measure

---

[123] On this point, see João Carlos Loureiro, 'Contribuição de Sustentabilidade & Companhia: Linhas para uma Discussão Constitucional ou a Arte de Morrer Ingloriamente em Sede de Fiscalização Preventiva I—Pensões: entre a Atualização e a Redução' (2016) 92 (2) Boletim da Faculdade de Direito 717; 'II—Sobre o(s) Modo(s) de Realização da Redução Retrospetiva dos Montantes de Pensões' (2017) 93 (1) Boletim da Faculdade de Direito 57.

[124] Arts 75 and 117 of the State Budget Law for 2014, Law No 83-C/2013 of 31 December 2013.

based on the violation of the equality principle. In addition to old-age benefits, the measures adopted during the crisis also contended with some social assistance legal regimes.

Still in 2014, we must also refer to the judicial challenge of a norm concerning healthcare benefits. A group of deputies of the left parties asked the CC for a declaration with generally binding force of the unconstitutionality of norms contained in the State Budget Law for 2014. They also challenged a norm that reverted 50 per cent of the income received from employers' contributions to ADSE to the state purse as being in breach of the Constitution. However, the Court decided, in its Decision No 572/2014, that these contributions were themselves made from state funds, and the norm's scope of the application did not impinge on the principles of the so-called 'Fiscal Constitution'. In other words, the Court said it was not in breach of either the principle of the unitary nature of the personal income tax or the principle of equality.

In 2015, under an *ex post facto* review process, article 6(1)(b), and its no 4, of Law No 13/2003 of 21 May, amended by Decree-Law No 133/2012 of 27 June were brought before the CC by the Ombudsman. According to these norms, both Portuguese citizens and the members of their households must legally reside in Portuguese territory for at least one year before they could apply for and receive the Social Insertion Income. In Decision No 141/2015,[125] the CC, by a vast majority of its justices, declared these two norms unconstitutional with generally binding force because they violated the principle of equality. It is important to note that, in its decision, the Court considered the Court of Justice of the European Union case law on social benefits of a strictly 'assistentialist' nature, according to which the Member States are not obliged to treat their nationals and those of other Member States equally.

The same norms were also brought before the CC under an *ex post facto* review process by the Attorney-General, but in this case because they subjected recognition of the right to the Social Insertion Income to the fulfilment of several requisites. One of those requisites was that if the applicant was not a national of a European Union (EU) Member State, a European Economic Area country, or another state with an agreement with the EU permitting the free movement of persons, he/she must have resided in Portugal legally for the previous three years. The same norm also denied the Social Insertion Income in cases in which the remaining members of the applicant's household (except for children below the age of three) had not also lived in Portugal for at least the last three years. The CC also declared this norm unconstitutional on both counts in its Decision No 296/2015 because the Portuguese Constitution requires an attitude of openness towards foreign citizens, and this difference of treatment was disproportionate.

---

[125] Fernández Sánchez (n 27).

2. Critical assessment of Portuguese constitutional case law

As is evident from the above, the Portuguese case law concerning, at the substantial level, the legislative reforms imposed by the economic and financial crisis is, as expected, that of the CC.

Other courts' judgments, namely those of the administrative courts, are mostly formal decisions, considering the courts are not competent to judge directly (abstractly) the challenge of the legal rules on the grounds of unconstitutionality, knowledge of which is restricted to the CC.[126] Although the diffuse and specific monitoring of all rules, including laws, by all courts, with an appeal to the CC, is enshrined in the Portuguese judicial order, the claims brought before the administrative courts did not challenge individual actions implementing specific legal rules on the grounds of their unconstitutionality.[127]

Therefore, although the Portuguese CC, unlike its European counterparts, enjoys the power to *review* the constitutionality of the legal norms, both *concretely* (on appeal against other courts' decisions) and *in abstract terms*, all relevant decisions delivered by the CC during the crisis concerned abstract control proceedings. In some cases, it was a *preventive* review (before the enactment by the President of the Republic, at his request); in other cases, a *consecutive* review (after the law has come into force, at the request of the President of the Republic, the Ombudsman, and opposition members of parliament).

The constitutionality issues arising from the adopted legislative measures concerned, particularly, the reduction of social benefits and old-age pensions. Although the Portuguese Constitution enshrines both property rights and the right to social security as fundamental rights, the Court did not assess the direct constraints on any of these rights. The CC did not find that the legislative measures resulted in the restriction of property rights, for two reasons.

First, because the Portuguese pension system is a pay-as-you-go system and not a capitalisation one; moreover, although it is a contributory scheme, calculation conditions were rather generous, so the amount of the pension paid could not be an object of property. It was not a matter of partial expropriation because, on the one hand, there was no removal of a particular legal position but rather a decision in general and abstract terms regarding the content of a category of rights. On the other hand, a property right is an *individual* (*personal*) right, and the right to a pension is a position with an active *social component*. From a genetic and a functional

---

[126] Only through the direct judicial review of concrete actions implementing the rules in question may the stakeholders carry out the incidental control of the constitutionality of the aforementioned legislative measures, to review its constitutionality and legality (arts 204 and 280 of the Constitution of the Portuguese Republic; arts 69 and following of the CC Framework Law, approved by Law No 28/82 of 15 November 1982; v Dec STA/Plenary of 20 May 2010, P 0390/09; Dec STA/Plenary of 07 December 2010, P 0798/10; and Dec STA/Plenary of 19 March 2015, P 0949/14).

[127] The requests concerned a segment of the law (pensions under the second pillar, established by private legal persons), but challenged the laws themselves and not individual implementing measures.

perspective, the right to a pension is a right to participate in a joint solidarity fund that is set up by the Government with the contributions of workers and employers and partially funded by the transfer of sums from the general State budget.

The second reason is that the Portuguese Constitution has in its portfolio a specific fundamental right, the right to social security, thus waiving the more generic property right. However, the Court does not see in these cases a direct restriction of the right to social security.

The right to receive a retirement pension was an expression of the right to social security granted to *all* under article 63 of the Constitution, embedded in the principle of dignity of the human person, in articles 1 and 2, and sought to guarantee, precisely, a decent human existence to all persons who have come to the end of their working life. So far, pension entitlement and the protection thereof do not exclude in advance the possible reduction of the exact pension amount by the legislator.[128] The Constitution guarantees the right to the pension, and not the right to a certain amount of a pension. Such amount is established by the administration, following the criteria that have been laid down by the legislator, but which have a less-than-constitutional value.[129]

Neither were the Decisions founded on the dignity of the human person, which is not a specific fundamental right in the case law of the CC but just a principle of 'jurisgenetic' value, characterising the constitutional status of the individual persons and the basis of the regulatory system of the fundamental rights.

Therefore, the CC did not address the issue of the constitutionality of the austerity measures as a restriction of fundamental subjective rights, which would require judicial inspection of the legislator's strict fulfilment of the principle of proportionality, in its three criteria: suitability, necessity, and proportionality in the strict sense.

It chose to compare the legislative measures with the principles of equality, proportionality, and the protection of legitimate trust, having formulated and applied a principle of 'equal proportionality'.[130]

This principle of proportional equality, which was new in Portuguese case law, is founded on the idea that inequality on the grounds of different circumstances is not immune to a proportionality judgment. Unequal treatment, albeit justified, must be proportionate to the reasons for such unequal treatment, and must not

---

[128] However, the Court found that some aspects of pension entitlement—such as the period of service counting for retirement—may be similar to rights, freedoms, and guarantees, thus being governed by the same rules as set out in art 18 of the Constitution (see Decision No 411/99).

[129] Notwithstanding the fact that the *confidence* in the preservation of the exact amount of the pension, set when entering into retirement, is legitimate and worthy of legal protection, particularly since the system sets a 'fixed benefit', whereby each pensioner is guaranteed a fixed rate of replacement of the reference salary.

[130] See Ravi Afonso Pereira, 'Igualdade e proporcionalidade: um comentário às decisões do Tribunal Constitucional sobre cortes salariais no setor público' (2013) 98 Revista Española de Derecho Constitucional 317–70.

be excessive. Consequently, the judgment concerning the reasonableness of the measure of difference is subject to the proportionality test.

In an overall assessment of the relevant case law, we find that, from the perspective of social rights, the CC is especially sensitive to two principles—the principle of equal proportionality and the principle of protection of legitimate expectations.

The decisions declaring the unconstitutionality of the restrictive measures were fundamentally based on the excess charges or sacrifices (over consecutive years) with which certain groups were burdened (civil servants and pensioners), compared to other social groups. Critics pointed out that such a judgment did not take into account these groups' privileges, namely health, compared to private workers of working age who were heavily hit by unemployment during the economic and financial crisis.

The CC seems to have always preferred, in terms of its constitutionality, to increase the tax burden (which grew as a result of the judgments of unconstitutionality) as a solution for the more universal and appropriate distribution of the costs of the crisis.

The principle of protection of legitimate expectations, namely of vested rights, was also applied: the CC awarded higher weight to the pension entitlement, requiring a stronger motive and a more structural purpose for limiting it, especially if permanent—in line with the maxim that *the more consistent the affected rights are, the stronger the reason must be for reviewing them.*

Weighing the interests against equal proportionality, the CC did not go into great depth regarding the community interests that justified the austerity measures. The Court accepted the circumstance of the serious financial crisis as a 'known fact' and did not value it legally. It considered it to be neither an 'exceptional economic status' equivalent to the state of emergency provided for in the Constitution, nor an international legal order arising from the MoU, whose Economic and Financial Adjustment Programme left some room for the national political choices.

Therefore, the CC did not regard the resolution of the financial crisis as the expression of a supreme national interest that should prevail over the private rights or interests of citizen groups. At an early stage, the CC did not declare or limit the effects of the declaration of unconstitutionality of the restrictive measures. He considered, above all, the exceptional and temporary nature of such measures, despite announcing the unconstitutional nature thereof in the following years, as it found that there was space and time to come up with alternatives.

On the other hand, in opposition to the legitimate expectations trustworthy of protection, the community value invoked in the case law, alongside financial sustainability, was particularly that of the sustainability of the social security system. The CC has not expressed high regard for the value of intergenerational justice or solidarity, which was also called to debate and would have made sense to ponder on, namely concerning the legislation that sought the convergence of the private and public social security systems.

Generally, the Court always claimed to acknowledge the legislator's own space, although it found that the latter should provide reasons of public interest for the measures taken.

Also, the method for applying the principles was clear and coherent, especially in the beginning. The Court enhanced the principle of proportional equality through a double test: first, by assessing the grounds for different treatment set out by the legislator between citizens who were targeted by the restrictive measures and others, to understand whether it was dispensable (negative test); afterward, by assessing the differentiating measures in a context of proportionality to see if they were within the scope of 'a fair measure of difference' or the 'limits of sacrifice' (positive test). Moreover, the violation of the principle of legitimate expectations (trust) implied that the result would be 'unacceptable, arbitrary or excessive'.

The CC tested compliance with the constitutional principles firmly. It did not limit itself to controlling the evidence of breach thereof, instead including considerations of need (existence of less restrictive options) or, in general, political judgments (purpose and scope of the measure in the framework of a public policy), establishing individual criteria for weighing the interests at stake, based on such considerations and judgment. That is what happened, for example, when it found that the legislator 'should have taken other measures of political and financial policy in general', or that legislative restriction could be justified only 'in the context of a broad strategic vision of government structure reform' ('systemic and global reform of social security').

Therefore, much of the doctrine (and, in the Court, the dissenting votes) criticised the methodology that was not entirely coherent and an attitude that became overly interventional in some decisions.

Despite all criticism, we cannot say that these decisions changed the Portuguese separation of powers model or even the balance between the sovereign powers. As some authors said,[131] the CC 'has gone beyond' its powers here and there, but not as much as to produce a relevant breach on its role as a 'negative legislator'.

We can also identify two other achievements from this period: first, the resilience of the Portuguese constitutional form of government; and, second, the inappropriate use (and abuse) of 'cavalier budgétaire' by the Portuguese Parliament.

The Portuguese constitutional form of government is a mix between parliamentary, presidential, and semi-presidential ('French') models. The government has an ordinary legislative power in all matters not constitutionally reserved to the parliament (mainly in public policies issues[132]). The President of the Republic has political veto power over legislative acts approved by parliament (laws) and the government (decree-laws), and parliament can overcome the presidential veto

---

[131] See Ribeiro and Coutinho (n 108).
[132] Art 198(1)(a) contains government's ordinary legislative power and arts 182 and 199(g) refer to government's power on conducting social and economic public policy.

(confirming the laws by special majorities) and control the government legislative acts (by changing their formulations or revoking them).

We can say that in Portugal passing laws in times of crisis—when the urgency of the situation calls for quick decisions—is no different from legislating in ordinary times, especially on economic, social, and cultural rights matters, because they are not part of the parliamentary legislative reserve.[133] So, government legislative acts can always be approved quickly and under a more straightforward procedure.

Still, it is worth noticing that during this period the government had majority support in parliament, which means that parliament could have straightforwardly approved those legislative acts, and, in fact, it had, although they were included in the annual budgetary law. Using the annual budgetary law to introduce changes in different legal regimes, sometimes on matters that are not even fiscal or tax issues ('cavalier budgétaire'), is common practice in Portugal[134] and has not yet been condemned by the CC.

That option can be explained, on the one hand, because the Government wanted to reinforce (even if apparently) the democratic legitimacy of the measures by their parliamentary approval and, on the other hand, by the intention to avoid any organic unconstitutionality if they finally could be considered as restricting rights, freedoms, and fundamental guarantees. Regardless of the government's intention, the use of the annual budgetary act to approve the main social measures of the MoU cannot be considered a novelty or a distinctive mark of this period.

3. The judicial protection of social rights in times of crisis

The question of the role of courts in protecting the fundamental rights is a universal issue of constitutionalism, and a particularly rough issue as far as social rights are concerned, considering that the standards of the constitutional judicial review of laws are indeterminate, and the fulfilment of the rights depends on choices about the allocation of limited funds. In the framework of social constitutionalism, courts are called upon to assess the democratic legislator's compliance with open constitutional principles and rules, by surveying public policies, which, in financial crises, tend to reduce social benefits.

The principle of the separation of powers, which is central today, is addressed in many ways all over the world, in different contexts (*common law* and *administrative*

---

[133] It would be different if the measures affected rights, freedoms, and guarantees, because restriction thereof is constitutionally reserved to parliamentary legislative acts (art 165(1)(b) Portuguese Constitution).

[134] The special nature and procedure of the annual budgetary act—government's exclusive initiative and the formal parliament act—explain this traditional practice in Portugal. To better understand the question see, for all, Tiago Duarte, *A Lei por Detrás do Orçamento* (Almedina 2007).

and civil law countries). Authors tend to group it into systems with a strong control (*supremacist*), weak control (*detached*), and medium control (*engaged*), depending on the courts' power to interfere with the democratic legislator.

In Portugal, as in many continental European countries, the idea of moderate control prevails—the rule of constitutional law is applied, but with due respect for the division of powers and self-restraint of the courts on issues with political implications, namely in setting and implementing public social policies—albeit with varying practical applications.

In the literature (and in the case law as well, taking into account dissenting votes in almost all court judgments), there are some differences regarding the role that courts should play, particularly the CC, in protecting the social benefit entitlements.[135]

The Portuguese Constitution explicitly protects individualised social rights (which is not the case in Germany, for example), and some authors defend that, when it comes to the democratic legislator's decisions limiting such fundamental rights, the legal arsenal that the Constitution provides to the judicial power must also be used. Thus, the CC should also exercise intensive control, and there should not be any room for judicial self-restraint. This position comes from the idea that, when the legislator fulfils a social right (for example, social security right), the reduction or limitation of the benefits guaranteed by law must be regarded as a restriction of a fundamental right (ie, that the implementation by law confers content on the constitutionally consecrated right). Furthermore, entitlements to benefits thus conferred enjoy reinforced extra protection under the right to property, consecrated in the Constitution in broad terms, generally comprising any economic right (and not only ownership according to civil law).[136]

However, the majority position is that, concerning the social rights to benefits, the CC must acknowledge the margin of appreciation of the legislator, who enjoys democratic preference whenever the Constitution uses general wording and does not establish or specify the content of the rights. The Court should exercise self-restraint and, respecting the principle of the separation of powers, carry out control limited to the evidence of the violation of the essential core of the right, in other words, the *bare essentials for a decent existence*, which is the absolute limit and not restricted to what is possible.

---

[135] We do not include social freedoms that historically would be included in social rights, such as, for example, the right to strike and trade union freedom.

[136] There is thus the view that the CC did well in the crisis case law, but performed poorly in the reasoning, as it should have decided that the right to a pension as a fundamental right incorporated the content that was given to it by law. Therefore, any limitation or withdrawal should be addressed as limiting the content of a fundamental right, applying the rules of art 18, set out for the rights, freedoms, and guarantees (rights with a determinable content according to the Constitution). Tight control by the Court would be justified only if a restriction of fundamental rights were to be considered and not within the context of control of options of public policies, where the legislator is entitled to a scope of freedom.

The same idea of self-constraint goes for the control of compliance with the applicable fundamental legal principles, in particular, the principles of equality, non-discrimination (and the prohibition precluding arbitrariness), proportionality (in all of its dimensions), and the protection of legitimate expectations. Under the principle of proportionality, the dimensions of action rule and control rule particularly stand out. In a state governed by the rule of law, all public powers, beginning with the political and legislative power, are obliged to seek the appropriate, necessary, and balanced solutions through their actions. The courts, however, only invalidate such solutions that are *unequivocally* inadequate, unnecessary, or unbalanced. Otherwise, the CC will ultimately become a ruler of last resort.

Of course, the level of the courts' supervision of the laws, especially that of the CC, is not fixed and varies according to the legislated matters.

In implementing the social benefit entitlements, generally speaking, policy-makers and legislators regard the 'multicentrality' of issues, the technicality of the subjects, and the flexibility of choices. There are reasonable alternative interpretations for the implementation of constitutional rules. Not having democratic legitimacy and political responsibility, nor enjoying, in general, technical expertise on such matters, courts should be limited to overseeing the legislator's actions. They should only invalidate democratic choices when given evidence of being unreasonable in terms of their grounds and measure. They should never assume the role of the legislator, choosing the best solution in its lieu.

Such prudential behaviour is particularly valuable in severe crises—economic and financial—where it is necessary to reduce state social benefits. In such cases, the Constitution is not suspended, but the values and interests must be weighed against the social and political reality. In controlling compliance with constitutional provisions and principles, the Court must grant the legislator more room for assessing and deciding, specifically in the use of the criterion of necessity, as long as the restrictive measures are temporary and are appropriate for addressing the problems. At the same time, they must be intransigent in the compliance with the constitutional limits, which are under a high level of judicial scrutiny, as they should be.

Finally, note that the theoretical and practical grounds for adequate control and self-restraint of the courts in protecting the social rights against the legislator do not result only from their lack of democratic (electoral) legitimisation and political accountability or the fact that they are not technically equipped to assess the political policies.

Such an attitude also represents the acknowledgement of the constitutional opening-up to social and political pluralism. Because of the different reasonable views on what is fair or unfair concerning policy and given the open discussion between such reasonable conceptions within the public arena: it is the legislative power, and not the judicial, that must make the decision about the way forward.

IV. Conclusion

In being unusually severe, the crisis forced restrictive measures that affected social rights in different ways and with different outcomes. Some of the measures were eventually reverted by the new socialist government for political reasons, even those that had not been intended to be temporary. Others did not pass through the sieve of the CC. So, the successive decisions of unconstitutionality resulted in the adoption of what were mostly tax measures for balancing the state budgets, playing down the initial requirements of the MoU regarding social cuts.

Despite the changes in the labour legislation and the social security schemes during the crisis years, Portugal ended up failing to implement structural reforms, especially of the social security system. Moreover, although the economic revival helped de-escalate the problem, it subsists, and it can hit rather hard if the economic and financial situation takes a turn for the worse.

The implications for constitutional law concerning the separation of powers were limited because in Portugal the government has ordinary legislative competence in such a broad manner that may enact decree-laws in the field of social protection without challenging the law-making powers of the Parliament.

However, the crisis brought new legal and constitutional contributions to the interpretation and implementation of the legal framework of social rights. Leading doctrinal positions have resulted from the case law. First, the right to a retirement pension has different levels of protection, meaning that the right to a fixed pension sum (ie, the amount fixed when the pensioner starts receiving that benefit) is not untouchable. In case of relevant public interest (either temporarily or even permanently, if occurring in the context of a structural reform), the ordinary legislator can sacrifice a certain pension amount. Second, only the minimum amount indispensable for ensuring a decent existence enjoys total protection in times of economic-financial crisis. Finally, the legitimate expectations of inviolability of benefits nurtured by those people who are entitled to receive benefits from the public budgets or bodies do not enjoy the same level of protection as those of people receiving sums from the private sector. Comparing the sacrifices imposed on both, one must focus on the principle of equal proportionality, which does not ignore the fact that civil service pensioners and employees are not subject to the same level of risk and precariousness.

9

A 'Bail-In' of Social Rights? The Cypriot Experience of the Financial Crisis

Constantinos Kombos and Athena Herodotou

I. Introduction

When the Republic of Cyprus (or Cyprus) became part of the eurozone system in January 2008, the prevailing view was that Cyprus had a long-standing welfare state system that provided a relatively close-knit social safety net.[1] The aims, tools, and

---

[1] Odysseas Christou, Christina Ioannou, and Anthos Shekeris, 'The Cypriot Welfare State at a Time of Crisis' in Klaus Schubert, Paloma de Villota, and Johanna Kuhlmann (eds), *Challenges to European Welfare Systems* (Springer 2016) 79–80.

Constantinos Kombos and Athena Herodotou, *A 'Bail-In' of Social Rights? The Cypriot Experience of the Financial Crisis*
In: *European Welfare State Constitutions after the Financial Crisis*. Edited by: Ulrich Becker and Anastasia Poulou,
Oxford University Press (2020). © The Contributors. DOI: 10.1093/oso/9780198851776.003.0009

approaches of that system were nonetheless directly affected by the global financial crisis of 2008. A new economic reality emerged and had the effect of restructuring the Cypriot economic model and, as a corollary, the national social model. The crisis manifested itself in the collapse of the banking sector and in the detrimental effects that the exposure to the ongoing Greek sovereign debt crisis had. As a result, the economy was negatively affected and the underlying anomalies of the Cypriot system were magnified.[2]

In terms of the timeline of events, on 25 June 2012 the Cypriot government submitted a request for stability support to the President of Eurogroup, as per article 13(1) of the Treaty establishing the European Stability Mechanism (ESM). On 25 March 2013, the Eurogroup agreed with the Cypriot authorities on the key elements of Cyprus's macroeconomic adjustment programme.[3] A few days later, the Eurogroup endorsed the Memorandum of Understanding on Specific Economic Policy Conditionality (the MoU) and the Financial Assistance Facility Agreement (the Loan Agreement), as agreed between the European Commission (on behalf of the ESM), the European Central Bank (ECB), and the International Monetary Fund (IMF)—the so-called Troika—and Cyprus.[4]

On the one hand, the Loan Agreement provided for a €10 billion financial assistance package towards Cyprus, with the ESM providing up to €9 billion and the IMF contributing around €1 billion. The MoU on Specific Economic Policy Conditionality, on the other hand, aimed at creating an economic adjustment programme to address short- and medium-term financial, structural, and fiscal challenges faced by Cyprus. Consequently, the MoU established a new economic policy for Cyprus based on three pillars: (1) measures to ensure the return of stability in the banking sector, (2) structural measures, with emphasis on the restructuring

---

[2] For an economic analysis of the Cypriot financial crisis, see Stavros A Zenios, 'The Cyprus Debt: Perfect Crisis and a Way Forward' (2013) 7(1) Cyprus Economic Policy Review 3; Alexander Apostolides, 'Beware of German Gifts Near Elections: How Cyprus got Here and Why it is Currently More Out than In the Eurozone' (2013) 8(3) Capital Markets Law Journal 300; Sofronis Clerides, 'The Collapse of the Cypriot Banking System: A Bird's Eye View' (2014) 8(2) Cyprus Economic Policy Review 3. See also, Demetra Arsalidou and Maria Krambia-Kapardis, 'Weak Corporate Governance can Lead to a Country's Financial Catastrophe: The Case of Cyprus' (2015) 4 Journal of Business Law 361. For a general analysis of the situation before the crisis (emerging imbalances), the crisis and the run-up to the Economic Adjustment Programme, and the Programme Design and objectives and its financing, see European Commission Directorate-General for Economic and Financial Affairs, *The Economic Adjustment Programme for Cyprus* (European Economy Occasional Paper 149, Brussels 2013) <http://ec.europa.eu/economy_finance/publications/occasional_paper/2013/pdf/ocp149_en.pdf> accessed 10 July 2019.

[3] Cyprus was the only case where the key elements of the adjustment programme were defined by Eurogroup before Troika reached staff-level agreement with Cypriot authorities; see Michael Ioannidis, 'EU Financial Assistance Conditionality after Two Pack' (2014) 74 Heidelberg Journal of International Law 61, 72.

[4] The Loan Agreement, and the therein attached MoU, were ratified by the Cypriot House of Representatives on 30 April 2013 with the Financial Assistance Facility Agreement (Ratifying) Law (1(III)/2013).

of the public sector, and (3) fiscal consolidation measures to correct the excessive government deficit.[5]

In other words, the Cypriot government, as the recipient state of the financial assistance and on the basis of the principle of strict conditionality, had to undertake a series of profound changes in its domestic economic and social policies. These changes inevitably affected employment, the social security schemes, the welfare system, pensions, healthcare, and public assistance. The structural and fiscal consolidation measures were in effect imposed on the understanding that they were necessary for achieving the long-term stability of public finances, as well as for supporting 'the diversification of the economy and to alleviate the adverse impact on jobs and growth arising from Cyprus's exposure to external shocks'.[6] A series of significant and substantial social protection reforms were voted into laws by the House of Representatives in December 2012, prior to the implementation of the MoU. Further measures were sought through the MoU, such as the introduction of cuts and reforms in salaries and pensions, reforms of social benefit schemes, and measures to contain the growth of health expenditure.

Overall, Cyprus struggled to ensure compliance with the terms resulting from the Loan Agreement and the MoU, while at the same time having to implement measures that restructured the pre-existing social protection system both in terms of its rationale and its content. Moreover, it must be noted that the relevant changes were required at a point when the bail-in had been introduced, thus creating a unique crisis in economic, social, and constitutional terms. The economic crisis in Cyprus had a direct and indirect impact on both the private and public economic areas, thus magnifying the short-term negative effect on the society. Citizens were in more need of the social safety net due to the collapse of the private part of the economy, while at the same time the public economics were now considerably constrained and under an obligation to reform the mechanics of the social provision.

II. The background of the Cypriot economic crisis and the adoption of the MoU

1. The Cypriot banking crisis and the need to restructure the welfare system

Until 2008, Cyprus had a relatively steady economy, with a surplus in its fiscal accounts. Despite the economic crisis in Europe, Cyprus did not take those preventive

---

[5] For the reasons for the excessive government deficit, see Athanasios Orphanides, 'What Happened in Cyprus? The Economic Consequences of the Last Communist Government in Europe' in Alexander Michaelides and Athanasios Orphanides (eds), *The Cyprus Bail-in: Policy Lessons from the Cyprus Economic Crisis* (Imperial College Press 2016); Christou, Ioannou, and Shekeris (n 1).

[6] European Commission Directorate-General for Economic and Financial Affairs (n 2) para 81.

measures necessary to insulate itself from the crisis and to prepare for the danger. The first signs of recession were detected in the Cypriot banking system in 2009. In May 2011, Cyprus was cut off from international capital markets and by the end of 2011 the Council of Ministers struck an agreement with the Russian Federation for a €2.5 billion emergency loan in order to help Cyprus maintain fiscal stability. However, this was not enough. In June 2012, the government submitted a request for stability support to the ESM and the IMF, yet the negotiations with Troika were prolonged and lasted for almost a year.

On 16 March 2013, the Eurogroup agreed to an unprecedented and drastic bundle of measures that centred on the idea of a 'bail-in' for €10 billion. Put differently, the Eurogroup accepted to provide financial assistance to Cyprus, but the amount provided would not be distributed for the recapitalisation of the Cypriot banks. Cyprus would have to recapitalise them—and secure an amount of approximately €5.8 billion—using its own means. The initial proposal for a bail-in provided for the imposition of a one-time levy of 9.9 per cent on deposits over €100,000 and a one-time levy of 6.75 per cent on deposits below €100,000. However, on 19 March 2013, the House of Representatives rejected it. On 21 March 2013, the ECB piled the pressure on the Cypriot government by warning it would cut off its emergency liquidity assistance after 25 March unless a programme was in place. This ultimatum meant that a failure to agree to terms would have led to the collapse of Cyprus's two largest banks, namely the Bank of Cyprus and the Cyprus Popular Bank (Laiki Bank). Consequently, the banking sector would have collapsed and Cyprus would have gone bankrupt because of a €30 billion liability that was unfunded and the exchequer would be unable to pay.

On 22 March 2013, the House of Representatives passed the Resolution of Credit and Other Institutions Law,[7] which was published in the Official Gazette on the same day.[8] On 25 March 2013, the government reached a revised agreement with Eurogroup on the key elements necessary for a future economic adjustment programme.[9] In the Eurogroup Statement on Cyprus, the Eurogroup warranted the financial assistance towards Cyprus of up to €10 billion to safeguard the country's financial stability, as well as to safeguard stability in the eurozone.[10] The Eurogroup

---

[7] Law 17(1)/2013.

[8] Official Gazette of the Republic of Cyprus, No 4379 of 22 March 2013. An unofficial translation of the law in English is available at <https://www.centralbank.cy/images/media/pdf/17_I_2013_EN_Resolution.pdf> accessed 10 July 2019.

[9] Michele Kambas and Karolina Tagaris, 'Cyprus Banks Remain Closed to Avert Run on Deposits' *Reuters* (Nicosia, 25 March 2013) <https://www.reuters.com/article/us-cyprus-parliament/cyprus-banks-remain-closed-to-avert-run-on-deposits-idUSBRE92G03I20130325> accessed 10 July 2019; 'Eurogroup Signs Off on Bailout Agreement Reached by Cyprus and Troika' *Ekathimerini* (Nicosia, 25 March 2013) <http://www.ekathimerini.com/149669/article/ekathimerini/news/eurogroup-signs-off-on-bailout-agreement-reached-by-cyprus-and-troika> accessed 10 July 2019.

[10] See Eurogroup Statement on Cyprus <https://www.consilium.europa.eu/uedocs/cms_data/docs/pressdata/en/ecofin/136487.pdf> accessed 10 July 2019.

reiterated that the €10 billion would not be used to recapitalise Laiki Bank and the Bank of Cyprus.

In return, Cyprus would take measures so as to secure the amount of €5.8 billion using its own means.[11] However, all deposits below €100,000 (known as insured deposits) were now to be safeguarded, in accordance with EU principles, and more specifically Directive 1994/19/EC on deposit guarantee schemes,[12] as amended by Directive 2009/14/EC.[13] To this end, Cyprus agreed to resolve Laiki Bank, the country's second largest bank at the time, levying all deposits larger than €100,000 (known as uninsured deposits) and levying 47.5 per cent of uninsured deposits in the Bank of Cyprus.[14] In other words, uninsured depositors of Laiki Bank lost everything and uninsured depositors of the Bank of Cyprus lost almost half of their deposits. In this manner, the 'bail-in' marked a departure from established practice and was a tool that was to be tested in a small-scale economy with minimal contagion capacity.

On 30 April 2013, the House of Representatives implemented the MoU into legislation and, like other states that accepted financial assistance, Cyprus was subject to strict conditionality. That required a number of reforms, including the restructure of the welfare system in a way that it would streamline the broad range of benefits provided, while preserving the viability of the social protection schemes and protecting the most vulnerable and disadvantaged people. Specifically, Cyprus committed to implement structural reforms to support its fiscal consolidation efforts, to ensure the sustainability and intra- and inter-generational fairness of its pension system, and to review and contain spending of the social insurance system and the social welfare schemes.[15] Furthermore, Cyprus undertook to minimise overlaps in benefits and improve targeting, and to prepare an action plan that would cover all social programmes, including social assistance and family

---

[11] With Directive 2014/59/EU of the European Parliament and of the Council establishing a framework for the recovery and resolution of credit institutions and investment firms (adopted on 15 May 2014 and entered into force on 2 July 2014) the creditor bail-in became an official banking resolution tool of choice within the EU.

[12] Directive 94/19/EC of the European Parliament and of the Council of 30 May 1994 on deposit-guarantee schemes.

[13] Directive 2009/14/EC of the European Parliament and of the Council of 11 March 2009 amending Directive 94/19/EC on deposit-guarantee schemes as regards the coverage level and the payout delay.

[14] The bail-in was based on two decrees adopted by the Central Bank of Cyprus, as the Resolution Authority of Cyprus, on the basis of the Law on Resolution of Credit and Other Institutions Law of 2013. The first decree (Decree No 103, published in the Official Gazette of the Republic of Cyprus, Annex III (I), No 4645, 769–80, of 29 March 2013) provided for the recapitalisation of the Bank of Cyprus, through a conversion of uninsured deposits into shares of the bank or into securities. The second decree (Decree No 104, published in the Official Gazette of the Republic of Cyprus, Annex III (I), No 4645, 781–88, of 29 March 2013) provided for the transfer of certain assets and liabilities, as well as insured deposits, of the Laiki Bank to the Bank of Cyprus and for the liquidation of uninsured deposits.

[15] Letter of intent, Memorandum of Economic and Financial Policies, and Technical Memorandum of Understanding of 29 April 2013, sent by the Republic of Cyprus to the IMF which describes the policies that Cyprus intends to implement in the context of its request for financial support from the IMF, paras 26–27 <https://www.imf.org/external/np/loi/2013/cyp/042913.pdf> accessed 10 July 2019.

benefits.[16] Therefore, this financial assistance conditionality—'the most advanced mechanism of European economic governance'[17]—forced Cyprus, as a recipient state, to undertake profound changes not only in its economic but also in its social policies, pressured by the need for timely lending. It is nonetheless noteworthy that a large number of the social reforms, which will be analysed below, were introduced prior to the signature of the MoU to secure the deal.

2. The uncertain legal nature of the MoU in the Cypriot legal order

The MoU, which formed the basis for financing Cyprus's deficits and substantive monetary needs, was ratified in the Cypriot legal order as an ordinary law in accordance with article 169(2) of the Constitution and it has been approached as an international treaty creating contractual obligations for Cyprus.[18] Nevertheless, it remains doubtful whether the MoU could come within the scope of article 169 of the Constitution. Firstly, it is unclear whether the MoU qualifies as an international treaty that needs ratification under article 169(2) of the Constitution. Secondly, article 169(1) refers to an international agreement with international organisations or other states and includes matters relating to commerce, economic cooperation (including payments and credit), and *modus vivendi*. Consequently, the MoU is not an agreement with another state and it remains doubtful whether it qualifies as an agreement with an international organisation.

In terms of procedural effect, an instrument placed within article 169(2) requires ratification through legislation whereas an instrument within article 169(1) shall be concluded under a decision of the Council of Ministers. Thus, if one assumes that the MoU falls within the scope of article 169(1), the MoU would not need legislative ratification but could have entered into force with a mere executive decision. This point raises a serious separation of powers issue, given that the executive power in effect seems to have delegated to the legislature a competence that the Constitution reserves for the executive. In reality, however, the choice of ratification under article 169(2) was the result of ambiguity, uncertainty, and cautiousness as to the proper meaning and scope of article 169 as the designated route for implementing the MoU in the domestic legal order. The Attorney-General opined that the Loan Agreement and the MoU could not have been implemented without

---

[16] ibid, para 28.
[17] Anastasia Poulou, 'Austerity and European Social Rights: How Can Courts Protect Europe's Lost Generation' (2014) 15 German Law Journal 1145, 1149.
[18] Art 169(2) of the Constitution, which provides that 'any other treaty, convention or international agreement shall be negotiated and signed under a decision of the Council of Ministers and shall only be operative and binding on the Republic when approved by a law made by the House of Representatives whereupon it shall be concluded'.

the approval by the House of Representatives, as they fell within the definition of an 'international treaty' under article 169(2). Moreover, the decision for legislative approval may have been influenced by the 2002 Revenue and Expenditure Management and Accounting Law, stipulating that, except for international loan agreements governed by article 169 of the Constitution, the conclusion of any other loan agreement by the state for an amount exceeding the total amount of one million Cypriot pounds shall not be binding on the Republic of Cyprus unless ratified by law in the House of Representatives.[19]

In either case, the effect on the status of the instrument is to have superior force vis-à-vis conflicting national law but not the Constitution, as per article 169(3). Therefore, in constitutional terms the MoU is viewed as a *sui generis* instrument that is arguably not expressly covered within article 169, yet which has a political content that materialises through national measures introduced for the purpose of complying with the MoU. It is argued that the MoU is to be approached on the basis of a contractual obligation that has dense political meaning due to the credibility of the state being at stake and which thus carries unprecedented binding power yet without necessarily having legally binding power in constitutional terms.

It is noteworthy that the Cypriot courts have refrained from analysing the MOU's legal nature. Both the Supreme Court (acting as Administrative Court) and the District Courts simply refer to the economic adjustment programme as a 'political agreement' or a 'political arrangement' between Cyprus and the Eurogroup.[20] For instance, in *Demetriou et al v Central Bank of Cyprus et al*,[21] the Supreme Court characterised the MoU as a 'political agreement for the establishment of an Economic Adjustment Programme'. The issue of the nature of the MoU was also raised before the Supreme Court in *Christodoulou et al v Central Bank of Cyprus et al*.[22] There, the applicants challenged the legality of Decrees 103 and 104 imposing the haircut of uninsured deposits. The applications were dismissed on a preliminary objection, as the matter held that the dispute fell in the sphere of private law, not of public (administrative) law, thus the proper course of action was for the depositors to instigate civil actions.[23]

What is interesting in *Christodoulou* is another preliminary objection raised by the respondent. Particularly, it was suggested that the MoU, on the basis of which Decrees 103 and 104 were issued, is an agreement of a political nature.

---

[19] Law 112(I)/2002, art 28(1). This law was repealed in 2014, after the conclusion of the Loan Agreement and the MoU.

[20] See, for example, *Christodoulou et al v Central Bank of Cyprus et al* (2013) 3 CLR 427; *Demetriou et al v Central Bank of Cyprus et al* Joined Cases nos 1034/2013 and others (9 October 2014); *Santis v Bank of Cyprus Public Company Ltd et al* App no 3005/13 (17 July 2013); *Green Power Energy Ltd v Cyprus Popular Bank Public Company Ltd et al* App no 4990/13 (30 April 2014).

[21] *Demetriou* (n 20).

[22] *Christodoulou* (n 20).

[23] See Christian Duve and Philip Wimalasena, 'Who Decides Whether Bail-in is Legal? What Comes After Cyprus and Greece?' (2015) 9(3) Law and Financial Markets Review 177.

Therefore, the argument goes, the Decrees constitute 'acts of government' ('*actes de gouvernment*') with the view of making 'the conclusion and materialization of *international treaties*, namely the MoU and the Loan Agreement, possible'.[24] The characterisation of the Decrees as 'acts of government' would mean that their content and the measures resulting from them escape judicial review. However, this comment was not examined by the majority decision in constitutional terms and the uncertainty of the exact legal status of the MoU remained unanswered. The majority decision simply stated that it would not elaborate on the issue as it had already found that it lacked jurisdiction and in any case the ruling on this issue would not have any practical consequence.[25] It is, however, noted that such a finding would have significant constitutional consequences in other situations, where in effect it could have resulted in pre-emption of judicial scrutiny.

More recently, in *Parklane Hotels Ltd et al v the Republic*,[26] the Administrative Court was called to decide on the constitutionality of the 2013 Property Taxation (Amending) Law.[27] The adoption of the contested Law was deemed necessary for gaining additional revenue from property taxation as per the MoU. While the Law was found constitutional, the Court briefly commented on the legal nature of the MoU. Particularly, the applicants referred to Greek jurisprudence and claimed that Memoranda of Understanding constitute political and governmental programmatic statements and contain no binding legal rules; and even if they were considered as binding international treaties, then such treaties have superior force over national law, but not over the Constitution. The Court distinguished between the Greek and the Cypriot MoU, indicating that the latter was the result of an agreement between the Cypriot government and Troika and it included a series of measures that should had been immediately implemented in order to secure financial support. Moreover, the MoU was published in the Official Gazette of the Republic (as part of the Financial Assistance Facility Agreement Law) in accordance with article 169(2) of the Constitution and, consequently, it was a legally binding international agreement.

Despite the Court's reference to the provisions of the Cypriot Constitution and the affirmation of the legally binding character of the MoU as an instrument with superior force over national legislation, the legal reasoning of this finding was insufficiently and hastily elaborated. Moreover, this was the finding of a court of first instance, while the Supreme Court has yet to comment in a holistic manner on the exact legal nature of the MoU in Cyprus.[28] Many and significant constitutional

---

[24] ibid (emphasis added).

[25] cf dissenting opinions of Judges Papadopoulou and Erotokritou in *Christodoulou* (n 20), who rejected the preliminary objections and held that the Decrees cannot be considered acts of the government.

[26] Joined Cases nos 6175/2013 and others (15 March 2019).

[27] Law 33 (I)/2013.

[28] On whether MoUs, or loan conditions, are legally binding, see Claire Kilpatrick, 'Are the Bailouts Immune to EU Social Challenge Because They Are Not EU Law?' (2014) 10 European Constitutional Law Review 393, 406–15.

points of both a procedural and substantive nature were bypassed in the case law, with interesting constitutional questions remaining unanswered.

III. Reforms in national social protection systems during the financial crisis

1. Overview of the national social protection and healthcare systems

a) Constitutional social protection

According to article 9 of the 1960 Constitution of Cyprus, '[e]very person has the right to a decent existence and to social security. A law shall provide for the protection of the workers, assistance to the poor and for a system of social insurance'.[29] Article 9 does not provide a definition over the notion of 'decent existence' but it has been interpreted as creating an obligation upon the state 'to create and maintain such conditions of living, of work and of health as *to enable every person to enjoy a standard of living adequate for the health and well-being of himself and his family*'.[30] Furthermore, article 9 establishes a constitutional duty upon the state to enact laws establishing a system of social protection aimed at protecting individuals in the event of unemployment, sickness, disability, widowhood, old age, or other similar circumstances.[31] Therefore, article 9 of the Constitution seems to be providing a general enablement clause that has, at the same time, a duty-bound core not to act beyond the benchmark set therein.

b) Overview of the social protection system

The Cypriot social protection scheme is regulated under the 2010 Social Insurance Law.[32] All persons gainfully employed in Cyprus (either as employees or as self-employed persons) are compulsorily covered by the scheme,[33] which is divided into two parts: the basic part, corresponding to the repealed flat-rate scheme, and the earnings-related part. The Social Insurance Scheme, as it is called, is financed by contributions paid by insured persons (employees), employers, and the state. Employers are liable to pay contributions to the Social Insurance, Annual Holidays

---

[29] For further analysis see Constantinos Kombos, 'Social Rights in the Republic of Cyprus' in Krzysztof Wojtyczek (ed), *Social and Economic Rights as Fundamental Rights* (Eleven International Publishing 2016) 57–86.

[30] Criton Tornaritis, 'The Social and Economic Rights under the Law of the Republic of Cyprus' in *Mélanges Marcel Bridel* (Lausanne 1968) <http://www.kypros.org/Documents/Tornaritis/docs/social.html> accessed 10 July 2019 (emphasis added).

[31] Achilles C Emilianides, *Cyprus (International Encyclopaedia of Laws: Constitutional Law Series)* (Kluwer Law International 2013) 174.

[32] Social Insurance Law of 2010 (59(I)/2010), as amended.

[33] ibid, arts 4 and 11.

with Pay, Redundancy, Human Resources Development, and Social Cohesion Funds. The Social Insurance Law envisages an increase of approximately 1.3 per cent every five years to the contribution rate of employees and employers.[34] All contributions are paid at the Social Insurance Services, a governmental body under the control and supervision of the Ministry of Labour, Welfare and Social Insurance. The obligation to pay contributions ceases when the insured person reaches the pensionable age (in principle, sixty-five years old).[35]

The Social Insurance Scheme provides for a number of periodical benefits, such as maternity allowance, sickness benefit, unemployment benefit, invalidity pension, statutory pension, widow's/widower's pension, orphan's benefit, missing person's allowance, and paternity allowance (introduced in 2017).[36] It further provides for a number of lump-sum benefits, such as maternity grant and funeral grant.[37] Finally, the Scheme provides for employment injury benefits, which include temporary incapacity (injury benefit), disability benefit, and death benefit.[38] The disability benefit may take the form of a lump-sum grant or a pension, depending on the degree of disablement.[39]

Employed persons are entitled to all aforementioned benefits, whereas self-employed persons are not entitled to unemployment benefits or to employment injury benefits.[40] Voluntarily insured persons working abroad for Cypriot employers are not entitled to employment injury benefits; other voluntarily insured persons are not entitled to maternity allowance, paternity allowance, sickness benefit, and unemployment benefit.[41] Therefore, the system is founded on the principle of residence of the worker and not of the employer.

All periodical benefits are comprised of the basic benefit and the supplementary benefit.[42] The basic benefit, which includes increases for dependants, is linked to the insurable earnings of the insured person in the basic insurance, while supplementary benefits are related to the insurable earnings of a person in the supplementary insurance.[43] The Social Insurance Services—which are responsible for the implementation of the governmental policy, schemes, and measures in the field of social insurance and the identification of social and economic needs that can be

---

[34] ibid, arts 5, 12, and 15.
[35] ibid, arts 2 and 16.
[36] ibid, pt III, arts 21–45.
[37] ibid.
[38] ibid, pt IV, arts 46–66.
[39] ibid, art 49. The disability grant is payable to employed persons suffering a loss of physical or mental faculty of a degree between 10 per cent and 19 per cent, while the disability pension is payable to those suffering a loss of 20 per cent and above.
[40] ibid, arts 24(2)(a) and 47.
[41] ibid, art 24(2)(b).
[42] ibid, art 21(2).
[43] Basic and supplementary benefits for every type of benefit are set out in detail in Annex IV of the Social Insurance Law of 2010, as amended.

confronted with social security—are responsible for the payment of the majority of these benefits and pensions.

In addition to the Social Insurance Services, the Ministry of Labour, Welfare and Social Insurance has also established the Social Welfare Services, which aim at safeguarding social cohesion and social solidarity, at providing social protection, at achieving social inclusion, and at combating poverty and social exclusion. Furthermore, the Department for Social Inclusion of Persons with Disabilities, which is also under the control of the Ministry of Labour, Welfare and Social Insurance, aims at improving the quality of life of persons with disabilities, at creating new prospects for their social inclusion through the design, coordination, and implementation of reforming policies, and at providing social benefits to persons with disabilities. The Ministry of Labour, Welfare and Social Insurance created the relatively new Welfare Benefits Administration Service, with the task of implementing and administering various social schemes, including the guaranteed minimum income, child benefit, mother's allowance, and the scheme for supporting pensioners with low income. Therefore, the system is headed by the Ministry of Labour, Welfare and Social Insurance and it can be characterised by complexity and administrative overlap that surely impact upon its efficiency. Finally, it should be noted that the social protection system in Cyprus has been influenced by EU law, as it adheres to its norms and policies in the fields of social inclusion and social protection.[44]

c) Overview of the healthcare system
The Cypriot healthcare system is comprised of two parallel delivery sectors, namely a public sector and a separate private sector.[45] These two delivery routes were for the most part mutually exclusive, until the recent healthcare reform. Now, the private sector supplements public benefits. Particularly, until May 2019, the public healthcare sector, administered by the Ministry of Health and financed by the state budget, provided free-of-charge services through six hospitals, four specialist centres, three rural hospitals, thirty-eight health centres, and other centres

---

[44] For instance, Cyprus implemented EU regulations on Social Security Coordination; see Regulation (EC) No 883/2004 of the European Parliament and of the Council of 29 April 2004 on the coordination of social security systems (2004) OJ L166, Regulation (EC) No 987/2009 of the European Parliament and of the Council of 16 September 2009 laying down the procedure for implementing Regulation (EC) No 883/2004 on the coordination of social security systems (2009) OJ L284/1, Regulation (EU) No 1231/2010 of the European Parliament and of the Council of 24 November 2010 extending Regulation (EC) No 883/2004 and Regulation (EC) No 987/2009 to nationals of third countries who are not already covered by these Regulations solely on the grounds of their nationality (2010) OJ L344/1, Regulation (EU) No 465/2012 of the European Parliament and of the Council of 22 May 2012 amending Regulation (EC) No 883/2004 on the coordination of social security systems and Regulation (EC) No 987/2009 laying down the procedure for implementing Regulation (EC) No 883/2004 (2012) OJ L149/4.

[45] See Haris Charalambous, 'Cancer Care in an Economically Torn Country: Cyprus' in Michael Silbermann (ed), *Cancer Care in Countries and Societies in Transition: Individualized Care in Focus* (Springer 2016) 164–66.

for primary services. However, the public sector services did not secure universal coverage. Approximately 83 per cent of the population had access to public health-care, while the rest of the population could only use public services after paying the relevant fees.[46] As regards the private healthcare sector, it is mostly financed by private out-of-pocket payments and its services are provided through, inter alia, private hospitals, clinics, diagnostic centres, and independent practitioners.[47]

In 2001, the House of Representatives enacted the General Healthcare System Law,[48] aiming at the introduction of a universal General Healthcare System (GHS) which would provide healthcare to all citizens. However, the introduction of such an arrangement did not take place until 2017. Until then, Cyprus had been char-acterised as the 'only EU member state that [lacked] a universal health system',[49] and its government was urged to take concrete steps towards implementing a re-form that would move the Cypriot healthcare system forward, while at the same time enabling the control of healthcare expenditure growth.[50] On 16 June 2017, the House of Representatives unanimously voted in favour of the implementation of the GHS, marking the beginning of a new era for Cyprus's healthcare system.[51] This newly established system is financed through contributions by the employers, employees/self-employed, pensioners, and the state.[52] The first phase of the system, concerning outpatient care provided by general practitioners, specialist doctors, pharmacies, and laboratories, came into force on 1 June 2019. The second phase and the complete implementation of the GHS will occur on 1 June 2020 with the introduction of inpatient services, accident and emergency department services, ambulance services, services by nurses, midwives, and allied health professionals, palliative care, medical rehabilitation, preventive dental care, and home visits.[53]

The implementation of the GHS in Cyprus is entrusted to the Health Insurance Organisation (HIO), a public legal body governed by a board of directors with tri-lateral representation from the government and the employers' and employees' unions. Healthcare services within the GHS are offered by all public and private healthcare providers contracted with the HIO. The beneficiaries of the new GHS are all persons who live in the areas controlled by the Republic of Cyprus and are

---

[46] Mamas Theodorou and others, 'Cyprus Health System Review' (2012) 14(6) Health Systems in Transition 1, 35.

[47] The inspection, regulation, and licensing of private hospitals, clinics, polyclinics, independent practitioners, etc is supervised by the Ministry of Health in accordance with the relevant legislation, such as the Private Hospitals (Establishment and Operation Control) Law (90(I)/2001), as amended, and the Registration of Medical Physicists Law (33(I)/2008), as amended.

[48] Law 89(I)/2001.

[49] Myria Antoniadou, 'Can Cyprus Overcome its Health-Care Challenges?' (2005) 365 The Lancet 1017, 1017.

[50] George Samoutis and Constantinos Paschalides, 'When will the Sun Shine on Cyprus's National Health Service?' (2011) 377 The Lancet 29, 29.

[51] General Healthcare System (Amending) Law (74(I)/2017).

[52] See arts 19 and 68(2)(b) of the 2001 General Healthcare System Law (n 48), as amended.

[53] ibid, art 22.

Cypriot citizens, European citizens residing and working in Cyprus or having acquired the right of permanent residence, third-country nationals who meet the requirements of national law, as well as those dependent on the above-mentioned categories.[54] It is thus evident that even persons without an income, such as the unemployed, children, students, soldiers, and public benefit recipients, will also have equal access to healthcare services.

2. Structural reforms and cuts

The financial crisis in Cyprus, lasting from 2012 to 2016,[55] caused a significant increase in unemployment and increased the percentage of people at risk of poverty and social exclusion, thus placing industrial relations under pressure.[56] Significant cuts were introduced in almost all social benefits. This is evident in an official financial report, according to which the expenditures for social protection (including old age, sickness, disability, unemployment, and housing) in 2014 amounted to €4,036.9 million, in comparison to €4,381.6 million in 2013.[57] As it is stated therein, it is noteworthy that it was the first reduction in the total social protection expenditure since 2000.[58] Nevertheless, the economic crisis also helped bring to the surface the need to address important gaps and weaknesses of the social protection system attributable to its projected long-term unsustainability.[59]

a) Old-age pension
In general, the pension schemes in Cyprus comprise the General Social Insurance Scheme (GSIS) and the occupational pension plans. All persons gainfully employed in Cyprus (as employees, self-employed, or voluntarily insured persons), both in the private and in the public sector, participate compulsorily in the earnings-related GSIS.[60] Old-age pension, or 'statutory pension' as it is now called,[61] is payable to all insured persons (employed, self-employed, or voluntarily

---

[54] ibid, art 16.

[55] Cyprus exited the economic adjustment programme, without a successor arrangement, on 7 March 2016.

[56] On industrial relations, see Constantinos Kombos, 'Trade Union Representation in Cyprus: the Right of Association' in Carmen La Macchia (ed), *Representing Employee Interests: Trade Union Systems Within the EU* (Bomarzo 2013) 101–35. See also, in general, Nicos Trimikliniotis, *Social and Employment Situation in Cyprus* (European Parliament Directorate General for Internal Policies, Policy Department A: Economic and Scientific Policy August 2012).

[57] Statistical Service, Ministry of Finance, 'Social Protection in Cyprus: Revenue and Expenditure 2014' (February 2017) General Social Statistics, Series III, Report No 11, 15.

[58] ibid.

[59] Christos Koutsampelas and Panos Pashardes, 'Social Protection in Cyprus: Overview and Challenges' (Cyprus Economic Policy Papers, No 05-17, September 2017) 7.

[60] Social Insurance Law of 2010, as amended, arts 35–39.

[61] The Social Insurance (Amending) Law (52(I)/2017) has replaced the term 'old-age pension' with the term 'statutory pension' throughout the basic Social Insurance Law of 2010.

insured persons) on reaching the pensionable age of sixty-five (for both males and females), provided that they meet the relevant insurance conditions. Insured persons are entitled to early retirement at the age of sixty-three if further statutory requirements are met,[62] while other groups of insured persons may also retire earlier.[63]

Those persons not entitled to statutory pension may receive a social pension, in accordance with the Provision of Social Pension Law of 1995.[64] If the person is not entitled to statutory pension or social pension, then he/she may be entitled to an old-age lump-sum payment at the age of sixty-eight if certain insurance conditions are met.[65] Finally, the Cypriot pension system also comprises the Government Employees Pension Scheme (GEPS), which provides supplementary pensions to civil servants, educational personnel, the police, and armed forces.[66] These old-age-related benefits have been extensively reformed, mostly for the purpose of preserving fiscal sustainability.[67]

More specifically, in 2012 the House of Representatives amended the Social Insurance Law and introduced article 35A providing for scaled reductions in statutory pensions.[68] The same amending legislation provided for the automatic adjustment of the statutory retirement age every five years, in accordance with the alteration to life expectancy, starting in 2018 for the period of 2018–2023.[69] In addition, stricter eligibility conditions were introduced in Annex III of the Social Insurance Law (regarding article 23 and insurance conditions for benefits). Accordingly, the minimum contributory period for a statutory pension would increase gradually over the period of January 2012 to January 2017, from ten to fifteen years. Furthermore, the yearly indexation of pensions, including statutory pension, was suspended from 1 January 2013 to 31 December 2016.[70] In regard to social pensions, the Provision of Social Pension Law was also amended in 2012 in order to explicitly provide that the social pension amount for the period of January 2013 to December 2016 would be equal to €336.28.

---

[62] Social Insurance Law of 2010, as amended, art 35.

[63] For instance, miners can retire earlier at the age of fifty-eight (see Social Insurance Law, as amended, art 36). Similarly, members of the police and the armed forces can retire earlier, if specific prerequisites relating to their rank and years of service are met (see the Pensions Law (97(I)/1997); the Members of the Armed Forces of the Republic (Retirement and Related Matters) (General Provisions) Law (215(I)/2012); the Retirement Benefits of Employees of the Public and Wider Public Sector, including Authorities of Local Government (Provisions of General Application) Law (216(I)/2012)).

[64] Law 25(I)/1995, as amended. The social pension is also available to those people that receive statutory pension, although it is considered very low, in accordance with arts (3)(1)(c) and 4(1) of the Provision of Social Pension Law of 1995, as amended. There are further requirements for becoming a beneficiary to the social pension, such as that the person should have resided in Cyprus for at least twenty years after the age of forty or for at least thirty-five years after the age of eighteen (see art 3(2)).

[65] Social Insurance Law of 2010, as amended, art 38.

[66] Pensions Law (97(I)/1997).

[67] Koutsampelas and Pashardes (n 59) 22.

[68] Social Insurance (Amending) Law (193(I)/2012).

[69] See definition of 'retirement age' in art 2 of the Social Insurance Law of 2010, as amended.

[70] Social Insurance Law of 2010, as amended, art 77(5).

Moreover, it can be argued that the GEPS was negatively impacted by the various reform initiatives. The Retirement Benefits of Employees of the Public and Wider Public Sector, including Authorities of Local Government (Provisions of General Application) Law of 2011 raised the contribution rate for the GEPS and closed it to new appointees in the public sector.[71] In 2012, further detailed changes were introduced to the GEPS[72] and included inter alia the pensionable age of public servants, which was gradually increased from sixty-three to sixty-five and, as from 2023, will be linked to life expectancy.[73] Finally, the legislation of 2012 introduced disincentives for early retirements (actuarial reduction)[74] and, at the same time, lump-sum pension benefits became taxable for the first time.[75]

Overall, the old-age related expenditures of Cyprus were as follows: in 2011, €1,734.9 million; in 2012, €1,925.7 million; in 2013, €1,934.9 million; and in 2014, €1,907 million. This indicates that following the implementation of the MoU in 2013, there was a significant decrease in the overall expenditures for old-age benefits.[76]

b) Social assistance

In its letter of intent to the IMF, Cyprus recognised that the existing social assistance system did not in all cases provide benefits to those who were most in need and that its administration had shortcomings.[77] Thus, in 2014 Cyprus introduced the guaranteed minimum income (GMI) Scheme, which regulates social assistance. The GMI Scheme is arguably the second most important social reform in recent years, following the introduction of the GHS, both in terms of philosophy and expenditure allocation.

It was introduced through the Guaranteed Minimum Income and Social Benefits Law[78] that replaced the public assistance scheme.[79] This reform aimed, firstly, at providing better support to groups who were exposed to the risk of poverty, including the working poor who were not recipients of any other income support benefit in the past, and, secondly, at improving the operational efficiency of

---

[71] Law 113(I)/2011, as amended, arts 4, 5, and 6.

[72] The Retirement Benefits of Employees of the Public and Wider Public Sector, including Authorities of Local Government (Provisions of General Application) Law of 2012 (216(I)/2012) abolished the Retirement Benefits of Employees of the Public and Wider Public Sector, including Authorities of Local Government (Provisions of General Application) Law of 2011.

[73] The Retirement Benefits of Employees of the Public and Wider Public Sector, including Authorities of Local Government (Provisions of General Application) Law of 2012 (n 72), art 9.

[74] ibid, art 11.

[75] ibid, art 8.

[76] Statistical Service, 'Social Protection in Cyprus: Revenue and Expenditure' (n 57) 31.

[77] Cyprus Letter of Intent to the International Monetary Fund (n 15), para 15.

[78] Law 109(I)/2014, as amended.

[79] According to art 39 of the Guaranteed Minimum Income Law of 2014, as amended, '[f]rom the date of the entry into force of this legislation, the provision of public assistance to any beneficiary of public assistance, as per the provisions of the Public Assistance and Services Law [95(I)/2006, as amended], is terminated'.

the overall system by eliminating duplicate benefits.[80] The GMI is a top-up benefit which is calculated as the difference between the basic and the family income[81] and its recipients can also receive a housing allowance when they are either renting property or living in a property on which they have taken out a mortgage.[82] In order for a person to be entitled to the GMI, he/she must satisfy a complex set of criteria relating to their age, nationality, residency, employment, and assets (regarding both moveable and immovable property).[83] It is this complexity of the system, combined with bureaucratic inefficiency, that has cast doubt on the effectiveness of the Scheme.

The introduction of the GMI Scheme has led to a dramatic fall in the number of eligible beneficiaries of social assistance. Prior to the reform, and pursuant to the Public Assistance and Services Law, 61,500 families were considered to meet the eligibility criteria; in March 2016, only 25,508 families met the requirements provided under the GMI Scheme.[84] The government has attributed this significant decrease to the lower-than-expected number of applications from retirees and to the high rejection of 63 per cent of the applications mostly on the account of assets and deposits that exceeded the statutory threshold.[85] Of the total number of households that received the GMI, 27 per cent were unemployed, 16 per cent were working poor, 21 per cent were pensioners, and 36 per cent were inactive due to disability, domestic care responsibilities, or other reasons.[86] Finally, the GMI Scheme created incentives for taking up work and introduced mechanisms for labour market reintegration, as it provided that recipients had to be registered with public employment services and had to be in search of a job if they were unemployed.

c) Family allowances

The Cypriot social security system provided for a number of family-related allowances. Prior to the financial crisis, some of the most important family allowances included the marriage grant, birth grant, funeral grant, maternity allowance, child

---

[80] Christos Koutsampelas, 'The Cypriot GMI Scheme and Comparisons with Other European Countries' (2016) 10(1) Cyprus Economic Policy Review 3, 3–4.

[81] Guaranteed Minimum Income Law, art 8(1). 'Basic income' is the pre-specified minimum threshold set by law, determined with the use of reference budget methods, such as food, clothing, health, household, and social needs of the recipient. 'Family income' is defined as the sum of the monetary income of all members of the family unit (art 12); incomes such as funeral, birth, student, or military grants, or benefits via the scheme for supporting pensioners with low income, are not taken into account (art 12(2)). For a more detailed analysis, see Koutsampelas and Pashardes (n 59) 15–16.

[82] Guaranteed Minimum Income Law, art 16. Note that the basic income is set at €480 per month for a single individual, increased by 50 per cent for every member of the family aged fourteen and over, and by 30 per cent for each child below the age of fourteen.

[83] ibid, arts 4, 5, 13, 14, 18, and 19.

[84] Consideration of Reports: Reports Submitted by the States Parties in accordance with arts 16 and 17 of the Covenant, sixth periodic report of Cyprus (Doc No E/C.12/2016/SR.53), Committee on Economic, Social and Cultural Rights (59th session), 22 September 2016, para 33.

[85] ibid.

[86] ibid, para 34.

allowance, single-parent allowance, student grant, mother allowance, and financial assistance to multi-child families. Family allowances were also affected by the financial crisis since some were abolished, others were modified, and others were indirectly affected. In general, a significant decrease of expenditures relating to family and child benefits had taken place. More specifically, in 2011 the total expenditure was €360.2 million; in 2012, the amount dropped to €286.4 million; in 2013, it was further reduced to €258.5 million, and in 2014 to €243.5 million.[87]

For instance, the marriage grant was abolished for weddings that took place on 1 January 2013 and thereafter, in accordance with the Social Insurance (Amending) Law of 2012.[88] In December 2012, the mother allowance (allowance for mothers with four or more children) was also repealed,[89] and its €22 million allocated budget was targeted to those in need.[90] However, the mother allowance was revived in 2017 through an executive decision of the Council of Ministers.[91] Other allowances, such as birth grant (provided to the mother of a newborn) and the financial assistance to multi-child families, were not affected by fiscal consolidation. The maternity allowance was also modified in a way so as to provide additional maternity allowance to mothers whose new-borns are hospitalised with medical problems.[92]

The child allowance, as regulated by the Child's Benefits Law,[93] was also reformed. In 2011, an amendment introduced the definition of 'dependent children' and the right to child allowance was made available to families with 'dependent children', rather than to 'families with children'.[94] In addition, the amendment introduced a limit as to the assets criteria for qualifying as a beneficiary[95] and in 2014 stricter income criteria were introduced, causing families with a gross income of over €59,000 to lose eligibility.[96] Finally, the student grant was also influenced by the financial crisis. In 2011 a new law was enacted[97] which provided that a student's family with an annual income of over €59,000 and/or asset of over €1,200,000 lost eligibility for the student grant. However, in 2015 a new law replaced the 2011

---

[87] Statistical Service, 'Social Protection in Cyprus: Revenue and Expenditure' (n 57) 31.

[88] Law 193(I)/2012, which amended art 27.

[89] Mother's Allowance (Repealing) Law (179(I)/2012) which repealed the Mother's Allowance Law (21(I)/2002), as amended.

[90] Consideration of Reports: Reports Submitted by the States Parties in accordance with arts 16 and 17 of the Covenant, sixth periodic report of Cyprus (Doc No E/C.12/2016/SR.54), Committee on Economic, Social and Cultural Rights (59th session), 23 September 2016, para 10.

[91] Council of Ministers, Scheme for the Provision of Multi-Child Mother Allowance, Decision No 82.519, 3 May 2017.

[92] Social Insurance Law of 2010, art 29(7), as amended by Law 37(I)/2012. Here, it should be noted that the Social Insurance Law of 2010 was amended in 2017 in order to provide for paternity allowance to insured husbands whose wife gives birth or who has a child through surrogacy or adopts a child up to the age of twelve years; Social Insurance Law of 2010, art 29A, as amended by Law 115(I)/2017.

[93] Law 167(1)/2002, as amended.

[94] See Child's Benefits Law, art 4(1), as amended by Law 189(I)/2011.

[95] ibid.

[96] Child's Benefits Law, Annex, as amended by Law 180(I) of 2012.

[97] Student Grant Law (188(I)/2011).

legislation and removed the gross income as a criterion; thus, now families with assets of over €1,200,000 are not eligible for the grant.[98]

d) Unemployment benefits

It is very interesting to note that the provisions regarding unemployment benefits were not affected by the financial crisis that hit Cyprus, and this illustrates social awareness and a continuing emphasis on social integration. At the same time, it will be misleading to detach unemployment benefits from the wider economic situation as it was unfolding at the time, since that situation triggered and accelerated the unemployment issue. Nonetheless, the unemployment benefit remained available to involuntarily unemployed persons between the ages of sixteen and sixty-five.[99] The duration of the payment of the unemployment benefit cannot exceed 156 days.[100] Thereafter, involuntarily unemployed persons can apply to receive the GMI, provided that they meet the required conditions as described above (III.2.b).

The total expenditure of the Republic of Cyprus regarding unemployment benefits had initially increased due to the impact of the financial crisis and the high rates of unemployment. In particular, in 2011 the amount spent on unemployment was €232.2 million; in 2012, €321.4 million; and in 2013, €358.4 million.[101] The state showed its commitment towards supporting the unemployed through the transfer of €170 million from the Supplementary Pensions Account of the Social Insurance Fund into the Unemployment Account, in order to cover the deficit of the latter for the years 2013–2014.[102] However, the total expenditure dropped to €272.8 million in 2014, to €215.9 million in 2015, and to €191.5 million in 2016, with the decrease being attributed to the reduction of the levels of unemployment.[103]

e) Healthcare

The healthcare system, as existed prior to the introduction of the GHS, was influenced significantly by the economic crisis, as the MoU made explicit recommendations for healthcare reforms. These recommendations were incorporated via the State Medical Institutions and Services General (Amending) Regulation (143 of 2013), in which no reference to the MoU was made. The Regulation introduced disincentives for using emergency care services in non-urgent situations, limited

---

[98] State Student Welfare Law (203(I)/2015).

[99] Social Insurance Law of 2010, as amended, arts 31, 32, and 34.

[100] ibid.

[101] Statistical Service, 'Social Protection in Cyprus: Revenue and Expenditure' (n 57) 31.

[102] See new art 99 of the Social Insurance Law introduced with the Social Insurance (Amending) Law (106(I)/2014).

[103] Statistical Service, Ministry of Finance, 'Social Protection in Cyprus: Revenue and Expenditure 2016' (February 2019) General Social Statistics, Series III, Report No 12, 15. This study notes that this decrease in unemployment benefits is primarily due to the respective decrease in the unemployment rate in 2016 to 12.9 per cent from 14.9 per cent in 2015 and from 16.1 per cent in 2014.

access to certain chronic disease patients, increased the fees for medical services for non-beneficiaries, and minimised the provision of medically unnecessary laboratory tests and pharmaceuticals. Access to public healthcare was restricted only to those who had contributed to social insurance for at least three years and who had settled all of their tax obligations.[104] Persons entitled to healthcare benefits, as well as non-beneficiaries, had to pay respective fees set by the Ministry of Health to use public services. Nevertheless, these developments did not discourage people from seeking public healthcare. On the contrary, the financial crisis led to an unprecedented workload increase for public hospitals, as people were avoiding the more expensive private out-of-pocket healthcare, leading to the inability of the public healthcare sector to cope with the large number of patients that public hospitals were receiving.

3. Grounds of justification and procedural particularities of the reforms

In general, the House of Representatives has exclusive power to legislate on all matters.[105] The legislative process regarding primary legislation can take two forms: through the tabling of a bill by the executive branch, or through the tabling of a Private Member's bill by a member of the House of Representatives.[106] All bills are published in the Official Gazette of the Republic, accompanied by a brief explanatory statement. These statements serve as valuable guidance, as they explain the reasons and the intentions behind the proposed legislative act, regardless of whether it is an enacting, amending, ratifying, or repealing legislation. Yet, in the case of these social policy reforms, the explanatory statements failed to provide a clear understanding as to the primary reason behind such reforms, namely the need to meet the strict conditionality requirements under the MoU, in order for Cyprus to receive the next instalment of the loan by Troika. The explanatory statements simply refer to the need of further reducing public expenditure.

Other laws may provide a ground of justification in their preamble. For instance, in the preamble to the 2012 Reduction in Remunerations and Pensions of Officials, Employees and Pensioners of the Public and Wider Public Sector Law it is stated that its enactment was necessary in order to reduce the public sector expenditure by reducing, among others, the salaries and pensions of officials, employees, and

---

[104] Medical Foundations and Services (Fees and Control) Law (40/1978), as amended, art 4(1). However, there were exceptions for particular vulnerable groups, such as beneficiaries of the GMI or of social pension, unemployed persons, and members of single-parent families.

[105] See pt IV (arts 61–85) of the Constitution of Cyprus, and especially art 61. The Communal Chambers had exclusive powers to legislate in relation to education and religious and family matters, as per arts 86–111 of the Constitution. However, their operation was suspended after the events of 1964 and their powers have been conferred (and are exercised) by the House of Representatives.

[106] Constitution of Cyprus, art 80.

pensioners of the public and wider public sector, due to the difficult financial situation and due to the need to avoid any further deterioration of the fiscal situation. Despite being enacted prior to the adoption of the MoU, this is one of the rare legislations relevant to social reforms envisaging a rather helpful preamble and setting the need for financial (and fiscal) stability as its ground of justification. Nonetheless, there was no reference to the temporal duration of the cuts, nor a clear explanation of the procedures followed for endorsing the particular rates for reducing salaries and pensions. The lack of such clear temporal duration of the cuts could have affected the ability of the judiciary to assess the proportionality and legality of the measures. Although the Cypriot courts examined the legality of this particular law, and found it unconstitutional, the issue of proportionality remained unanswered.[107]

This approach can be contrasted with the preamble to the Law on the Restrictive Measures to Transactions,[108] where the legislator makes explicit reference to articles 63 and 65 of the Treaty on the Functioning of the European Union as enabling Member States to adopt measures which are necessary for reasons of public order and public security, and characterises the restrictive measures as necessary for ensuring financial stability and for avoiding any destabilising tendencies that may cause serious problems to the Cypriot economy. Therefore, in the latter case the legislator ties reforms in with the obligations of Cyprus as a Member State of the EU and, specifically, with the derogation provisions relating to the free movement of capital. That was necessary because the restrictions impacted on the EU's fundamental economic freedoms whereas the social reforms were viewed as having only an internal dimension.

As for the procedure of the adoption of the budget, the Minister of Finance presents a draft to the Council of Ministers, and if it is approved it is submitted to the Parliamentary Committee of Finance as the 'Budget Bill'.[109] At that stage, it is common for amendments to be proposed by the Parliamentary Committee of Finance after political negotiations, and, if agreed by the Minister, they are then introduced in the Budget Bill.[110] This process is considered to be highly political

---

[107] See *Avgousti et al v the Republic* Joined Cases nos 898/2013 and others (27 November 2018) and *Nicolaidi et al v the Republic* Joined Cases nos 98/2013 and others (29 March 2019), analysed below in IV.2.b. Note also that an amendment of the Law in 2018 (Law 94(I)/2018) introduced a temporal duration of the reductions, lasting from July 2018 until January 2023, along with a very detailed preamble elaborating on the background and the need of such measures.

[108] Law 12(I)/2013.

[109] Constitution of Cyprus, art 167.

[110] Note that art 80(2) of the Cypriot Constitution envisages that the House of Representatives cannot increase the expenses provided for in the budget. It can, however, decrease the state's income. All remunerations, pensions, and grants are charged on the Consolidated Fund of the Republic (ibid, art 166). No expenditure can be met from the Consolidated Fund or other Public Funds except upon the authority of a warrant by the Minister of Finance, but no warrant can be issued unless such expenditure has been adopted in the budget for the financial year to which the warrant relates in the budget (ibid, art 168).

and aims at guaranteeing the positive outcome of the voting before the plenary session of the House of Representatives, which will be called to either approve or reject the proposed Bill by simple majority.[111]

These customary and informal rules of prior consultation and cooperation between the executive and legislative branch, with a view of reaching a political consensus for approving the budget, were affected by the MoU and the strict conditionality requirements.[112] The executive coordinated with Troika to formulate the latter's restrictions and requirements into national rules. Absence of the necessary consensus by Troika due to any alteration of the original draft would result in failure to meet the strict conditionality requirements and, subsequently, the scheduled financing would be halted. Consequently, while the parliamentary process was not formally and directly affected as a result of the MoU, the legislature's law-making autonomy was *de facto* constrained.

In essence, the House of Representative simply passed the bills tabled before it by the Council of Ministers hastily without any amendments, in order to secure Troika's consent and timely lending. This time pressure is more than evident in a Report of the Parliamentary Committee on Finance regarding the amending bill tabled by the executive regarding the retirement of civil servants and members of the armed forces, dated 19 December 2012, even before the adoption of the MoU.[113] As it is noted therein, it was necessary for Cyprus to implement specific reforms, for securing an agreement between the Cypriot Government and Troika. The Committee stressed that it did not have the necessary and desirable time for examining such legislative acts or for engaging in social dialogue. Nevertheless, due to the critical situation, it had to cooperate with the executive and adopt the proposed measures with a 'fast-track' procedure.

---

[111] Constantinos Kombos, 'The Impact of the Economic Crisis on the Functioning of Institutions: the Cypriot Experience' in Ronaldo Tarchi (ed), *Crisi economica ed impatto sulle istituzioni nazionali* (www. federalismi.it, numero speciale 26 2016) 7–8.

[112] For an in-depth analysis of the impact of the MoU on the constitutional and institutional setting; see Kombos, ibid.

[113] Report of the Parliamentary Committee on Finance for the bills of the 'Retirement Benefits of Employees of the Public and Wider Public Sector, including Authorities of Local Government (Provisions of General Application) Law of 2012' and the 'Members of the Armed Forces of the Republic (Retirement and Related Matters) (Provisions of General Application) Law of 2012' <http://www2.parliament.cy/parliamentgr/008_05e/008_05_3876.htm> accessed 10 July 2019 (in Greek).

IV. Social protection reforms before Cypriot courts: a constitutional approach

1. Legal basis for challenging social protection cuts and reforms

People (such as beneficiaries of social benefits, allowances, and grants and employees of the public and wider public sector) whose legitimate interests were adversely and directly affected by these social protection reforms could challenge incidentally the constitutionality of the legislative cuts and reforms or the legitimacy of the decisions of the executive or legislative power, by filing a recourse before the Administrative Court pursuant to article 146 of the Constitution.[114] In *Pancyprian Organization of Large Families et al v Attorney-General*,[115] the Nicosia District Court reaffirmed that the only venue for challenging the constitutionality of cuts of social benefits, such as the child's benefit and the student grant, is via a recourse to the Administrative Court.[116]

2. Social protection cuts and reforms: the human rights dimension

The assessment of the constitutionality of the social protection cuts and reforms introduced as fiscal consolidation measures was very much delayed in Cyprus, causing insecurity and uncertainty, especially to the government and employees and pensioners of the public and wider public sector. Some of the applications challenging the constitutionality of social protection reforms were filed against legislation predating the adoption of the MoU (ie in 2011 and 2012) and others following its adoption (ie 2013 and onwards). The first two decisions were issued by the Supreme Court (acting as the Administrative Court) in 2014. Nevertheless, this significant and promising development was followed by a prolonged silence. Thus, by 2017, the great majority of judicial decisions relating to social protection

---

[114] Art 146(1), as amended, provides that the Administrative Court has 'exclusive jurisdiction to decide in the first instance on a recourse made to it on a complaint that a decision, an act or omission of any organ, authority or person, exercising any executive or administrative authority is contrary to any of the provisions of this Constitution or of any law or is made in excess or in abuse of powers vested in such organ or authority or person'. It should be noted that the Administrative Court was established in January 2016, through the amendment of art 146 of the Constitution (see the Eighth Amendment of the Constitution Law (130(I)/2015) and the Establishment and Operation of an Administrative Court Law (131(I)/2015). Prior to this amendment all recourses were filed before the Supreme Court.

[115] App no 6914/2012 (22 March 2017).

[116] See also, *Patsalosavvi-Leontiou v the Republic* (1997) 3 CLR 70 and *Electricity Authority of Cyprus v Filiastidi* (2003) 3 CLR 342, where the Plenary of the Supreme Court reaffirmed that the proper procedure for challenging decisions related to social security benefits is through filing a recourse to the Administrative Court.

dealt with the legality of executive decisions either to reject an application for receiving social benefits, grants, or pensions or to approve an application for a reduced amount of what the applicants believed they were entitled to.[117]

The Cypriot Courts' inaction was brought to an end in 2018, as they resumed delivering judgments in the field of such cuts and reforms, causing alarm to the government. The following analysis will examine these cases and proceed to an assessment of the judiciary's reaction to the crisis-related reforms from a constitutional and human rights law perspective. What is noteworthy is that the vast majority of the decisions focused on the alleged violation of the right to property, as stipulated in article 23 of the Constitution, and none of the claims was based on the right to a decent existence and to social security, as per article 9.

a) The initial judicial approach: the *Charalambous* and *Koutselini-Ioannidou* cases

The first case relevant to cuts attributed to the financial crisis, albeit introduced prior to the adoption of the MoU, is *Charalambous et al v the Republic*.[118] In 2011, the House of Representatives passed the Special Contribution for Officials, Employees and Pensioners of the Public Sector and Wider Public Sector Law.[119] According to the provisions of this law, as amended,[120] public officials, employees, and pensioners were obliged to pay 'special contributions'.[121] These special contributions were extended so as to apply until 2016.[122]

The applicants, all public officials and employees (no pensioners were involved in this case), requested the Supreme Court (acting as the Administrative Court) to declare the law unconstitutional and, thus, null and void. The applicants alleged that the law was contrary to article 23 of the Constitution (right to property), as well as to article 1 of the First Additional Protocol to the European Convention on Human Rights (ECHR). The applicants further claimed that articles 24 (obligation of every person to contribute towards the public burden according to their financial means), 26 (right to enter into a contract), and 28 (principle of equality and non-discrimination) of the Constitution were also violated. According to

---

[117] See, for instance, *Kakoulli v Ministry of Labour, Welfare and Social Insurance (Department of Social Services)* App no 426/2015 (31 December 2015); *Andreou v Ministry of Labour, Welfare and Social Insurance (Social Welfare Services)* App no 5894/2013 (11 September 2014); *Andreas Christou et al v the Republic* App no 346/2011 (4 October 2012); *Demourtsidou v the Republic* App no 5808/2013 (10 February 2016); *Charalambous v the Republic* App no 6462/2013 (30 December 2015).

[118] Joined Cases nos 1480/2011 and others (11 June 2014).

[119] Law 112(I)/2011.

[120] The law was amended in December 2011, with Law 193(I)/2011.

[121] Officials, employees, and pensioners of the public sector with a monthly salary or pension that exceeded €2,500 were obliged to contribute 2.5 per cent of their monthly income or pension. Those public officials, employees, and pensioners whose income or pension exceeded €3,501 were requested to contribute 3 per cent and those whose income or pension exceeded €4,501 were obliged to contribute 3.5 per cent.

[122] The Special Contribution for Officials, Employees and Pensioners of the Public Sector and Wider Public Sector (Amending) Law (184(I)/2012).

the applicants, their salary was an asset and a property right, which was unlawfully restricted in violation of the Constitution and the First Additional Protocol. Furthermore, they argued that the law failed to provide them with just compensation for the loss of their property. The respondents submitted that the limitation imposed through the challenged law was based on grounds of public interest or of public benefit (*utilité publique*). Therefore, and as the preamble of the contested law prescribed, these cuts were necessary and aimed at the reduction of public expenditures, in order to deal with the fiscal challenges of the Cypriot economy.

The majority decision, citing a number of EU instruments (treaties, opinions, recommendations, regulations), indicated that Cyprus adopted these measures in consultation with the competent EU organs, in order to harmonise with the political and economic objectives set by the EU. The Supreme Court held that there was no violation of articles 24 and 28 of the Constitution, as the legislator was entitled to first target the employees and pensioners of the public sector due to the serious problems of the public finances. This was a political choice which could not be assessed by the Court.[123] And in any case, the House of Representatives had enacted a similar legislation for special contributions by employees in the private sector.[124]

As for the right to property envisaged in article 23 of the Constitution, the majority indicated that it is not an absolute right. It may be subjected to those limitations specifically provided in article 23(3); ie those which are absolutely necessary in the interest of (a) public safety or (b) public health or (c) public morals or (d) town and country planning or (e) *development and utilisation of the property for the promotion of the public benefit or for the protection of the rights of others.*[125] The

---

[123] On this issue the Supreme Court reaffirmed its previous case law, holding that the principle of equality must be balanced with the economic situation and fiscal policy in place at the time, and that the state has the discretion in times of extreme economic crisis to take measures targeting specific groups of the population without necessarily violating the principle of equal treatment; see Constantinos Kombos and Stéphanie Laulhé Shaelou, 'The Cypriot Constitution Under the Impact of EU Law: An Asymmetrical Formation' in Anneli Albi and Samo Bardutzky (eds), *National Constitutions in European and Global Governance: Democracy, Rights, the Rule of Law* (Springer 2019) 1396.

[124] For reasons of equal treatment and non-discrimination, four months after the adoption of the Special Contribution for Officials, Employees and Pensioners of the Public Sector and Wider Public Sector Law, the House of Representatives enacted parallel legislation for employees of the private sector; see the Special Contribution for Employees, Pensioners and Self-Employed of the Private Sector Law (202(I)/2011).

[125] In particular, art 23 of the Constitution provides:

(1) Every person, alone or jointly with others, has the right to acquire own, possess, enjoy or dispose of any movable or immovable property and has the right to respect for such right.

The right of the Republic to underground water, minerals and antiquities is reserved.

(2) No deprivation or restriction or limitation of any such right shall be made except as provided in this Article.

(3) Restrictions or limitations which are absolutely necessary in the interest of the public safety or the public health or the public morals or the town and country planning or the development and utilization of any property to the promotion of the public benefit or for the protection of the rights of others may be imposed by law on the exercise of such right. Just compensation shall be promptly paid for any such restrictions or limitations which materially decrease the economic value of such property: such compensation to be determined in case of disagreement by a civil court.

majority held that the cuts introduced in salaries and pensions, as special contributions, could not be justified on grounds of public benefit under article 23(3), as this provision links the promotion of public benefit with the imposition of restrictions or limitations to the property for development and utilisation purposes; it does not link public benefit with public interest and the need to overcome the economic crisis.

However, the majority rather ambiguously continued to add in the same paragraph that the salary may be a property right, yet it does not guarantee any right to a salary of a particular amount. They held that the aim of article 23 regarding the right to a salary is to prevent any arbitrary, and without legislative regulation, infringement of the core of the right to salary or the arbitrary and substantial decrease of the salary. Thus, the relatively small special contribution cuts of the rate, of 1.5 per cent to 3.5 per cent of the gross monthly salary, did not amount to an arbitrary intervention to the right to property, as it did not neutralise the right nor affect the core of the right to a salary.[126] Consequently, the applicants' argument that the special contribution constitutes a breach of article 23 of the Constitution was rejected by the Court. Similarly, the Court rejected the claim that public interest, as a ground for enacting the referred legislation, was insufficiently justified and indicated that it was not necessary for a preamble or an explanatory statement to refer to the full background of the enactment of the law.[127] In other words, the Supreme Court acknowledged that the salary falls within the definition of 'property', as protected by article 23. Moreover, it clearly recognised that article 23(3) does not provide for a limitation of the right to property for consolidating the public finances as a ground of public benefit; therefore, such limitation is not permissible. Nevertheless, the Court took a surprising turn and indicated that since the reduction of the salary introduced by the law was insignificant, it did not amount to a deprivation of the right. The Court's approach can only be described as confusing, since it is unclear why the Court chose to proceed with the examination of the effect of the limitation on the core of the right, from the moment that it had already established that the limitation was impermissible under the Constitution.

The dissenting judges (Nathanael, Parparinos, and Liatsos) adopted a different approach and found the contested law in violation of articles 23, 24, 26, and 28 of the Constitution. In relation to the right to property, the dissenting judges stressed that article 23 does not allow for deprivation or limitation of salaries or pensions,

---

[126] On this issue, the Supreme Court cited a Portuguese case, where cuts of up to 10 per cent, imposed due to the serious economic crisis, were not considered essential so as to constitute a deprivation of the basic right; see *Diário da República*, 396/2011 (17 October 2011).

[127] In the particular case, the preamble was found satisfactory. It is noteworthy that the Court also noted that: 'not even the fact that the preamble of the Law does not explicitly refer to grounds of public interest, to the [Stability and Growth Pact] which is binding on Cyprus as a member of the Eurozone or to the rest of EU legislation concerning the broader obligations of Cyprus as an EU member for fiscal discipline and stability, may have an impact on the validity of the Law' (translation by the authors).

unless the limitation is based on the grounds laid down in paragraph 3. Moreover, they held that the justification provided in the preamble (invoking public interest) was vague, general, over-simplified, and insufficient and they were unable to judicially scrutinise the law. In their conclusion, the three judges observed that 'it is important to stress that the alignment with the constitutional prescriptions, especially in times of crisis, is even more imperative. Consequently, despite the need of the state for economic recovery—which is understandable, especially in the light of the current circumstances—it cannot override the Constitution by breaching the property rights of its citizens.'[128]

Four months after the *Charalambous* decision, the Supreme Court was called to examine the constitutionality of the 2011 Pensions of State Officials (General Principles) Law[129] in *Koutselini-Ioannidou et al v the Republic*.[130] The applicants raised the issue of unconstitutionality of the said law, which provided for the abolition of multiple pensions and the suspension of receiving pension when a person reached the pensionable age, yet he/she continued to hold a public position or office. More specifically, article 3(b) of the said law stipulated that when pensioners assumed any public office, service, or post, their pensions were suspended for the duration of their term. The applicants' submission was that article 3(b) breached articles 23 and 28 of the Constitution, as well as article 1 of the First Additional Protocol to the ECHR. The respondents claimed that article 3(b) did not result in the deprivation of property or any other right; rather, it was a temporary suspension. Alternatively, the respondents supported that if there was a deprivation of the right to property, it was justified on the grounds of public interest.

Regarding pension as a property right, the majority of the Supreme Court explained that once a person reaches the retirement age the right to pension is crystallised and it is then protected under article 23 of the Constitution. The Court reaffirmed that article 23 is not absolute, as it can be limited, restricted, or even deprived by law as per paragraphs 2 and 3 of article 23. The necessity of every limitation or deprivation must be elaborated in the relevant legislation and the explanatory statement of its adoption. In the event that the limitation is permissible and the right is restricted to a substantial extent, there is an obligation for just compensation.

The Supreme Court further analysed the relationship between article 23 of the Constitution and article 1 of the first additional protocol and held that the latter allows limitations on the grounds of public interest, whereas the former does not. By referring to *Charalambous*, the Court stated that the limitation of the right to property for the development and utilisation of property for the promotion of the public benefit found in article 23(3) was not identical but stricter than the limitation of the

---

[128] Translation by the authors.
[129] Law 88(I)/2011.
[130] Joined Cases nos 740/11 and others, 7 October 2014.

right on the grounds of public interest. Therefore, the Cypriot Constitution affords greater protection to the right to property than the ECHR and its First Additional Protocol.

In the case at hand, the Court ruled that article 3(b) of the Pensions of State Officials (General Principles) Law did not amount to a mere suspension of the right, but essentially to the loss of the right to pension, for as long as the pensioners held another public position. Moreover, article 3(b) of the law entered a limitation to the right to property on the grounds of public interest or public benefit, which are not envisaged in the Constitution. Consequently, the Court found that the contested law violated article 23 of the Constitution and refrained from analysing further human rights violations, as the law was already found to be unconstitutional.[131]

In their dissenting decision, Judges Pampallis, Paschalides, and Christodoulou (who were in the majority decision in *Charalambous*) held that the Law was in conformity with the Constitution. More specifically, the dissenting judges stressed that the adoption of the law was necessary in order to achieve institutional and economic restructuring, to consolidate public finances, and to comply with EU obligations. The dissenting decision concluded that the law under examination did not deprive or restrict the right to pension of the applicants, in the context of article 23(3) of the Constitution. The suspension of the pension was the result of willingly assuming another public office and a temporary measure. Finally, the three dissenting judges held that the suspension of pensions was not contrary to article 28 of the Constitution, as they did not have sufficient evidence that would allow them to examine such allegation.

The *Koutselini-Ioannidou* judgment was unpopular, caused public outcry, and received heavy criticism by the media. It is true that the *Charalambous* and *Koutselini-Ioannidou* decisions, both decided by the full bench of the Supreme Court in a relatively short period of time, could be differentiated at first glance. In *Charalambous*, the reduction in salaries and pensions, as a special contribution,

---

[131] cf Judgment of 20 September 2016, *Ledra Advertising Ltd and Others v European Commission and European Central Bank (ECB)*, Joined Cases C-8/15 P to C-10/15 P, EU:C:2016:701, paras 69–75, where the Court of Justice of the EU confirmed that art 17 of the Charter (right to property) may be restricted, provided that 'the restrictions *genuinely meet objectives of general interest* and do not constitute, in relation to the aim pursued, a disproportionate and intolerable interference, impairing the very substance of the right' (emphasis added). The Court concluded that the Cypriot MoU corresponded to an objective of general interest pursued by the EU, namely the objective of ensuring the stability of the banking system of the euro area as a whole. Thus, the measures for recapitalisation of the Cypriot banking system provided for in the MoU did not constitute a disproportionate and intolerable interference impairing the very substance of the appellants' right to property. For an analysis of Cypriot cases before the CJEU, see Paul Dermine, 'The End of Impunity? The Legal Duties of "Borrowed" EU Institutions under the European Stability Mechanism Framework: ECJ 20 September 2016, Case C-8/15 to C-10/15, Ledra Advertising et al. v European Commission and European Central Bank' (2017) 13(2) European Constitutional Law Review 369; Anastasia Poulou, 'The Liability of the EU in the ESM framework' (2017) 24(1) Maastricht Journal of European and Comparative Law 127; Anastasia Karatzia, 'Cypriot Depositors Before the Court of Justice of the European Union: Knocking on the Wrong Door?' (2015) 26(2) King's Law Journal 175.

was relatively small and did not neutralise the right nor affect the core of the right to property. In *Koutselini-Ioannidou* the limitation introduced by the challenged law amounted to a neutralisation of the core of the right to property and a deprivation that could not survive the test of necessity and proportionality. Nevertheless, this understanding would have been correct if the Court had applied the same steps and had found that the limitations were permissible under the Constitution.

In particular, and as it will be analysed below, *Koutselini-Ioannidou* has been interpreted by subsequent case law as envisaging a two-step approach for the examination of the constitutionality of a limitation to the right to property: first, the Court should examine whether the limitation was permissible as per article 23(3) of the Constitution and, if it was permissible, it would then examine the substance and legality of such limitation. However, this was not the approach in *Charalambous*. As already noted, the Court found that the limitation was not permissible and yet found the contested law constitutional. Consequently, the exact relation between the two cases remains uncertain. Are the two decisions in conflict? Or did the *Koutselini-Ioannidou* decision overturn *Charalambous*? Unfortunately, the Cypriot case law failed to provide any guidance as to this point.

b) Social protection cuts and reforms and the right to property

The *Charalambous* and *Koutselini-Ioannidou* decisions were followed by a prolonged silence by the Administrative Court in relation to the numerous pending applications challenging social protection cuts and reforms. The situation changed four years later, in November 2018, when the Administrative Court delivered its decision on the constitutionality of allowance reductions and allowance abolitions of 211 applicants working with the 24-hour shift system in the public service (firefighters and nurses) and the police, by virtue of the 2014 Budget Law.[132] Particularly, in *Christodoulidou et al v the Republic*[133] the Administrative Court rejected almost all applications, with the exception of seven applications submitted by nurses, which were found in breach of the principle of equal treatment.[134] All applicants argued that the reductions and abolition of benefits should be declared in breach of articles 9, 24, and 28 of the Constitution, as well as article 1 of the First Additional Protocol to the ECHR. The applicants failed to raise any claims on the grounds of article 23 of the Constitution. The Administrative Court examined the facts that led to the abolition or reduction of the relevant allowances and indicated

---

[132] Law 52(II)/2013.

[133] *Christodoulidou et al v the Republic* Joined Case Nos 441/2014 and others (12 November 2018).

[134] As for the seven successful applications, the Administrative Court held that the distinction between nurses in closed mental health hospitals and other mental health nurses and the abolition of the hazardous work allowance for the latter violated the principle of equality and art 28(1) of the Constitution. This was due to arbitrary differentiations between nurses of the same category and the absence of any study justifying such distinction.

that the state was in a great financial crisis and had an obligation to implement the MoU, in order to cope with the financial crisis.

The applicants alleged that article 1 of the First Additional Protocol was violated since the allowances at hand formed part of their monthly salary. At this point, the Court referred to *Charalambous* and reaffirmed its finding that the right to property as found in article 23 of the Constitution encompasses the salary as well as legitimate expectations. Subsequently, it referred to *Koutselini-Ioannidou* and its finding that article 23 of the Constitution affords a wider protection to property than the First Additional Protocol, since it does not allow limitations on grounds of public interest and public benefit. However, the Court concluded that it could not adjudicate on whether the Budget Law was in violation of article 23, as this claim was not raised by the applicants. In relation to article 1 of the First Additional Protocol, the Court held that the intervention to the right to property, through the reduction and abolition of allowances, was justified on grounds of public interest and it was necessary and appropriate to achieve cost savings and a balanced budget for government expenditure. Additionally, the Court found that the 25 per cent reduction in shift allowances and 33.3 per cent in the overtime allowance calculation formula was not a disproportionate restriction on the property right of the total remuneration, taking into account the financial benefit resulting from that restriction and the fact that a variety of other cuts in the salaries, allowances, and pensions of all categories of civil servants and public pensioners ensured the saving of millions and reduced the budget deficit. As a result, the Court found that the reductions and abolition of certain allowances did not violate article 1 of the First Additional Protocol.

Two weeks later, in *Avgousti et al v the Republic*,[135] the Administrative Court examined the constitutionality of reductions in the pensions of public and wider public sector employees. The 115 applicants claimed that the 2012 Reduction in Remunerations and Pensions of Officials, Employees and Pensioners of the Public and Wider Public Sector Law,[136] as amended in 2013, contravened article 23(3) of the Constitution and article 1 of the First Additional Protocol to the ECHR. More specifically, they supported that article 23(3) does not enlist public interest as a legitimate ground for restricting the right to property. On the other hand, the respondents claimed that the enactment of the contested law was necessary in order to reduce the expenditure of the public and wider public sector and to avoid a further deterioration of the fiscal situation during a difficult financial situation as per the preliminary agreement and later the MoU. The Court referred to both *Charalambous* and *Koutselini-Ioannidou* decisions and laid out the test to be applied for examining the constitutionality of the limitation of the right to property (including the right to pension). The Court is to first examine whether the limitation was permissible under

---

[135] *Avgousti* (n 107).
[136] Law 168(I)/2012.

article 23(3) of the Constitution and, if it was permissible, it must examine the substance and legality of such limitation. When applying the first limb of the test, the Court reaffirmed that limitations on property rights for the consolidation of public finances and avoidance of their further deterioration on the grounds of public interest or public benefit are not permissible under article 23(3) of the Constitution. Thus, the Court did not apply the second limb of the test and declared the law unconstitutional. The *Avgousti* case caused alarm to the Ministry of Finance as the implementation of the decision would mean that the government would be obliged to reimburse the reductions in pensions, costing the state millions of euros per year. Consequently, the Attorney-General of the Republic and the Minister of Finance appealed the decision of the Administrative Court (V). An important aspect of *Avgousti* is the analysis of the exact relation between article 23 of the Constitution and article 1 of the First Additional Protocol. By drawing from *Charalambous* and *Koutselini-Ioannidou*, the Court explained that the two provisions afford different levels of protection to the right to property; yet, the fact that the Protocol permits limitations on the grounds of public interest or public benefit does not make such limitations permissible under the Constitution. This understanding derives from article 53 of the ECHR, providing that nothing in the Convention shall be construed as limiting or derogating from any of the human rights and fundamental freedoms which may be ensured under the laws of any party.[137] Given that the Constitution affords a greater protection to the right to property (by permitting limitations on stricter grounds), the Cypriot courts cannot allow a limitation on the grounds of public interest, which by nature limits the right to a greater extent than under the Constitution.[138]

On 29 March 2019, the Administrative Court issued three significant decisions, with great economic implications, on the constitutionality of laws imposing different forms of cuts and reforms to the salaries of employees of the public and wider public sector as a result of the preliminary agreement and the MoU. In *Nicolaidi et al v the Republic*,[139] the Court was called to determine whether the reductions in the salaries of the applicants (employees of the public and wider public sector) imposed by the 2012 Reduction in Remunerations and Pensions of Officials, Employees and Pensioners of the Public Service and of the Wider Public Sector Law,[140] as amended in 2013, were in violation of article 23.[141] In other words, in *Nicolaidi* the Court assessed the same law as in *Avgousti*; however, this case focused

---

[137] The same approach and understanding was adopted regarding the relation between the Cypriot Constitution and arts 17 of the Charter of Fundamental Rights of the European Union (the right to property and its limitation on grounds of public interest) and 53 (level of protection).

[138] The two-step test was reaffirmed in *Hadjipanagiotis et al v the Republic* App no 6182/2013 (28 December 2018).

[139] Joined Cases nos 98/2013 and others (29 March 2019).

[140] Law 168(I)/2012.

[141] It should be noted that, similarly to the rest of the case law following the same line, the applicants based their claim of unconstitutionality not just on art 23 of the Constitution, but also on arts 9, 24, 26, and 28 of the Constitution and on art 1 of the First Additional Protocol. However, the Court starts the

on salaries rather than on pensions. By applying the reasoning of *Charalambous* and *Koutselini-Ioannidou*, yet not the two-limb test of *Avgousti*, the Administrative Court held that salaries fall within the definition of 'property' of article 23 and, therefore, are constitutionally protected. Nonetheless, the preamble of the contested law indicated that the limitation imposed on the salaries of the applicants was justified on the grounds of public interest or public benefit, which is not permissible under the Constitution. As a result, the Court held the law unconstitutional and did not proceed to examine any further aspects of the matter.

In *Koundourou et al v the Republic*,[142] the second decision issued on the same day, the Administrative Court examined the constitutionality of the 2011 Law on the Non-Concession of Increases in Salaries and of Indexation Increases,[143] and its compatibility with the right to property. As its name suggests, this law provided for the non-concession of the indexation increases and increases in salaries until 2016. According to its preamble, the law was adopted in order to prevent any further deterioration of the public finances and to secure the correct functioning of the public service, as required by public interest. The Court first affirmed that the increases in salaries and indexation increases are part of the employees' gross salary and fall within the definition of property. Failure to grant these increases from 2011 until 2016 as provided by the contested law constitutes a deprivation. Having cited the entire reasoning of *Nicolaidi*, the Court simply concluded that the law under examination in *Koundourou* imposed a limitation and/or deprivation on the applicants' salaries on the grounds of public interest, which is not permitted under article 23 of the Constitution. Therefore, this law was also found unconstitutional.

Finally, in *Filippou et al v the Republic*[144] the Court examined the constitutionality of the 2011 Law on Retirement Benefits for Employees in the Public and Wider Public Sector,[145] which provided for a cut of the gross salary of these employees, as a contribution to the Consolidated Fund of the Republic. The aim of the law was to restrain the expenses of the public sector occupational pension scheme (GEPS). The Court analysed the right to property once more, reaffirmed that the salary is protected under article 23, and held that in the case under examination there was a limitation of the right on the grounds of public interest, which

---

assessment with art 23 of the Constitution, and if the law under examination is found unconstitutional, then the Court refrains from examining the rest of the grounds.

[142] Joined Cases nos 611/2012 and others (29 March 2019).
[143] Non-Concession of Increases in Salaries and of Indexation Increases of Officers and Employees' Salaries and of Pensioners' Pensions of the Public and Wider Public Sector Law (192(I)/2011).
[144] Joined Cases nos 1713/2011 and others (29 March 2019).
[145] Law 113(I)/2011. This Law was amended, abolished, and replaced with the Retirement Benefits of Employees in the Public and Wider Public Sector, including the Local Authorities Law (Provisions of General Implementation) (216(I)/2012).

is not permissible under the Constitution. Consequently, this law was also declared unconstitutional.[146]

In so surmising, the Administrative Court delivered three decisions with the exact same reasoning holding that the approach of the House of Representatives to adopt laws limiting the right to property of employees of the public and wider public sector, through cuts and reforms, on the grounds of public benefit or public interest was unconstitutional. The economic consequences of these decisions caused frustration to the government and especially to the Ministry of Finance, as they essentially meant that the state must compensate employees of the public and wider public sector with more than €2 billion. As expected, the government appealed against the three decisions of the Administrative Court and at the same time requested the Court to issue an order for stay of execution of these first instance judgments until the adjudication of the appeals. Both the request for an order and the appeals were pending before the full bench of the Supreme Court until spring 2020 (V).

c) Assessing the Cypriot courts' approach to social protection reforms and human rights violations

It has become evident from the above analysis that the Cypriot case law relating to the cuts and reforms introduced as austerity measures, both before and after the adoption of the MoU, dealt primarily with property rights of employees or pensioners of the public and wider public sector. The first group of judicial decisions, namely *Charalambous* and *Koutselini-Ioannidou*, was decided by the full bench of the Supreme Court (acting as the then Administrative Court) and provided some valuable guidance for the interpretation of the constitutionally protected right to property in the context of social rights and austerity measures. In particular, *Charalambous* established, first, that the salary is a property right protected under article 23 of the Constitution but that this does not guarantee any right to a salary of a particular amount and, second, that article 23(3) does not permit a limitation of the right to property for consolidating public finances as a ground of public benefit. *Koutselini-Ioannidou*, on the other hand, established, first, that the right to pension crystallises and comes under the protection of article 23 once the employee reaches the retirement age and, second, that the Cypriot Constitution affords greater protection to property than does the First Additional Protocol to the ECHR.

The second group of judicial decisions, from *Christodoulidou* onwards, has been issued from the newly established Administrative Court and all decisions refer to the reasoning of both *Charalambous* and *Koutselini-Ioannidou* as authoritative. Yet, they fail to elaborate on the exact relationship between the two decisions and

---

[146] See also the relevant case law in *Spiridaki v the Republic* App no 830/2017 (28 June 20019), *Petridi v the Republic* App no 320/2015 (29 July 2019), which reaffirm *Charalambous* (n 117), *Koutselini-Ioannidou*, *Avgousti* (n 107), and *Nicolaidi* (n 107).

the different approaches used when examining the constitutionality of the limitations to the right to property. This ostensible weakness can be justified, taking into account that *Charalambous* and *Koutselini-Ioannidou* were decided by the full bench of the Supreme Court, Cyprus's highest court, and the administrative judges are bound to follow its rulings (*stare decisis*). Can it be that the ruling in *Koutselini-Ioannidou* takes precedence over *Charalambous* as it was decided at a later stage? This seems to be the practice of the Administrative Court in subsequent case law, as it implicitly adheres to the test established in *Koutselini-Ioannidou* and correctly examines the substance of any limitation only when such limitation is permissible under article 23(3).

Indeed, the *Charalambous/Koutselini-Ioannidou* judicial enigma can only be resolved in favour of the latter decision, since in *Charalambous* the Supreme Court should have found the contested law unconstitutional from the moment that the limitation was not permissible. In any case, legal certainty demands the adoption of and adherence to a comprehensive test for the assessment of any alleged unconstitutional deprivation or limitation of the right to property. Drawing from the text of article 23 of the Constitution and the relevant domestic and international case law, it is submitted that when such an allegation arises, the Court should assess a series of issues. As preliminary points, the Court must, first, establish that the contested legal right that is the subject of the recourse (salary, pension, special allowances, etc) falls within the definition of 'property' of article 23 and is thus constitutionally protected. The second preliminary point is that the Court must further establish the existence of an actual interference with the right to property.

After ascertaining these two points, the Court should then proceed to apply the typical human rights tripartite test to ensure the conformity of the deprivation or limitation with article 23 of the Constitution. First, the Court must assess whether the limitation is prescribed by law. Second, it must examine whether the limitation pursues a legitimate aim, as identified by article 23 itself, and is therefore permissible under the Constitution. In the event that the deprivation or limitation is not permissible under the Constitution, the Court must find the law (or the relevant provision) imposing such deprivation or limitation unconstitutional. If, however, the deprivation or limitation is permissible, the Court must then proceed to the third step of the test and examine the necessity of the limitation and the proportionality of the measure to the goal sought. Only then can deprivations or limitations of the right to property be found constitutional under article 23.

As a final remark, it should be noted that the approach of the Supreme Court of Cyprus towards the Constitution has always been formalistic, with the judges adhering to the letter of the Constitution.[147] In the cases examined above (and with

---

[147] See the formalistic approach followed by the majority of the Supreme Court in *Christodoulou* (n 20), regarding the legality of the measures adopted to impose the bail-in; cf dissenting decision of Judge Erotokritou; see Constantinos Kombos, *The Impact of EU Law on Cypriot Public Law* (Sakkoulas 2015).

the exception of *Charalambous*) such formalistic approach coincidentally worked in favour of human rights. However, this is not always the case, as there were other occasions where this strict adherence to the constitutional text was detrimental for the effective protection of human rights.[148] Thus, it is submitted that the Cypriot courts should embrace a more lenient human-rights-based approach when interpreting the limitations or restrictions of fundamental rights and liberties. This view is supported by the case law of the courts themselves holding that 'legislation involving interference with Fundamental Rights and Liberties safeguarded under the Constitution, ..., and their construction is governed by the settled principle that such provisions should be construed, in case of doubt, in favour of the said Rights and Liberties'.[149]

3. Separation of powers and judges' remunerations

The Supreme Court, in *Fylactou et al v the Republic*[150] (filed before the adoption of the MoU), held unanimously that the cuts imposed on the remuneration of judges in an effort to help the economy through two legislative acts—the Special Contribution Officers Employees and Pensioners of the State and Public Sector Law and the Pension Benefits for Government Employees and Employees of Public Sector including Local Authorities (Provisions of General Application) Law—were in breach of article 158(3) of the Constitution providing that 'the remuneration and other conditions of service of any such judge shall not be altered to his disadvantage after his appointment'.[151] In the initial submissions, the respondent argued that according to the principle of natural justice the Supreme Court judges should be excluded from the case as adjudicators, as any decision would directly affect their interests. The Attorney-General stressed that this claim was not one of personal bias from the judges, but one from the point of justice being done as

---

[148] See *Aziz v the Republic* (2001) 3 CLR 501 and the right to vote; *President v House of Representatives*, Reference no 2/2016 (7 July 2017) and positive discrimination.

[149] *Fina (Cyprus) Ltd of Nicosia v the Republic* (1962–1963) 4 RSCC 26, 33. See also art 33 of the Constitution providing that fundamental rights and liberties guaranteed by the Constitution shall not be subjected to any other limitations or restrictions than those provided therein, while such limitations and restriction shall be interpreted strictly and shall not be applied for any purpose other than those for which they have been prescribed.

[150] (2013) 3 CLR 565.

[151] This decision was later reaffirmed by a series of appeals filed by current and retired Supreme Court judges where the Administrative Court held that the reductions of their remunerations and pensions, in accordance with the 2013 Budget Law (59(II)/2012), were inconsistent with arts 158(3) and 153(12) of the Constitution; see *Papadopoulou v the Republic* App no 620/2014 (19 December 2018), *Parparinou v the Republic* App no 1375/2017 (30 May 2019), *Hadjihambis et al v the Republic* App no 1680/2015 (3 June 2019), *Hadjihambis v the Republic* App no 1187/2014 (3 June 2019), *Paschalides v the Republic* App no 526/2015 (3 June 2019), *Paschalides v the Republic* App no 235/2015 (3 June 2019), *Pamballi v the Republic* App no 440/2017 (4 June 2019), *Nicolatos v the Republic* App no 439/2017 (26 June 2019), *Pouyiourou v the Republic* App no 982/2018 (4 July 2019), *Kleanthous v the Republic* App no 1291/2018 (14 June 2019), *Michaelidou v the Republic* App no 527/2017 (29 July 2019).

understood by an objective observer. However, this argument was subsequently retracted.

The respondent also claimed that the troublesome economic situation of the country demanded all citizens to contribute in accordance with their means. Thus, it would be a failure if the judges were exempted from these austerity measures. The Supreme Court characterised this argument as emotional, poor in terms of legal arguments, and as being an unjust attack against the applicants (judges). The Supreme Court found itself in a difficult and unpleasant situation. Yet, as the 'guardian of the Constitution' with the duty of interpreting and preserving its provisions, it did not have a choice, other than deciding on the case before it. The Court emphasised the cardinal role of the separation of powers in the Cypriot Constitution, as evidenced by article 158 of the Constitution aiming at safeguarding the independence and impartiality of the judiciary. The contested laws were considered to amount to an alteration of the remuneration of the judges to their disadvantage and were found in breach of article 158 and the principle of the separation of powers.[152]

V. Conclusion

It has become evident that the economic crisis affected the Cypriot social protection system extensively. Social reforms and cuts were implemented both before the adoption of the MoU, with the view of mitigating the effects of the crisis and entering into an agreement with Troika for financial support, and after its adoption, adhering to the strict conditionality requirements. The social reforms aimed at correcting the excessive government deficit and the unsustainable social protection system, at eliminating the existing shortcomings of the system, at protecting those who were most in need (such as the working poor), at allocating resources in a more efficient way, and at creating incentives for taking up work.

The assessment of the legality of the social protection cuts and reforms adopted as austerity measures in Cyprus is rather limited, one-dimensional, unclear, and disappointing. All relevant case law relates to the salary and pensions of employees and pensioners of the public and wider public sector, with the exception of the salary of judges; there is no case law assessing the constitutionality of any other social protection reform. Moreover, the Cypriot courts addressed the claims raised by the applicants based on the right to property and confined their reasoning to the violation of article 23; alleged violations of other constitutionally protected rights have been examined occasionally and to a lesser extent. The relationship between the approaches followed in *Charalambous* and *Koutselini-Ioannidou* for examining the constitutionality of the contested laws remains vague and unclear.

---

[152] See also *Laoutas v the Republic* (2001) 3 CLR 40.

Consequently, the Cypriot courts failed to provide not only a legal analysis of the relationship between austerity measures and human rights other than the right to property but also a clear analysis and understanding of the right to property.

In any case, the legality of these social protection cuts and reforms introduced through legislation in order to meet the strict conditionality requirements for timely lending was pending before the Supreme Court until very recently.[153] The expectation was that the court would, on the occasion of the appeals filed against *Avgousti, Nicolaidi, Koundourou,* and *Filippou,* address the gaps and weaknesses of the previous case law and would at least establish a clear test for assessing the constitutionality of deprivations or limitations to the right to property. The court's dilemma was to either reaffirm its previous interpretation of the right to property as provided in article 23 of the Constitution, thus adopting a pro-human rights approach, or to reverse the Administrative Court's decisions by introducing a new interpretation or mechanism for enabling limitations of human rights on grounds not encompassed in the Constitution. Unfortunately, in a split decision that has attracted criticism the Court chose the latter. The overall impact of the decision remains to be seen.

---

[153] At the time of editing of this work, the majority of the Supreme Court reversed the findings of the Administrative Court in the cases analysed above (*Avgousti* (n 107), *Nicolaidi* (n 107), *Koundourou* (n 142), and *Filippou* (n 144)) upholding the relevant laws and the restriction of the right to property as constitutional; see *Republic v Avgousti et al* App nos 177/18, 75/19, 76/19, 77/19, 79/19, 80/19, 84/19, and 85/19 (10 April 2020).

10

The Outcome of the Financial Crisis in Italy

A Sea Change for the Doctrine of Social Rights

Matteo De Nes and Andrea Pin

I. Introduction

The global crisis was a turning point for law, economy, welfare, and politics in Italy. It seems fair to say that the way the economic breakdown hit Italy and the way the country reacted will have a lasting impact for years to come. The economy shrunk; the welfare system entered critical status; the crisis hit the job market, pensions, and other safety nets, to which the state responded with drastic reforms; a technocracy-driven government replaced volatile political majorities; and the need to reassure capital markets and the European Union (EU) prompted constitutional reforms and froze the process of decentralisation of powers from the state

Matteo De Nes and Andrea Pin, *The Outcome of the Financial Crisis in Italy* In: *European Welfare State Constitutions after the Financial Crisis*. Edited by: Ulrich Becker and Anastasia Poulou, Oxford University Press (2020). © The Contributors.
DOI: 10.1093/oso/9780198851776.003.0010

to local bodies. The crisis and the dramatic changes in response to it triggered vast popular reactions, which culminated in huge resentment and have paved the way for a Euro-sceptical political agenda. The crisis has ultimately left Italy with fewer resources, less welfare protection, a sceptical view of supranational institutions and of globalisation, new political subjects, and a deeper, albeit contested, role of courts in balancing social rights with austerity measures.

What really made an impact on Italian legal and political thinking was how institutions reacted to the economic crisis. After a short overview of the constitutional protection of social rights, this chapter will track the constitutional and legislative reforms that were put in place to counter the crisis, explore the political and cultural contours that backed them, and finally consider how the Constitutional Court reacted to them.

The trajectory of the post-crisis legal measures in Italy has undergone two major phases. The first phase spanned roughly from 2011 through 2015; the second started fading only in 2020, when the Covid-19 pandemic forced state institutions to reconsider their agenda.

Between 2008 and 2011, the state was able to intervene in the economy, tempering the social effects of the crisis. In 2011, such countermeasures became unsustainable because of the already weak fiscal status of Italian institutions, absent any serious attempt to reform the welfare state, re-launch the economy, and fight inefficiencies. It was 2011 when the crisis affected the law, the economy, and social rights in Italy, and the EU pushed national institutions to implement structural reforms.[1] In 2011, the weak centre-right political majority, which had already been in the spotlight for a while, collapsed under both the pressure of the crisis and of EU and international criticism of the government's failure to address the crisis.

In 2011, in the haste of fighting both economic and fiscal crisis, an emergency government coalition put a series of profound reforms in place. Although they heavily impacted social rights, the measures that the coalition passed were ultimately approved by the Constitutional Court, which safeguards constitutional values through judicial review of legislation.[2] Soon thereafter, with the 2012 'Fiscal Compact', the EU consolidated an approach to the crisis that combined economic liberalisation,[3] welfare austerity, and increased taxation for the eurozone states that were in a difficult fiscal situation.[4] This EU response to the crisis seemed to reinforce the Italian approach, and ensured a sort of political 'honeymoon period', during which actors across the political spectrum and the judiciary viewed economic and fiscal reforms rather favourably.

---

[1] The 'distinctive EU approach' to the crisis has been investigated by Erika Szyszczak '"Europe Isn't Working in Europe": Reform and Modernisation of the European Welfare State in the Wake of the Economic Crisis' (2015) 38 Fordham Int'l LJ 1193.

[2] On the usefulness of judicial review in defending social rights, Matthias Klatt, 'Positive Rights: Who Decides? Judicial Review in Balance' (2015) 13 Int'l J Const L 354.

[3] As to the long-established 'market ideology' of the EU, Danny Nicol, 'Europe's *Lochner* Moment' (2011) 2 Pub L 308, 319.

[4] Szyszczak (n 1) 1213.

The 'honeymoon' ended in 2015. Probably sensing general dissatisfaction about the backsliding of welfare services in a time of crisis, with no significant success on the economic front, both the parliament and the Constitutional Court started to heighten their protection of social rights, questioning their prior, basic approach that considered austerity measures necessary both to protect social rights and to boost the economy. Indeed, statistical data give a worrying picture of the country. The most telling is probably the poverty rate: from 2005 to 2015, the Italian population in absolute poverty dramatically increased by 140 per cent.[5]

Finally, after the 2018 parliamentary elections, the *Movimento 5 Stelle* (Five Stars Movement) and the *Lega* (League) joined forces in a Euro-sceptical government coalition. They set out for an ambitious package of counter-reforms in social policy, which they implemented between the end of 2018 and the beginning of 2019.

This chapter tracks down the political consequences of the economic crisis' outbreak. It then describes the austerity measures put in place to counter the economic and welfare collapse, together with the relevant case law of the Constitutional Court. It finally considers the main aspects of the post-2018 political agenda.

II. Background

1. The 2011 ECB letter, the political crisis, and the decline of social rights

During 2011, Italy faced a deep sovereign debt crisis, as well as a significant deficit in the balance of payments. These events aggravated the exceeding Italian public deficit, which had already become a matter of concern. Indeed, cuts in public expenditures were already being implemented as early as 2010.[6]

In 2011, financial markets hesitated to purchase government bonds and interest rates increased considerably, as the state public debt began to be considered unsustainable. European financial institutions worried that the collapse of Italian public finance could destabilise the whole Eurozone and trigger a pan-Euro crisis, and they pushed for fiscal, economic, and institutional reforms. They did not recommend, however, that the country undergo an official programme of financial assistance, similar to those of Greece, Spain, Portugal, Ireland, or Cyprus. The EU institutions rather followed an informal procedure, aimed at influencing domestic structural fiscal and financial reforms without legally imposing them.

---

[5] Certified by the Italian National Institute for Statistics (ISTAT). Elena Granaglia, 'La povertà oggi in Italia. Recenti tendenze e quattro nodi critici' (2017) 2 Questione giustizia 19 <http://questionegiustizia. it/rivista/2017-2.php> accessed 29 August 2019.

[6] Specifically with the *decreto legge* 31 May 2010 n 78 in *Gazzetta Ufficiale* 31 May 2010 n 125 suppl ord n 114.

On 5 August 2011, the then-President of the European Central Bank (ECB), Jean-Claude Trichet, and his imminent successor, Mario Draghi (who was leading the Italian Central Bank at the time and had already been appointed to the ECB Presidency), privately sent a letter to the then-President of the Council of Ministries, Silvio Berlusconi. The letter urged the Italian government to adopt severe austerity measures and structural reforms as soon as possible to restore investors' confidence. Specifically, the letter stated the necessity of some specific measures: (a) full liberalisation of local public services; (b) reform of collective wage agreements, encouraging more flexible solutions; (c) reform of job contract legislation, to make dismissals less onerous; (d) increase in the sustainability of public finance and reduction of the public deficit and public debt (at central and local levels); (e) increase in the retirement age; (f) reduction of civil servant recruitment and, if necessary, salaries; (g) automatic cuts to politically discretionary expenditures; (h) fostering of efficiency of public bodies; and (i) abolition of the provinces. Moreover, the ECB warmly encouraged the government to accelerate the reform process using decree-laws that sidestepped lengthily parliamentary debates. Because the decree-law is an act that has the force of law, it is passed by the government only under extraordinarily urgent circumstances and must be confirmed by the parliament within sixty days.[7] Its adoption would have sped up the reforms and put them before parliament as a fait accompli. Finally, the ECB encouraged a constitutional reform to set budget rules that would standardise fiscal and financial constraints. Clearly, the package of reforms that the ECB urged Italy to enact went beyond the urgency of the crisis, as they were sweeping and structural in nature.

The ECB implicitly granted its financial support, namely by purchasing state bonds in the financial markets, subject to the condition that these reforms be implemented.[8]

The ECB letter remained undisclosed to the parliament and the public until 29 September 2011, when a newspaper disclosed it.[9] When it was released, the Italian Government's already weak position worsened; it was understood as proof that Italy was being driven according to an ECB secret agenda or, alternatively, that the government did not enjoy a good international reputation, as it was given direct and precise prescriptions and warnings. The further disclosure that then-government-leader Silvio Berlusconi had bowed to the letter's specific requests with a letter in response promising that Italy would comply with the requests caused the dwindling political majority that backed the government to collapse.[10]

---

[7] Art 77 of the Italian Constitution.

[8] Federico Losurdo, 'Austerità e riforme strutturali nella crisi dell'ordine di Maastricht' (2014) 14 RDSS 581, 588–89.

[9] Corriere della Sera, 29 September 2011 <https://www.corriere.it> accessed 29 August 2019.

[10] Gerardo Pelosi and Isabella Bufacchi, 'Ecco il testo della lettera che l'Italia ha inviato alla UE: licenziamenti facili in caso di crisi e pensioni a 67 anni dal 2026' Il Sole 24 Ore (26 October 2011) <https://st.ilsole24ore.com> accessed 29 August 2019.

The whole correspondence between the ECB's leaders and the Italian government was subject to fierce doctrinal criticism. Italian constitutional scholarship considered the letter an unconventional instrument of political pressure.[11] The ECB letter could not be defined as soft law because it was completely outside any Italian, European, or international legal scheme.

Critics likewise targeted the procedure and the contents of the letter. It was secretly sent to the government and it was extremely detailed in listing fiscal and financial policies to be adopted. It concretely bypassed the Italian parliament, despite the fact that the measures encouraged by the letter had to be implemented through parliamentary legislation. In November 2011, Silvio Berlusconi resigned, and the government faced international concerns and mixed national reactions, which oscillated between anxieties that Italy could not repay its public debt and anger that external forces were driving Italian politics through a sort of 'project fear' based on the economy and fiscal crisis. The President of the Italian Republic, Giorgio Napolitano, filled the institutional vacuum by stimulating the creation of a government that would address the necessity of reforms to avoid the worsening of the fiscal crisis.

A former EU Commissioner and respected economist, Mario Monti, was considered the right pick to form a government that, by listening to the call of the EU institutions, would address the fiscal and economic crisis. As Monti was not an active politician, President Napolitano first exercised his presidential power by appointing Mario Monti as Senator for life. Once a member of the parliament, Monti had the ability to conduct negotiations with parliamentary groups.[12]

In the end, Napolitano appointed Mario Monti as the new President of the Council of Ministries. Monti's Council of Ministries was composed of experts who were well versed in the critical issues at stake in the ECB letter but had not been elected to the parliament. The primary, explicit goal of the new government was restoring the country's financial credibility to prevent further financial storms and the bankruptcy under the pressure of Italy's public debt. The new government assured that Italy would implement the necessary measures suggested in the ECB letter.

By the time Mario Monti took the helm of the government, it had become apparent how and to what extent the ECB warnings would affect Italian economic and fiscal policies. Although Italy was not involved in any official programme of financial assistance granted by the so-called European 'rescue funds' (the European

---

[11] Massimo Luciani, 'L'equilibrio di bilancio e i principi fondamentali: la prospettiva del controllo di costituzionalità' *Corte costituzionale* (22 November 2013) 11 <http://www.cortecostituzionale.it/> accessed 29 August 2019. Andrea Morrone, 'Crisi economica e integrazione politica in Europa' (2014) 3 Rivista AIC 2 <http://www.rivistaaic.it/it/> accessed 29 August 2019. Elisa Olivito, 'Crisi economico-finanziaria ed equilibri costituzionali. Qualche spunto a partire dalla lettera della BCE al governo italiano' (2014) 1 Rivista AIC <http://www.rivistaaic.it/it/> accessed 29 August 2019.

[12] 'Mario Monti nominato senatore a vita. La mossa del Colle, il via libera del premier' *La Repubblica* (9 November 2011) <http://www.repubblica.it> accessed 29 August 2019.

Financial Stabilisation Mechanism, the European Financial Stability Facility, and the European Stability Mechanism), the ECB letter's recommended measures mirrored those enshrined in the well-known Memoranda of Understanding that the applicant states had to implement in order to be included in the rescue programmes. Such measures required macroeconomic adjustments of payment balances through the reduction of domestic demand, which inevitably implied a reduction in wages and welfare expenditures.

The series of events that took place from the fiscal crisis to the ECB letter and the fall of the Berlusconi government to the inception of the Monti government had two main drivers: avoiding the Scylla of financial default on one hand and the Charybdis of the rescue programme on the other. In other words, the road to Italian reforms mirrored the spirit and structure of the Economic and Monetary Union (EMU), precisely to avoid Italy relinquishing direct control of its policies to the EMU itself.

The Monti government did not merely address the urgency of fiscal crisis through ad hoc measures. It took a structural approach, under the belief that this was necessary to the financial stability of the state within the EMU macroeconomic governance. The government enacted a series of structural reforms through the decree-law, which, as mentioned above, is a powerful legal tool.

A first set of measures, intended to avoid the fiscal collapse, went under the name *Salva Italia* (Save Italy).[13] A second set of reforms meant to boost economic growth was nicknamed *Cresci Italia* (Italy, Grow).[14] Both decree-laws were put in place within a very small interval of time, with very little debate, and under the pressure of the circumstances. In sum, emergency and urgency dictated structural reforms that should have been developed under less pressing circumstances.

The reform that epitomises all the others is the constitutionalisation of the so-called 'golden rule' of a balanced budget, passed in 2012 (constitutional law n 1/ 2012).[15] But huge reforms affected all the main components of the welfare state, the labour market, and job contract regulation. Many such reforms have outlived the Monti government and the emergency phase to which it responded. In 2013, new parliamentary elections were held. Mario Monti ran with a party that he funded shortly before the election day; he gained a small number of seats and virtually disappeared from the political stage.

---

[13] *Decreto legge* 6 December 2011 n 201 in *Gazzetta Ufficiale* 6 December 2011 n 284 suppl ord n 251, converted in *legge* 22 December 2011 n 214 in *Gazzetta Ufficiale* 27 December 2011 n 300 suppl ord n 276.

[14] *Decreto legge* 24 January 2012 n 1 in *Gazzetta Ufficiale* 24 January 2012 n 19 suppl ord n 18, converted in *legge* 24 March 2012 n 27 in *Gazzetta Ufficiale* 24 March 2012 n 71 suppl ord n 53.

[15] *Legge costituzionale* 20 April 2012 n 1 in *Gazzetta Ufficiale* 23 April 2012 n 95.

2. The constitutionalisation of the balanced budget rule

The 1948 constitutional provisions on the public budget did not reflect any specific economic theory or identifiable doctrine of public finance.[16] The annual budget could be in balance, in deficit, or in surplus, depending on the political discretion of the government, which submits the budget, and the parliament, which approves it. The only constraint on decisions affecting public finance was the following: 'any law involving new or increased expenditure shall provide for the resources to cover such expenditure' (article 81, paragraph 3, Italian Constitution).[17] Such a rule is still in place, but the constitutional context has changed since 2012, and its meaning must be gleaned in light of this novelty. Until 2012, the constitutional obligation to guarantee economic and social rights went hand in hand with neutral and flexible rules for the public budget, which allowed for different economic and fiscal policies.[18]

The 2012 constitutional change draws on pre-existing financial constraints, however. Already in the early 1990s, after the Treaty of Maastricht and its European Stability and Growth Pact entered into force, state budgetary policies started to account for financial constraints on the public deficit and public debt in order to comply with EU regulations.

Indeed, because of the Stability and Growth Pact, since the end of the 1990s Italian lawmakers have imposed financial restrictions on every local authority. Numerous provisions, for example, have imposed limitations on the recruitment of government employees, a general prohibition of deficit spending unless under exceptional circumstances, limits to current expenditures, and the reservation of specific amounts of financial resources to achieve the Maastricht parameters on public deficit and public debt.[19] The state has put constraints on the autonomy of local authorities, which is protected under the Italian Constitution,[20] by over-stretching its domain over finances of the whole public sector.[21] In short, before the global crisis, the external constraint dynamic developed not only from the

---

[16] Sergio Bartole, 'Art. 81' in Giuseppe Branca (ed), *Commentario alla Costituzione. La formazione delle leggi. Art. 76-82* (Zanichelli-Il Foro Italiano 1979). Massimo Luciani, 'Economia nel diritto costituzionale' in *Digesto delle discipline pubblicistiche* (Utet 1990). Massimo Luciani, 'Unità nazionale e struttura economica. La prospettiva della Costituzione repubblicana' (2011) 4 Diritto e società 636. Guido Rivosecchi, 'L'equilibrio di bilancio: dalla riforma costituzionale alla giustiziabilità' (2016) 3 Rivista AIC <http://www.rivistaaic.it/it/> accessed 29 August 2019.

[17] Paolo De Ioanna, *Parlamento e spesa pubblica* (Il Mulino 1993).

[18] Omar Chessa, 'Pareggio strutturale di bilancio, keynesismo e unione monetaria' (2016) 36 Quaderni costituzionali 455, 472.

[19] Dario Immordino, 'L'autonomia finanziaria a dieci anni dalla riforma costituzionale' (2011) 39 Le Regioni 415, 433–34.

[20] Art 119 of the Italian Constitution.

[21] Art 117, para 3 of the Italian Constitution.

supranational level to the national level, but also from the central government to local authorities, in cascading fashion.

The outbreak of the 2008 financial crisis prompted the tightening of such constraints, bringing them to the constitutional level in the span of four years. With the crisis, the Euro Plus Pact, the Fiscal Compact, the EU directives, and the regulations enshrined in the Six Pack and in the Two Pack converged in the neo-liberal logic that has characterised the European Continent since the Maastricht Treaty and discouraged public spending and debt in time of crisis.

In 2012, the Monti cabinet submitted to the parliament a constitutional reform proposal aimed at entrenching the balanced budget rule within the Constitution. The pressure of financial emergency quickly persuaded the parliament to adopt a reform that would put shackles on the spending power of public institutions and converted the parliamentary process into a landslide. The parliament thus approved the bill in a very short time. As a result, a relevant constitutional change that incorporated a specific economic doctrine, with a foreseeably wide impact on the domestic welfare system, took place under the pressure of emergency. The considerable effects on the effective protection of social rights were hardly subject to contemplation; how the new rule would balance rights and resources remained largely unexplored.

Specifically, constitutional law n 1/2012 amended several articles of the Italian Constitution, detailing the new budget rules in meticulous fashion that is rather uncommon to the Italian tradition of constitutional drafting.

The new first and second paragraphs of article 81 of the Italian Constitution, which traditionally focus on the state budget and balance sheet, now read, '[t]he State shall balance revenue and expenditure in its budget, taking into account the adverse and favourable phases of the economic cycle'. Moreover, '[n]o recourse shall be made to borrowing except for the purpose of taking account of the effects of the economic cycle or, subject to authorization by the two Houses approved by an absolute majority vote of their Members, in exceptional circumstances'.

According to article 97 of the Italian Constitution as amended in 2012, '[g]eneral government entities, in accordance with European Union law, shall ensure balanced budgets and the sustainability of public debt'. Moreover, the new first paragraph of article 119 states that local authorities, namely municipalities, provinces, metropolitan cities, and regions 'shall have revenue and expenditure autonomy, subject to the obligation to balance their budgets, and shall contribute to ensuring compliance with the economic and financial constraints imposed under European Union law'.

Constitutional law n 1/2012 did not specify the meaning of words and concepts such as 'balancing revenue and expenditure' in public entities' budgets. The parliament passed law n 243/2012 shortly thereafter to clarify that the state budget equilibrium is the 'medium-term objective'.[22] Such a medium-term objective is 'the

---

[22] Art 3, para 2 *legge* 24 December 2012 n 243 in *Gazzetta Ufficiale* 15 January 2013 n 12.

value of the structural balance determined on the basis of the criteria established by the European Union'.[23] In turn, the structural balance is 'the consolidated balance sheet corrected for the effects of the economic cycle ... defined in accordance with European Union law'.[24]

From a theoretical perspective, such legal changes have left considerable leeway to balance revenue and expenditure according to economic cycles.[25] Indeed, the 'golden rule' of a balanced budget that has been constitutionalised does not deal with actual revenue and expenditure, but it rather focuses on the costs and the revenue that could potentially be secured by existing production capacity. In other words, it considers the level of revenue that taxation provides if the production system operates at full speed.[26] This formula defers the identification of that level to political negotiations, as the government and the EU must agree in quantifying the potential Italian gross domestic product (GDP).

The piece of legislation that activated the new constitutional rule, however, draws a sharp distinction between the state and local authorities. Under law n 243/2012, the state retains significant leeway in light of the effects of the economic cycle. Conversely, local bodies must achieve a predetermined balanced budget.[27] Consequently, localities are facing grater difficulties in granting social services of paramount importance, as they must provide healthcare and social assistance.

The 2012 constitutional reform and its implementation law n 243/2012 have had powerful consequences on the relationship between domestic and supranational institutions, as well as on the balance between the legislative and the executive powers. As to the relationship between Italian and EU institutions, it domesticated external constraints. Such constraints were already grounded in the Treaty of Maastricht and the Stability and Growth Pact and enjoyed constitutional protection.[28] But constitutional law n 1/2012 was surely an important paradigm shift. This reform did more than impose respect for EU fiscal rules on Italy. It expressly constitutionalised a neo-liberal formula, which became the prism through which the constitutional protection of fundamental social rights had to be examined. Squaring the longstanding tradition of social rights enshrined in the Constitution and the new rules for the budget became the business of the Constitutional Court. The 2012 constitutional reform did not simply constitutionalise neo-liberalism; it judicialised it.

---

[23] ibid art 2, para 1, lett e.

[24] ibid art 2, para 1, lett d.

[25] Luciani, 'L'equilibrio di bilancio e i principi fondamentali' (n 11) 21.

[26] Chessa (n 18) 458.

[27] Art 9, para 1, *legge* n 243/2012 (n 22). Luca Antonini, 'Armonizzazione contabile e autonomia finanziaria degli enti territoriali' (2017) 1 Rivista AIC <http://www.rivistaaic.it/it/> accessed 29 August 2019.

[28] Art 117 of the Italian Constitution, as amended in 2001, states that 'Legislative powers shall be vested in the state and the regions in compliance with the Constitution and with the constraints deriving from EU-legislation and international obligations'.

As to the relationship between the legislative and the executive power, the constitutional reform, together with the new EU economic governance architecture, substantially marginalised the role of the parliament in drawing up fiscal and financial policies.[29] Budget policies are now negotiated between the government and the EU Commission during the whole financial year. This has cut the parliament off from strategic budgetary decisions, inevitably affecting the balance between the executive and legislative powers of the State.[30]

III. Reforms in national security systems

1. Preliminary remarks: social security and the healthcare system in Italy

Like several other European social constitutions drafted after the end of World War II, the Italian Constitution directly provides a significant set of social rights, which are strongly related to the fundamental principles of social dignity and equality enshrined in article 3 of the Constitution. Specifically, the second paragraph of article 3 states that '[i]t is the duty of the Republic to remove the economic and social obstacles which by limiting the freedom and equality of citizens, prevent the full development of the human person and the effective participation of all workers in the political, economic and social organization of the country'. Such a crucial principle represents the assumption of social rights granted by the Constitution, such as workers' rights (articles 1, 4, 35, 36, 37, 38, 39, 40), the right to healthcare (article 32), the right to maintenance and social assistance (article 38), the rights of people with disabilities (article 38), and the right to education (articles 33 and 34).[31]

The constitutional literature has generally considered social rights justiciable and enforceable.[32] On one hand, alleged violations of social rights can be argued in ordinary and administrative courts if public bodies fail in fulfilling relevant legislative provisions; on the other hand, any domestic judge can call the Italian

---

[29] On the role of the Italian Parliament within the EU, Nicola Lupo and Giovanni Piccirilli, *The Italian Parliament in the European Union* (Hart 2017). Nicola Lupo and Guido Rivosecchi, 'Valutare le politiche di bilancio: il ruolo del Parlamento' (2016) 22 Diritto pubblico 333. On the role of the Italian parliament in the budgetary decision-making process: Chiara Bergonzini, *Parlamento e decisioni di bilancio* (Franco Angeli 2014).

[30] Chiara Bergonzini, 'Manovra di bilancio 2019: quando si finisce col fare a meno del Parlamento' (2019) 39 Quaderni costituzionali 162.

[31] Although the right to education is generally included among social rights by the Italian constitutional literature—eg Vezio Crisafulli, 'La scuola nella Costituzione' (1956) 6 Rivista trimestrale di diritto pubblico 55; Umberto Pototschnig, 'Istruzione (diritto alla)' in *Enciclopedia del diritto* (Giuffrè 1973)—the present country report will not address the education system as it is outside the scope of the present book.

[32] Aldo Carosi, 'Prestazioni sociali e vincolo di bilancio' *Corte costituzionale* (7 October 2016) <http://www.cortecostituzionale.it> accessed 29 August 2019.

Constitutional Court to state whether a legislative provision jeopardises a social right granted by the Constitution.

The central government and the local authorities (regions, provinces, and commons) share the constitutional obligation to implement a pervasive and inclusive welfare system. Local, regional, and state authorities differ in terms of the powers that the Constitution accords to each of them, as different levels of government control different aspects of the Italian welfare system. Yet they all play an important role in it, and a series of legal and constitutional reforms between the late 1990s and early 2000s has provided them with more powers in social matters.

The state has exclusive legislative power to determine the 'basic level of benefits relating to civil and social entitlements to be guaranteed throughout the national territory' (article 117, paragraph 2 of the Italian Constitution). Such power enables the state to set minimum standards of welfare services and to prevent excessive gaps in social protection across different areas of the country. The state also has exclusive legislative power over social security (old-age and unemployment benefits) and in regulating job contracts[33] (article 117, paragraph 2).

In contrast, concurrent legislation between state and regions applies to job protection and safety, as well as to health protection (article 117, paragraph 3). In these matters, 'legislative powers are vested in the Regions, except for the determination of the fundamental principles, which are laid down in State legislation' (article 117, paragraph 3).

Regions have exclusive legislative power in all subject matters that are not expressly attributed to the state. In terms of social rights, this rule means that regions can legislate in all the other fields of social services and social assistance. This power extends to any social benefit, such as economic allowances for people with disabilities, support for the aged and persons who are not self-sufficient, and school and university fellowships, just to name a few.

Through social insurance contributions and tax revenues, the state finances old-age and unemployment benefits through the *Istituto Nazionale della Previdenza Sociale*—INPS (National Institute of Social Security), which is a public authority supervised by the Ministry of Labour and Social Policy. Management of the healthcare system and active labour market policy are entrusted to regions, while municipalities have a duty to provide all other forms of social assistance.

According to the Constitution, local authorities perform their duties using different financial resources: they set and levy taxes and collect revenues of their own, in compliance with the Constitution and according to the principles of coordination of public finance within the tax-power limits that are fixed by the state. They also share in revenues from state taxes related to their respective territories.

---

[33] This power is part of the state competence in civil law (art 117, para 2, lett l of the Italian Constitution).

Moreover, the state distributes the resources of an equalisation fund for the terri-tories with lower per-capita tax-raising capacities.[34]

Despite the revenue and expenditure autonomy granted by the Italian Constitution, however, the resources that are made available to regions and muni-cipalities still largely depend on choices made by the state due to three powers that it enjoys. First, the state has the power to coordinate the public finance of all public institutions. Second, it establishes the total amount of financial resources devoted to local authorities. Third, as it holds the ultimate international responsibility for state budget performances, it can put constraints on sub-national levels of govern-ment to ensure that budget goals are achieved.

The overall constitutional context is one of a modern, deeply decentralised wel-fare state with strong social rights protection. When the crisis hit, however, decen-tralisation was still in the making—especially in the tax sector—and funding for social expenditures was already in distress due to the ever-growing public debt.

2. Reform (and counter-reform) of the pension system

The post-crisis measures had powerful, durable effects on pensions and unemploy-ment benefits. But the crisis actually boosted measures in this field that were long due before 2008. Although many governments tinkered with pensions for decades, in 2013, pension expenditures skyrocketed at 16.3 per cent of GDP—the highest in Europe.[35] The global collapse of the economy forced the government to consider the sustainability of pension treatments almost from scratch, despite the unpopu-larity of the subject.

As pensions are an important part of public expenditures, increased longevity and the declining birth rate have been a matter of concern for decades. Alongside Scandinavian countries, Italy has the highest life expectancy in Europe.[36] Paying for retirement has become increasingly difficult, as the number of childbirths per woman is extremely low and below the substitution ratio.[37] The demographic out-look is rather grim now, for the number of people who cannot sustain themselves and who rely on others to survive will increase from 28.4 per cent in 2009 to 58.5 per cent in 2060.[38]

---

[34] Art 119, para 2 of the Italian Constitution.
[35] Marcello Minenna, 'Le condizionalità imposte dal *Fiscal compact* e gli impatti sul sistema previdenziale italiano' (2014) 14 RDSS 33.
[36] According to 2010 statistics. Denard Veshi, 'Le sfide del futuro: i costi della vecchiaia e il *long term care*' (2013) 13 RDSS 369, 370.
[37] ibid 371.
[38] ibid.

The anti-crisis measures justified and accelerated processes that were initiated long before the crisis. Since the early 1990s, several legislative reforms have tried to transform a system of retirement based on the working wage into one based on individual contributions to the social security system, which would be more sustainable and carve out room for voluntary retirement plans.[39] This reform was supposed to also have positive spillover effects on the market of voluntary plans and push individuals to invest money in financial enterprises.

Post-2008 urgency triggered drastic measures of reform[40] and hampered the widespread opposition that normally awaits them;[41] the Monti government started its activities on 16 November 2011 and adopted the *Salva Italia* decree-law n 201/2011 on December 6. This decree-law tried to obtain fresh resources and grant sustainability to public finances, but it mostly heeded the ECB's call.

The breadth of *Salva Italia*'s measures and their social and economic impact made this decree the most significant austerity package implemented during the financial crisis. It contained numerous provisions, including a significant increase in taxation (specifically on real estate, fuel, waste, luxury cars, and boats, as well as an increase in value added tax), liberalisations, remarkable cuts in provinces' expenditures, and pension reform.[42]

The decree spelled out its connection to the EU constraints by affirming that its provisions were 'intended to ensure compliance with the international commitments and the European Union, to respect budgetary constraints, economic and financial stability'. In terms of retirement treatments, it explicitly aimed at 'strengthen[ing] the long-term sustainability of the pension system in terms of the incidence of social security expenditure on gross domestic product.'[43]

The pension reform (better known as the *Monti-Fornero* reform, after the name of the Minister for Labour) became law in a very short time. The parliament rapidly confirmed the decree on 22 December by passing law n 214/2011. The whole parliamentary process, which took only a couple of weeks despite a two-month deadline, raised some doubts about the effectiveness of parliamentary control over such a long and complex measure.

Several principles inspired the retirement benefit reform: intergenerational convergence; abolition of privileges; very small exceptions only for the weakest categories of workers; flexibility in access to pension benefits; incentives to postpone retirements; adaptation of minimum treatment requirements to increase

---

[39] Maurizio Cinelli, *Diritto della previdenza sociale* (Giappichelli 2016) 530.

[40] Minenna (n 35) 38.

[41] The reforms were enacted after little or no parliamentary debate and without hearing the labour unions first. Francesca Fedele and Adriano Morrone, 'La legislazione sociale del 2011 tra crisi della finanza pubblica e riforma delle pensioni' (2012) 12 RDSS 105, 131.

[42] The pension reform had been introduced by arts 6, 21, 24 of *decreto legge* n 201/2011 (n 13).

[43] Art 24, *decreto legge* n 201/2011 (n 13). Pasquale Sandulli, 'Il sistema pensionistico tra una manovra e l'altra' (2012) 12 RDSS 1, 7–8.

longevity; and the simplification, harmonisation, and inexpensiveness of different pension regimes.[44]

The reform developed around five pillars. The *Monti-Fornero* reform (a) unified the institutions that provide security services, incorporating the *Istituto Nazionale di previdenza e assistenza per i dipendenti dell'amministrazione pubblica*—INPDAP (National Institute of Social Security and Assistance for Public Administration Employees) and other institutes within the INPS; (b) reformed the system of individual contributions to post-retirement pensions; (c) raised the minimum retirement age; (d) recalculated pension treatments based on individual contributions; and (e) accorded full inflation adjustment only to smaller pensions.[45]

A tax, which took the name of 'solidarity contribution',[46] was levied on larger pensions, while self-employed persons had to pay larger sums of contributions to receive post-retirement payments.[47] Pre-existing legal trends grew in scale; retirement treatments were now generally based on actual individual contributions instead of pre-retirement wage.[48] This change disconnected post-retirement treatment from pre-retirement salary and tied it to the sum of contributions workers paid.

Finally, the retirement age was raised. Albeit gradually, the system is progressively raising the retirement age to sixty-seven, effective in 2021.[49] Twenty years of individual contributions will become a standard requirement to receive pension treatments.[50] As retirement age adapts to changes in life expectancy,[51] this age will probably increase further, hitting seventy in 2050.[52]

The reform also amended the seniority pensions regime. This is a unique feature of the Italian social protection system, as it allows workers to retire after a number of years of work, regardless of their age.[53] Seniority pensions made their appearance in Italy to reward people for their contribution to national well-being, rather than as a social benefit. As they became increasingly expensive for the Treasury, several legislative measures started tightening seniority pension requirements as early as 1995.[54] But the *Monti-Fornero* reform abandoned this system and simplified the scenario. Workers could enjoy retirement benefits after forty-two

---

[44] Art 24, para 1, *decreto legge* n 201/2011 (n 13).
[45] More specifically, only pensions that did not exceed three times the basic treatment received full adjustment. Fedele and Morrone (n 41) 130–31. Additional measures were the significant increase in the number of the population that was left out of retirement plans and the freezing of the mechanism that adjusts pensions to inflation. Minenna (n 35) 43.
[46] Fedele and Morrone (n 41) 133.
[47] ibid 134.
[48] ibid 135.
[49] ibid 136.
[50] Cinelli, *Diritto della previdenza sociale* (n 39) 560.
[51] Art 12, *legge* 30 July 2010 n 122 in *Gazzetta Ufficiale* 30 July 2010 n 176 suppl ord n 174.
[52] Cinelli, *Diritto della previdenza sociale* (n 39) 559.
[53] ibid 526–33.
[54] ibid 572.

years of work if they were men, forty-one if they were women.[55] The minimum age was fixed at sixty-two years old; before reaching sixty-two, workers could still enjoy seniority, but with significant cuts.[56]

These drastic measures were taken in such a hurry that a sizeable group of people who had negotiated with the state and their employers for pre-pension treatment in accordance with the previous regime found themselves with neither jobs nor pensions. As the *Monti-Fornero* reform did not really afford a grace period, such former employees did not meet the new requirements to enjoy any treatment.[57] They found themselves jobless in circumstances of high unemployment, and their conditions were worse than those of the rest of the population because they were rather aged. This was clearly a side effect of the hurry in which the changes were made, to the extent that it was exceptionally hard for the government to get a realistic figure of those affected for a long while.[58]

Moreover, as the Italian Court of Audit later confirmed, the rapidity of the reform has also affected the quality of statistical measurements on which the pension reform-based treatments were quantified. Contrary to prior belief, in the medium- and long-term, the reform may heavily affect retired people, as the individual contribution-based calculation, together with discontinuous career paths, could lead to insufficient pension benefits.[59]

Building upon the criticisms against the new retirement pension regime, the 2018–2019 government led by *Lega* and *Movimento 5 Stelle* tinkered with it. At the end of 2018, after a long negotiation between the government and the EU Commission,[60] the parliament passed the 2019 budgetary law, which established a fund aimed at financing an experimental programme of pre-retirement.[61] The subsequent decree-law n 4/2019 enacted a the new regime for the years 2019–2021 (so-called *pensione quota 100*—pension quota 100). This provisional regime allows pre-retirement for workers who have reached the age of sixty-two, after thirty-eight years of work, with no penalties for the retirement allowance.[62] The same decree-law also provides a specific regime for women, who may decide to retire at the age of fifty-eight (if employees) or fifty-nine (if self-employed) after thirty-five years of work.[63]

[55] Fedele and Morrone (n 41) 136.

[56] Cinelli, *Diritto della previdenza sociale* (n 39) 573.

[57] Minenna (n 35) 46.

[58] Giorgio Santini and others, 'La riforma delle pensioni' (2012) 46(3) Economia & Lavoro 123.

[59] Corte dei Conti, 'Rapporto 2017 sul coordinamento della finanza pubblica' (April 2017) 195 <http://www.corteconti.it/> accessed 29 August 2019.

[60] During this negotiation, an excessive debt procedure was avoided at the last moment. Guido Rivosecchi, 'Manovra di bilancio 2019: la rientrata procedura di infrazione per debito eccessivo' (2019) 39 Quaderni costituzionali 155.

[61] Art 1, para 256, *legge* 30 December 2018 n 145 in *Gazzetta Ufficiale* 31 December 2018 n 301 suppl ord n 62.

[62] Art 14, *decreto legge* 28 January 2019 n 4 in *Gazzetta Ufficiale* 28 January 2019 n 23, converted in *legge* 28 March 2019 n 26 in *Gazzetta Ufficiale* 29 March 2019 n 75.

[63] Art 16, ibid.

This process of counter-reform is ongoing and the ordinary regime prescribed by the *Monti-Fornero* law is still in place. But it is hard to predict whether it will remain in force or will also be replaced with a new regime, since the austerity measures adopted in this field during the crisis are now considered politically unsustainable.

3. Reform of labour market regulation and unemployment benefits

The ideological underpinnings of the Italian governments' anti-crisis policies reflected onto unemployment measures. Ideally, the political agenda that drove that phase considered unemployment a temporary status, which the Italian economy would overcome by shrinking the public deficit and debt and pursuing a massive liberalisation process. Resurrecting the national economy and putting public expenditures in check, in the medium run, should have created more job opportunities. As a result, the Monti government's reforms dared to reduce unemployment protection in a time of crisis,[64] under the belief that this would later encourage re-employment and economic recovery.

As time passed, it became clear that the political agenda of the Monti government did not meet the expectations of quick economic recovery, and the unemployment rate deteriorated. At the 2013 parliamentary elections, Monti and the political party he formed virtually disappeared from the political scenario. Shortly after the 2013 elections, the new President of the Council, Matteo Renzi,[65] put a series of reforms in place that, even in Italian, went under the English name of the 'Jobs Act'.[66] This title was supposed to give the reform a modernising, pro-economy political appeal. Within the package of measures it implemented, the most noticeable reform consisted of an exceptional rule intended to promote employment.

The normal rule that had been in place for decades prohibits companies with more than fifteen employees from terminating a job contract without a 'just reason'

---

[64] *Legge* 28 June 2012 n 92 in *Gazzetta Ufficiale* 3 July 2012 n 153 suppl ord n 136. Simonetta Renga, 'La "riforma" degli ammortizzatori sociali' (2012) 26 Lavoro e diritto 621.

[65] The post-elections political coalition first elected Enrico Letta as government leader; after few months Matteo Renzi replaced him.

[66] The so-called 'Jobs Act' consists of the *decreto legge* 20 March 2014 n 34 in *Gazzetta Ufficiale* 20 March 2014 n 66, converted in *legge* 16 May 2014 n 78 in *Gazzetta Ufficiale* 19 May 2014 n 114; *legge delega* 10 December 2014 n 183 in *Gazzetta Ufficiale* 15 December 2014 n 290; eight legislative-decrees: *decreti legislativi* 4 March 2015 n 22 (on unemployment benefits) and n 23 (on job contracts) in *Gazzetta Ufficiale* 6 March 2015 n 54; *decreti legislativi* 15 June 2015 n 80 (on maternity benefits) and n 81 (on jobs contracts) in *Gazzetta Ufficiale* 24 June 2015 n 144 suppl ord n 34; *decreti legislativi* 14 September 2015 n 148 (on unemployment benefits), n 149 (on labour inspectorates), n 150 (reform of employment services), and n 151 (on equal opportunities) in *Gazzetta Ufficiale* 23 September 2015 n 221 suppl ord n 53.

(based on the employee's behaviour) or without a 'justified objective reason'. A 'just reason' normally consists of an employee's misbehaviour, while financial difficulties or technological innovations may amount to a 'justified objective reason'. Per the article 18 of the so-called *Statuto dei lavoratori* (Workers' Statute), in case of unlawful dismissal the employee must be reintegrated and receive compensation for the damage he/she suffered (in a few minor cases, only compensation is required).[67] This rule has shielded employees from job uncertainties and fluctuations of the economy. The flip side is that the rule has probably discouraged companies from hiring new employees, unless they had a reasonable expectation that their enterprise would grow and flourish. This had created tensions between the employees, who enjoyed the benefit of the rule and did not want it to be changed, and those seeking employment, who were adversely affected by the rule.

The most advertised part of the 'Jobs Act' consisted in breaking away from this rule that prohibits terminating employees. The 'Act', in fact, has introduced a new regime for job contracts signed after 7 March 2015, when the 'Act' entered into force. As a general rule, the new regime allows employers to terminate a contract without justification, so long as they compensate the employees. The reintegration operates only under certain circumstances, such as when the dismissal took place only orally, or was motivated by discrimination.[68]

The 'Jobs Act' has also introduced a new regulation of unemployment benefits, maintaining and emphasising the traditional distinction between external and internal benefits (depending on whether the beneficiary is set outside or inside the labour market). In case of involuntary unemployment, external benefits are granted by social insurance for employment (*Nuova assicurazione sociale per l'impego*).[69] On the other hand, specific income assistance is also granted while the employment relationship is still in place, through the *Cassa integrazione guadagni* and the *Fondi bilaterali di solidarietà* (the internal benefits).[70]

Here it is not possible to analyse in depth the complex regulation of these unemployment and income-assistance treatments, but it is worth highlighting the main features of the reforms implemented in the field during the financial crisis.

With regard to social insurance for involuntary unemployment, the main innovation concerns the duration of the benefit,[71] which is commensurate to the individual contribution of the applicant up to a maximum of two years, even if

---

[67] Art 18, *legge* 20 May 1970 n 300 in *Gazzetta Ufficiale* 27 May 1970 n 131, as amended by *legge* n 92/2012 (n 64). Maria Vittoria Ballestrero and Gisella De Simone, *Diritto del lavoro* (Giappichelli 2017) 520–83.

[68] Arts 3 and 4, *decreto legislativo* n 23/2015 (n 66).

[69] Art 2, *legge* n 92/2012 (n 64), adopted under the Monti Government, which introduced some minimal changes in the previous unemployment protection regime (dating back to 1919). Subsequently, the regulation in this field has been amended by one of the legislative-decrees in the 'Jobs Act': art 3, *decreto legislativo* n 22/2015 (n 66).

[70] *Legge* n 92/2012 (n 64) and *decreto legislativo* n 148/2015 (n 66).

[71] Art 5, *decreto legislativo* n 22/2015 (n 66).

non-continuous. Moreover, the amount of the benefit is initially set at seventy-five per cent of the average wage of the previous two years; afterwards, this amount decreases to a certain percentage per month.[72] The 'Jobs Act' has emphasised the role of a specific benefit requirement introduced by the Monti government, namely the availability of work. Indeed, the recipient shall lose the benefit if he/she refuses a job offer that pays more than twenty per cent of the unemployment allowance, when the workplace is set within fifty kilometres of his/her residence.[73] The reform pushes the unemployed to accept a new job more than the previous rule; before the 'Jobs Act', the new job offer was compared to the amount of the last wage and not to unemployment allowances.

The 'Jobs Act' has also innovated in the field of income assistance. It has reduced the maximum period protected by income assistance per single employee from six years to two. Assistance in the case of employer bankruptcy has been abolished.[74]

The *Cassa integrazione guadagni* is a traditional tool of income assistance that helps people facing temporary suspensions or a reduction in business activities. It operates under conditions strictly prescribed by law and is funded by both the state budget and contributions paid by employers and employees. Alongside this traditional tool the 'Act' also introduced bilateral solidarity funds (*Fondi bilaterali di solidarietà*), which are state funds that operate in fields not covered by traditional income assistance. However, benefits granted by bilateral solidarity funds are subject to the establishment of specific financial reserves, and are available only to the extent allowed by the state budget's status.[75] This provision directly derives from the balanced budget rule now enshrined in the Italian Constitution, and it raises concerns because it conditions its effectiveness on the status of the state budget.[76]

Moreover, the 'Jobs Act' has conditioned income assistance on some requirements that the beneficiary worker must respect. Specifically, the recipient might have to attend training or upgrading courses, as well as be involved in community service activities in his/her municipality of residence.[77] Severe sanctions await one who breaches these duties, in particular the loss of eligibility for income assistance.

4. The healthcare system and its underfunding

The Italian Constitution embeds a universalistic model of healthcare, as required by the principles of dignity (article 2 of the Italian Constitution) and equality

---

[72] Art 4, ibid.
[73] Art 25, *decreto legislativo* n 150/2015 (n 66).
[74] Michele Miscione, 'La Cassa integrazione dopo il Jobs Act' (2016) 15 Diritto & Pratica del Lavoro 921.
[75] Art 35, *decreto legislativo* n 148/2015 (n 66).
[76] Cinelli, *Diritto della previdenza sociale* (n 39) 358–59.
[77] Art 26, *decreto legislativo* n 150/2015 (n 66).

(article 3) as well as by the imperative that '[t]he Republic ... safeguard health as a fundamental right of the individual and as a collective interest and ... guarantee free medical care to the indigent' (article 32).

Between the early 1990s and the mid-2000s, the *Servizio Sanitario Nazionale* (National Health Service) established in 1978 underwent a strong decentralisation.[78] This process gradually increased the regional competences through ordinary laws,[79] and reached its apex with the 2001 constitutional reform.[80] The reform entrusted regions with the legislative power on health protection,[81] while reserving to the state the power to establish a basic threshold for healthcare services that must be provided throughout the national territories. Finally, per the 2001 reform, if a region lacks funds to cover its healthcare expenses, additional resources will cover the gap.[82] The basic levels of healthcare were established for the first time in 2001 and recently updated in 2017.[83]

Despite the new 2001 regional powers and financial mechanisms, the traditionally wide discrepancies in the level of services provided in different regions did not decrease. Some regions experienced a very high level of inefficiency and a very low level of services, while others were optimal both in their budget and service performances. The state was also responsible for such disfunction. As it never identified the optimal costs for each healthcare service, it was unable to identify whether a region was in true need of financial help or was simply wasting resources. For years the state struggled to close the gap among regions, some of which kept their poor performance in terms of services, while increasing their public debts for which the state was internationally responsible. All in all, the state bore the financial burden of the unequal performances among regions, since it had to cover considerable regional deficits in health expenditures during the first decade of the new millennium.[84]

The economic and fiscal crisis exacerbated these phenomena and cast clouds over the full actuation of the 2001 constitutional reform. The application of long-awaited fiscal federalism, which should have endowed local autonomies with substantial levying powers, virtually disappeared from the agenda.

---

[78] *Legge* 23 December 1978 n 833 in *Gazzetta Ufficiale* 28 December 1978 n 360.

[79] *Decreto legislativo* 30 December 1992 n 502 in *Gazzetta Ufficiale* 30 December 1992 n 305 suppl ord n 137; *decreto legislativo* 7 December 1993 n 517 in *Gazzetta Ufficiale* 15 December 1993 n 293 suppl ord n 113; *decreto legislativo* 19 June 1999 n 229 in *Gazzetta Ufficiale* 16 July 1999 n 165 suppl ord n 132.

[80] *Legge costituzionale* 18 October 2001 n 3 in *Gazzetta Ufficiale* 24 October 2001 n 248.

[81] Art 117, para 3 of the Italian Constitution.

[82] Art 117, para 2 and art 119 of the Italian Constitution.

[83] *Decreto del Presidente del Consiglio dei ministri* 29 November 2001 in *Gazzetta Ufficiale* 8 February 2002 n 33; *decreto del Presidente del Consiglio dei ministri* 12 January 2017 in *Gazzetta Ufficiale* 18 March 2017 n 65.

[84] Luca Antonini, *Federalismo all'italiana* (Marsilio 2013). Ettore Jorio, 'L'extra deficit sanitario: tra un sistema di controllo conflittuale e piani di rientro non propriamente adeguati' (2008) Federalismi <http://www.federalismi.it/> accessed 29 August 2019.

Under the pressure of the crisis, through annual budget laws the state cut the fiscal resources it gave to regions in need and put strong, detailed constraints on the legislative powers of all the regions, including those that had performed well in terms of both budget and welfare. Such anti-crisis measures strongly affected the healthcare system, which the ECB letter had emphasised as needing deep review, with specific regard to efficiency indicators. Austerity measures have underfunded healthcare services during the last decade; public healthcare expenditure has increased only by an average of one per cent per year, while in the other eurozone countries the increase amounts to an average of 3.8 per cent per year.[85] Specifically, from 2002 to 2005 the Italian healthcare expenditure grew by an average of 6.8 per cent per year, from 2006 to 2010 by an average of 2.8 per cent per year, and from 2011 to 2017 by an average of 0.5 per cent per year.[86]

Even if the Italian healthcare system has maintained an appreciable level of quality,[87] its underfunding appears dramatic, and it has already surfaced at the societal level. Longer waiting times now are required to access public health services, and citizens often delay or renounce necessary treatments.[88] Limited public financial resources have forced hospitals to ration healthcare services.[89] Private expenditure for healthcare services has significantly increased, broadening social gaps and inequalities:[90] in 2014, 9.5 per cent of the population renounced health treatments due to economic reasons or inefficiencies of the public healthcare systems.[91] This had happened while the main developed countries allocated more and more resources to health, following a trend that reflects the increase in health demand, linked to the increase in well-being and the ageing of the population.[92] Moreover, since scientific and technological innovations are instrumental to secure the high quality of a healthcare system nowadays, the underfunding is likely to have more negative effects on Italian healthcare.

However, the 2018–2019 government coalition has confirmed its counter-trend agenda also in healthcare services. The public expenditures in the field have started to increase again since then, similar to the other western countries. Such expenses

---

[85] RBM—Censis, 'VII rapporto sulla sanità pubblica, privata, intermedia' (2017) 18 <http://www.censis.it/> accessed 29 August 2019. Ufficio Parlamentare di Bilancio (UPB), 'La revisione della spesa pubblica: il caso della sanità' (Focus tematico n 9, 21 December 2015) <http://www.upbilancio.it/> accessed 29 August 2019. Antonio Giulio de Belvis and others, 'The Financial Crisis in Italy: Implications for the Healthcare Sector' (2012) 106 Health Policy 10.

[86] Ministero dell'economia e delle finanze, Ragioneria generale dello Stato, 'Il monitoraggio della spesa sanitaria' (Roma, November 2018) 53 <http://www.quotidianosanita.it> accessed 29 August 2019.

[87] OECD, 'Health at a Glance 2017: OECD Indicators, How does Italy Compare?' <http://www.oecd.org> accessed 29 August 2019.

[88] RBM—Censis (n 85) 157–58.

[89] UPB (n 85).

[90] RBM—Censis (n 85) 153 and 161.

[91] Rapporto Istat 2015, 'La situazione del Paese' <http://www.istat.it> accessed 29 August 2019.

[92] UPB (n 85).

grew 1.6 per cent in 2018, hit 2.3 per cent in 2019, and are expected to increase by an average of 1.4 per cent per year between 2020 and 2022.[93]

5. Social assistance under stress

The crisis and austerity tandem brought to the surface the unresolved disputed over the nature and the span of constitutionally protected social assistance. According to article 38, paragraph 1, of the Italian Constitution, '[e]very citizen unable to work and without the necessary means of subsistence has a right to maintenance and social assistance'. Notwithstanding such provision, for decades Italy has never implemented a general and universal social protection scheme for non-workers; the universal access to healthcare service was an exception.[94] Only in the late 1990s did the legislature start to address this issue.

The 1998 legislation gave a very capacious definition of social assistance. It included all of the activities related to the provision of (free or paid) services aimed at removing situations of need and difficulty that people face in their life. It excluded only the services covered by the social security system—which essentially consists of pensions and unemployment treatments—and the healthcare system.[95] The area of social assistance services thus encompasses allowances against absolute poverty, benefits for disadvantage people and people with disabilities, and family allowances.

Pursuant to constitutional provisions, social assistance should be decentralised and the largest share of resources for social protection should be allocated to local communities.[96] However, the resources made available by the state budget decreased dramatically during austerity. Funding dropped from €1.884 billion per year in 2004 to €42.9 million in 2012, then slowly bounced back to €297.41 million in 2014.[97] This underfunding worsened the average level of social assistance, with the paradoxical result that public institutions provided less services to the people in need exactly when they needed it most.[98]

Only in 2017 did the legislature try to reverse the trend of shrinking social benefits by adopting a comprehensive measure against poverty, the so-called *reddito di inclusione* (inclusion income). This tool aimed to support the poorest sections

---

[93] Senato della Repubblica, Camera dei Deputati, 'Dossier 2019, Documento di economia e finanza (DEF) 2019' 44 <http://www.quotidianosanita.it> accessed 29 August 2019.

[94] Mattia Persiani, 'Diritto della sicurezza sociale' in *Enciclopedia del diritto, Annali IV* (Giuffrè 2011) 450–51.

[95] Art 128, *decreto legislativo* 31 March 1998 n 112 in *Gazzetta Ufficiale* 21 April 1998 n 92 suppl ord n 77.

[96] *Legge* 27 December 1997 n 449 in *Gazzetta Ufficiale* 30 December 1997 n 302 suppl ord n 255, and *legge* 8 November 2000 n 328 in *Gazzetta Ufficiale* 13 November 2000 n 265 suppl ord n 186.

[97] Francesca Biondi Dal Monte and Vincenzo Casamassima, 'Le Regioni e i servizi sociali a tredici anni dalla riforma del Titolo V' (2014) 42 Le Regioni 1065, 1102–03.

[98] Monica Delsignore, 'I servizi sociali nella crisi economica' (2018) 26 Diritto amministrativo 587.

of the population through monetary allowances.[99] The initial amount of this fund was €1.8 billion per year, and was expected to increase progressively, reaching €2.8 billion starting in 2020.[100] Despite its financial relevance, the *reddito di inclusione* covered only absolute poverty; it did not address other relevant issues, such as shrinking healthcare treatments or waning social assistance services, which were also largely affecting the middle class.

Subsequently, the 2018–2019 Government coalition adopted a measure aimed at fighting poverty and unemployment at once. The *Movimento 5 Stelle–Lega* coalition introduced a basic income, which went under the name of *reddito di cittadinanza* and replaced the previous *reddito di inclusione*. The *reddito di cittadinanza* is strictly linked with the economic status of the recipient and the job opportunities. The government was able to successfully push this project through the parliament, and the 2019 budgetary law finally funded this ambitious measure with around €7 billion in 2019, €8 billion in 2020, and €8.3 billion from 2021.[101] Together with the counter-reform of the pension system, this basic income was certainly a pillar of the *Lega* and *Movimento 5 Stelle* coalition's expansionary fiscal and financial agenda.

The *reddito di cittadinanza* is still at an embryonic stage and is supposed to expand over time. For the time being, it is difficult to predict its financial impact in the long run. However, its relevance for the state budget is undoubtable, since, compared to other unemployment benefits, it addresses a wider pool of beneficiaries and has a bigger allowance amount.

Finally, from the 1990s until the early 2010s, the Italian system of welfare had also undergone profound changes in its mixture of private and public providers of welfare services. Although non-profit organisations have always operated within the Italian domain, it was only in the 1990s that they gained recognition. Between the late-1990s and early-2000s, their importance gained traction, as they appeared to be more flexible and efficient than public institutions, and both the state and regions entrusted them with more powers to act and with a more significant role as service providers.

The 2001 constitutional reform constitutionalised the principle of subsidiarity, thereby magnifying the non-profits' role once more. At the local, regional, and national levels, private service providers drew attention and received help from public institutions.[102] A 'Law on the Third Sector'[103] was passed to secure

---

[99] *Legge* 15 March 2017 n 33 in *Gazzetta Ufficiale* 24 March 2017 n 70. Vincenzo Casamassima and Elena Vivaldi, 'Ius existentiae e politiche di contrasto alla povertà' (2018) 38 Quaderni costituzionali 115.

[100] Art 1, para 197, *legge* 27 December 2017 n 205 in *Gazzetta Ufficiale* 29 December 2017 n 302 suppl ord n 62 (annual budget law for 2018).

[101] Art 1, para 255, *legge* n 145/2018 (n 61), 2019 budgetary law. The *decreto legge* n 4/2019 (n 62) later intervened again in the subject.

[102] Biondi Dal Monte and Casamassima (n 97) 1081 and 1090.

[103] *Legge* n 328/2000 (n 96).

non-profit activities with an authority that would both patrol their policies and give them voice.[104]

During the crisis, the scenario has changed dramatically. Although service cuts have pushed people to seek services from private providers more than they did before, the Agency for the Third Sector was closed, and non-profit activities were de-prioritised. The further reforms that later ensued in the field never quite reinstated the Third Sector in its pre-crisis central role.

IV. Human rights affected by social security reforms: the jurisprudence of the Italian Constitutional Court

The 2012 constitutional reform entrenched neo-liberal economic theory within the text of the Italian Constitution, domesticating external constraints deriving from the European Monetary Union. The reform strengthened the legitimacy of austerity policies already in place, but also had the effect of increasing the political and social tensions and concerns about the protection of fundamental social rights enshrined in the Italian Constitution.

The Italian Constitutional Court has played a pivotal role in addressing such tensions, before and after the constitutional amendment's passage. The Court has had to hear cases revolving around the state's duty to grant social rights, such as pensions and public workers' salaries, or, alternatively, the preservation of the regional and local welfare nets, vis-à-vis budgetary constraints such as healthcare and social assistance.

The copious case law of the Italian Constitutional Court on these matters can be grouped into two phases: the first lasting from the beginning of the debt crisis in 2011 until 2014; the second from 2015 to the present. Indeed, during the first phase it maintained an initial deference to legislative power, but then the Court slowly moved into the second phase, in which it subjected fiscal and financial constraints to a stricter scrutiny.

1. From 2011 to 2014: the Constitutional Court and the de-prioritisation of social rights

At first, the Constitutional Court largely endorsed the state's approach to the crisis and legitimised the reduction of social security and healthcare services under the

---

[104] Stefano Zamagni, *Libro bianco sul Terzo settore* (Il Mulino 2011).

pressure of the emergency. Moreover, the Court legitimised the state policy of blocking wage increases for specific categories of civil servants (in particular for university employees),[105] declaring unconstitutional only the cutting of magistrates' and public administration managers' salaries.[106]

The most significant judgments in this phase concerned financial relationships between the central state and regions, because the very first target of austerity policies was local spending power.[107] However, as described above, this power is strictly linked to the provision of healthcare services and social assistance. In other words, by cutting regional resources, the state was putting crucial welfare nets in danger. This risk was later confirmed by the Italian Court of Auditors, which affirmed that the central state imposed upon local authorities a disproportionate financial consolidation, potentially undermining the protection of an essential level of social rights.[108]

The Constitutional Court, however, upheld the heavy state measures that curtailed regional autonomy and reduced part of the welfare system.

First, the Court legitimised detailed provisions that undermined the autonomy of regions in light of the critical conditions of the Italian economy; extreme circumstances called for extreme measures, notwithstanding the constitutional provisions on the allocation of competences.[109] The gravity of the circumstances thus justified the erosion of regional autonomy.

Second, the Court reasoned that the state bears ultimate responsibility for the overall performance of the whole country under the lens of EU institutions. This argument reinforced the previous observation of the emergency status of Italian public finances and confirmed that the state could intervene in regional matters to ensure the financial sustainability of the institutions.[110] Several times, the Court stated that 'whilst the primary addressee of the requirements imposed on public finances is the State, they must inevitably affect all institutional bodies that contribute to the formation of the consolidated budget of the public administrations, in relation to which it is necessary to verify compliance with the commitments

---

[105] Corte cost n 304/2013 and n 310/2013 (all judgments of the Court are available at <http://www.cortecostituzionale.it/> accessed 29 August 2019).

[106] Corte cost n 116/2013 and n 223/2012.

[107] Franco Gallo, 'Federalismo fiscale e vincolo del pareggio di bilancio' (2014) Astrid rassegna. Elena di Carpegna Brivio 'Quali prospettive per le autonomie locali dopo l'introduzione dell'equilibrio di bilancio?' (2015) Federalismi <http://www.federalismi.it/> accessed 29 August 2019. Bergonzini, *Parlamento e decisioni di bilancio* (n 29) 161. Andrea Morrone, 'Pareggio di bilancio e Stato costituzionale' (2013) 27 Lavoro e diritto 357, 375.

[108] Corte dei Conti, sez. Autonomie, 'Relazione sulla gestione finanziaria degli enti territoriali 2013' (December 2014), VII and 15 <http://www.corteconti.it> accessed 29 August 2019.

[109] Corte cost n 16/2010, n 198/2012, n 205/2013. Andrea Morrone, 'Garanzia della Costituzione e crisi economica' in Marilisa D'Amico and Francesca Biondi (eds), *Diritti sociali e crisi economica* (Franco Angeli 2017) 25, 31–32. Massimiliano Boni, '2010-2015: cinque anni di giurisprudenza costituzionale sulla decretazione anticrisi' (2015) Federalismi <http://www.federalismi.it/> accessed 29 August 2019.

[110] The case law that uses this argument is copious. See eg Corte cost n 326/2010, n 232/2011, n 148/2012, n 52/2010, n 16/2010, n 60/2013, n 22/2014, n 88/2014, n 188/2014.

made on European and supranational level'.[111] The Court maximised the state's constitutional competence in setting principles of coordination of public finance and the taxation system,[112] overriding the constitutional distribution of powers between the state and the regions, to the extent that some warned about the state's 'omnivorous competence'.[113]

Third, the 2012 budgetary constitutional reform pushed the Court to consider social rights in light of long-term sustainability and a sound budget. Specifically, the Court stated that entrenching the principle of the sustainability of public debt within the Constitution implied a formal responsibility under principles of solidarity and equality. Such responsibility fell upon the institutions, as well as each taxpayer towards each other, including those from future generations.[114]

These three components coalesced in re-centralising local and regional powers and reducing welfare services between 2011 and 2015. The only limit set by the Court upon the legislature concerned the temporal effects of cuts to local spending power; because the funding reductions were considered necessary in an emergency, they had to be temporary and limited to specific budget years.[115] This statement obviously legitimised a serious detriment to the provision of social services in the short-term.[116]

Due also to the Constitutional Court's approach, regional discrepancies in wealth and public services probably widened under the austerity period. Regions and local bodies, which are the main service providers, have continued to provide welfare opportunities[117] in light of decreasing resources. The outcome has exacerbated regional gaps between wealthy areas and those reliant on state aid. For instance, in 2014 the Calabria region had €26 per person to spend per year, compared with €304 in the areas located in the Province of Trento,[118] which enjoys special autonomy status and is comparable to a region.

The post-crisis lack of resources might have had an even more durable impact on the country. The per-person expenditure for healthcare places Italy at the bottom of the list of the Organization for Economic Co-operation and Development (OECD)

---

[111] Corte cost n 88/2014, n 40/2014, n 39/2014, n 138/2013. Guido Rivosecchi, 'Ragionando sull'introduzione dell'equilibrio di bilancio, tra incompiuta attuazione della riforma e anticipazioni della giurisprudenza costituzionale' (2016) 4 Forum di Quaderni costituzionali <http://www.forumcostituzionale.it/wordpress/> accessed 29 August 2019.

[112] Art 117, para 3 of the Italian Constitution.

[113] Rivosecchi, 'Ragionando sull'introduzione dell'equilibrio di bilancio' (n 111) 5. In similar terms Aldo Carosi, 'La Corte costituzionale tra autonomie territoriali, coordinamento finanziario e garanzia dei diritti' (2017) 4 Rivista AIC 2 <http://www.rivistaaic.it/it/> accessed 29 August 2019.

[114] Corte cost n 88/2014.

[115] Corte cost n 79/2014, n 193/2012, n 205/2013, n 229/2013, n 236/2013, n 22/2014, n 23/2014. Luca Antonini, 'Introduzione. I vincoli costituzionali al pareggio di bilancio tra (indebiti) condizionamenti delle dottrine economiche e (possibili) prospettive' in Luca Antonini (ed), La domanda inevasa, (Il Mulino 2016) 46–47.

[116] ibid.

[117] Biondi Dal Monte and Casamassima (n 97) 1085.

[118] ibid 1081 and 1103.

countries,[119] and the decline of resources might have already been felt in terms of life expectancy, which dropped in 2015 for the first time in the history of the Italian state.[120]

2. From 2015 to present: the (slow) recovery of social rights

In 2015, when the economic crisis was still hitting the country, the Constitutional Court took a fresh look at the status of welfare and at fiscal performance; more importantly, it reconsidered its exercise in balancing rights and the budget. Consequently, it began deeply scrutinising pieces of legislation that reduced welfare services, under the assumption that '[i]t is the guarantee of inviolable rights that must condition the budget, whilst conversely the need for budgetary equilibrium cannot condition the requirement to provide such services'.[121]

The Constitutional Court case law took this new path with respect to both central and local welfare obligations. This approach led to stricter scrutiny of state measures and more pervasive inquiry into real social needs. It did so using sophisticated arguments in balancing fundamental social rights and budgetary needs.

The main driver of this sea change in the Court's case law probably was the persistence of economic stagnation. The unsatisfactory fiscal and economic performances likely prompted the Court to reconsider the role of the economic crisis. It lost its appeal as the paramount justification for curtailing social rights.

This new approach brought about new arguments, which the Court elaborated *ex novo* and utilised alongside arguments already existing in the Court's jurisprudence. This toolkit mostly consisted in: (a) the mitigation of the impact of specific Court judgments; (b) the principle that budgetary constraints need adequate justification; (c) the attempt to progressively define the core of social rights that cannot be undermined by the legislature; (d) the principle of reasonableness.

a) The mitigation of the impact of specific Court judgments
Judgments of the Italian Constitutional Court usually have retroactive effects.[122] Only very occasionally, in a small number of cases throughout its history, the Court had managed these effects by stating that specific decisions operate only

---

[119] Lorenza Violini, 'Salute, sanità e Regioni: un quadro di crescente complessità tecnica, politica e finanziaria' (2015) 43 Le Regioni 1019, 1022.

[120] ibid 1020.

[121] Corte cost n 275/2016. Andrea Longo, 'Una concezione del bilancio costituzionalmente orientata: prime riflessioni sulla sentenza della Corte costituzionale n. 275 del 2016' (2017) Federalismi <http://www.federalismi.it/> accessed 29 August 2019.

[122] Gustavo Zagrebelsky and Valeria Marcenò, *Giustizia costituzionale* (Il Mulino 2012) 347.

prospectively and not retroactively.[123] However, the Court never explicitly affirmed its power to govern the effects of its decision until the famous judgment n 10/2015.[124]

This judgment represents a milestone of the 'crisis jurisprudence', because in it the Court started to more deeply scrutinise legislation through the principles of reasonableness and proportionality. The Court declared unconstitutional an extra taxation on oil companies, but only prospectively. Consequently, oil companies had no rights to any refund from the state. This was an important innovation in constitutional adjudication, because traditionally the Court would have annulled the extra tax retroactively and the state would have had to reimburse the oil companies for the 2008–2015 period, the full period of time the law had been in effect.[125]

In this case, the Court foresaw that reimbursing the oil companies would have aggravated the fiscal status and worsened the protection of social rights. Mitigating the effects of the judgment meant keeping the budget balance sound and therefore preserving resources necessary to fulfil the institutional obligation of mutual solidarity and equality among Italian citizens (articles 2 and 3 of the Italian Constitution). The Court found that the detriment to the oil companies' right to property it caused was reasonable. Indeed, the Court stated that 'the overall consequences of the repeal of the contested provision with retroactive effect would end up requiring an unreasonable redistribution of wealth ... This would thus result in irremediable detriment to the requirements of social solidarity, and hence a serious violation of Articles 2 and 3 of the Constitution.'

In a later judgment (n 178/2015), the Court again used its power to mitigate the effects of its own rulings, but in a different way. In this case, it struck down a legislative provision that had frozen labour negotiations in the field of public employment for a duration it found excessive, adding that this decision's effects would operate only prospectively and not retroactively.[126] In contrast with judgment n

[123] Erik Longo and Andrea Pin, 'An Evolution in "Italian Style": The Constitutional Court Says it will Govern the Effects of its Judgments (and will Use the Proportionality Test to Do It)' (Int'l J Const L Blog, 20 March 2015) <http://www.iconnectblog.com/2015/03/an-evolution-in-italian-style-the-constitutional-court-says-it-will-govern-the-effects-of-its-judgments-and-will-use-the-proportionality-test-to-do-it> accessed 29 August 2019.

[124] This judgment prompted an intense debate among scholars, divided between those in favour of and against the decision. See eg Adele Anzon, 'La corte costituzionale "esce allo scoperto" e limita l'efficacia retroattiva delle proprie pronunzie di accoglimento' (2015) 2 Rivista AIC <http://www.rivistaaic.it/it/> accessed 29 August 2019; Luca Antonini, 'Forzatura dei principi versus modulazione temporale degli effetti della sentenza' (2015) 35 Quaderni costituzionali 718; Andrea Pin and Erik Longo, 'Dalla sentenza n. 10 alla n. 70 del 2015: quando la giustizia costituzionale diventa imprevedibile' (2015) 35 Quaderni costituzionali 697.

[125] Longo and Pin, 'An Evolution in "Italian Style"' (n 123).

[126] Antonio Ruggeri, 'La Corte costituzionale e la gestione sempre più "sregolata" dei suoi processi' (2015) Questione giustizia <http://questionegiustizia.it/> accessed 29 August 2019. Roberto Pinardi, 'La Consulta ed il blocco degli stipendi pubblici: una sentenza di "incostituzionalità sopravvenuta"?' (2015) Forum di Quaderni costituzionali <http://www.forumcostituzionale.it/wordpress/> accessed 29 August 2019. Maria Mocchegiani, 'La tecnica decisoria della sentenza 178 del 2015: dubbi e perplessità' (2015) Forum di Quaderni costituzionali <http://www.forumcostituzionale.it/wordpress/> accessed 29 August 2019.

10/2015, the Court directly balanced budgetary needs with social rights, rather than with the right to property. It was easy for the Court to root its decision in the workers' right to labour negotiations and trade union freedom, which is protected under article 39 of the Italian Constitution.

The Court, however, did not adhere to the previous seminal decision on the oil companies' taxation. It did not fully articulate the reasons for mitigating the effects of its judgment, merely stating that 'the sacrifice of the fundamental right protected under Article 39 of the Constitution [wa]s no longer tolerable. [T]he structural nature of the suspension of bargaining procedures ha[d] been made fully evident', to the extent that the suspension had 'become unconstitutional on a supervening *ex post* basis', and consequently the effect of the judgment would only follow the moment the decision was released.

Mitigation of the effect of its judgments now is within the arsenal of the Constitutional Court. Mitigation gives it more leeway and a higher degree of freedom in adjudicating financial disputes, because the Court can now tap the duty to preserve a sound budget into the effects of its judgments, instead of weighing it against the protection of social rights and denying their existence. So far, however, the inconsistent jurisprudence of the Court on this point has not provided this practice a solid and clear foundation.

b) Budgetary constraints and the need of adequate justification

In the famous judgment n 70/2015, the Constitutional Court struck down a law which had limited the annual revaluation increase for larger retirement pensions adopted by the *Salva Italia* decree-law.[127] It stated that such legislation was 'limited to a generic reference to the "contingent financial situation"', whilst the overall design of the legislation does not establish why financial requirements should necessarily prevail over the rights affected by the balancing operation, against which such highly invasive initiatives are adopted'. In other words, the Court stated that while the right to an adequate pension was not absolute, balancing it with budgetary requirements must be justified in detail. This judgment, as is normal for the Italian Constitutional Court's rulings, had retroactive effects and prompted an intense debate among scholars. Some authors remarked on the innovative character of the judgment, which gave full pre-eminence to social rights over budgetary needs and austerity policies.[128] On the contrary, other scholars were critical because in this case the Court did not simply consider the budgetary implications of reimbursing

---

[127] *Decreto legge* n 201/2011 (n 13).

[128] Silvana Sciarra, 'Alcune linee di tendenza della recente giurisprudenza costituzionale in materia di rapporto di lavoro e previdenza' *Corte costituzionale* (16 October 2015) <http://www.cortecostituzionale.it> accessed 29 August 2019. Giovanni Guiglia, 'La Corte costituzionale e l'adeguatezza delle pensioni al tempo della crisi' (2016) Federalismi <http://www.federalismi.it/> accessed 29 August 2019.

the eligible retirees.[129] It is beyond doubt, however, that this was the first instance in which the Court clearly detached itself from the previous 'crisis jurisprudence'. The takeaway from the judgment, in fact, is that a balanced budget is not a winner-take-all principle;[130] conversely, budgetary constraints that could jeopardise social rights need adequate and detailed justification.

It did not take long before the Court developed this line of reasoning further. In its judgment n 188/2015 it stated that an in-depth preliminary collection of data and information must be attached to any law regarding public finance. Therefore, the Court may assess technical and illustrative reports, which the government drafts in support of a bill, when it scrutinises fiscal and financial measures.

In cases revolving around issues of federalism, the Constitutional Court has been, on average, more deferential toward the state's constraint policies. It has kept a favourable approach towards state cuts in regions' and local authorities' welfare services, grounding them in the state's power to coordinate the national public finance, which the Court has interpreted in a rather broad fashion.[131]

The sea change in the Constitutional Court's approach to austerity, however, has also affected the state's power to control local public finance. Again in 2015, the Court started to scrutinise state legislative provisions in this field more pervasively, paying more attention also to local autonomy in providing social services. The Court has progressively assessed the state's power to coordinate public finances of local authority in light of the principles of reasonableness and proportionality.[132]

This new approach has developed a type of scrutiny that considers the concrete impact of fiscal and financial policies on regional welfare. Indeed, the Court has stated that regions may present evidence that financial restrictions prescribed by the state inhibit them from providing public services related to constitutional social rights. Once verified, the state legislation that threatens such local functions must be declared unconstitutional.

Such a bold rule, however, remains only theoretical. Although numerous judgments have confirmed this new type of scrutiny,[133] the Court has rarely found that a region was able to provide evidence of an impossibility of securing social rights. Even the means through which regions can demonstrate the impossibility of providing a minimum standard of social services are still obscure.

---

[129] Augusto Barbera, 'La sentenza relativa al blocco pensionistico: una brutta pagina per la Corte' (2015) 2 Rivista AIC <http://www.rivistaaic.it/it/> accessed 29 August 2019. Andrea Morrone, 'Ragionevolezza a rovescio: l'ingiustizia della sentenza n. 70/2015 della Corte costituzionale' (2015) Federalismi <http://www.federalismi.it/> accessed 29 August 2019.

[130] Giulio M. Salerno, 'La sentenza n. 70 del 2015: una pronuncia non a sorpresa e da rispettare integralmente' (2015) Federalismi <http://www.federalismi.it/> accessed 29 August 2019.

[131] Corte cost n 77/2015, n 152/2015, n 227/2015, n 160/2016, n 202/2016, n 106/2017, n 135/2017, n 190/2017.

[132] Corte cost n 250/2015, n 272/2015.

[133] Corte cost n 65/2016, n 127/2016, n 151/2016, n 205/2016, n 154/2017, n 169/2017.

Despite such critical aspects, overall the Court is now assessing the relationship between social rights and budgetary needs with greater attention. It considers the financial performance of regions in light of the social services they render to the community.[134]

c) The hard core of social rights

The economic crisis pushed the Constitutional Court to further develop a balancing theory that already existed in its jurisprudence. To some extent, the financial breakdown compelled the Court to sharpen its techniques.

In the last three decades, before the principle of budget equilibrium was entrenched in the Constitution, the Italian Constitutional Court occasionally stated that budgetary equilibrium represented a constitutional value.[135] On this basis, the Court created a specific theory to balance budgetary needs with social rights. This theory assumed that social rights were 'financially-affected',[136] although they also enjoyed a hard core.[137] This twofold observation meant that social rights could be limited to make public finances sustainable; but this could happen only within limits, as a minimum protection for social rights had to be guaranteed in any case.

These theoretical categories, which resonate well with comparative constitutional doctrines,[138] have allowed the Court to balance social rights and budgetary needs in the context of social protection.[139] This approach gave the legislature some—but not complete—latitude to make fiscal and financial decisions.

At first glance, this theory seems to respect the boundaries of judicial and legislative powers. It does have some flaws, however. The concept of the 'hard core' of social rights is vague and probably debatable altogether. This is confirmed by the Constitutional Court's case law, which has defined the hard core of certain rights quite inconsistently.[140] This means that if the national economic condition is stagnant or in regression, the hard core runs the risk of being defined narrowly.

However, the Court has recently tried to specify the content of the 'hard core' of social rights on the basis of a specific constitutional provision, enshrined in article

---

[134] Corte cost n 247/2017, n 186/2016. Luca Antonini, 'La Corte costituzionale a difesa dell'autonomia finanziaria: il bilancio è un bene pubblico e l'equilibrio di bilancio non si persegue con tecnicismi contabili espropriativi' (2018) 1 Rivista AIC <http://www.rivistaaic.it/it/> accessed 29 August 2019.

[135] Corte cost n 10/2016 and n 260/1990.

[136] Corte cost n 356/1992, n 78/1995, n 88/1995. Giacinto della Cananea, 'Finanza e amministrazione pubblica' in Giacinto della Cananea and Marco Dugato (eds), *Diritto amministrativo e Corte costituzionale* (Edizioni Scientifiche Italiane 2006) 148.

[137] Corte cost n 309/1999, n 376/2000, n 252/2001. Donato Messineo, *La garanzia del 'contenuto essenziale' dei diritti fondamentali. Dalla tutela della dignità umana ai livelli essenziali delle prestazioni* (Giappichelli 2012).

[138] David Bilchitz, 'Socio-Economic Rights, Economic Crisis, and Legal Doctrine' (2014) 12 Int'l J Const L 710.

[139] In the field of healthcare protection: Corte cost n 309/1999.

[140] Carmela Salazar, *Dal riconoscimento alla garanzia dei diritti sociali* (Giappichelli 2000) 129. Maurizio Cinelli, 'Condizionamenti finanziari e diritti sociali: la giurisprudenza costituzionale tra vecchi e nuovi equilibri' (2019) 19 RDSS 1, 24–25.

117 of the Italian Constitution. This provision gives the central state the power to determine the 'basic level of benefits relating to civil and social entitlements to be guaranteed throughout the national territory'.

While acknowledging the discretion of the legislature, the Court has emphasised that such basic levels shall be identified and quantified according to the principle of reasonableness. The Court itself retains power to scrutinise the reasonableness of the state's determination. Consequently, the levels of benefits should be adequate, looking to social services that must be provided to fully protect fundamental rights. At the moment, however, this type of scrutiny remains largely theoretical. The legislature has failed to establish the basic levels of many benefits, hence the Court cannot assess their reasonableness.

The potential of such scrutiny is very high. In a judgment on healthcare funding, n 169/2017, the Court said that once the legislature has identified the basic level for a certain social service, the legislature cannot forfeit it through broad, national reductions in public expenditure.[141] Therefore, once they are identified and quantified, the basic levels of benefits become the very hard core of the rights involved, which cannot be underfunded by the legislature. This principle, which the Court has spelled out in the context of healthcare services, is capable of being applied to every social right. This means that by identifying a certain basic level of social rights, the state's hands will be tied from making cuts in that field.

The Constitutional Court has reiterated this approach time and again since then. For example, judgment n 83/2019 stated that transport and general assistance are core components of the right to access educational services for people with disabilities, which are run by regions. Per the judgment, the state must reserve an adequate, precise, and predictable amount of financial resources for the regions to carry out this activities.

d) The principle of reasonableness
In the jurisprudence of the Italian Constitutional Court, the reasonableness of scrutiny derives from the constitutional principle of equality.[142] Through this principle, the Court assesses the rationality and the consistency of a legislative provision. During the economic crisis, judicial review of legislation has generally adopted this standard to scrutinise pieces of legislation under the lenses of multiple constitutional provisions.

In a 2017 judgment, the Court adopted the principle of reasonableness in the field of pensioners' rights. As analysed before, the *Salva Italia* decree-law, issued

---

[141] Aldo Carosi, 'La Corte costituzionale tra autonomie territoriali' (n 113). Luca Antonini, 'Il diritto alla salute e la spesa costituzionalmente necessaria: la giurisprudenza costituzionale accende il faro della Corte' (2017) Federalismi <http://www.federalismi.it/> accessed 29 August 2019.

[142] Livio Paladin, 'Ragionevolezza (principio di)' in *Enciclopedia del diritto* (Giuffrè 1997). Gino Scaccia, *Gli 'strumenti' della ragionevolezza nel giudizio costituzionale* (Giuffrè 2000). Andrea Morrone, *Il custode della ragionevolezza* (Giuffrè 2001).

by the Monti government, limited the annual revaluation increase for old-age pensions. The Court struck down this provision in aforementioned judgment n 70/2015 (see IV.2.b). In the aftermath of the judgment, the legislature amended the stated austerity measure.[143] However, because of budgetary needs, it defined the revaluation of annual pensions on a gradual scale; smaller pensions with a smaller base amount would receive a higher percentage of annual revaluation, while larger pensions would benefit from a lower percentage of annual revaluation.

The Constitutional Court was called to rule again. In this case, it found that the new provision, though not in full compliance with the previous judgment of the Court, was reasonable. Indeed, in judgment n 250/2017, the Court said that budgetary needs could be preserved through partial and temporary sacrifice of the interest of pensioners to protect the purchasing power of their benefits.[144] Therefore, the Court stated, the legislature had lawfully prioritised low pensions by giving precedence to them in the context of scarce public resource.

While largely saving the legislation under scrutiny, the Constitutional Court set the ground for a new jurisprudential wave. In fact, it emphasised that reasonableness and proportionality scrutiny are context-dependent. This meant that, in order to review the legislation, it had to contrast the relevant provisions with the financial circumstances and objective data. Thus, the Court affirmed its power to balance rules in light of the economic and social scenarios within which they had to be enforced.

Although apparently in favour of austerity, the new Court's logic watered down the importance of the recently enacted constitutional provisions on fiscal and financial constraints. Since it was called to balance rules with fiscal constraints, economic needs, and social distress, the Court gave a new meaning and spirit to article 81 of the Italian Constitution, which enshrines the neo-liberal golden rule of budget equilibrium. With its judgment n 61/2018, the Court stated that the requirement of budget equilibrium shall not operate mechanically, but in a flexible and anti-cyclical fashion. This statement revolutionised the institutional approach to the crisis. Rather than legitimising austerity measures, it boosted a new political agenda, based on expansive fiscal policies in times of crisis.

V. Conclusion

The impact of the global economic crisis on the Italian economic and social infrastructures has been huge. Albeit at different pace, the government and the

---

[143] *Decreto legge* 21 May 2015 n 65 in *Gazzetta Ufficiale* 21 May 2015 n 116, converted in *legge* 17 July 2015 n 109 in *Gazzetta Ufficiale* 20 July 2015 n 166.

[144] Andrea Michieli and Filippo Pizzolato, 'La Corte garante della complessità nel bilanciamento tra diritti sociali ed esigenze finanziarie' (2018) 38 Quaderni costituzionali 201.

parliament, on one hand, and the Constitutional Court, on the other, have processed the crisis and the measures to counter it in ways that seem to have left a lasting mark on the political, institutional, and constitutional culture of Italy.

In 2008–2011 national institutions tried to cope with the critical economic and financial scenario. Their attempts did not manage to stabilise the economy, but eroded the fragile national budget and increased the public debt. Slowly but steadily, the crisis reached the core of the agenda, prompting the political institutions to take more radical measures.

The sequencing of the anti-crisis measures and their impact on social rights starts in 2011, when the institutions tackled the economic crisis and the rampant national debt with a neo-liberal logic and austerity policies. On a theoretical level, the core notions and the structure of social protection remained formally intact and strictly linked to the constitutional principle of substantial equality. On a practical level, national legislation downsized the welfare state and undermined the effectiveness of social rights. It increased the retirement age in order to ease the pension treatments' weight on public debts; it made the labour market more flexible, thus spreading uncertainties among job-seekers; draconian cuts affected healthcare and social assistance; national institutions put shackles on regions' and local bodies' spending powers; taxation increased in the apex of the crisis.[145] From an institutional point of view, this set of new policies enjoyed large parliamentary support and a favourable view from the Constitutional Court, and it was secured through the 2012 constitutional reform that passed the budget equilibrium rule.

However, since 2015 wide scepticism arose about the effectiveness of the austerity measures. New coalitions set out to mitigate the impact of such measures and the Constitutional Court started scrutinising welfare cuts and tax increases more closely.

Finally, the 2018 parliamentary elections' results marked a visible reversal-of-course in Italian politics. The post-2011 neo-liberal logic, its belief in austerity measures, and the trust in the EU's handling of the continental crisis gave way to a new scenario. Despite significant gaps in their political views, both *Lega* and *Movimento 5 Stelle* called for more welfare protection, lower taxes, and expansive economic policies.[146]

The 2018–2019 government coalition was based on a clearly anti-austerity agenda. Its core components consisted in dismantling the *Monti-Fornero* pension reform, introducing a basic income, increasing the public expenditure for the welfare state in general, and reducing the tax burden. This programme

---

[145] Alberto Alesina, Carlo Favero, and Francesco Giavazzi, *Austerity. When It Works and When It Doesn't* (Princeton University Press 2019) 138–40.

[146] On the theoretical differences between the 'invisible hand' approach and the logic of coordinating social activities through authority: Nick Barber, *The Principles of Constitutionalism* (OUP 2018) 250–54.

also required a deep reconsideration of the EU-imposed constraints on public spending as well as of the 2012 constitutional amendment on the budget equilibrium. The government was, in fact, very vocal in advocating a new, flexible interpretation of both, thereby creating serious tensions with EU institutions.

The Italian journey between 2011 and 2018 did not leave its political and constitutional culture untouched. The early appreciation of austerity changed considerably between a first phase (from 2011 to 2015) and a second phase (from 2015 to present). The first phase saw fiscal and economic policies and the Constitutional Court sharing the view that economic and welfare austerity and the re-centralisation of policies that had been decentralised for decades were necessary to protect the sustainability of the Italian budget and the economy. The widespread view was that such measures would be temporary. In the long run, Italians would enjoy the benefit of economic growth and of social rights.

Within the second phase, the Constitutional Court has adopted a less complacent view of austerity measures. Since 2015, the Court has repeatedly stated it would shield social rights against disproportionate austerity measures. The Court has expressed a different view of how economic and fiscal crises should be handled, largely abandoning the idea that shrinking the state, protecting the budget, and freezing the welfare state would help resurrect the economy, which, in turn, would help recover tax revenues and restore the welfare net.

The new Court's view of the crisis has been more theoretical than practical, so far. Despite its bold affirmations about the priority of social rights, it has only occasionally struck down key austerity measures. It is hard to predict how far the Court will go in dismantling legislation that has constrained regional powers and reduced welfare services, and, even more fundamentally, in determining whether it may legitimately scrutinise fiscal and economic policies in depth.

The Court approach seems to have fluctuated together with Italian political culture. When state policies espoused neo-liberal theories, the Court did not challenge them. When the neo-liberal euphoria lost much of its political appeal and dissatisfied the public, the Constitutional Court also detached itself from it, leaving room for a bolder affirmation of social rights. It would be unfair, however, to read the Court's approach as opportunistic. It may be the case that the Court simply lacks the capacity for an independent assessment of economic and fiscal measures. It seems to rely on the prevailing existing economic doctrines or on widespread political beliefs.

How the Court reads economic policies has become extremely relevant after the 2012 constitutional amendment that introduced the rule of a balanced budget, which certainly is the most enduring legacy of the austerity period. This 'golden rule' can be read as subordinating the protection of social rights to budgetary constraints. Although the Court has lately prioritised social rights—or at least stated it would do so—instead of putting a sound budget first, it must still play with the same constitutional rule in place.

It is still too early to foresee how the interpretation of the balanced budget rule will look like in the future. As of early 2019, however, it seems that the Court is endorsing significant centralisations of competences from regions to the state, while reconsidering austerity thoroughly. Within a single judgment, the Constitutional Court found that the 2012 constitutional amendment gives the state crucial powers in managing and coordinating national economic policies, inevitably affecting also the autonomy of local authorities,[147] but that it may also command 'anti-cyclical policies', aimed at 'counteracting the depression of economic activities'.[148]

Perhaps these are mere dicta, which will soon lose their teeth in constitutional adjudication. But the anti-cyclical reading of article 81 sounds prospectively as a sea change in constitutional interpretation, given the previous austerity-oriented jurisprudence.

It is unclear how the constitutional rule of the budget equilibrium will affect future constitutional adjudication, in light of scepticism that has grown around the political movements that have backed the rule. The post-crisis emergency has left a constitutional clause that outlives the doctrine that shaped it. Its interpretation is a big question for the Constitutional Court, for legal scholars, and for the future of social rights.

---

[147] Corte cost n 61/2018.
[148] ibid.

11

The Predominance of a 'Strong' Economy over a 'Weak' Social Constitution

The Legacy of the Financial Crisis in Spain

Juan Antonio Maldonado Molina and Juan Romero Coronado

I. Introduction

The economic crisis has had a strong impact on the Spanish social protection system in its different modalities, ie the social welfare system, health system, long-term care system, and social services systems. The economic resources allocated to social protection were frozen, both in terms of per capita expenditure[1] and in

---

[1] Expenditure on social protection benefits per capita has decreased slightly in the years of the crisis. So, 2010: €5,715.8; 2011: €5,801.42; 2012: €5,662.98; 2013: €5,676.13; 2014: €5,668.43; 2015: €5,730.88 . Source of data in <http://appsso.eurostat.ec.europa.eu/nui/show.do?dataset=spr_exp_sum&lang=en> accessed 19 March 2018.

Juan Antonio Maldonado Molina and Juan Romero Coronado, *The Predominance of a 'Strong' Economy over a 'Weak' Social Constitution* In: *European Welfare State Constitutions after the Financial Crisis.* Edited by: Ulrich Becker and Anastasia Poulou, Oxford University Press (2020). © The Contributors. DOI: 10.1093/oso/9780198851776.003.0011

terms of percentage of gross domestic product (GDP),[2] given that the formula to fight against this crisis was the containment of public expenditure, also preventing debt, following the guidelines agreed by the countries of the eurozone[3] to ensure the stability of the common currency.

The international treaties and the Treaty on the Functioning of the European Union oblige these countries to reduce the public deficit. Nevertheless, they do not indicate how to do it, leaving freedom to each member state.[4] In Spain, it was decided to reform the main protective structures with the purpose of reducing costs, which has resulted in a decrease in the level of protection. This policy of containment took place precisely at a time when the demand for coverage was increasing, both because of the social problems arising from the crisis and because of the increase in average life expectancy that has been occurring in current societies.

Together with the singular reforms on every protective system, it must be emphasised that in 2011 a reform of the Spanish Constitution took place, indicating that '[a]ll public administrations will conform its actions to the principle of budgetary stability', linking the maximum structural deficit to 'the limits established by the European Union for their member states' (article 135). The reform of this article was extraordinary in all respects. Consider, in this regard, that the Spanish Constitution had only been reformed once since its approval in 1978. Furthermore, this can be described as an 'express reform', passed expeditiously and without the public being consulted via a referendum.[5] Despite the urgency in its approval, its entry into force was postponed until 2020. However, if there is any unique element, it is the fact that 'it was not truly the result of an autonomous decision, rationally adopted by the Government and the main opposition group, but on the contrary, the necessary result of the economic and financial conditions of the time and, definitely, of the demands coming from Europe'.[6]

---

[2] The percentage of expenditure according to the GDP is lower than the average of the countries of the eurozone, having been reduced, since the amount per beneficiary has been frozen while the GDP has been increasing. So, 2010: 24.6 per cent; 2011: 25.3 per cent; 2012: 25.5 per cent; 2013: 25.8 per cent; 2014: 25.4 per cent; 2015: 24.6 per cent. Source of data in <http://ec.europa.eu/eurostat/tgm/table.do?tab=table&init=1&language=en&pcode=tps00098&plugin=1> accessed 19 March 2018.

Expenditure on health and social protection has increased in 2018 compared to 2017, but only in absolute terms, since in proportion to GDP it has been reduced. Thus, they have gone from 6 per cent to 5.8 per cent (health) and from 16.5 per cent to 16.2 per cent (social protection) <http://www.europapress.es/economia/macroeconomia-00338/noticia-gobierno-aprueba-martes-presupuestos-2018-rebajas-irpf-subidas-pensionistas-20180325102632.html> accessed 27 March 2018.

[3] Treaty on Stability, Coordination and Governance in the Economic and Monetary Union; Treaty Establishing the European Stability Mechanism (ESM).

[4] Cristina Sánchez-Rodas Navarro, 'About the (In)Competence of the European Institutions to Reform the Public Systems of National Pensions in the Light of the EU Law and the International Treaties' (2018) 10 Cuadernos de Derecho Transnacional 396, <https://doi.org/10.20318/cdt.2018.4127> accessed 19 March 2018.

[5] Since the parliamentary consensus was so high, the percentage of parliamentarians required to request the referendum was not reached (10 per cent of the members of either House).

[6] Antonio Bar Cedrón, 'La reforma constitucional y la Gobernanza Económica de la Unión Europea' (2012) 30 Teoría y Realidad Constitucional 60 <http://revistas.uned.es/index.php/TRC/article/view/7002/6700> accessed 20 March 2018.

Organic Law 2/2012, of 27 April, on budgetary stability and financial sustainability develops this constitutional mandate and includes within its scope of application the National Social Security Administrations (article 2.1.d), which must maintain a balanced or budgetary surplus situation. Nevertheless, the National Social Security Administration is exceptionally allowed to incur 'a structural deficit in accordance with the objectives and conditions provided in the Social Security Reserve Fund regulations. In this case, the maximum structural deficit permitted for the central administration shall be reduced by the same amount as the Social Security deficit' (article 11.5). Thus, the National Social Security Administration is also subject to the principle of budgetary stability, despite the fact that, given its social purpose of solidarity, it is irrational to expect that a social protection system should aspire to a surplus or even to a budgetary equilibrium. Therefore, a deficit is permitted here, but contingent upon it being transferred to the central government.

Evidently then, both because of the 2011 constitutional reform and its legal development in 2012, the Spanish constitutional panorama is one where social and economic clauses coexist. The economic provisions, however, prevail, creating an imbalance between the social and the economic. We are, therefore, faced with the predominance of a 'strong' economic constitution over a 'weak' social constitution, the latter being subordinated to the economic rationale of controlling the public deficit (Monereo Pérez).[7]

It is true that the economy always sets limits because resources, by definition, are scarce. Already in 1994 the Spanish Constitutional Court (TC) recalled that 'Social Security rights as social benefit rights that involve a considerable financial burden are of legal content and they inescapably require legislative intermediation. It is up to the legislator, according to the situations of need and the financial means available, to determine the protective action to be dispensed by the public social welfare system and the conditions for access to benefits and for their loss. This feature of entitlement to benefits that require a solid financial base and an administration of scarce resources allow the legislator a wide freedom of configuration.'[8]

However, a different issue to the rational distribution of resources is the fact that budget stability is achieved at the expense of respecting social rights, which are the main hallmark of European states. It should not be forgotten that article 1.1 of the Spanish Constitution includes the clause of the social and democratic 'State of Law'. Based on this idea, certain actors have proposed to include in the Constitution a clause referring to the Union and the express link to the European Convention on Human Rights, the (Revised) European Social Charter,[9] as well as

---

[7] José Luis Monereo Pérez, 'La Ley de Presupuestos Generales del Estado para 2015 y su incidencia en materia de Seguridad Social: La persistencia de las políticas de austeridad y de racionalización del gasto público y sus consecuencias' (2015) 2 Revista de Derecho de la Seguridad Social 12.

[8] [1994] 126 STC 5 (TC).

[9] Arts 1, 2, 3, 4, 11, 12, 13, 19, and 23.

the Charter of Fundamental Rights of the European Union[10] (something that is already possible through article 10.2 of the European Constitution).[11] With this, following Monereo Pérez, the right to social security would be enshrined as a fundamental social right, identifying a nucleus or redoubt unavailable to the legislator, which operates as an 'institutional guarantee' (in the terms that the TC already declared in the STC 32/1981), so that it must be preserved 'in recognisable terms' in line with the image that the social conscience has of it in each time and place, being outside the economic cycles and the imbalances of public expenditure.

II. Characterisation of the reforms

1. As to the form: the 'making-of': the governmentalisation of the reform process

Formally, the government has resorted to the systematic use of the royal decree-law[12] as a legislative instrument to implement not only temporary reforms but also eminently permanent structural reforms. As has happened in other countries, they are framed within the well-known phenomenon of 'governmentalisation'.[13]

Thus, except for the reforms relating to pensions (which are structural and long-term), all have been approved by royal decree-law, which is a type of rule that, although it has the status of law, is not dictated by the legislative but by the executive power in case of extraordinary and urgent necessity, being validated by the parliament afterwards. However, this exceptional mechanism has been abused. In fact, even one of the reforms that affected pensions was approved in this way,[14] moving away from something that in Spain was a tradition. Namely, that pension reforms were approved with the consensus of social agents and the entirety of the most representative parliamentary groups.

In any case, a measure is being used extensively that must remain exceptional. The urgency and exceptional nature of the situation was invoked to distort the separation of powers to the detriment of the development of new laws through parliament.[15]

---

[10] Arts 5, 15, 16, 27, 31, 34, and 35.

[11] Monereo Pérez, 'La Ley de Presupuestos Generales del Estado para 2015 y su incidencia en materia de Seguridad Social' (n 7) 12.

[12] Art 86.1 of the Spanish Constitution of 1978 allows the government to pass a royal decree-law without normal parliamentary approval as a temporary legislative provision if measures must be implemented urgently.

[13] A well-known term coined by Foucault. Michel Foucault, *Seguridad, Territorio y Población* (Akal 2008) 116, 117.

[14] Royal Decree-law 5/2013, of 15 March, on measures to favour the continuity of the working life of older workers and to promote active ageing.

[15] José Luis Monereo Pérez, 'El derecho de la Seguridad Social en una coyuntura crítica' (2014) 1 Revista de Derecho de la Seguridad Social 13.

2. On the substance: arguments used to justify the reforms

The arguments that justify the reforms are of four types, which occasionally converge in the same rules:

a) Financial stability

Those reforms are not conjunctural reforms, but structural ones. In this regard, two types of reforms are included. Some reforms seek financial balance, such as the ones approved in the matter of health expenditure cuts[16] and long-term care expenditure.[17] Other reforms try to adapt the finances to demographic evolution.[18]

b) Economic emergency

The respective reforms are conjunctural reforms, which are applied only in the short term (a budgetary exercise, for example) and which rely on the inability to cope with costs, due to an extraordinary and urgent need to meet the objective of the public deficit. Within this group, we would have (1) freezing of the pensions update,[19] (2) temporary suspension of protection for less severe degrees of

---

[16] Royal Decree-law 16/2012, of 20 April, on urgent measures to guarantee the sustainability of the National Health System and improve the quality and safety of its benefits: in its Explanatory Preamble it says 'All the countries of the European Union are analyzing and adopting measures that allow optimizing their care and pharmaceutical models and, especially, their pharmaceutical expenditure and weight in health spending. The implementation of measures in this area is very intense, especially in those countries hardest hit by the financial and economic crisis'.

[17] Royal Decree-law 20/2012, of 13 July, on measures to guarantee budgetary stability and promote competitiveness. In its Explanatory Preamble, it says:

> The recession that the Spanish economy began to experience in 2008, and the economic policy followed at the time to face it, led to the accumulation of some macroeconomic unsustainable imbalances. Insofar as these imbalances are only partially solved, recovery from a path of stable growth in our country is not feasible. This was evident throughout 2011, when, after several quarters of slight recovery, the Spanish economy proved to be intensely vulnerable to the deterioration of the euro-zone and returned to immerse in a recessive period.
> ... The new structural reforms are also key not only to guarantee that our country adapts its productive structure and is prepared optimally for the following expansive phase of the cycle, but to generate additional growth and partially compensate in this way the restrictive impact of the fiscal short-term policy. In the medium term, both types of reforms will combine effects in the same direction and will be unequivocally positive to restore growth in the economy, production and employment.

[18] Law 27/2011, of 1 August, on updating, adaptation, and modernisation of the social welfare system; Royal Decree-law 5/2013, of 15 March (n 14); Law 23/2013, of 23 December, regulatory of the Sustainability Factor and of the Revaluation Index of the Social Security Pension System. The latter states: 'The unfavorable demographic evolution is accompanied by an intense economic crisis that has anticipated several years the emergence of deficits in the Social Security accounts, which has added economic tensions in the short term despite the extremely important effort of funding derived from the Government's decision that the state budget assumes one hundred percent of the cost of non-contributory benefits'.

[19] Royal Decree-law 28/2012, of 30 November, on consolidation measures and guarantee of the social welfare system, whose Explanatory Preamble states:

> The crisis is assuming a high deficit of the Social Welfare system during 2012, with the consequent liquidity stresses that will be marked next December 2012, in which the two

dependence, within long-term care,[20] and (3) suspension of the paternity leave extension.[21]

c) Gaining the confidence of the financial markets

The majority of the reforms (especially in the years 2010 to 2013) had a motivation that is rarely acknowledged explicitly and formally: they ultimately sought to overcome the crisis of confidence in financial markets in the eurozone, markets which reacted with a strong tightening of conditions of financing of private agents. There was only one reform in Spain that recognised it in its Explanatory Preamble: Royal Decree-law 20/2012, of July 13, on measures to guarantee budget stability and promote competitiveness.

Therefore, financial equilibrium was not the only principle to inspire the reforms; the aim was also 'to raise the credibility of financial markets', as expressly stated in the Statement of Reasons[22] of the Royal Decree-law 20/2012, of 13 July, which has been the most devastating social-rights norm resulting from the crisis, affecting long-term care and unemployment benefits. The need to obtain financing, financial aid, from private markets has been put ahead of the maintenance of the social rights of citizenship.

d) Implementing policies of the European Union

It can be stated that EU institutions make reform guidelines, which from another point of view also means that they can serve as an 'alibi' for Member States cutting

---

monthly payments have to be paid, ordinary and extraordinary, of pensions of the Social Security.
    ... This circumstance, together with others such as the need to comply with the objective of the public deficit, requires as an extraordinary and urgent need to cancel the updating of pensions in 2012 and suspend the revaluation of pensions for the year of 2013 ...'.

[20] Royal Decree-law 8/2010, of 20 May, by which extraordinary measures are adopted to reduce the public deficit. In its Explanatory Preamble it indicates, 'The hardness and depth of the economic crisis has led all the industrialized countries to make a significant tax effort to relieve the consequences of the crisis and preserve the levels reached of development and well-being. Nevertheless, as a result of this essential expansive fiscal policy, public finances have suffered a serious deterioration that now needs to be corrected as an essential requirement to reach a solid and lasting economic recovery'.

[21] Law 39/2010, of 22 December, on General State Budgets for the year 2011; Royal Decree-law 20/2011, of 30 December, on urgent measures in budgetary, tributary, and financial matters for the correction of the excessive public deficit; Law 2/2012, of 27 April, on budgetary stability and financial sustainability; Law 17/2012, of 27 December, on General State Budgets for the year 2013; Law 22/2013, of 23 December, on General State Budgets for the year 2014; Law 36/2014, of 26 December, on General State Budgets for the year 2015; Law 48/2015, of 29 October, on the General State Budgets for the year 2016.

[22] Literally, it states: 'To the imbalances that have yet to be resolved in the Spanish economy have been joined on this occasion a crisis of confidence in the financial markets, to which different institutional problems of the euro zone are not alien. The most immediate consequence of this instability in the markets has been a strong tightening of financing conditions of private agents. Essential in overcoming this situation will be not only the design of an economic policy strategy that contains the appropriate elements in the present context, but also its articulation in the medium term in a credible way and able to arouse the credibility of financial markets'.

the public protection system, as this constitutes the main measure suggested by the Union guidelines. Rationalisation is raised to community strategy. Practically all the Explanatory Preambles about reforms refer to the Union, to indicate that they are reforms that are being adopted in all Member States, to point out that they are policies approved in Councils of the Union, or directly to denote that they fall within the commitments of the excessive deficit framework established by the European Union.

This does not mean that the approved measures, in a singular way, are imposed,[23] but all measures are supported by policies of the European Union. The revision of the standards that approved the main restrictive reforms of social rights shows that—formally and also at the most foundational level—it is the imposition of financial equilibrium (imposed because it is a principle assumed as a mandate of the European Union) that marks economic policy. Thus:

- Royal Decree-law 8/2010, of 20 May, by which extraordinary measures are adopted to reduce the public deficit.[24]
- Law 27/2011, of 1 August, on updating, adaptation, and modernisation of the social welfare system.[25]
- Royal Decree-law 16/2012, of 24 April, on urgent measures to guarantee the sustainability of the National Health System and improve the quality and safety of its benefits.[26]
- Royal Decree-law 20/2012, of 13 July, on measures to guarantee budgetary stability and promote competitiveness.[27]

---

[23] Navarro (n 4).

[24] 'The commitment of the Government of Spain to the sustainability of its public finances was reflected in the update of the Stability and Growth Plan 2010–2013, approved by the Council of Ministers on 29 January 2010. It establishes as an objective, in accordance with the Excessive Deficit Procedure opened by the European Union, the reduction of the deficit for the whole of the Public Administrations up to 3 percent of the gross domestic product'. 'However, the evolution of the economic situation, as well as the commitments made by our country within the European Union in defence of the Monetary Union and the economies of the eurozone, makes it necessary to anticipate some of the measures provided for these scenarios in order to accelerate the path of fiscal consolidation, thus restoring markets confidence in meeting the deficit reduction prospects'.

[25] 'This situation is not specific to Spain, but common to the rest of the countries around us. The European Councils of Lisbon, Stockholm, Gothenburg, Barcelona, Brussels, up to the most recent, promote as priorities the prolongation of the working life and the discouraging of early retirement. Countries in our environment have made legal reforms in the sense of reducing stimuli to the premature abandonment of the active life and some have established the legal age 67 years'.

[26] 'All the countries of the European Union are analyzing and adopting measures that allow optimizing their health care and pharmaceutical models and, in particular, pharmaceutical expenditure and its weight in health spending. The implementation of measures in this area is very intense, especially in the countries that the financial and economic crisis have hit with more intensity'.

[27] 'The mentioned strategy is fundamentally based on two axes: the fiscal consolidation and the impulse of new structural reforms. The measures of fiscal adjustment are indispensable at this point as reinforcement of those already included in the last Update of the Stability and Growth Program 2012–2015 to guarantee that Spain strictly meets its fiscal commitments within the frame of Excessive Deficit established by the European Union. In addition, they turn out to be necessary to recover the confidence and the credibility of the public administrations. . . .

- Royal Decree-law 28/2012, of 30 November, on consolidation measures and guarantee of the social welfare system.[28]
- Royal Decree-law 5/2013, of 15 March, on measures to favour the continuity of the working life of older workers and to promote active ageing.[29]
- Law 23/2013, of 23 December, regulatory of the Sustainability Factor and the Revaluation Index of the Social Security Pension System.[30]

Paradoxically, the European Parliament does not hold the European Union responsible for restrictive reforms, but rather the Member States themselves. Thus, in the European Parliament resolution of 14 January 2014 on social protection for all, including self-employed workers, after pointing out that social security is a strictly national competence,[31] in its recital d) it states that 'to overcome the crisis, certain Member States have slashed public expending drastically at the same time as demand for social protection was increasing as a result of the rise in unemployment; that Allocations from national budgets to achieve coverage of social services have been further stretched as contributions have fallen in the wake of wide-scale job losses or wage cuts, which place the European social market economy at a real risk'. In this way, the states hold the European Union responsible, and the European Union holds the states responsible. The third party is always responsible.

The modification of the fiscal path foreseen by Spain in the Stability and Growth Program 2012–2015 has been given by the meeting of the ECOFIN of last 10 July. In this meeting, the EU Ministers of Economy decided to grant to Spain a one-year extension to correct its excessive deficit and bring it below 3 % of the GDP. This decision, therefore, leads to the modification of the Excessive Deficit Recommendation issued by the European Council of November 30, 2009, setting 2013 as a deadline for achievement of a deficit of the Public Administrations of 3 % of the GDP'.

[28] 'In light of the impact of the crisis on the set of public accounts, and specifically on the Social Welfare System, a set of measures to ensure the economic viability of such a system has been undertaken for years. As continuation to the already approved reforms, the Government has pledged a set of additional measures that penetrate into the reforms and are orientated to the fulfilment of the recommendations adopted for Spain in the European Council held on the 28th and 29th of June, 2012'.
[29] 'The present Royal Decree-Law addresses these issues through measures in the field of early retirement, partial retirement, compatibility between active life and pension, the fight against fraud and employment policies. These measures allow the recommendations of the Council of the EU of 10 July 2012 to be met, in the field of the sustainability of the pension system and the promotion of active ageing'.
[30] 'This law is consistent with the various recommendations contained in several instruments and documents of the institutions of the European Union, such as the "White Paper 2012: An Agenda for adequate, safe and sustainable pensions", supplemented by other documents such as the "Aging report 2012" or "Adequacy of Pensions in the EU 2010–2050", all of them framed within the Europe Strategy 2020, which constitutes the reference for the coordination of economic policies of the Member States and the scope from which a policy guidance and coordination of efforts to face the challenge of ageing and its impact on social protection systems'.
[31] Considering the European Parliament resolution of 14 January 2014 on social protection for all, including self-employed workers <http://www.europarl.europa.eu/sides/getDoc.do?pubRef=-//EP//TEXT+TA+P7-TA-2014-0014+0+DOC+XML+V0//EN> accessed 25 March 2018.

III. The structural reforms

The economic crisis has meant a reform of all social protection systems with important modifications, which in some cases have had such an impact that, in practice, those systems have been so weakened that their efficiency has even been doubted. This has happened especially with the new long-term care system (the so-called System for Personal Autonomy and Care of Dependent Adults—SAAD), implemented in 2007, a few years before the crisis, and which, being the least consolidated, has been the most affected.[32]

Along with the SAAD, the other most affected system has been social security with regard to the retirement pension, which was reformed into the three key elements that defined it: (a) retirement age, promoting a delay in the age of cessation of activity; (b) the amount, with a reduction of the amount when calculating pension benefits over longer time periods; and (c) penalising and hindering access to early retirement.

In addition to these two systems (long-term care and pensions), the health system has also suffered restrictions due to the economic crisis. Let us develop these issues.

We will focus on legislative reforms from 2010 to 2015, as the temporary framework in which reforms that have their origin—direct or indirect—in the economic crisis are approved.[33] During this period two political parties governed in Spain: the PSOE (until December 2011) and the Partido Popular (PP) (from that date until June 2018).

1. The retirement pension

a) Early reforms

The PSOE Executive Commission addressed cuts in spending on pensions following two rules. The first was precisely the norm by which it was assumed that the cost containment policy was adequate to overcome the economic crisis.[34] The second had a greater impact and was agreed both by social partners[35] and rest of the political parties: the retirement reform.[36]

---

[32] A detailed analysis of all these reforms, in Juan Antonio Maldonado Molina, 'El reformado Sistema de Dependencia' (2015) 71 Revista de Derecho Social 79.

[33] It is not easy to determine the beginning and end of the economic cycle of crisis in Spain but the first restrictive measures were approved in May 2010.

[34] Royal Decree-law 8/2010, of 20 May (n 20).

[35] 'Social pact for growth, employment and the guarantee of pensions' signed on 2 February 2011 by the government and the social partners, whose pt II refers to the Agreement for the reform and strengthening of the public pension system.

[36] Law 27/2011, of 1 August (n 18).

aa) No revaluation of pensions
The Spanish social welfare system, as stated in article 50 of the Constitution, must guarantee that the purchasing power of pensions is maintained. This was guaranteed by the annual revaluation of pensions, whereby they increased every year according to the increase in the Consumer Prices Index (CPI).

But in May 2010, within the extraordinary measures approved for the reduction of the public deficit with Royal Decree-law 8/2010, it was agreed to exceptionally suspend the revaluation of contributory pensions for the year 2011.[37] As we will see later on, this was only a preview of other more drastic measures in terms of revaluation, since in December 2013 a new revaluation technique was approved, which in practice means that, since then, an annual pensions increase of 0.25 per cent would be provided regardless of the increase in the CPI.

bb) Reform of the retirement pension
Law 27/2011, of 1 August, on updating, adaptation, and modernisation of the social welfare system (in force since 1 January 1 2013) was a complete reformulation of the retirement pensions, in which three aspects were modified: the ordinary age of retirement; the early retirement; and the amount of pension, modifying the regulatory base and the applicable percentage (elements used to calculate the amount according to the working life that the worker has accrued).

These three modifications reflect the same purpose: to reduce the costs of the system, guaranteeing its financial sustainability.[38] We will succinctly expose such reforms,[39] but focus only on the age and the amount, since the reform in Law 27/2011 relating to early retirement did not enter into force, having been amended by the PP government in 2013.

(1) Reform of the pensionable age The pensionable age was redefined, breaking with the parameters that had been kept in our country since 1919.[40] It was not merely an increase in the retirement age, but pension entitlements were now determined on two criteria: one based on age (the age at which old age will allegedly have materialised and that, therefore, follows one of the classic foundations of old-age protection: sixty-seven years old), and one based on lifetime workplace pension contributions (which takes into account the right to benefits as its foundation

---

[37] It was not a measure applied to all pensions, since the revaluation of pensions of lower amounts was maintained (benefits with minimum complements and non-contributory pensions, among others).

[38] Therefore, in the economic report that accompanied the draft law, it is pointed out that all these measures would imply a saving of the social welfare system of 0.1 per cent GDP in 2015; 0.3 per cent GDP in 2020; 1.4 per cent GDP in 2030 and 2.8 per cent GDP in 2040.

[39] For a global analysis, see José Luis Monereo Pérez and Juan Antonio Maldonado Molina, 'La reforma de la jubilación' (2012) 29–30 Revista General de Derecho del Trabajo y de la Seguridad Social.

[40] Juan Antonio Maldonado Molina, 'Jubilación, retiro y vejez. Conceptuación general' (2011) 57 La edad de Jubilación 85.

and is ultimately used to calculate an individual's official retirement age: sixty-five years old). This allows the retirement age to be made more flexible. In this way, a single legal age of reference is dispensed with, and two are used depending on the worker's contribution period.[41]

However, it is assumed that demographic factors may increase the retirement age further. For this reason, and as a 'sustainability factor', it was expected that 'from 2027 the fundamental parameters of the system will be revised by the differences between the evolution of life expectancy at 67 years old of the population in the year in which the revision is carried out and the life expectancy at 67 years in 2027. Such reviews will be carried out every five years using for this purpose the forecasts made by government agencies'. Therefore, Law 27/2011 was not limited to raising the age of retirement, but also sends a clear message, which is that the retirement age can be contingent, and this is only a first step in light of possible future modifications. It opened the door to a parametric system, but without clarifying what parameters could have an impact. Finally, when the sustainability factor was regulated in 2013, this model was not considered for retirement age, but for the initial amount and for the revaluation.

(2) **Reform of the quantity** The contributory pension for retirement is calculated by taking the amount of the salary being replaced as a base ('the regulatory base') and applying a percentage. Before the reform, the regulatory base was estimated by averaging contributions provided in the previous fifteen years. The percentage was obtained on the number of contributing years with a variation from 50 per cent with fifteen contributing years up to 100 per cent with thirty-five years of contributions.

The reform of 2011 modified both elements, resulting in a reduction of the amount of the pension. Thus, the period that composes its regulatory base was increased to cover the previous twenty-five years. Obviously, despite the base's update mechanism, it is a measure that will produce a widespread reduction in the amount of the pensions.[42]

Where there are gaps in an individual's employment history, a method called 'integration of gaps' is applied (whereby the months in which there was no contribution are completed by the minimum base of contribution). But it also has been the object of an important reform. In this way, until 1 January 2013, the integration

---

[41] A new concept is used; it is the 'working life', which is considered complete with thirty-eight years and six months contributed to the system (with some transitory rules that begin at thirty-five years of contribution). Outside of this case, the retirement age is located in sixty-seven years old (age progressively reached with transitory rules).

[42] Unlike the increase in age in case of a working life of less than thirty-eight and a half years, which does not affect those who prove a long working life, changes in the regulatory base do affect the insured as a whole, since the norm is that the bases are increasing throughout one's work life.

of gaps was total: all gaps were completed with one hundred per cent of the minimum base. Since that date, the forty-eight monthly payments with most recent gaps will be integrated with one hundred per cent, and the rest of the possible gaps will be integrated with 50 per cent of the minimum base. These are more restrictive rules, which reflect the principle of tax payment instead of solidarity and have a very clear gender impact, as is expressly assumed in the Economic Report of the Law, which reflected how the new rules of integration of gaps had a higher incidence in women than in men.[43]

The second element used for the calculation of the pension is the percentage. Law 27/2011 modified the percentages to be applied to the regulatory base, so that to obtain 100 per cent of the pension it was necessary to contribute thirty-seven years (instead of thirty-five, which was the working life that previously gave rights to the full pension). This resulted in a reduction in the pensions of those whose working life is shorter (mainly women).

b) Decisive reforms

aa) Consolidation measures and measures to favour the continuity of the working life

Royal Decree-law 28/2012, of 30 November, on consolidation measures and guarantee of the social welfare system regulation, suspended the revaluation of contributory pensions for 2013,[44] and left its update without effect for the year 2012.

The PSOE government and the PP agreed not only to defer the retirement age, but to put a limit on early retirement. However, the limitations proposed by the PSOE executive in Law 27/2011 (and that should have entered into force on 1 January 2013) seemed insufficient to the PP, and were suspended in December 2012 for three months. In March 2013, the Royal Decree-law 5/2013, of 15 March, on measures to favour the continuity of the working life of older workers and to promote active ageing, modified early and partial retirement. In both cases, access requirements were toughened and the penalty for voluntarily early retirement was increased. In the case of partial early retirement, certain especially discouraging measures were approved, which is also contrary to the promotion of gradual and flexible retirement.[45]

---

[43] Juan Antonio Maldonado Molina, 'La pensión de jubilación ordinaria. Concepto, requisitos y cuantía' (2017) II Tratado de Seguridad Social 73.

[44] Notwithstanding the foregoing, pensions will 'increase' in 2013 by 1 per cent generally or 2 per cent if not exceeding €1,000 per month.

[45] Juan Antonio Maldonado Molina, 'La acumulación de la jornada del jubilado parcialmente' (2018) 418 Revista de Trabajo y Seguridad Social 43.

bb) Sustainability factor and revaluation index of the public pension system
With Law 23/2013, of 23 December, a parametric reform is introduced for the first time in the Spanish social welfare system. So, it introduces two new rules:[46]

(1) Application of a sustainability factor to the initial amount The initial amount of the contributory retirement pension will no longer be entirely determined in proportion to the contributions, but the amount will vary according to the evolution of the life expectancy of the pensioners (and, consequently, of the time over which the pension is expected to be received). The sustainability factor adjusts the initial retirement pension so that the total received throughout the life of a pensioner who has access to the pension system for a certain number of years and likely will have a greater life expectancy is equivalent to that received by someone who retired at an earlier time.[47] According to the Explanatory Preamble of the law, its purpose is to maintain proportionality between contributions to the system and expected benefits, ensuring to present and future generations the perception of adequate and sufficient pensions. The law says that this factor deals with the risk associated with the increase in longevity and adjusts intergenerational equity, although only with respect to retirement pensions.

However, Law 6/2018, of 3rd July, on the PGE (General State Budgets—Spanish acronym) for 2018, redrafted the unique final disposition of Royal Legislative Decree 8/2015, establishing 'Application of the sustainability factor regulated in article 211 for the Consolidated Text will be carried out once the Follow-up and Assessment Commission of the Toledo Pacts reaches an agreement regarding application of the measures necessary to ensure system sustainability. In any event; however, its coming into force shall be no later than 1st January 2023.'

Consequently, a delay was approved so it does not become effective until 2023, when an agreement should have been reached by the Follow-up and Assessment Commission of the Toledo Agreements. This Agreement may be to maintain what was provided initially or to amend or delete it directly, whereby it would not be

---

[46] For an in-depth analysis of this important reform, see Miguel Rodríguez-Piñero, Bravo Ferrer, and María Emilia Casas Baamonde, 'El factor de sostenibilidad de las pensiones de jubilación y la garantía de la suficiencia económica de los ciudadanos durante la tercera edad' (2014) 5 Revista Relaciones Laborales 1; José Luis Monereo Pérez and Juan Antonio Fernández Bernat, 'El factor de sostenibilidad en España: ¿un nuevo paso para el cambio silencioso de modelo de pensiones públicas?' (2013) 62 Revista de Derecho Social 209; Borja Suárez Corujo, 'Las increíbles pensiones menguantes: la metamorfosis del sistema público de pensiones a través del factor de sostenibilidad' (2014) 5 Revista Relaciones Laborales 131.

[47] Putting it concisely, it functions as follows: how much life expectancy has increased at sixty-seven will be calculated in a specific five-year period (in 2019 [year initially provided] the life expectancy variation between 2012 and 2017; in 2024, the variation between 2017 and 2022; and so on); that percentage is applied to the amount that would normally correspond to the worker, since it is understood that the amount that results from applying the legal rules corresponds to a specific demographic situation; and should this vary, then the calculation initially foreseen should vary.

effective in 2023 either, although the drafting of the PGE Law for 2018 appears to suggest the government would not waive its becoming effective.

(2) Mechanism of automatic adjustment on revaluation of pensions The Spanish social security system, according to article 50 of the Constitution, must ensure the purchasing power of pensions, which was articulated with the periodical revaluation of said pensions. Thus, they were increased annually pursuant to the increase indicated by the CPI.

A new formula was introduced, which is no longer linked to the CPI but instead depends on the financial evolution of the system (with minimum and maximum limits). The revaluation will be based on the income and expenditure of the system. In practice, it implies that pensions will only be increased by a maximum of 0.25 per cent regardless of the increase in the cost of living.[48] This has provoked a great social response, mobilising the collectivity of pensioners, who for the first time in decades have taken to the streets to speak out against such an increase.[49]

This new formula became effective in 2014. During its first years of validity it passed under the radar since the economic scenario was deflation, so despite pensions being revalued 0.25 per cent there was no loss of purchasing power. However, it was from 2017 when the senior citizens' collectives became aware of what had been passed in December 2013, when the CPI started to greatly overtake the approved pension increase, leading to a loss of purchasing power among the pensioners' collective. This led, as we all know, to an unexpected social response, ie for the first time in decades the pensioners' collective took their protest to the streets.

Social pressure forced the government to increase the amount of pensions for 2018 and 2019. PGE Law 6/2018, of 6 July, obviously did not intend to suspend, much less abolish, General Social Security Law (GSSL) article 56, since (contrary to what happened with Law 23/2013) prior consensus had been sought within the Toledo Pact and, moreover, it was an extended PGE law.[50] That is why it only provides some extraordinary increases under the expression 'additional pension increase'[51] for 2018 and 2019, as a transitory measure, since (as the Statement of Reasons provides) that was 'without forgetting the Toledo Pact Commission of Follow-up and Assessment of Agreements is responsible for analysing the situation of the Social Security System and

---

[48] In no case may the result obtained give rise to an annual increase of pensions that is (as a lower limit) less than 0.25 per cent or (as an upper limit) higher than the percentage variation of the CPI in the annual period prior to December of the year, plus 0.50 per cent.

[49] cf <https://elpais.com/elpais/2018/03/17/album/1521280369_757173.html> accessed 24 March 2018.

[50] As the previous government could not present the PGE draft bill for 2018 at least three months prior to the expiry of that corresponding to 2017, the previous one was extended. Therefore, the 2018 PGE Law only regulates those dispositions which respect TC doctrine over eventual contents, together with its necessary contents.

[51] Fifty-first additional disposition of 2018 PGE Law 6/2018.

establishing recommendations which guarantee its medium-/long-term financial sustainability'.[52]

Both questions were affected by Royal Decree-law 28/2018, which revised the 2018 increase (going for a total of 1.7 per cent, instead of the 1.6 per cent approved, leading to a compensatory payment of 0.1 per cent) and set some ad hoc rules for 2019, suspending application of GSSL article 58; unlike in 2018—where an additional increase over that provided by GSSL article 58 (which was not suspended) was passed—said rule is done away with.

2. Long-term care

Social assistance is the responsibility of the Autonomous Communities (regional governments) and local entities. They have not been subject to any reform directly, although they have suffered during the crisis due to budget cuts.

Within this category it is necessary to analyse long-term care which, as we have indicated, is included in SAAD, which began operation in Spain in 2007 (Law 39/2006). Since May 2010, SAAD was a target of the first budget cuts. An overview of such reforms shows not only how the reforms try to correct the deficiencies observed in the early years (such as the regional imbalances), or a 'lower' reduction in costs, but the authentic pillars of the system are affected: the financing of the Autonomous Communities is suspended and the compulsory insurance of informal caregivers is eliminated (until May 2019), as well as a reduction in their benefits.

All these cuts (introduced from 2010 to 2013, though those of 2012 are especially important) have cracked the pillars of the SAAD as it was conceived in 2006. These reforms and the ones undertaken at the end of 2013 allow us to talk about a new SAAD, a SAAD of minimums, in which the State returns to ignore its responsibilities for the care of dependents, laying the foundations for coverage to be restricted again to the family area (but as an informal, unrecognised sector), or in the private sphere for those with the highest purchasing power.

It can be argued that this series of cuts and nine rule[53] changes in the field of dependent adult care has blurred the

---

[52] The PGE Law for 2018 does not admit to Law 23/2013 being unfair, but rather it explains the pension increases in the 'context of economic growth and compliance with the goals of budget stability'; however, it admits it should be amended, referring to agreements reached in the Toledo Agreement Follow-up & Assessment Commission, which guarantee elimination of the social security system deficit. Meanwhile, it simply establishes 'a transitory pension increase regime for 2018, and where appropriate 2019'.

[53] Royal Decree-law 8/2010, of 20 May (n 20); Royal Decree-law 20/2011, of 30 December (n 21); Law 2/2012, of 29 June; Royal Decree-law 20/2012, of 13 July (n 17); Law 17/2012, of 27 December (n 21); Law 22/2013, of 23 December (n 21); Royal Decree-law 1050/2013, of 27 December; Royal Decree-law 1051/2013, of 27 December; Law 36/2014, of 26 December (n 21).

boundaries so much that it represents a completely different SAAD model.[54]

Economically, they have fulfilled the aim with which they were conceived: to reduce the government budget deficit.[55] From a social point of view, the reading is quite different, as from the point of view of employment. The care of dependent adults is no longer a sector of employment[56] because, to achieve the reduction of the deficit, the professional caregiver sector has been suffocated.[57]

The SAAD functions as an autonomous system funded by the state (covering services provided by regional and local entities, financed in part by the state depending on the number of beneficiaries). The services provided are of two types: services (home help, telecare, among others); and economic, with the payment of a benefit to family caregivers, whose activity was recognised, considering them insured in the social welfare system (paying their contributions), and they are compensated with an economic benefit.

After the reform, the work done by the family members is no longer recognised (in fact, since 2012 to 2019 they no longer get paid the contribution), losing what was perceived as an achievement from the point of view of social justice. The reform has had a positive aspect; it encourages the professionalisation of long-term care, which is important because it allows families to be freed from the task of caring for their dependents, as well as creating employment in the sector. Unfortunately, the professionalisation is not being carried out, so what has really happened is a turning back in which the relatives are the ones who take care of the dependents, but without the financial support that they received from 2007 to 2012.[58] The

---

[54] Juan Antonio Maldonado Molina, 'El Sistema para la Autonomía y Atención a la Dependencia tras sus reformas' (2014) Prevención y Protección de la Dependencia: un enfoque transdisciplinar 182.

[55] If we analyse the information published on 30 April 2013 by the Spanish government in *National Program of Reforms 2013*, 'with the application of these measures spending has been reduced at 599 million euros in 2012, there being estimated an additional reduction of 1,108 million in 2013 and of 571 million additional Euros in 2014' (p 23).

[56] The Commission of the European Communities, in the White Paper on 'Growth, competitiveness, employment. Challenges and ways forward into the 21st century', by listing the sectors that are considered employment fields, already included home help for the elderly and disabled people, health care, meal preparation, and housework <https://publications.europa.eu/en/publication-detail/-/publication/0d563bc1-f17e-48ab-bb2a-9dd9a31d5004/language-en> (p 22) accessed 26 March 2018.

[57] Employment has been created, but less than expected. As stated in the 'Informe de la comisión para el análisis de la situación actual del sistema de la dependencia, de su sostenibilidad y de los actuales mecanismos de financiación, para evaluar su adecuación a las necesidades asociadas a la dependencia' (6 October 2017), Law 39/2006 was expected to create 104,469 new jobs in 2007 and reach 262,735 new jobs in 2010. However, 'since the entry into force of the Dependency Law, on 1 January 2007 to December 2016, employment in the Social Services System, to which Care of Dependent Adults belongs, has experienced growth, a total of 162,539 new affiliations' (p 140) <http://www.dependencia.imserso.es/interpresent2/groups/imserso/documents/binario/inf_comision_analisis_20171006.pdf> accessed 26 March 2018.

[58] If we consider the data published on 30th April 2013 by the Spanish government in the *National Program of Reforms 2013*, 'with application of these measures, expenditure was reduced by 599 million euros in 2012, estimating an additional reduction of 1,108 million in 2013 and a further 571 million euros in 2014' (p 23).

amount of economic benefit has been reduced by between 15 per cent and 25 per cent (depending on the degree of dependence and type of benefit), and equally the level of services has also reduced. That is, the number of hours of home help service to which each beneficiary is entitled was reduced.

3. Family allowances

Article 39 of the Spanish Constitution states that authorities ensure the social, economic, and legal protection of the family. Despite this, if there is a protective branch with insufficient coverage, then it is family benefits.

Already before the crisis, the protective strength of this branch was very weak and the expenditure reduction of these years has stopped (and even suppressed) some of the measures that were beginning to apply in our system before the crisis. This happened with the Law 35/2007, which established a benefit for the stimulus of the birth rate of €2,500 for the birth or adoption of a child, a benefit that was repealed by article 7 Royal Decree-law 8/2010, of 20 May, adopting extraordinary measures to reduce the public deficit.

Together with this measure, which directly reduced the familiar coverage, there was another benefit that was indirectly affected. Namely, paternity leave. Indeed, in 2009 it was an extension of the duration of paternity leave was approved from thirteen days to four weeks,[59] which would come into force on 1 January 2011. Nevertheless, the economic crisis and the need to reduce spending provoked the suspension of this measure year after year until 2015.[60]

4. Unemployment

Article 41 of the Spanish Constitution contemplates unemployment benefit as a specific benefit that provides coverage for situations of need for all citizens.

In Spain, unemployment protection is structured at two levels: the contributory and the social assistance security level. Nevertheless, the social assistance security level is also determined by the accreditation of a minimal period of contribution, resulting in a blurring of the contributory and assistance levels. Both levels have been affected by reforms motivated by the economic crisis.

---

[59] Law 9/2009, of 6 October.
[60] Thus it was suspended on seven occasions. The first time by Law 39/2010, of 22 December, on General State Budgets for 2011 and the last by Law 48/2015, of 29 October, on General State Budgets for 2016.

The Royal Decree-law 20/2012, of 13 July, on measures to guarantee budgetary stability and promote competitiveness, introduced substantial modifications in unemployment protection, reforming and questioning, in numerous aspects, the model existing up to that moment.

With regard to contributory unemployment, it offered an income replacement that ranged from seventy per cent for the first six months of unemployment to sixty per cent from the seventh month up to a maximum of twenty-four months. The Royal Decree-law 20/2012 modified these percentages by reducing the percentage to fifty per cent of the regulatory base from the seventh month. Together with this measure, the contribution of the management entity to social security that corresponds to the worker in the situation of unemployment was partially abolished.

As for unemployment benefits, the special subsidy for those over forty-five years of age that have exhausted their contributory benefit has been eliminated and the minimum age to access early retirement subsidies has increased from fifty-two to fifty-five years old.

Unemployment insurance is predicated on stable employment, not on precarious working patterns, for which a precarious coverage is contemplated.[61] Data on the number and type of beneficiaries support this statement. Thus, it is striking how, despite the high unemployment rate, there has been a reduction in spending on social benefits, which according to the Economic and Social Council responds to the shorter periods of receipt of social benefits[62] and the lower number of beneficiaries,[63] which in turn is due to the improvement in employment,[64] but also due to the concerning regression of the extent of protection provided by the system: never, until 2014, had our unemployment benefit system left such a large number of people without coverage. If the year 2014 ended with a decrease in the unemployment rate, in terms of unemployment protection, the lowest coverage rate in recent years was reached, offering protection to only 58.85 per cent of the unemployed, representing almost a twenty-point decrease since 2010, the year in which it reached its maximum value.[65]

---

[61] Juan Antonio Maldonado Molina, 'La protección por desempleo de los trabajadores precarios' (2015) La protección por desempleo en España.

[62] Consejo Económico y Social, *Memoria sobre la Situación Socioeconómica y Laboral. Spain 2014* (CES 2015) 21.

[63] During 2014, the system reached an average volume of 2,542,977 beneficiaries of unemployment benefits, which means a decrease of 11.2 per cent compared to the previous year. On average, the number of beneficiaries of contributory benefits was 1,059,799 and of welfare benefits 1, 221,390. If in 2008 one out of every three unemployed people with coverage received a welfare benefit, at the end of 2014 it was almost one in two (this is due to the long-term unemployed who saw their contributory unemployment extinguished).

[64] Of those who left benefits, 64.5 per cent was accounted for by their return to the labour market.

[65] Consejo Económico y Social (n 62) 617.

5. Healthcare

The Royal Decree-law 16/2012, of 14 April, on urgent measures to guarantee the sustainability of the National Health System and improve the quality and safety of benefits, affected the health system trying to contain spending, at the same time as reordering the benefits package. It constitutes a 'health counter reform'[66] in the sense that it represented a setback for all the reforms approved in this area in the previous two decades, which had aimed to extend the subjective and objective scope of health coverage, being also approved without consensus, as had been the usual practice. With this reform we have sought to save €7,267 million.

Among the most controversial measures that it introduced are:

a) When defining beneficiaries, it returns to the notion of 'insured' instead of 'right holders', which weakens the principle of universality in healthcare insurance. It excludes health coverage for foreigners in irregular situations, except in cases of vital emergency.[67] Those left out of the healthcare system are allowed to receive such services by paying the costs or signing a special agreement that acts like private insurance, and at a high price.[68] Until 2012, the principle of universality had no exceptions, with the entire population being covered, including foreigners in an irregular situation. However, the reform approved that year omitted this group. Faced with this, the regional governments within their legislative powers decided not to assume this limitation, extending protection to everyone again, within their legislative powers. However, the TC has declared that the Autonomous Communities do not have competence to do so, admitting that the right to effective protection of health may be subject to general interests, those that the state legislator deems convenient at the time. Finally, after Royal Decree-law 7/2018, of July 27, both foreigners who are legally residing in Spain and those who are not registered or authorised as residents in Spain have the right to health protection and healthcare in Spain; the same conditions as people with Spanish nationality, provided that said persons meet certain requirements.[69]

---

[66] As the TC stated, the Royal Decree-law 16/2012 'is a twist on the previous policy of progressive extension of free or subsidized health care from the creation of the National Health System' (FJ-8 of the STC 139/2016), since the criteria for delimiting the entitlement of the right of access to health benefits, now selected, are different from those established in the previous drafting of art 3 of Law 16/2003, which addressed different parameters such as those related to the holder's residence in Spanish territory.

[67] Law developed by regulation by Royal Decree 1192/2012, of 3 August, which regulates the status of insureds and beneficiaries for the purposes of health care in Spain charged to public funds through the National Health System.

[68] Victoria Rodríguez-Rico Roldán, 'El derecho a la asistencia sanitaria de los extranjeros en situación irregular' (2015) 5 Revista de Derecho de la Seguridad Social 97.

[69] Juan Antonio Maldonado Molina, 'The Exclusion of Foreigners in an Irregular Situation from the Right to Health Care in Spain' (2019) 1 Issues in the Justiciability of the Right to Health 28.

b) Part of the services portfolio becomes a co-payment. This measure penalises the chronically ill and those on the lowest incomes.

c) The percentage of co-payment for pharmaceutical benefits is increased, and an important group of medicines is excluded from financing. Thus, the pharmaceutical benefits are divided into two main categories depending on whether they are provided to hospital patients[70] or outpatients.[71] For the latter, there has always been a co-payment in certain situations. But after the 2012 reform, the co-payment extends even to pensioners. Therefore, until 24 April 2012, workers had to pay 40 per cent of the cost of the medicine,[72] which was completely free for pensioners.[73] From this date onwards, medicines free of charge are suppressed for most pensioners. They will only be free for non-contributory pension beneficiaries, setting a minimum participation percentage for the rest of 10 per cent except for the pensioners of the highest acquisitive capacity (though for all there is marked a maximum monthly limit on the amount they have to pay).

IV. Interpretation by the Constitutional Court

The TC has validated the form and the content of the legislative measures, as none of these restrictive reforms has been considered unconstitutional by it. In Spain, this legislative approach has therefore been legitimised by our constitutional court. The TC has validated the government's use of the Royal Decree-Law on very permissive grounds (SSTC 16 July 2014).

1. Constitutional evaluation of the procedural aspects of the reforms

These government reforms have not only diminished the social support for due process guarantee, but they have reinforced the primacy of the economy and have highlighted the role of the government as manager of the public to the detriment of Parliament. So these reforms have not only reduced social and legal guarantees, but have also reinforced the protagonism of the economy, underlining the role of the government as public administrator.

---

[70] It is part of what is called the basic common services portfolio of the National Health System, which is fully funded with no co-payment if hospitalized. It is around 30 per cent of the total pharmaceutical expenditure.

[71] It is part of the additional common portfolio, which is subject to funding limits, including the co-payment of the beneficiary.

[72] Public employees integrated in special regimes, 30 per cent.

[73] Except for public employees with special regimes who paid 30 per cent.

The use of the royal decree-law has the negative effect of a reduction of the 'legal-social guarantee',[74] although this has not prevented the TC from admitting its use based on a broad interpretation of article 86 of the Spanish Constitution, considering that the limits and requirements set forth in article 86 of the Spanish Constitution have been respected (extraordinary and urgent need) when 'an extraordinary situation in cases of problematic economic situations'[75] occurs. It has supposed a certain break in the distribution of powers with a distortion of the natural mechanisms that create standards, on the grounds that it was necessary to take extraordinary measures urgently and immediately (but in many cases has exceeded the causal limits that article 86 of the Constitution imposes). In any case, emergency laws have played the leading role in the reforms of the system stemming from the economic crisis.

2. Constitutional evaluation of pension reform

The Royal Decree-law 28/2012, of 30 November, on consolidation measures and guarantee of the social welfare system, suspended the revaluation of contributory pensions for 2013,[76] and left without effect its update for the year 2012. These reforms reached the TC,[77] which analysed whether these measures constituted a violation of the non-retroactivity of unfavourable rules.[78] In this regard, the TC[79] considered that when Royal Decree-law 28/2012 was approved, there was no

[74] José Luis Monereo Pérez, 'El derecho del Trabajo y el legislador de la crisis económica. Técnica legislativa y política del Derecho Social' (2014) 38 Revista General de Derecho del Trabajo y de la Seguridad Social 1.

[75] The urgency of the matter requires an immediate reaction to the assumption on which an action is intended, and this action should be reflected in 'an immediate regulatory action' that cannot be postponed in time or even to the approval of a law by urgent procedure (STC 29/1982, FJ 3), therefore the effects pursued by such action must be immediate. On these requirements, see—among others—the STC 137/2011, FJ 4.

[76] Notwithstanding the foregoing, pensions will 'increase' in 2013 by 1 per cent generally or 2 per cent if not exceeding €1,000 per month.

[77] The appeal was lodged by 146 Members of various parliamentary groups, representing more than 13 million voters compared to 10,830,693 from the PP, author of the appealed and controversial rule.

[78] The appeal is based on the fact that art 50 of the Constitution contains a very clear and precise mandate addressed to the State, stating that 'the public authorities will guarantee, through appropriate and periodically updated pensions, economic sufficiency for citizens during the third age'. Therefore, the duty to revalue pensions periodically is not the result of the sovereign decision of the legislative branch but constitutes a rigorous development of the constitutional mandate, so that the legislator does not have unlimited freedom to suppress the revaluation mechanism. It cannot ignore the set of constitutional requirements. In addition to the substantive issue, the recurrent parliamentarians considered that the suspension in extremis of the updating of pensions through the use of the Royal Decree-law was a violation of the Constitution because it exceeded the exceptional circumstances for which such a rule is enabled.

[79] [2015] 49 STC (TC) and [2015] 144 STC (TC). About them, see Borja Suárez Corujo, 'La suspensión del mecanismo de actualización de las pensiones y la decepcionante sentencia del Tribunal Constitucional 49/2015, de 5 de marzo' (2015) 2 Revista de las Relaciones Laborales 185; José Ignacio García Ninet and Jesús Barceló Fernández, '¿El imparable declive de la revalorización/actualización de las pensiones?: notas al hilo de la STC (pleno) 49/2015, de 5 de marzo de 2015' (2015) 4 Revista de

consolidated right, accepted and integrated in the pensioner's background, but a mere expectation,[80] so it rejected the argument that article 9.3 of the Constitution had been violated, which includes the non-retroactivity of sanctions that are not favourable or restrictive of individual rights.

The TC resolved that articles 9.3 and 33 of the Spanish Constitution were not violated, because the legislator has a certain margin regarding the updating of pensions depending on the economic possibilities of the system.[81] And, to reach this conclusion, it relies on previous constitutional doctrine, which summarises four points:

- 'It is up to the legislator to determine the scope of the right of citizens to obtain and the correlative obligation of the public authorities to grant a pension during the third age, establishing the requirements and conditions that are needed to make this right effective';[82]
- Article 50 of the Constitution tends 'to eradicate situations of need, which must be determined and assessed, taking into account the general context in which they occur and in connection with economic circumstances, the availability at the moment and needs of different social groups. It cannot be excluded, therefore, that the legislator, assessing the relative importance of the situations of need to be met, regulates, in response to the indicated circumstances, the level and conditions of the benefits to be made or modifies them to adapt them to the needs of the moment';[83]
- Article 50 of the Constitution does not require that each and every one of the vested pension commitments experience an annual increase. The 'periodic update guarantee does not necessarily imply the annual increase of all pensions. By setting a limit to the payment of new pensions or by denying the updating for a time of those that exceed this limit, the legislator does not exceed the scope of the functions that correspond to him in the assessment of those socioeconomic circumstances that condition the adaptation and updating of the pension system';[84]

Derecho de la Seguridad Social, Laborum 147; José Luis Monereo Pérez and Juan Antonio Fernández Bernat, 'Revalorización y actualización de pensiones: la STC 49/2015, de 5 de marzo de 2015' (2016) Extra 1 Revista de Derecho de la Seguridad Social 15.

[80] This makes art 33.3 of the Constitution inapplicable, which refers to the fact that 'no one shall be deprived of their property and rights except for justified cause of public utility or social interest, through the appropriate compensation and in accordance with the law'.

[81] The TC considered that the fact that the Law provided that when the CPI was higher than expected such revaluation must be updated 'in accordance with the provisions of the respective General State Budget Law' (art 48.2 General Social Security Act of 1994) is to recognize the legislator has a margin to approach the updating of pensions depending on the economic possibilities of the System, while also trying to administer limited economic means for a large number of social needs.

[82] [1987] 144 STC 3 (TC).

[83] [1987] 127 STC 4 (TC).

[84] [1987] 134 STC 5 (TC).

- The limitation of the update of the purchasing power of higher pensions, 'as it is based on the requirements derived from the control of public expenditure and the principle of solidarity, enjoys an objective and reasonable justification'.[85]

3. Constitutional evaluation of health reform

In addition, faced with these reforms, some Autonomous Communities reacted with their own legislative[86] developments, which tried to restore the rights prior to the reform. However, the central government presented a conflict of competence to the TC, which found in favour of the state. In all cases, the TC restricted itself to analysing the distribution of powers, without going on to assess whether the substantive right to healthcare was violated or not.

In these sentences, the TC interprets what should be considered as basic legislation, preventing regional developments that improve the state minimum if what is to be improved is the entitlement to the right, differentiating consequently the subjective scope (which should not be improved) and the objective (which can be improved).[87] Therefore, regional improvement cannot take place in the subjective scope of the law, since this area in fact constitutes the core of regulation that guarantees equality at the state level.

As we have indicated, the government reform of 2012 supposed a turn in the previous policy of progressive extension of free or subsidised healthcare, a declared constitutional turn.[88]

But, in addition, in the sentences at the end of 2017, it is the TC that takes another turn, distinguishing for the first time the subjective elements of the objectives in the determination of the notion of 'basic legislation' and preventing regional developments that improve the state minimum, if what they want to improve is the ownership of the right. The interpretation given by the TC also implies a step backwards because it denies the fundamental nature of the right to health contained in the Constitution. Literally, it was held that 'the right to health established by Article 43 of the Spanish Constitution is a mandate that has been constitutionally enunciated as a guiding principle and not as a fundamental right, and, therefore, it is the legislator who has to determine the appropriate techniques to carry them out'.

---

[85] [1990] 100 STC 3 (TC).

[86] Basque Country [2017] 134 STC (TC); Navarre [2017] 140 STC (TC); Valencian Region [2017] 145 STC (TC); Navarre [2018] 17 & 18 SSTC (TC).

[87] About these statements, see Juan Antonio Maldonado Molina, 'La distribución de competencias como límite a la efectiva protección de la salud: Sentencias TC 134/2017, de 16 de noviembre; 140/2017, de 30 de noviembre; y 145/2017, de 14 de diciembre' (2018) 20 Revista Foro, Journal of Legal and Social Sciences of the Complutense University of Madrid 305.

[88] [2016] 139 STC (TC); [2017] 33 STC (TC); [2017] 63 STC (TC); [2017] 64 STC (TC); [2017] 98 STC (TC).

This interpretation, ultimately, subsumes the effective promotion of the right to health to general interests, but considers that general interests are those that the state legislator deems convenient. Thus, a regional regulatory framework that would effectively implement article 43 of the Constitution would risk becoming unconstitutional if the improvement it made in the basic regulations were contradictory to the central government's political guidelines that, apart from emptying of content to the Autonomous Community, make the declaration of a social and democratic state of right devoid of interest, since it would prioritise the distribution of competence to the maximum development of social rights. And it cannot be forgotten that the right to health is a fundamental social right linked to the right to life and human dignity.

These sentences include a dissenting vote,[89] which disagrees with the decision when considering that the state minimum (previously universal) 'is now susceptible to improvement by the Autonomous Communities, with basis on the principle of autonomy and specific foundation in the regional competition of legislative development in matters of health', so it considered that it was fully constitutional for a Community to legislate such minimums.[90]

But they also question whether the constitutionality of a standard can be assessed only in strictly competitive terms, considering that 'the effectiveness of the right to health protection should have presided over the interpretation of the competing areas of competency, in order to support, among the diverse possible interpretations, those that reasonably allow to fulfil the mandate proclaimed in Article 43 of the Spanish Constitution and reach their objectives'. They understand that this is 'an idea that has been outlined in constitutional jurisprudence, but which unfortunately has not yet gained the necessary relevance in its widespread application. The Constitution can only be understood and interpreted correctly when it is understood as a unit'.[91] Clearly this dissenting vote represents a plea in favour of the defence of the material right to health as a hallmark of the welfare state.[92]

---

[89] From the Magistrates Mr Fernando Valdés Dal-Ré, Mr Juan Antonio Xiol Ríos, Mr Cándido Conde-Pumpido Tourón, and Ms María Luisa Balaguer Callejón. In sentences 140/2017 and 145/2017 they are sent to those formulated in the STC 134/2017.

[90] They consider that this interpretation is clearly disruptive in the way it has been maintained. Literally, they say 'we express resounding disagreement with that excessive notion of the basics, which does not differ substantially from an exclusive legislative competence of the State. It undermines in this way a more than consolidated constitutional doctrine on the shared normative competences in a State of plural structure'. Advancing on this idea, they recall that 'what is forbidden to the regional legislator is precisely the opposite: it cannot worsen the financing regime of the pharmaceutical benefit, making it more burdensome for the user'.

[91] [1988] 227 STC 13 (TC); [2002] 239 STC 3 (TC); [2011] 30 STC 5 (TC); [2015] 233 STC 2 (TC).

[92] The following paragraph is especially eloquent: 'As a result of this normative involution, that outstanding legislator that is the Government has placed in brackets the exhausting but steady process of construction and consolidation in the Spanish society of the Welfare State. On this side, the conception of the Welfare State, characteristic of the most advanced social constitutionalism, has been supplanted in order to achieve presumed objectives such as economic efficiency and rationalization by the Workfare State'.

Therefore the vote denounces the situation whereby Autonomous Communities, having openly and directly addressed the problem (via regulatory intervention), are now the subject of litigation raised by the central government, while others (most of them) 'chose extreme and camouflaged political options of an indirect and informal nature, in the style of issuing instructions to the health centres under their jurisdiction to provide all citizens, regardless of their legal status or nationality, with the precise health services to guarantee their right to health, free of charge', which of course does not guarantee the equality of all Spanish citizens, nor guarantee the principle of legal security.

V. Conclusion

The economic crisis has led to a series of restrictive reforms that have reduced the level of social protection in all areas. Pensions, healthcare, long-term care, unemployment, social assistance, and family benefits currently offer a lower protection level than before the crisis, so less protection compared to pre-crisis levels. As we have said the TC has endorsed the substance of these reforms. But also the form, since none of the restrictive reforms of rights has been considered to be unconstitutional by the Spanish High Court.

The motivation for such reforms has focused on the pursuit of financial balance, arguing that the only way to save the Social Protection Systems is to ensure that they are economically sustainable. The reforms were motivated by the search for economic stability, based on the argument that the only way to save social protection systems is to make them economically viable. But along with that aim—formally declared—implicitly what has really been sought is to reassure the financial markets, giving preference to the tranquillity of those who provide financial support rather than to the social peace that a rights-based regime provides. Besides the formally declared objective, the real objective was to rebuild the confidence of the financial markets, preferring to allay them rather than achieve the social tranquillity provided by a social protection system guaranteeing well-being. The restriction of social rights has certainly not been motivated by 'social reasons', but formally all the reforms have been justified by 'reasons' of an essentially economic-financial nature. The economic rationality of public deficit control has been superimposed on the maintenance of social rights, even on those recognised constitutionally. From the social perspective, what has taken place is a clear reduction of the protection conferred in the pre-existing legal model and, with it, a regression in the legal guarantee of the social subjective rights to social protection enshrined in article 41 of the Spanish Constitution.

Most of these reforms have been characterised by the executive, not parliament, driving them, so that in the plane of the technical regulations a systematic use of the royal decree-law has been resorted to as a legislative instrument to perform not only circumstantial but also essentially structural and permanent reforms. The majority of these reforms stem from the Spanish government and not its parliament. In other words, the government has resorted to the systematic use of the royal decree-law[93] as a legislative instrument to implement not only temporary reforms but also eminently permanent structural reforms. This has led to the fracturing of the separation of powers, distorting the natural mechanisms for creating legislation, contending that extraordinary measures must be taken with extreme urgency (often exceeding the causal limitations established in article 86 of the Spanish Constitution).

The Spanish Constitution was reformed in 2011, with the introduction of the principle of budgetary stability in article 135. Organic Law 2/2012, of 27 April, on budgetary stability and financial sustainability develops this constitutional mandate and includes its application to the National Social Security Administration (article 2.1.d), which must maintain a balanced budget or even produce a surplus. Nevertheless, exceptionally, the National Social Security Administration may incur 'a structural deficit subject to the purposes and conditions established in the Social Security Reserve Fund Regulations'. In such event, the maximum structural deficit permitted for the central government shall be reduced 'in the same amount as the deficit of the Social Security Administration' (article 11.5). Thus, the National Social Security Administration is also subject to the principle of budgetary stability, despite the fact that, given its social purpose of solidarity, it is irrational to expect a social protection system to aspire to a surplus or even to budgetary equilibrium. Therefore, its deficit is permitted, but contingent upon it being transferred to the central government's deficit.

Evidently then, after the 2011 constitutional reform and its application in 2012 legislation, the Spanish constitutional panorama is one where social and economic provisions coexist. The economic provisions, however, prevail, creating an imbalance between the social and the economic. We are, therefore, faced with the predominance of a 'strong' economic constitution over a 'weak' social constitution, the latter being subordinated to the economic rationale of controlling the budget deficit.

We understand that this imbalance between the economic and the social is a mistake. The social protection systems can also be drivers of economic dynamism, even of economic recovery. Consider that the economic capacity of pensioners affects consumption. In part the idea of active ageing is also based on this understanding, since social benefits make possible that a part of the population preserve the purchasing power that places them as 'consumers', avoiding not only social exclusion, but also the potential slower economic growth posed by an ageing

---

[93] Art 86.1 of the Spanish Constitution of 1978 allows the government to pass a royal decree-law without normal parliamentary approval as a temporary legislative provision if measures must be implemented urgently. This royal decree-law must be signed by the king.

population. Similarly, long-term care and healthcare are important sources of employment. Therefore, we should avoid apocalyptic diagnostics that present the new demographic scenarios as 'problems' since they can be 'opportunities' in which social protection systems help to maintain a sustainable balance between the 'social reason' and the 'economic reason'.[94]

Access to the social welfare system is a fundamental right which, in accordance with European Union law, constitutes a key element of the European social model, as underlined in the European Parliament resolution of 14 January 2014 on social protection for all, including self-employed workers.[95]

The arrival of the new government in June 2018 brought with it the recovery of the rights lost in the matter at the time of the crisis. After the passing of Royal Decree-law 7/2018, of 27 July, both foreigners who are legally residing in Spain (article 3.1 Law 16/2003) and those who are not registered or authorised as residents of Spain have the right to the protection of health and healthcare under the same conditions as people with Spanish nationality.[96]

Therefore, the origins of the reform of 2012 can be traced back to the economic crisis at that time. This in turn gave rise to the jurisprudential doctrine that we analysed in this chapter (the judicialisation of healthcare for foreigners in Spain). It should not be forgotten, however, that thanks to the legislative reform approved on 27 July 2018 the jurisprudential analysis has lost its relevance as the universal right to healthcare in Spain has been recognised once again. After Royal Decree-law 7/2018, of 27 July, on universal access to the national health system, a giant step has been taken in the real universality of healthcare, without which the system could still be reproached—especially considering the state of affairs in the period just after August 2012—for staying in a theoretical universality.

---

[94] Monereo Pérez, 'La Ley de Presupuestos Generales del Estado para 2015 y su incidencia en materia de Seguridad Social' (n 7) 11.

[95] European Parliament resolution of 14 January 2014 on social protection for all, including self-employed workers <https://www.europarl.europa.eu/sides/getDoc.do?pubRef=-//EP//TEXT+TA+P7-TA-2014-0014+0+DOC+XML+V0//EN> accessed 24 March 2018.

[96] Provided that said persons meet all of the following requirements: (a) They are not obliged to prove the compulsory coverage of health care by other means, by virtue of the provisions of European Union law, bilateral agreements, and other applicable regulations; (b) They are unable to export the right to health coverage from their country of origin or provenance; (c) There is no third party obliged to pay.

12

Conclusions from a
Comparative Perspective

Ulrich Becker

I. Legacy of the reforms with respect to social protection

1. Facts: social protection reforms

Beginning with a summary of the facts, one can observe that, when comparing the situations before and after the financial crisis, a broad range of changes have occurred in almost all areas of social protection. As this crisis was directly concerned with financial resources and the balancing of state budgets, it does not come as a surprise that particularly those social protection systems with the largest budgets have been affected.

a) Pensions and healthcare

This first holds true for *old-age pension* systems. Most countries provide for a combination of different forms of systems, which leads to a functional mix of two or three tiers of social security (also often called 'pillars'). Reforms concerned, generally speaking, both the regular basis consisting of public pay-as-you-go (PAYG) schemes and additional systems which had been in place in different forms and

Ulrich Becker, *Conclusions from a Comparative Perspective* In: *European Welfare State Constitutions after the Financial Crisis*. Edited by: Ulrich Becker and Anastasia Poulou, Oxford University Press (2020). © The Contributors.
DOI: 10.1093/oso/9780198851776.003.0012

for different groups of persons. The reports provide accounts of the various and numerous measures that were taken during the financial crisis. These measures were country-specific, sometimes more, sometimes less complex combinations of changes, which were always dependent on the pre-existing overall architecture of the respective national old-age security system and on the different economic situations in each country. Yet, they followed similar patterns and pathways. These measures included: raising the pension age,[1] changing the contribution conditions for pensions,[2] lowering the pension levels,[3] and, less prominently, raising contribution rates;[4] universalising the basic public schemes,[5] sometimes also additional schemes,[6] and dismantling specific schemes with rather generous benefits for specific persons,[7] in some cases abolishing special pensions[8] and reorganising the mixture of PAYG- and capital-funded schemes;[9] and reducing pre-retirement arrangements.[10] In terms of more specific measures, there were also cutbacks in particular pension benefits,[11] new contribution obligations for pensioners,[12] the freezing of pension indexations,[13] and limitations to the accumulation of different pensions or of pensions with income from several employment relations.[14]

Second, *healthcare reforms* were undertaken in almost all countries under investigation. When it comes to the provision of benefits in kind and services—which is by far the most important part of any healthcare system and requires a rather complex infrastructure in which hospitals, physicians, and other health practitioners provide stationary and ambulatory treatment, as well as pharmaceutical and medical products—this can be organised either in the form of an insurance system[15] or a national service.[16] Although systems of the latter kind are mainly financed from taxes, they are, as a rule, also based on contributions and not without conditions for coverage. In reality, and depending on the criteria chosen for the

---

[1] Ch 3, II.1; Ch 5, II.2.a; Ch 6, II.2; Ch 7, II.2.a; Ch 8, II.2.a.bb; Ch 9, III.2.a; Ch 10, III.2; Ch 11, III.1.a.
[2] Ch 7, II.2.a; Ch 9, III.2.a; Ch 10, III.2; Ch 11, III.1.a.
[3] Ch 5, II.1.b; Ch 6, II.2; Ch 11, III.1.b (sustainability factor).
[4] Ch 6, II.2.
[5] Ch 5, II.2.a; Ch 10, III.2.
[6] Ch 6, II.2.
[7] Ch 7, II.2; Ch 9, III.2.a.
[8] Ch 5, II.2.a.
[9] Abolishing the compulsory second private pillar in *Hungary*, Ch 2, II.1.a, and reducing contribution rates for the second tier in *Latvia*, Ch 4, II.2; but we can also observe a strengthening of the second tier through raised contributions to the compulsory private and capital-funded system in *Romania*, Ch 5, II.2.a. See for the reduction of reserved assets in *Greece* Ch 6, II.2.
[10] Ch 3, II.1.b; Ch 5, II.1.b; Ch 6, II.2; Ch 8, II.2.a.bb; Ch 10, III.2; Ch 11, III.1.b.
[11] Of non-contributory and universal payments in *Ireland*, Ch 7, II.2.a; of Christmas and Easter allowances for pensioners younger than sixty years in *Greece*, Ch 6, II.2; of thirteenth- and fourteenth-month pensions in *Portugal*, Ch 8, II.2.a.bb.
[12] See the 'solidarity levy for the unemployed' in *Greece*, Ch 6, II.2., the 'extraordinary solidarity contribution' in *Portugal*, Ch 8, II.2.a.bb, and the 'solidarity contribution' in *Italy*, Ch 10, III.2.
[13] Ch 7, II.2; Ch 8, II.2.a.bb; Ch 9, III.2.a; Ch 10, III.2 (partially for higher pensions); Ch 11, III.1.a.
[14] Ch 5, II.2.a.
[15] Ch 3, II.1.
[16] Ch 4, II.1; Ch 6, II.3; Ch 7, II.2.a; Ch 8, II.1.c; Ch 10, III.4; Ch 11, III.5.

categorisation of systems, some healthcare systems can be regarded as a mixture of the two types of public systems.[17] They are complemented by private healthcare. Notwithstanding their classification, healthcare systems were affected by the financial crisis. In most countries the respective reforms were not as diverse as those effected for old-age security, and money saving or cost containment was paramount. Still, in most cases they also consisted of more than one measure. First, there were budget cuts,[18] realised through the reduction of state subsidies in some cases,[19] in other cases through a decrease in contribution rates[20] or lower contributions, with an increase in unemployment becoming a common feature;[21] second, co-payments were raised.[22] In some instances, access to healthcare services became more difficult, or was altogether barred, for a considerable percentage of the population.[23] At the same time, there were also efforts to increase both the efficiency and the effectiveness of healthcare systems.[24] *Cyprus* introduced a new hybrid system based on contributions that, for the first time, provided comprehensive coverage.[25]

b) Unemployment and familiy benefits

Most replacement benefits and allowances in support of specific groups of persons also underwent changes.[26] In this regard, a more complex and diverse picture emerges.

Special attention must be paid to benefits granted in cases of *unemployment*, as unemployment was a major issue during the crisis. In most countries, both cuts—concerning the amount[27] and the duration[28] of benefit payments—and changes in the benefit requirements were effected.[29] They sometimes concerned all benefits notwithstanding their financial source,[30] and sometimes non-contributory benefits only.[31] In *Spain*, contributory unemployment benefits were reduced from the seventh month onward,[32] with the intention of putting economic pressure on

---

[17] Ch 5, II.2.d.

[18] Ch 4, II.2; Ch 6, II.3; Ch 10, III.4.

[19] With a parallel increase in contributions, Ch 8, II.2.e.bb.

[20] Ch 5, II.2.d.

[21] Ch 3, II.3, although the contribution rate was lowered, and the healthcare taxes were increased.

[22] Ch 4, II.2; Ch 7, II.2.e; Ch 11, III.5.

[23] Ch 6, II.3; Ch 7, II.2.e; Ch 11, III.5.

[24] By the unification of different funds, the introduction of new procedures for the purchasing of pharmaceuticals and other products, and better monitoring of healthcare providers, Ch 6, II.3.

[25] Still in the phase of implementation, Ch 9, III.1.c.

[26] See for changes from disability pension to rehabilitation pension in *Hungary* Ch 3, II.4; for reductions of sickness benefits in *Portugal* Ch 8, II.2.e.aa; for cuts and, as a consequence, the introduction of a new system for long-term care in *Spain* Ch 11, III.2.

[27] Ch 5, II.2.b.

[28] Ch 3, II.6.

[29] Ch 7, II.2.d; in Romania, the change of calculation basis of 2011 has not been implemented, Ch 5, II.2.b.

[30] Ch 7, II.2.d.

[31] Ch 11, III.4.

[32] Ch 11, III.4.

jobseekers—which, however, can hardly work in times where there is simply a lack of jobs on offer.[33] It is remarkable that some countries found ways to act against this trend of curtailments. In *Cyprus*, the state moved money from a pension fund to the unemployment fund.[34] *Portugal* increased benefits as well as coverage, and also facilitated access to unemployment benefits.[35] In *Italy*, a new benefits scheme was introduced. While it entered into effect towards the end of the financial crisis,[36] and comes with restrictions typically associated with activation policies, it has also replaced a widely ineffective system.

The manifold *family allowances* experienced cutbacks and some restructuring,[37] and this holds true for most countries even if the actual role they play in the context of social protection differs.[38] As with unemployment benefits, at least some improvements have also been reported.[39]

c) Social assistance

An analysis of changes in *social assistance* leads to the most differentiated results. In *Ireland*, there were no structural changes, but drastic reductions in supplementary welfare allowance.[40] In *Portugal*, reforms led both to a reduction in benefit amounts and to efforts to improve the quality of life.[41] *Latvia* saw a moderate rise in benefits.[42] In *Romania*, some special benefits were suspended until 2016, whereas the level of the monthly guaranteed minimum income was slightly increased.[43] A distinction between social security and social assistance was introduced in *Greece*, and different measures aimed to alleviate the minimisation of the welfare state.[44] After the end of the financial crisis, a new universal system of social assistance came into being. *Cyprus* set up a new guaranteed minimum income scheme with some activation elements, even though complex conditions led to severe problems with effectiveness and to a decrease in the number of social assistance recipients.[45] *Italy*, which had never had an effective system of social assistance, first undertook budget cuts, but also introduced new social assistance schemes in 2017.[46]

---

[33] Whereas other countries followed activation policies earlier; see for the 'Road to Work' programme introduced in 2009 in *Hungary* Ch 3, II.6.

[34] Ch 9, III.2.d.

[35] Ch 8, II.2.d.

[36] Ch 10, III.3.

[37] Ch 5, II.2.c; Ch 7, II.2.c; Ch 8, II.2.c; Ch 9, III.2.c.

[38] See for a rather marginal role in *Spain* Ch 11, III.3.

[39] In *Hungary* in the context of the overall welfare policy of the *Fidesz* government, Ch 3, II.5; in *Cyprus* for particularly vulnerable persons, Ch 9, III.2.c.

[40] Ch 7, II.2.b.

[41] Ch 8, II.2.b.

[42] Ch 4, II.2.

[43] Ch 5, II.2.e.

[44] Ch 6, II.2.

[45] Ch 9, III.2.b.

[46] Ch 10, III.5.

2. Reasons: financial crisis and other drivers

In theory, one can distinguish between three different reasons for reforms. First, crisis-related reforms, which aimed at maintaining a budget balance and/or at reducing expenditure on benefits schemes, and which were based on the considerations and observations of those responsible for the creation and implementation of such schemes; namely national parliaments and other national actors (intrinsic crisis-related reforms). The respective reforms often made reference to the need for economic stability and for reassuring financial markets.[47] In some cases, they started before the intervention of external institutions.[48] In *Hungary*, it was clearly an autonomous decision to abolish the capital-funded second pillar of old-age security because of the state budget deficit.[49] Second, reforms can be directly linked to the intervention of third parties (extrinsic crisis-related reforms). In our context such interventions took the form of conditionalities that were associated with the provision of loans and laid down in Memoranda of Understanding (MoU) and of policy recommendations made by European Union (EU) institutions. In several cases, the influence of such reasons is easy to identify[50] and, as the country reports show, these cases increased with the number and duration of financial support that was received from the external institutions. In other cases, we can see an overlap between extrinsic crisis-related reforms and the first category; when their outcome may well have been in line with the assessment of national actors. Although it is clear that even here European and international institutions had a considerable impact, this is somewhat obfuscated by the fact that national institutions, which had to implement the respective conditionalities, did not always expressly state their motives[51] or concurrently relied on different reasons.[52] In other words, these cases call for political responsibility to be attributed to the European and international institutions (even if this does not imply legal responsibility or causality at the same time, see II.2.a). The influence of such reasons can be seen in *Italy,* where budget consolidation had begun before the financial crisis and was then informally influenced by the European Central Bank,[53] and in *Spain,* where reforms were supported by the EU.[54] Third, reforms may also be based on reasons other than the temporarily relevant budgetary situations, like reactions to foreseeable long-term developments such as demographic processes or changes in social policies

---

[47] See Ch 7, II.2; Ch 8, II.3; Ch 11, II.2.c.
[48] See Ch 8, II.3.
[49] Ch 3, II.3.
[50] See Ch 7, II.2; Ch 8, II.3; even if measures had been taken beforehand in order to facilitate the signing of MoUs, see Ch 9, II.2.
[51] See Ch 5, II.1; but see also Ch 9, III.3.
[52] See Ch 4, II.3.b, Ch 7, II.2.
[53] Ch 10, II.1.
[54] Ch 11, II.2.d.

(non-crisis-related reforms). The new healthcare system in *Cyprus* has been introduced in order to extend coverage to the whole population.[55]

Of course, the first and third reasons are strongly interrelated.[56] Social protection is always based on financial redistributions, be it in the form of contributions
or taxes. This is why there are always good reasons to worry about the efficiency of
protection systems. But this is also why, more generally, it is not easy to differentiate
between economic and other reasons for reforms. Reacting to an ageing population, for example, always means dealing with a threat to the financial sustainability
of social protection. And activation policies are never merely about strengthening
individual freedoms and individual self-responsibility, about improving the participation of persons with disabilities,[57] or about improving gender equality. To the
contrary, they always aim at various economic effects that may help reduce benefits
or raise the overall productivity by increasing labour market participation, based
on the assumption that individual behaviour can be influenced by economic incentives and sanctions.

Against this background, one could attempt to distinguish between different
reasons for reform, not on the basis of motives, but rather according to the short-
term effects of the measures.[58] In this respect, it could be argued that crisis-related
reforms were those which had an immediate effect on expenditure, that is to say
cuts in benefits claims and in the budget of social protection systems; whereas non-
crisis-related reforms were those which were concerned with the structure of social protection systems even though the latter had not been on the political agenda
of national governments. That might be regarded as the catalytic effect of a crisis,
which often gives the final impetus for those reforms which are painful and, thus,
unpopular.

It has to be added that even the extrinsic crisis-related reforms cannot be reduced to merely financial cutbacks with immediate effect. They also encompassed
structural reforms, which were requested in several MoU by the European and
international institutions.[59] With this request, the institutions wanted to make sure
that measures would be taken in order to stabilise the financial situation in the
long run and, as part of this, also to guarantee the financial sustainability of the
social protection systems. Lastly, we can also observe the different steps taken to
influence structural reform, from the first MoU asking for such reforms, and subsequent MoUs putting emphasis on their effective implementation.[60]

---

[55] Whereas the MoU made much less far-reaching recommendations, see Ch 9, III.1.c and III.2.e.
[56] See also Ch 5, I.
[57] See the example of *Hungary*, where changes from disability pensions to rehabilitation pensions
were also made with the goal of strengthening reintegration (Ch 3, II.4).
[58] See also Ch 11, II.2.
[59] See Ch 4, II.3.a; Ch 7, II.2.
[60] See Ch 6, II.2.

The overall conclusion is that a clear-cut distinction cannot be based on either motives or the substance of reforms. The financial crisis generated an urgency around budgetary consolidation measures and, in most countries, this coincided with a general social policy orientation that tried to enhance the financial sustainability of the social protection systems.[61] In most cases, austerity measures at least raised the pressure to reduce spending, and thus to reduce social benefits. Some MoUs recommended very specific and concrete measures to reform social protection and their implementation was closely monitored. Where reforms had already been on the political agenda before,[62] the crisis could still have had a specific impact. It sped up and/or consolidated several of the previously planned structural changes.[63]

3. Outcome: cutbacks and structural changes

A financial crisis puts extraordinary pressure on social protection systems. On the one hand, it makes all the inefficiencies and weaknesses of those systems visible. On the other, it necessitates short-term reactions and immediate cuts in expenditure where structural changes are necessary in order to put social protection on a reliable and sustainable foundation.

In most countries, the manifold reforms of old-age pension systems were both structural reforms and cutbacks at the same time.[64] The former, such as raising the pension age and changing contribution conditions, aimed at reacting to societal and labour market changes. The latter very often concerned benefits which seemed to be additional rather than 'merited' (ie non-contributory benefits),[65] or part of a more privileged security arrangement (in particular old-age security in the public sector).[66] A combination of specific temporary measures and structural reforms was also common in the field of healthcare reforms and in the context of many other social protection systems[67] (see above, I.1).

---

[61] See Ch 8, II.3. More generally (and including other case studies) Stefano Civitarese Matteucci and Simon Halliday, 'Constitutional Law and Social Welfare After the Economic Crisis' in Francesco Merloni and Alessandra Pioggia (eds), *European Democratic Institutions and Administrations, Cohesion and Innovation in Times of Economic Crisis* (Springer and Giappichelli Editore 2018) 149, 166.

[62] See Ch 1, II.1.

[63] See for some of the reforms in *Ireland* Ch 7, IV; for fruitless previous efforts to reform in *Greece* Ch 6, II. In this respect, it is certainly true that challenges to social protection systems faced due to demographic change and increased international competition were of a general nature and concerned all European countries; however, some of them had already accomplished parts of the necessary adaptations to their social protection systems before the crisis hit the economy. See also Ch 10, III.2.

[64] But see for a preponderance of benefit cuts also Ch 4, II.2.

[65] See Ch 7, II.2.a.

[66] See Ch 7, II.2.a.

[67] See Ch 7, IV.

A rather predictable outcome of the reforms was the decrease of mandatory capital-funded pension systems. *Hungary* abolished its second tier that had been created following the outdated World Bank model of the late 1980s—even though it did so to address an acute liquidity squeeze and not so much in order to pursue new reform strategies.[68] In *Latvia*, the amount of contributions dedicated to the capital-funded tier of protection was heavily reduced.[69] Nevertheless, we can also observe contrary developments, as for instance in *Romania*, where the reaction was not to lower but to raise contributions to the compulsory private and capital-funded system.[70]

The question remains whether the structural reforms were of a permanent nature, and whether they have been implemented properly[71] or at least partly re-reformed after the financial crisis.[72] There are examples of both outcomes, and this shows that the search for appropriate solutions for the adaptation of social protection systems remains an important issue which requires discussion independent from the additional economic pressure emanating from the financial crisis.

What could be observed during this crisis was a certain loss of social rights,[73] either due to cutbacks or due to the haste with which structural reforms were implemented.[74] The situation remains problematic to this day, especially with regard to healthcare provision since, in general, healthcare systems are still largely underfunded.[75]

The welfare state has also struggled, as in times of financial crisis there is an increased demand for social protection when fewer resources are available.[76] One would expect that resulting problems play a particular role for those who are already in a precarious situation, and that, as a result, new groups of vulnerable persons can be identified.[77] In this context, it is remarkable that a couple of European countries tried to take countermeasures by strengthening their social assistance schemes, in some cases already during the crisis, in other cases as a lesson learned from the crisis (see above, I.1.c).

---

[68] Ch 3, II.2.a.

[69] Ch 4, II.3.a.

[70] Ch 5, II.2.a.

[71] See for doubts in *Portugal* Ch 8, IV.

[72] See Ch 8, I; Ch 10, III.2; without a clear strategy Ch 11, III.1.b.

[73] Although every state has been affected differently, see Ch 6, I. It seems that the *Romanian* welfare state has not changed very much, due to temporary restrictions on the one hand and the relatively low level of benefits on the other, Ch 5, V.

[74] Ch 10, III.2.

[75] See for serious problems in *Italy* Ch 10, III.4.

[76] Ch 7, II.2.f.

[77] Ch 7, II.2.f.

II. Legacy of the reforms with respect to
constitutional law

1. The role of constitutional law and adjudication

a) Overview

From a comparative perspective, there are remarkable differences concerning the question whether the above-mentioned processes of social law reforms were controlled by courts applying constitutional and/or international law.[78]

In *Hungary*, no cases were reported. This may be an outcome of the profound constitutional reform which took place in 2011. The new 'Fundamental Law' is not so much a result of the financial crisis as of an overall political process. It led to major changes as far as the protection of social rights and the role of the Constitutional Court are concerned: the right to social security became a state objective, and social insurance is not expressly mentioned in the Constitution any more. At the same time, access to the Constitutional Court was restricted.[79] Similar reasons, namely difficulties in accessing the court and no constitutional protection of the right to social protection and healthcare, led to a dearth of cases challenging crisis-related social protection reforms in *Ireland*.[80] Nevertheless, cases dealing with the rights to property and to equality, as well as with legitimate expectations, give some hints on the interrelation between crisis and legal doctrine.

In most of the other countries, *constitutional courts* had the opportunity to decide on social protection reforms. In *Latvia*, the Constitutional Court, which is accessible both to members of the parliament and to individuals, took six decisions, and it is not by chance that five of them dealt with old-age pensions, and three of the latter ones with specific schemes for public services; only one concerned another branch of social protection, namely parental allowance.[81] A similar situation emerged in *Romania*, where constitutional control was rather comprehensive as a result of most social protection reforms coming before the Constitutional Court, which exercised both an a priori and an a posteriori control.[82] Here too the more relevant cases concerned pensions, although the Constitutional Court also had the opportunity to review cutbacks of other social benefits. In *Portugal*, the Constitutional Court is competent to control constitutionality from concrete and abstract perspectives[83] and accompanied the country's series of social protection reforms with decisions, first primarily concerning cuts in pension rights in

---

[78] And there are still cases pending, see Ch 9, V.
[79] Ch 3, III.2.
[80] Ch 3, III.
[81] Ch 4, III.1.a.
[82] Ch 5, III.
[83] And also a priori under certain conditions, Ch 8, III.2.

2012; then in 2013 with two decisions on additional respective cuts, but also on additional contribution obligations; in 2014 with two decisions on solidarity and sustainability contributions; and in 2015 with its decisions on restrictions of access for specific groups of persons to social assistance.[84] This led to several corrections, whereas in *Spain*, the Constitutional Court in its decision in 2015 on pension reforms left the respective legislative measures untouched and further decided, in the context of healthcare, that regions had to respect the core legislation of the federation.[85] The Constitutional Court in *Italy* first accepted austerity measures, especially with their consequences for the regions and the federal structure of state.[86] However, from 2015 onwards, it enhanced judicial review first in two cases on pension indexation and cuts in pension rights and then concerning the basic level of benefits relating to civil and social entitlement, which must be guaranteed throughout the national territory.[87]

Control of constitutionality in *Cyprus* is exercised by the Supreme Court, which is accessible to individuals in its role as administrative court by means of appeal. Two cases on the levying of additional contributions and the non-cumulation of pensions with other pensions, and their suspension while earning from public employment, were decided in 2014. Subsequent decisions did not follow before November 2018 and were issued by the Administrative Court, which had been established in 2016;[88] they concerned the reduction of allowances and pensions, as well as of salaries and occupational pensions in the public sector.[89] Similarly, it is the Council of State, acting as the supreme administrative court, which had to decide on the constitutionality of social protection reforms in *Greece*.[90] The Council of State turned out to be accessible for all relevant social groups.[91] In 2012, it upheld reductions of allowances and pensions, and in 2014 cuts in the healthcare budget.[92] Yet, it issued a series of decisions in 2015 that summarised the austerity measures undertaken since the beginning of the financial crisis and imposed on pensioners and came to the result that the cutbacks were disproportionate.[93] In 2016 it also stressed the obligation to provide sufficient health services.[94] Later on, it again accepted the reduction of an end-of-employment benefit characterised as pension benefit, and also the introduction of the new old-age pension system.[95]

---

[84] Ch 8, III.1.
[85] Ch 11, IV.2 and 3.
[86] Ch 10, IV.1.
[87] Ch 10, IV.2.
[88] Ch 9, IV.1 and 2.
[89] Those decisions were reviewed by the Supreme Court in April 2020, Ch 9, V.
[90] Ch 6, III.3.
[91] Ch 6, III.5.
[92] Ch 6, III.4.a and III.6.
[93] Ch 6, III.4.b.
[94] Ch 6, III.6.
[95] Ch 6, III.4.c.

b) Objects and rights

The overview makes clear that a control of pension reforms was at the centre of judicial constitutional review. Reductions of healthcare budgets, although constituting an important part of the austerity measures (see above, I.1.a), were a rarer object of adjudication. They came before the constitutional courts in *Italy* and in *Spain* in the context of regional powers,[96] and before the State Council in *Greece* both as a general measure of reform and in the form of certain restrictions for the provision of pharmaceuticals;[97] a special case in *Ireland* only concerned a service provider who had a contract with the state to deliver services at a rate that underwent reductions during the crisis.[98] Most of the other social benefits were either not under scrutiny or only formed part of a general control of reforms;[99] there were only two cases that dealt respectively with family benefits[100] and with unemployment benefits.[101]

The fundamental rights involved mirror the objects of adjudication. In some cases, the principle of equality played a role.[102] It led to corrections of some reductions of social benefits,[103] but also was more generally relevant in *Portugal* in the form of a newly developed principle of proportional equality.[104] The protection of legitimate expectations[105] and of legal certainty,[106] or the rule of law more generally, were taken into consideration in a series of cases, sometimes as own legal bases for judicial review,[107] sometimes as part of other and more specific constitutional provisions. The right to a minimum subsistence has been acknowledged in *Greece* and *Portugal*.[108]

A very noteworthy fact is that the protection of acquired rights, and in particular of pension rights, is guaranteed on the basis of different constitutional provisions. Theoretically, the constitutional right to property, article 1 of Protocol 1 of the European Convention on Human Rights (ECHR), and, where available, the right to social security or the right to adequate pensions could all be relevant and form independent legal yardsticks. Yet, they have rarely been used together, at least

---

[96]   Ch 10, IV.1 and 2.c; Ch 11, IV.3.
[97]   Ch 6, III.6.
[98]   Ch 3, III.
[99]   Ch 5, III.1.
[100]   Ch 4, III.1.
[101]   Ch 5, III.3.
[102]   See also Ch 4, III.1.b; Ch 7, III.2.
[103]   Ch 8, III.1.c; Ch 9, IV.2.b.
[104]   In Portugal. Ch 8, III.1.a and b.
[105]   In the context of an increase of contribution rates in *Portugal*, Ch 8, III.1.b.
[106]   In all cases in *Latvia*, Ch 4, III.1.b; in the context of a revaluation of pension entitlements in *Portugal*, Ch 8, III.1.b.
[107]   Also in *Romania* if social benefits were not protected by the Constitution, although the Constitutional Court rejected the arguments that their cutbacks violated the rule of law and the principle of equality, Ch 5, III.4.
[108]   Ch 6, III.2.b, based on the right to dignity; Ch 8, III.1.b, based on a combination of the right to dignity and the right to social security.

not in a balanced and elaborated manner. There were different reasons for that. At the beginning, there was some uncertainty on whether pension rights could be qualified as property in *Greece*,[109] and they have, in fact, not been regarded as property in *Portugal*.[110] In *Latvia*, the right to social security served as *lex specialis* in relation to the right to property, without, however, neglecting the role of the ECHR;[111] in *Romania* the right to pensions was at least more relevant[112] and in *Italy* the right to social security also played a more important role than the right to property.[113] Nevertheless, the different approaches opened up the way to a proportionality test. Although it is conceivable that this divergence influenced the weight ascribed to the legal positions of the persons affected by the reforms,[114] it does not appear to have played a decisive role in the outcomes of constitutional control (see below, II.2).

c) Inter- and supranational sources

National courts made reference to different sources from outside the national legal jurisdiction, namely to EU law,[115] the International Covenant on Economic, Social and Cultural Rights, and the European Social Charter.[116] Whereas most of these sources were scarcely used and merely mentioned, without playing a decisive role, the case of the ECHR is different. This does not come as a surprise, for both formal and substantial reasons. First, the ECHR forms an integral part of many European constitutions, sometimes expressly mentioned in this role, sometimes through the interpretation of national provisions. Second, as the great majority of the cases dealt with the protection of acquired social rights, the 'negative dimension' of fundamental rights[117] was at stake because their consideration nearly always led to the question of whether reductions of benefits led to an interference with individual positions protected by these rights and whether such interferences could be justified. As a potentially relevant fundamental right, the courts discussed the right to property (and to possession, article 1 of Protocol 1) without going beyond this traditional approach.[118]

---

[109] Dafni Diliagka, *The Legality of Public Pension Reforms in Times of Financial Crisis* (Nomos 2018) 107–09.

[110] For the reasons see Ch 8, III.2.

[111] Ch 4, III.2.a.

[112] Ch 5, III.2.b; see for a comparable situation in *Spain* Ch 11, IV.2.

[113] Ch 10, V.

[114] See Ch 8, III.2.

[115] But not substantially to the Charter of Fundamental Rights due to its art 51, see Ch 6, III.4.a and below, II.2.a.

[116] Ch 4, III.4.

[117] Ch 2, II.2.c.

[118] See for possible alternatives (arts 8 and 2 ECHR) Ingrid Leijten, 'The Right to Minimum Subsistence and Property Protection Under the ECHR: Never the Twain Shall Meet?' (2019) 4 European Journal of Social Security 307, 322–23.

It is remarkable that the interpretation of article 1 of Protocol 1 still varies considerably from court to court—although the case law of the European Court of Human Rights (ECtHR) was always taken into account. This might be partly due to inconsistencies within its jurisprudence. In particular, it is still unclear under what conditions 'legitimate expectations' are protected, ie when there is a 'direct link between the level of contributions and the benefits awarded'. Similarly, confusion remains around the acceptance of the ECtHR that states can amend their social protection legislation if this complies with the proportionality or 'fair balance' test, and around whether there is a clear concept of a 'core minimum' of property rights.[119] But the divergent reception at the national level is also due to a restricted number and variety of cases. As far as the outcome is concerned, some cases demonstrate a wide interpretation of the notion that the ECHR does not guarantee social rights as such,[120] while others invoke the concept of 'core rights' without elaborating its actual meaning.[121] In sum, there is still much room left to develop an—increasingly necessary—common interpretation of equivalent fundamental rights enshrined within national constitutions, the ECHR, and EU law.[122]

2. Impact of the constitution on welfare state reforms

Although the legal character of MoUs was not left without discussion—in particular with regard to the question of whether they needed transformation, and in this context the participation of Parliament[123]—and although it was clear that the MoUs put at least political pressure on national governments and even sometimes requested concrete measures of social protection reforms (above, I.2),[124] courts held the national legislators accountable for the respective reforms.[125] This opened the way for constitutional review at the national level, regardless of the extent to which the actions of EU bodies could also be subjected to review by the ECJ.[126]

Such control led, in most countries where it has been actually exercised (see II.1.a), to the acceptance of several complaints brought before courts. The exception is *Spain*; this may be due to a certain reluctance on the part of the Constitutional Court,[127] but if one considers that judicial review has over time experienced a

---

[119] These uncertainties become clearly visible in *Béláné Nagy v Hungary* App no 53080/13 (ECtHR, 13 December 2016) paras 105–26, with separate opinion of judge Wojtyczek (paras 2–9) and separate opinion of judges Nussberger, Hirvelä, Bianku, Yudkivska, Møse, Lemmens, and O'Leary (paras 4–21).
[120] Ch 4, III.2.a; Ch 5, III.2.b.aa.
[121] Ch 4, III.2.a.
[122] See Ulrich Becker, 'Grundrechte der Arbeit in Europa – zu Funktionen, Verschränkungen und Konfliktlinien vernetzter Grundrechtsordnungen' (2019) 5 Europarecht 469–501.
[123] Ch 4, II.3.c; Ch 9, II.2.
[124] Together with EU legal sources, Ch 2, IV.
[125] Ch 6, II.4.a; Ch 8, III.2.
[126] Ch 2, V.
[127] And the introduction of a 'budget stability clause' into the Constitution, see Ch 11, IV.2. and V.

development in other countries during the crisis, it could also be attributable to the relatively short period of austerity measures taken. In *Italy*, the Constitutional Court struck down limitations of the revaluation of pensions;[128] as did the *Latvian* Constitutional Court in three decisions on cutbacks in pension rights, where it held that the respective restrictions of the right to social security and to legal certainty were disproportionate;[129] as well as the *Romanian* Constitutional Court, which argued that cutbacks in already acquired rights to pensions financed from contributions would violate the constitutional right to pensions, which is enshrined as a fundamental right.[130] The Supreme Court of *Cyprus* saw in the anti-cumulation provisions concerning pensions, as well as in the reductions of pensions, salaries, and occupational pensions in the public sector, interferences with the right to property, which could not be justified as this right had no limitation clause with regard to public interest.[131] Whereas in the last three countries mentioned the judgements align with a series of similar cases, the picture is different and shows more variations in *Portugal*. Here, the unequal burden concerning the first and second reductions of pensions was seen as a violation of proportional equality; the additional contributions levied on unemployment and sickness benefits were regarded as a violation of the right to a minimum level of subsistence; the recalculation of retirement entitlements was a breach of legitimate expectations; and imposing sustainability contributions was a breach of legal certainty; finally, the reduction of survivors' pensions, when accumulated with other pensions, was, again, a violation of the equality principle.[132]

When social protection reforms underwent corrections by judicial decisions, those decisions of unconstitutionality were accorded the necessary respect and have been implemented.[133] They led to adaptations in the programming of the reform process, even if they did not, for obvious reasons, make the task of stabilising budgets easier: at the end, they provoked further measures at the international[134] and national level.[135]

3. Economic pressure and legal doctrine

When adopting social protection reforms at the national level, crisis-related changes may affect legislative procedures in two different ways: first, as an effect of special urgency, and second, as a shift within the separation of powers, as

---

[128] Ch 10, IV.2.a and c.
[129] Ch 4, III.2.
[130] Ch 5, III.2.b.
[131] Ch 9, IV.2.
[132] Ch 8, III.1.
[133] See for a case of self-restricted effect Ch 8, III.1.a.
[134] See Ch 5, I and V.
[135] See for the introduction of a new pension system Ch 6, II.2; for tax measures Ch 8, IV.

traditionally conceived. The experiences made during the time of financial crisis vary broadly. In some countries, no changes were observed.[136] In others, it seems as if the procedure was, at times, sped up.[137] As a simple fact, this does not raise legal concerns. Things are different when—possibly also in connection with accelerated procedures—the separation of powers is concerned. Whereas in some countries only informal consultations were cut short,[138] or the parliament was even deliberately involved to enhance democratic legitimation,[139] the situation must be subjected to more critical assessments in others.[140] This holds especially true if not only single violations of procedural rules were reported[141] but also legislation based on governmental decrees was used in a systematic way, even if not criticised by courts,[142] and thus undermined the role of parliaments—in particular in cases in which the necessary negotiations with international institutions had sometimes already led to a considerable narrowing of the discretion available to the national legislature. It should be added that the respective strategies to strengthen the role of governments first took place where the national constitutions provided a suitable framework, and also where it had been used previously in order to come to decisions on social protection reforms. Bearing that in mind, it seems as if the actual handling of the separation of powers was rather a question of legal and political culture than of crisis-driven urgency.

A similar result can be drawn from our inquiries with regard to 'justification patterns': the requirements posed by courts for the justification of interferences with fundamental rights and, more to the point, the application of the proportionality test. Most courts have accepted that the financial crisis put specific pressure on national governments and led to a specific emergency situation. Generally speaking, they also accepted that legislators had a certain margin of appreciation when it came to the appropriateness of measures taken to react to the crisis.[143] Nevertheless, they did not cast aside the general rules associated with proportionality tests, and they set limits to social protection reforms.

From a doctrinal point of view, the decisions were less convincing where they were based on the assumption that some fundamental rights had a more or less absolute character. Such an approach may be understandable when it comes to the independence of the judiciary, which was, in fact, appealed to in two countries to protect judges against cuts in their pension rights.[144] But it is more than

---

[136] Ch 7, III.
[137] Ch 4, II.3.c.
[138] Ch 9, III.3.
[139] Ch 8, III.2.
[140] See for the question whether loan agreements needed ratification Ch 4, II.3.c.
[141] See for the emergency procedure in *Romania*, which was generally accepted, although the Constitutional Court in one case held its use to be unconstitutional as fundamental rights were concerned, Ch 5, III.1.
[142] Ch 6, III.1; Ch 10, II.2; Ch 11, II.1 and 5.
[143] See Ch 4, III.2; Ch 5, III.2; Ch 6, III.5; Ch 7, III.2; more reluctant Ch 8, III.2.
[144] Ch 5, III.2.c; Ch 9, IV.3.

questionable when a statutory right to a pension becomes untouchable in practice. This does not only hold true when other rights to social benefits, though also protected by constitutional provisions, do not enjoy the same judicial protection.[145] More generally, it is necessary to elaborate clear rules for the conditions under which cutbacks in social benefits can be justified,[146] without regard to whether the benefits come under the scope of application of the right to property or the right to social security. In this context, courts must also make clear how they apply the proportionality test, and they should follow all doctrinal rules in a consistent manner.[147]

Apart from these flaws, most courts have developed a convincing position towards the protection of social rights.[148] They have respected the primacy of the legislature without giving it total leeway. They have asked for plausible reasoning, and they are more and more prepared to weigh the arguments put forward by governments in order to find a balance between social protection and financial necessities.[149] It is a step forward for social rights protection[150] to lead to such a legal discourse, even if corrections of legislative measures are then restricted to relatively few cases of formal failures, unequal treatment, and extreme circumstances. Social rights allow the judiciary to play an important role in imposing checks and balances. Therefore, and particularly in times of crises, one can draw an overall conclusion: social rights and their protection by constitutional law matter.

III. The financial crisis and the constitution of European welfare states

(1) Reactions to the financial crisis reveal the basic principles and structures concerning the relation between the economy and social protection, as they try to readjust this relationship. In this respect, they are directly concerned with the foundations of political communities and their societal order—in contrast to reactions to other crises, like natural catastrophes or pandemic diseases, although it goes without saying that the capability of communities to react to the latter crises in an appropriate way very much depends on a stable relationship between the economy and social protection.

---

[145] See Ch 5, III.3.

[146] See criticism in Ch 9, IV.2.c and V.

[147] See criticism in Ch 4, III.3 and IV.

[148] See Ch 8, III.3 and IV. See for more (and too) sceptical assumptions as far as social rights in a narrow sense are concerned Antonia Baraggia and Maria Elena Gennusa, 'Social Rights Protection in Europe in Times of Crisis: "A Tale of Two Cities"' (2017) 11 ICL Journal 479, 505.

[149] Even in the context of constitutional provisions on balanced budgets; see Ch 10, IV; for a more pessimistic assessment Ch 11, I and V.

[150] See for discussions on the introduction of social rights into the constitution Ch 7, III.4; for a proposal to strengthen these rights Ch 11, I.

Societies based on individual freedoms and equality both need market economies and social protection, and the one depends on the other, which also means that neither prevails over the other.[151] That it is paramount to find the right balance is what we are experiencing now: the present challenge to contain the coronavirus also puts emphasis on the crucial role of well-working healthcare systems, and on the fact that past cutbacks on healthcare expenditure may have multiplied these challenges.[152]

(2) Social policy reactions to the financial crisis correspond to what one would expect from crisis-driven politics in general: they consist of a mixture of cutbacks of benefits as immediate remedies, and of structural changes as possible solutions in the longer term. This could be observed in all countries even if the mixture was different and nation-specific; it varied in particular in the extent to which a country was affected, and also in the duration of the actual critical situation.

It also becomes clear that crisis-driven reactions come with their own disadvantages. As for short-term reactions, the problem is that social rights have to be restricted in times in which they are specifically needed. Some countries tried to solve the problem by putting more emphasis on unemployment and social assistance benefits. This points at a certain strategic change: it is not by chance that in the aftermath of the financial crisis universal social assistance systems were set up in those countries that did not have such systems effectively in place at the beginning of this century. That does not mean the birth of new 'minimum welfare' states: a universal guarantee of subsistence is a necessary foundation for all developed welfare states. As for other long-term reactions, in particular structural changes in old-age security and healthcare systems, it is still open how and whether they will last. The crisis might have helped to implement them partially and temporarily. But it certainly does not spare the respective countries the debates and political compromises that are unavoidable in order to reform social protection thoughtfully and thoroughly.

(3) Whether constitutional control is effected, and to what extent, is a question of institutional settings and the legal culture behind them. In most countries it actually took place during the financial crisis, yet with different intensities. Over time, and with increasing duration of the austerity measures, the role of constitutional control seems to have augmented in at least those states that were affected most.[153]

---

[151] It should also be noted that the term 'neo-liberalism' has a very different meaning if its use is compared between countries with different institutional settings, see Marion Fourcade-Gourinchas and Sarah L. Babb, 'The Rebirth of the Liberal Creed: Paths to Neoliberalism in Four Countries' (2002) 108(3) American Journal of Sociology 533–79. See for the argument that governments should be 'accountable for . . . regulating the market and redistributing resources' Ignacio Sainz. 'Rights in Recession? Challenges for Economic and Social Rights Enforcement in Times of Crisis' (2009) 1(2) Journal of Human Rights Practice 277, 287.

[152] See Ch 10, IV.1.

[153] See for a non-linear development, but a very remarkable 'second phase' of adjudication, Ch 6, III.4.b and c; further Ch 8, III.1 and Ch 10, IV.

The question remains whether this is due to a certain impatience as structural changes of social protection systems need time in order to show visible results, whether it is caused by a changing overall political situation that often does not leave legal assessments untouched, or whether it is a systemic reaction in the sense of reviewing measures more thoroughly if they were put on judges' desks repeatedly. Much speaks for the latter position, although courts dealing with concrete cases will often not be able to take the cumulative effect of a series of social benefits reductions into account.[154] That means that constitutional control also works according to its own mechanisms in the field of social rights. The financial crisis has not weakened the constitutional backbone of welfare states, but rather resurrected the role of social rights.

Yet, it is obvious that constitutions primarily protect acquired rights, at least when it comes to actually defending social rights against austerity measures. It is not by chance that most cases dealt with cuts in pension benefits, although courts based their outcomes on different legal provisions, and they also revealed a spectrum of differing levels of 'strictness' as regards protection, especially in relation to the conditions for justifying restrictions on the rights concerned. The case law of all courts was silent in relation to the programmatic dimension of social rights, and this missing part is well illustrated by the fact that the right to healthcare of individuals, although affected in more than one country by the austerity measures, has nowhere been the subject of a court decision. That may be an expression of judicial self-constraint; but it also shows, in parallel to the findings for social policy, that times of crises are not the best times for making progress with the conceptualisation of complex matters.

(4) During the financial crisis we experienced different assessments of whether budgetary restraints could be taken into account without violating social rights.[155] In its aftermath, those differences persist when it comes to answering the question of how to balance economic freedoms and social rights properly. That may not be unexpected as social and economic policies still belong to the core field of national policies. But these policies are not only a matter of 'common concern'.[156] They need more than coordination: they need a common understanding.

The financial crisis left the EU, and in particular the Economic and Monetary Union, without an institutional solution that could help to avoid similar situations and to bridge the ever growing disparities between the Member States. The lack of a European solution becomes clearly visible now, in times of a new crisis. The pathway to find such a solution may not lead to new and stable institutional settings, although some well-constructed ways of more financial transfers between the Member States seem advisable. At least for the time being, the solution may

---

[154] Ch 6, III.3.
[155] See Ch 6, IV; Ch 10, V; Ch 11, V.
[156] Art 121(1) TFEU for economic policies.

rather lie in spontaneous initiatives of financial support—a strategy also followed at the national level with respect to crisis-related measures of compensation.[157] But even if this were true—there is one overall lesson which should be learned from the financial crisis, the observance of which would also help overcome the pandemic crisis: we need a substantial and commonly accepted agreement on how to balance the economy and social protection in the future.

[157] See Ulrich Becker, *Soziales Entschädigungsrecht* (Nomos 2018) 135–38 for social policy reactions to flood damage in Germany. Denmark has—obviously in order to shift from legal to political decisions—changed the provision on compensation in its epidemics law (*epidemiloven*) <https://www.retsinformation.dk/Forms/R0710.aspx?id=213436> accessed 15 April 2020.

Index

For the benefit of digital users, indexed terms that span two pages (e.g., 52–53) may, on occasion, appear on only one of those pages.